THE BANKING SITUATION

THE BANKING SITUATION

American Post-War Problems and Developments

BY

H. PARKER WILLIS

PROFESSOR OF BANKING
COLUMBIA UNIVERSITY

AND

JOHN M. CHAPMAN

ASSISTANT PROFESSOR OF BANKING
COLUMBIA UNIVERSITY

NEW YORK : MORNINGSIDE HEIGHTS
COLUMBIA UNIVERSITY PRESS
M·CM·XXXIV

WITH THE COLLABORATION OF

JOHN G. BECKER
FREDERICK W. JONES
N. GILBERT RIDDLE
JULES I. BOGEN
J. A. GRISWOLD
LOUIS SHERE
SCHROEDER BOULTON
V. D. KAZAKÉVICH
ELI TASH
WILLIAM ALLEN DAY
A. WILFRED MAY
CAROLINE WHITNEY

PUBLISHED 1934

PRINTED IN THE UNITED STATES OF AMERICA
GEORGE BANTA PUBLISHING COMPANY · MENASHA, WISCONSIN

PREFACE

The following pages have been written as the result of a study of banking conditions in the United States initiated at the opening of the academic year 1932-1933. In May 1932 the Social Science Research Council made a grant to the Department of Banking, School of Business, Columbia University, designed to cover the expenses of statistical and clerical work in the making of "A General Survey of the Position of Banking in the United States"; and the work, after being planned during the summer of 1932, was actually undertaken in the autumn of that year. The present volume is the outgrowth of studies made during the months since the date named.

In planning the banking survey thus provided for, decision was reached to carry on the inquiry as a coöperative undertaking, to be shared in by the members of the Banking Seminar. At the opening of the Seminar for the year 1932-1933, the project of such a survey was outlined to the members and the latter were invited to select phases of the banking situation for special study and analysis. The topics thus distributed were definitely assigned to the various members and these were supervised in their choice of material and in the formulation of the plan of investigation. This supervision continued throughout the year, with regular Seminar consultations, and has resulted in producing a large body of statistical and other material bearing upon the current condition of American banking.

At the time that these phases of the work were being undertaken in the Banking Seminar, a small staff was organized for the purpose of carrying on independent statistical studies, and secondarily of aiding the various investigators in the preparation of such data as might be necessary for the completion of their work. This statistical work has been continued throughout the year and has resulted in the collection of a considerable amount of new material and the retabulation of much that was already easily available in published reports, but had not been computed upon a uniform basis of a kind permitting satisfactory comparisons to be made between different periods and different types of activity.

In finally completing the survey the editors have also made extensive use of the data collected by the Senate Committee on Banking, to which one of these acted as adviser during the years 1930 to 1932 inclusive. The task immediately before the Committee was the preparation of the Banking bill of 1932, passed by the Senate on June 16, 1933; and the data prepared at the request of the Committee and originally published, largely, in the hearings (Hearings, Sen. Res. 71, 71st Cong., 3d sess., Pts. I-VII) had been availed of. Much of the material contained in these hearings was necessarily first published by the Committee in its original form and without much statistical and other analysis. Such analysis could properly be supplied only through nonofficial study and discussion, as has been attempted in this volume.

Still further valuable data were obtained from the Banking Survey of 1925-1926, conducted in those years with the participation of the editors of this volume and with the use of funds which were then supplied by a committee of bankers who desired a complete investigation of the banking situation, with particular reference to bank failures and branch banking. The results of the inquiry in question were filed at the time with the Senate Banking Committee, were furnished by the latter to the Federal Reserve Board, and through it to the committees of the reserve system which, within the past three years, have been studying the reserve question and the branch and failure problems as well as a variety of other topics. These latter studies of the Federal Reserve Board and system have never yet been published, while the earlier data compiled in the banking inquiry of 1925-1926, though filed in the spring of 1926 with the Senate Banking Committee, thus becoming a public document, have continued to be available only in typewritten form and thus to only a very few students of the banking question.

Acknowledgment should be made to the Senate Banking and Currency Committee and through it to the Federal Reserve

Board for the use of the unpublished volumes representing the work of the committees of the Federal Reserve system above referred to, which as to be noted, were during the spring of 1933, filed with the Senate Banking and Currency Committee as a public document. Wherever material, drawn from these studies prepared under the auspices of the Federal Reserve system, has been employed in the preparation of the present discussion, the fact is specifically noted and acknowledgment made to the particular phase of the Federal Reserve study involved.

In the study presented in these pages, such portions of the material collected in 1925-1926 as are still germane to the topic now under consideration have been amplified and brought down to date and their results embodied. The volume herewith is thus a composite of the material obtained through the banking survey of 1925-1926, of the statistical data of the Senate Banking Committee 1930 to 1932 inclusive, and of the Banking Seminar, Columbia University, during the year 1932-1933, with such additional matter drawn from the work of the Committee of the Reserve System as is indicated here and there.

In thus combining and consolidating the mass of data which had been made available in various quarters, as already indicated, it obviously has been out of the question to furnish more than very condensed statements upon many of the points at issue. There has been no effort to supply a primarily statistical or encyclopedic treatment of the situation, but rather to furnish a general review of the essential facts and figures necessary to form a judgment of outstanding banking problems in the United States. While no attempt has been made to popularize the material, or to give it an appeal to a very wide audience, the aim has been constantly kept in mind to supply a sufficient body of background data to enable the ordinary intelligent reader to gain a clear conception of the major factors involved in each of the principal phases of the banking situation and to shape his opinions accordingly.

Where a considerable number of persons have collaborated in the preparation of a detailed piece of work, it is not always easy, or even possible, to make complete acknowledgment of the assistance rendered by each of them. In this volume, however, the attempt is made at each point where an important contribution has been made by a member of the Banking Seminar to assign due credit through footnote references. On the title page is furnished a list of those members of the Seminar who have contributed considerably to the volume. These contributions have been specifically acknowledged at the appropriate points. Special mention should also be made of the courtesies extended and information furnished by Hon. J. A. Broderick, Superintendent of Banking, State of New York.

COLUMBIA UNIVERSITY THE EDITORS
May 15, 1934

CONTENTS

PART I: A CRISIS IN AMERICAN BANKING

BY H. PARKER WILLIS

PART II: STRUCTURE

PART III: CONTROL

PART IV: BANK PORTFOLIOS

PART V: CENTRAL BANKING

TABLES

CHARTS

PART I

A CRISIS IN AMERICAN BANKING

BY

H. PARKER WILLIS

CHAPTER I

THE COLLAPSE OF AMERICAN BANKING

INTRODUCTION

For several years past it has been evident, even to casual students of banking and of the general industrial situation in the United States, that a fundamental reform or reorganization was inevitably necessary. The inadequacy of the American banking mechanism to provide for the requirements of business had long been evident. It had been necessary to permit the existence of extensive innovations in banking practice, not sanctioned by the experience of older nations. These are exemplified in the custom of dividing the accommodation of the larger business enterprises among a considerable number of banking institutions, thereby preventing the latter from gaining the complete knowledge of individual and corporate affairs, and of the basis for credit that would otherwise have been deemed necessary. The constant recurrence of bank failures for a long time has been another outstanding phase of the situation. This failure habit has been minimized on the ground that it represented sporadic conditions or local bad management. It was in the latter part of the decade 1920-1930, for the first time recognized as the outgrowth of fundamentally wrong organization in American banking, and hence subject to correction only through far-reaching and thorough reform.

The weakness and apparent unsuccess of the Federal Reserve system in its effort to control dangerous tendencies, denied or minimized for a decade after the close of the World War, was at length brought into glaring prominence by the collapse of 1929 and the depression which followed that event. These conditions were only slowly appreciated as being parts of a larger whole, and the legislation of Congress subsequent to the adoption of the Federal Reserve Act had been correctly assessed as merely a series of incidental and patchwork changes in enactments already upon the statute books. Nevertheless the real nature of the conditions underlying the banking problem, as just stated, were not popularly recognized, and the rank and file of the commercial public still has only a vague notion of the true nature of the factors underlying the banking difficulties prior to 1933.

Forces affecting American banking which had for a long time been in the making came to a head in February, 1933. These elements were of a fundamental nature; they had long been recognized and their danger noted by those concerned with the study of banking and financial conditions. Little, if any, attention had been paid to such warnings by either bankers or public men. There prevailed the belief that the situation, if left to itself, would recover its balance; and that difficulties and dangers would thus once more prove self-corrective. Accordingly, the measures which were taken during the years 1931 and 1932, for the improvement of banking conditions, were entirely of the sort classified as "relief," and in no case partook of reconstruction, reform, or improvement.

The state of things revealed by the breakdown of 1933 has shown that such hopeful expectations were not well founded; and that there is need for complete rectification and reconstruction, even of the very foundation upon which the present-day banking system of the United States rests. The case calls for thorough reconsideration of the theories upon which American banking has been based, as well as of the technique by which it has been conducted. The test of "soundness" in any banking system is always afforded by its ability to withstand the onslaughts which develop as the result of friction inside the economic mechanism, as well as those that are due to changes of a more profound nature in relationships of economic groups. Such a test the American banking structure has not found itself able to withstand, and the questions have thus inevitably arisen, (1) what must be done to adapt our banking system to immediate necessities and, (2) what changes of a longer-range variety must be attempted in order to make it responsive to the dictates of soundness and safety, thereby reducing the danger that there may be a recurrence of the banking difficulties which have been conspicuous since 1929.

Problems that are thus forced upon the attention of the observer must necessarily be given a first place in the study of the condition of American banking at the present moment. Their urgency is, however, rendered greater, particularly as compared with the conditions presented during former periods of collapse, when we remember that, for the past twenty years, the United States has been equipped with a central banking system comprising twelve separate institutions—the Federal Reserve banks—bound together in such a way as to make a single central system of great power; and that this system has, nevertheless, failed to safeguard the nation against a breakdown. Evidently the difficulties which American banking has had to face have not been those that were directly attributable to a faulty or defective system of local banking, or to mismanagement. They plainly involve, as well, fundamental questions of central banking, and they require a treatment which shall include within itself a discussion of the central-banking relationships of the banking system as a whole, as well as the international aspects of our Reserve system.

The holding of nearly 40 per cent of the monetary gold of the world by the reserve system, and suspension of gold redemption, notwithstanding the existence of this vast reserve in the hands of the central organization lends special importance and point to the character of the financial situation of the moment. It both emphasizes the unsatisfactory character of the relationship between the central-banking system of the United States and the underlying or local banks, and at the same time it calls attention to the lack of a proper mechanism of trusteeship for the fulfillment of the obligations of a system which has come into the control of so large a proportion of the world's gold. The problem of banking in the United States thus becomes a question of both commercial and central-banking structure and management, as well as of the restoration of international financial soundness. It is also a very practical issue in the rebuilding of the economic mechanism which, for a variety of reasons, has already become seriously broken.[1]

In its banking aspect the national economy of the United States demands a thorough reconstruction if the nation is to be provided with this support which it needs in order to resume effective functioning.

First Indications of Unsoundness

The implication that American banking is practically in a state of collapse, inevitably raises the question, first of all, when, and under what conditions, the breakdown first showed itself. To make fair answer to this query it is necessary to refer to previous conditions. For some years there have been evidences of banking weakness.

These first showed themselves, in conclusive and unmistakable form, in the growth of failures to a proportion affording indubitable indication of an unsound condition. Such failures began not long after the collapse of 1920 which reflected largely the effects of the World War. Upon them were superimposed those of the abuses of credit and business which followed the struggle. There need, however, be no doubt that the unsound and inflationary financing of the war had tremendously weakened the resisting power of the banking system of the United States by changing its methods and by filling it with long-term Government paper holdings. Thus the basis had been laid for a gradual disintegration which was to follow the earliest indications of inadequacy.

Beginning with the year 1922, bank failures had attracted the attention of students of American conditions. While practically no heed was given to them by those in authority, they continued to afford warning signals, in increasing degrees of severity, up to the collapse of 1933. The Comptroller of the Currency has furnished the summary review of the decade 1921-1930 presented on the following page.

[1] Since the paragraphs above were written the Government of the United States has assumed title to this gold stock. The action so ordered emphasizes and does not alter the opinions expressed.

These failures had been generally disregarded; prior to the panic of 1929 they were treated as mere superficial symptoms of local excess or error. After the panic the number of failures greatly increased and eventually resulted in the gradual establishment of conditions that amounted to local moratoria. Banks in various parts of the country, with or without the consent of their depositors and other customers, had begun to "ration" their creditors so that they paid only a fraction of what might be demanded of them, when and as withdrawals were requested. The rapid spread of this situation through the Western and Midwestern states was tacitly overlooked, and the press at large paid practically no attention to it. Such an attitude seems to date back to the autumn of 1931 when, during the organization of a National Credit Corporation for the purpose of providing mutual aid among banks, the attempt to silence controversy or criticism became more strenuous than at any previous time. Since then the means of access, for the ordinary man, to data that would enable him to judge and to formulate conclusions as to the nature of the events occurring in the banking world have become less and less adequate. Data relating to bank failures were discontinued by the Federal Reserve Board during the spring of 1933 and have not been resumed. Other authentic data have been greatly reduced in number.

	All Banks	National Banks	State Member Banks	State Non-member Banks
Suspended	6,968	925	257	5,786
Reopened	797	98	27	672
	6,171	827	230	5,114

The immense number of bank failures during the year 1931 totaling, in the aggregate, nearly 2,300 of all sorts and classes (equal to 15 per cent in number of all institutions) should have afforded conclusive evidence of the necessity for complete and thorough reorganization of the banking system. But it apparently afforded, instead, only a further stimulus for intensifying the disposition to cover the occurrences by providing what was termed "relief." Accordingly, the creation of the Reconstruction Finance Corporation (January-February, 1932), with its extended series of loans to hard-pressed banking institutions, totaling, by the close of 1932, to nearly $850,000,000, was a logical method of carrying still further a plan of action which had already been proven inadequate. Indeed, there is, as now appears, abundant reason for the opinion that the Reconstruction Finance Corporation loans must be regarded as one of the factors in bringing about a still further deterioration of bank assets.

Meanwhile, the government had, either directly or through mere inactivity and refusal to act, frustrated the corrective measures that had been brought forward. The so-called "Glass bill" of 1931, which sought to provide a means for the liquidation of failed institutions without the necessity of long delay for the depositor, and which proposed many other banking reforms, had been definitely and effectively opposed by the national administration in 1931-1932. The measure had been prevented from coming before Congress a sufficient length of time prior to the close of the session in July, 1932 to permit any action, whether favorable or otherwise. Nothing had been offered as a substitute, so that the year 1932 closed with a more threatening banking situation and a less hopeful outlook for remedial action than had been evident at any previous moment. That a major collapse of banking was inevitable had become evident to many minds with the opening of the year 1933. Not only had the banks of the country, as already observed, become less and less liquid, and showed less and less ability to meet the demands of their depositors in many parts of the country, but they were also, in large numbers of cases, failing or refusing, or finding themselves unable to supply active businesses with the funds they required to maintain their service to the community.[2]

The question how long the banking system could avoid a general closing, or, as some feared, a general condition of bankruptcy, was present in many minds, and was the subject of private discussion in numerous banking institutions and admin-

[2] For collateral evidence on this subject the reader is referred to the *Reports of the National Industrial Conference Board,* issued during the year 1932, and containing the results of an investigation into the conditions under which banking credit was extended to would-be borrowers.

istrative offices. The belief that Congress would ultimately be prevailed upon to take some measure toward the relief of the situation buoyed up many, but as the winter advanced it grew plainer than ever that no such hopes were likely to be realized. Gradually the question, uppermost in many minds during the month of February, 1933, came to be rather when and in what form the breakdown would show itself, than the issue whether it would appear at all. Apart from continued failures of isolated banks, the first definite indication of mass collapse of the banking system had been afforded by the so-called "holiday" declared by the governor of Nevada on October 31, 1932. The Executive of the state, by proclamation, exempted all banks from making payments to depositors over a period of 12 days. Thus, the situation which, as already seen, had been widely prevalent in numerous other commonwealths of the West and Midwest, had received official sanction.

This extreme step, never before known in American financial history, was followed, within a few weeks by the temporary holiday of like sort, lasting only a day or two in early February, by which the state of Louisiana aided the banks of the city of New Orleans. On February 14 these events were followed by a proclamation on the part of the governor of Michigan which closed the banks of that state for a period of eight days (later extended four days) and forbade their meeting the demands of depositors. The holiday plan—the constitutionality of which is subject to doubt—spread steadily from state to state, taking, in some localities, a voluntary form and in others being made mandatory upon the entire body of banking institutions.

Beginning with the state of Michigan, the notion of bank holidays, or relief to the banks from the necessity of continuing to meet their obligations to creditors, grew rapidly. It had taken a good while to achieve a condition of the public mind that would tolerate such a policy. The American public had been educated to expect, under penalty of suspension or receivership, immediate payment, upon sight, of demand liabilities, and even of liabilities potentially subject to delay, such as time deposits in commercial banks. Yet, the gradual appearance of difficulties in many states, as well as the lessons learned from expedients resorted to abroad, had unquestionably brought about a considerable change of mentality over large areas of the nation. The "holiday" notion accordingly spread with amazing rapidity, and, at various dates within the two weeks following its appearance, had added to the number of states subject to it, until, on the first of March, it had affected, in one way or another, fully thirty states in seven of which actual bank holidays had been declared.

The legislation which had been adopted in these states—largely without consideration or debate—star chamber proceedings being employed on the pretense that action must be speedy and secret in order to prevent popular panic—was of three major sorts:

1. In some states, as in Michigan, there was a general executive order either preceding legislative action which later legalized it, or preceded by such action, forbidding for a designated period of time local banks, subject to state jurisdiction, to pay out funds at the request of depositors.

2. In other states, legislation enacted, or executive orders issued, permitted banks to notify their depositors at will of a determination not to meet claims of the latter in a proportion greater than that indicated by the degree of liquidity of the bank. In some cases, such a decision was to be reached by the banks acting individually; in others, only with the assent and approval of the local superintendent of banking, or the banking department.

3. In still other states, action was taken designating the percentage up to which depositors might draw, thus specifying the degree of liquidity that was to be considered uniform for the entire body of banks in the state.

It was almost at once evident that such measures involved serious potential difficulties and dangers not apparent on the surface. There was, to begin with, the fact that state authorities were not able constitutionally to dictate to the national banks within their borders the course of action the latter should pursue, while the national banks, themselves, would be committing an act of technical bankrupty were they to follow the lead of the state authorities. In order to rectify this difficult situation, Congress, late in February, 1933, adopted an act in which permission was given to national banks to coöperate with the authorities of states by adapting themselves to local conditions. The Comptroller's office, moreover, issued a proposed draft of a uniform act and recommended it to the various state legislatures should the latter feel inclined to take action toward the establishment of a bank holiday for institutions within their borders.

More important than the legal or constitutional difficulty for which a remedy was thus sought, was the fact that, in many cases, the national banks, or some of them, had no wish to join in the holiday provisions of the localities in which they were situated. They had, in such cases, kept themselves in position to meet all claims to which they might be subject, and they desired naturally to demonstrate to depositors and customers their ability to meet and overcome the obstacles of the time, both as a service to such customers and as an evidence of their own trustworthiness. There followed what was deemed, in some instances, the necessity or desirability of coercing, by various methods, the sounder banks of the community into acceptation of the standard thought essential for the less liquid and less well-managed institutions.

Moreover, there was, in not a few instances, a practical difficulty of management under the new conditions, particularly in those states where a complete or nearly complete suspension of payments had been effected. It was speedily evident that, through lack of currency, the business of several communities was likely to be brought almost to a stop. The issue of some form of local medium of exchange was thus essential, and such a medium was afforded by substitute money of various classes, among which the so-called clearing house certificate, the token, and others of more or less local effectiveness, were conspicuous. It remained true that, as the holiday spread rapidly over the country, there was less and less possibility of maintaining inter-community trading and exchange of goods. A national currency was lacking. This difficulty became more and more pronounced as the suspension became more and more widespread, and eventually reached its climax when the United States itself, on March 5, declared a general banking holiday to last for four days. Events leading up to the latter situation must, however, receive some detailed attention before we go further with the review of the situation created by the holiday.

The proclamation of a national banking holiday by the President of the United States had been preceded by the development of some very serious conditions. Discussion of the necessity and desirability of the holiday, itself, will, in future times, probably center around these conditions. It will have largely to do with the presumed results that may be expected by commentators to have made themselves inevitable, thereby rendering the banking holiday itself more or less unavoidable. Perhaps the most significant of these incidental or ancillary elements in the case was presented by the transfer of funds out of New York to the interior. This factor in the situation needs careful analysis. At the time when the resolution was reached to declare a banking holiday in New York (4:15 A.M. on March 4), it was estimated that the total amount owed by New York banks to correspondents in New York and in other places was about 900 million dollars, and perhaps 800 millions to the out-of-town banks alone. This large amount even represented a drawing-down of about 750 million from the peak which is presumed to have been 1,650 million dollars at maximum (February 1).[3] As interior banks had come to feel the pressure exerted by their depositors more and more keenly, they had been more and more disposed—or had thought themselves compelled—to draw upon their correspondent banks for funds. At the time the bulk of their funds were unquestionably concentrated in New York City; and, hence, a steady call upon New York City banks to supply funds to those in the "country."

It must not be supposed, of course, that New York City banks stood alone in this respect. The larger banks of the country in such cities as Chicago, San Francisco, Kansas City, St. Louis, and others felt the same kind of pressure. But, since they, themselves,

[3] Official figures state "due to banks" by New York at reporting member banks as $690 millions on March 8. This would mean $960 millions total withdrawn.

were in many cases large holders of claims upon New York banks, the tendency was to transfer or "reflect" the pressure from these points in the interior to New York correspondents already referred to. This pressure, then, necessitated realization on the part of the banks which were subjected to it or (what became the same thing) rediscounting with local Federal Reserve banks. However the funds were obtained, they represented a draft made by the larger banks of the various communities, either upon one another (by selling their securities to buyers who paid for them with drafts on their deposits in other banks), or upon the funds accumulated in the Reserve banks.

There was an obvious limit to the extent to which such realization could successfully take place. The attempt to sell securities in the open market has usually driven the price of these securities to low levels, while the attempt to obtain funds through rediscounting at Reserve banks was impeded by the fact that the supply of eligible paper was, in some cases at least, not adequate; in other cases the Reserve banks had begun to fear that they would not be able to continue the extension of accommodation. Some of them had been neglectful and careless in failing to provide themselves with the necessary amount of Federal Reserve notes, so that they were actually unable to meet rediscounting demands intended to increase the supply of currency on hand in local banks. This difficulty of meeting a demand which might run up (as already seen) to as much as 960 million dollars was naturally a serious consideration with the New York banks, and was proportionately so with banks in other centers.

Another factor in the case (which was less conspicuous so far as the average observer was concerned, but which nevertheless was of serious proportions) was furnished by the foreign exchange situation. Payments to foreign countries had for a year or two previously been a serious problem with Federal Reserve banks, as well as with some of the large private banking houses of New York. The demands of the French, Swiss, and Dutch bankers who had been in the habit of holding their reserve balances partly in the form of gold, earmarked, or invested in bankers' acceptances in New York, had led, during the autumn of 1931 and winter of 1932, to a loss of gold amounting to some 750 million dollars. Other shipments of gold had taken place, and while they had been largely restored by imports of other gold (which by January 1, 1933 had brought total gold holdings back near to the level of the beginning of 1932) further large exports of gold repeating the former outflow were very much feared.

It was quite true that the withdrawals made by foreign countries had already so greatly reduced their balances in the United States as to leave the latter far less subject to the danger of export of gold than had previously been the case. However, private investors had (to some extent) likewise become alarmed, and were exporting their capital in the form of gold, a process which, if continued for any great length of time, might result in exhausting the national gold supply. Moreover, large private bankers had, for some time past, been firm in the conviction that the United States would be driven off the gold standard. They had been making foreign commitments in dollars (selling dollars "short," while buying sterling with the proceeds). That is to say, they were becoming large holders of sterling deposits or claims and were paying for them with claims to American gold dollars, a process which meant that they were giving to foreigners the right to draw from the United States a corresponding amount of gold, in excess of the sums which would naturally have been exported as the result of commercial payments, or the withdrawal of foreign balances normally held in the United States.

This situation had thrown Federal Reserve managers into a condition bordering on panic. They had never developed and trained an adequate foreign exchange staff, and were not in a position to undertake, with the prospects of success, dealings which would be necessary if they were to meet and overcome the dangers arising out of this potential drain of gold. Accordingly, the effect of the conditions already described was naturally that of tending to impress Reserve bankers with the desirability of surrendering the gold standard, in fact, by suspending direct gold payments.

A third factor to which attention has already been incidentally given, but which probably deserves more weight than has usually been allotted to it, was furnished by the extensive hoarding of currency, and the substitution of local media of exchange known as "scrip," throughout the country. While there are no authentic figures either as to the amount of scrip thus issued, or as to the total of currency hoarded, it would seem likely that the latter—which had been estimated by President Hoover's administration about a year previously at $1,500,000,000—had fully doubled in amount. The issue of scrip had probably been made in sums sufficient in the aggregate to take the place of the currency withdrawn from circulation. It would not be surprising if a total of one billion in scrip had been actually issued—if we include scrip in the more appropriate sense of the term (clearing-house certificates and other similar expedients). According to report, the New York Clearing House within a few days after the suspension of the banks had printed, and had on hand in warehouse, $100,000,000 of clearing-house certificates.

The effect of these issues in different parts of the country was felt in several ways. On the one hand they tended to make actual currency less necessary and rendered it more mobile, and hence, more likely to be presented for conversion into cash, especially by those who desired to hoard gold. The scrip also tended to inspire distrust on the part of those who were compelled to use it, and hence helped to render the general banking instrumentalities of the country less responsive. Psychologically the reliance upon these expedients operated to reduce confidence in the general solvency of the community. These considerations throw light upon the actual closing of the banks of the country which was finally decreed on the fifth of March, after the change of administration at Washington had become an accomplished fact. The question whether such a closing was or was not "necessary," will, for a long time, be debated. In the following pages, considerations tending to throw light upon the extent of such necessity will be marshaled. It is not necessary at this point to express any opinion upon this subject.

It is, however, evident that the central question regarding American banking was not whether the several state systems would or would not have to close or suspend payments, but was whether the twelve Federal Reserve banks would find it necessary to do so. Granting that they did not encounter or recognize such a necessity, it was equally plain that the action to be taken by the several state systems, or even by the national system, was of secondary importance. Even if the banks of New York City, the chief financial center of the country, found themselves obliged to close, the step thus to be taken was, after all, certain to be of relatively short life and secondary importance, however significant temporarily, or in the "short run," it might be. The Federal Reserve system had been entrusted with the function of maintaining liquidity; and if its constituent member banks were not in position to maintain their own liquidity, the system itself, if able to keep its notes converted into gold on demand, would yet be able to keep the nation upon the gold standard pending the time when a deliberate determination to give up that system of currency might be arrived at. It would, likewise, be able to keep international indebtedness payable in gold, and would, at the same time, enable the government of the United States to meet its obligations in standard coin as it was by every obligation, expressed or implied, moral and actual, in duty bound to do.

Why should not the Federal Reserve system have been successful in meeting such an obligation? The nation, at the opening of March, 1933, possessed fully 40 per cent of the monetary gold supply of the world at large with a total stock estimated officially at about $4,400,000,000. Whether this great figure may be taken as an accurate record of the real stock of gold possessed by the country may be questioned, since it includes a figure, designed to allow for hoarding, whose accuracy is open to considerable doubt. The subsequent deposits of gold made in Federal Reserve banks after the adoption of legislation by Congress, requiring such deposits, has emphasized the uncertainties which previously existed with respect to this point. It is probable that the amount actually held by the United States and its citizens, including the sums hoarded, was not less than $4,500,000,000 at the opening of March, 1933.[4] Of this great sum, two-thirds, approximately, was held in the vaults of Federal Reserve banks which, at the beginning of March, 1933, reported a total of not far from $3,100,000,000 actually on hand. Fears of a European drain, general among reserve bankers during the year preceding, had proven mythical. The close of the year 1932 found the country with fifty millions more gold actually visible than at the beginning, and with unquestionably as much of the metal really in the hands of the public as on the first of January, 1932. The nation was not only strong in gold, but it possessed a favorable trade balance for the year of nearly $300,000,000, had outstanding at least $12,000,000,000 of foreign investments, in addition to the much-discussed war debt, and was in position to collect probably half of the total of the interest nominally produced by its private claims on foreigners.

By discounting and buying immense sums of government obligations in the endeavor to assist the Treasury in keeping outstanding, at low rates, as large a volume of current indebtedness as possible, while at the same time endeavoring to raise prices by adding to the market supply of funds as much free credit as it could command, the Reserve system had, moreover, reduced its potential usefulness to its members. During the late spring and early summer of 1932 it had, against the warnings of all conservative observers, purchased in open market some $1,200,000,000 of government obligations, so that its total stock on hand of such obligations was close to $2,000,000,000 at the end of February, 1933. Its outstanding note issue was steadily increasing, because many creditors of banks, seeing the latter likely to encounter difficulty, and realizing the frozen condition of the reserve institutions, themselves, took occasion to draw upon the former for redemption of deposit claims. In the endeavor to meet such claims, the member banks readily obtained discount accommodation from the reserve institutions, largely against government bonds, partly against the miscellaneous obligations rendered discountable under the terms of the remedial legislation of 1932; and thus, the outstanding volume of Federal

[4] The Federal Reserve Board figure is $4,282,000,000 for March 1933.

Reserve notes had risen at opening of March, 1933, to a total of near $4,000,000,000 (later to $4,293,000,000 on March 15). Further increase of this vast outstanding currency volume was naturally feared by critics. The position, apparently buttressed impregnably by the great gold holding of the system, was, in fact, weakened by the inflation and asset deterioration that had occurred, and there was reason to fear the consequences of the excesses and blunders of management which had characterized past months.

And yet, the status of the Reserve system should have been strong enough to resist any demands originating in the ordinary course of business. Foreign countries were not in position to weaken it. They had already ear-marked about all the gold to which they could successfully lay claim without crippling their American balances. Though it was estimated that net foreign balances totaled, on behalf of foreign creditors of every class, perhaps $750,000,000 at the opening of March, there was little of this sum that could be used as a means of actually withdrawing gold. Already, during the year 1932, the reserve system had withstood drafts of that description, and foreign countries had moved their gold to their own shores, or had deposited it under earmark in New York. The danger lay entirely in the possibility of domestic withdrawals of gold, or in a flight of capital which might result in eventual shipments. Immediate withdrawals for domestic hoarding were, of course, minor in importance.

One other factor was of greater immediate significance. A speculation in foreign exchange had, as seen above, developed during the immediately preceding months, and had resulted in piling up claims for foreign currencies which the reserve bank was finding it needful to meet in earmarked gold. Speculators in New York bought sterling; and the British government, in pursuance of its policy of maintaining a relative degree of stability in the pound sterling, bought the dollars offered for the sterling—almost necessarily so—with the result that they earmarked a corresponding amount of metal. It was here, if anywhere, that the reserve system found itself endangered. Yet, it should have been possible, through the use of central-banking methods—if necessary, with coöperation of the foreign central banks, as in former years—to offset and cancel the effects of such transactions and demands.

Whatever the cause of the action by the reserve system at the time of the collapse of American banking, early in March, it is clear that steps leading to such action were taken by, and with the advice, and probably at the earnest request or even demand, of some, at least, of the reserve authorities. Thus by the morning of the fourth of March, when New York banks (frightened by heavy withdrawals from savings banks and inclined also to fear the effects of interior withdrawals of currency, initiated by interior banks which needed such currency and drew upon their New York balances) demanded a "moratorium" or "holiday," they found the reserve system eager to join them in the disposition to abdicate from duty. The result was the decision, during the early hours of the fourth of March, to close both the Reserve Bank of New York and the local New York banks. This decision immediately resulted in the suspension of all banking activity during Saturday, March 4, and was continued by the President of the United States in a proclamation issued on the night of the fifth of March and effective therefore, at the hour of opening for business on Monday, the 6th.

The proclamation in question was issued by virtue of the existence of the "trading with the enemy act" of 1917, which bestowed upon the President of the United States power to take steps of drastic character because of the then prevailing emergency resulting from the conflict with Germany. The outstanding orders contained in the proclamation in question led to the suspension of gold redemption by closing all banks, including the reserve banks, and to the discontinuance of shipments of gold abroad. It likewise forbade hoarding or retention of gold or gold certificates by individuals, and called for the redeposit of such forms of standard money with the reserve institutions. It declared a national bank holiday for four days; and, Congress then meeting and confirming the powers assumed by the President, the holiday was further continued until the 13th, 14th, and 15th in the case of three different groups of banks into which the banking system of the country had been sub-divided.

Foremost among implications of this policy, of course, was

the practical suspension of the gold standard of the United States, and the bestowal of the quality of irredeemability upon the currency. Next was the closing of the banks of the country. Third in importance was the suspension of many business establishments which found themselves unable to get the funds they needed or even to obtain the use of the actual balances they had on deposit for the purpose of paying workers or purchasing material. The closing was disastrous to the foreign credit of the United States. Inevitably it called attention to the complaints with respect to the management of banking in the United States. It demonstrated, beyond a peradventure, that what had been asserted concerning the dangers inherent in banking as currently conducted under the American system of organization and management prevalent for some years past had been well founded. It called attention to the necessity for some steps designed to bring about a restored condition of solvency, and it emphasized the neglect of which both Congress and preceding administrations since the close of the war had been guilty, in their failure to take the necessary measures of correction. It summoned the nation to action.

CHAPTER II

TEMPORARY REMEDIES

The emergency which had sprung up in American banking, outlined in the previous chapter, necessarily called for instant relief. Inasmuch as the banking system was in suspense, and inasmuch as convertibility into the standard of value, temporarily at least, had been suspended, it was necessary to supply some kind of actual circulating medium, and to afford a means by which, to some extent, the banking system should be enabled to function.

A first care of the new administration at Washington was obviously that of supplying a temporary basis of procedure for business and industry. Several courses of action were evidently possible: (1) to permit local associations of bankers to proceed to the institution of local currencies; (2) to undertake the issue of a national emergency currency which should provide a basis for the doing of business throughout the country; (3) to modify the Federal Reserve Act and to place the Reserve banks in charge of the actual task of supplying a circulating medium, or (4) to issue emergency currency within the Reserve system. All these expedients were apparently given considerable thought by those who were vested with the responsibility at the time. Local clearing-house associations were at first encouraged to issue their own currency, and, as a substitute, the national government considered the propriety and advisability of putting into circulation its own issue of something like clearing-house certificates, or of giving powers of circulation to the clearing-house certificates that were in process of being issued by the associations of the various cities. The final decision, however, to use the facilities and machinery of the Reserve banks was in fact the only feasible one, and the only one likely to supply what was needed.

In reaching this obvious decision several valuable days were lost in choosing between conflicting policies. The national administration, however, eventually submitted to Congress on the ninth of March, a bill to provide for the immediate emergency and designed to accomplish several objects as follows:

1. In the first place, it ratified the acts of the President undertaken since the suspension of the banks, the bank holiday, and the administrative steps that had accompanied them. It renewed and in some particulars extended the powers of the President in these matters and authorized him to take extreme steps against the hoarding or withdrawal of coin from circulation. (Act, March 10, Sec. 1.)

2. It further provided for the issue of new notes to which the familiar title "Federal Reserve Bank Notes," already possessed by an older issue of currency put out by the Reserve banks, was attached. These new bank notes were, like their predecessors, to require no specie reserve and to be issued through Reserve banks in the same way as the old ones. They were now, however, to be issued not only against government obligations but also against almost any other assets of banks that might be considered expedient by reserve banks. (*Ibid.,* Title IV.)

3. The Act further provided for the issue or establishment of a new way of dealing with banks which were in no proper condition to continue in operation. Functionaries were to be named to whom the title "conservators" was assigned. (*Ibid.,* Title II.)

4. In order to provide for the reorganization of banks under conditions which rendered it very difficult, if not impossible, to obtain new capital, the Act permitted the reorganization of the capital structure in such a way as to create an issue of preferred stock, free of double liability and constituting a prior claim upon the assets. The holders of this preferred stock were to be (as a rule) either depositors in the institutions, who converted their claims against it into preferred stock upon terms worked out by agreements, or, in some cases, members of the general public who were induced to supply real cash. It was recognized, however, that in many cases, it would not be possible to obtain the funds needed by either of these methods and, accordingly, the law permitted the making of advances by the Reconstruction Finance Corporation—such advances to be used in the purchase of preferred stock of the banks thus subject to reorganization. (*Ibid.,* Title III.)

There was at first, unavoidably, a considerable amount of uncertainty with reference to the designation of banks which were to be allowed to open, and the segregation of those to whom conservators were to be appointed, or which were to go into receivers' hands. The office of the Comptroller of the Currency was in no condition to give valuable suggestions with reference to the choice of banks for "conservation" because of defective oversight and examination reports. Although some assistance was obtained from the abler of the national bank examiners, it was undoubtedly true that the work of classifying and judging the banks had to be performed with only the most meagre data upon which to found an opinion. Eventually, however, the banks were divided roughly into three general classes:

a) Those which were authorized to open without reservation, and with obligation to pay their depositors in full upon demand; in this class or group of banks the number was probably about 9,000–10,000.

b) A group of institutions which, although under no official control or direction, were permitted to open upon a restricted basis with notice to their depositors that withdrawals must not exceed a specified percentage of the amounts credited to the individual depositor; banks of this class probably numbered about 5,000.

c) A group of banks which was placed in the hands of the so-called "conservators" with instructions to perform certain limited functions and with permission to receive new deposits at the will of depositors; such funds to be kept in cash or invested in government bonds, but in any case to be maintained as a separate and independent fund subject to the orders of the depositor and hence not to be mingled with the other funds of the bank in question. This group of banks probably numbered in the neighborhood of 3,000 to 4,000.

d) Banks finally and definitely closed, numbering about 1,000.

The total thus indicated for all banks was about 18,000–19,000, and is naturally somewhat a matter of conjecture. The official figures furnished by the Comptroller of the Currency during the year 1932 relating to conditions at the end of June of that year, showed a total of 19,163 banks all told, operating under national and state charters and including both national and state private banks and mutual savings banks. Inasmuch as the total number of recorded failures during the remaining six months of 1932 and the first two months (January and February) of 1933 was approximately 1,200, it would seem likely that the total remaining banks technically solvent and still open for business on the first of March, 1933, may have been in the neighborhood of 18,000, a figure which corresponds roughly with the number of banks in the several groupings already indicated.

It is far more difficult to apportion the deposit liabilities of the country among these different classes of banks. Unofficial estimates were made from time to time during the few weeks succeeding the bank holiday and perhaps the best semi-official estimate then furnished was that of taking the total deposit liabilities of the banks of the country as about 40 billion dollars at the opening of March; the close of that month found banks operating unrestrictedly and without limitation representing perhaps 10 billion dollars of demand deposits and 20 billion dollars of time deposits as against previous figures of 14 billion demand and 24 billion of time deposits; the remaining 2 billion as being unclassified. What would seem to be certain was that between 4 and 6 billion dollars of deposits of every kind had been rendered unavailable to the depositors. If we should add to this the deposits which had become only partly available through restrictions upon withdrawals, we shall probably be driven to the conclusion that the figures representing deposits "tied up" or rendered unavailable would need to be increased by fully 50 per cent above the figure prior to the "holiday."

These estimates are necessarily conjectural and approximate, pending the completion of the process of reclassifying banks—a process which required a period of several months for its completion and fulfillment. It is, at all events, beyond question that a very substantial percentage of the immediate buying power of the community represented by deposits in banks had been entirely cut off—certainly for the time being and over an indefinite period, much of it perhaps permanently.

The superficial facts of the situation created by the Government must now be outlined. First of all, the closing of so many banks necessarily left a large number of places—towns and villages—without any banking facilities whatever, while many more were left without adequate banking facilities. This change evidently involved a corresponding change in the type of payment employed by the community. Checks and drafts were evidently unavailable as a means of settlement in communities thus separated from their ordinary credit accommodations. The result necessarily was a considerable enlargement of the extent of reliance on note currency and a tendency to hold note currency in the hands of the population very much longer than would normally have been the case.

This "hoarding," occurring prior to the holiday but increased as it was by the later action of the Government in permanently closing so many banks, had naturally created a need for circulation which had to be met and provided for by the issue of new types of note currency. How the necessity was met will shortly be discussed. At this point it is sufficient only to note that the condition which gave rise to the so-called hoarding tendency was the outgrowth of an important change in the practice of banking and of the methods of transferring goods and services. More important than this change in technique, was the fact that the closing of so many banks not only tended to reduce the amount of physical facilities already practically available, but also had the effect of changing the character of the business of the banks that remained open. This change in the character of business was due to the fact that bank customers were in many cases no longer borrowers on business paper, but, in so far as they borrowed at all, were required to supply collateral. That situation has already been referred to in Chapter I, but requires notice at this point as a phase of the post-holiday changes of banking structure.

Since in many cases, the banks were not willing to lend, even upon such collateral, the banks found a large part of their business consisting in liquidation of paper or securities, either on their own account or for the account of their customers. In not a few cases banks, which were in rather poor condition, continued to feel the withdrawals made by neighboring banks desirous of recovering the full amount of their claims against the weak banks. Even those that were tolerably strong were inclined to maintain themselves in an unnecessarily high condition of liquidity, which, in practice, meant that they refused to advance loans to members of the community who would otherwise have received them. The study of the National Industrial Conference Board shows a very widespread refusal of credit, and this refusal of credit became much more marked after the bank holiday than it had been prior to that date. What was done, therefore, had the effect of tying up not only large quantities of business funds but, also, of putting much larger amounts out of reach by rendering the institutions which controlled them temporarily indisposed to place resources at the service of those who would normally have been borrowers.

Perhaps the most serious phase of the situation was, however, found in the fact that a good many banks which ought not to have been opened at all were allowed to resume business. Many more which ought to have been immediately placed in the hands of receivers in order to liquidate them were given an intermediate status by nominating conservators, who differed from receivers chiefly in the amount of latitude granted them for reorganization of the banks and the addition of new capital. Banks belonging to this category found, in many instances, that it was necessary for them to close once more—this time to remain closed. In most states, the local banking authorities, who had, generally speaking, been granted the power to decide whether given banks were to be reopened or to remain closed, had been too generous or optimistic in their decisions. They accordingly found it necessary to revoke the permission they had granted and to place the banks in the hands of conservators, or, in not a few instances, to order them—as already stated—definitely into the hands of receivers. This necessity of retracing steps already taken, and of reclosing a good many institutions was, of course, tantamount to a confession that mistakes of judgment had occurred, and that it was now necessary to rectify them by adopting an exactly opposite policy. The effect of this conduct on the public was in many instances to destroy its "confidence," and to lead not a few persons to continue the practice of keeping their needed funds in their own hands in the form of circulating notes. As a result, the banking situation soon showed signs of weakening. These were emphasized by several different factors, as follows:

a) It proved extremely difficult to raise new capital in the various localities where such capital was required as a condition precedent to the reopening of banks.

b) In many instances, banks which had reopened found themselves continuously drawn upon by the depositors, sometimes because of lack of confidence and more often because the depositors needed funds for the payment of their own expenses.

c) As a result of this condition, country banks were disposed to draw more or less steadily or heavily upon their city correspondents.

d) Banks in the hands of creditors or conservators, as well, of course, as those in the hands of receivers, found it necessary to arrange, as soon as possible, for at least moderate payments to depositors, and in so doing found it imperative in not a few instances, to try to sell their security holdings on the Stock Exchange. In so far as they were successful, the sales so made were, of course, settled by means of checks on the metropolitan banks, which meant that the latter were steadily called upon to assist in the liquidation of the portfolios of the banks in the country and in the smaller towns. The metropolitan banks were thus steadily weakened as a result of the effort to maintain payments, or declare dividends on behalf of depositors in interior institutions.

e) Because of the reduced state of activity in business, funds paid out to depositors came back very slowly to the banks in the form of new deposits made by manufacturers and others, who would ordinarily have received funds from the community in payment for goods purchased.

It is well to stop at this point to inquire whether the action which had been taken was practically the only course which had been open to the national administration or, if not, what other expedients it might have employed in an effort to combat the disintegrating tendencies that had been at work. As has been seen, in our first chapter, the decision of the New York banks to suspend payments on the third of March practically forced upon the national government the necessity—whether it would or not—of suspending payments for at least a brief banking holiday, so that the question here under discussion may be narrowed for a moment to a consideration of what other remedies might have been applied as compared with those actually undertaken.

The closing of the banks having been rendered unavoidable, the real question at issue was that of determining the conditions upon which a reopening might occur. Obviously the main point involved in this matter was how to secure the continued payment of the deposit liabilities of the banks in as large a proportion as reasonably was to be expected of them. An answer to this question had been afforded tentatively by the so-called "Glass bill," passed by the Senate during the preceding winter (February, 1933) in which it had been proposed that a liquidating corporation be created, with instructions to take over and pay off (in bank credit) deposit claims of all closed institutions. This operation would merely have meant the transfer of the deposit payments of a closed bank to some bank still able to remain open, so that the only difference, so far as the depositor was concerned, would have been the marking down of the face value of the claim from its former amount to a lesser sum set by the extent to which the assets of the original depository bank had depreciated. Failure to make such provision by the Glass bill, or by some other method, implied the limitation of the buying power of the community in the way already indicated. It was a condition such as might, by analogy, have been produced by a surgeon who, after making an amputation, failed to stanch the flow of blood.

The unwholesome conditions existing in the deposit structure of the country might have been reduced, but the reduction was attended by so serious a reflex effect upon the individual that the change gained by the removal was dearly paid for. The action taken, at all events, showed clearly enough, once more, that mere relief measures would not fill the requirements of the existing conditions, and that much more strenuous steps must be taken for the purpose of correcting the underlying difficulties which had themselves been primarily responsible for the evils complained of.

It is now necessary to pause for a moment to glance at the situation as affecting the reserve banking institutions of the country.

CHAPTER III

BASIS OF BANKING

Any survey of banking in the United States or elsewhere, which passes beyond the limits of a mere survey of conditions on the part of individual institutions, early finds itself compelled to take account of some general problems of central banking. These underlie the entire banking problem. According as one or the other of the conflicting analyses or views of the theory by which they are controlled may be accepted, does the individual conclude that banking in general is "sound" or the reverse. This basic factor in the situation calls for a brief statement of the theoretic basis which is thought of as underlying any banking system and of the Reserve system in particular.

Banking is often conceived of as a process of conserving or protecting money, accompanied by the lending of it to borrowers who are then expected to repay it at designated times, and "safety" in banking is by such observers thought of as the making of these loans in such a way as to insure the return of an equal amount of money. In fact there is no basis for any such conception of banking in modern industrial societies, and the present survey of banking presupposes an entirely different view. The essential function of banking, as the industry is today organized, has little to do with money, the connection being found only in the extent to which banking is able to insure conversion of claims into money upon demand. Banking, before business has progressed far, and before industrial civilization has reached a high point, finds itself occupied largely with estimating the relative supplies of, and demands for specified goods, and hence their ability to command other goods in exchange. The banker practically marks supplies of goods with the valuation at which he thinks they will exchange, and he places upon his books a corresponding indication in the form of "deposits" or claims, upon him, which he guarantees by undertaking to keep redeemable upon demand, in money.

According to the success with which he makes his advances and the wisdom with which he selects commodities thus to be offset, one against the other, does he succeed in "clearing" balances on his books without actually resorting to money. His "deposits" are the outgrowth of the recognition of exchange value resultant from, or inherent in, given ownership of goods. His "assets" are the obligations undertaken by his customers to protect him by eventually putting him in funds. Such funds must be equal to the amount that he has guaranteed as the worth of the commodities presented to him as a basis for lending. From this brief survey it is clear that the banker is essentially one who concerns himself with facilitating the movement of goods into actual consumption, the basis of his loans being found in the consuming power of the community. When this consuming power is greatly reduced, the ability of the banker to convert his deposits is correspondingly lessened. Conversely, when the consuming power of the community is increased, goods move more rapidly and prices tend to rise. At such times the banker is likely to think of himself as being able more easily than he expected to meet obligations.

There is another and opposing school of banking thought which has in late years more and more tended to reject this view of the function and duty of the banker. It includes all those who think of the banker as ultimately occupied with the duty of providing capital for production. To those reasoners the soundness of banking seems best tested by the ability of the bank to effect the sale of assets rather than by the ability of bank customers to obtain the liquidation of their holdings of goods. It has been common among writers on banking in recent years to assert that the idea of liquidity in bank assets was largely misconceived, and that the ability to convert bank assets or deposits into money depended upon the maintenance of a satisfactory market for the obligations which the bank was holding. From this point of view it would not have mattered whether a given bank, for example, one lending to the Anaconda Copper Company, let us say, had limited its advances to the amount for which copper in current course of production could unquestionably be sold, or whether the bank had made these loans upon a basis determined by the reproduction, or perhaps cost, value of the plant of the concern. The real test from the standpoint of those who argue that bank soundness depends upon "shiftability" is found in the maintenance of a wide and diversified market for investment securities.

A necessary corollary from this briefly-stated view of conflicting notions of the theory of banking is found in the functions to be assigned to central banking. Those who believe in the older idea of liquidity necessarily view the central bank as having a primary function to perform in the maintenance of a portfolio consisting exclusively, or at least predominantly, of paper growing out of operations of exchange of goods—that is to say, of consumption. Those who believe in the so-called shiftability theory naturally look upon the central bank as having a sound portfolio if the loans it has made are secured by obligations—no matter of what duration—which can undoubtedly be sold at any time for enough to meet the obligations incurred by the borrowers or discounters at Reserve banks. These two points of view, opposed as they are one to another, have been evident in their operation since the organization of the Federal Reserve system. The system, itself, bottomed as it was on British practice and developed upon the basis afforded by British-banking thought, was from the first organized with the idea of banking liquidity as its controlling motive. Its constituent act forbade the making of loans for the purpose of speculation or the carrying of investment securities, and directed that rediscounting by the Reserve banks be done solely for the purpose of effecting the exchange of goods. Indeed, every safeguard that was possible was applied in the framing of the act with a view to preventing it from surrendering the fundamental standard of liquidity to which it had been subjected in the first instance.

The coming on of the World War and the early necessity, to which the Reserve banks were subjected, of devoting themselves almost wholly to the financing of government bonds, forced abandonment of the fundamental theory upon which the system had been organized, and imperceptibly it has shifted the management of Reserve banks away from the older basis, placing it upon the newer foundation of investment banking theory with a portfolio concept dominated by the idea of "shiftability." It was an easy transition, after the war was over, from a portfolio, presumably composed of government bonds purchased at the dictates of "patriotism," and whose liquidity was due to the fact that a nation with large buying and producing power stood ready to support the government by purchasing and holding these bonds, to a situation in which the central-banking system was conceived of as dealing largely in such bonds and in advancing its funds for any purpose for which they might be desired or needed, provided only that such loans were secured or protected by government obligations possessing the theoretical liquidity or convertibility to which reference has just been made. Speculation was thus given an entrée into the Federal Reserve system, and the underlying basis of its existence was altered.

During the decade 1920-1930, Reserve banking authorities seldom allowed themselves to fall back upon, or even to take very seriously, the original principle upon which the system had been organized, and a very large portion of their portfolios came to consist either of securities primarily, or of loans protected by such securities as collateral. The outcome was to make the Reserve banks dependent quite as truly as any other banks upon the ability of the community to purchase, pay for, and hold or absorb issues of bonds, stocks and other securities. Accordingly, when the strength of the financial structure was put to a test, as it was in 1929, the result was to force it to fall back upon a dependence on general conditions in the stock market.

The reasons which give rise to the changes thus indicated in the character of the Federal Reserve system require lengthy and careful survey for their complete comprehension.

Such a survey has been afforded in later chapters of the present volume (Parts V and VI). It is desired here merely to discuss in general terms the effects of the system's policies which had been reflected in this condition immediately prior to the breakdown of 1933. And yet, some brief reference must be made to the underlying factors in the case which motivated the development.

As the change, to which reference has already been made, gradually came about in the structure of the Federal Reserve system, the character of its portfolio necessarily underwent considerable alteration. There had been an assumption in official quarters, for many years, that it was safe and prudent for banks to engage their resources very largely in loans upon stock exchange securities, provided only that these loans were well protected, and that a large margin of safety was preserved between the nominal face amount of the loans and the technical quoted value of the securities by which they were protected.

True, this point of view had never been openly accepted by the Federal Reserve system. In the original Federal Reserve Act, the conception of banking liquidity as the outgrowth of loans based upon consumption needs represented by "self-liquidating paper" had been accepted, and during the first years of the system had been adhered to. The financing of the World War had necessarily brought a great change into this type of central-banking practice, since it had inevitably made the portfolios of the Reserve banks to consist largely of the Government's own paper or of obligations of member banks with Government bonds used as collateral. When the war was over the Federal Reserve Board and the Treasury authorities of that period did endeavor to improve the portfolios of both the Reserve banks and the member banks, and had partially succeeded in doing so.

The result was that after the commercial crisis of 1920-1921, Reserve banks found themselves in a comparatively liquid condition with relatively small portfolios of government paper and with a continuous inward flow of gold which tended very strongly to promote the strength of their position. The volume of their business, however, tended to be small. Controlled as they were by the desire to exert a large influence in the market and to exhibit large profits from year to year (a habit which had become confirmed during the war years), the Reserve banks now began to give themselves more and more to the financing of speculation. Such operations had been, as we have seen, prohibited under the Federal Reserve Act, but that act had left a technical loophole by permitting Reserve banks to finance to any extent the paper of the government.

In 1916, upon the pretense that the legislation would merely advance the technical convenience of the members of the system, the Reserve Board had given its assent to, and had obtained the enactment of, a proposal originating in New York City by which member banks were allowed to borrow from Reserve banks upon their own direct notes with eligible paper used as collateral instead of discounting the paper in the usual way. The effect of this war-time change was to permit a great growth of direct member-bank notes secured by government obligations, and after the war, with the public debt of twenty-seven billion dollars outstanding and widely diffused, it was a strong temptation to the Reserve banks to continue discounting such member-bank obligations with government collateral regardless of the purpose of the loan. As a result these obligations had come to constitute the accepted vehicle through which the Reserve banks advanced funds for the financing of speculative stock market transactions.

The years 1921-1929 were years of tremendous stock market expansion and they were also years in which enormous loans were made by American citizens to foreigners for the purpose of upbuilding and reconstructing the business of these foreign countries. Individuals and corporations came more and more to avoid borrowing at banks, and to substitute therefor the practice of providing themselves with working capital in the stock market. In a large majority of cases, the securities so issued were not paid for, but were "carried" by means of bank loans, and it was suggested that such carrying was unavoidable—that it indeed, represented a "new era" in American finance. This new era was to be one in which the business enterprise would no longer be dependent upon the bank, and would resort to the public in order to satisfy its needs for capital, while the public in meeting these requirements, would at the same time establish a claim upon the profits of industry, thereby theoretically becoming partners in the enterprise. The shallowness of all this hasty explanation is now sufficiently apparent, but it needs to be remembered that during the years in question, the lines of reasoning thus developed had become widely accepted, and the premises upon which they were based had taken deep root in public opinion.

As a result the great change already referred to, in the composition of the portfolios of member banks throughout the country, had become definitely confirmed. This change was most concretely represented by the growth, in many banks, of large holdings of securities, often found upon examination to consist of second-grade bonds and, in some cases, where state laws permitted it, of stocks. Some larger banks which had become deeply engaged (with the Federal Reserve banks) in the issuance of acceptances which, during the year just before the panic of October, 1929, had come to include not less than $1,600,000,000 of paper, most of it, at times, in the hands of the Reserve system, were finding their portfolios largely occupied with these acceptances, with loans upon direct paper offered by member banks which meant, in effect, on government securities, and with obligations of a contingent sort, which, if actually presented by foreign creditor countries, must necessarily have brought severe pressure to bear upon the Reserve institutions. All this may be briefly summed up in the statement that between 1921 and 1929 the Reserve system was in the singular position of having an enormous gold reserve, both absolutely and relatively, while at the same time its assets consisted of values which in the last analysis, were of doubtful liquidating power. At the time of the panic of 1929, and the tremendous shifts and changes which occurred as a result of the vast alterations in the stock market, the weakness of the system became fully revealed. The larger banks for themselves endeavored to stabilize the stock market to a certain small extent, but their efforts were ineffectual, and the reserve banks were obliged to play a considerable part in assisting banks to care for the needs of their customers, by lending to them and by buying back government securities from bankers who needed to realize cash.

An attempt to restore "prosperity" by cutting discount rates was undertaken as soon as the first force of the panic had passed by, and eventually resulted in bringing down the rediscount rate at the Reserve Bank of New York to 1.5 per cent. With corresponding decreases at the Reserve banks of the interior, acceptance rates likewise fell to very low figures and every effort was made to induce the member banks to maintain, in some measure at least, the large amount of extensions of credit which they had previously carried. This policy, however, was unsuccessful, and the business paper of the member banks fell away rapidly; at the same time, the amount of their rediscounts at the Federal Reserve banks likewise declined. In the years 1930-1931, the business of the Reserve system came to consist very largely of loans upon government securities accompanied by very large holdings of the same kind of paper, although outstanding acceptances continued substantially large in amount up to the middle of the year 1931.

The fallacious view that it was the duty of the Reserve banks to assist the market by pushing out credit through what were called "open market purchases" had been widely preached both by bankers and politicians, and as a result, Reserve institutions found themselves constantly importuned not only to keep rates low but also to buy heavily in the open market. After the collapse of German credit in July, 1931, and again after the abandonment of the gold standard by Great Britain in September of the same year, the policy of the Reserve banks in these particulars became more and more positive and well-marked. The situation was masked, to a considerable degree, by the presence of the large gold holdings already described, while the discouragement of the community with the stock-market prospects led to a decided falling off of speculative demand and inability on the part of the Reserve system to stimulate an improvement of sentiment and of borrowing.

The question was asked throughout the bank holiday and in the period of difficulty which preceded it: "Has not the Reserve banking system the strength to assist the existing banks out of their present difficulties? Was not the system created for that express purpose, among others? Is it not true that the Reserve banking system is the possessor of a large portion of the monetary gold in the world? Should it not then be in a position to assist in alleviating, if not actually warding off, dangers to the banking system already manifested?" These questions were reiterated during the bank holiday, by reason of the fact that the holiday had affected not only so-called "weak" banks but all others, so that the query rose in many minds whether the difficulties from which the nation was suffering were not probably the result of faulty structure rather than of localized bad banking. These questions must be answered in the future by those who attempt to reason about the banking features of the year 1933. A short sketch of the conditions existing in the Reserve system at the time of the breakdown is therefore essential. It involves a brief reference to matters already described which must now be reviewed from another angle.

Withdrawal of gold, accompanied by revival of hoarding and great shifts of capital, characteristic in Europe after the breakdowns in Germany and in England, had more or less spread to the United States, where hoarding began to develop itself on a very definite basis during the latter part of the year 1931. A sharp run on the gold of the Reserve system grew out of the effort of France to take home that part of her reserve of the metal which had been invested in this country in acceptances, and the outcome was the loss of more than seven hundred million dollars of gold by the Reserve system during the autumn of 1931 and spring of 1932. The middle of 1932 found the Reserve system's gold depleted and a substantial amount of hoarding in progress throughout the country, partly due to doubt and dissatisfaction with the business situation, partly the result of lack of confidence in the government, but fundamentally the consequence of the policy of the Reserve banks and the habit of pushing credit out into use through the purchase of government bonds. Deficits in the public treasury, which had become pronounced in 1931, grew to tremendous proportions during 1932. The deficit for the fiscal year 1932 amounted to close to three billion dollars. The Treasury Department was unwilling to borrow on long term, and consequently supplied its needs by borrowing from member banks—the Reserve banks being then called upon to support the bonds by free rediscounting and by extensive open market operations.

These conditions inevitably tended, more and more, to weaken the position of the Reserve banks; and when, in the spring of 1932, it was announced that the necessities of the Treasury and the constantly declining course of commodity prices had led the Reserve institutions to undertake the policy of open-market operations, already sketched, on a larger scale than ever before, the announcement was received with apprehension by many thoughtful observers. We have already noted that, during the months of April, May, and June, 1932, the Reserve banks purchased nearly $1,200,000,000 Government securities and paid for them in the form of credits on their books.

It is now appropriate to note some credit results of this open-market policy. As the funds could not be used by the member banks in loans to customers, owing to the continuous decline in the volume of business, the effect of the policy of the Reserve banks was to create a large body of so-called "excess reserves"—book balances which they were carrying in favor of their member banks and which the latter might have used as they saw fit, at any time. They were in fact expected to use these reserves in larger loans to customers, which the latter did not demand. This was not a healthy state of affairs. It led neither to advance in commodities nor in securities. Excess reserves were further aggravated by the fact that gold was again flowing back to the United States, after the tremendous withdrawals of which we have already spoken, and, by the close of the year 1932, the Reserve banks held very nearly as much as they possessed at the opening of the year, their total stock of the metal on January 1, 1933, being approximately three billion dollars, while their reserve ratio was in the neighborhood of 65 per cent. There was an excess of "credit"—largely nonliquid—and a decline of borrowing demand.

It was with these conditions prevalent that the Reserve system entered the year 1933. As we have just seen, the system had recovered its gold and was now in possession of as large a stock as it had, with one or two exceptions, ever had. It was overburdened with government obligations, and with loans of member banks based upon such obligations. On the other hand, the great withdrawals of gold had reduced the balances held by foreign countries in the United States and, hence, had correspondingly lessened their power to draw gold away from the United States. The total of American securities said to be in possession of foreigners at the close of 1932 was estimated at approximately $2,500,000,000, whereas American claims upon foreign countries, even after the great transformations of preceding years, must have been easily four times that amount without regard to the so-called war debts totaling, it appeared, well toward twelve billion dollars or more. Moreover, the United States, in spite of all the vicissitudes of foreign trade, had maintained a so-called "favorable" merchandise balance, and was in position to enlarge this balance still further whenever it chose, by the establishment of less onerous conditions for the governing of international business. The position was thus strong, although vitiated in many ways by the open market policy which had the habit of protecting speculative borrowers when and as required, and the constant burden of the Treasury and its financing which had grown more and more onerous as the months had gone by. Under such conditions, the Reserve system approached the end of February, at which time it was to be subjected to the final test imposed by the coming bank holiday.

There is no conclusive evidence that the bank holiday had been for some time definitely contemplated by Federal Reserve banks, or that any particular preparation for it was made. Nothing in the statements of the Federal Reserve Board or the Federal Reserve banks—either public or private—indicated any consciousness of the seriousness of the situation. When the breakdown first occurred in Michigan, as has already been mentioned, the local Reserve bank (Chicago district) found itself unable or indisposed to assist to any great extent, and short of actual supplies of notes with which to meet the emergency to which it was exposed.

Other Reserve banks were not in a position to be of much assistance. They had already been greatly enlarging the note issue in response to the demands of their members, who, in order to fulfill the necessities of customers, resorted to the Reserve banks for accommodation, and obtained it through the issue of notes which they speedily paid out to such customers.

Reserve banks had not anticipated any such development, and they even found themselves short of notes at the time when the crisis came on. It was necessary in not a few cases for them to pay out gold certificates, although they had previously been using every effort to get in these certificates. Such paper payments were made because the gold certificates were actually available and could be used to satisfy the demand for currency, notwithstanding the fact that the Reserve banks regretted the necessity of disbursing them because they were claims upon gold.

As a result of all these factors, toward the end of February, the Reserve ratio tended to sink very markedly and fell temporarily, far below the legally established 40 per cent required of Reserve banks as the proportion necessarily to be borne by gold on hand to outstanding circulating notes. It was in these circumstances that the Reserve system finally came face to face with the question of a national moratorium or suspension of banking payments.

The question whether the Reserve banking system "ought" to have "gone off gold" along with the other banks, and the allied question whether it "could" have maintained its responsibility for redemption independently, will undoubtedly long be debated as the crux in the recent banking history of the United States. It is a question which cannot be settled offhand, but which must be dealt with as the result of thorough analysis of the policies of the Reserve system over a long period of years. Such opinions are never to be regarded as the outgrowth of immediate or standard performance but they must be treated as the product of circumstances slowly maturing and gradually developing themselves in connection with business changes.

CHAPTER IV

BANKING REFORM AND BANKING LEGISLATION

The general condition of banking in the United States which has been set forth in the foregoing pages obviously offers many problems of a pressing nature. Dispassionate review of these problems will undoubtedly produce the conviction, in some cases, that they have been the outgrowth of changing economic conditions, and of new relationships in business and in trade, as a result of which there has been a reorganization and readjustment of such relationship; but, while considering this "natural" character of a part, at least, of what has taken place, fair review of the situation will also bring the conviction that many of the problems that we now encounter in American banking have not been unavoidable, but have been the outgrowth of hasty legislation, undue concessions to special interests, and inadequate supervision on the part of those entrusted with the control and regulation of banking.

To those who recognize any measure of truth in the general indictment of the situation thus outlined, the question must naturally occur: Why it is that the United States, perhaps the wealthiest country in the world, perhaps also that country in which the widest distribution of income has taken place, should have suffered particularly from such adverse conditions? A glance around the world shows clearly that, while there have been many countries which have suffered from depreciated currency, unstable exchange, repudiation of debts, and general economic disturbances, there is none possessed of anything like the wealth of the United States, or even, advantageously situated, that has ever thought itself subjected to any such necessity. In many ways, the condition of banking in the United States is unique, and the wonder that nothing should have been done to check the advent of the state of affairs thus depicted must be correspondingly unique. It is, therefore, worthwhile to note, in a general way, what are the principal factors that control banking legislation in the United States; and the principal obstacles in the way of obtaining sound and satisfactory action. To this may then be added a survey of the most recent legislation of Congress, designed to set forth the real conditions as they exist at the present moment, as a result of current action on the part of the legislative body.

In most countries, legislation on the subject of banking—a technical and highly specialized occupation—originates in one of two ways. It may, first of all, be proposed by the administration of the country. In parliamentary nations, where the members of the cabinet are, from time to time, drawn from the legislative body, the latter then remaining, in effect, a controlling factor to which the various political groups must report and be responsible, it has been the custom to frame codes of financial and banking legislation which are then submitted to the legislative body for adoption. In some other countries, of which Canada may be taken as an example, the banking community itself succeeds in exercising a general jurisdiction over the conditions that surround its own operation; and has the wisdom, from time to time, to acquiesce in changes designed to give the public what may be demanded by circumstances, even though such changes may not always appear advantageous to the members of the banking community itself. The decennial revision of the Canadian Banking Act has tended to keep that document up to date, and to fit it for use as a reliance by the community, in the belief that evils or defects in it, when detected, will be rather promptly overcome and rectified, through the incorporation of remedial measures at the time of the next revision.

In the United States, we have not been willing to assent to either of these methods. A review of American financial legislation from the Civil War down to 1933, reveals not a single occasion upon which the Federal administration has projected and brought before the legislative body any major change in the fundamentals of currency or banking or both, or has secured the adoption of such legislation. On the other hand, American bankers have practically never been willing to agree among themselves upon necessary changes in banking laws, or to assume the position of sponsoring or advocating such changes. The American Bankers' Association has seldom, if ever, taken any position with regard to banking laws except to oppose or antagonize what was being proposed, and though it has actually at times given its endorsement to some measure of a partial or limited sort, the Association has often reversed its position; in other cases it has been obliged to admit the existence of a very representative minority whose point of view was far from coinciding with that of the larger body of members. All this may be summed up in the statement that, while American bankers have usually had a very great negative influence upon Federal banking legislation, they have not, for many years, exerted any constructive influence, or shown any initiative in recommending or bringing to the statute books, decisive measures of legislation.

The consequence of this situation has been that banking legislation in the United States has been sporadic—a thing of shreds and patches—sometimes good, but more frequently ill-adapted to its purpose or incomplete in its operation. In the case of most of the major legislation of recent years, a beginning has been made by some group of special interests, usually masked behind a body of "business men"—sometimes subsidized by the banks of the country—sometimes by other elements. Occasionally members of Congress, impressed by the necessity of change in legislation, have exerted themselves to secure the enactment of measures which, in thir opinion, would tend to promote a better state of affairs. The Federal Reserve Act was the outgrowth of such an endeavor on the part of members of Congress, although it would probably never have reached the statute book had it not been for the whole-hearted support of President Woodrow Wilson. The Banking Act of 1933 was, in like measure, the product of a very small number of persons not engaged in business or in banking, but chiefly interested to secure a helpful improvement in banking law.

It is easy to see how this characteristic method of banking legislation, prevalent in the United States, has tended to bring about the conditions which exist at the present moment. Not for many years has it been possible to carry through Congress any enactment which did not, in some measure, succeed in uniting the different factions or conflicting groups of interests behind it. When there has been a sufficient agreement among opposing groups to permit the formulation and introduction of legislation, it has usually been necessary to make concessions—sometimes of a dangerous and injurious sort—sometimes of a kind which merely postponed necessary reform, or which rendered the proposed legislation ineffectual. Thus, for example, in the Federal Reserve Act, it was thought unavoidable to placate banking institutions by granting to members the right to take savings deposits (time deposits), and to engage in fiduciary operations. The Banking Act of 1933, in like measure, was obliged to include a joint guarantee of bank deposits at the last moment as the price of the enactment of any corrective or restrictive clauses in the law.

From all this, the inference must be drawn that banking legislation in the United States is seldom, if ever, able to go to the root of the problems at which it aims; and is usually blocked of its main purpose by the unfortunate necessity of admitting concessions in its terms which go far toward nullifying the benefits of other portions of the law, or which in some cases absolutely run counter to successful administration of it. Coming sporadically, and depending upon the necessity for the expression of sudden public opinion in its favor, as it thus does, American banking legislation is often ill-timed, inadequate, and not especially well adapted to the situation which it contemplates, and, generally speaking, given to compromises in its terms.

A survey of the factors entering into the framing of American banking legislation would, moreover, be incomplete, if it omitted to recognize the fact that in American politics there has always been a set of primary popular ideas or prejudices which have been quite as consciously used for the purpose of directing national public opinion and of inducing it to work along specified lines. One such shibboleth is found in the idea of monopoly. For many years past politicians have been in the habit of appealing in every way possible to the fears of the rank and file of the American public with regard to the danger of monopoly, or of acquisition of power by special interests. The so-called "anti-trust agitation," in many of its extreme or absurd manifestations, hostility to any kind of centralization of capital or control, and the opposition to equity in the taxation of "creditor classes," all furnish illustrations of these varying methods of appealing to public prejudices, which have been widely availed of in the course of our banking development, as well as in connection with other movements.

To the growth of prejudice of this kind, may be attributed, for example, the antagonism largely felt toward branch banking, the widespread objection to central banking of any kind, overcome only after the utmost difficulty at the time of the passage of the Federal Reserve Act, the prejudice against really vigorous and stringent examination of banking institutions, and the preferential treatment of local bankers, notwithstanding their methods have been open at times, to question on the ground of honesty, or on the ground of legality. The result has been that, in the American banking system, have been perpetuated many long-existing abuses, evils and unscientific phases, all of which have tended greatly to restrict the development of correct methods of enforcement of sound professional ethics. Notwithstanding these conditions, there is probably no country of the world in which there is a greater approach to the real existence of a so-called "money trust" than the United States. Nor is there any country in which there is less assurance of nonpartisanship and fairness in the extension of credit by banks to individuals or corporations.

To these facts almost all business men bear witness—although seldom willing to express themselves in public—while the history of Congressional legislation shows the actual technique by which desirable legislation is so emasculated as to make it worse than nothing. It is seldom that there can be any actually frank Congressional debate upon currency or banking questions, viewed from the standpoint of merit; and, in recent years, most such discussions have been largely personal recriminations or an appeal to prejudice based on "anti-trust" and other allied ideas, or an effort to stir up popular prejudice or imaginary fears of one sort or another. For many years it was the practice of the banking community to secure the "pigeon-holing," or ignoring, of new legislation by the familiar methods of legislative obstruction and control.

When these forms of opposition lost their force or were unsuccessful, proposed changes of law were often either referred to committees around which special interests clustered, or they were made by legislators who were determined to prevent any further growth or development of arguments of the kind thus contemplated. In other cases, such legislation was allowed to reach a fairly advanced stage, and then was called up for "hearing" before some committee, at which time a joint onslaught by banking interests developed for the purpose not of improving or strengthening the legislation, but merely of rendering it ridiculous, or at any rate unpopular, and of relegating it to the background. Recent legislation is full of illustrations of this sort, one or two of which will presently be considered.

The question is thus seriously raised whether it may not be possible, at some early date in the future, to bring about definite self-conscious action on the part of the political authorities in connection with duly constituted representatives of the various banking interests, for the purpose of considering and definitely agreeing upon, proposed changes in legislation, with a view to having such changes specifically debated before the legislative body and either defeated or adopted as the result of evidence and argument, rather than through political trickery or dissimulation. Such a result can be brought about only through the establishment of some recognized agency, authorized to speak for the financial community, in coöperation with an administration which regards itself as definitely called upon to take the helm, and give expression to enactments which are neither "radical" nor "protective" with regard to favorite interests, and which are intended to bring about a stronger, better, and generally more efficient, financial structure. How this situation may be realized is a question which embodies and consolidates the various aspects of the so-called "banking problem" into one.

Most persons recognize that, in a very unusual degree, the

panic of 1929 was the outgrowth of bad management of credit, and of the banking institutions through which credit was developed and applied. Even those who shared most freely in the debauch of speculation which preceded 1929 were willing enough to admit, in private discussion, the fact that essential changes were called for in the structure of American banking. When admitting such necessity, however, these same interests were usually inclined to say, frankly, that it was their desire to defer any action on it as long as possible, because of the fact that even the discussion of legislation tended to "upset" conditions and to throw the market into a fever of uncertainty. From such uncertainty it could emerge only with considerable damage, or, perhaps, be subjected to discredit which would result in the collapse of values. Because of this attitude, not merely on the part of the rank and file of bankers, both "commercial" and "investment," but also of political and other leaders, as well as of the community at large, it was never possible during the decade 1919 to 1929, to secure any extensive and thorough attention in Congress whatever for pending banking problems.

The two outstanding enactments of those ten years were the Agricultural Credits Act of 1923, and the so-called McFadden Act of 1927, the former designed to establish a hybrid type of short-term agricultural credit lending institution whose major effect was to deepen and further the confusion and danger already existing in agricultural lending, while the purpose of the McFadden Act was that of providing a means for the splitting up of bank stocks or the declaring of stock dividends by banks, and thus the furtherance of speculation, while at the same time feeding the general speculative mania by admitting commercial banks to the investment banking business, and permitting them to engage a substantial part of their savings (time deposits) in loans upon real estate. These two enactments—the one belonging to the administration of President Harding, and the other to that of President Coolidge—must be regarded as nothing more than the surface manifestations of speculation and unsound financial demands.

Of the various amendments to the Federal Reserve Act

adopted during the ten years in question, there was not one which was calculated to strengthen the legislation or to protect public or private credit against attack. On the contrary, practically all were designed to weaken the protection of the banking system at some point, and to subject it to risk or hazard in the effort to grant greater latitude in the borrowing of funds for speculative purposes, or in the easing of restrictions already resting upon the banking institutions.

It was thus without any support or assistance from the financial community, and certainly without any from the then national administration, that the United States Senate passed in July, 1930, a piece of legislation entitled "Senate Resolution No. 71," which had been introduced some weeks previously by Senator Carter Glass, of Virginia, and had been favorably reported by the Senate Banking Committee. The legislation in question authorized the Committee to undertake an official investigation into the general financial situation, and to engage the services of experts and otherwise to provide itself with facilities for forming a judgment upon existing banking conditions with a view to recommending such legislation as might be deemed necessary for their correction and improvement. The Committee was given power to subpoena persons and papers, and generally to do all that was necessary to make its inquiries effective. Acting under the terms of this resolution, the Committee named a subcommittee of which Senator Glass was named Chairman, and of which the chairman of the General Committee was an ex-officio member; and this subcommittee initiated and carried on a series of hearings during the months of January and February, 1931.

It also sent to bankers throughout the country, as well as to others who were likely to be possessed of the necessary information, a list of questions designed to elicit the information required by the Committee in the course of its investigations, and presumably to be helpful in the formulation of a piece of legislation intended for presentation to Congress. The hearings included three general classes of witnesses. First of all, an attempt was made to obtain the opinions of the administrators of Federal Reserve banks with regard to the working of those banks themselves and with reference to the existing relationships between them and their members. With a view to obtaining full information on this subject, a very thorough questionnaire was sent to each Federal Reserve bank, and was answered by each, the replies being thus embodied in a separate brochure which appeared as part of the hearings subsequently published. Certain officers of the Federal Reserve banks were then called to the witness stand, while those who had expressed a desire to be heard also were given the opportunity to testify. The hearings concerning the Federal Reserve system, opened with these official and semi-official witnesses, to whom were added the Comptroller of the Currency.

It is worthy of record at this point that the order of witnesses at the hearing was not the result of the decision of the Committee, but of the wish expressed by members of the Federal Reserve Board to give their testimony prior to the hearing of statements of officers of any Federal Reserve banks. The members of the Board were particularly desirous of stating their views with respect to the policy of the Board, and through it of the Federal Reserve system, with regard to the control of credit during the years 1927-1929—the period during which the panic of 1929 was in the process of developing. Unquestionably, it was their feeling that they had been subjected to severe popular criticism, and also that the officers of sundry Federal Reserve banks had directly and indirectly propagated in the public mind an attitude of unfriendliness or criticism toward the Federal Reserve Board. It was their thought, through a public and systematic setting forth of what they had done, to bring about a more correct public understanding of the real elements of the problem of Federal Reserve credit as presented during the years in question.

Although not directly expressing the desire to be heard, it was also clear that the Comptroller of the Currency felt it incumbent upon himself to offer some kind of explanation of the remarkable record of bank failures which, though the climax was not yet reached, was already so far advanced as to receive the attention of the entire civilized world and to be regarded by thoughtful men as one of the major contributing causes of the panic of 1929. The first group of witnesses, then, consisting of Federal bank administrators and officials of reserve banks, may be regarded as having provided, in conjunction with the elaborate questionnaire already referred to, the basis for a knowledge of the conditions, both superficial and underlying, that control in the Federal Reserve system.

A second group of witnesses included the actual managers or responsible officers of so-called "stock exchange banks," the banks which had been primarily concerned in the use of commercial bank funds, for the purpose of promoting stock exchange and other speculation and which, through the organization of auxiliary corporations (the so-called "affiliates"), had been successful in avoiding or evading the prohibitions of the national banking law and of the Federal Reserve Act in their application to investment banking and to securities speculation. In conjunction with this group of witnesses, the Committee had likewise sent out a set of questionnaires addressed to the principal banks throughout the country, which were then concerned in the operation of the so-called affiliates. In these questionnaires, an immense amount of data relating to actual transactions, losses, profits, and stock market relationships had been accumulated, although published without the actual names of the enterprises from which they were gathered, or of the persons concerned in the management and operation of such enterprises.

A third group of witnesses included outside experts, economists, and authorities upon various phases of the banking situation, and might be regarded as having viewed the developments from an impersonal and more or less impartial standpoint. These, therefore, were presumably in a position to express an authoritative opinion, without bias, upon various measures that might be taken with a view to the introduction of satisfactory legislation for correcting the most outstanding evils that might be regarded as having led up to the panic of 1929. Along with the testimony of these witnesses, there was received by the Committee the results of several other questionnaires sent out to appropriate persons and designed to ascertain the actual facts with regard to the study of banking portfolios, the control and examination of banks, and a variety of other matters.

It was upon the basis of the information thus collected that the Subcommittee of the Senate Banking Committe began its work.

The method of working pursued by the Committee is now worthy of careful review. Since it was not desired to carry into effect the preconceived ideas or prejudices of any member of the Committee or of its staff, but rather to formulate and project a law which would correspond in general terms to the existing requirements of the banking system, and would hold out some promise of general correction of evils, it was plain that the first necessary step was to be found in an analysis of the testimony that has been furnished, or received by, the Committee, and of the data collected by it; and that if possible, this analysis should be so framed as to indicate the causes or factors to be regarded as chiefly instrumental in bringing on the panic of 1929, thereby suggesting their own remedies.

At the same time, it was regarded as the duty of the Committee to make a complete and careful list of the suggestions, ideas for legislation, or remedial action that had been brought before it, either in the open or public hearings or in executive hearings, or through communications received by members of the Committee from private persons.

We may now devote ourselves, first of all, to a review of the analysis made by the Committee and its counsel. The first point to which this análysis was naturally directed has to do with the actual condition of credit, and the trend of its development during the post-war period in which the conditions that gave rise to the panic of 1929 had developed. In analyzing this condition of credit, through the study of the data already referred to, the Committee found practically no disagreement among the different classes or groups of witnesses when the testimony was stripped of all evasion and qualification. The witnesses agreed that there had been, during the years in question, a very serious and widespread misapplication of banking credit or, in other words, a use of banking loans and advances which, if made with a foresight developed in accordance with the known principles of sound banking, would not have been sanctioned. This misapplication of credit, according to the testimony, had taken shape chiefly in the following ways:

a) Through the application of bank funds in over-large quantities to the actual purchase of long time securities.

b) Through the creation of large "lines" of credit based upon securities owned or partly owned by bank borrowers.

c) Through the inordinate enlargement of "brokers' loans" —a form of advance made by banks upon stock exchange securities as collateral in favor of brokers who expected to lend the funds thus acquired to their customers upon margin, in order to enable the latter to engage in further speculation.

d) Through the extension of an excessive amount of consumers' credit by the discounting of paper growing out of sales made upon the "instalment plan." Such credit was found to have been advanced in some industries, especially where financial organization had been developed for the purpose of furnishing the basis for protecting the loans so made; the result being to consolidate great quantities of claims upon future income in the form of nominally liquid paper which, however, depended entirely upon the maintenance of the current flow of incomes and wages.

e) Through the misuse of the so-called bankers' acceptance which, originating as a means of guaranteeing the soundness and liquidity of actual available paper representing exchange, had come to represent what were practically collateral loans placed upon goods largely in storage at home or abroad.

f) Through the extension of enormous lines of credit upon real estate security of one sort or another, sometimes in the form of loans upon bonds, and sometimes in the form of purchases of real estate, and at other times through the discounting of paper based upon direct real-estate mortgages.

The effect of this misapplication of credit was reflected, according to the data placed before the Committee and as interpreted by it, in two ways:

1. The enlargement of the outstanding "total deposits" of the

banks from a figure of less than $13,000,000,000, in 1920, to a figure of over $21,000,000,000 at the close of the year 1929—ten years later; and

2. In the shifting of an immense proportion of this deposit line out of the form of "demand" and into the form of "time," deposit liabilities; whereas, the time deposits which had constituted 26 per cent of the total at the beginning of 1920, constituted 34.5 per cent at the end of the period closing 1929.

With reference to the sources of this credit—which had figured so largely in the creation of "frozen assets"—the data furnished the Committee appeared to indicate three major origins, as follows:

a) The inflow of an immense amount of gold from abroad, representing payments made to cover the difference between exports of all kinds and imports of all kinds. This growth in gold holdings carried the total from $2,400,000,000 at the beginning of 1920, to $4,400,000,000 at the end of 1929.

b) The "release" of reserves, producing potential expansion of credit by the shifting of deposits from the "demand" form to the "time" form; (reserves against demand deposits being 7, 10, and 13 per cent according to the location of the bank, while against time deposits they were uniformly 3 per cent).

c) The gradual evolution of methods of avoiding the maintenance of any excess reserves, as for example, through the establishment of a market for "Federal funds," in which those banks which had surpluses of reserves mutually sold such surpluses to banks that were deficient, thereby spreading out reserve balances and keeping them close to the minimum line required by law.

d) Adoption by the Reserve banks of a policy of hoarding gold and keeping it away from the public. This, although not consistently followed throughout the whole period (being sometimes interrupted by an equally lax disposition to pay out gold or its representatives) was, nevertheless, characteristic of reserve policy, and had the effect of withdrawing gold from circulation, and thereby of establishing an unnaturally large bank reserve, with the corresponding tendency to build up thereon an undoubtedly inflated body of credit obligations.

A review of changes in the banking structure which had taken place during the preceding decade, as studied by the Committee, seems to show that the following outstanding alterations had taken place:

a) An extraordinary drift toward reduction in the number of banking institutions from a maximum of about 31,000 in the year 1921 to a total of about 22,000 at the end of 1929.

b) A tendency to increase the number of large-sized institutions as a result of mergers, frequently brought about for purely stock-jobbing purposes, with a view to making profits through the expansion of the values of bank stocks.

c) The transference of bank stocks from the position of closely-held, slow-moving, conservative investments to the position of a speculative, low-priced (the Act of 1927 permitted banks to cut down the par value of their shares and not a few reduced it to as low as $10), rapidly-shifting medium of semi-gambling transactions—few stock holders paying much attention to the rates of dividend but being concerned chiefly in the great fluctuations of quoted values which had been brought about.

d) The gradual growth of branch banking upon a very limited scale within the areas to which it had been confined by provisions of law.

e) The introduction of what was known as "group banking" or ownership of banks by holding companies, thereby resulting in making such banks mutually interdependent; hence, in certain circumstances, especially liable to failure.

f) The establishment of "affiliated" companies, organized under state law and designed to permit banks with which they were connected to undertake banking transactions of various kinds quite evidently outside of the intended scope of the National Banking Act or of contemporary state banking laws.

Summed up, these changes in structure might be regarded as simply indicating a trend toward a more speculative, less responsible, and on the whole more highly concentrated form of banking in the United States. The concentration however, was in the main, unwholesome, since it tended to produce less rather than more stability, contrary to the conditions established by similar tendencies in foreign countries.

From the standpoint of internal banking conditions, the evidence submitted to the Committee appeared to show that the following conditions were generally characteristic:

a) A "frozen" status in the portfolios of the banks, owing to the fact that assets mainly consisted of paper of extended maturity, or paper whose realization, although nominally provided for at relatively earlier dates, was in reality entirely dependent upon maintenance of an existing market condition (as for example, in the automobile trade).

b) A close dependence upon the stock market, by reason of the enormous volume of brokers' loans which had been developed (running close to 8 billion dollars during the later part of 1929); these loans being subject to call, and hence likely to impel a sudden and exceptional strain upon the banks, as they did during the October panic in 1929.

These conditions might be summed up in the statement that the evidence before the Committee showed a marked increase in instability, uncertainty, and lack of security in the banking system.

The Committee had, as already seen, devoted considerable attention to conditions in the Federal Reserve system, as differentiated from the commercial banking system of the country. So, in analyzing the testimony before it, the Committee necessarily sought to form its own opinion as to what changes had taken place in the Federal Reserve system. These were found to be substantially as follows:

a) A decline in commercial paper holdings of the members of the system, and, coördinate therewith, a decline in the practice of discounting with reserve banks.

b) An increase in the practice of open market operations at reserve banks, and a growing tendency on the part of member banks to depend upon the results of these open market operations as a means of supplying themselves with funds; sometimes directly, sometimes through the Federal fund market, or in other ways.

c) A continuing and steady enlargement of the dependence of the reserve system upon the stock market borrowing demand, as shown by the extent of the loans made by reserve banks to borrowers (under the so-called 15-day clause) which permitted lending of bank funds upon the member bank's own note supported by eligible paper as collateral, such paper being usually governmental securities of various kinds).

d) An increasing tendency on the part of the reserve system to lend chiefly to small groups of large city banks in the immediate neighborhood of the larger reserve banks, and the tendency to subordinate all else thereto.

e) The development of the practice, on the part of the Reserve system, of leaving to the Federal Reserve Bank of New York power to control and direct the open-market operations of the system (partly corrected through the action of the other Reserve banks in changing the method of controlling open-market operations). It thereby acquiesced in the practice of leaving to the Reserve Bank of New York the management of foreign relations. As a result, foreign funds had been largely engaged in frozen paper ("revolving" bankers' acceptances and other of the same level), with the guarantee of the Federal Reserve Bank of New York which, of course, meant the guarantee of the system.

Summed up, this evidence plainly implied that the Reserve system had itself been tending to fall into a "frozen" position, the bulk of its loans being based upon long-term paper, whose convertibility depended entirely upon the stock market. And yet in spite of its enormous and imposing gold reserve, it was in a weak position because of the liability of its being called upon by foreigners who imagined that their funds were liquid, when they had, in reality, been invested in long-term paper which the Reserve system had guaranteed to be convertible into gold.

The general situation thus revealed, was naturally of a complex character. It suggested to many minds the instability of the entire banking system and the need of a complete and thorough reorganization of it—root and branch. There were members of the Committee who tentatively leaned to the view that what was needed was a complete revision of the entire structure of banking in the United States, in order to obtain a greater degree of responsibility, reliability, and solvency. These views, however, did not prevail. It was the opinion of the Committee, after careful consideration, that the proper method of procedure to be pursued would be that of attempting to rectify the objectionable conditions, individually and severally, by ascertaining what could be done toward removing the causes which underlay the difficulties; and by seeing to it that, so far as practicable, the evil influences which had worked together to bring on the state of things complained of might be alleviated or removed. The adoption of this point of view was of great importance. It signified that the Committee had practically made up its mind not to attempt a far-reaching or thorough-going piece of work, but rather to attempt the patching up of the old structure and recognition of the basis of banking already existing, as on the whole, satisfactory; or at any rate likely to be more nearly satisfactory than any other that was likely to be devised.

The tacit agreement thus to enact a remedial rather than a constructive statute was partly dictated by political considerations. President Hoover, then at the head of the Administration in charge of the country, had, from the outset of his administration, been believed unfavorable to reform. Efforts to initiate new banking legislation in the House of Representatives, soon after his accession to office, had been crushed by "packing" the banking committee and making every effort to prevent the enactment of remedial measures relating to branches. Secretary Mills, who succeeded Secretary Mellon as the head of the Treasury Department, was believed hostile to any extensive or seriously beneficial measure. The Republican party, then in power, in the House of Representatives and, technically at least, possessed of a majority in the Senate, was not friendly to banking changes. It was evident that if any very incisive measure should be proposed, it could succeed only by getting the approval of the Administration, or by representing so general a demand for remedial action that it could not be resisted. A few members of the Banking Committee were of the opinion that no such situation could be produced and the adoption of the act assured. These considerations, gradually but strongly, tended to stimulate support of a plan to adopt a purely corrective piece of legislation.

The decision to attempt the kind of banking bill just described was, as has been seen, the most fundamental and most important step that could have been taken. It implied that the method to be pursued in preparing the new measure should, indeed must, be that of compiling the remedies that had been proposed in various quarters for the correction of known and admitted evils, such as those already described, and the formulation of enactments intended to correct or cure such evils. In getting ready to carry through this plan the Committee, through its counsel, undertook a careful compilation of the projects definitely recommended to it, either in the public hearings or the executive sessions at which witnesses had been heard when they preferred to testify in private, or the answers to questionnaires sent out by the Committee, and the correspondence with which members of the Committee had been deluged. Multitudinous suggstions were thus obtained, but the majority of them may be stated as follows:

A. Reorganization of structure

1. Restoration of $100 par value as required unit for shares of stock in national (and member) banks.
2. Enlargement of minimum capitalization of national (and member) banks.
3. Requirement of materially larger surplus of national (and member) banks.
4. Requirement of a definite proportional relationship between bank capital (and surplus) and demand deposits carried.
5. Extension of power to establish branches.
6. Prohibition of group banking.
7. Prohibition of power of banks with branches or control of other banks to exert more than a specified amount of voting power in Federal Reserve banks.
8. Change in methods of taxing banks.
9. Alteration of relations with correspondents.

B. Modification of operating methods

1. Prohibition of brokers' loans or regulation in some way of the increasing volume of such loans.
2. Prohibition of margin trading or a modification of margin trading in such a way as to take the burden of financing speculation off the banks.
3. Limitation of the amount of bank funds to be invested in securities.
4. Restriction of the total volume of loans to be made by banks on collateral securities.
5. Limitation of loans to be made by groups or classes of banks for security speculation.
6. Restriction of conditions under which banks might borrow from Reserve banks in order to reduce stock market lending with reserve funds as a basis.
7. Control of the efficiency of bank officers by granting extensive powers of removal.

C. Reserve banking

1. Curtailment of power to lend on what was practically stock exchange collateral under the 15-day clause.
2. Systematization and legalization of open market control.
3. Publicity and responsibility with relation to foreign central banks.
4. Definition of open market powers.
5. Abolition of practice on the part of Reserve banks of guaranteeing investments of foreign central banks held in the United States.
6. Alteration of power of Reserve banks to trade in acceptances.
7. Increase in Reserve Bank's responsibility for the condition of members.

D. General problems of banking system

1. Complete separation of investment from commercial banking.
2. Enlargement of reserve requirements so as to protect time deposits and other credit.
3. Limitation of deposits growing out of actual business to institutions engaged in commercial business and to them only.
4. Entire abolition of affiliates.

5. Control and examination of affiliates.
6. Guaranty of bank deposits.
7. Establishment of joint responsibility for liquidation of assets in failed banks.
8. Creation of broader reserve system by the admission of new classes of members, e.g. mutual savings banks, and others.
9. Complete reorganization of banking system, by taking time deposit business out of the hands of national banks or compelling national banks to surrender trust and investment business to state chartered banks, and probably to transfer to the latter control of savings deposit business.
10. Action establishing branches of Reserve banks in foreign countries.

CHAPTER V

THE GLASS BILL

These major suggestions evidently constituted an enormous field for consideration and action, but they by no means exhausted the list of recommendations or suggestions that had come to the Committee. They were, in fact, only the principal or "key" suggestions; for nearly every one of them suggested a group of other recommendations constituting additions to, or modification of, these major ideas and affording a further development and elaboration of these underlying thoughts. The classification which has been given above, however, was adopted for the purpose of simplifying the great body of suggestions offered by witnesses and advisers; and each one of these groups was further subclassified for immediate reference and use in connection with the process of drafting.

The outline of the program having thus been definitely drawn up, conversations among members of the Committee were initiated for the purpose of indicating the lines along which to proceed. In this determination, of course, the chairman of the subcommittee played the commanding part. The decisions finally arrived at constituted the basis for the work of the technical adviser of the Committee in actually putting the bill together. The outgrowth of these conversations was reflected in conclusions somewhat as follows:

1. Since the present situation evidently centers around a faulty use of credit, the fundamental element in the new legislation must be an effort to correct this faulty use. Such effort seemingly must concern itself with the character and extent of the banks' investments in securities, and the conditions under which their loans are to be made on securities. Such a conclusion, however, would be forceful only if validated by providing for general rectification of conditions of bank lending. This rectification must concern itself with the character of the portfolio of the member banks, and must then be made to cover also

the conditions under which they obtain credit from the Federal Reserve banks.

Starting with this as the fundamental idea, the new act, accordingly, devoted itself, first of all, to the whole question of loans upon, and holdings of, securities. It divided its proposals into two main groups, one of which sought to give the Reserve Board at Washington the power to shut down on, or limit, the undue expansion of security loans. This was to be accomplished by authorizing the Board to fix the percentage of bank loans in the aggregate which might be made upon securities. Moreover, in order to make this policy effective, so-called "outside loans" made by non-bankers to brokers were forbidden, with the notion that loans to brokers would accordingly be made by member banks upon their own responsibility and without being subject to the disturbing influences which must come through the interposition of outside lenders in the market. That necessarily was a great departure from anything previously attempted in the national banking act. It should be noted at this point that the national banking act, adopted in 1863-1864, was a measure representative of the mid-century ideas of banking, and concerned itself almost entirely with commercial and other short-time paper.

There was, at the time, very little in the way of a stock market or money market in the United States, while these markets in Europe were rudimentary; and banks were not inclined to engage themselves over-heavily in stock exchange lending or securities' purchases. Accordingly, the National Bank Act ignored the securities market entirely; and thus the securities side of the bank portfolio came to be regulated, so far as it was at all under control—by administrative measures taken by the Comptroller of the Currency. The securities side of national banking legislation, in other words, had never been developed to anything like the extent which had been attempted in the control of commercial paper. It was felt by the Committee that not only considerations of soundness, but also those of fairness, as between the different classes of borrowers, should naturally sanction a proposal to try to subject the two sides of the bank's lending to somewhat similar conditions or restriction. On this, if upon no other ground, it would be legitimate to attempt some such type of control as has just been generally pointed out. Accordingly, the Glass bill, as the new measure had begun to be termed, undertook to limit the character of bonds that could be bought by banks, sought to prevent banks from putting too large a proportion of their funds into any one issue of bonds, attempted, as we have seen, to prevent undue extension of loans upon bonds and stocks, and incidentally proposed to require revaluation and reorganization of the real estate loan portfolios of the lender banks.

2. While thus placing in the forefront the whole question of the use of credit by members, the Committee, of course, recognized that one of the major troubles in the whole situation had evidently been the failure of the Reserve system (although originally organized as a mechanism for credit supervision) to fulfill its duty. Accordingly, the new measure sought to require that loans made by Reserve banks to members upon eligible paper used as collateral, should not be made if the members were planning to use the funds for the purpose of enlarging their loans to speculators in the stock market. Accordingly, further increase of the loans under the so-called "15-day clause" was to be suspended if any member bank should be found to be enlarging its collateral loans during the period in which it was still holding advances from its Reserve bank.

However, the Committee fully realized that mere efforts looking to the better control of credit in the future might easily be unsuccessful, as in the past, through shrewd contrivance of the managers of Reserve and member banks, and that public opinion obviously demanded some kind of assurance of the greater safety of individual funds in banks. To this problem the Committee accordingly addressed itself.

3. For many years past, there had been a general demand for what was called the "guaranteeing of bank deposits." The term was a misnomer—advocates of the plan having in mind rather, a guaranteeing of bank assets. The idea was based upon the thought that it should be possible to compel all existing banks,

having outstanding deposits, to contribute to an insurance fund whose proceeds should be employed for the purpose of paying off the deposit liabilities of any bank which might find itself deficient in assets and hence unable to meet the claims of its depositors in full. This notion had been the basis of demand, and of agitation supporting such demand, in many of the Western states, for years preceding, and had resulted in guaranty-of-deposits plans actually tested in several states, but always without much success. This lack of success had frequently been explained by advocates of the guaranty of deposits with the statement that the experiment had not been tried on a sufficiently broad scale, and that an adequate test of it could be obtained only through the institution of a generally compulsory guaranty that should be national in its scope. Accordingly, the Committee had had before it many plans projected by banking reformers, calling for such a guaranty of deposits.

Chairman Glass had never believed in the efficacy of this expedient, but he had been strongly impressed by the suffering and inconvenience inflicted upon the community at large through the numerous bank failures of past years and the unsatisfactory methods that had been employed in national bank receiverships. It was a fact that receiverships were in the habit of extending anywhere from a few months to as long as twenty-one years, and that on the average, as stated by the Comptroller, they were at the time running to a period of about six years. Recognizing that in bank failures the source of difficulty and losses is not primarily found in lack of assets, but is found in the fact that the resources of depositors are tied up and rendered unavailable for long periods, during which there is a corresponding drag in the process of liquidation, the Committee joined with Chairman Glass in concluding that the remedial measures most calculated to help the situation would be found in the development of a better system of receiverships, and in the furnishing of an assurance that bank depositors would be able to obtain the liquidation of their actual claims upon banks in so far as represented by bona fide assets. In the opinion of the Committee, liquidating power and not guaranty was demanded. It was, accordingly, determined to introduce into the new measure a plan for the establishment of a liquidating corporation whose duty it should be, immediately upon the failure of a member bank (except in those cases where some provision of state law might prevent a state-chartered institution from being dealt with in this manner) to secure an approximately correct valuation of its assets. As soon as possible thereafter the liquidating corporation should provide for the purchase of the bank's assets, either in whole or in part—preferably in as large a part as possible—paying to the receiver of the bank the proceeds in available funds. The receiver was then to disburse the funds so placed in his hands in satisfaction of the claims of depositors, thus insuring an almost immediate settlement within a short time upon the basis of the estimated worth of the bank's assets.

The plan evidently presented difficulties in connection with the valuation of the assets, which in the case of many failures is open to serious question. Accordingly, the project determined upon by the Committee provided for subsequent revaluation and the return to the bank of any surplus which might be realized by the liquidating corporation over and above the price at which the assets had been purchased, deducting, of course, the liquidating fees involved in the operation. The effect of the plan, if carried into practical operation, would have been to strip the receivership system of much of its evil, by necessarily shortening the period of receiverships, and eliminating a large proportion of the political appointments and "graft" of a localized character invariably associated with them. The plan would not have returned to the depositor dollar for dollar of his claims—in a large proportion of cases there was no reason why it should, since the claims on the banks were not "deposits" of "money," as often supposed, but were credits that had been written up on the books of the banks as a result of loans made by or through negotiations with the "depositor" or borrower. This project, therefore, was considered by the Committee entirely adequate to the protection of the bank depositor against most of the evils to which he had been subject, while leaving him still with a measure of individual responsibility for the protection of his claims through the selection of a well-qualified bank as to whose condition he kept more or less informed. To make it fully inclusive the Committee added provisions enabling groups of banks to borrow on their joint notes, in cases of emergency, at Reserve banks.

4. Continuing further in its fundamental review of the relationship between the public and the banks, the Committee recognized several distinct lines of approach, each of which called for careful treatment. The first was unquestionably the separation of investment from commercial banking. As things stood, an outstanding fact in the situation was that through the organization of the so-called "affiliates," banks ordinarily chartered for the purpose of carrying on commercial undertakings—or, in the case of trust companies, caring for fiduciary operations—had definitely gone into the stock and bond business. Starting with the issue of bonds as their major activity, the affiliates had gradually passed, during a tolerably brief period of years, to the financing and issuing of preferred stock, and then to the issuing and financing of common stock. From such activities they had then passed to stock market operations, including the purchase or "accumulation" of stocks in the market which seemed to be low in price, or were susceptible of being advanced in price by manipulation. Thus, working with the funds of the parent organizations, they had become intermediaries through which the savings of the public—since most commercial banks were now permitted to receive time or savings accounts—were siphoned off into the stock market, there to furnish the basis of operations intended for the speculative profit of those who had engineered them.

The inquiries of the Committee had not disclosed with anything like exactitude the total number of affiliates in the United States, though its number was believed to be in the neighborhood of 750. It was certain, in all events, that the larger banks in most of the principal cities were in some way connected with organizations of the sort, and that the trend had of recent years tended to spread. It appeared to the Committee that only in one of two ways could this danger be corrected: first, by placing the affiliates under strict federal supervision; second, by effecting an absolute divorce between the parent banks and affiliates. There was probably no member of the Committee that entertained any direct regard for the interests of the system which had thus inflicted upon the country, during the decade of 1919–1929, such outrageous wrong and suffering, but there was, unquestionably, some difference of opinion as to the policies that might be followed in obtaining an effective curb upon the evil. Three such courses in practice, accordingly, suggested themselves: (1) severe inspection and regulation of the affiliates under penalty of expulsion of the parent bank from the Federal Reserve system should the desired inspection be refused; (2) organization of the affiliates under Federal charters with penalties applied to member banks if they permitted themselves to operate in conjunction with any affiliate not federally chartered; (3) complete separation of the affiliates from the parent banks.

These three proposals were accordingly presented to the subcommittee and by it carefully considered. Such consideration led to fairly prompt rejection of the second of the three alternatives—that of federal incorporation of the affiliate. It was true that such federal incorporation had already been proposed and strongly advocated as a means of improving the situation created by the organization of railway affiliates or holding companies, but the Committee recognized that to propose a comprehensive plan for such federal incorporation would be a task of lengthy character, while it was hoped the proposed Glass bill might find a fairly prompt reception—of course, if it were held to more simple terms. Of the two remaining proposals, that which called for federal inspection and constant examination of the affiliates and for the control of relationships between the parent banks and its associate companies including regulation of transactions and operations in the stock of the parent banks carried on by the affiliates, first commended itself to the Committee, and a plan for the attainment of this end was incorporated into the first draft of the measure. Further consideration shortly led to the elimination of this project. Members of the Committee had received great numbers of letters from citizens of all classes who were outraged by what they considered the injustice to which they had been subjected through the affiliate system and who demanded absolute elimination of it—root and branch—from the national banking and Federal Reserve system.

Accordingly, it was determined to set aside the original plan and to substitute that of completely separating parent banks from their affiliate enterprises. Provisions to this effect were ordered incorporated into the bill and this step was promptly taken; such separation, however, was found to be a rather difficult matter. The affiliates had always been perfectly legal, regularly established enterprises, operating under state laws. Congress then could only attack them by prescribing the relationships which might or might not exist between corporations (banks) under its jurisdiction and the state corporations (affiliates). These relationships were speedily recognized as being: (1) ownership, (2) lending operations of various kinds, (3) direction through common boards or committees, or (4) joint stock representation. Actual ownership of the stock of these corporations was already controlled by the National Banking Act, while in the case of state member banks, nothing that Congress could do would affect their legal rights in such matters.

5. It was, accordingly, determined first to separate the stock of national and member banks from the stock of affiliates in those companies where, as had frequently been true, the two certificates of stock were only simultaneously transferable. Further, it was directed that the various schemes of control through trustees and the like should be terminated, and that after a period of two years, the separation of ownership and direction should thus become complete. It was, of course, recognized that nothing in the enactment thus proposed would prevent the existence of an identical body of stockholders in the case of a bank and an affiliate, but it was believed that this identity would shortly disappear, and that, while friendly relationships would doubtless continue between given groups of enterprises, Congress would have done its utmost if it brought about an actual separation of the stocks, and of the directorates, of the concerns affected. In addition, it was thought necessary that there should be specific

limitation of the loans to be made by banks to their affiliates, so that such loans would be limited by the same restrictions and conditions that would be applied in the case of any loan made by banks in similar circumstances. With these provisions, accordingly, the Committee then passed to the consideration of another aspect of the question of the use of bank funds in support of speculation.

It was recognized that in nothing that had thus far been determined was there anything that would in the slightest degree interfere with the excessive application of ordinary bank resources in the stock market. Further, it was plain that although the banks might in some cases be considerably restricted in the amount of their commitments by the fact that their accommodations at reserve banks were not to be used for the purpose of enlarging security loans, they might at times simply fall back upon the reserve banks for the financing of their ordinary commercial business and devote themselves, as often in the past, to the almost exclusive financing of the stock market through the use of their own funds. It was, therefore, thought best, after a good deal of deliberation, to invest the Federal Reserve Board with the power of determining what percentage of the bank's total credit might be at any given time employed in the making of loans upon collateral security. Necessarily, it was recognized that, in many cases, such loans were not at all intended for the purpose of speculating in the securities used for collateral, but that, in numerous cases, the securities were merely placed behind the loan in order to insure the bank against loss; the loan itself being intended for a definitely commercial purpose, although given additional protection in the way indicated. This point had been emphasized with tiresome reiteration by Reserve bank officials during the hearings on the bill and was, moreover, obvious. The Committee itself, before the hearings began, had presented to banks and bankers a questionnaire in which inquiry was made with regard to the purpose of their security loans and had received frank and full answers from those who were thus addressed.

The exercise of the power thus granted was evidently one that must be carried out with circumspection and after due investigation. Yet, in its theoretical aspect it did not differ in any way from the other principles of the National Banking Act designed to prevent the undue concentration of risks through the taking on of commercial loans that had shown themselves excessive. Accordingly, the exercise of this power by each Federal Reserve District was considered by the Committee to be the most effective way of directly reaching a situation which, in its opinion, had become one of intolerable danger. While it was recognized that the Federal Reserve Board had, in the past, shown little or no courage or initiative in the use of the great powers already bestowed upon it, the addition of this one would at least place definitely the responsibility for failure to apply an early check to the process of misapplying bank credit, which had been so pronounced a feature of the period before each of the great financial crises of recent years. It would always be possible to demand of the Board that it exercise its authority, and while it might prove to be true as in the past that the Board would, in such cases, take the part of the speculative community (as had been done by Governor Young, for example, in his defense of brokers' loans in February, 1928), the necessity of shouldering the responsibility for subsequent mishaps could not be avoided. This provision, was, therefore, inserted in the bill with the full and actual approval of every member of the subcommittee—some members indeed expressing the fear that the section as so drafted was not strong enough, and accompanying it with a pious hope that something of more effective character might later be added.

6. Having thus definitely sought to close the avenues through which bank funds had been escaping into hasty and ill-judged speculation in stocks and bonds, the Committee next devoted itself to protecting in better form the savings of the community placed in the hands of the banks. It recognized that the Federal Reserve Act, in providing for the taking of time deposits by national banks, and the State legislatures by extending this permission to their own banks, in many instances, had doubtless committed serious blunders. Abstractly, the most effective way

to correct these blunders would seem to be that of refusing to banks the authority to receive time deposits. To take any such step would, however, have caused an enormous inconvenience. Precisely what its results might have been in those parts of the country that were not provided with savings banks was a matter open to question. Such drastic action would certainly have necessitated a tremendous and far-reaching change in the banking situation. Accordingly, the Committee determined not to follow this line of approach to the evil, rightly recognizing that it is seldom possible to turn back the course of evolution, and by merely revoking authority once granted, to create a situation of a new sort. There was, however, no doubting the fact that the public was deeply dissatisfied with the tremendously high risk involved in the placing of their funds in banks, and that terrible and wide-spread suffering had been caused through the tying up and loss of such funds through the closing of banks.

7. It seemed best to seek alleviation of these evils by two methods: (1) the raising of the reserve required against time deposits in such a way as to eliminate the artificial inducement to the carrying of such deposits, and (2) the segregating, in some measure at least, of the assets of banks which represented their savings and time deposit liabilities from those which represented their demand deposit liabilities. Both measures would be exceedingly distasteful to the banking community.

For long years past, the banks had been using every possible means to bring about the enlargement of their savings, or time deposits, as compared with their demand deposit liabilities. Depositors had been offered substantial rates of interest as an inducement to shift demand deposits into time deposits; and the banks, also, as a result of practical necessity or as a means of competition, had fallen into the habit of paying time and savings deposits on demand, seldom invoking the period of postponement which under the law they were permitted to apply. The major reasons for these inducements had been found in the fact that, whereas ordinary demand deposits had to be protected by reserve balances amounting to 7, 10, and 13 per cent according to the location of the bank, time and savings deposits called for but a three per cent reserve. In these circumstances, the process of transfer had proceeded rapidly with the result that, at the beginning of 1930, the proportion existing between time and demand deposits, in the banks of the nation as a whole, was approximately one and one-half of time deposits to one of demand. Time deposits, in other words, were 150 per cent of demand deposits.

Reviewing the situation, the Committee came to the conclusion that probably the fairest measure of reform would be simply to place the deposits upon a uniform reserve basis; thereby eliminating discrimination between time and demand liabilities and making it a matter of indifference so far as reserves were concerned, from the standpoint of the bank, in which form (time or demand) its obligations were stated. Viewed in this way, the legitimate objection to the proposal could be only that it would imply the necessity for suddenly building up a very large addition to reserves at a time when reserves had been reduced to a very low figure. In order to meet this possible objection, the Committee determined to spread out the process of increasing the reserve behind time deposits over a series of years, thereby giving to the banks abundant opportunity for preparation. By way of further protection of the savings deposits, it was moreover determined to give them a prior lien upon assets, so that it would no longer be possible, as had often been the case in the past, for a group of demand depositors possessed of private information, or perhaps only conjecturing that a given bank was in a weak position, to withdraw their claims against it, thereby leaving it to close with a clientele consisting only, or largely, of time depositors.

8. The care thus bestowed upon the time depositor could evidently be warranted only by the elimination of the elements of danger affecting the demand depositor which were the result of deficient reserve and other protection. The studies made on behalf of the Committee had conclusively shown that reserve protection had been allowed to run down in a rather remarkable way during preceding years. The Federal Reserve Act had originally been framed in its reserve provisions as a result of a

compromise, or tacit agreement, arrived at with the stock market or investment interests of the country. These had more or less rightfully asserted in past years that the support furnished by banks of the country belonged to them as well as to anyone else; and that, provided they could give good security, they were as much entitled as anyone to the services of the banks. Accordingly, when it was proposed in the Federal Reserve Act to place the reserves of the member banks in the hands of the Reserve banks, which were prohibited from lending for speculative or investment purposes, the interests so affected were up in arms against the proposal. Eventually the framers of the Federal Reserve Act, recognizing that the new measure, if successful at all, would make a given unit of reserve eventually more efficient than had been the case previously, determined to cut reserve balances from the figures originally named, so that in place of being 25 per cent in central reserve cities, they were made 18 per cent while corresponding changes were made in the other groups of banks.

After the United States entered the war, inflation propaganda became general, and the Federal Reserve Board, consciously yielding to it, recommended to Congress that the reserves be further cut, making them 13 per cent for banks situated in central reserve cities, 10 per cent for banks in other reserve cities, and 7 per cent for banks elsewhere. At the same time, all requirements relating to the holding of a vault cash reserve were eliminated; and thus, the sums carried in Reserve banks were made the sole and only required reserves of the nation so far as member banks were concerned. It was, of course, assumed at the time that, whereas some banks would doubtless be operated close to their reserve minima, others would, as in former years, be possessed of surplus reserves, so that the exceedingly narrow percentages which had been fixed in the Federal Reserve Act as thus amended during the war, were not thought of as necessarily representing actual reserves. After the war, however, the practice of open market dealings eventually gave rise to what was called a system of trading in "Federal funds," and these funds were nothing more nor less than balances upon the books of Federal Reserve banks. In this trading it was the practice of banks with excess amounts to their credit to sell or transfer their excess to the account of less fortunately-situated banks, so that the latter filled up their deficits from the surpluses of the stronger banks. As a result the minimum required reserve was always approximately the reserve that was carried in Reserve banks; or, as Governor Young once expressed the matter in a letter to a critic: There was no such thing as a surplus reserve. This condition inevitably subjected weak banks to a very severe stress at times, since, in the circumstances just depicted, they often found it hard to get assistance from their correspondents.

Most of the banks were continuously thus "loaned up," and the reserve requirement of the Federal Reserve Act was largely neutralized in its effect. For example, if bank "A" found itself in need of—let us say—$50,000 to make good a deficit in its reserve account, it might resort to any one of several alternatives. Thus, it might sell bonds of which it happened to be possessed and with the proceeds fill up its balance, or, it might go with eligible paper to the Federal Reserve bank of its district and obtain a rediscount; or it might purchase federal funds in the open market. Normally it would be inclined to follow the cheapest of these alternative courses, and that was almost invariably the purchase of federal funds. Thus the influence of the federal funds market was toward the further tying up of bank resources in investment securities, and, generally speaking, toward the "freezing" of bank portfolios; while at the same time it tended toward the curtailment of the rediscounting business of Federal Reserve banks, and drove them more and more into the open market as a field for the use of their own resources. It was a part of the general speculative unsoundness of the period. The banking subcommittee had not in this case, as it had not in most others, thought that mere prohibition would be wise; and it therefore determined merely to regulate the Federal funds market. It provided, accordingly, that there should be a fixed relationship between the rate at which sales of federal funds should be made and the rediscount rate at the Federal Reserve bank at the time, the effort being to bring about a unification or standardization of money market practices or charges, thereby strengthening the reserve position of the country as a whole by tending to bring about a greater degree of liquidity in the banking situation.

9. These provisions probably became known in some more or less accurate form to the Federal Reserve Board. At all events, the Governor of that board communicated to the subcommittee in November, 1931, the substance of a report relating to reserves, which was the outcome of the work of a Committee of Federal Reserve bankers appointed some years before. This Committee had been slowly investigating the reserve situation of the country and attempting to reach a basis of agreement with regard to an alteration of the reserve bases of the nation. It had had to recognize that the reserve situation was not satisfactory, and was not so regarded by any competent critic. It had also had strongly brought to its attention the fact that the country was, at the opening of the panic of 1929, upon an exceedingly narrow reserve basis. It was true that the immense gold importations of the country had been placed in the Reserve banks, and had there created an impressive hoard of gold, amounting at times to about three billion dollars—a sum far in excess of any ever accumulated by any banking system; but it was also true that, at the breaking out of the panic of 1929, this immense body of reserves represented much less than 5 per cent of the outstanding deposit claims of the banks of the country.

Bankers, recognizing clearly enough that they would soon be brought face to face with a stringent condition, and having exhausted every resource of ingenuity to release reserves by the conversion of time into demand deposits, were now pressing hard upon the reserve bank authorities for a reduction of reserve requirements. The Committee of the Reserve banks, to which reference has already been made, was undoubtedly aware of this pressure, and was unwilling to propose the natural expedient (that which the subcommittee of the Senate Banking Committee had already determined upon) of requiring an enlargement of actual reserves. The Reserve Bank Committee had, as a substitute, finally resolved upon a new plan in which the volume of reserves to be carried was to be determined, not as a percentage of the outstanding amount of deposits, but as a percentage of the velocity of deposits. Thus, for example, if under the old system with an outstanding demand liability of $100 a bank found itself obliged to keep 13 per cent or $13 as a reserve, under the new plan if the velocity or turnover of deposits has been ascertained as—say—5, the total to be protected would be 100 times 5, or $500, the reserve to be held against it would be $65, if the old percentage were adhered to. The Committee now proposed to cut the old percentage to a minimum of 5 so that in the case of the illustration just given the required protection would be, say $25. It would, however, be proportionately less than this as the turnover shrank. Thus, if normal turnover were 2.5, the reserve requirement would be $12.50, or approximately what it would have been under the old system, and if it fell to 1, it would be only $5.

A specious argument was presented that speculative banks located in the larger cities were those of highest turnover, and that consequently they would be the institutions called upon to maintain highest reserves, while country banks in small places with limited turnover and long term assets would not be required to maintain much reserves. The project as recommended by the Governor of the Federal Reserve Board to the Committee turned out upon examination to be full of danger, and to contain some serious technical blunders, and the Committee determined, for the present at least, to lay it aside with the understanding that it recognize the possibility of a percentage of velocity as conceivably a better way of ascertaining reserve than the old method. The decision referred to left the Committee, however, with the two proposals already referred to: the raising of reserves against time deposits, but regulation of the Federal-funds market with, of course, the partial segregation of assets against savings deposits by way of protection of the "small" man.

In this way the Committee felt that it had practically disposed of the more serious of the issues growing out of the misuse of credit during the decade 1919-1929, and the stock market debauch which had accompanied it. The adoption of these purely protective, or as they might be called "emergency," measures, was not, however, sufficient to remedy the underlying evils that had been brought to its attention and it had, therefore, to consider the question how far it was willing to go in making the proposed act a general means of reform rather than a mere emergency measure designed to limit danger and head off the hazards of the situation for the time being. This general problem, large as it was, naturally received a great deal of attention at Committee meetings and finally culminated in the decision not to attempt the fundamental reorganization of the banking system at the time, but to make the measure one of transition or temporary relief, in the thought that at a later date the time might be more propitious for general action. Such a decision, however, could not, in the nature of the case, exempt the Committee entirely from making some legislative provisions designed to enable its projects to "fit in" to the structure or framework of banking already existing. Perhaps the most urgent matter which thus presented itself as an outgrowth of the corrective provisions already agreed upon was that which related to what was called "group banking."

10. There had come into existence in many parts of the country holding companies organized under state laws and responsible to no one, whose mission it was to acquire and hold the stock of banks. Practice had led to the organization of these holding companies in states distant from the scene of their activities. Thus, for example, in the Northwest, two corporations organized under the laws of Delaware had acquired between them the stock of upward of 300 banks, which they operated as they chose, and for whose operation they were responsible to no one. The individual banking units themselves were subject, of course, to the national or state authorities, but it was evident that the responsibility for them was no longer lodged in individual or local stockholders. The Committee, accordingly, determined to deal in some way with this state of affairs, and it recognized three phases of it as particularly falling within its jurisdiction: (1) the fact that, under the holding-company system, the double

liability of stockholders provided in most banking laws, had practically disappeared; (2) the fact that the holding-company organization might, and in some cases actually did, give to a single holding-company group domination of the Federal Reserve bank in the district; (3) the fact that a "string" of holding-company banks might easily shift from one to another assets or balances and thus present to local examiners an appearance of strength which they did not possess.

It was determined to deprive such holding companies of the power of voting stock in the various banking units under their control, unless amenable to Federal inspection, and, likewise, to deprive such controlled units of the power of voting in the election of directors of Federal Reserve banks. Abstractly, the Committee saw that what it had already determined, with regard to the security affiliates, would seem likewise to commit it to a similar course of action with regard to bank holding company affiliates—the more so as it appeared that, among the group banks of the Northwest, there were included a number of security affiliates of the same kind that had already been prohibited. It had before it a rather complex problem—that of tolerating and continuing the existence of the bank holding-company affiliate, and at the same time of administering equal justice by subjecting it to the same terms and conditions that had already been made applicable to the security affiliate; and, furthermore, of insuring that the existence of such bank holding-company affiliates should in no wise infringe upon the efficiency or safety of the banks included in the "group."

The problem was political as well as economic and financial, for the reason that Chairman Norbeck (Senator from South Dakota) represented a region of country in which the affiliates had taken deep root, so that he had among his constituents influential bodies of voters both for and against the group system. After a full discussion with Mr. Norbeck it was agreed by the Committee to undertake to tolerate the group banks (holding-company affiliates) but only upon the conditions: (1) that they surrender their voting power in Reserve banks; (2) that they undertake to build up a satisfactory balance of assets designed to provide for stockholders' double liability; and (3) that they submit to examination by national authorities and to the preparation of combined statements designed to exhibit the simultaneous situation of all the banks included within a group. These provisions were, accordingly, embodied in the first draft of the new bill. There remained now one rather serious and difficult problem, partly long term or structural in its nature, partly immediate, or emergency. This was the question of branch banking.

The branch banking question had for many years past been one of the most sharply controversial issues in American public life—so far at least as related to financial problems. The numerous small banks throughout the country had succeeded in creating the impression that expansion of branch banking would result in subjecting them to competition of so severe a nature that it could not be endured and that consequently they would fall into the hands of a so-called "money trust." On the other hand, the larger banks of the cities, although in some cases friendly to branch banking, were in other cases inclined to the opinion that the introduction of the proposed system would be hurtful to their interests, necessitating their investing extensively in the establishment of branch systems in order to prevent competitors from gaining advantage of them. Some had already invested heavily in the extension of correspondent relationships with the small banks, and they did not care to undertake further warfare which they thought might at best have the effect of merely changing the hold they already had upon the small banks into another type of influence without adding to the profit-making possibilities of their organization.

Advocacy of branch banking had been maintained largely by publicists and public men whose interest in it was entirely academic. After the panic of 1929, a new element entered the situation. Some proprietors, owners of group banks, reached the conclusion that it would be profitable for them to convert their controlled institutions into branches of one central organization. These, however, were comparatively few in number and the major influence politically, so far as Congress was concerned, was quite uniformly on the side of the existing or unit banking system, and was against branch banking. Chairman Glass of the subcommittee had been a recognized advocate of branch banking and was convinced that, through the extension of branch banking, a sounder and safer type of organization would be obtained. He also thought that the gradual conversion of the groups and chains into branch systems would be a more practicable and effective disposal of them than could be attained through any effort to break them up or dissolve them into their former constituent elements. In this view, nearly all of the other members of the subcommittee concurred with Mr. Glass, although Senator Norbeck, the Chairman of the Banking and Currency Committee entertained an opposite view, deferring to the sentiment of the small unit bankers of his own part of the country. The Committee thus had a rather difficult problem to settle within its own ranks.

Discussion of branch banking culminated in acceptance by all members, except Senator Norbeck, of a plan for permitting the extension of branch banking throughout the territory of those states in which a national bank might be situated. Congress, of course, could not give to state banks any power relating to branch banking not already enjoyed by them under their state charters. The plan to bestow a state-wide branch-banking power was immediately met by opponents with the proposal that, in lieu thereof, the Committee merely grant power to extend branch banking on a state-wide basis in those states which already permitted branch banking to their own institutions. This, of course, would have limited the power to create branches very materially as there was not more than a handful of such states at the time, so that in the majority of commonwealths the new legislation would have confronted a situation in which no extension was possible without the consent of the local state legislature. There would have been little advantage in any such step, and every member of the Comittee, with the exception of Senator Norbeck, was accordingly inclined to look for a more liberal method of dealing with the situation.

Unfortunately a canvass of opinion in the House of Representatives showed very clearly that broad branch banking provisions would be unlikely to receive any support, and that, if made an integral part of a new bill, they would be likely to lead to the defeat of the latter. There seemed to be no choice, therefore, broad branch-banking provisions apparently signifying, as Congress then stood, an insurmountable obstacle to the legislation. As it was evident that the new measure, if framed along any such lines as those already proposed, would raise up against itself a host of enemies, the idea of incorporating liberal branch-banking provisions into the Act tended to lose ground with the members of the Committee. Eventually a tentative compromise was framed by inserting in the bill a section which undertook to extend the branch-banking power on a state-wide basis, in such states as had no laws prohibiting branch banking.

Although the foregoing provisions constituted the major elements in the Glass bill, there were certain others which were thought necessary or desirable either for the purpose of correcting manifest errors or doubtful situations which had already come into existence, or for the purpose of rendering the working of the Act smoother than it would otherwise be. Among such must be reckoned the section of the law which sought to regulate rates of interest at banks in order to supplement the provision on that subject already incorporated into state law. The section abrogated the authority granted to national banks in 1927, to issue stock of a par value of less than $100, and prohibited investment and other private bankers against the carrying of deposits placed with them by corporations engaged in interstate business. This latter provision had been intended primarily for the purpose of preventing the siphoning off of deposits in incorporated banks into private institutions which would, as in the past, feed them into stock exchange loans.

With regard to the Reserve system the proposed law undertook little toward the change already determined on as necessary for the correction of the excess of speculative credit, save the elimination of one or two rather serious abuses which had admittedly crept into Federal Reserve practice. One of these had to do with the foreign relations of Federal Reserve banks. For several years past it had been the practice of the Federal Reserve Bank of New York to take upon itself authority to represent the entire system in foreign negotiations, and this assumption, usually "winked at," or tolerated, by the Federal Reserve Board, largely through a desire on the part of the latter not to have to assume responsibility in foreign matters, had grown into a practice of representing the Reserve Bank of New York in other countries as practically the manager or head of the system—the other Reserve banks being thought of as "interior banks," or branches, or auxiliaries of the Federal Reserve Bank of New York. In order to correct this misunderstanding, the new Act carried a section providing that no negotiations with other central banks should be conducted except with the knowledge and consent of the Federal Reserve Board.

The other Reserve banking situation which seemed to call for attention lay in the fact that, as with foreign transactions, so with domestic open market operations, the Reserve Bank of New York had been allowed to assume an authority which did not belong to it. This authority had frequently been exercised to the disadvantage of the interior banks, and of late years under conditions which had evidently elicited their disapproval. Because of such disapproval the interior banks had insisted upon reorganizing the mechanism for the control of open market operations and had established a general Open Market Committee consisting of one member from each Reserve District, whose function it was to direct the conduct of open-market operations. A careful review of the situation led the subcommittee to the opinion that by all odds the best step it could take would be to consolidate or recognize the system of technique which had thus been developed by the Reserve banks themselves as the result of harsh experience. It was plain to thoughtful minds that there could be little or no assurance of continued maintenance of the new system along the lines that had been mapped out unless something were done to confirm or stereotype it. Accordingly, the Act undertook to amalgamate into law the existing provisions of the agreement under which open-market operations were then being carried on, and the proposed bill carried a section expressed in language nearly identical with that of the constitution of the open-market committee which had already been filed with the Committee during the public hearings.

CHAPTER VI

THE BANKING ACT OF 1933

The Glass bill was introduced into the Senate and thus made public on January 21, 1932—a little more than a year after initiation of the public hearings and inquiries which had been instituted toward the close of 1930. The question has often been asked whether the bill thus constructed was the exclusive work of some particular person who had embodied in it special ideas of his own, and what was the official support or approval of it. This is a matter which deserves some consideration.

President Hoover, the then chief executive of the United States, was inclined, during the campaign of 1932, to refer occasionally to banking reform as a policy or program which had enjoyed his own special approval or recommendation. In his speech of acceptance of August, 1932, he had inserted a sentence which thus referred to banking reform, although he had not mentioned exactly what he included under that head. A careful scrutiny of his published speeches and addresses, however, fails to disclose any advocacy of new banking legislation, and it was a matter of common knowledge in Congress that, at the outset of his administration, it had been the wish of the Treasury Department, presumably with Mr. Hoover's assent, to have matters so arranged that legislation relating to branch banking and to other kindred matters would not make its appearance on the floor. The membership of the Committee on Banking and Currency in the House had been rearranged accordingly, and it had proven impossible to obtain any definite action in the lower house of Congress.

Secretary Mellon, meanwhile, had given place to Mr. Ogden Mills at the head of the Treasury Department, but there was no reason to expect a more favorable attitude on the part of Mr. Mills than there had been on the part of his predecessor.

The banking situation had greatly changed since the subcommittee had begun its labors. The numerous failures, embarrassments and financial difficulties which had been characteristic since long before the panic of 1929 had deepened into a chronic condition during 1930, and had been aggravated and brought to a head by the reflex influence of the financial collapse of Germany in 1931, as well as by the subsequent suspension, in 1931, of gold payments by Great Britain. President Hoover had thought it necessary, as early as October, 1931, to bring forward and place before members of Congress, carefully chosen so as to represent the two major parties, in an informal meeting at the White House, projects for the improvement of the financial situation.

Of these the outstanding one was the plan for the so-called National Credit Corporation which was set on foot during the autumn of 1931, and had begun to make some small advance toward the beginning of December of that same year. The National Credit Corporation was supposed to possess a capital contributed by banks throughout the country, and was intended to undertake loans based upon collateral security which ordinarily would not prove acceptable to banks, although in the long run they might perhaps be liquidated. The corporation was also expected to make loans in behalf of groups of banks which it was thought would be willing to coöperate, guaranteeing one another, as had been the habit of clearing houses in times past. President Hoover, however, encountered utmost difficulty in securing any considerable measure of activity on the part of the corporation in question, and the number of bank failures, which had already grown very large before the enterprise was thought of, increased at a rapid pace during the later months of the year, so that, by the close of December, such failures had reached the unprecedented total of 2298. The President had thus come to recognize the unavoidable character of banking change and of the need for strengthening of the banking structure; and it is probable that, at the time of the introduction of the Glass measure in January, 1932, his mind was more genuinely open with regard to the whole question than it had been at any date prior thereto. Much the same was true of the Federal Reserve Board, which, although for a long time past it had recommended nothing in the way of remedial action, had at length come to life with the Reserve plan for basing computations on deposit velocity already sketched in the foregoing pages.[1]

Knowing of the ill-concealed hostility of the White House, of the Federal Reserve Board, of the Treasury Department, and of the Comptroller of the Currency toward anything in the way of banking changes it had been the feeling of Chairman Glass that there would be little use in seeking the advice or suggestion of any of them regarding the new bill. The subcommittee desired however, largely as a matter of record, that the bill should be submitted to a representative of the Administration, and, accordingly, it had been placed in the hands of the Comptroller of the Currency during the last week of 1931. Consideration of the measure during the succeeding fortnight or more convinced the Comptroller that he would have nothing to do with it, and through his deputy he informed the Committee that he could not even allow himself to make a written statement about the measure, so strong was his feeling of opposition. Thus, it may be said that the Glass bill, when it appeared in public, came not only without approval of the Administration, but also with every reason to suppose that it would meet with a hostile reception. Such in effect proved to be the case.

The Comptroller of the Currency's office had begun an attack on the bill through the press, and in one way or another, the national Administration generally followed suit. President Hoover effectually anticipated the Glass bill by suddenly insisting that the Banking and Currency Committee devote itself to what was called an immediately available remedial measure. He, therefore, ordered sent to both houses of Congress a plan for a further remedial step. This was the so-called Reconstruction Finance Corporation. The bill creating it had been prepared in the Federal Reserve Board under the general direction of the Governor of that organization, and paralleled closely the lines of the War Finance Corporation Act which had been used during the World War as a medium for financing banks that were hard pressed and had no eligible paper; and had from time to

[1] See Chap. V, pp. 76-78.

time been given an additional lease of life by Congressional action until it had finally worn itself out and been discarded. President Hoover now urged the readoption of this old and discarded expedient in the form of a new measure, drafted as already described. Senator Glass and his subcommittee were well aware that it was quite out of question to obtain the attention of Congress for two financial measures of primary importance at one and at the same time. They accordingly determined to yield the right of way to the new measure thus presented as an emergency plan. The Reconstruction Finance Corporation was consequently granted a prior place in the discussion; the Bill creating it passed through various hearings, was amended and finally enacted by the Senate. This action seemed to leave the way clear for consideration of the Glass bill.

By this time the larger banks of New York and other places had definitely taken alarm and were exerting themselves to their utmost to prevent the consideration of the Glass measure. Since it had made its appearance on the floor of the Banking and Currency Committee in the form of a report from the subcommittee there had been opposition, and this antagonism had not come, as was expected, solely from the conservative Republican side of the Committee, but had also been actively shared in by the so-called Progressive Republicans as well as by Democratic members. In fact, it at first seemed as if the Glass measure had hardly any friends; and the proposal to subject it to hearings, obviously with a view to delay, instead of taking it up section by section for consideration, seemed to meet with favor. A change however soon occurred as the bill was studied. It seemed as if the Glass measure might perhaps be brought to a definite vote; and so imminent was the danger of its passage in that event, that it was deemed worthy of closest attention by the Federal Reserve Bank of New York, the Treasury Department, and various of the larger commercial banks—all coöperating to bring about a withholding of the measure.

Sundry bankers visited members of the Committee in an endeavor to explain to them the dangers of the legislation; the Governor of the Reserve Board and the Secretary of the Treasury in lengthy conversation with President Hoover urged on the latter need of opposition to the Glass measure. President Hoover, however, did not think it well to attempt any direct action. His prestige in Congress was already at low ebb and he probably realized that any such step on his part would meet with a rebuff. He therefore resorted to indirect methods of influencing the course of events. Summoning Chairman Glass to the White House late in January, 1932, he requested that Mr. Glass consent to a revision of the bill to be carried out by properly qualified "experts." He was, he said, fully in sympathy with the idea of enacting some legislation provided it could be properly shaped, but he had been informed that the Glass bill—probably without the knowledge or realization of the Chairman of the Committee—had assumed a radical and dangerous form, in addition to the fact that it had been carelessly prepared and contained unworkable provisions. Mr. Hoover, moreover, represented the same point of view in conversation with sundry Republican members of the subcommittee, who felt themselves bound to support the wishes of the President of the United States, notwithstanding they had already shared largely in the preparation of the details of the measure and voted to report it.

In these circumstances Chairman Glass thought it wise to say to the chief executive that he would be glad to have such a review if made as the President suggested by nonpartisan experts of high standing. President Hoover thereupon designated two persons—the one an officer of the Federal Reserve Bank of New York who had already been very active against the Glass bill, both through the press and otherwise, the other a member of the statistical staff of the Federal Reserve Board who had exerted himself in similar ways against the measure. The two were directed to consult with the subcommittee and did so. Chairman Glass thereupon referred the bill to the Presidential appointees with the request that they consider it and report in writing as soon as possible with reference to its terms. Calling to their assistance other representatives of the Federal Bank of New York, of the Treasury, and of the Federal Reserve Board, the two referees already chosen now prepared a survey of the Glass measure, section by section. They might have saved trouble had they simply stated in a sentence that they were opposed to the entire bill, for there was practically not a section of the whole measure as it then stood which they did not denounce as either unworkable, dangerous to the public credit, injurious to the banking system at large or in some way undesirable. An interesting feature of the presentation was that one of its most pungent paragraphs was directed against the section in the Glass bill which had proposed to enact into law the existing provisions of actual practice with regard to open market operations. Consideration of this memorandum led to a lengthy reply in answer to which came a further memorandum embodying material on portions of the Glass bill which had not been available at the time of the first memorandum or which represented afterthoughts and later suggestions. It was of the same nature as the first memorandum, and was accompanied by a proposed revision of the Glass bill, which would have provided for practically a totally different piece of legislation, with little or no relationship to the subject matter of the plan originally put forward by the subcommittee.

Perusal of these lengthy and detailed statements had persuaded the members of the subcommittee that the effort put forward on behalf of President Hoover by the so-called experts was without force, and they were about to report their opinion to this effect when the Administration in February, 1932, diverted attention from the proposals of the Banking Committee by putting forward another "emergency" measure. This emergency proposal, subsequently hastily put through Congress and enacted without much discussion, was what later became known as the "Glass-Steagall bill." It was (1) a plan for relieving Federal Reserve banks of the necessity of keeping gold as previously behind their notes, and (2) of relieving member banks of the necessity of "putting" up eligible paper as collateral when they desired accommodation. The measure was brought forward upon the pretense that it would ward off a threatening banking crisis, and that without it a general collapse of nation-wide proportions would be inevitable. Although Chairman Glass had little faith in the representations which were thus made by the White House, and although he recognized the insincere character of most of what was said on the subject, he believed it to be the course of prudence to allow this bill to supersede the Glass measure in its place before the Banking and Currency Committee and to endeavor, through reasoning, to secure a correction of its terms and the elimination of the more hazardous of its features.

After lengthy discussion and negotiation he eventually succeeded in introducing extensive amendments into it so that it was robbed of not a few of the dangers inherent in the White House draft, although it continued to permit Federal Reserve banks to transfer, from the custody of reserve agents to the banking departments of the several institutions, the entire amount of gold previously held by the Reserve agents for the protection of the notes. This left the notes subject merely to the protection of ordinary banking reserves of 40 per cent gold which the Reserve institutions had been required from the first to carry in the banking departments. It was a very decided weakening of the protection and liquidity of reserve notes. Experience has furnished abundant reason for thinking that there was no necessity whatever for its adoption, although it had been put forward as a matter of the utmost urgency, for investigation clearly showed that the reserve banks were amply able to furnish all the export gold for which they were likely to be called upon, while the new issue of notes under the measure amounted, on the first of the following July, to only about 150 million dollars paralleled by a corresponding retirement of old reserve notes. The Glass-Steagall Act was unquestionably the "red herring" drawn across the trail of banking legislation. It did, however serve this purpose well, for it retarded the further consideration of the Glass measure; and it was not until well into March, 1932, that the Banking and Currency Committee eventually voted to report the revised Glass bill, portions of which providing special rediscount arrangements, had been enacted in the Glass-Steagall measure.

The action so taken advanced the campaign of discussion by an important step. The revised Glass bill, obnoxious as it was, both to the Administration and to the larger banks of the country, had now overcome many of the prejudices and obstacles which had been placed in its path, and apparently had a clear road before it to a vote in the Senate. There was every reason to think that the session then in progress would last long enough to permit the new measure to obtain consideration on the floor, so that as a result members of the Senate would be subjected to the disagreeable alternative of having to vote for or against it, and perhaps of having to state their opinion one way or another. It was evidently time for the opposition bankers to exert their strongest efforts, and this they proceeded to do. A general nation-wide campaign, engineered by the American Bankers' Association, was set on foot for the purpose of demanding hearings on the Glass bill. This was upon the ground that no consideration and no hearings had been devoted to the subject before—the bankers ignoring the facts that they had systematically shirked the invitations to appear before the Currency and Banking Committee which had been extended to them, and that the American Bankers Association and the Investment Bankers Association had declined to express any opinion whatever upon the major phases of the legislation as presented to them through their officers. There was thus no occasion for any such hearings—a fact unquestionably recognized by all except those who were determined to obtain a further postponement of the day of reckoning with banking legislation.

Chairman Glass, however, was of the opinion that persistent and steady pressure, with acquiescence in any demand that appeared to have force, no matter how unreasonable, was the wisest method of following out his campaign. He reintroduced the Glass bill with all amendments, this time as Senate No. 4115, and under this number, hearings were ordered before the full Banking and Currency Committee. They extended through the later part of March and into early April, and presented opportunity for the appearance of various bankers and representatives of banking associations to testify, practically to a uniform purport, namely, that there was no section in the Glass bill and none of its proposals that were either desirable, beneficial, or likely to afford a remedy for existing conditions. So monotonous was the continuous reiterations of these statements, that Mr. Glass jocosely stated his opinion that the witnesses had all attended a "bankers night school" designed to coach them for their appearances before the Committee.

The Federal Reserve Board, however, which had thus far been silent—apparently only anxious to avoid sharing in the discussion of the Glass Bill—had at length been compelled to assume a position. It refused to assent to most of the extraordinary statements that had been made by the Committee of review appointed by President Hoover, consisting of its own subordinates or staff members—and it eventually took the Glass bill up for serious consideration and discussion among its own membership. The result was the appearance of the Governor of the Board before the Committee early in April, 1932, with a series of proposals which were designed to embody the considered views of the Board. In a formal letter accompanying the testimony of the Governor, the Board said:

> The Federal Reserve Board is in sympathy with the purpose of the bill to strengthen the supervision of the Federal Reserve System over general credit conditions and to invest the Federal Reserve authorities with certain disciplinary powers in relation to banks that pursue unsafe and unsound policies or abuse the privileges of membership. The Board's recommendations on this subject are incorporated in its proposed revision of sections 3 and 29 of the bill.
>
> With respect to the section of the bill dealing with open-market operations, the Board calls attention to the fact that there is already in existence an open-market committee on which each of the Federal Reserve banks has representation. This has come about as the result of natural development. The Board believes that it would be inadvisable to disturb this development by crystallizing into law any particular procedure. The Board believes that nothing further is necessary or advisable at this time than an amendment clarifying its power of supervision over open-market operations of the Federal Reserve banks and their relationships with foreign banks, as set out in the Board's memorandum.
>
> The Board is not in sympathy with the provisions of the bill discriminating against member-bank collateral notes. Experience shows that the particular instrument on which Federal Reserve credit is

obtained is not an adequate test of the use to be made by the member bank of the proceeds of the credit and that an attempt to control speculation through restrictions on member-bank collateral notes would not be effective in accomplishing the purpose of this section of the bill. Indeed, it probably would interfere seriously with the convenient and economical operation of the System. In this connection the Federal Reserve Board desires to renew the recommendation made in its annual reports for several years, that the maturity for which advances may be made to member banks on their promissory notes secured by paper which is eligible for discount be increased from 15 to 90 days. Such an amendment would be especially helpful to country banks.

The Board is of the opinion that the adoption of a system of reserves based on velocity of accounts as well as on their volume, as recommended by the System's committee on reserves, would be an important step in strengthening the influence that the Federal Reserve System could exert in the direction of sound credit conditions. The section of the bill dealing with reserves would accentuate rather than reduce the inequalities that have grown up in the distribution of reserves between different classes of member banks. The Board also believes it should not be overlooked that this section of the bill would exert a tightening influence on credit conditions at times when it would be contrary to the public interest.

The Board is in favor of establishing a liquidating corporation, but proposes to limit the scope of its operations to member banks and suggests a different method of financing it, together with certain changes in the provisions for its administration.

With respect to affiliates the Board believes that important reforms to be accomplished at the present time are the granting of power to the supervisory authorities to obtain reports and to make examinations of all affiliates of member banks and the prescribing of limitations on the loans that a member bank may make to its affiliates. The Board realizes that many evils have developed through the operation of affiliates connected with member banks, particularly affiliates dealing in securities. The Board's memorandum contains a draft of a provision for the separation of such affiliates after a lapse of 3 years.

It should be recognized that effective supervision of banking in this country has been seriously hampered by the competition between member and nonmember banks, and that the establishment of a unified system of banking under national supervision is essential to fundamental banking reform.

Together with this testimony on behalf of the Federal Reserve Board, should probably also be placed the testimony of the Board of Directors of the Federal Reserve Bank of New York through the Governor of that institution. The Board of Directors in question filed a lengthy letter, practically amounting to a plea for noninterference with existing methods of financing through the stock market, but offering no constructive suggestions on the ground that the moment was not an expedient one for the modification of banking laws.

A review of the changes officially suggested by the Federal Reserve Board was at once taken in hand at the end of the hearings, and Chairman Glass determined to introduce into the definition of the term "affiliate," some changes which had been urged by the Board. The original definition of the term had been taken from definitions which had been prepared for the legislature of the State of New York by a committee of bankers, advised by eminent counsel who had carefully formulated the terms to be used in describing those companies. The changes suggested by the Board in these particulars were not very far-reaching and seemed intended to attain substantially the same object as the contested original definition. They were, therefore, accepted. On the other hand Chairman Glass introduced minor modifications into the language of the sections relating to discount of speculative paper by Federal Reserve Banks, and into the section relating to the organization of the open market committee. Practically all of the other suggestions made by the Reserve Board were laid aside, or in some cases a nominal compliance in unimportant details was undertaken. One change of some significance was the addition to the bill of a section authorizing the removal of incompetent or undesirable bank officers after proper hearing and decision by designated authorities. From the bill, also, there disappeared the provisions relating to the complete separation of investment and commercial banking, the nonacceptance of deposits by private banks, the restrictions upon real-estate lending, and the orders for the revaluation of real-estate mortgages, while in other particulars the bill underwent substantial softening. So amended, it was again "voted out" by the Banking and Currency Committee and made its appearance on the floor of the Senate in April, 1932.

The measure had again advanced to a position of importance and the banking interests determined to resort to a final weapon. Members of the Senate formed a combination in May and June, designed, through "filibustering," to prevent the legislation from coming to a vote. The session was now drawing rapidly to a close with a great deal of unfinished and very urgent business still to be attended to. The filibuster undoubtedly brought into grave danger the prospects of the measure so far as the immediate session of Congress was concerned. President Hoover, on the other hand, had practically won a silent victory, since it was out of the question that the bill, after going through the Senate could also receive attention in the House of Representatives. The influence of the Administration had been strong enough to prevent any stirrings toward the introduction of a similar bill in the lower chamber. Chairman Glass, however, persevered in the endeavor to bring the bill to a vote. He succeeded in obtaining a preferred position for the measure so as to insure its discussion whenever an interruption in the current of business might take place, and thus occasional consideration of the generalities of the bill was now and again possible. However, as the session drew to its close in early July, 1932, the ruling political clique determined to prevent further agitation of the banking question, and this they did by displacing the Glass bill from its preferred position, thereby carrying it over to the next winter session.

The victory of the Democratic party under the leadership of Governor Franklin D. Roosevelt of New York became almost a certainty early in the summer. The election resulted in a sweeping victory of unprecedented proportions for Mr. Roosevelt, and therewith came the necessity of reconsidering and realigning the views of the different parties on the major public questions. There remained, however, a possibility of action on the Glass bill before the expiration of the old Congress, which, under

American constitutional law, as it then stood, had a continued life until March 4, 1933. It was evident to Mr. Glass and to others, particularly in view of the disappointing experiences during the later months of the preceding session, that it was not likely anything would be accomplished except through the direct expression of a wish on the part of Mr. Roosevelt. The President-elect and his advisers had been giving considerable thought and study to the Glass bill.

Not long after the announcement of the election results, in November, 1932, they communicated with Senator Glass and advised him of the wish of the President-elect to have the Glass bill adopted, if possible, during the coming short session. There were sections in the bill which were not altogether approved by the President-elect—among them, especially, the branch banking provisions. Yet, the measure seemed to him of some promise and he desired to see its enactment, even if it should later be found desirable to attempt a broader and more ambitious piece of legislation. With this assurance Senator Glass proposed, early in the short session, to have the Senate take up the Glass bill where it had been dropped six months before. This desire on his part, however, proved impossible of realization for the reason that the question of a default upon the international public debts had become urgent with the approach of the day when the next installment payment was to be made—about the middle of December. President Hoover had sought to defer the taking of any definite position on this question until after the election, and in this he had been successful, but the consideration of the matter could now no longer be postponed, and it, accordingly, became necessary to reach a decision about it, giving the pros and cons on its various aspects. In this the national administration was wholly absorbed during the major part of December. It was only after the post-holiday reassembling that Senator Glass succeeded in obtaining agreement for the further consideration of the banking bill, now reintroduced as Senate No. 4412, and finally in passing the measure in the upper chamber on January 10, 1933. In the meantime, a new difficulty had presented itself.

Banking conditions, as we have seen, had been bad for many years, and had grown steadily worse as the depression following the panic of 1929 had deepened. They had reached a peak of disaster, it was thought, with the terrible failure record of 1931. Many had supposed that the Reconstruction Finance Corporation, which had begun active work about the opening of March, 1932, would immediately and effectually alleviate these evils, but as the year 1932 drew to a close it became apparent that much of what had ben done by the Corporation had sufficed merely to intensify and to stereotype existing banking conditions. The uncertainty and anxiety of the community about banking prospects became intense shortly after the presidential election, because of realization that a deadlock between the two political parties had now been established, and that nothing was likely to be attempted until after March fourth.

The failure of the Treasury Department to relieve the fiscal situation by placing a large refunding loan before the end of 1932 was a cause of anxiety, and those fully instructed on the situation and the banking conditions which grew out of this neglect were of the opinion that something serious in the way of a break-down, or collapse, was imminent. Early in the year 1932, these difficulties came to a practical head through the establishment of the bank suspensions or holidays in parts of the country which we have studied at an earlier point. An emergency banking act—hastily drafted, without much consideration, by unskillful hands—was signed by the President on March 10, thus relieving the Reserve banks, which had closed simultaneously with others on March 4, of the necessity of making further payments in specie, while it left the reopening of the rank and file of the banks to be determined by the Administration. This reopening was necessarily arranged for as rapidly as might be possible; banks resumed payment in the larger cities first, followed by more remote institutions, until all that were presumably able to pay their obligations, in whole or in part, to depositors on demand had been restored to business activity. There remained closed between four and five thousand banks out of an estimated total of about 18,000 presumably open at the beginning of March, 1933.[2]

The arrangements of the moratorium and of the reopening of banks took much time, and in the meanwhile the new Administration had apparently given no thought whatever to banking. It had, in fact, apparently repented of its assurances to Mr. Glass, for although it was understood that the President-elect had expressed to the leaders of the House of Representatives a desire that the Glass bill should be adopted if possible in the short session, they made no definite motion toward that end.

The Banking and Currency Committee—a continuing body, since the Senate does not come to an end and reorganize with an outgoing administration, or at the end of a designated term of office, as is the case with the House of Representatives—had, however, merely accepted some new members and designated a new chairman early in March, 1933, as the result of the change of party control. Mr. Norbeck was succeeded by Senator Fletcher of Florida, while the Committee itself reappointed the subcommittee on banking (which had gone out of existence when the Glass bill had been reported), naming Senator Glass once more as its chairman. The membership of the subcommittee was slightly changed, Senator McAdoo—newly elected from California—now taking the place of one of the former members. The Glass bill was reintroduced in the form adopted as Senate bill No. 4412, and was referred to the new subcommittee. After awaiting the pleasure of the administration and receiving no indication thereof, the subcommittee, which had naturally felt the same pressure from constituents and public opinion that had made itself apparent during the two years preceding, resolved to proceed with the consideration of the measure and again to report it. Facing a new political situation, however, it was evident that a further amendment and reorganization of the bill would be essential. The changes which had taken place both in the Senate and in the House had led to the elimination of a banking and financial influence which had been dominant dur-

[2] On August 15 it was announced that about 2,800 of these banks remained closed.

ing the preceding régime, but had substituted the domination of other elements which professed a desire for legislation directed against property owners and property-holding in general by providing for the transfer of billions through currency depreciation. These elements had already secured the enactment of the so-called Inflation Bill which invested the President of the United States with power to issue greenbacks, coin silver at a ratio of 16 to 1, and direct Reserve banks to undertake immense open-market operations, as well as to reduce the content of the gold dollar—while it had likewise provided for other anomalies and extreme measures previously thought impossible. One phenomenon produced by the early part of the session had been the appearance of a large brood of bills providing for the guaranty of deposits, a proposal which had already taken very deep root in the House of Representatives. It became evident to Chairman Glass that some one of these bills would doubtless go through Congress, and that the Glass bill would probably succeed in passing only in the event that it were willing to compromise with this guaranty of deposits project. Mr. Glass, accordingly, determined to introduce into the measure a modification of the guaranty of deposits plan, and at the same time to restore to it a number of the desirable features which had been eliminated during the preceding session under pressure of the Hoover administration. The plan embodied in the original bill, therefore, for a liquidating corporation was taken up and broadened. It now appeared as a project for the establishment of a bank deposit insurance corporation whose mission it should be to take charge of and liquidate the assets of insolvent banks and, at the same time, to insure depositors against loss by collecting from solvent banks a specified percentage of their deposits and paying the same to the depositors of insolvent institutions. Two variations of this scheme had been presented in the several bills that were before Congress—the first calling for a government guaranty of deposits, in which the total cost rested upon the Treasury, the other calling for a guaranty provided for by levies upon the several banks. Mr. Glass was successful in securing the adoption of the latter, although he compromised to the extent of permitting the government to supply 150 million dollars—the estimated amount that had been taken from the member banks through the fact that the excess earnings of Reserve banks above 6 per cent on their capital stock had been paid to the government as a franchise tax, notwithstanding as it was claimed, that the Reserve banks had always performed services for the government without charge and that that should have exempted them from the payment of any such levy. Therefore, the proposed guaranty of bank deposits, eventually embodied in the bill, represented a conservative modification of the more extreme of the guaranty plans that were before Congress, although Chairman Glass undoubtedly regretted the necessity of incorporating any such measure into the bill.

Included in the new form of the Glass bill, however, was again the order to bring about a complete separation of investment and commercial banking, by forbidding their simultaneous pursuit by any single institution. The bill, moreover, ordered the complete separation of affiliates from parent banks and limited the time for such separation to a single year. At various points restrictions and limitations which had, perforce, been dropped from the original Glass bill, were now reintroduced. It was regrettable that in this process of reconstruction, Mr. Glass should have found it out of the question to improve upon the branch banking provision in the earlier forms of the Glass bill. Such a change was, however, impossible from the first; and as the bill was finally reported, its terms were, if anything, less favorable to branch banking than those of the final draft of the bill in the preceding Congress.

It was an ironical development that the Glass bill, after passing through this long series of transformations and compromises, should now in its later stages find itself unaided by the administration upon which it had counted for support. Nevertheless, it shortly appeared that the Roosevelt administration was anything but favorable to the new measure. The new Secretary of the Treasury, Mr. William E. Woodin, who had taken office in the Roosevelt administration, had been for several years a Director of the Federal Reserve Bank of New York. He now, under the influence of the latter institution, wrote to the subcommittee on banking a letter expressive of his opposition to the Glass bill, reiterating some of the objections which had been urged in the discarded memorandum prepared by the two advisers which had been appointed by President Hoover to review the measure. He was particularly antipathetic to the idea of losing his own place on the Federal Reserve Board, and he objected especially to the other provisions designed to modify the working of the Federal Reserve Act which had been proposed by the Glass Committee. In a hearing before the Committee Mr. Woodin failed to make good these points of view; but as a personal concession to him the Committee finally allowed him to retain his membership on the Federal Reserve Board, rejecting, however, all of the other criticisms which he had offered.

The modified bill was reported by the subcommittee and then by the Committee in full, but it now encountered the indifference, if not the hostility, of the President. Feeling at last that some definite expression of their views was called for, the banks of New York united in a joint letter to him in which they protested vigorously against the guaranty of deposits provision, and indicated a general dislike of the whole legislation. This may have influenced his mind. Even to get the bill adopted in either house was difficult if not impossible, and advocates of the measure had again made up their minds that the legislation must await a more convenient season when the revelations developed by another subcommittee, concerning undesirable or dangerous practices on the part of investment bankers, tended to give an impetus to the demand for the Glass measure. That was hardly reasonable since its provisions, tending to correct the investment banking situation were small and were merely incidents in a series of much more extensive and far-reaching proposals.

Legislation, however, is seldom dictated by purely logical considerations. It had been intended to adjourn Congress upon a certain date, but friction developing between it and the Executive, a few days of grace were afforded; and the added impetus of the investment-banking inquiry already referred to was sufficient to give the Glass bill adequate momentum to carry it to the statute books in the closing hours of the session, on June 16, 1933. President Roosevelt received the news with the assurance to the public that it was the best legislation of its kind since the adoption of the Federal Reserve Act, and promptly affixed his signature when the measure reached the Executive desk—thus definitely converting it into law, on June 16, 1933.

The Glass bill, as thus adopted, undoubtedly represents in its history an epitome of the conditions under which banking legislation has been initiated and carried forward for more than a century of American history. The review of it thus given is worthy of note, not merely because of its intrinsic interest, but because of the commentary it affords upon the technique and methods of most financial legislation in the United States. The conditions thus set forth are not those that can ever be expected to conduce to efficiency, adequacy, or promptness in the enactment of such legislation, but they should undoubtedly be brought to a close at as early a date as possible.

CHAPTER VII

THE FUTURE

Most of the discussion thus far devoted to the so-called "Glass bill," or Banking Act of 1933 as it is now to be known, has had to do with the negative or prohibitory provisions of that measure. Important as these may be in detail we must now recognize that the sections which direct a guaranty of bank deposits, like those which command a separation of investment from commercial banking, are to be treated as those which are of fundamental character. Their significance far transcends the ordinary guaranty. If fully and consistently carried out, they will produce changes in the current organization of banking that will transform it in essential respects. The significance of the measure in these detailed particulars can hardly be overestimated. Yet a closer scrutiny shows that, important as they are, they cannot be considered the ultimately significant elements in it. It is only when the terms of the new Act are studied in their relation to current financial conditions that we realize how, if the measure be permitted to become fully operative, it may transform the entire banking system of the United States.

This revolutionary quality in the Glass bill was not by any means so evident in its earlier drafts as in its later phases, but it was present, and, as we shall see, has been arrived at, perhaps unexpectedly to some of those who were chiefly responsible for it, through a route quite different from the one originally planned. Yet it was never possible to induce the generality of our bankers to take more than a casual interest in the project. Refusing to recognize the need for some essential reforms, particularly in the matter of the divorcement of the "security affiliates," as well as in other particulars, they turned a cold shoulder to the measure in its first stages, believing that it could be "killed" by Executive disapproval. Even when, in the spring of 1932, they began to manifest a belated interest in the subject, it was still only with the notion of killing the measure, or of securing its amendment in details which they had marked as particularly disagreeable or distasteful to themselves and their own interests.

They were obviously wrong in believing that the public at large cared little about what was done regarding the banks; and doubly wrong in the opinion that there would be insufficient force behind the measure to secure its passage. Even at the last, thinking that they had a strong bulwark in the reported disapproval by, or indifference of, President Roosevelt toward the Glass measure they counted, up to the final moment of passage, upon failure or possibly a veto, only to hear from the White House the, to them, astonishing statement that the measure represented the best banking legislation since the adoption of the Federal Reserve Act. When they, however, had time to study the provisions of the completed legislation in greater detail many were surprised to recognize the implications of the Act. Some of them at once proposed a movement for the repeal or amendment of its terms at the coming Congress. At the American Bankers Association sessions in Chicago during the last week of September, elaborate discussion of plans and prospects occurred with semi-official advice from representatives of the Administration to accept the new law and make the best of it.

Regardless of such amendment they were face to face with the necessity of accepting, and providing for, a radical transformation in the entire structure of the banking system of the United States—one which they probably could not avoid. What they can do is to shape the ways and means by which this transformation occurs, and so to mitigate its injurious effects upon existing banks. Will they now at length view the situation constructively; and will they then turn to a careful analysis of their own position and of the action that should be taken from a system standpoint, so that all—including the customers of the various institutions—may be protected; or will they continue the highly individualistic and local attitude that has been characteristic of them in the past? It is fundamentally necessary that this question be answered in favor of constructive action, since only in that way will serious disaster to our financial structure be averted. The question is no longer whether the Glass bill was wise at the outset, or whether its provisions have been well constructed or not. The measure has become a fact, and must be reckoned with as such. Present evils might have been corrected in another way, but have not been. The nation must follow the cruder and more difficult course which the politicians have marked out.

Let us see exactly wherein the transformations that have been suggested above are to be found—how they are likely to be produced. And in studying the situation, let us consider first a few very fundamental background facts in the case. Of these the outstanding is that the banks of the country, taken as an aggregate, had no capital and surplus prior to the aid extended to them by the Reconstruction Finance Corporation late in 1933. This condition was admitted at the opening of the spring of 1933 for it was then common knowledge among bank administrators that, if bank assets were to be "marked down" to true value, there would be left no equity for shareholders. There were, indeed, not a few strong and well-managed banks here and there whose capitals and surpluses were intact or nearly so, but they were far more than offset by the great multitude whose assets had been enormously reduced in value through the shrinkage of stock-market quotations. Of late, there has been a reduction in the activity of current discussion of banking conditions; and some have supposed that it betokened a serious change for the better in the general outlook. The closing of a large number of institutions, thus taking them definitely out of the field of active banks, has naturally reduced the number of current bank failures, yet enough have continued to show (especially when we recall that it had been asserted that all weak banks had been wiped out) that the basic elements of weakness in the situation have continued. The advance in stock-market prices for the second grade bonds and other securities of the types held by many banks have not sufficed to change their position very materially.

Such advances, even at their utmost, have not nearly made up the gap between solvency and failure that had been previously noted, while the banks themselves, when seeking to take advantage of the higher prices and "unload" their holdings have frequently found the market "thin," and the demand for such securities entirely inadequate to take off more than a fraction of the offered supply. Even when it has had some strength it has been only at decidedly lower prices than those nominally current. Besides this difficult balance-sheet situation of the banks, is the further basic element in the case, that the sale of bank stock is today a most difficult matter. Not only does the position of the average bank with a balance sheet known to be "marked up," by grace usually of the banking authorities, frighten away the ordinary investor, but the changes in banking, and the extraordinarily doubtful attitude of the community toward all banking institutions, necessarily cause many to hesitate about assuming the liabilities which are theoretically inherent in bank stock ownership. Add to these two underlying considerations affecting the profitableness of the banking situation, the fact that, as any one with half an eye can now see, the new legislation on banking greatly changes the terms and conditions upon which banking must be conducted—and it is apparent that the background conditions of the occupation have greatly altered.

Coming into a banking world thus weakened and transformed by the results of the credit debauch of the past ten years and more, the Banking Act of 1933 provides among others the following important changes in conditions:

1. A general guarantee of bank deposits, constituting a liability upon all the banks in the nation.

2. A prohibition of the payment of interest on demand deposits and an official regulation of interest upon time deposits; hence a far reaching alteration of the terms of competition both between banks themselves and between the banks on the one hand and the investment market on the other.

3. A complete separation of commercial from investment banking.

4. A doubling of the minimum capital of (future) banks.

5. A recognition of the system of chain or group banking, at the same time that branch banking is continued as a prohibited banking method.

These elements in the new bank act are thus singled out not because they are the only, or necessarily the most important phases of the legislation taken individually, but because they constitute a series of measures linked together exerting a combined influence and thus to be considered as constituting a radical transformation in the foundations of American banking. Let us see what these legislative innovations actually signify.

The new Banking Act provides[1] that, under its terms, a deposit guaranty corporation shall be established, and that to this corporation all banks shall contribute in proportion to their deposits. The guaranty, however, applies only to banks that have been examined and found eligible for the benefits of the new undertaking. According to the terms of the legislation (Section 12B, subsection J):

> Every member bank shall apply to the corporation for class A stock of the corporation. . . . Upon receipt of such application, the corporation shall request the Federal Reserve Board, in the case of a state member bank, or the Comptroller of the Currency in the case of a national bank, to certify upon the basis of a thorough examination of such bank whether the assets of the applying bank are adequate to enable it to meet all of its liabilities to depositors and other creditors as shown by the books of the bank. . . . If such certification be in the negative the corporation shall deny such application.

This clearly meant that if, after careful examination by the constituted authorities, a given bank shall be found to be possessed of assets inadequate to meet the claims of its depositors and other creditors, it shall be denied membership in the depositors' guaranty scheme. Obviously, the first care of those entrusted with the duty of administering the new law was to determine the meaning of the ambiguous language used in the statute. The Board of Directors of the new insurance corporation was named in July, and later in September made an unofficial announcement that banks' assets were adequate to enable them to qualify for the benefits of the temporary insurance fund (until June, 1934) whenever appraised at a value sufficient probably to meet de-

[1] The Federal Reserve Board has published elaborate regulations for the application of the new act, in *Federal Reserve Bulletin,* August, 1933.

positors' claims. On this basis it was possible to admit a large majority of the banks to temporary guaranty on January 1, 1934, though even then probably 400–500 institutions had to be excluded—how many, the authorities declined to make known either by name or number. The question of admission to the permanent fund (July, 1934), however, remained.

We may now make various suppositions. Assume:[2] that this act is enforced strictly and honestly without political or other favoritism in accordance with its terms. In such a case, evidently, the authorities must ultimately exclude from the enjoyment of the guaranty scheme a large number of banks. Thus guaranty will, in such case, apply only to a relatively small number of large, solvent banks which will guarantee one another, and will constitute a nucleus of soundness in our system. This possibly would be the most desirable, though the least likely, outcome of the new legislation. Such a nucleus would then be surrounded by a large outer circle of banks, known to have been rejected because of their unsoundness or unworthiness for the guaranty owing to their inability to show assets "adequate to enable" them to meet all of "their liabilities to depositors and other creditors." What would become of the banks in this outer circle? Various conjectures as to their fate would be in order, were it not that the act definitely provides for them. "If any national bank shall not have become a Class A stockholder of the corporation on or before July 1, 1934, the Comptroller of the Currency shall appoint a receiver or conservator therefor in accordance with the provisions of existing law"; and again "If any state member bank shall not have become a Class A stockholder of the corporation on or before July 1, 1934, the Federal Reserve Board shall terminate its membership in the Federal Reserve System."

These are stern provisions in existing circumstances. They must mean that this new law, if literally and truthfully applied, will close a large number of the banks of the country, and will leave the nation with scarcely any banks over large areas. Such a situation would be conceivable—would perhaps amount mere-

[2] The Board of the Corporation has ruled that "other creditors" does not include stockholders. Continuation of the temporary fund until July 1, 1935, is now proposed.

ly to a mandate to introduce the Canadian branch-banking system at once and without preparation—were it not that the act, after bitter struggle in Congress has refused to enlarge the permitted area of branch banking, save through the consent of the states, and then only in a way that must necessarily cripple the operation of the branch system and prevent it from becoming nationally effective. The outcome, therefore, of the legislation, if (once more) honestly enforced, would have been to disestablish the Federal Reserve System so far as the rank and file of members are concerned, driving these members into the state systems of banking, there to become non-guaranteed independent units operating under the local laws, and leaving the Reserve System to consist of a few large solvent banks which mutually guarantee one another. As already stated, this, in some ways, might be a consummation devoutly to be wished by the theoretic observer were it not for the handicaps imposed upon branch banking which, even under the most careful and liberal management, must deprive many places of any banking facilities whatever, pending at least action by state legislatures providing for its use within their limits.

Such an outcome was in our practical policies, nearly unthinkable. Accordingly the authorities have thought best to administer the act thus far with Pickwickian interpretation of its provisions, so that the "adequate assets" mean simply assets that perhaps are adequate to meet the demands of depositors (without regard to stockholders)—always provided the latter do not attempt a "run." In this case even, the certifying authorities have manifestly had to come to some serious compromises with their own official consciences. Let us not accuse them of any dishonesty, or greater insincerity than that which has already been exhibited by them. As is well known, the banking authorities, both national and in many of the states, have for more than a year past been disposed to permit banks to "mark up" their assets, or rather to keep them "marked up," on their books, in order that such banks might not be compelled to show an impairment of resources so great as to compel an immediate closing.

In as much as the banking authorities have been inclined for the present to accept the same view of the "adequacy" of assets that has prevailed for a year or two past, what shall we then expect? We can hardly suppose that there will be merely a situation in which some banks are singled out for execution, though not notoriously in worse condition than their neighbors; but we must anticipate that some more or less general policy applicable to all—politics being what they are—will be accepted. It must be a policy which will permit banks in average good condition—banks not worse than the general average of our banking institutions—to enjoy permanent guaranty. This is the probable outcome of the situation, and even that interpretation of the Act, if fully and strictly applied, will mean of necessity the closing of many institutions which have in recent months been permitted to keep open their doors and to vegetate on as best they can in their respective communities.

One other outcome may, however, be given some consideration, namely: that institutions not in very good condition, or possessed of "adequate assets" to meet their liabilities, be continued in the privileges of the guaranty, provided that they are able to obtain the endorsement or underwriting of some other bank of known responsibility. In such a case, the banking authorities would be in effect interpreting the "adequacy" of assets to include such a guarantee or assurance on the part of another bank—just as Secretary of the Treasury Woodin, during spring of 1933, on the advice of his Treasury counsel, included in the assets of the Harriman National Bank of New York, a letter written by the New York Clearing House and vaguely asserting an intent to protect depositors in that bank from loss.

In what circumstances, however, would large strong banks, or solvent banks generally, be disposed to grant such an assurance or guaranty? Obviously only on some basis that would eventually reimburse them; and this could be only the virtual ownership of the guaranteed bank's assets and "plant." The attempt to introduce such a régime as thus contemplated would amount to the extension of group banking on a national scale under the provisions liberally made for it in the Banking Act of 1933—a hybrid kind of branch banking, subject to government supervision and examination. The question whether the larger banks of the country would go into this sort of affiliate business, and would organize state corporations for the purpose of owning and operating "strings" of smaller banks may be questioned. Yet that is a possibility; and it is apparently about the only way, short of extraordinary laxity in the interpretation and in the administration of the terms of the new Act by which the nation could be provided with a normal supply of banking facilities in its various towns and villages.

It is now apparent, from what has been said, that the enforcement of the new Act implies certain alternatives: (1) continuance of the individual banks as at present, with doubtful portfolios and a danger of failure, but with the other banks of the nation which are still solvent, and in some cases liquid, obliged to assume general responsibility for them; or: (2) complete reorganization of the system in which the larger banks practically buy and take over the smaller institutions in vast numbers; or: (3) reduction of the Federal Reserve system to a mere nucleus in numbers with a surrounding body of banks either dubbed "insolvent" by the banking authorities as having "inadequate" assets to meet their obligations or admitted to the guaranty on basis of temporary toleration; or (4) participation of the government in ownership through the purchase of preferred stock. It was this last course of action that was attempted and is now being tried by the government through the purchase at the close of 1933 of some $600,000,000 worth of preferred stock in over 3000 banks—a number still steadily increasing. Does this mean permanent participation by the government in our banking? There is no answer as yet and until there be, the situation is evidently indeterminable.

Whichever course of action may be the one actually pursued, it is clear that the result must be, in one way or another, to make the larger and more solvent institutions responsible for the assets of all the banks in the country; it is the assets and not the "deposits" of the banks that are guaranteed. Such responsibility may come about through steady redemption when failure occurs, as under (1); or through concentration of ownership, as under (2);

or through indefinite and indirect responsibility, as under (3); or through public participation as under (4), the funds for government ownership being borrowed from the larger banks. The new Act requires either a general and determined action, on the part of the population at large designed to provide the capital for the recapitalization and refurnishing of the local or unit banks of the country, or else a general transformation in which the large banks shall become the responsible operators of the entire banking system. The community is asked to abandon or preserve its "unit bank system."

How will the country accept and regard this alternative? We have already observed the present attitude of the nation toward the purchase of bank stock. It is not likely, as things stand, that we shall see a general movement toward the purchase of new bank stock merely in obedience to the abstract motive of supplying the funds wherewith to recharter and reëstablish the banks which have so largely fallen into disrepute. It is much more probable that banks found on the margin of solvency shall be granted license to proceed on their way, and that the larger banks shall, in that fashion, be saddled with the duty of meeting the losses that must be incurred in the large number of prospective bank failures that are still to be dealt with, owing to the fact that our institutions are so devoid of capital and so uncertain in the character of their assets. Can the relatively few banks that are thus solvent and liquid fairly and properly assume the responsibility that Congress has placed upon them and supply either the capital needed to re-capitalize the small banks—thereafter owning them themselves, through holding companies, or to buy them out and take them over "lock, stock, and barrel," or to pay for the deficiencies in their assets when failures occur?

It is unreasonable to suppose that the large banks can do any such thing. Equally unreasonable is it to expect them to undertake it, unless they be permitted to initiate fully and freely a widely-diffused branch-banking type of organization, and this the struggle over the Glass bill renders unlikely, certainly for the early future. Assuming that the full administration of the Act proves slow, the banks undertaking to feel their way and to take no drastic action until it can be ascertained exactly what losses the new measure will subject them to, it must be taken for granted that the measure will bring about not, as alleged by some, a much greater laxity in the operation of banks; but, on the contrary, a disposition on the part of many to keep watch upon others and to handicap the others in every way, since only by such means may they count upon holding losses down to a more reasonable figure. This attitude, if adopted, will be fully warranted and could not be objected to even by the most convinced advocate of lax administration in banking or of "easy money."

Inasmuch as the political pressure upon the banks to make unduly hazardous loans is already great, and inasmuch as the banks have been restrained in the agricultural districts, heretofore, by the danger of direct loss, it may be expected that hereafter the restraint upon them exerted by the other banks through supervision of various kinds, refusal of loans designed to "carry" or relieve them when they show first signs of trouble, and in various similar ways, will be opposed to the influence of the political authorities. Thus one effect of the new law may be to sharpen the issues already open between the bankers and the politicians.

One topic incidentally mentioned in the foregoing discussion must, before leaving this phase of the situation, be given more direct study. The prohibition of interest on demand deposits must be expected to work a large change in the correspondent relationship between the smaller banks of the interior and the larger city institutions. That such will be the case, the haste of certain erstwhile city bank opponents of branch banking to recant their earlier views gives eloquent testimony. As yet, the figures covering the city bank deposits of country banks are insufficient to permit the formation of a positive judgment as to the more essential elements in the case. They seem already to show a strong tendency on the part of the smaller banks to withdraw their funds from the city institutions and to cause a decisive shrinkage in total deposits as reported. In this tendency, the smaller banks will be confirmed by the fact that city institutions are, by the Banking Act, forbidden to act as the agents through whom other banks may place funds in the stock market. Thus a fundamentally important change in interbank relationships is imposed upon the other great alterations and innovations made necessary by the elements in the legislation already sketched. That this alteration would in itself be easily enough made may be true, but, taken in combination with the changes necessitated by the other elements in the legislation, the case is different. We must necessarily look to this phase of the enactment as unavoidably rendering the whole prospect more complex and difficult to deal with. Large transfers of funds out of the city banks which have held them in the past, and into other institutions, or perhaps to the reserve banks, with corresponding changes in the means by which spare bank funds are kept invested, cannot but work a very considerable alteration in the money market position, and must eventually result in some financial readjustments whose significance will not fully appear until later on.

Finally, it is worthy of note that the provision of the new law raising the minimum of future capitalization of banks in the national system (and, by implication, the capitalization of the member banks of the Federal Reserve system) to $50,000, or double its present amount, while desirable in itself, comes at a time—in conjunction with the other far-reaching changes just reviewed, when it will tend to render still more difficult the recapitalization of the banking system of the country. It would be hard enough to get the system recapitalized with the old minimum capital. It will be considerably more difficult to secure the capital required under the revised regulations of the law as to capitalization. Thus it is a tremendous dose of bank reorganization that the new legislation has afforded. For this very reason the original framers of the Glass measure had discarded not a few of the proposals which now, in a far more drastic shape, have been incorporated into the final draft as lately enacted as law.

It ought not to be overlooked in estimating the future prospects of this legislation that it will almost inevitably alter, in essential particulars, the management of the Federal Reserve system. The changing of the banking structure, if achieved by either of the three main methods already outlined, or by some combination of them, must have its profound effect upon the make-up of the banking system and its organization for the early future. One thing that was early shown by the investigation which accompanied the preparation of the Banking Act of 1933 was the fact that the smaller banks of the country were certainly not receiving much direct benefit from the operation of the system, but were supporting it with practically no return. The altered structure of banking which seems likely to be developed under the new Banking Act must accordingly leave the weaker banks of the country in a better position from the standpoint of service, than they have had heretofore. They will certainly not continue in a position in which they receive little or no service from the reserve banks, and at the same time go on bearing the costs of the system, unless there be some greater return to them than that which they have heretofore enjoyed. That such is the case has been evident for a good while, partly through the steady shrinking of the membership of the system, partly through the constant, and more or less well-reasoned complaints uttered by the members of the system, partly through the fact that the Reserve banks themselves were able to show so little in the way of real or direct service to their members as revealed in their statements and reports. It is a situation that has required remedy, and the need of such remedy is now brought forcefully to the front through the terms of the new legislation as well as through the situation to which it has given rise.

It is less obvious, but equally true, that the new legislation will, if enforced, result in a reduction of service on the part of the Reserve banks to their larger members. For a good while past, the chief activities of the Reserve banks in direct dealing with their members have consisted in their loans and advances to the city banks upon the direct notes of the latter collateraled by so-called eligible paper, which in fact consisted of government obligations of one sort or another. Under the terms of the Banking Act of 1933, such advances are henceforward to be prohibited, should there be evidence that such member banks are increasing the amount of their own loans upon collateral security (i.e., for the financing of speculation) during the period in which they have money out by way of advances to members. Remove this type of service, and of course the utility of the Reserve banks to their members will be largely reduced or will disappear. It would seem, then, that accurate and faithful enforcement of the new legislation will tend to render the Reserve banks as little useful to the large city members as they have long been to the country banks. This would leave, as an open question growing out of the enactment: What is to be the place of the Reserve Banking system in the new banking world which will be created should the outworking of the Act be approximately that which has been foreshadowed? It is an important issue; for obviously no such system can long exist unless able to render some real constructive service to those for whose use it was supposedly intended.

For a good while past it has been observed that the Reserve system was steadily developing into a purely governmental, or government-financing, type of banking system or arrangement. This observation has been based upon the fact, well recognized by all, that the Reserve system was devoting itself almost exclusively, to government operations or to operations designed for the carrying out of the purposes of the Treasury Department. That this is the chief or essential mission of the Reserve banks has indeed been asserted by leading members of the present national administration, and they have attempted, confessedly, to "crush" the Federal Reserve Board because of its presumed tendency to stand in the way of the complete attainment of some such object. A long step in this direction has indeed been taken in the so-called devaluation act, adopted in January, 1934, whereby many of the powers of the Board are in effect transferred to the Treasury. To deprive the Reserve System of what for reasons of circumstance and bad management, has become in recent years the major occupation of the system—the financing of speculation—means that the strong drift toward making it a medium more and more exclusively for the financing of

Treasury operations will be further intensified. There can, indeed, be no other outcome.

How far then will the banks which own and, in theory, operate, the system be inclined to support it merely as a Treasury agency? This is a serious and difficult question—one which ought to be firmly and frankly faced, and definitely answered. The immediate necessity is that of finding some specific field of banking service for the Federal Reserve system. Today it stands as a menace rather than as an assistance to the banks of the country, the more so because its existence opens the way for such recommendations as have constantly been offered, since the opening of the present administration, looking to the nationalization of the system. One such suggestion was lately offered before the New York State Bankers Association when a member of the so-called "brain trust" suggested (neglecting the fact that the member banks today own the reserve banks and have contributed their entire funds) that the reserve banks should become (with the use of what means of purchase was not stated) owners of the member banks, thus establishing a completely government-owned and operated system of banking in the United States. Such vagaries and suggestions for what appears to be thought of as expropriation will be more and more frequent as the system has less and less to do. One way out of the present situation would be furnished by bringing the system more closely into contact with the individual by permitting the Reserve banks to engage in operations of the type that are undertaken by practically all other central banks. This is a sharply controverted point, yet in some way the system must be given a definite field of occupation since its development and the circumstances of the time have so largely destroyed that with which it started, and since the new law has now cut it off from the speculative field of activity which it had itself developed.

The Banking Act of 1933 thus invokes, although less acutely and directly than in the field of individual banking, a crisis in the history of the Federal Reserve system. How will the system meet this issue, and how will it adapt itself to aid the other banks in overcoming and solving the new problems which events have thrust forward for settlement after a long period of incubation during which they have had but little attention from those whose chief care they should have been? The answer must be derived from a careful study of the facts and figures which reveal the conditions surrounding our banking system and determining its reconstruction. With these we now proceed to deal.[1]

[1] A considerable portion of the foregoing Chapter (Chapter VII) was published as an article in the *Commercial and Financial Chronicle* for August 26, 1933.

PART II

STRUCTURE

CHAPTER VIII

PRESENT POSITION OF THE BANKING SYSTEM OF THE UNITED STATES[1]

We may now devote ourselves to a sketch of some of the most important changes that have taken place in the banking system of the United States. This chapter will deal primarily with alterations in banking structure and will endeavor to point out the principal lines of change in the development of the various phases of banking. Such changes relate to the structure of banking and its division between different types of institution, or to alterations in the average size and capitalization of banking units, or to the distribution of banking establishments throughout the country. These elements all enter into the general development of the banking system and have an important bearing upon the shape and form that it eventually assumes. After this general survey has been completed, an attempt will be made to show how some of the major types of banking institutions have grown up and gradually taken their present form, and to indicate the chief problems by which they have been confronted during this development. A preliminary outline of structure is, however, necessary as a background to later and more specific analysis.

I. Nature of Banking Statistics

Before beginning a review of the structure of American banking, it is appropriate to indicate the source of our information and the nature of banking statistics used. Most of the tables given in this chapter have been compiled from the *Annual Reports of the Comptroller of the Currency* or computed on the basis of data published in these Reports. This does not mean,

[1] This chapter was prepared by V. D. Kazakévich. The material on the Distribution of Banks, by sizes, has been taken, as is indicated in the text, from the as yet unpublished Report of the Committee of the Federal Reserve System on Group, Chain and Branch Banking. The rest of the data has been compiled by V. D. Kazakévich with the assistance of Messrs. J. Torpats and G. Wittmann, and a clerical staff furnished by the Emergency Work Bureau of Columbia University.

however, that the statistical information so presented can be obtained by the reader by direct reference to the Reports, as the presentation of the figures often changes from year to year—the same information appearing in different tables and under new titles; certain tabulations are discontinued after a period of years and others added; while the data are often subdivided in a different fashion and summary figures include new items or omit old ones. In order to build up a comparable series it is often necessary to undertake a considerable amount of recomputing in order to eliminate changes in the method of presentation. Most of the information assembled in this chapter is scattered through a number of annual editions, so that to the process of recomputation was added that of assembling the data.

Although the *Annual Reports of the Comptroller of the Currency* are not only the official government source for banking information, but also probably the most complete set of banking statistics in existence, there still remains the question how completely they cover the field and whether all of the data they present are entirely reliable. The office of the Comptroller receives directly the reports for the national-banking system; for information relating to institutions chartered by the various states, it has to rely on other sources.[2]

[2] Methods are explained in Vol. I, pp. 87-88 of the 1917 Report as follows:

"It appears that the first official attempt to collect statistics relating to banking in the United States was made in 1833 by the Secreary of the Treasury in compliance with a resolution of the House of Representatives adopted July 10, 1832, as follows:

'Resolved, That the Secretary of the Treasury be directed to lay before this House, at the next and each successive session of Congress, copies of such statements or returns, showing the capital, circulation, discounts, specie, deposits, and condition of the different State banks and banking companies as may have been communicated to the legislatures, governors, or other officers of the several States within the year, and made public; and where such statements can not be obtained, such other authentic information as will best suit the deficiency.'

"In conformity with this resolution, and up to 1863, inclusive, the Secretary of the Treasury submitted to Congress such information relating to the condition of banks as he had been able to obtain. In his annual report on the condition of the banks for 1863, the Secretary stated that the action of Congress requiring regular returns from banks of their circulation and deposits, with reference to the internal revenue to be collected on account of them, would probably supersede the necessity of a compilation from statements or returns under State laws, and suggested the expediency of rescinding the resolution of July 10, 1832, and this suggestion presumably received favorable consideration, as no reports to Congress on the condition of State banks were made by the Secretary subsequent to 1863.

The thoroughness with which the entire field of banking is covered by the office of the Comptroller varies moreover from year to year. It is possible, in some instances, to check the degree of completeness of the official figures.

The Reports of the Comptroller of the Currency for the years 1900, 1901, and 1902 publish figures of the total number of banks provided by the Commissioner of Internal Revenue. These figures originated during the Spanish-American War as a result of the "War Revenue Act of June 13, 1898."[3] If we compare the figures of the total number of banks compiled by the Comptroller and those given by the Bureau of Internal Revenue, the following discrepancies are shown:

NUMBER OF BANKS

	Comptroller's Figures	Bureau of Internal Revenue Figures
1900	10,382	13,325
1901	11,406	14,455
1902	12,424	15,387

"From 1864 to 1882 semiannual returns for taxation purposes were made to the Commissioner of Internal Revenue relating to the capital and deposits of banks.

"By act of Congress dated February 19, 1873, as amended by act of February 18, 1875 (sec. 333, U.S.R.S.), the Comptroller of the Currency is required to collect and publish in his annual report to Congress:

'A statement exhibiting under appropriate heads the resources and liabilities and condition of the banks, banking companies, and savings banks organized under the laws of the several States and Territories; such information to be obtained by the Comptroller from the reports made by such banks, banking companies, and savings banks to the legislatures or officers of the different States and Territories, and where such reports can not be obtained, the deficiency to be supplied from such other authentic sources as may be available.'

"From 1873 to 1908 the Comptroller obtained statistics relating to banks other than national from the State bank superintendents, supplementing these returns by correspondence with individual banks in States where no provision was made for periodical returns. From 1909 to 1915, inclusive, while the work of revising the monetary system was in progress, this information was obtained from special individual reports secured by correspondence with the banks and through the coöperation of the State bank superintendents.

"Information relative to the condition of State banks for the years 1916 and 1917 has been obtained largely from compilations made by the various State superintendents of banking."

[3] Section 2 of this act provided for the imposition of a tax of $50 on banks with a capital of $25,000 or less, and of $2 on each additional $1,000 in excess of $25,000 (the surplus fund was included in the amount of capital).

It is clear that about one-fourth of all the banks that paid the War tax on capital never did send in any report to the office of the Comptroller. When the office of the Comptroller of the Currency attempted in 1873, for the first time, to comply with the provisions of the act of Congress relating to state bank statistics, returns from only nine states could be obtained.[4] The coverage increased with time and in 1900 the office of the Comptroller states that the banks reporting represent practically 83 per cent of the banking capital of the country.[5]

The first reasonably complete figures may be had as of April 28, 1909, when the National Monetary Commission made a canvass of all the banks in the United States. The results of that survey were published in the 1909 Report of the Comptroller in place of the usual mid-year figures. Only in 1912 did the Comptroller begin to publish a combined balance sheet for all banks other than national, and, starting with 1921 for state (commercial) banks.

It is clear that, even relative to the total number of banks, the official figures are far from complete, and it is difficult to say what the degree of accuracy is even for the years of the World War. Undoubtedly, for the early years of the present century, the data given in this chapter (or anywhere else) are strongly biased so far as completeness goes in favor of national banks.

In addition to the lack of completeness, the official figures suffer from various other defects. In 1921, for instance, stock savings banks did not report for the state of California; again in 1932 the Comptroller gives the resources of all private banks in the country as equaling $55,418,000, while Messrs. J. P. Morgan & Co. report to the United States Senate that their resources amounted in that year to $424,708,000. Thus, the resources of one private bank were in that year more than eight times greater than the total in which they presumably should have been included. In 1931 the Comptroller listed 284 private banks, while the Committee of the Federal Reserve System on Group, Chain and Branch Banking includes, for the same year, 504 private banks. We could, if necessary, give many more similar examples,

[4] *Annual Report of the Comptroller of the Currency,* 1903, Vol. I, p. 44.
[5] *Ibid.,* 1900, Vol. I, p. xxxviii.

but those here presented are sufficient to indicate the inadequacy of existing banking information and the misleading character of a great many official figures.

In spite of all that, we still base our survey of the structure of the American banking system on these figures, for the reason that, all shortcomings notwithstanding, the data published every year by the office of the Comptroller are still the best and most complete of all existing sources. Under the existing system of unit banking and of dual supervision, it would probably be difficult to obtain a more complete and accurate picture. Therefore, although many figures given in this chapter must contain considerable margins of error, the data as a whole do present, we believe, a fairly accurate picture of the general changes in structure, and particularly of prevailing trends.

II. Distribution of Numbers, Capital Funds, and Resources

In a survey of any banking system a beginning is best made through the medium of a general descriptive presentation showing how the main facts relating to the scope of the system developed over a period of years and how they stand, as a result of this process, as shown by the latest available data. In this discussion, it has been deemed best to present the data covering a considerable number of years—from 1900 to 1932—in order that sufficient basis for comparison may be furnished. During this period extensive changes took place in banking, as we can observe from the figures given in Table 1.

Because of the magnitude of these changes, it is difficult to trace the interrelation of various types of banks from the actual figures. In order to bring out the relative position of the different institutions more clearly, the figures for the number, capital funds, and resources of various kinds of banks have been reduced to a percentage basis—expressed as a percentage of their totals for each year—thus rendering comparisons easier. As a result, Table 2 offers a percentage distribution of the numbers, capital funds, and resources of all banks in the United States, classified by types of banks.

A reference to Table 2 shows definite tendencies in the com-

TABLE 1

CHANGES IN THE NUMBER, CAPITAL FUNDS AND RESOURCES OF BANKS IN THE UNITED STATES 1900-1932*

(By type of bank)

	NUMBER				CAPITAL FUNDS (in millions)				RESOURCES (in millions)			
	1900	Highest		1932	1900	Highest		1932	1900	Highest		1932
	No.	No.	Year	No.	$	$	Year	$	$	$	Year	$
All Banks	10,382	30,812	'21	19,163	1,907	10,013	'30	8,093	10,786	74,020	'30	57,245
National Banks	3,732	8,249	'22	6,150	1,013	3,881	'30	3,131	4,944	29,117	'30	22,368
All Others	6,650	22,658	'21	13,013	894	6,132	'30	4,962	5,842	44,903	'30	34,877
State Commercial	4,369	18,875	'21	10,455	367	2,198	'29	1,460	1,760	16,824	'29	9,479
Loan & Trust Cos.	290	1,680	'25	1,235	275	2,880	'30	2,362	1,330	17,703	'30	13,119
Mutual Savings	652	678	'07	594	196	1,134	'31	1,043	2,336	11,192	'31	11,134
Stock Savings	350	1,529	'15	502	31	161	'15	87	289	2,196	'26	1,090
Private Banks	989	1,497	'09	227	25	43	'09	10	127	266	'19	55

* Compiled on the basis of data abstracted from the *Annaul Reports of the Comptroller of the Currency.*

The largest number and the highest capitalization of private banks are found in 1909; this is the year of the survey conducted by the National Monetary Commission. In all probability during the later years the Reports of the Comptroller did not cover all the private banks in existence. In reference to the reliability of data on private banks even as late as 1932, see page 124 of the text.

position of the aggregate number of banks as we get further away from the year 1900. In 1900 nearly 36 per cent of all banks were national and 42 per cent were state chartered banks of a commercial type comparable with the national. The relative importance of the number of state commercial banks increased till, in 1921, this type of bank reached 61 per cent of the aggregate number of all banks, while in the same year national banks declined to about 27 per cent of the total. Beginning with 1922 the trend reversed itself and by 1932 the national banks had reached 32 per cent of the total, while the state-chartered commercial institutions had dropped to 55 per cent. From Table 1 we may see also that loan and trust companies comprised only about 3 per cent of all banks in 1900, but rose steadily to over 6 per cent in 1932. During the same period—1900 to 1932—both mutual savings banks and private banks showed a decline in numbers relative to the aggregate number of banks in the country, while the number of stock savings banks was around 3 per cent of the aggregate in 1900 as well as in 1932.

If we reduce the actual figures for capital funds of various types of banks to a percentage basis, we notice at once from Table 2 that the distribution of capital funds follows somewhat different lines from that of numbers. In 1900 the national system accounted for 53 per cent of the aggregate capital funds of all banks; this ratio declined steadily for thirty-three years until, in 1932, national banks contained only 39 per cent of the total capitalization of all banks. Capital funds of state commercial banks increased from 19 per cent of the aggregate at the beginning of the period, to 29 per cent in 1921; after that they once more declined, reaching 18 per cent of the total capitalization of banks by 1932. As measured by this share of total capital funds, loan and trust companies and mutual savings banks grew in relative importance during the post-war decade; by 1932 their capital funds reached 29 per cent and 13 per cent of the capitalization of all banks in the country.

Analyzing the distribution of resources given in Table 2 on the same basis, we observe, in the case of national banks, a relative decline in resources—from 46 per cent of the aggregate

TABLE 2

PERCENTAGE DISTRIBUTION OF NUMBERS, CAPITAL FUNDS AND RESOURCES OF ALL BANKS IN THE UNITED STATES AMONG THE VARIOUS TYPES OF BANKS*

NUMBERS

YEAR	National	Other Than National	State Commercial	Loan & Trust	Mutual Savings	Stock Savings	Private
	%	%	%	%	%	%	%
1900	35.9	64.1	42.1	2.8	6.3	3.4	9.5
1901	36.5	63.5	43.7	2.9	5.8	3.0	8.0
1902	36.5	63.5	43.4	3.4	5.3	3.1	8.4
1903	36.1	63.9	43.6	3.9	4.8	3.1	8.6
1904	35.9	64.1	46.6	3.9	4.5	3.3	5.8
1905	34.5	65.5	47.5	4.2	4.1	3.5	6.3
1906	33.8	66.2	49.5	4.1	3.8	3.6	5.2
1907	32.8	67.4	50.5	4.0	3.4	3.7	5.8
1908	32.0	68.0	52.6	3.9	3.2	3.6	4.7
1909	30.6	69.4	50.3	4.8	2.9	4.7	6.7
1910	30.9	69.1	52.7	4.7	2.8	4.9	4.0
1911	29.8	70.2	52.7	5.1	2.6	5.1	4.6
1912	29.3	70.7	53.1	5.6	2.5	5.1	4.4
1913	28.8	71.2	53.9	5.8	2.4	5.2	3.9
1914	28.1	71.9	54.2	5.8	2.4	5.5	4.0
1915	28.1	71.9	53.9	6.1	2.3	5.6	3.8
1916	27.5	72.5	56.2	5.8	2.3	4.5	3.7
1917	27.2	72.8	57.2	5.8	2.2	4.2	3.4
1918	26.7	73.3	57.5	5.8	2.2	4.1	3.8
1919	26.7	73.3	59.1	4.7	2.1	3.8	3.5
1920	26.6	73.4	60.4	4.7	2.1	3.6	2.7
1921	26.5	73.5	61.3	4.8	2.0	3.2	2.3
1922	27.1	72.9	60.0	5.1	2.0	3.5	2.2
1923	27.3	72.7	59.8	5.4	2.0	3.4	2.0
1924	27.5	72.5	59.4	5.7	2.1	3.4	1.9
1925	28.0	72.0	58.9	5.8	2.1	3.4	1.8
1926	28.4	71.6	58.6	5.9	2.2	3.2	1.8
1927	28.8	71.2	58.0	6.1	2.3	3.1	1.7
1928	29.3	70.7	57.5	6.2	2.3	3.0	1.5
1929	29.8	70.2	57.0	6.3	2.4	2.9	1.5
1930	30.1	69.9	56.4	6.5	2.5	3.0	1.5
1931	30.8	69.2	55.5	6.7	2.7	3.0	1.3
1932	32.1	67.9	54.5	6.5	3.1	2.6	1.2

* Percentages do not add exactly to 100.0. This table has been computed on the basis of data abstracted from the *Annual Reports of the Comptroller of the Currency*.

TABLE 2 *(Continued)*

PERCENTAGE DISTRIBUTION OF NUMBERS, CAPITAL FUNDS AND RESOURCES OF ALL BANKS IN THE UNITED STATES AMONG THE VARIOUS TYPES OF BANKS*

CAPITAL FUNDS

YEAR	National	Other Than National	State Commercial	Loan & Trust	Mutual Savings	Stock Savings	Private
	%	%	%	%	%	%	%
1900	53.1	46.9	19.2	14.4	10.3	1.6	1.3
1901	52.3	47.7	19.8	15.0	10.1	1.5	1.3
1902	51.5	48.5	19.1	17.6	9.0	1.3	1.4
1903	49.5	50.5	19.0	21.1	7.9	1.3	1.2
1904	49.0	51.0	20.7	20.6	7.5	1.3	0.9
1905	48.5	51.5	20.6	20.9	7.5	1.4	1.1
1906	47.7	52.3	21.5	21.2	7.1	1.5	0.9
1907	48.1	51.9	22.6	20.2	6.4	1.6	1.1
1908	47.4	52.6	22.9	19.7	7.5	1.6	0.9
1909	47.6	52.4	18.2	23.6	6.8	2.7	1.2
1910	48.3	51.7	18.0	22.6	7.5	2.8	0.7
1911	48.1	51.9	17.8	23.0	7.2	3.0	0.8
1912	47.5	52.5	17.5	23.5	7.6	3.1	0.9
1913	47.1	52.9	17.7	23.6	7.6	3.3	0.7
1914	46.5	53.5	18.3	23.4	7.6	3.4	0.8
1915	46.4	53.6	18.1	23.2	7.9	3.5	0.7
1916	45.6	54.4	20.0	23.5	7.7	2.6	0.6
1917	45.3	54.7	20.4	23.4	7.8	2.5	0.6
1918	45.5	54.5	21.0	23.1	7.4	2.3	0.6
1919	45.4	54.6	25.5	19.1	7.3	2.0	0.6
1920	45.3	54.7	27.4	17.9	6.9	2.0	0.5
1921	44.0	56.0	29.2	18.3	7.0	1.1	0.4
1922	43.3	56.7	27.2	18.4	8.5	2.1	0.4
1923	42.3	57.7	26.9	19.6	8.9	2.1	0.4
1924	41.3	58.7	26.6	20.3	9.3	2.1	0.3
1925	40.4	59.6	26.3	20.8	10.2	2.0	0.3
1926	39.6	60.4	26.2	21.4	10.7	2.0	0.3
1927	39.2	60.8	25.2	22.6	11.1	1.6	0.3
1928	40.1	59.9	23.3	23.7	11.2	1.4	0.2
1929	37.8	62.2	23.1	27.4	10.2	1.2	0.2
1930	38.8	61.2	20.6	28.8	10.5	1.1	0.2
1931	38.3	61.7	19.2	29.3	12.0	1.1	0.1
1932	38.7	61.3	18.0	29.2	12.9	1.1	0.1

* Percentages do not add exactly to 100.0. This table has been computed on the basis of data abstracted from the *Annual Reports of the Comptroller of the Currency.*

TABLE 2 *(Continued)*

PERCENTAGE DISTRIBUTION OF NUMBERS, CAPITAL FUNDS AND RESOURCES OF ALL BANKS IN THE UNITED STATES AMONG THE VARIOUS TYPES OF BANKS*

RESOURCES

YEAR	National	Other Than National	State Commercial	Loan & Trust	Mutual Savings	Stock Savings	Private
	%	%	%	%	%	%	%
1900	45.8	54.2	16.3	12.3	21.7	2.7	1.2
1901	45.9	54.1	17.5	13.1	20.0	2.3	1.2
1902	45.0	55.0	17.3	14.8	19.4	2.3	1.3
1903	44.0	56.0	17.4	16.1	19.0	2.4	1.2
1904	43.8	56.2	18.8	15.7	18.5	2.4	0.8
1905	43.3	56.7	18.9	16.9	17.5	2.4	1.0
1906	42.9	57.1	20.3	16.3	17.3	2.5	0.8
1907	43.1	56.9	21.0	15.6	16.7	2.6	1.0
1908	44.5	55.5	20.6	14.6	17.0	2.4	0.8
1909	44.4	55.6	15.8	19.3	16.1	3.2	1.2
1910	44.1	55.9	16.5	18.8	16.3	3.7	0.7
1911	43.9	56.1	15.9	19.7	15.9	3.8	0.8
1912	43.5	56.5	15.5	20.4	15.7	4.0	0.8
1913	42.9	57.1	16.1	19.9	16.0	4.4	0.7
1914	42.6	57.4	16.1	20.4	15.8	4.4	0.7
1915	42.4	57.6	15.8	21.1	15.5	4.5	0.6
1916	43.2	56.8	17.2	21.8	14.1	3.2	0.6
1917	43.9	56.1	18.3	21.3	13.0	3.0	0.5
1918	45.1	54.9	19.2	20.4	11.8	2.9	0.6
1919	44.6	55.4	24.6	16.7	10.9	2.7	0.6
1920	44.1	55.9	26.4	15.7	10.6	2.8	0.4
1921	41.3	58.7	28.6	16.5	12.2	1.1	0.4
1922	41.1	58.9	25.9	16.9	12.6	3.1	0.4
1923	39.8	60.2	26.2	17.6	12.8	3.3	0.3
1924	39.5	60.5	25.9	18.1	12.9	3.4	0.3
1925	39.2	60.8	25.7	18.6	12.8	3.4	0.3
1926	39.0	61.0	25.5	18.8	13.0	3.4	0.3
1927	39.0	61.0	24.3	20.5	13.2	2.7	0.2
1928	39.8	60.2	22.8	21.3	13.5	2.4	0.2
1929	38.0	62.0	23.3	22.4	13.9	2.2	0.2
1930	39.3	60.7	20.6	23.9	13.9	2.1	0.2
1931	39.4	60.6	18.7	24.0	15.9	1.9	0.1
1932	39.1	60.9	16.6	22.9	19.4	1.9	0.1

* Percentages do not add exactly to 100.0. This table has been computed on the basis of data abstracted from the *Annual Reports of the Comptroller of the Currency.*

bank resources in 1900 to 39 per cent in 1932—similar to the decline in capital funds. Resources of state commercial banks rose from 16 per cent of total resources of all banks in 1900 to 29 per cent in 1921, and then declined to 17 per cent in 1932; the change in the distribution of resources coincided in this case with the trend in the distribution of numbers and capital funds. The percentage of total banking resources, represented by the resources of loan and trust companies, doubled during the thirty-three years studied, increasing from 12 per cent in 1900 to 23 per cent in 1932. This tendency corresponds to the changes that took place in the share of total numbers and capital funds of all banks, made up by numbers and capitalization of trust companies. Resources of mutual savings banks increased, during the post-war decade, from 11 per cent of the resources of all banks in 1920 to 19 per cent in 1932, while from 1900 up to the end of the war their relative importance was declining.

The percentual course of development thus presented fails to bring out one especially important feature of the situation as represented by figures of numbers and dollar amounts of capital funds and resources. While, through the thirty-three years covered, capital funds and resources increased, in the period from 1900 to 1921 there also took place a very rapid increase in the number of banks—from 10,382 to 30,812—due largely to the growth in commercial institutions, both national and state. Since that time, in spite of a continued growth up to the present depression in dollar amounts of capital funds and resources, the total number of banks was decreasing, and by 1932 had declined to about two-thirds of the 1921 number. By 1932 national banks declined by about 25 per cent and state commercial banks by nearly 50 per cent of their 1921 number. Throughout the period, from 1900 to 1932, the number of mutual savings banks underwent very little change; their resources declined from 22 per cent of aggregate banking resources in 1900 to around 11 per cent in 1920, and rose to 19 per cent in 1932. The increase in the numbers of trust companies was comparatively moderate, but they gained both in dollar amounts of resources and in respect to their share of the resources of all banks.

Both the rapid increase in the total number of banks up to 1921 and the drastic decline after that year must, therefore, be attributed to the wide fluctuations in the number of commercial institutions. The outstanding feature of development, especially during the past ten years, has been, in addition to the declining tendency in the number of commercial banks, a very rapid growth in the resources, in dollar amounts as well as relative to total resources of all banks, of institutions other than those chartered as commercial banks. In June, 1932, of the total number of 19,163 institutions, about 32 per cent were national banks, the remainder being made up of state-chartered institutions of various kinds among which 10,455, or 54.5 per cent of all banks, were state commercial banks; 1,235, or 6.5 per cent, were organized as trust companies, 594, or 3.1 per cent, mutual savings banks; and 502, or 2.6 per cent, stock savings banks. At the same time the combined resources of national and state commercial banks accounted in 1932 for only slightly over one-half (55.7 per cent) of the aggregate resources of all banks, as against 70.5 per cent in 1920.

III. Average Capitalization and Resources

Quite as important as the general change in number which has reduced the aggregate of banks from nearly 31,000 in 1921 to about 18,000 at the time of the nation-wide bank holiday in March, 1933, is the change which has taken place in capitalization. There has been, not only a very substantial increase in the amount of capital funds, but also a general drift toward increase in the average capitalization of each institution. This tendency, however, has been irregular and much slower than the increase in the prevailing size of the unit in the basic industries throughout the country. Since 1929 this tendency to grow shows a falling off, owing in all probability to failures and other disturbances of capital structure brought about by the depression. In Table 3 there have been computed the average capital funds and resources of banks in the United States during the thirty-three years covered by the three preceding tables, with the design of comparing especially the conditions of growth that have made themselves evident among the different classes of banks.[6]

In 1932 the average capitalization for all banks equalled $422,000 as compared to $184,000 in 1900. While, at the end of the same period, national banks had $509,000, as against $271,000 at the beginning, state-chartered banks of a commercial type comparable to national had, in 1932, an average capitalization of only $140,000, as compared to $84,000 in 1900. In 1932 the highest average capitalization was found among institutions not chartered primarily as commercial banks; loan and trust companies show average capital funds of $1,912,000 and mutual savings banks, of $1,756,000; at the same time we may note that the capitalization of stock savings banks is only slightly above that of state-chartered commercial banks.

At this point it is appropriate to compare the average capitalization of various classes of banks with their average resources also presented in Table 3. In 1932 the average resources of national banks equalled $2,987,000, as compared to $905,000 for state commercial banks. All through the thirty-three years covered, banking institutions of primarily non-commercial nature possessed much higher average resources than commercial banks; in 1932 the resources of loan and trust companies averaged $10,623,000 per unit and those of mutual savings banks, $18,744,000. Stock savings banks follow, in respect to resources, the trend of national banks, while their average capitalization, as already indicated, is only slightly above that of state commercial institutions.

If we compare the relationship of resources to capitalization among the various classes of banks, we observe from Table 4 that the ratio between capital funds and resources of commercial institutions has been rising since the beginning of the war. In spite of the wide differences in average capitalization and resources between national and state chartered commercial institutions, their ratios follow each other quite closely. In 1932 the

[6] The size of banks is very far from being uniform, so that the dispersion around the average capitalization must be extremely wide; we must keep this in mind in evaluating the significance of the figures presented in Table 3.

TABLE 3

AVERAGE CAPITAL FUNDS AND RESOURCES OF VARIOUS TYPES OF BANKS*

(In thousands of dollars)

CAPITAL FUNDS

YEAR	All Banks	National	Other Than National	State Comm.	Loan & Trust	Mutual Savings	Stock Savings	Pri-vate
1900	184	271	134	84	949	300	89	25
1901	178	255	134	81	915	311	85	28
1902	185	261	141	82	972	316	79	30
1903	190	260	150	83	1,031	314	78	26
1904	185	253	148	82	970	309	74	29
1905	177	248	139	77	888	326	74	31
1906	174	246	138	76	895	327	71	31
1907	169	250	130	76	849	316	74	32
1908	165	244	127	72	825	389	73	30
1909	162	251	122	58	793	387	92	29
1910	166	259	124	57	793	453	97	31
1911	165	266	122	56	739	458	96	29
1912	166	269	123	55	695	501	101	32
1913	167	274	124	55	678	530	107	30
1914	165	272	123	56	660	529	102	34
1915	168	277	125	56	634	571	105	32
1916	168	278	126	60	673	570	96	26
1917	175	292	132	62	713	612	104	29
1918	176	300	130	64	702	599	98	29
1919	187	318	139	81	755	641	101	33
1920	202	343	151	92	773	681	112	37
1921	206	343	157	98	790	716	70	37
1922	216	345	168	98	782	905	131	41
1923	226	349	179	101	810	978	136	40
1924	240	361	195	107	862	1,074	151	38
1925	255	368	211	114	908	1,227	154	41
1926	277	387	234	124	1,007	1,342	169	46
1927	306	416	261	133	1,138	1,489	159	45
1928	339	464	288	138	1,289	1,624	162	46
1929	375	477	332	152	1,620	1,590	156	56
1930	416	535	364	152	1,841	1,738	160	48
1931	429	533	383	149	1,889	1,889	158	47
1932	422	509	381	140	1,912	1,756	173	46

* Computed on the basis of data abstracted from the *Annual Reports of the Comptroller of the Currency.*

ratio for the average national institution was 7.15, and that for an average state commercial bank, 6.46. Loan and trust companies have, on the average, a ratio lower than that of commer-

TABLE 3 (*Continued*)

AVERAGE CAPITAL FUNDS AND RESOURCES OF VARIOUS TYPES OF BANKS*

(In thousands of dollars)

RESOURCES

YEAR	All Banks	National	Other Than National	State Comm.	Loan & Trust	Mutual Stock	Stock Savings	Pri-vate
1900	1,039	1,325	878	403	4,587	3,584	824	128
1901	1,083	1,363	923	434	4,835	3,738	834	163
1902	1,076	1,325	932	428	4,756	3,943	799	163
1903	1,045	1,273	917	418	4,329	4,140	801	144
1904	1,023	1,249	897	414	4,069	4,219	731	145
1905	1,031	1,293	893	409	4,198	4,442	705	161
1906	1,014	1,286	874	415	3,988	4,623	700	155
1907	995	1,318	839	413	3,868	4,830	689	171
1908	917	1,277	748	359	3,403	4,929	615	160
1909	938	1,359	752	295	3,771	5,288	639	164
1910	972	1,385	787	304	3,865	5,725	740	171
1911	969	1,427	774	291	3,729	5,925	712	164
1912	992	1,473	793	291	3,622	6,237	769	177
1913	989	1,477	792	296	3,382	6,589	827	180
1914	1,008	1,526	805	300	3,510	6,708	816	185
1915	1,027	1,551	823	301	3,530	6,856	810	171
1916	1,173	1,838	920	359	4,376	7,312	832	179
1917	1,330	2,142	1,025	426	4,913	7,735	952	211
1918	1,410	2,382	1,057	471	4,983	7,710	991	217
1919	1,635	2,728	1,236	679	5,781	8,314	1,168	262
1920	1,761	2,915	1,342	770	5,909	9,063	1,386	266
1921	1,612	2,516	1,287	752	5,550	9,695	570	248
1922	1,659	2,510	1,342	717	5,506	10,261	1,486	276
1923	1,791	2,610	1,483	785	5,782	11,173	1,740	274
1924	1,947	2,791	1,626	850	6,204	12,014	1,943	270
1925	2,152	3,017	1,816	941	6,884	12,951	2,153	297
1926	2,306	3,173	1,962	1,005	7,370	13,584	2,430	352
1927	2,518	3,410	2,157	1,056	8,497	14,581	2,154	351
1928	2,730	3,707	2,325	1,080	9,327	15,728	2,158	367
1929	2,849	3,641	2,514	1,165	10,047	16,377	2,128	400
1930	3,074	4,015	2,669	1,124	11,319	16,989	2,130	317
1931	3,181	4,062	2,788	1,069	11,478	18,653	2,020	289
1932	2,987	3,637	2,680	905	10,623	18,744	2,172	244

* Computed on the basis of data abstracted from the *Annual Reports of the Comptroller of the Currency.*

cial banks, the figure for 1932 being 5.56. The highest ratios between capital funds and resources are found in savings institutions—10.67 for mutual savings banks, and 12.55 for stock savings banks, in 1932. During the thirty-three years covered, the ratios for the average mutual savings banks tended to decline, owing to a very rapid growth in capitalization, while the relation between capitalization and resources of the average stock-savings-bank unit showed a tendency to increase.

It may be well to point out here that very often data for national banks are compared with figures for all banks other than national, which easily gives the impression that both systems developed along more or less parallel lines. A procedure similar to this was followed in the study made by the Committee of the Federal Reserve System on Group, Chain and Branch Banking. In this instance both the average capitalization and the average resources, as well as the ratios between these two figures for the average unit of all banks other than national, may be found in Tables 3 and 4; but in the text we have brought out the comparison between commercial institutions operating under the National Banking Act and those chartered by the various states. The figures for all banks other than national are so strongly biased by the inclusion of savings institutions, as well as the tremendous growth of trust companies, that on this basis alone, it would be possible to reach the erroneous conclusion that the trend of commercial banking, both inside and outside of the national system, has followed approximately similar lines. From the figures as they are presented here it is clear that, although the ratio of capital funds to resources is approximately similar in commercial banks whether state or national, the national banks have throughout the thirty-three years studied, a much higher average capitalization, as well as greater average resources, per unit, than do state-chartered commercial institutions.

IV. Distribution of Banks by Size

The data given in the Reports of the Comptroller of the Currency on the distribution of banks by sizes is rather fragmentary and covers only the national system. Therefore, the material for this section was taken from a study of banks by size groups made by the Committee of the Federal Reserve System on Group, Chain and Branch Banking.

TABLE 4

RATIO OF AVERAGE CAPITAL FUNDS TO AVERAGE RESOURCES*

YEAR	All Banks	National	Other Than Natl.	State Comm.	Loan & Trust	Mutual Savings Stock	Stock Savings	Private
1900	5.65	4.89	6.55	4.80	4.83	11.95	9.26	5.12
1901	6.08	5.35	6.89	5.36	5.28	12.02	9.81	5.82
1902	5.82	5.08	6.61	5.22	4.89	12.48	10.11	5.43
1903	5.50	4.90	6.11	5.04	4.20	13.18	10.27	5.54
1904	5.53	4.94	6.06	5.05	4.19	13.65	9.88	5.00
1905	5.82	5.21	6.42	5.31	4.73	13.63	9.53	5.19
1906	5.83	5.23	6.33	5.46	4.46	14.14	9.86	5.00
1907	5.89	5.27	6.45	5.43	4.56	15.28	9.31	5.34
1908	5.56	5.23	5.89	4.99	4.12	12.67	8.42	5.33
1909	5.79	5.41	6.16	5.09	4.76	13.66	6.95	5.66
1910	5.86	5.35	6.35	5.33	4.87	12.64	7.63	5.52
1911	5.87	5.36	6.34	5.20	5.05	12.94	7.42	5.66
1912	5.98	5.48	6.45	5.29	5.21	12.45	7.61	5.53
1913	5.92	5.39	6.39	5.38	4.99	12.43	7.73	6.00
1914	6.11	5.61	6.54	5.36	5.32	12.68	8.00	5.44
1915	6.11	5.60	6.58	5.38	5.57	12.01	7.71	5.34
1916	6.98	6.61	7.30	5.98	6.50	12.83	8.67	6.88
1917	7.60	7.34	7.77	6.87	6.89	12.64	9.15	7.28
1918	8.01	7.94	8.13	7.36	7.10	12.87	10.11	7.48
1919	8.74	8.58	8.89	8.38	7.66	12.97	11.56	7.94
1920	8.72	8.50	8.89	8.37	7.64	13.31	12.38	7.19
1921	7.83	7.34	8.20	7.67	7.03	13.54	8.14	6.70
1922	7.68	7.28	7.99	7.32	7.04	11.34	11.34	6.73
1923	7.92	7.48	8.28	7.77	7.14	11.42	12.79	6.85
1924	8.11	7.73	8.34	7.94	7.20	11.19	12.87	7.11
1925	8.44	8.20	8.61	8.25	7.58	10.56	13.98	7.24
1926	8.32	8.20	8.38	8.10	7.32	10.12	14.38	7.65
1927	8.23	8.20	8.26	7.94	7.47	9.79	13.55	7.80
1928	8.05	7.99	8.07	7.83	7.24	9.68	13.32	7.98
1929	7.60	7.63	7.57	7.66	6.20	10.30	13.64	7.14
1930	7.39	7.50	7.33	7.39	6.15	9.78	13.31	6.60
1931	7.41	7.62	7.28	7.17	6.08	9.87	12.78	6.15
1932	7.08	7.15	7.03	6.46	5.56	10.67	12.55	5.30

* Computed on the basis of data abstracted from the *Annual Reports of the Comptroller of the Currency.*

Although the size of capital stock is not the best measure for the size of a bank, it is possible to classify banks on that basis for a longer period of time than following any other measure of size. Table 5, prepared by the Federal Reserve Committee, shows the approximate number of state and national banks falling into two size groups by ten or eleven year intervals since 1877.

TABLE 5

DISTRIBUTION OF INCORPORATED BANKS*

(By size of capital stock)

YEAR	STATE BANKS		NATIONAL BANKS		STATE AND NATIONAL BANKS	
	Less than $50,000	$50,000 and over	Less than $50,000	$50,000 and over	Less than $50,000	$50,000 and over
				Number		
1877	187	634	—	2,080	187	2,714
1888	747	1,043	—	3,144	747	4,187
1899	2,529	1,578	—	3,579	2,529	5,157
1909	9,042	3,536	2,197	4,773	11,239	8,309
1920	14,429	6,432	2,605	5,419	17,034	11,851
1930	9,695	5,924	1,992	5,255	11,687	11,179
				Percentage of Total		
1877	22.8	77.2	—	100.0	6.4	93.6
1888	41.7	58.3	—	100.0	15.1	84.9
1899	61.6	38.4	—	100.0	32.9	67.1
1909	71.9	28.1	31.5	68.5	57.5	42.5
1920	69.2	30.8	32.5	67.5	59.0	41.0
1930	62.1	37.9	27.5	72.5	51.1	48.9

* Figures for 1877, 1888, 1899, and 1909 from Barnett, "State Banks and Trust Companies Since the Passage of the National Bank Act," *Publications of the National Monetary Commission,* Vol. VII, pp. 212, 222, 231, and 257. Figures for 1920 and 1930 were collected by the Committee on Branch, Group and Chain Banking with the coöperation of the Federal Reserve banks and state banking departments. The 1920 figures include 386 banks in Illinois which were classed as private banks on June 30 of that year, most of which had been converted to state banks by the end of the year on account of a law prohibiting the operation of private banks after January 1, 1921.

In classifying active state banks by size groups, whenever individual reports for June 30 were not obtainable, figures for the nearest available data were used. For this reason the totals in the table showing the distribution of banks by size groups in 1920 and 1930, differ somewhat from similar figures in the comptroller's reports. The State bank figures used were either supplied by the State banking departments or compiled from their published reports.

For 1909, 1920, and 1930 trust companies are included with State banks.

The Committee of the Federal Reserve system points out that:

The most striking feature of these figures is the increase each decade down to 1920 in the number of State banks with less than $50,000 of capital stock. Banks of this size constituted 23 per cent of all State banks in 1877, but in 1920 they had risen to 69 per cent of the total.

In 1877 all of the national banks and 77 per cent of the State banks had $50,000 or more of capital stock. By 1899 only 38 per cent

TABLE 6

DISTRIBUTION OF STATE AND NATIONAL BANKS IN 1920 AND 1930

(By size groups)

SIZE GROUP LOANS AND INVESTMENTS	ALL BANKS		NATIONAL BANKS		STATE BANKS	
	1920	1930	1920	1930	1920	1930
			Number			
Under $150,000	6,548	4,839	345	335	6,203	4,504
150,000–250,000	5,114	3,510	759	701	4,355	2,809
250,000–500,000	6,977	4,966	2,029	1,591	4,948	3,375
500,000–750,000	3,172	2,362	1,315	968	1,857	1,394
750,000–1,000,000	1,819	1,552	861	767	958	785
1,000,000–2,000,000	2,733	2,600	1,423	1,320	1,310	1,280
2,000,000–5,000,000	1,573	1,887	811	1,014	762	873
5,000,000–10,000,000	508	595	260	307	248	288
10,000,000–50,000,000	369	454	184	202	185	252
50,000,000 and over	72	101	37	42	35	59
Total	28,885	22,866	8,024	7,247	20,861	15,619
			Percentage of Total			
Under $150,000	22.7	21.2	4.3	4.6	29.7	28.8
150,000–250,000	17.7	15.3	9.5	9.7	20.9	18.0
250,000–500,000	24.1	21.7	25.3	21.9	23.7	21.6
500,000–750,000	11.0	10.3	16.4	13.4	8.9	8.9
750,000–1,000,000	6.3	6.8	10.7	10.6	4.6	5.0
1,000,000–2,000,000	9.5	11.4	17.7	18.2	6.3	8.2
2,000,000–5,000,000	5.4	8.3	10.1	14.0	3.6	5.6
5,000,000–10,000,000	1.8	2.6	3.2	4.2	1.2	1.9
10,000,000–50,000,000	1.3	2.0	2.3	2.8	0.9	1.6
50,000,000 and over	0.2	0.4	0.5	0.6	0.2	0.4
Total	100.0	100.0	100.0	100.0	100.0	100.0

See note, Table 5.

of the State banks had this amount of capital, and by 1909 only 28 per cent. In 1900 the National Bank Act was amended to permit the organization of national banks with only $25,000 of capital stock in towns of less than 3,000 population. By 1909 about 31 per cent of the national banks had less than $50,000 capital stock, but this percentage had increased only slightly by 1920. In the latter year the number of national banks with less than $50,000 of capital stock was only 2,605 in comparison with 14,429 State banks.

Loans and investments are a better measure of the size of a bank than capital stock. The Federal Reserve Committee made an analysis of the distribution of banks by size as measured by loans and investments for the period 1920 to 1930; the results of that investigation are presented in Table 6.

The following interpretation of the results of this classification of all banks according to size of their loans and investments is given in the Report of the Committee:

While there was a net decline of 21 per cent during the ten-years in the number of banks, this decline occurred in the groups of banks with less than $2,000,000 of loans and investments, and principally among those with less than $750,000 of loans and investments.

The result of these changes was to decrease the percentage of the total banks in the smaller size groups in 1930, as compared with 1920 and to increase the percentage in the larger size groups. Notwithstanding these changes, however, there was still in 1930 a larger preponderance of small banks—over 13,000 banks, or 58 per cent, having loans and investments of less than $500,000, while 8,400, or 37 per cent, had loans and investments of $500,00 to $5,000,000 and 1,150, or 5 per cent had loans and investments of $5,000,000 or more.

In comparing the size distributions of the national and state bank groups, the Committee points out that:

Of the State banks, about 30 per cent both in 1920 and in 1930, and of the national banks, 4 per cent in 1920 and 5 per cent in 1930, had loans and investments of less than $150,000. In the former year 74 per cent of the State banks, and in the latter year 68 per cent, had loans and investments of less than $500,000, while for national banks the corresponding figures were 39 per cent and 36 per cent. In 1920 about 23 per cent, and in 1930 about 28 per cent, of the State banks had loans and investments between $500,000 and $5,000,000 while about 55 per cent of the national banks in 1920 and 56 per cent in 1930 had loans and investments between $500,000 and $5,000,000. Two per cent of the State banks in 1920 and 4 per cent in 1930 had more than $5,000,000 of loans and investments; for national banks the correspondent figures were 6 per cent and 8 per cent.

When the numbers of State and national banks with less than

$500,000 of loans and investments are compared, it appears that in 1920 there were 18,639 of these banks, of which 15,506, or 83 per cent, were State banks, and 3,133 or 17 per cent, were national banks. By 1930 the number had been reduced to 13,315, of which 80 per cent were State banks and 20 per cent were national banks.

Among medium sized banks the field has been about equally divided between the State and the national banks. Of the 9,297 banks in 1920 with from $500,000 to $5,000,000 of loans and investments, 53 per cent had State charters. By 1930 the number of banks of this size had been reduced to 8,401 in number, with 52 per cent having State charters.

Among large banks also, the field is about equally divided between the national and the State systems. In 1920 there were 949 banks with more than $5,000,000 of loans and investments, of which 49 per cent had State charters; while in 1930 there were 1,150 banks of this size, with 52 per cent of them under State charters.

Further comparison between the State and national systems is possible by noting the number in each size group in Table 6. State banks predominated over national banks, both in 1920 and 1930, in all size groups with less than $1,000,000 of loans and investments. National banks predominated over State banks in number in the size groups between $1,000,000 and $10,000,000 of loans and investments. Among banks with over $10,000,000, however, there were more with State charters than with national charters in 1930.

The percentage changes in the number of State and of national banks during the decade from 1920 to 1930, also shown in Table 6 throw considerable light on changes in the relative importance of State and national banks. In all size groups with less than $2,000,000 of loans and investments, there were declines during the decade in the number both of State and national banks. In size groups with more than $2,000,000 of loans and investments there were increases in the numbers of both State and national banks. Among banks with less than $500,000 of loans and investments, the rates of decline were far greater among State banks than among national banks; while among the State banks with more than $10,000,000 of loans and investments, the rate of increase among the State banks was greater than among the national banks. Only among banks of from $2,000,000 to $10,000,000 of loans and investments did the national banks increase during the decade more rapidly than the State banks.

Thus the number of State banks not only exceeds the number of national banks among the larger banks, but this excess increased during the period 1920-1930. At the same time their predominance slowly diminished among small banks, due to the higher suspension rates among State than among national banks.

The Committee on Group, Chain and Branch Banks also prepared a table giving the distribution of banks by sizes and according to geographic location, which is reproduced below:

TABLE 7

PERCENTAGE DISTRIBUTION OF BANKS IN 1920 AND 1930

(By size of loans and investments and by geographic divisions)

	STATE AND NATIONAL BANKS									
SIZE GROUP LOANS AND INVESTMENTS	New England	Middle Atlantic	North Central	Southern Mountain	Southeastern	Southwestern	Western Grain	Rocky Mountain	Pacific Coast	Total
	1920									
	%	%	%	%	%	%	%	%	%	%
Under $150,000	2.3	3.4	14.2	26.0	30.3	32.7	29.2	29.4	13.8	22.7
150,000–250,000	4.1	5.0	17.1	17.0	18.3	19.4	22.8	20.5	13.4	17.7
250,000–500,000	11.9	16.5	26.6	24.5	22.1	23.8	27.4	21.6	23.3	24.1
500,000–750,000	12.9	12.5	13.2	10.3	10.6	9.7	9.5	9.7	14.0	11.0
750,000–1,000,000	10.2	11.8	8.2	6.7	5.3	4.4	4.0	5.0	7.8	6.3
1,000,000–2,000,000	23.5	22.7	11.2	9.0	8.4	5.3	4.5	7.2	14.5	9.5
2,000,000–5,000,000	22.5	16.2	6.0	3.7	3.7	3.3	1.6	5.2	7.5	5.4
5,000,000–10,000,000	7.3	6.2	1.9	1.9	0.6	0.7	0.5	1.1	2.5	1.8
10,000,000–50,000,000	4.5	4.5	1.3	0.9	0.7	0.7	0.4	0.3	2.8	1.3
50,000,000 and over	0.8	1.2	0.3	—	—	0.03	0.1	—	0.4	0.2
Total	100.0	100.0	100.0	100.0	100.0	100.0	100.0	100.0	100.0	100.0
	1930									
	%	%	%	%	%	%	%	%	%	%
Under $150,000	2.3	1.0	12.3	23.2	33.2	35.4	32.8	23.1	13.1	21.2
150,000–250,000	1.6	3.4	15.8	16.0	15.7	18.5	21.3	18.3	13.7	15.3
250,000–500,000	6.3	12.7	24.7	21.7	19.3	22.4	25.2	25.2	25.0	21.7
500,000–750,000	9.5	11.1	12.7	12.7	9.9	8.3	8.1	9.9	11.7	10.3
750,000–1,000,000	7.9	9.9	8.3	6.6	5.9	5.1	4.4	6.7	9.0	6.8
1,000,000–2,000,000	24.2	24.6	13.4	11.2	8.9	4.8	4.7	7.5	13.3	11.4
2,000,000–5,000,000	29.0	22.7	8.0	5.1	4.9	3.2	2.4	6.3	8.7	8.3
5,000,000–10,000,000	10.7	7.3	2.7	1.7	1.0	1.2	0.6	1.7	2.2	2.6
10,000,000–50,000,000	7.7	5.8	1.7	1.8	1.1	1.0	0.4	1.3	1.8	2.0
50,000,000 and over	0.8	1.5	0.4	—	0.1	0.1	0.1	—	1.5	0.4
Total	100.0	100.0	100.0	100.0	100.0	100.0	100.0	100.0	100.0	100.0

See note, Table 5.

In commenting on the geographic distribution of banks of various sizes, the Report of the Committee points out that:

> The small banks are located primarily in the agricultural regions of the South and Middle West. The large banks are located principally in the Northeastern part of the country, including the North Central States.
>
> In the New England and Middle Atlantic States, where there is a preponderance of urban, commercial, and industrial activity, the proportion of small banks was low both in 1920 and 1930, and the proportion of large banks was high. Moreover, in all size groups of less than $1,000,000 of loans and investments in these two divisions, the number of banks was less in 1930 than in 1920, and in all size groups with more than $2,000,000 the number was greater in 1930 than in 1920.
>
> In the groups of States where there is a preponderance of rural and agricultural activities, the picture becomes almost directly the opposite of that in the commercial States. The banks with less than $150,000 loans and investments constituted the most numerous class, and in three out of the five groups of States they were relatively more numerous in 1930 than in 1920. Moreover, there was no pronounced tendency for the proportion of large banks to increase. In all the groups of agricultural States, the bulk of the banks in 1930 still had loans and investments of less than $500,000.

The concentration of banking business in institutions of larger size can be observed from the following figures computed by the Committee and representing the ratio of the loans and investments of the twenty largest banks in the United States to loans and investments of all banks:

1900—15.1	1926—15.7	1929—21.2
1920—13.8	1927—17.1	1930—24.8
1925—15.2	1928—18.1	1931—27.3

The distribution of numbers of banks and loans and investments of banks according to sizes of communities, also based on the Report of the Federal Reserve Committee, is presented in Table 8. Relative to this distribution the Report states:

> The great majority of banks, both in 1920 and in 1930 were located in small towns. In 1930 a fourth of all the banks were located

in towns of less than 500 population, while 61 per cent were located in towns of less than 2,500 population. Twenty-six per cent of all banks were located in towns of from 2,500 to 25,000 population in 1930, this percentage being slightly greater than in 1920. Only 13 per cent of all incorporated banks in 1930 were located in cities of more than 25,000 inhabitants. Only about half of these, or 7 per cent of all banks, were located in cities of more than 100,000 population.

The distribution of the loans and investments of these banks is vastly different. In 1930 the banks in towns of under 2,500 popula-

TABLE 8

DISTRIBUTION OF THE NUMBER OF BANKS AND OF LOANS AND INVESTMENTS BY SIZE OF TOWN AND IN PERCENTAGE OF TOTAL

POPULATION OF TOWN	NUMBER		LOANS AND INVESTMENTS	
	1920	1930	1920	1930
	%	%	%	%
Under 500	28.6	25.0	3.8	2.1
500–1,000	17.8	16.9	4.1	2.5
1,000–2,500	19.6	19.0	7.2	4.7
2,500–5,000	10.5	10.9	6.0	4.5
5,000–10,000	7.0	8.0	5.9	4.9
10,000–25,000	6.0	7.0	7.9	7.3
25,000–50,000	2.6	3.3	5.4	5.2
50,000–100,000	2.2	2.5	6.3	5.7
100,000 and over	5.7	7.4	53.4	63.1
	100.0	100.0	100.0	100.0

See note, Table 5.

tion embracing 61 per cent of the total number, had only 9 per cent of the total loans and investments. The banks in towns of from 2,500 to 25,000 population, 26 per cent of the total number of banks, had only 17 per cent of the total loans and investments. The banks in cities of more than 100,000 inhabitants, only 7 per cent of the total number, had 63 per cent of the total loans and investments.

On the basis of the data presented in this section, we can see that banking institutions of small size still predominate numerically over large units. In spite of that, the greater portion of the banking business of the country is concentrated in large banks. The figures also show that up to about 1920 the small units were increasing relative to the total number of banks, but that during the third decade of the present century the large banks began to form an increasingly greater percentage of the total number.

The small state banks decrease in numbers more rapidly than the national banks of the same size. The small banking units show no diminution in the percentage they form of the total in agricultural states, while in the industrial regions a marked shift toward institutions of larger size is noticeable.

During the period 1920 to 1930 there took place among large state institutions a more rapid growth, both in numbers and in the amount of business handled, than among national banks of the same size.

Further comments on this decline of the national banking system can be found in the last section of this chapter. For a study of the decline of the small bank, the reader is referred to Chapter IX, which is devoted to that subject.

V. Geographic Distribution of Banks

This sketch of the relative position of various types of banking institutions would be incomplete without an accompanying survey of the geographic distribution of numbers and resources. Table 9 presents a picture of the changes in the numbers and resources of banks that took place in the various sections of the country from the time of the survey conducted by the National Monetary Commission, or from 1909 to 1932.

Table 9 shows that in all parts of the country the number of banks first increased and then declined, while resources continued to grow practically up to the present depression. In the second section of this chapter we reduced the distribution of numbers, capital funds, and resources among various types of banks to a percentage basis, so as to bring out more clearly the interrelations of various institutions. The same procedure has been followed here. In Table 10 is presented the percentage distribution of the numbers and resources of banks, according to the geographic subdivisions of the country as adopted by the United States Census. This table covers the period from 1909 to 1932 and gives an idea of the changing importance of various parts of the country from the banking standpoint.

TABLE 9

CHANGES IN THE NUMBER AND RESOURCES OF BANKS IN THE UNITED STATES: 1909-1932

(By groups of states)

GROUPS OF STATES	ALL BANKS				NATIONAL BANKS				ALL OTHERS			
		Highest				Highest				Highest		
	1909	No.	Year	1932	1909	No.	Year	1932	1909	No.	Year	1932
						Number						
New England	1,080	1,133	'21	994	483	483	'09	350	597	724	'21	644
Middle Atlantic	2,436	3,359	'27	2,719	1,402	1,732	'28	1,527	1,034	1,647	'26	1,192
East No. Central	4,251	5,887	'23	4,089	1,259	1,398	'23	1,011	2,992	4,499	'24	3,078
West No. Central	6,413	9,128	'21	4,640	1,362	1,593	'21	1,052	5,051	7,535	'21	3,588
South Atlantic	2,257	3,344	'21	1,780	591	748	'23	491	1,666	2,605	'21	1,289
East So. Central	1,662	1,900	'24	1,323	342	387	'27	298	1,320	1,518	'23	1,025
West So. Central	2,357	3,347	'21	2,036	848	1,154	'25	814	1,509	2,312	'21	1,222
Mountain	858	1,592	'20	731	312	526	'21	270	546	1,073	'20	461
Pacific	1,132	1,469	'18	791	287	501	'21	332	845	1,036	'18	459
Possessions	45	70	'29	60	7	7	'14	5	38	64	'29	55
United States	22,491	30,812	'21	19,163	6,893	8,249	'22	6,150	15,598	22,658	'21	13,013

TABLE 9 *(Continued)*

GROUPS OF STATES	ALL BANKS				NATIONAL BANKS				ALL OTHERS			
	1909	Highest		1932	1909	Highest		1932	1909	Highest		1932
	$	$	Year	$	$	$	Year	$	$	$	Year	$
	Resources (In millions of dollars)											
New England	2,694	8,359	'28	7,063	818	2,520	'30	1,966	1,875	5,707	'29	5,097
Middle Atlantic	8,724	33,067	'30	26,246	3,707	11,935	'30	8,565	5,018	21,132	'30	17,681
East No. Central	3,409	13,124	'29	8,734	1,690	4,562	'28	3,427	1,719	8,947	'29	5,307
West No. Central	2,218	5,932	'20	3,536	1,151	2,628	'20	1,806	1,066	3,301	'20	1,729
South Atlantic	1,163	4,405	'26	3,193	567	2,001	'27	1,405	597	2,461	'26	1,789
East So. Central	552	1,918	'29	1,235	268	939	'29	678	285	979	'29	556
West So. Central	693	2,816	'29	1,955	438	1,784	'29	1,282	255	1,167	'20	674
Mountain	429	1,245	'20	784	272	685	'20	475	156	561	'20	310
Pacific	1,155	5,145	'30	4,174	454	3,183	'31	2,722	701	2,965	'26	1,451
Possessions	58	367	'29	325	4	44	'30	42	54	352	'29	283
United States	21,095	74,020	'30	57,245	9,369	29,117	'30	22,368	11,726	44,904	'30	34,877

Compiled on the basis of data abstracted from the *Annual Reports of the Comptroller of the Currency*. The figures in this column do not add to the total, as the peak was reached in the various groups of states in different years.

TABLE 10

PERCENTAGE DISTRIBUTION OF NUMBERS AND RESOURCES OF BANKS ACCORDING TO GEOGRAPHIC AREAS, DURING THE YEARS 1909-1932

GROUPS OF STATES	ALL BANKS					NATIONAL SYSTEM					ALL OTHERS				
	Highest		Lowest		Avge.	Highest		Lowest		Avge.	Highest		Lowest		Avge.
	%	Year	%	Year	%	%	Year	%	Year	%	%	Year	%	Year	%
								Number							
New England	5.2	'32	3.7	'23	4.1	7.0	'09	4.9	'23	5.5	5.0	'32	3.2	'21	3.6
Middle Atlantic	14.2	'32	9.9	'17	11.1	24.8	'32	19.4	'20	20.9	9.4	'31	5.9	'14	7.2
East No. Central	22.0	'30	18.1	'10	19.6	18.3	'09	16.4	'32	17.4	23.9	'30	18.0	'10	20.4
West No. Central	30.4	'19	24.2	'32	28.2	19.8	'09	17.1	'32	18.8	34.4	'19	27.6	'32	32.0
South Atlantic	11.2	'13	9.2	'31	10.5	9.4	'16	8.0	'32	8.9	12.0	'13	9.5	'31	11.1
East So. Central	7.4	'09	6.1	'19	6.6	5.1	'14	4.5	'20	4.9	8.5	'09	6.6	'18	7.3
West So. Central	11.5	'14	10.2	'31	10.7	14.4	'26	11.4	'10	13.1	11.0	'14	8.8	'27	9.8
Mountain	5.3	'20	3.6	'27	4.3	6.5	'20	4.4	'30	5.0	4.9	'20	3.3	'27	4.0
Pacific	5.4	'13	4.1	'32	4.7	6.1	'21	4.2	'09	5.6	5.6	'10	3.5	'29	4.4

TABLE 10 (*Continued*)

GROUPS OF STATES	ALL BANKS					NATIONAL SYSTEM					ALL OTHERS				
	Highest		Lowest		Avge.	Highest		Lowest		Avge.	Highest		Lowest		Avge.
	%	Year	%	Year	%	%	Year	%	Year	%	%	Year	%	Year	%
						Resources									
New England	12.8	'09	10.1	'20	11.4	8.8	'32	7.0	'20	8.0	16.0	'09	12.0	'25	13.9
Middle Atlantic	45.9	'32	36.9	'20	40.4	41.0	'30	36.6	'13	39.0	50.7	'32	35.8	'20	41.3
East No. Central	18.5	'26	15.3	'32	17.4	18.8	'13	14.3	'31	17.0	20.0	'29	14.1	'10	17.6
West No. Central	11.4	'19	6.2	'32	9.4	12.3	'09	7.7	'30	10.3	11.5	'19	5.0	'32	8.8
South Atlantic	6.8	'25	5.4	'31	6.2	7.7	'25	6.0	'30	6.9	6.6	'21	5.0	'31	5.6
East So. Central	2.8	'23	2.2	'31	2.6	3.4	'29	2.7	'17	3.0	2.8	'20	1.6	'32	2.4
West So. Central	5.0	'20	3.3	'09	3.9	6.5	'29	4.6	'10	5.7	3.9	'20	1.9	'32	2.6
Mountain	2.5	'17	1.4	'32	1.9	3.0	'17	2.1	'30	2.6	2.0	'17	0.9	'32	1.4
Pacific	7.3	'32	5.5	'09	6.5	12.2	'32	4.9	'09	7.4	7.5	'26	4.1	'31	5.9

The method of compiling this table may be more clearly understood if we trace the steps followed in obtaining the percentages for the number of "All Banks" for any one of the nine geographic areas. The actual figures of the numbers of banks were abstracted by states and by years from the *Annual Reports of the Comptroller of the Currency*. A total for the particular group of states was obtained for every year and expressed as a percentage of the grand total for the number of banks in the country in the corresponding years. As a result, twenty-four percentages were obtained for each year from 1909 to 1932. In the table we present the highest and the lowest of these twenty-four percentage figures, as well as the average for the entire period covered.

The same process was repeated with the number of national banks for each group of states. They were expressed as percentages of the total number of National banks in the country for every one of the twenty-four years covered. The percentage distribution of the numbers of "All Other" banks has been compiled on the same basis. Exactly similar procedure was employed in obtaining the percentage distributions of resources for "All Banks," "National System," and "All Others."

Because of the fact that the data on banks operating in the Possessions (Hawaii, Porto Rico, Alaska, and the Philippines) do not appear in these tables, the figures in the "Average" column do not add up exactly to 100.0.

Table 10 extends back for a sufficient number of years to show the changes that have been taking place in the distribution of numbers and resources, as well as the different form which the apportionment of numbers takes as compared to that of resources. If we look at the distribution of numbers and resources separately, we notice the surprising minor nature of the shifts that took place in the course of twenty-four years. The largest concentration of numbers of banks is not found in the sections of the country having the greatest portion of banking resources. Resources are concentrated on the Atlantic seaboard where only a comparatively minor part of the total number of banks is located.

The greatest concentration of national banks is found in the Middle Atlantic, East North Central, and West North Central States; while about one-third of all state institutions is grouped in the West North Central States. Both in the case of national and state institutions, the distribution of resources does not coincide with the allotment of numbers.

In 1932 nearly one-half of all the resources of national banks were in the three Middle Atlantic States; while in the West South Central States, where around 10 per cent of the national banks were located, there could be found only about 2.5 per cent of their aggregate resources. In the case of state institutions, the largest concentration of resources also is found in the same three Middle Atlantic States, where their numbers are less than 10 per cent of all state banks in the country; while in the West North Central States, where the largest portion of the number of state banks is still located, resources of state institutions amounted in 1932 to only 4.96 per cent of the aggregate resources of all State banks.

The greatest changes in the percentage of resources allotted to a group of states occur—with the exception of the Mountain and Pacific states, where both numbers and resources vary widely relative to the aggregate—in the sections of the country where the percentages of numbers are comparatively stable. Reversely, the share of the total number allotted to a group of states fluctuates widely where resources are more stable relative to the aggregate.

TABLE 11

COEFFICIENTS OF VARIATION FOR THE PERCENTAGE DISTRIBUTION OF NUMBERS AND RESOURCES, 1909-1932

GROUPS OF STATES	NUMBERS			RESOURCES		
	All Banks	Natl.	Other Than Natl.	All Banks	Natl.	Other Than Natl.
New England	9.87	11.00	12.17	7.13	6.30	9.70
Middle Atlantic	12.55	7.42	16.29	5.69	2.81	8.76
East No. Central	7.12	2.36	10.26	4.65	7.62	10.00
West No. Central	6.33	5.20	6.08	17.66	16.16	21.53
South Atlantic	5.34	3.89	5.76	7.71	8.06	8.13
East So. Central	5.43	12.41	6.92	7.35	5.93	12.52
West So. Central	2.74	6.01	6.93	11.13	11.04	18.09
Mountain	12.01	13.43	12.95	17.23	11.79	22.87
Pacific	9.25	7.74	16.20	7.53	29.41	15.35

The above figures are coefficients of variation, the use of which was introduced by Karl Pearson. This measure is significant only for purposes of comparison. For instance, we see that the coefficient for the number of all banks in New England is 9.87 and for the South Atlantic States 5.34. This means that the percentage which the New England banks form of the total number of banks has, over the period of twenty-four years, been more variable than that of the South Atlantic States and that the difference in the degree of change in these two groups of states is represented by the relationship of 9.87 to 5.34. For the Middle Atlantic States the coefficient for the number of National banks is 7.42, as against that of 16.29 for banks other than National. This means that the percentage of all national banks located in the Middle Atlantic States was more than twice as stable as the percentages of all banks other than National for the same states which show a variability more than twice as large.

The method of computing the coefficient of variation is as follows: For each year from 1909 to 1932, and for each group of states we have a percentage representing the portion of the total found in the particular section of the country. We obtain an average percentage for each group of states for twenty-four years (the arithmetic mean of twenty-four percentage figures). Then the difference between this average and every one of the twenty-four percentage figures is obtained and squared. From the sum of the squares of the differences we derive the standard deviation (the root-mean-square deviation). Finally, the standard deviation is expressed as a percentage of the average (the arithmetic mean) which gives us the coefficient of variation which shows in one figure the degree of change as measured from the average (the arithmetic mean). This coefficient is a percentage and can therefore be compared to other similar coefficients which show the degrees of fluctuation around their averages.

This tendency can be observed more clearly from Table 11 in which the extent of fluctuations in the percentages of numbers and resources found in a group of states over a period of twenty-four years are represented by one figure, so that we can contrast the amplitude of the change for various parts of the country in the apportionment of numbers of banks and banking resources, for all banks, as well as by type of banks.

Large fluctuations in the percentage of numbers allotted to each section of the country are found, as we may see from Table 11, in the case of both national and state institutions in the Mountain and the Pacific States—the newer sections of the country—where the growth of banking has been extremely rapid in the twenty-four years covered. The percentages of national banks show a high variation in New England, where the importance of the national banking system was declining, while the percentages of the total number of state institutions fluctuated most in the Middle Atlantic States, where banks other than national were gaining in importance.

We may see also from Table 11 that the fluctuations in the percentages of resources allotted to groups of states are somewhat wider than those for numbers. The portion of resources of all banks, other than national, found in the East and West South Central, Mountain, and Pacific States, shows considerable variability. These are the regions where the actual number of banks had very radically changed. In the Pacific States the shift of large institutions from one jurisdiction to another accounts for the unsteadiness of the percentage of resources in the two systems, while the percentages for all banks are much more stable.

In the West North Central States the large variation in the percentages of resources must be attributed to very extensive shrinkage in the number of banks, largely due to failures. Wide fluctuations in the share of total resources apportioned to a section of the country seem to take place in those sections where there occurred extensive changes in the actual number of banks; these changes, however, are not fully reflected in the percentage distribution of numbers and in the degree of variability of percentages of each group of states. Apparently both the rate of increase and that of decline in numbers were rather uniform throughout the country.

We may, therefore, conclude that definite shifts in the geographic distribution of banks, as measured by numbers and resources, did occur during the twenty-four years studied, but that the banking structure shows a greater homogeneity than is generally believed. The changes in the share of numbers and resources held by the various sections of the country progress from year to year with a marked degree of independence of each other, but the widest fluctuation in the percentages of resources seems to occur in localities where the greatest changes in the actual number of banks have taken place. In spite of the tremendous expansion in the total number of banks—from 1909 to 1921—and a very rapid and not less intense shrinkage—from 1922 to 1932—the proportion of the aggregate numbers and resources allotted to each group of states shows a much greater stability than one might expect. Both the rise and the decline in total numbers seems to have progressed at about the same rate throughout the country and the same may be said relative of the steady growth of resources. Apparently the elements of homogeneity inherent in any closely knit and interdependent country, such as the United States, permeated the development of the banking mechanism even in spite of the existence of a unit banking system.

VI. The Decline of the National System[7]

After surveying the subdivision of banking resources among various types of banks, the changes undergone by each class of banks, and the distribution of banking throughout the various sections of the country, there remains the problem of the relative importance of the national system as against the institutions chartered under the laws of the different states. The original idea of the National Bank Act was that all banking should be organized under the national system; the 10 per cent tax on the notes of banks operating under State jurisdictions was expected to bring about a large movement of state institutions toward national organization. When state banks found means of continuing in the banking business through the extension of

[7] This subject has already been discussed indirectly in Section IV of this chapter on the Distribution of Banks by Size. The reader is referred to Table 6 and the accompanying text on p. 139.

commercial credit it was considered that the national banking system served a useful purpose in affording a means of readjusting, or "equalizing," the banking facilities of the country by permitting the creation of national institutions where local banking was inadequate. It was then thought that the two systems could exist side by side supplementing each other. In reality, competition between the two systems very quickly arose, banks shifting from national jurisdiction and taking out state charters and vice versa, depending on which of the systems offered the greatest latitude in bank operation. The distribution of numbers, capital funds and resources of all banks in the country between the two systems may be observed from Table 2.

This table shows that for thirty-three years the national system has been steadily losing ground against the banks operating under state charters. Even if we take into consideration the fact that in the earlier years the coverage of state institutions was incomplete, still, the general tendency must be correctly represented, as the percentages for the year 1909 based on the Report of the National Monetary Commission do not show a break in the general trend. Only in the three years—1930, 1931, and 1932—does the national system begin to show a slight gain over all banks other than national due to the greater number of failures among state-chartered institutions.

The decline of the national banking system, which to a certain extent may be attributed to the fact that banks have taken out state charters, is mainly due to the tremendous growth of loan and trust companies and savings banks. It may be further illustrated through the method used in Table 12. This tabulation presents, in dollars and cents, the resources found in the national system per each dollar of resources located in all banks other than national. For the entire country the resources of national banks were, in 1909, equal to 80 cents per dollar in state institutions; this proportion declined steadily till it reached 61 cents in 1929; only during the depression years did the relationship change slightly in favor of national banks; for each dollar of resources in state-chartered institutions, the national banks had 65 cents in resources in 1931.

The national system can claim a larger share of banking resources throughout the twenty-four-year period only in the West South Central and the Mountain States. The same holds true of

TABLE 12

RATIO OF RESOURCES OF NATIONAL BANKS TO RESOURCES OF ALL BANKS OTHER THAN NATIONAL

THE AMOUNT OF NATIONAL BANK RESOURCES IN DOLLARS AND CENTS FOR EACH DOLLAR OF RESOURCES IN ALL BANKS OTHER THAN NATIONAL

(By groups of states, by years)

YEAR	New England	Middle Atlantic	East North Central	West North Central	South Atlantic	East South Central	West South Central	Mountain	Pacific	Total Possessions	All United States
1909	.44	.74	.98	1.08	.95	.94	1.72	1.74	.65	.07	.80
1910	.41	.69	1.05	1.01	.99	1.12	1.58	1.59	.82	.09	.79
1911	.41	.73	.94	.99	.94	.93	1.59	1.53	.82	.07	.78
1912	.42	.70	.92	.97	.94	.90	1.59	1.48	.82	.06	.77
1913	.40	.69	.87	.92	.90	.92	1.61	1.34	.79	.08	.75
1914	.39	.70	.84	.88	.90	.98	1.47	1.30	.75	.08	.74
1915	.38	.70	.83	.87	.92	1.10	1.52	1.29	.76	.08	.74
1916	.40	.75	.81	.87	.91	1.08	1.57	1.22	.78	.07	.76
1917	.39	.79	.81	.88	.91	1.01	1.59	1.16	.82	.05	.78
1918	.45	.86	.85	.81	.96	.94	1.47	1.19	.85	.04	.82
1919	.46	.84	.79	.78	1.00	.92	1.41	1.17	.86	.03	.80
1920	.44	.84	.75	.80	.86	.83	1.29	1.22	.88	.03	.79
1921	.40	.75	.64	.69	.86	.87	1.22	1.24	.75	.03	.70
1922	.41	.73	.62	.70	.85	.86	1.48	1.23	.71	.03	.70
1923	.45	.64	.59	.71	.82	.86	1.50	1.26	.66	.04	.66
1924	.43	.65	.59	.74	.81	.87	1.47	1.43	.55	.04	.65
1925	.44	.64	.55	.76	.80	.88	1.63	1.37	.55	.04	.65
1926	.44	.63	.54	.79	.79	.88	1.64	1.37	.54	.04	.64
1927	.39	.59	.52	.82	.87	.96	1.73	1.34	.98	.05	.64
1928	.37	.60	.54	.85	.85	.99	1.81	1.28	1.31	.05	.66
1929	.40	.52	.47	.88	.82	.96	1.73	1.26	1.46	.04	.61
1930	.45	.56	.49	.86	.79	1.06	1.78	1.28	1.53	.16	.65
1931	.43	.54	.52	.94	.79	1.18	1.85	1.35	1.83	.14	.65
1932	.39	.48	.65	1.04	.79	1.22	1.90	1.53	1.88	.15	.64

Computed on the basis of data abstracted from the *Annual Reports of the Comptroller of the Currency.*

the Pacific States after 1928 because of the transfer of the Bank of Italy and other banks to the national system. In New England the resources of national banks fluctuate around 40 per cent of the resources of all banks other than national for the entire period under observation. With this one exception the national system was definitely holding a decreasing portion of the total bank resources of the country, throughout its industrial sections and the Atlantic seaboard. Apparently the competition between the two types of chartered banks, as well as the rapid development of banking institutions not primarily organized for commercial purposes, has been bringing about a marked redistribution of banking resources that has resulted in the concentration of a much larger portion of the banking assets of the country outside of the national system.

Summary

In concluding this survey it is well to repeat once more what was said about the nature of the statistics at the beginning of this chapter.

1. The figures presented here are the best and most complete data available at present, but they are still far from perfection. Therefore, we should look upon the statistical review just concluded as indicative of certain definite trends and allow for substantial margins of error in the case of individual figures.

2. The number of banks grew very rapidly during the first two decades of the present century, while in the third decade there occurred a very marked shrinkage. Both these tendencies were due to the expansion and contraction of the number of commercial banks.

3. Capital funds and resources of all types of chartered banking institutions increased during the period 1900 to 1932, but the outstanding feature of this development was the growth, both in capitalization and resources of trust companies—institutions not primarily chartered for commercial purposes—and savings banks.

4. Average capital funds and resources per banking unit increased more slowly in the case of commercial banks than in that of trust companies and savings institutions. Therefore the average trust company and savings banks represent a much larger banking unit than do commercial banks, especially if measured by average resources.

5. The ratio between average capitalization and resources is higher in savings institutions than in commercial banks, but trust companies show a lower ratio than either national or state-commercial banks.

6. The vast majority of the banks of the country still are small banks, but the small units are decreasing in numbers while the large institutions are increasing. Small state institutions decrease more rapidly than do national banks of the same size. The small banking units do not show any tendency to diminish in the agricultural sections of the country, while, in industrial regions, the small banks form a definitely smaller percentage of the total in 1930 as compared to 1920. The vast majority of banking institutions is still located in small towns, while more than half of the business is found in cities of larger size and more than a quarter in the twenty largest institutions.

7. Geographically the distribution of banking resources differs very radically from that of numbers. The greatest concentration of the numbers of banks is not found in the same sections of the country which account for the largest portions of resources and vice versa.

8. The greatest fluctuations in the share of resources allotted to a section are found in groups of states where the actual number of banks has changed most. The rate at which both numbers and resources grow or decline seems to be fairly uniform throughout the country. This unexpected degree of homogeneity in banking trends accounts for the fact that over a period of years, the geographic distribution of numbers and resources of banks is much more stable than one would have expected.

9. As measured by resources, the national system has definitely declined in importance as compared with state institutions. This is due to the tremendous expansion of primarily noncommercial institutions, such as trust companies and savings banks.

10. The data on the changes that have taken place in the size distribution of commercial banks indicate that there is a definite tendency toward larger banking units.

CHAPTER IX

PROCESS BY WHICH PRESENT CONDITIONS HAVE DEVELOPED[1]

In the preceding chapter we reviewed the institutional framework of the banking system as it stood prior to the banking crisis of 1933 and the changes that have been taking place during the past two decades. We may now turn to the underlying causes instrumental in the shaping of the existing banking structure. In this connection the most important tendencies are treated in separate chapters. The present discussion is followed by a presentation of the intermingling of banking functions (Chapter X—Commercial, Investment, and Other Types of Banking) and by a review of fiduciary activities of financial institutions (Chapter XI—Development of Fiduciary Banking). Savings banking (Chapter XII—Savings Banking) is then considered; followed by a presentation of the problem of bank failures (Chapter XIII—Bank Failures). Before beginning to review these phenomena separately, it is imperative to dwell at some length on one general tendency that permeates the institutional framework. This chapter deals with the one tendency, which may be summarized as the decline of the small bank.

In the figures of the preceding chapter we presented a picture of the distribution of banks by sizes, based on the statistical material assembled by the Committee of the Federal Reserve System on Group, Chain and Branch Banking. It brought out the fact that the size distribution of banks, measured both by capital and loans and investment, is changing, and that the small banks are diminishing in numbers as well as in importance. (Tables 5, 6, 7, and 8). It was also made clear that an increasingly large portion of the banking business is concentrated in the larger

[1] The matter included in this chapter is not available in the ordinary official sources and, in order to complete the other studies presented in this volume, some of the text has been excerpted and adapted by V. D. Kazakévich from the *Report of the Committee of the Federal Reserve System on Group, Chain and Branch Banking.*

banking units, but that in spite of all, a very large percentage of the banks of the country is still composed of institutions of small size.

This gradual structural change may be linked to a variety of causes such as the expansion of noncommercial financial institutions, the intermingling of banking functions, the epidemic of failures among small banks, as well as to changes in banking practice. Here we confine ourselves to the problem of whether there exist any inherent causes in the banking business, as it progressed during the post-war decade, that would favor the large unit and discriminate against the small bank. In order to reach conclusions we trace the distribution of net profits, and deficits by sizes of banks, as well as the extent of insufficiencies of earnings by banks of various sizes and geographic location. We shall also review the comparative costs involved in operating a small and a large bank, and the relative difference in the amount of capital needed to operate banking units of various sizes.

The Committee of the Reserve system presents the following comments on the general trend in net profits of national banks, accompanied by Table 13, covering the years 1890-1931.

The average rate of net profits on invested capital for the national banks during the ten years, 1921-1930, was 7.3 per cent. For the fiscal year ending June 30, 1931, however, the rate of net profits of national banks dropped to 1.4 per cent. For the fiscal year 1932 national banks as a whole reported a net deficit of $140,071,000.

From 1905 to 1915 the trend of net profits was downward. From 1921 to 1928 the trend was upward. During 1921-1930 the rate of net profits of national banks was lower than in the twenty years, 1901-1920. The rate of net profits of national banks at 7.3 per cent during the decade ending with 1930 compares with an average of 8.3 per cent during the years 1901-1910. Although there was a declining tendency in the net profits of national banks after the early part of this century, the rapid rise during the war years offset the pronounced decline from 1907 to 1914 and the average net profits for the second decade were equal to those of the first.

The trends of net profits of national banks which gives the annual rate of net profits on invested capital of all national banks from 1890 to 1931 is illustrated in Table 13:

TABLE 13

RATE OF NET PROFITS ON INVESTED CAPITAL OF NATIONAL BANKS 1890-1931

YEAR	RATE OF NET PROFITS ON INVESTED CAPITAL (*per cent*)	YEAR	RATE OF NET PROFITS ON INVESTED CAPITAL (*per cent*)
1890	7.71	1911	8.12
1891	7.67	1912	7.51
1892	6.59	1913	7.87
1893	6.68	1914	7.28
1894	4.19	1915	6.03
1895	4.75	1916	7.49
1896	5.06	1917	8.84
1897	4.60	1918	9.44
1898	5.24	1919	10.17
1899	5.74	1920	10.76
1900	8.61	1921	7.73
1901	7.70	1922	6.45
1902	9.00	1923	7.08
1903	8.55	1924	6.71
1904	8.37	1925	7.54
1905	7.53	1926	8.07
1906	8.55	1927	7.79
1907	9.49	1928	7.57
1908	7.87	1929	8.21
1909	7.52	1930	6.19
1910	8.33	1931	1.40

I. Profits and Deficit

In the studies of the Report of the Committee of the Federal Reserve System on Chain, Group and Branch Banking, dealing with banking profits are presented data showing the numbers of national banks grouped according to size and rate of net profits, as well as the percentage distribution by size of banks of all institutions reporting a net deficit or net profits of less than 6 per cent on invested capital. The percentage distribution of the number of national banks among the groups showing various rates of net profits, and by size of banks follows. Similar data are presented according to geographic subdivisions of the country and the changes are traced through the years 1926 to 1930. Finally, a comparison is made with the results shown by the Iowa State Banks. From these condensed abstracts a clear picture of the changes in the earnings of various-size groups of banks is furnished, as follows:

Net Profits of Small and Large Banks

During the five years 1926-1930 the average annual number of national banks which rendered earnings reports was 7,403. Of these 4,000, or somewhat more than half, on the average annually earned 6 per cent or more on their invested capital; 1,396, or nearly one-fifth, earned less than 6 per cent but as much as 3 per cent; 836, or

TABLE 14

NUMBER OF NATIONAL BANKS RENDERING EARNINGS REPORTS, GROUPED BY SIZE OF LOANS AND INVESTMENTS AND BY RATE OF NET PROFITS ON INVESTED CAPITAL—AVERAGE 1926-1930

SIZE GROUP LOANS AND INVESTMENTS	AVERAGE ANNUAL NUMBER OF NATIONAL BANKS REPORTING				
	Net deficits or no net profits	Net deficits or net profits of less than 3 per cent	Net deficits or net profits of less than 6 per cent	Net profits of 6 per cent or more	Total
Under $150,000	123	189	261	92	353
150,000–250,000	207	321	460	281	741
250,000–500,000	333	539	853	766	1,619
500,000–750,000	153	273	471	582	1,053
750,000–1,000,000	96	177	318	407	725
1,000,000–2,000,000	140	273	533	797	1,330
2,000,000–5,000,000	86	163	344	675	1,019
5,000,000–10,000,000	21	44	97	215	312
10,000,000–50,000,000	11	25	58	153	211
50,000,000 and over	1	3	8	32	40
Total	1.171	2,007	3,403	4,000	7,403

about one-ninth, earned less than 3 per cent; and 1,171, or about one-sixth, earned no net profits or had annual net deficits.

Of the 1,171 banks, which annually on the average reported net deficits or no net profits, 57 per cent had less than $500,000 of loans and investments and about 78 per cent had loans and investments of less than $1,000,000. These percentages change somewhat for banks showing net deficits or net profits of less than 3 per cent or less than 6 per cent, but they reveal essentially the same fact, that a large proportion of the banks that had unsatisfactory rates of net profits during the period were institutions with limited resources. The following Table 14 gives for various size groups the average number of national banks submitting annual earnings reports during 1926-30, and the average number reporting specified rates of net profits on invested capital.

The next Table 15 shows for each of the 10 designated size groups the number of banks per hundred that reported, over the period 1926-1930, net deficits or less than 6 per cent net profits annually on invested capital. It brings out the fact that among banks in the smallest size group three in four failed to realize as much as 6 per cent, while among banks in the next largest size group the proportion was about 3 banks in 5, in the next about 1 bank in 2 and among the others from about 4 in 10 to about 2 in 10.

TABLE 15

PERCENTAGE OF NATIONAL BANKS GROUPED BY SIZE OF LOANS AND INVESTMENTS REPORTING ANNUAL NET DEFICITS OR NET PROFITS OF LESS THAN 6 PER CENT ON INVESTED CAPITAL

AVERAGE 1926-1930

SIZE GROUP LOANS AND INVESTMENTS	PERCENTAGE
Under $150,000	73.9
150,000–250,000	62.1
250,000–500,000	52.7
500,000–750,000	44.7
750,000–1,000,000	43.9
1,000,000–2,000,000	40.1
2,000,000–5,000,000	33.8
5,000,000–10,000,000	31.1
10,000,000–50,000,000	27.6
50,000,000 and over	19.8
Average—all groups	46.0

The smallest banks, those with less than $150,000 of loans and investments, made the worst comparative showing. In this size group more than half of the banks reported either less than 3 per cent net profits on invested capital, no net profits, or net deficits. In the next largest size group, that comprising banks with loans and investments of $150,000 to $250,000, the corresponding proportion was more than 2 banks in 5, and in the next largest it was about 1 bank in 3.

In the smallest size group, that for banks having loans and investments of less than $150,000, one out of every three banks reported during this period net deficits or no net profits, and in all three of the size groups of less than $500,000 of loans and investments the proportionate number of banks that had net deficits or no net profits was above the average for all national banks. During this five year period the total number of national banks in these three size groups represented about 37 per cent of all national banks in the country and about 3.5 per cent of the total loans and investments of all national banks in 1930.

The following Table 16 gives the complete percentage distribution of national banks in size groups according to rates of net profits on invested capital, representing the average of the years 1926-1930.

TABLE 16

PERCENTAGE DISTRIBUTION OF NATIONAL BANKS GROUPED BY SIZE OF LOANS AND INVESTMENTS AND BY RATE OF NET PROFITS ON INVESTED CAPITAL—AVERAGE 1926-1930

SIZE GROUP LOANS AND INVESTMENTS	TOTAL	REPORTING NET TOTAL DEFICITS OR NO NET PROFITS		REPORTING NET PROFITS				
		6% or more	0.0% to 5.9%	Less than 3%	3% to 5.9%	6% to 8.9%	9% to 11.9%	12% and over
Under $150,000	100%	14.6	20.4	18.8	20.2	13.8	7.0	5.3
150,000–250,000	100	11.3	16.7	15.3	18.8	17.5	9.9	10.6
250,000–500,000	100	8.7	11.9	12.8	19.4	20.8	13.5	13.1
500,000–750,000	100	5.9	8.7	11.4	18.8	23.8	15.1	16.4
750,000–1,000,000	100	5.7	7.5	11.2	19.5	24.2	16.2	15.7
1,000,000–2,000,000	100	4.0	6.6	10.0	19.5	25.6	17.8	16.5
2,000,000–5,000,000	100	3.2	5.2	7.6	17.7	26.9	20.6	18.8
5,000,000–10,000,000	100	2.3	4.5	7.2	17.2	28.7	21.6	18.6
10,000,000–50,000,000	100	1.9	3.4	6.5	15.8	29.9	25.1	17.5
50,000,000 and over	100	1.0	1.5	4.6	12.7	31.5	28.9	19.8
Average—all groups	100	6.4	9.4	11.3	18.9	23.2	15.8	15.0

Geographic Comparison

In order to have enough banks in some size groups to make a percentage distribution of value, it was necessary to effect certain geographic combinations. The New England and Middle Atlantic groups were combined to represent the industrial area heretofore presented, while the Western Grain and Southwestern States were used in combination as representing an agricultural area. In order to show roughly what conditions have been in the remaining portions of the United States, three other groups are given. North Central States are combined as one group; the Southern Mountain and Southeastern States form a second; and the Rocky Mountain and Pacific Coast States, a third.

TABLE 17

PERCENTAGES OF NATIONAL BANKS GROUPED BY SIZE OF LOANS AND INVESTMENTS AND BY GEOGRAPHIC DIVISIONS REPORTING NET DEFICITS OR NET PROFITS OF LESS THAN 3 PER CENT ON INVESTED CAPITAL—AVERAGE 1926-1930

	NORTH-EASTERN	MID-CONTINENT		SOUTH-EASTERN	WESTERN
SIZE GROUP LOANS AND INVESTMENTS	New England and Middle Atlantic States	Western Grain and South-western States	North Central States	Southern Mountain and South-eastern States	Rocky Mountain and Pacific Coast States
Under $150,000	51.7	51.4	53.5	57.7	63.3
150,000–250,000	32.5	47.8	31.5	36.4	49.4
250,000–500,000	24.2	38.4	32.9	26.4	34.6
500,000–750,000	19.1	32.9	25.8	23.3	26.9
750,000–1,000,000	18.7	31.5	24.4	25.3	24.9
1,000,000–2,000,000	15.2	30.6	22.0	20.7	25.0
2,000,000–5,000,000	12.8	18.2	17.0	20.7	23.8
5,000,000 and over	12.2	11.2	9.6	17.0	18.9
Average—all groups	16.9	37.0	25.2	24.7	32.5

New England: Maine, New Hampshire, Vermont, Massachusetts, Rhode Island, Connecticut.

Middle Atlantic: New York, New Jersey, Delaware, Pennsylvania, Maryland, District of Columbia.

Western Grain: Minnesota, North Dakota, South Dakota, Iowa, Nebraska, Missouri, Kansas.

Southwestern: Louisiana, Texas, Arkansas, Oklahoma.

North Central: Michigan, Wisconsin, Illinois, Indiana, Ohio.

Southern Mountain: West Virginia, Virginia, Kentucky, Tennessee.

Southeastern: North Carolina, South Carolina, Georgia, Florida, Alabama, Mississippi.

Rocky Mountain: Montana, Idaho, Wyoming, Colorado, New Mexico, Arizona, Utah, Nevada.

Pacific Coast: Washington, Oregon, California.

The average experience for all size groups was best in the Northeast, where 17 out of 100 banks failed to return as much as 3 per cent on invested capital. The Mid-continent experience was lowest with 37 out of 100 banks in the low profits groups.

The Western States made the poorest showing of all the geographic divisions in three of the size groups. Nineteen out of every 100 banks with portfolios of $5,000,000 and over reported annual net deficits or net profits of less than 3 per cent. The two groups of smallest banks also showed poorer earnings in the Western States than anywhere else. In the Southeastern and Southern Mountain States the large banks also made a relatively poor showing.

If the size group $150,000–$250,000 is compared with that of $5,000,000 or more, the situation may be summarized by saying that the proportion of banks with unsatisfactory net profits was more than four times as great among the smaller banks as among the larger ones in the Mid-continent States; more than three times as great in the North Central States; and between two and three times as great in the Northeast, Southeast, and West.

There are, of course, many profitable small banks in all localities, some highly profitable ones. The experience of the five years, however, was that the probabilities of profitable operation are much lower for smaller banks than for larger ones.

Net Profits by Years

Of the five years included in this survey, the poorest net profits were shown in 1930 and the best in 1928. This is illustrated in Table 18 (see page 166). Forty out of every 100 national banks reported net deficits or net profits of less than 3 per cent in 1930, while in 1928 the figure was 22 out of every 100. In three of the five major geographical groupings 1930 afforded the worst experience during the five years. The Mid-continent and the Western States, on the other hand, showed the highest proportion of unsuccessful banks in 1926, while in both cases the experience in 1930 was but a trifle better.

The Northeastern States, the most highly industrialized area, showed a much better experience than any other region in every year, except 1930. In that year there were more unprofitable banks in the Northeastern region than the average for the whole country. The North Central States also made a poor record in 1930. The agricultural difficulties of earlier years were reflected in the large proportion of unprofitable banks in the Mid-continent, and Western States in 1926 and 1927.

TABLE 18

PERCENTAGE OF NATIONAL BANKS GROUPED BY GEOGRAPHIC DIVISIONS REPORTING NET DEFICITS OR NET PROFITS OF LESS THAN 3 PER CENT ON INVESTED CAPITAL, 1926-1930

GEOGRAPHIC DIVISION	AVERAGE 1926-1930	1926	1927	1928	1929	1930
Northeastern	16.9	7.8	8.7	10.3	16.2	42.0
Southeastern	24.7	18.3	21.3	22.3	26.0	37.2
North Central	25.2	15.7	21.8	20.5	26.8	42.6
Mid-continent	37.0	42.6	38.8	33.0	29.4	41.2
Western	32.5	37.3	34.1	28.8	27.0	34.9
Average—all groups	27.1	24.6	24.5	22.5	24.4	40.6

Iowa State Bank Experience

When the Iowa State bank experience is compared with the national banks in the Mid-continent States it will be observed from Table 19 that the proportion of smaller State banks showing unsatisfactory returns was even larger than among national banks.

Sixty-two per cent of the Iowa State banks in the smallest-size group reported net deficits or net profits of less than 3 per cent. This corresponds to 51 per cent of the Mid-continent national banks. In the second-size group the per cent of banks reporting net deficits or net profits of less than 3 per cent was 53 for the State banks and 48 for national banks, and in the third size group it was 45 for State banks compared with 38 for national banks. Among State banks of Iowa with loans and investments of $2,000,000 and over, 23 out of 100 reported net deficits or earned less than 3 per cent annually, while among national banks in the Mid-continent States 18 out of 100 of those with loans and investments of $2,000,000–$5,000,000 reported net deficits or net profits of less than 3 per cent.

This analysis of profitableness of national banks shows very clearly that the largest profits were earned by the banking units of larger size. The greatest percentage of banks showing deficits or low earnings is found among the small banks. The highest percentage of small banks showing a deficit or small earnings is located in the agricultural states. We also compared the national bank with the state banks in Iowa, the experience of small state banks having been even more unsatisfactory than that of small national banks in the mid-continental states.

We may thus conclude on the basis of the data assembled by the Committee of the Federal Reserve system, as well as from other sources, that the small banking unit shows smaller rates than the large bank and that during the period 1926 to 1930 an increasing percentage of small banks became unprofitable. The Committee of the Federal Reserve system on Group, Chain and Branch Banking attempted also to allocate the causes which account for the increasing unprofitableness of the small banks, to which we devote the second half of this chapter.

TABLE 19

PERCENTAGE DISTRIBUTION OF IOWA STATE BANKS GROUPED BY SIZES OF LOANS AND INVESTMENTS AND BY RATE OF NET PROFITS ON INVESTED CAPITAL—AVERAGE 1926-1930

SIZE GROUP LOANS AND INVESTMENFS	TOTAL	REPORTING NET DEFICITS OR NO NET PROFITS		REPORTING NET PROFITS				
		6% or more	0.0% to 5.9%	Less than 3%	3% to 5.9%	6% to 8.9%	9% to 11.9%	12% and over
Under $150,000	100%	19.0	23.1	20.3	16.7	13.1	4.4	3.4
150,000–250,000	100	14.3	19.8	18.8	16.9	12.5	10.4	7.3
250,000–500,000	100	10.4	18.5	16.1	17.9	16.1	9.5	11.3
500,000–750,000	100	7.5	12.8	16.1	20.2	18.6	12.0	12.9
750,000–1,000,000	100	6.2	12.0	16.9	17.8	19.4	10.7	16.9
1,000,000–2,000,000	100	7.9	10.6	17.6	18.5	19.8	14.1	11.5
2,000,000 and over	100	3.1	10.0	10.0	25.0	23.8	9.4	18.8
Average—all groups	100	12.5	18.3	17.6	17.9	15.4	9.1	9.2

II. Reasons for the Decline of the Small Bank

In order to single out the items which are responsible for the increasing percentage of small banks unable to show any profits or which operate only with very meager net returns, the Committee of the Federal Reserve system made an analysis of the operating costs in banking units of various size.[2] In presenting

[2] Several of the Reserve banks have done pioneer work in this field—notably the Reserve Bank of Boston.

the results obtained by the committee we first show the results obtained from the comparison of gross earnings and net profits for the same size groups of banks. After that we turn our attention to operating expenses per $100 of loans and investments in small and large banks. Net profits and capitalization per $100 of loans and investments, as well as net profits per $100 of invested capital are then taken up. Finally, we trace the same factors by size of bank and according to geographic location.

This information collected by the Federal Reserve Committee shows at what a disadvantage the small bank finds itself from the operative point of view as compared with the larger banking unit, and furnishes a conclusive explanation for the decline of the small bank.

Gross Earnings and Net Profits

The smaller banks made larger annual gross earnings per $100 of loans and investments than the larger banks. Net profits per $100 of loans and investments, however, were lower for the smaller banks than for the larger ones. The figures are given in Table 20 below:

TABLE 20

ANNUAL GROSS EARNINGS AND NET PROFITS PER $100 OF LOANS AND INVESTMENTS OF NATIONAL BANKS GROUPED BY SIZE OF LOANS AND INVESTMENTS—AVERAGE 1926-1930

SIZE GROUP LOANS AND INVESTMENTS	GROSS EARNINGS	NET PROFITS
Under $150,000	$9.18	$0.02
150,000–250,000	8.06	0.50
250,000–500,000	7.35	0.70
500,000–750,000	6.99	0.98
750,000–1,000,000	6.74	0.99
1,000,000–2,000,000	6.58	1.05
2,000,000–5,000,000	6.55	1.13
5,000,000–10,000,000	6.37	1.14
10,000,000–50,000,000	6.39	1.21
50,000,000 and over	6.09	1.37

The typical bank in the size group $150,000-$250,000 reported annually more than $8 gross earnings per $100 of loans and investments but retained only fifty cents as net profits. On the other hand, the typical bank of $10,000,000-$50,000,000 reported only about $6.40 gross earnings but retained $1.20 as net profits.

Operating Expenses

The larger banks had better net results because their salaries and wages, other expenses, and net losses were all lower in proportion to their loans and investments than in the case of the smaller banks.

The load of interest on deposits increases until a size of $5,000,000 of loans and investments is reached. With respect to salaries and wages and other expenses the movement is in the opposite direction. The load of salaries and wages declines rapidly until a size of $1,000,000 loans and investments is reached, after which there is much less contrast between groups. This is also true of other expenses. As in many manufacturing activities, so also in banking, unit

TABLE 21

ANNUAL EXPENSES AND NET LOSSES PER $100 OF LOANS AND INVESTMENTS OF NATIONAL BANKS GROUPED BY SIZE OF LOANS AND INVESTMENTS—AVERAGE 1926-1930

SIZE GROUP LOANS AND INVESTMENTS	INTEREST ON DEPOSITS	SALARIES AND WAGES	OTHER EXPENSES	NET LOSSES
Under $150,000	$1.34	$3.32	$2.81	$1.69
150,000–250,000	1.74	2.46	2.04	1.33
250,000–500,000	1.97	1.95	1.61	1.13
500,000–750,000	2.04	1.66	1.40	0.91
750,000–1,000,000	2.08	1.51	1.30	0.86
1,000,000–2,000,000	2.18	1.38	1.20	0.75
2,000,000–5,000,000	2.24	1.31	1.18	0.70
5,000,000–10,000,000	2.28	1.19	1.15	0.62
10,000,000–50,000,000	2.17	1.22	1.19	0.59
50,000,000 and over	2.00	1.10	1.08	0.53

costs appear, up to a certain point, to decrease with large-scale activity. Banks with $1,000,000 loans and investments and over appear to have had most of the operating advantages possessed by the larger banks.

Comparing the size group $150,000-$250,000 with the $10,000,000-$50,000,000 group, the typical bank in the former group had an average cost for salaries and wages over the five years of $2.46 per $100 of loans and investments as against $1.22 for the typical bank in the other group. Other expenses for the first group amounted to $2.04, compared with $1.19 for the second group. Net losses for the first group were $1.33, and for the second group, fifty-nine cents.

The banks in the smallest places, perhaps, do not always face as much competition for customers' funds as those in the larger cities, but the smallest banks could not afford even the load of interest on deposits which they were carrying. Their other items of expenses were so high relatively that their final result was unsatisfactory. The table [22] shown below indicates that after paying interest on deposits the smaller banks had remaining from $5 to $7 annually per $100 of loans and investments, while the larger banks had little more than $4. However, the larger banks, having smaller expenses

TABLE 22

ANNUAL GROSS EARNINGS LESS INTEREST ON DEPOSITS AND NET EARNINGS (BEFORE LOSSES) PER $100 OF LOANS AND INVESTMENTS OF NATIONAL BANKS GROUPED BY SIZE OF LOANS AND INVESTMENTS—AVERAGE 1926-1930

SIZE GROUP LOANS AND INVESTMENTS	GROSS EARNINGS LESS INTEREST ON DEPOSITS	NET EARNINGS (BEFORE LOSSES) *
Under $150,000	$7.84	$1.71
150,000–250,000	6.32	1.83
250,000–500,000	5.38	1.82
500,000–750,000	4.95	1.89
750,000–1,000,000	4.66	1.85
1,000,000–2,000,000	4.40	1.81
2,000,000–5,000,000	4.31	1.83
5,000,000–10,000,000	4.09	1.75
10,000,000–50,000,000	4.22	1.80
50,000,000 and over	4.09	1.90

* After payment of interest on deposits, wages, and other expenses but before provision for losses.

per $100 of loans and investments, showed about the same net earnings (before losses) as the small banks. The smaller net losses of the larger banks, however, led to their better showing in net profits.

Rate of Profits and Capitalization Per Unit of Business

The rates of net profits on invested capital of banks by size groups differ not only because of the varying rates of net profits per $100 of loans and investments but also by reason of the relation of loans and investments to invested capital.

These figures raise the serious question why small banks operate with a higher capital base than large banks. Under the National Bank Act, banks in towns of a population in excess of 6,000 but not in excess of 50,000 must have a capital of $100,000. In towns the population of which exceeds 3,000 but does not exceed 6,000 the minimum capital may be $50,000; in towns the population of which does not exceed 3,000, minimum capital must equal $25,000. All national banks are required before declaring a dividend, to carry 10 per cent of their net profits to surplus until the surplus is equal to 20 per cent of capital.

TABLE 23

ANNUAL NET PROFITS AND INVESTED CAPITAL PER $100 OF LOANS AND INVESTMENTS AND NET PROFITS PER $100 OF INVESTED CAPITAL OF NATIONAL BANKS GROUPED BY SIZE OF LOANS AND INVESTMENTS—AVERAGE 1926-1930*

SIZE GROUP LOANS AND INVESTMENTS	NET PROFITS PER $100 OF LOANS AND INVESTMENTS	INVESTED CAPITAL PER $100 OF LOANS AND INVESTMENTS	NET PROFITS PER $100 OF INVESTED CAPITAL
Under $150,000	$0.02	$32.87	$0.08
150,000–250,000	0.50	22.71	2.06
250,000–500,000	0.70	19.36	3.87
500,000–750,000	0.98	18.29	5.61
750,000–1,000,000	0.99	17.82	5.83
1,000,000–2,000,000	1.05	16.97	6.56
2,000,000–5,000,000	1.13	16.05	7.47
5,000,000–10,000,000	1.14	15.64	7.76
10,000,000–50,000,000	1.21	15.64	8.27
50,000,000 and over	1.37	17.09	8.64

* If figures in column 1 are divided by figures in column 2, the results will not exactly equal column 3, owing to the fact that ratios given for groups of banks are not the ratios that would be obtained by treating all banks in a group as one big bank, but are ratios typical of the group obtained by averaging the ratios of all the banks in the group, giving each bank a weight of one.

At $6.00 of invested capital per $100 of loans and investments, a ratio sustained by many of the larger banks, the minimum amount of loans and investments of a $30,000 invested capital bank would be $187,500; an invested capital of $120,000 would support $750,000 in loans and investments. There were, in 1930, 300 national banks which had less than $150,000 of loans and investments, and doubtless there are now many larger banks trying to live where they cannot accumulate a volume of business sufficient to cover expenses and losses. To show satisfactory results banks must have a large enough volume of business to support the amount of their invested capital.

Geographic Comparison

In order to determine how items of earnings and expenses vary in an industrial area as contrasted with an agricultural area, comparisons have been made between the Northeastern States and the Mid-continent States. Gross earnings per $100 of loans and investments in the Northeastern States vary little from small bank to large bank. In Mid-continent States, on the other hand, the rate of gross earnings is substantially higher for smaller banks than for the larger banks. The fact that both the rates on customers' loans and the proportion of funds invested in such loans are higher in the Mid-continent

TABLE 24

ANNUAL GROSS EARNINGS AND NET PROFITS PER $100 OF LOANS AND INVESTMENTS OF NATIONAL BANKS IN NORTHEASTERN AND MID-CONTINENT STATES, BANKS GROUPED BY SIZE OF LOANS AND INVESTMENTS—AVERAGE 1926-1930

	GROSS EARNINGS		NET PROFITS	
SIZE GROUP LOANS AND INVESTMENTS	North-eastern States	Mid-conti-nent States	North-eastern States	Mid-conti-nent States
Under $150,000	$6.40	$9.83	$0.28*	$0.03
150,000–250,000	6.32	8.69	0.96	0.34
250,000–500,000	6.29	7.98	1.11	0.55
500,000–750,000	6.32	7.64	1.31	0.83
750,000–1,000,000	6.33	7.31	1.27	0.81
1,000,000–2,000,000	6.27	7.15	1.27	0.82
2,000,000–5,000,000	6.28	7.01	1.24	1.02
5,000,000 and over	6.15	6.62	1.21	1.12

* Net deficits.

States than in the Northeastern States is doubtless reflected in the higher gross earnings in the former region.

Table 25 brings out the variations in expense items and net losses between banks in the Northeastern States and the Mid-continent States. As to interest on deposits, there was little difference; but for salaries and wages, other expenses, and net losses decided contrasts appear. In the Mid-continent States net losses were larger through all size groups than in the Northeast. In loss experience, however, large banks of the Mid-continent States make almost as favorable a record as the Northeastern banks. Most small bank groups in the Northeast compare favorably with large banks there,

TABLE 25

ANNUAL EXPENSES AND NET LOSSES PER $100 OF LOANS AND INVESTMENTS OF NATIONAL BANKS IN NORTHEASTERN AND MID-CONTINENT STATES, BANKS GROUPED BY SIZE OF LOANS AND INVESTMENTS ANNUAL EXPENSES AND NET LOSSES PER $100 OF AVERAGE 1926-1930

SIZE GROUP AND INVESTMENTS	INTEREST ON DEPOSITS		SALARIES AND WAGES		OTHER EXPENSES		NET LOSSES	
	North-eastern States	Mid-continent States	North-eastern States	Mid-continent States	North-eastern States	Mid-continent States	North-eastern States	Mid-continent States
Under $150,000	$1.39	$1.27	$2.12	$3.63	$2.05	$2.95	$1.11	$1.96
150,000–250.000	1.56	1.75	1.76	2.71	1.48	2.22	0.57	1.66
250,000–500,000	1.90	2.00	1.43	2.22	1.23	1.78	0.61	1.43
500,000–750,000	2.01	2.12	1.30	1.93	1.12	1.55	0.59	1.19
750,000–1,000,000	2.12	2.09	1.21	1.83	1.09	1.44	0.63	1.14
1,000,000–2,000,000	2.28	2.12	1.15	1.70	1.01	1.41	0.56	1.11
2,000,000–5,000,000	2.39	2.08	1.09	1.60	0.99	1.42	0.56	0.90
5,000,000 and over	2.33	2.13	1.05	1.36	1.00	1.35	0.55	0.66

but the small banks of the Mid-continent States did not make such a good showing.

In the matter of operating expenses there is again a sharp contrast between the small banks of the Northeast and the Mid-continent States. It takes much less in salaries and wages in a year to handle $100 of business measured in loans and investments in the small banks of the Northeast than in those of the Mid-continent States. This is true also of other expenses.

Summary

1. In the five-year period, 1926 to 1930, a greater percentage of small national banks shows a deficit or low net earnings than do banks of larger size. High net profits are found mostly among large institutions.

2. In the agricultural sections of the country deficits or low net profits are more frequent among small national banks than in the industrial regions. This tendency of small banks to be less profitable, or to operate at a loss, has increased in the agricultural states over the years 1926 to 1930. The experience of state banks in Iowa shows a similar decline of small banking units.

3. Small national banks show considerably greater gross earnings than do large banks. But owing to the fact that salaries, wages, and other expenses are much higher per unit of business in a small bank, as compared to a large one, the net profits increase with the size of the institution.

4. Gross earnings, excluding only interest on deposits, are higher in small banks than in large ones. Net earnings prior to the deduction of losses do not differ greatly in banks of various sizes. The low net earnings and deficits in the small national banks are caused by relatively high losses and greater operating cost.

5. Net profits per $100 of loans and investments are much higher in large national banks than in small institutions. The same applies to net profits per $100 of invested capital. At the same time the small banking unit has a greater capitalization per $100 of loans and investments as compared to large institutions.

6. The gross earnings of national banks in the North Eastern

states do not vary with the size of the institution. In the mid-continental states they are high in small banks. Net profits of small banks are low in both regions; in the North Eastern states banks with loans and investments under $150,000 as a group show a deficit. The operating expenses of small banks are high in both cases; in the mid-continental states they reduce the high gross profits to a low rate of net earnings.

7. We may, therefore, conclude that the small banks require relatively a greater amount of capital and have higher operating expenses than large institutions. These factors reduce the gross earnings, if they are high, to low net profits or, if the gross earnings are low, to a deficit. Throughout the country deficit and insufficient earnings are found in much greater proportion among small institutions. The small bank is most unprofitable in the agricultural regions of the country where the largest number of small institutions is still located.

CHAPTER X

COMMERCIAL, INVESTMENT, AND OTHER TYPES OF BANKING[1]

In the foregoing discussion constant reference has been made to commercial banking as distinct from other types of operation. It is now necessary to devote some attention to the clarification of this thought, and to specify more in detail the conditions under which the banking system of the United States has developed to its present stage. In tables already presented, banking institutions have been classified as: national, state commercial, loan and trust, mutual savings, stock savings, and private banks. The reason for the differentiation which has occurred between these various types of institutions, and the basis of their relationship one to another, is plainly a fundamental question in a study of the organization of American banking.

ORIGIN OF DIFFERENTIATION

A glance over the history of banking shows that banking has passed through different experiences in different countries and that the distinction between commercial and investment banking is by no means uniform throughout the world. Neither is it true, as is sometimes stated, that commercial banking usually precedes the development of investment banking, or vice versa. The order of development, as between different types of banking in different parts of the world, depends upon local conditions, and upon the circumstances which control the organization and growth of banking and its relation to business enterprise. In the United States,,after a varied banking experience up to the time of Civil War, the country entered upon what was practically a new era, with a federalized banking system organized under the so-called "National" act, and devoted to facilitating what was then called "business." By business as distinct from agriculture,

[1] Prepared by H. Parker Willis.

was meant primarily the bringing forward and disposal of goods, and the National Bank Act was chiefly concerned with the conditions under which this process of exchange might be facilitated. Its fundamental interest apparently lay in the field of note issue, and the conditions under which the supply of notes was to be controlled and regulated. Not a few of the provisions of the National Bank Act were fundamentally restrictive, their object being to prevent the overlending of funds in given directions upon security which was represented by goods that might or might not prove salable. Little or nothing in the National Bank Act related to the control of investment operations by national banks and the Act moreover contained hardly anything designed to regulate the extent to which the funds of the bank should be used in the purchase of long-term securities or bonds.

After the adoption of the National Bank Act the various states remodeled their banking laws following, in a general way, the lead of the national system, and, while not in all cases paralleling it precisely, yet organizing their systems along lines of very similar character. The result of these acts of legislation was to build up in the United States between the years 1864 and about 1884—a twenty-year period—two coördinate systems of banking: the one national and the other state in origin, both being commercial in their nature and neither taking account of the investment side of banking to more than a very casual extent. After about the year 1884, the development of loan and trust companies, as they were then called, became important, and the succeeding twenty years witnessed a definite growth of these companies. The development of mutual savings banks was much older than either the national or state systems dating, in the New England States, back to about the year 1816. Stock savings banks began to make their appearance in considerable numbers from about 1875 onward, while private banking houses, which devoted themselves chiefly to investment operations, had existed in one form or another from the beginning of organized business in the colonies, and had definitely reached an important stage of development by the year 1875.

Question of Investment Banking

It was, from the beginning, more or less of a question how far the so-called commercial banks should be allowed to engage in what we now call "investment banking." In the development of the western states there was, from the outset, as in most new countries, a great need for capital, and a disposition to obtain it wherever it could be had. This led to the making of loans by so-called commercial banks which, although technically based upon the notes of borrowers, were in truth real-estate loans, being often secured by mortgages directly placed in the hands of the bank and in other cases by mortgages which were made in favor of, and held by, officers of the institution who thus practically acted for it in the creation of capital loans. The unsatisfactory character of this type of portfolio was early recognized by national bank examiners, and in a less degree by those of the states, but lack of a satisfactorily organized capital market prevented the authorities from interfering in any direct or serious manner with the tendencies which were thus exhibited in actual practice.

Accordingly, the tendency of investment banking to develop as a parasitic growth, drawing its support from commercial banking and constituting a diversion of the funds of the latter, notwithstanding that they were normally called for as a means of liquidating demand obligations, presented numerous elements of danger, which did not, however, secure recognition at an early date. As often happens in financial development, it was an incidental phase of investment banking which originally operated to bring to the front the hazards that were involved in the maintenance of commercial and investment banking as phases of the activity of the same institution. Stock-market borrowing had naturally developed as the market for securities became more and more widely developed after the Civil War. By about 1885, various evils in connection with the use of bank funds in supporting the market had become well recognized, and from that time onward, the tendency to employ the surplus funds of banks in connection with loans on securities tended to become a more and more pressing form of banking evil. A decade of development brought it, in the middle of the '90s, to a fairly advanced stage, and it continued to assume a more and more menacing aspect at the opening of the World War, just prior to which the Federal Reserve Act had been adopted in an effort to maintain the self-dependence of the commercial banking structure of the United States, and to avoid the absorption of too large a proportion of commercial banks' funds in connection with speculation.

Effect of the World War

The World War, with its presumed necessity for the use of all available banking resources in supporting and placing the obligations of the government, led to a very great development of investment banking, and immediately after the war the processes of extending and universalizing the corporate form of business organizations, already well marked prior to the opening of the struggle, took on a new and greatly developed life. During the decade 1920-1930, the expansion of the number of shares and securities of all kinds listed on the New York Stock Exchange, as well as on other exchanges, was notably contemporaneous with the vast expansion of loans and credit at banks for the purpose of permitting the issue, carrying, and speculation in such securities. The panic of 1929 found the banks of the country with portfolios very heavily overburdened with securities of every kind and, of course, with loans based upon, or collateraled by, securities.

It may be inferred from what has just been said that much of the development already referred to had taken place in consequence of the lack of regulation and the general absence of control, which had been characteristic of American banking on its investment side ever since the Civil War. This was doubtless true, but the fact remains that in practically all countries—even in Great Britain, the classical country of commercial banking—there had been, for a good many years past, doubt as to whether the older principles of banking, based upon the idea of dealings in commercial paper, had not become more or less obsolete. Not a few British economists had urged that the methods of the Germans (in whose banking system it had been customary for larger banks to devote themselves in no small measure to the financing of industrial needs for capital) should be transplanted to Great Britain; while in the United States, the financing of industrial enterprises came rapidly to center around the banks of the country.

The problem, however, of keeping such operations from decreasing the safety of commercial banking and from preventing depositors from obtaining the protection they required had always been recognized, and continues today to be a fundamental issue in connection with the whole question of banking structure. Thus, at the present moment, even after several decades of discussion and of more or less continuous readjustment, the country still finds itself with a banking system not yet fully integrated, and in which great confusion of function as between investment and commercial banking exists. A survey of banking at the present moment, therefore, inevitably leads to the conclusion that one of the earliest problems to be met and dealt with in rendering American banking safer and more conservative must be the decision as to what is to be done with regard to the classification of banks and the assignment of definite types of undertakings to them.

Commercial vs. Investment Functions

In studying this problem practically, let us note first of all the present position of the banks of the United States in connection with this question of commercial and investment operations. In so doing we will glance first at the national banks. National banks in their origin were supposed to do a demand-deposit business, and it was not until the adoption of the Federal Reserve Act that distinct regulation was given to the undertaking of savings-deposit business on their part. Savings deposits in the form of time deposits or time certificates of deposit had, of course, for a long time constituted an important activity at national banks, but the definite recognition of their functions in this field had not been attained, and was considerably interfered with, in many states, by the existence of state laws which limited the use of the word "savings" to banks that were subject to savings legislation and control. In the Federal Reserve Act, permission was granted for the taking of time deposits and it was not long before this authority was copied by state legislatures which were pressed to grant to banks organized under their jurisdiction the same powers which were possessed by national banks operating in competition with them.

The taking of savings, of course, implies the placing of savings deposits in some sort of portfolio investment corresponding roughly to the maturity of the savings or time deposits themselves. Yet the Federal Reserve Act made no specification as to the form of investment which should thus be considered appropriate, save that it contained some rather limited qualifications to be imposed upon real-estate loan operations undertaken by national institutions. The question evidently would not have been of first importance if the savings or time deposits had not assumed any very great importance in volume. They came speedily to occupy an important position, however, and the situation was aggravated by the fact that in the Federal Reserve Act the error had been committed of reducing the reserve to be carried behind time or savings deposits, so that there was an inducement to classify funds as "savings" or "time," rather than as demand, in order to get the advantage of the lessened reserve and the smaller expense entailed thereby. This same tendency was at work among state institutions, so that during the years after the adoption of the Federal Reserve Act an immense expansion in time deposits occurred, with the result that by the year 1930 fully three-fifths of all member bank deposits had come to be classified under the heads of time or savings deposits.

SECURITY AFFILIATES[2]

With this transition in the character of national bank portfolios, there was going on a similar change in state institutions. Their operations were likewise changing for reasons already indicated, and, eventually, state and national banks had come to occupy a foremost position as buyers of new issues of securities. They thus constituted, in an important sense, a fundamental market for bonds, and were accepted as such throughout the country. Investment banking itself had in the meanwhile taken

[2] Material on security affiliates used in this chapter is from Part VII, *Senate Banking Committee Hearings of 1932*, prepared by Dr. J. I. Bogen.

on a new form in connection with banking through the organization of what were called "security affiliates." The first security affiliate on record was organized in 1908 by the First National Bank of New York City. The method adopted in organizing this company was subsequently followed as a model by many other banks. The First Security Co. was organized as a corporation endowed with general powers, having a capitalization of $10,000,000—equal to that of the bank. The bank then declared a cash dividend of 100 per cent, which, however, was not actually disbursed to its stockholders. Instead, with the prior approval of the shareholders, this sum was directly subscribed to the stock of the security corporation, which was thus made fully paid, and was deposited under a trust of which six senior officers of the bank were made trustees. Shareholders of the bank then had indorsed on their stock certificates a statement that they had a beneficial interest in an equal number of shares of the security affiliate, which were to be inseparable from those of the bank.

The National City Bank, also of New York City, followed the lead of the First National in 1911, and during the following decade, many of the other large banks in the city, and in other centers, adopted similar policies. The significance of bank-security affiliates and their operations was known to the public in only a most general way, until the failure of the Bank of United States in December, 1930, clearly indicated the disastrous results that could follow upon a flagrant abuse of this device, such as took place in that case.

A great diversity of practice exists among the banks possessing security affiliates as to methods of organizing and operating them. Little standardization is noted in this field—a fact which makes generalizations concerning such organizations difficult. In defining a security affiliate for its questionnaire, the Senate subcommittee of the Committee on Banking and Currency of 1930-32, stated:

1. A part or all of the stock of which is deposited in trust for the benefit of stockholders of the bank; or

For the purpose of this questionnaire, a security affiliate shall be defined as a corporation:

2. The shares of which are sold in units in combination with shares of the bank; or

3. A controlling interest in which is held by the same interests which control the bank; or

4. A controlling interest in which is held by the bank; or

5. A controlling interest in which is held by some other security affiliate of the bank.[3]

[3] A more detailed definition is presented in the report of the commission appointed by Governor Roosevelt, of New York State, to make a study of the banking law of the State, which resulted in making security affiliates of State banks and trust companies subject to examination by the superintendent of banks in order to determine more fully the position of such institutions. The proposal of the commission was:

For the purpose of determining whether a corporation is subject to examination by the superintendent of banks in order to obtain full information as to the financial condition of a bank or trust company, there shall be deemed to be affiliated with a bank or trust company:

1. Any corporation of which such bank or trust company directly or indirectly owns or controls a majority of the voting shares of its capital stock or a lesser number of such shares if such lesser number shall amount to more than 50 per cent of the shares voted for the selection of directors at the preceding annual meeting of such corporation; or any corporation of which such bank or trust company in any other manner directly or indirectly controls the election of a majority of its board of directors.

2. Any corporation which directly or indirectly owns or controls a majority of the shares of capital stock of such bank or trust company or a lesser number of shares if such less number shall amount to more than 50 per cent of the shares voted for the election of directors at the preceding annual meeting of such bank or trust company; or any corporation which in any other manner directly or indirectly controls the election of a majority of the board of directors of such bank or trust company;

Any corporation of which a majority of the voting shares of its capital stock, or a lesser number of shares if such lesser number shall amount to more than 50 per cent of the shares voted for the election of directors at the preceding annual meeting of such corporation is directly or indirectly owned or controlled by the same, or substantially the same, stockholders as directly or indirectly own or control a majority of the shares of capital stock of such corporation subject to the provisions of this chapter or a lesser number of shares, if such lesser number shall amount to more than 50 per cent of the shares voted for the election of directors at the preceding annual meeting of such bank or trust company; *Provided, however,* That either *a)* there shall then exist, or within the preceding 2-year period have existed, business transactions or relations (of any kind, character, or description other than stock ownership) between such corporation and such bank or trust company, or *b)* such bank or trust company shall then own, have outstanding loans secured in whole or in part by, or be in any manner interested in the stock or securities of such corporation or in any property in which such corporation is in any way or to any extent interested or within the preceding 2-year period shall have had such ownership, loans, or interest.

3. Any corporation the election of a majority of the board of directors of which is or may be directly or indirectly controlled by any instrumentality,

The definition used by the subcommittee would cover virtually every usual case, with the exception of bank-holding companies, in which case the security company controls the bank, instead of the reverse.

---

agency or arrangement that directly or indirectly controls the election of a majority of the board of directors of such bank or trust company.

Any corporation a majority of the directors of which shall be directors of such bank or trust company or of which a majority of the executive committee of its board of directors are directors of such bank or trust company.

Any corporation the board of directors of which shall comprise a majority of the board of directors of such bank or trust company or the executive committee of the board of directors of which shall comprise a majority of the executive committee of such bank or trust company.

Any corporation all or substantially all of whose executive officers are executive officers of such bank or trust company.

Any corporation whose executive officers comprise substantially all of the executive officers of such bank or trust company.

Any corporation the business or policy of which is dominated or controlled, in whole or in part, by a bank or trust company, whether by contract or otherwise.

Any corporation which dominates or controls, in whole or in part, the business or policy of a bank or trust company whether by contract or otherwise: *Provided, however,* That either *a)* there shall then exist, or within the preceding 2-year period have existed, business transactions or relations (of any kind, character, or description) between such corporation and such bank or trust company, or *b)* such bank or trust company shall then own, have outstanding loans secured in whole or in part by, or be in any manner interested in the stock or securities of such corporation or in any property in which such corporation is in any way or to any extent interested, or within the preceding 2-year period shall have had such ownership, loans, or interest.

4. Any corporation, association, or partnership having business transactions or relations with a bank or trust company the examination of which on application of the superintendent of banks and on notice to such company shall be determined by a justice of the Supreme Court to be necessary or expedient in order to ascertain whether the capital of a bank or trust company is impaired or whether the safety of depositors with such bank or trust company has been imperiled.

For all the purposes of the foregoing definition—

All corporations similarly owned or controlled shall be regarded as a single corporation and if as a single corporation subject to examination each such corporation shall be deemed to be an affiliated corporation.

Stock held in the name of nominees of any bank, trust company, or other corporation or otherwise for the benefit of any bank, trust company or other corporation shall be deemed to be stock owned or controlled by such bank, trust company, or other corporation.

The above definition is considerably broader than that used by the subcommittee in its questionnaire. If literally applied, however, it would take in all kinds of enterprises in the management of which banks take an active interest, for it includes "any corporation" where the bank "directly or indirectly controls the election of a majority of its board of directors." A somewhat different definition is employed in the Banking Act of 1933.

Methods of Organizing Affiliates

There are four common methods whereby banks may provide capital for their security affiliates. These are:

1. Declaration of a cash dividend by the bank, which is specifically utilized to subscribe pro rata for shares in the security affiliate. This, as has already been seen, was the method adopted by the First National Bank in organizing its pioneer security affiliate, and has been the most common procedure since. In that case each stockholder specifically authorized the utilization of his dividend for this purpose. In later cases such action has been authorized by a general vote of shareholders, thus avoiding the necessity for unanimous consent in advance.

An interesting question is raised by the possibility of individual shareholders refusing to waive their cash dividend, and insisting upon receiving it in lieu of the stock of the affiliate. No such instance of refusal is on record, however.

2. Organization of the affiliate as a wholly owned subsidiary of the bank, through the bank subscribing for its shares. This method is possible only where the bank has the right to purchase stocks. In New York State, where trust companies have such a privilege, several of the large security companies affiliated with banks are directly owned subsidiaries of trust companies.

3. Offering of new bank stock to existing shareholders at a large premium over the par value, part or all of the premium being actually subscribed to stock of the affiliate. Thus, a bank whose shares are selling at $700 each may offer additional shares to its shareholders at $500, of which $200 will be allocated to the capital and the surplus of the bank and the balance of $300 utilized to subscribe to the stock of the security affiliate.

4. Direct offering of stock in the security affiliate to the bank's shareholders. This method has been least favored, except for the organization of investment trusts under the auspices of the banks, because it does not facilitate the establishment and maintenance of identity of shareholders for the bank and the security affiliate.

In practice one of the major problems in the organization of a security affiliate is the permanent maintenance of identity of shareholding interests in the two institutions. The usual methods whereby this is accomplished are the following:

1. The stock of the affiliate is deposited in trust for the proportionate interest of the shareholders of the bank. It is customary to indicate this proportionate interest on the certificates of the bank's shares. Since no shares of stock of the security affiliate go into public circulation, it does not become possible to transfer them to other names than those of the bank's stockholders.

2. The stock of the affiliate is printed on the same certificate with the stock of the bank, so that the two are transferred together. Suitable provisions appear on the certificate and elsewhere to prevent a valid transfer of one equity without the other. Where this is done the security affiliate has a list of stockholders of record which is the equivalent of the shareholders' list of the bank. Technical disadvantages, such as dual transfer taxes, etc., have been advanced by lawyers as militating against this method in comparison with the first.

3. The stock of the affiliate is fully owned, except for directors' qualifying shares, if needed by the bank, where the power to own such shares is given by law—as with trust companies and state banks in certain jurisdictions.

The security affiliates may be organized in any state, and several of them operated by New York banks are organized in Delaware, because of the more satisfactory charters that are available there. The directors and officials of the security affiliate may or may not hold similar posts in the bank. In some cases, a completely different set of individuals hold such posts in the two affiliated institutions, but it goes without saying that, through identity of stock ownership, there is identity of real control over the two.

An analysis of the operations of a number of typical security affiliates reveals a wide variety of activities. The more important functions which they exercise are the following:

1. Wholesalers of security issues, purchasing entire offerings or participating in purchase and banking groups which acquire whole issues of securities from governmental bodies or corporations.

2. Retailers of securities, maintaining corps of salesmen and often branches in other states than that in which the bank operates for the distribution of stocks and bonds to institutions and private investors.

3. Holding and finance companies, carrying blocks of securities for control or otherwise, which the bank could not or would not list among its own investments.

4. Investment trusts, buying and selling securities acquired purely for investment of speculative purposes.

5. An assets realization company, to take over from the parent bank loans and investments which prove doubtful or nonliquid.

6. A medium for supporting the market for the bank's own stock.

7. A real-estate holding company.

In most cases the security affiliates have exercised a combination of these functions, and in some instances they have exercised all of them. A majority of the banks possessing security affiliates have but one such organization, but in other cases more than one such corporation has been organized, at times with a specialization or function among them. Where a group of affiliates is built up in this way, their affairs frequently become interlocked through mutual loans and stockholdings, so as to make any subsequent separation difficult, even if thought desirable. The Banking Act of 1933 now directs the complete separation of banks from their affiliates, but this order applies, of course, only to member banks.

Savings and Investments

The savings banks of the country have naturally performed an important function in the service of investment banking which has been particularly marked in connection with the financing of city real estate. Controlled, in most of the states where they exist, by detailed and meticulous acts of law and administrative regulation, designed to afford general control of the classes of securities in which they may place their funds, the savings banks work along much narrower lines and are at the same time much more intensive in their operations than are commercial banks in any of their aspects. In a later chapter the development of savings banking will be fully reviewed, and it is necessary at this point only to refer briefly to it as a special phase of investment-banking development.

By private banking is meant that type of banking which is usually carried on by unincorporated firms and which, as is exemplified in New York and other financial centers, has chiefly for its object the bringing out of new issues and the placing of them in the hands of investors.

The question as to how far these different types of banking have tended to continue independent and how far they have become integrated or entwined with one another is obviously one of the most serious issues involved in the consideration of what is called "the banking problem." As we have seen, investment banking in its proper sense has, especially since the adoption of the McFadden Act of 1927, come to be clearly interdependent with the whole structure of commercial banking, while savings operations permitted under the Federal Reserve Act have grown more and more important as a phase of the transactions of national and state commercial banks. The competition between different grades of government for the organization of banks under their several jurisdictions, with the development of taxable capacity which accompanied such organization, has tended to accelerate and accentuate the tendency to fusion which would in any case have exhibited itself. In so far as figures representing organization under the different groups of laws governing banking throw light upon the scope and character of this development, they are depicted in the tables already given at an earlier point (Chapter VIII), showing by percentage relationships relative growth of national and state banks, trust companies, savings institutions and private partnerships. The question is thus plainly brought before the inquirer, whether at the present moment the tendency toward the fusion of functions in which savings, investment, and commercial banking are combined, shall be allowed to continue or whether effort shall be made to bring about a complete separation of these operations, one from the other. As to this question, two views or theories widely prevail; the one holding that the most important needs of banking will be developed by recognizing the tendency toward fusion of functions, and the other holding that efforts should be made to react toward the idea of an individualized banking system with operations carefully classified and separated, one from another. It is this latter conception that lay at the root of the so-called Glass bill, adopted as the Banking Act of June 16, 1933.

An Inevitable Development

The introduction of investment banking and of the financing of speculation into the field of national banking came about (as has been seen above) as a more or less "natural," or inevitable, development—given the general corporate conditions leading up to it as just outlined. Nations do not, unfortunately, shape their banking systems upon logical and predetermined lines, with a view to bringing about satisfactory organization; but they are prone to work from hand to mouth and to change their financial systems as circumstances change, or as current needs require. The great corporate development of the United States and the gradual shift in the form and extent of concentration of industry tended (as we have seen) to make business more and more directly dependent upon sales of securities negotiated with the public, and especially in later years to help make them independent of direct accommodation from banks.

In another way, however, the commercial or national bank has tended to enter the investment field and to become closely involved with operations in securities. Trust companies, as we have already noted, had begun to make their appearance in a well-organized form and in considerable numbers as early as the '70s, with a rather material enlargement during the succeeding decade. They had made enough progress during the twenty years from 1890 to 1910 to attract the envious regard of commercial banks so that when the Federal Reserve Act came up for discussion one of the urgent requests made by the banks of the country was that they should be permitted to take on trust company functions.

Grant of "Trust" Functions

There was a certain amount of justification in this demand in the fact that the exercise of fiduciary functions in the case of large establishments had become a matter of onerous responsibility and called also for a specialized knowledge which was possessed by relatively few persons, so that some good reason existed for the request that national banks be allowed to enter the trust company field. In studying the demands of the banks for this privilege, Congress, however, recognized two distinct situations, or phases, of the problem. The first was furnished by the necessity of the banks for an opportunity to enlarge their incomes, and it was thought that this end might be met by permitting them to enter the field of corporate trust functions, acting as registrar, transfer agent, depositary, disbursing officer or fiscal agent. Into this field Congress was ready to allow the commercial banks to enter. The other phase of the fiduciary problem was seen in the request of the banks that they be allowed to take on also what was called "individual trusts"—the duty of acting as executor, administrator, guardian, and generally, as the supervising agent through which the investment of trust funds is carried out. Into this latter field Congress was reluctant to admit the banks, partly because of doubt as to whether the courts would sustain its action in so doing (should it grant the application of the bankers for the exercise of these powers) and partly, also, because it felt that such investment functions were not likely to be well exercised by commercial banks of the ordinary type.

The Federal Reserve Act eventually granted the corporate trust powers and these, in due course of time, were upheld by the Supreme Court, whereupon an amendment to the Federal Reserve Act recognized the right of national banks to engage in any kind of trust function that they might see fit, whether individual or corporate. Thus, by the close of the World War, the national banks were fully launched upon the function of providing trust services, and it was not long before various states imitated the action of Congress by legislating to permit their own state banks to undertake the same functions that had thus been given over to the national institutions.

Transformation of Banking

The result of these changes was speedily seen in a further transformation of the scope of American banking. Not only was it gradually being transformed by its relationship to the stock market and its assumption of investment banking functions, but it now began to develop rapidly along the line of fiduciary duty, thereby still further bringing about the admixture of banking types, which in the beginning of the national banking system (and still more under the British banking system—its prototype) had been regarded as adverse to the proper management of commercial banking. National institutions were in many cases strategically placed for the acquisition of such business and, as a result, they began to take on very large volumes of fiduciary business, not only competing with the trust companies for the business that already existed but also seeking to develop as much of it as possible *de novo*.

Although at first the number of institutions which applied to the Federal Reserve Board for power to undertake the establishment of trust departments was small, it soon began to expand; and during the decade 1920-1930, the number of national banks vested with trust powers largely increased, whereas in 1917 the total number of national banks holding permits to engage in fiduciary business was only 481, the number so recognized was 2,329 in 1932, and this, in spite of the heavy failures of preceding years, was only a very slight recession from the peak level (2,461) which had been reached in 1929. Considerable profits also were being made by national banks from their fiduciary activities, as is clearly evident from the reports of the Comptroller of the Currency. Although the state banks had not acquired trust powers nearly as rapidly as had the national—because of the fact that under state laws the organization of trust companies on an independent basis had already for some years been authorized—there was, nevertheless, considerable expansion of trust-company powers on the part of state commercial banks through the decade in question.

It is thus evident that from the fiduciary side the steady changes introduced into commercial banking must be reckoned as of very great moment, and that these changes took place after the close of the World War at a time when it was already true that very great alterations were in prospect, owing to the fundamental changes in corporate and other financing which had been necessitated by the conditions growing out of the struggle. Eventually, therefore, the transformation that was occurring in American banking must be assigned, not merely to fortuitous condi tions or even to changes taking place under the pressure of competition among banks—as has been the case in the investment field, but must be attributed also to voluntary changes produced by legislation at the instance of banks desirous of gaining access to new and more profitable fields of work. This factor sufficiently explains the advent of fiduciary banking as a phase of what had originally been organized as commercial banking.

General Banking Alterations

The changes which have been outlined are, in their main features, already well known. What is less well recognized is the effect that they have produced upon the general banking situation. It is clear that their fundamental influence has been that of altering the scope of banking. In so far as this has been true, their influence has been to lessen the efficiency of the banks along their own appropriate lines and to diffuse their activities over a field for which they were perhaps not sufficiently equipped. There is, however, another aspect of the matter which is of even greater interest from the present standpoint. This is found in the competition which has always existed between the state and national legislative bodies for the organization of banks. Such competition naturally becomes more intense when the different institutions are permitted to engage in substantially similar types of operation. So long as the state institutions remained practically the only occupants of the fiduciary field, there was nothing to be feared from the competition of state legislatures with Congress in laying down the methods of control and subjecting them to unduly lax restrictions only. There was always this danger in so far as related to the commercial operations of state and national banks, although it was less acute soon after the organization of the national-banking system when the use of note currency was the accepted method of financing certain types of transactions, and deposit credit constituted only a secondary phase of activity.

Competition between state and national commercial banks began to be intense as note currency sank into the background and as the deposit function assumed first place as a form of lending. Such competition, however, was eventually intensified by both the entrance of the national banks into the investment-banking field as well as by their advent as fiduciary organizations. Taken together with the increased effort of national institutions to expand their savings or time-deposit departments, these innovations brought about a condition of almost complete competition or parallelism between the different institutions. The result was that as state legislation gradually granted to their own banks powers precisely parallel to those of the national institutions, there developed a complete competitive state of things. This was followed by a strong tendency to reduce the severity of examination and to relax the restrictions of law in order to eliminate any obstacles which might otherwise have been thought likely to interfere with the attracting of banks into either the state or national banking system, as the case might be. Thus, there developed during the latter part of the decade 1920-1930, an exaggerated form of an evil which had already been for some time recognized—the effort of state and national legislatures to attract banks to their own jurisdictions. Not only was the intermixture of deposit and investment banking rendered more complete by the assumption of fiduciary functions, but the exemption of the resultant institutions from restrictions at a time when conditions were calling urgently for greater care and oversight and greater severity of control rather than for less, necessarily made for unsoundness in the banking system. This brought to the front with unusual urgency the question whether it was not necessary that a realignment take place regarding the incorporation and oversight of the different types of institutions.[4]

Dangers of Situation

During the investigations made by the Senate Banking Committee in 1930-31-32, the dangers growing out of the combination of functions to which reference has just been made, were

[4] This subject of fiduciary banking is discussed in greater detail in Chapter XI of the present study.

clearly cited and attention was called to the fact that a revision was now urgent. One form of such readjustment was suggested by Mr. Owen D. Young, who recommended that Congress, through the exercise of its currency functions and general power over money, should compel all banks which undertake to receive deposits subject to demand and to the drawing of checks, to organize under Federal supervision. At the same time Mr. Young implied that national banks surrender their newly acquired fiduciary functions and content themselves with the performance of "straight" commercial (deposit) banking.

Thus would have been turned over once more all fiduciary functions to trust companies, likewise under state law, and for such a retransfer there was the more warrant in that the laws of property, inheritance, land holding, etc., are the products of the state legislatures and must be recognized by national banks, even when vested with the trust functions, as the ultimate regulator of their activities. In the same way the Young proposal would have resulted, it may be supposed, in transferring to state organized institutions investment-banking operations which the McFadden Act of 1927, had expressly conferred upon national banks. Savings activities of every kind, the holding of time deposits and all related business would presumably have gone also to state institutions. These changes would have been so far-reaching as to involve a practical revolution in the banking structure of the United States. They would have meant that national banks must completely transform the scope of their activities, while many state banks would have had to give up their charters and convert themselves into national institutions by recharter. The resultant operations would have been necessarily of a kind requiring several years for completion and during the period of transition would have entailed a good deal of disorganization. The resultant situation, if fully accomplished, would undoubtedly have been very much more logical than the state of things existing today, but the degree of success that might be expected to be attained in carrying it through and the extent of friction involved in such action would unquestionably have been such as to cause hesitancy on the part of prudent legislators.

General National Incorporation

Alternative with any such far-reaching plan is the idea suggested from various other sources to the Senate Committee and discussed not only before it but elsewhere, for the enactment of a general national law of banking incorporation, which would practically drive out from the exercise of the check and deposit business the state-chartered institutions, and which would in that way compel them indirectly to apply for national charters. This plan, presented to the Federal Reserve Board by the Senate Committee on Banking, was taken under advisement of the Board with a view to preparation of a form of law designed to put it into effect; but the resultant enactment, although often promised, has never made its appearance. Presumably it would have limited itself entirely to the "unification" of the banking system, its object being to bring all banks enjoying the deposit and checking function under Federal control, and to make them members of the Federal Reserve system; the outcome, therefore, being to give to the latter system a complete jurisdiction over the entire situation and a unity of power in connection with the establishment of new bank credit, which it had not otherwise possessed. This plan, in the comparatively crude and preliminary forms thus far assumed by it, has had nothing definite to say with respect to the question, by what banks the fiduciary functions or the taking of savings or time deposits should be carried on; but the assumption is evident in many minds that even under the unified banking system contemplated, it might well be that the exercise of noncommercial duties would still be permitted through the banking institutions thus united under the Federal Reserve system.

The only gain through so-called unification, which in that case could be definitely recognized, would be that of obtaining a theoretical identity of legislative control and of putting an end to the injurious competition which has of late years existed between national and state legislatures in connection with the holding out of inducements to bankers to organize under one or the other system as the case might be. The question must be asked if any such change, involving as it must somewhat the same problems of organization and somewhat the same long-drawn-out difficulties of application that had been recognized in the case of the so-called Young plan, would cause the gains to be effected to be really worth the price which would have to be paid in acquiring them. To this a different answer will necessarily be given by different observers according to the importance assigned by one or another to the desirability of a unified Federal Reserve system with the assumed control over credit that would result therefrom.

Unification of Banking

This subject has been considered in great detail by a committee of the Federal Reserve system which has been engaged during the past few years in reviewing the banking situation in the United States. In a report entitled *The Dual Banking System in the United States* dealing chiefly with the competitive aspects of the present situation as outlined above (filed with the Senate Banking Committee as a public document in 1933), the Federal Reserve group summarizes the situation as follows:

> The division of authority between the nation and State governments in chartering and supervising banks has been an important factor in: (1) the granting of an excessive number of charters and the consequent establishment of too many small banks; (2) the relaxing of the standards set up in the National Bank Act for commercial banks and the gradual extension of the powers of national banks; (3) the retarding of the development of effective standards of supervision in both State and national systems; and (4) the hampering of the work of the Federal Reserve banks in maintaining proper standards for membership and in promoting sound banking policy.

Excessive Chartering of Banks

The rapid growth in the number of banks in the country between the middle eighties and 1920 resulted in part from a number of favorable economic factors and in part from the competition between the State and national banking systems in the granting of charters. Prices and land values were rising during the greater part of the period and the agricultural communities were increasingly prosperous. Bank profits were relatively high during the early years of this century. The growth in the number of small banks had legislative encouragement in the lax provisions of State laws, permitting in some States the organization of incorporated banks with capital as low as $10,000, and in one State with a capital of only $5,000. In fact several States had no capital requirements at all for many years. There was little restraint upon the number of new bank organizations. Authorities in several States were without legal power to deny an application for a charter, even when they felt it was desirable to do so. In some States there was no banking department until well into the present century, and charters might be issued by judges or other officials whose main responsibilities lay in other fields.

An important factor in the increase in the number of small banks, however, was the competition between the State and national systems in the granting of charters. One of the first efforts of the national system to meet the competition of State banks was the reduction in 1900 of the minimum capital requirement from $50,000 to $25,000. After that there was a rapid growth in the number of both national and State banks, but the number of State banks continued to increase more rapidly. By 1920 there were two and one-half times as many State banks in operation as national banks.

The national supervisory authorities, as well as those of some of the States, have long been empowered to refuse charters at their discretion, if for any reason the proposed banks were not deemed reasonably certain of becoming sound and stable institutions. But both classes of supervisory agencies have been solicitous for the relative importance in numbers and resources of the banks under their respective jurisdictions, and this fact has had an important bearing upon the exercise of their discretionary powers.

Unsupported Banks

Too many banks were chartered in communities which could not support a bank, or in communities in which banking facilities were already ample. Many towns ranging in population from 200 to 1,000 had two or three banks or even more. In fact this was not an uncommon condition in many agricultural states around 1920. In the entire Western Grain States, for example, the population per bank was only 1,363 and in the two Dakotas the population per bank was less than 1,000 as contrasted with a population of nearly 10,000 per bank in New England.

The great majority of banks in existence in 1920 were small institutions. Over 6,500 of them had loans and investments of less than $150,000 each, and nearly 19,000 had loans and investments of less than $500,000 each. About 83 per cent of these 19,000 small banks were operating under State charter. In addition there were about 1,350 private banks in operation at that time, most of which were also small institutions.

Charters were granted frequently with little or no regard to the qualifications of the applicants. In many cases the men running these banks knew little about the principles or practices of banking. Many of the new banks were not only foredoomed to failure but were also likely to imperil the existence of other banking institutions. The establishment of such large numbers of small banks has in itself presented many problems, the principal of which are the difficulties of making adequate earnings, of providing reasonably competent management, and the inherent difficulties of exercising proper supervision over a large number of small institutions.

Effect of Small Capitalization

Some indication of the consequences of the small capital requirements for banks may be had from the fact that, of the 1,336 national banks which suspended in the eleven-year period 1921-1931, no less than 545, or over 40 per cent of the total, were institutions with capital of under $50,000. Of the combined total of 8,916 national and State banks which suspended during the same period, 5,987, or over 67 per cent, had capital of less than $50,000. The assumption would not be justified that all these smaller banks would have avoided suspension had their size been larger; there have been other elements of weakness in the banking structure, attributable also in large part to dual control, which have affected large and small banks alike. Many fairly large institutions, with capital up to $500,000 and more, have suspended; but the fact remains that the very small banks have been particularly vulnerable.

In chartering large numbers of small institutions, the banking departments have created vested interests which now make up the strongest element in opposition to the measures proposed for strengthening the banking structure. Numerically the small banks are the dominant part of the various banking associations and their political influence is great. Banks with loans and investments of less than $500,000 each still constituted well over half of the banks in the country in 1930 when the latest classification of all banks by size was made.

Relaxation of Restrictions on National Banks

Lowering the minimum capital requirement in 1900 was the first important measure of the national banking system to meet the competition of State banks. Another occurred in 1913 when the Federal Reserve Act authorized national banks not situated in reserve or central cities to make loans on improved and unencumbered farm land within their Federal reserve districts.

Prior to 1913 national banks had been forbidden to make loans against the security of real estate. State banks everywhere could do so, however, and in most instances without any stipulated restrictions as to the amount of the loans, their duration, or the quality of the mortgages securing them. The prohibition against real-estate loans by national banks was removed in 1913 with respect to farm land, and in the course of the ensuing fourteen years, culminating with the passage of the McFadden Act in 1927, restrictions were further relaxed, until finally all national banks were permitted to make loans against any kind of improved real estate extending up to five years and in aggregate amounts up to 50 per cent of their time deposits.

While the tendency to invest funds in long-term loans of a capital nature was accelerated by the growth of time deposits in banks doing both a commercial and savings business, these deposits have almost invariably been payable and actually paid on demand. This is true not only in the United States but also in England and Canada. In the latter countries, however, the fact that time deposits in commercial banks are in effect payable on demand is recognized as of basic importance in determining the manner in which such deposits are invested. In England bank loans of a capital nature are frowned upon as a matter of traditional principle; in Canada the banking laws contain prohibitions against loans secured by real estate and other capital assets, similar to the prohibition of real-estate loans by national banks in the United States prior to 1913. The significance of the removal of this restriction upon national banks lies in the fact that definite legal sanction has been given to a departure from the principles originally laid down as necessary for sound commercial banking practice.

Other measures of relaxation have occurred in connection with loans to single borrowers. Prior to 1906 the amount of such a loan by a national bank was limited to 10 per cent of the paid-up and unimpaired capital of the bank. In many States there were no limitations of this character upon State chartered institutions; in others the limitation applied to both capital and surplus. To improve the competitive position of national banks, the Federal law was amended in 1906 so as to make the 10 per cent limitation apply to both capital and surplus, provided the amount did not exceed 30 per cent of the capital stock alone. Most of the State laws, however, provided numerous exceptions to such limitations for State banks. To meet this situation the restriction on national banks was further relaxed by a series of amendments in 1918, 1919, and 1927.

These relaxations from the original National Bank Act have grown out of State bank competition. The less stringent laws of many of the States have been inducements for banks to operate under State charter, to such an extent that the resulting development has threatened to destroy or weaken the power of the national system. The Federal Government has elected, not to preserve the spirit of its own institutions through restraining the action of the States, but to attempt to solve the problem by removing restrictions on national banks.

In two other important matters Federal legislation has followed the lead of the States; namely, in the granting of fiduciary powers and branch-banking privileges. In both cases, however, the powers granted to national banks are not uniform throughout the country but are adjusted to the standards set by the various States. In 1913, with the passage of the Federal Reserve Act, the Federal Reserve Board was authorized to grant limited trust powers to national banks "when not in contravention of State or local law." As a result of this act and a series of amendments in 1918, 1922, and 1927, all the varied fiduciary functions of trust companies are now commonly performed by national banks.

Various other changes in Federal legislation have removed restrictions on national banks or extended their powers. Among these are: the authorization for national banks in towns of under 5,000 inhabitants to act as insurance agents and as brokers for real-estate loans; the lowering of reserve requirements against both time and demand deposits; and the authorization for Federal reserve members, including national banks, to issue bankers' acceptances. All these measures have been passed at least in part for the purpose of enabling national banks to compete with State chartered institutions. This purpose, in fact, has dominated the development of Federal banking legislation to such an extent that most of the important amendments to the national banking law since 1913 have been enacted in response to the competitive situation inherent in the dual banking system.

Dual Control and Supervision

Bank officials and directors are likely to resent criticism, and the ease with which they may escape existing supervision by changing from one system to the other greatly reduces the effectiveness of examining authorities. While there can be no doubt that bank supervision in general is on a higher plane than it was twenty years ago, it is nevertheless a fact that dual control of banking has tended to keep down the standards of supervision, as well as of banking law.

Effective supervision has been handicapped largely by two factors: In the first place, the supervisory authorities, whether national or State, have not been endowed with adequate powers; and in the second place, they have been unable to make full and effective use of such powers as have been granted them. To what extent the failure of legislative bodies to grant adequate powers is due to the dual system is difficult to determine, but the inability of supervisors to make full and effective use of such powers as they have arises out of the fact that banks are able to avoid the supervision of one system by leaving it and entering the other.

From the establishment of the national banking system in 1863 to the present time, successive Comptrollers of the Currency have placed before Congress recommendations for the improvement of banking supervision, by specifying certain standards and providing adequate powers and penalties for their enforcement. Thus it was recommended by the first comptroller that the failure of a national bank be declared *prima facie* fraudulent and that the officers and directors be made personally responsible as well as punishable criminally unless upon investigation it was found that the bank's affairs had been honestly administered. In 1887 it was recommended that penalties be imposed for the making of loans contrary to law; in 1895, that the comptroller be authorized, with the approval of the Secretary of the Treasury and after a hearing, to remove officers and directors for mismanagement or violations of law; in 1914, that the comptroller be authorized to penalize both banks and their officers by appropriate fines for violation of the law and failure to comply with his regulations; and in 1931, that a board composed of the Secretary of the Treasury, the governor of the Federal Reserve Board, and the comptroller should have power to remove officers or directors of banks who persistently violated the law or who continued unsafe and unsound practices. Congress has adopted none of these recommendations.

An important duty of both national and State supervisory authorities is to recommend legislation designed to improve the safety standards of banking. They are hampered, however, by the competitive situation into which they are forced by the existence of dual control. The dilemma of State supervisors in recommending banking legislation was described by the commissioner of banks of Massachusetts when he stated in 1929 that in passing State legislation care is exercised that nothing is done to drive State banks into the national system. That similar considerations have frequently influenced the Congress of the United States is evident from the record of legislation actually passed and the proposed measures defeated.

State Banks and the Federal Reserve System

Soon after its organization the Federal Reserve Board expressed its hope that a unified system of banking would develop through the Federal reserve system and stated that, "There can be but one American credit system of nation-wide extent, and it will fall short of satisfying the business judgment and expectation of the country and fail of attaining its full potentialities if it rests upon an incomplete foundation and leaves out of its membership any considerable part of the banking strength of the country."

The board extended liberal terms of admission to State banks, including the right to withdraw from membership on twelve months' notice. The State banks, however, were apprehensive of changes in the attitude of the board and hesitated about applying for membership. By June, 1917, only 53 State institutions had joined. Consequently certain amendments were passed by Congress in 1917 to encourage applications for membership by State banks.

Most of the provisions in the 1917 amendments dealing with State bank membership followed the spirit of the regulations issued by the board in 1915, which they extended. State bank members were permitted to withdraw from the system on six months' written notice to the Federal Reserve Board. They retained their full charter and statutory rights subject to the restrictions of the Federal Reserve Act, and regulations of the board relative thereto. Their examination and supervision were delegated to the Federal reserve banks and board, which, in turn, were authorized to accept reports and examinations from State supervisory authorities in lieu of those of their own examiners. Furthermore, State member banks were relieved of the restrictions upon national banks as to the amount which could be loaned to one person, firm, or corporation, subject, however, to the restriction that if the State bank had loaned to any one borrower more than the limitations governing a national bank, none of the paper of the borrower so accommodated could be rediscounted at the Federal Reserve banks.

In spite of these concessions, only about 800 of the 12,000 State commercial banks belonged to the Federal Reserve system in 1932. These 800 members included most of the very large State banks, however, and had about 58 per cent of the loans and investments of all State banks and trust companies. It is noteworthy, on the other hand, that in the large-size groups the number of nonmember banks has grown faster since 1920 than the number of member State banks. From 1920 to 1930 the number of nonmember banks with loans and investments of $10,000,000 to $50,000,000 increased from 64 to 128, while member State banks in the same size group increased from 121 to 124. The number of nonmember banks with loans and investments of $50,000,000 and over increased from 3 to 10 during the same period, while member State banks of that size increased from 32 to 49.

Competition between the two banking systems, resulting in an overbanked condition and relaxed standards, has materially hampered the effective functioning of Federal instrumentalities, i.e., the national banking system and the Federal Reserve system. This has been in some measure responsible for the development of unsound banking practices, the ineffectiveness of supervision, and the serious banking difficulties during the past twelve years.

Problem of Better Control

It is now possible to state in clearer terms the question that is raised as a result of the gradual intermingling of commercial, investment, and industrial banking that has constituted so striking a feature of the past fifteen years in American financial life. This problem consists in the attainment of a better control over the conduct of banking, and in this form it must be subdivided into two distinct sections: *a*) How to insure the safeguarding of individual funds carried as demand deposits in banks, if these banks are to be permitted to engage in the various activities that are now open to most institutions; and *b*) how to bring about a unification of control of institutions in such a way as either once more to simplify or separate the field of their functional activity, or to subject them to uniform standards of supervision or management which shall be such as to prevent competitive lowering of legislative regulations.

It is evident that no absolute answer can be given to the question stated in this two-fold form. A purely theoretical or dogmatic solution is comparatively easy—and is suggested by the so-called Young Plan—calling for the separation of banking functions already referred to. Apart from its actual practical difficulty, involving as it does the restoration of a condition of banking not in line with developments of recent years, and calling, therefore, for a complete reorganization of banking portfolios and assets, there remains the question whether any such simple and straightforward way of solving the problem will actually bring the solution that is desired. Whether such a solution can be attained by the methods indicated or not is a query that must depend for answer upon the actual banking needs of the community as they are seen reflected at the present time.

In the form assumed by American corporate life at present, it may well be doubted whether a purely commercial bank of the original British type is in position to render the utmost service to its clients. A negative answer by no means tends to defend or palliate the evils that have presented themselves to the American banking field during recent years. At most, such an answer merely rejects the notion that basic simplification will bring about the desired reform and substitute for it the thought that reorganization of banking conditions rather than an attempt to restore them to a preëxisting state is the more promising as well as the more serviceable method of bringing about a restoration of tolerable conditions.

It seems evident that in finding an answer to this broad general problem of banking structure, the inquirer must begin his search by surveying with some care the situation that has developed in the several branches of banking that exist as well developed activities at the present time. We may, therefore, turn our attention next to a survey of the growth and evolution of some of the major types of banking institutions in the United States and their general significance.

CHAPTER XI

DEVELOPMENT OF FIDUCIARY BANKING[1]

The handling of fiduciary business by incorporated institutions is a distinctive feature of American banking development. Corporate trustees or trust companies, which performed at first only fiduciary functions, later developed an extensive commercial banking business, while national banks and state commercial banks entered the trust field, so that now three types of banks handle trust funds. Owing to the absence of data on the total amount of trust business carried by trust companies and state commercial banks, it is impossible to obtain an aggregate figure for the volume of trust business in existence. It is also impossible to say what part of the aggregate is handled by commercial banks. However, trust companies report regularly on their commercial banking activities and adequate information is published relative to trust departments of national banks. There are however very few up-to-date statistics on the investment of trust funds; to get an idea how trust funds are placed we must use sample data taken either from groups of institutions or specific sections of the country. This chapter opens with a review of the growth of the trust company as an institution and the nature of their commercial banking business. It then takes up the activi-

[1] This chapter has been compiled by V. D. Kazakévich, using material from the work done by Messrs. William Allen Day and N. Gilbert Riddle. The figures on the growth of trust companies, their banking portfolios, the fiduciary activities of national banks, and the investment of trust funds by Massachusetts trust companies, have been assembled by Mr. Day while a member of the Banking Seminar. The results of this investigation under the title "A Statistical Study of the Changing Position of the Trust Company" were submitted by Mr. Day, in the spring of 1933, to the Faculty of Political Science, Columbia University and accepted in partial fulfillment of the requirements for the Degree of Master of Arts.

The analysis of the composition of investments in 184 trusts has been made by Mr. Riddle and represents a part of a larger study on trust companies to be published. Mr. Riddle's manuscript was submitted in the spring of 1933 under the title "The Investment Policy of Trust Institutions" to the Faculty of Political Science, Columbia University, and accepted in partial fulfillment of the requirements for the Degree of Doctor of Philosophy.

ties of the trust departments of national banks, and finally analyzes the composition of fiduciary portfolios on the basis of sample material.

I. The Growth of Trust Companies[2]

The first corporation in the United States that received legislative sanction to act as a fiduciary was, according to reliable reports, the Farmers Fire Insurance and Loan Company, chartered on February 28, 1828.[3] Until some time after the Civil War, comparatively few new trust companies were chartered, as there was very little corporate business. The operations of these early companies consisted mainly of dealings growing out of the management of personal trusts. Only in the last three decades of the nineteenth century, did the rapid expansion of the corporate form of organization bring about the development of corporate trust business. During the 'eighties, there began a branching out of trust companies into the commercial-banking field, followed by an expansion of fiduciary activities on the part of commercial banks which, in the post-war era, practically obliterated the distinction between commercial and trust institutions. Increase in the total amount of trust business handled, and, a parallel expansion into an entirely new sphere—that of commercial banking—brought about a tremendous growth in aggregate capitalization and resources, illustrated by Table 26. It is also to be noted from this table that the total number of trust companies did not change very materially during the past twenty years, although capital funds and resources increased continuously up to the beginning of the present depression.

Relative to all other types of banks and to the banking system as a whole, trust companies occupy a rather singular position, certain aspects of which have already been treated in Chapter

[2] By "resources" of trust companies is meant the resources reported to the banking supervisory authorities. These resources cover the commercial banking activities of trust institutions, but omit fiduciary funds. Throughout this first section on the growth of trust companies, "resources" of fiduciary institutions are used in that sense only.

[3] This institution was later known as the Farmers Loan and Trust Company of New York which, on January 30, 1929, became affiliated with the National City Bank of New York under a plan of reorganization whereby its name was changed to the City Bank-Farmers Trust Company.

VIII entitled the "Present Position of the Banking System of the United States." The number of existing trust companies is comparatively small; on June 30, 1932, they comprised only one-fifteenth of the total number of banks operating in the country. At the same time their capitalization equalled about one-third of the capital funds of all banks, and their resources were close to one-fourth of aggregate banking resources in the United States. This is accounted for by the fact that the average capitalization of a trust company is nearly four times as large, and the resources approximately three times as great, as those of an average na-

TABLE 26

GROWTH OF LOAN AND TRUST COMPANIES*

YEAR	NUMBER	CAPITAL FUNDS (in millions of dollars)	RESOURCES (in millions of dollars)
1875	35	29	123
1876	38	30	128
1877	39	31	124
1878	35	31	111
1879	32	30	112
1880	30	29	127
1881	31	30	157
1882	32	36	195
1883	34	38	212
1884	35	44	240
1885	40	46	248
1886	42	52	278
1887	58	64	319
1888	120	89	384
1889	120	98	441
1890	149	118	504
1891	171	135	537
1892	168	142	600
1893	228	166	727
1894	224	172	705
1895	242	194	807
1896	260	195	855
1897	251	196	844
1898	246	199	942
1899	260	210	1,072
1900	290	275	1,330
1901	334	306	1,615

* Abstracted from the *Annual Reports of the Comptroller of the Currency.*

TABLE 26 *(Continued)*

YEAR	NUMBER	CAPITAL FUNDS (in millions of dollars)	RESOURCES (in millions of dollars)
1902	417	405	1,683
1903	531	547	2,299
1904	585	568	2,380
1905	683	607	2,867
1906	742	664	2,959
1907	794	674	3,071
1908	842	694	2,866
1909	1,079	856	4,069
1910	1,091	865	4,217
1911	1,251	925	4,665
1912	1,410	980	5,107
1913	1,515	1,027	5,124
1914	1,564	1,033	5,490
1915	1,664	1,054	5,873
1916	1,606	1,081	7,028
1917	1,608	1,147	7,900
1918	1,669	1,172	8,317
1919	1,377	1,039	7,960
1920	1,408	1,088	8,320
1921	1,474	1,165	8,181
1922	1,550	1,213	8,534
1923	1,643	1,331	9,499
1924	1,664	1,434	10,324
1925	1,680	1,526	11,566
1926	1,656	1,667	12,205
1927	1,647	1,874	13,995
1928	1,633	2,105	15,231
1929	1,608	2,604	16,155
1930	1,564	2,880	17,703
1931	1,469	2,775	16,861
1932	1,235	2,362	13,119

tional bank. Commercial-banking institutions, national and state combined, outnumbered in 1932 all trust companies at the rate of about thirteen to one. The movement toward an increase in the average size of the trust company unit became especially strong after the close of the World War, trust companies expanding their resources without increasing proportionately in numbers. From 1921 to 1932 the number of commercial banks decreased by more than ten thousand; the average size of the commercial banking unit increased, while commercial banks, both national and state, extended their activities into the trust field; but in spite of all these changes trust companies expanded so rapidly that an increasing percentage of aggregate capitalization and resources of all banks is found in institutions chartered as trust companies.

In addition to large average size, another distinctive feature of trust companies is their geographic concentration in certain areas of the country. The largest number of trust companies is found in the Eastern states, with New England next in importance.[4] More than three-quarters of the resources of all trust companies are in the Eastern states; in the Middle West, where a large number of trust companies is located, their resources amount to less than 10 per cent of the aggregate resources of trust institutions throughout the United States. This indicates that, not only is the greatest number, and the major share of resources, of trust companies concentrated in the Eastern states and in New England, but that most of the large trust institutions are also located in the same area; while the trust companies spread out over the rest of the country—with a secondary center of concentration, so far as numbers go, in the Middle West—are predominantly of a much smaller size. The large average size of trust companies as compared to commercial banks must, therefore, be mainly attributed to the presence of a number of large institutions in the Eastern and New England states, and does not, in all probability, apply in the same degree to the trust companies located elsewhere.

A similar picture presents itself if we compare the number and resources of trust companies in a particular section of the country, with the number and resources of all the banks operating in the same area. In the Eastern states, while only about one-fifth of all the banks are chartered as trust companies, the resources of trust institutions comprise some two-fifths of the resources of all banks in that part of the country. In New England, the number of trust companies is slightly above one-quarter of the total number of banking institutions, while the resources of trust companies amount to somewhat less than one-quarter of the

[4] The Comptroller of the Currency includes under the caption of Eastern states, New York, New Jersey, Pennsylvania, Delaware, Maryland, and District of Columbia.

aggregate resources of the New England banks. Outside of these two areas, institutions chartered as trust companies form a comparatively small percentage of both the numbers and resources of all the banks. This further emphasizes the fact that, while in 1932 nearly 23 per cent of the aggregate banking resources of the country were in trust companies, the number of which was only about 6 per cent of the number of all banks, trust institutions of a much larger size than the average commercial bank were the rule and not the exception, probably only in a limited area, namely, in the Eastern states, and in New England.

II. Commercial Banking Business of Trust Companies[5]

At present we must regard the trust company as being in the commercial-banking business, competing with national and state commercial banks, due to the expansion of the banking departments of trust institutions. This trend has become especially pronounced during the past fifteen years, and the composition of the portfolios of trust companies, as given in Table 27, has a marked similarity to the distribution of loans and investments in national banks and the banking system as a whole.

The relationship between loans and investments changes from year to year in the case of trust companies, national banks, and the entire banking system (inclusive of savings institutions and private banks), but the fluctuations coincide quite closely in all three groups of banks. Apparently the same factors influence trust institutions as well as commercial banks, because the nature of their business has become quite similar.

If we compare the composition of the bond holdings of trust companies with that of commercial banks, certain differences are apparent although the tendency to enlarge or to diminish the volume of these holdings is very similar in both cases. In 1919 the investment portfolio of trust companies consisted largely of two items: United States Government securities constituting 9.5 per cent of all investments, and nonclassified items accounting for 85.7 per cent of the total. In 1921—a depression year—the un-

[5] Throughout this section the terms "assets," "loans," "investments," and "portfolio," when applied to trust companies, refer to the commercial banking departments of fiduciary institutions and have no reference to fiduciary funds.

classified items dropped to 41.9 per cent, with United States Government securities, state, county, and municipal bonds and railroad bonds increasing in importance. In 1922 the nonclassified securities grew once more to 63.4 per cent of all bond holdings. With the coming of the present depression the nonclassified securities dropped to 27.3 per cent in 1931, and to 19.9 per cent in 1932; while a proportionate increase took place in the holdings of other types, especially in those of United States Government bonds which reached 33.0 per cent of the total in 1931, and increased further in 1932 to 44.8 per cent.

TABLE 27

DISTRIBUTION OF ASSETS IN TRUST COMPANIES, NATIONAL BANKS AND IN THE ENTIRE BANKING SYSTEM*

	LOANS AS A PERCENTAGE OF LOANS AND INVESTMENTS			INVESTMENTS AS A PERCENTAGE OF LOANS AND INVESTMENTS		
	Trust Companies	National Banks	All Banks in the U. S. A.	Trust Companies	National Banks	All Banks in the U. S. A.
1919	66.4	68.5	67.2	33.6	31.5	32.8
1920	70.5	76.5	73.1	29.5	23.5	26.9
1921	68.5	74.9	71.6	31.5	25.1	28.4
1922	64.9	71.1	68.7	35.1	28.9	31.3
1923	67.3	70.0	68.6	32.7	30.0	31.4
1924	65.5	70.0	68.4	34.5	30.0	31.6
1925	68.3	68.9	68.3	31.7	31.1	31.7
1926	70.3	69.7	69.2	29.7	30.3	30.8
1927	67.6	68.6	67.9	32.4	31.4	32.1
1928	67.7	67.9	67.4	32.3	32.1	32.6
1929	72.8	69.0	70.0	27.2	31.0	30.0
1930	70.8	68.4	68.8	29.2	31.6	31.2
1931	62.7	63.2	63.2	37.3	36.8	36.8
1932	57.9	58.8	60.0	42.1	41.2	40.0

* The figures for national banks do not take account of real estate owned other than bank buildings while the data for trust companies and all banks include this item. These percentages have been computed on the basis of data abstracted from the *Annual Reports of the Comptroller of the Currency*.

The distribution of investment holdings of trust companies, given in Table 28, shows, if compared to that of national banks, first of all the extremely large proportion of nonclassified securities held by trust institutions. This is an additional indication of the inadequate manner in which banking records are kept; it prevents the making of a more thorough comparison of the investment of assets by these two types of institutions. Probably trust companies invest their resources more heavily in bonds of industrial corporations and short-term notes of various kinds than do national banks, but if that is so, the fact is concealed by

TABLE 28

PERCENTAGES OF TOTAL INVESTMENTS OF TRUST COMPANIES AND NATIONAL BANKS*

	UNITED STATES GOVERNMENT SECURITIES		STATE, COUNTY AND MUNICIPAL BONDS		RAILROAD BONDS		ALL OTHER BONDS NOT CLASSIFIED	
	Trust Comp.	Natl. Banks†	Trust Comp.	Natl. Banks	Trust Comp.	Natl. Banks	Trust Comp.	Natl. Banks
1919	9.5	49.1	1.0	6.4	1.9	8.2	85.7	6.1
1920	12.9	37.3	1.9	8.1	8.5	9.9	69.2	7.4
1921	22.9	32.2	7.0	9.8	16.6	10.1	41.9	8.8
1922	13.6	34.0	3.7	9.1	10.6	10.7	63.4	9.3
1923	15.5	38.4	2.9	7.9	10.1	9.9	64.1	10.3
1924	12.5	33.7	2.7	9.8	9.1	11.2	67.9	11.2
1925	12.3	32.7	3.1	10.4	10.2	11.8	66.4	12.2
1926	12.1	30.9	4.4	11.1	9.7	10.8	64.7	13.2
1927	10.4	30.2	5.9	11.6	7.5	10.3	67.0	14.2
1928	9.6	31.1	5.9	11.8	6.6	9.5	68.4	14.4
1929	10.4	32.1	4.4	11.4	13.1	8.9	66.0	13.2
1930	9.4	30.3	3.6	11.5	11.8	9.6	68.7	12.9
1931	33.0	33.7	9.3	13.0	15.2	9.4	27.3	11.6
1932	44.8	37.3	9.3	14.3	12.8	9.1	19.9	9.5

* These percentage figures are based on data abstracted from the *Annual Reports of the Comptroller of the Currency.*

† United States Government Securities held over and above the amount of such bonds pledged to secure National Bank Notes.

the generalized vagueness of the statistical information furnished by the office of the Comptroller.

We may, however, conclude on the basis of Table 28 that, during so-called prosperous times, trust companies hold in their portfolios relatively fewer United States Government bonds than do national banks. In depressions—both in that of the early twenties and the present depression—trust companies increased their holdings not only of state, county, and municipal, but also of railroad, securities. National banks also purchased more bonds of various local government bodies, but did not increase the proportion of their investments in railroad securities. In the present depression, trust institutions began to shift their assets into United States Government bonds earlier than did the national banks. In 1930 this type of security comprised only 9.4 per cent of their total investment holdings; in 1931 the percentage rose to 33.0. Both in the case of national banks and that of the entire banking system, the marked increase in United States bonds held was noted in 1932. This prior shift toward greater convertibility of investment portfolios in the case of trust companies can probably be explained by the fact that they are geographically concentrated around financial centers. Large

TABLE 29

PERCENTAGES OF TOTAL LOANS

	REAL ESTATE LOANS		LOANS ON SECURITIES	
	Banking Departments of Trust Companies	National Banks	Banking Departments of Trust Companies	National Banks
1930	13.8	9.9	47.8	37.8
1931	16.0	12.0	43.1	35.4
1932	21.0	15.9	34.8	32.9

banks are in a better position to change from one type of investment to another. The tendency toward heavy purchases of United States Government securities appeared in institutions located in, or near the financial centers. Trust companies have "switched" their investment policy at an earlier date than have national banks.

If the composition of loans made by trust companies be compared with that of national banks we observe, just as in the case of investments, that certain tendencies prevailing among national banks are found in an accelerated form in the case of trust institutions.

In the case of both loans on real estate and loans secured by stocks and bonds, the percentage of total loans that these categories comprise is somewhat higher in trust companies than in national banks. The tendency to loan on investment collateral instead of self-liquidating commercial assets has been more pronounced in recent years among national banks located in large cities than in so-called country banks. As the average trust company is larger than the average national bank, this tendency is also more pronounced in the case of trust institutions.

III. Fiduciary Activities of National Banks

The introductory paragraph of this chapter pointed out the impossibility of segregating the data for trust business handled by commercial banks, because of the fact that there are no published records of the total amount of fiduciary business held by state commercial banks. We can, however, consider to what extent one part of the commercial-banking system, namely the national banks, has entered the trust field.

In 1913 national banks were permitted to exercise trust powers through the passage of the Federal Reserve Act. Such a provision was included in the Act after a great deal of agitation on the part of national banks and bankers, who asserted that they must have the right to open trust departments and handle fiduciary transactions in order to be in position to meet effectively the competition of trust companies with banking departments. The extent to which national banks—institutions chartered primarily to engage in commercial banking—have availed themselves of this privilege can be seen from Table 30.

It will be observed from this table that in 1914, during which the Federal Reserve system opened, no permits were granted, but that since then there has been a rapid growth in the number of permits issued; during the period from 1915 to 1929 the number of national banks empowered to act as fiduciaries increased from 356 to 2461. A decrease in the number of new permits issued occurred in the years 1930, 1931, and 1932, and the number of banks holding permits declined both in 1931 and 1932. This was owing, probably, to the spread of bank failures and to a general retrenchment tendency brought about by the depression. At the same time a larger share of national banks that have gone out of existence must have been institutions that did not hold permits to exercise fiduciary powers; because, as to be seen from Table 31, the percentage of the total number of national banks that operate trust departments has been increasing throughout the country.

TABLE 30

ORIGINAL AND SUPPLEMENTARY PERMITS TO EXERCISE FIDUCIARY POWERS GRANTED TO NATIONAL BANKS FROM 1914 TO 1932, INCLUSIVE*

YEAR	ORIGINAL PERMITS GRANTED DURING YEAR	SUPPLEMENTARY PERMITS GRANTED DURING YEAR	TOTAL NUMBER OF PERMITS GRANTED DURING YEAR	TOTAL NUMBER OF NATIONAL BANKS HOLDING PERMITS AS OF DECEMBER 31†
1914	None	None	None	None
1915	356	"	356	356
1916	125	"	125	476
1917	112	"	112	570
1918	138	45	183	708
1919	372	137	509	1,074
1920	247	25	272	1,294
1921	134	14	148	1,410
1922	161	16	177	1,547
1923	182	19	201	1,696
1924	154	20	174	1,802
1925	178	13	191	1,951
1926	207	20	227	2,103
1927	215	74	289	2,264
1928	185	42	227	2,391
1929	165	25	190	2,461
1930	111	21	132	2,465
1931	41	7	48	2,329
1932	33	15	48	2,192

* Source: Obtained directly from the Federal Reserve Board.

† It will be observed that, if the total number of banks holding permits at the end of any year, and the number of permits granted during the succeeding year are added, the total will not agree with the total number of banks holding permits at the end of that year, the difference being because of deductions made during the year on account of banks closed, liquidated or having surrendered their permits.

It is to be noted that the number of national banks that have taken out permits is larger than the number of banks actually exercising trust powers. During the four years 1929 to 1932, the percentage of national banks that did hold permits and made use of their right to exercise trust powers increased: 79 per cent of the national banks possessing trust powers had trust departments in 1932, as against 71 per cent in 1929. Only slightly over one-third of all national banks have taken out permits to conduct trust business, but, as most of the large units had entered the trust field, institutions holding permits in 1932 included 81.4 per cent of the aggregate capital, and 83.0 per cent of the total resources of the national system.

TABLE 31

NUMBER OF NATIONAL BANKS OPERATING TRUST DEPARTMENTS, EXPRESSED AS A PERCENTAGE OF THE TOTAL NUMBER OF NATIONAL BANKS*

FEDERAL RESERVE DISTRICTS	1929	1930	1931	1932
	%	%	%	%
Boston	44.74	49.04	53.39	55.33
New York	35.49	39.01	40.88	43.05
Philadelphia	35.57	38.39	40.33	42.16
Cleveland	18.47	19.94	22.35	23.12
Richmond	29.80	32.51	36.04	38.59
Atlanta	26.23	27.73	27.83	30.07
Chicago	28.13	31.33	32.39	34.47
St. Louis	20.89	22.67	24.27	25.41
Minneapolis	7.44	8.72	11.65	12.60
Kansas City	12.01	12.87	14.54	15.35
Dallas	8.85	10.63	11.55	11.78
San Francisco	19.07	19.92	20.97	23.80
All National Banks	23.01	25.22	27.27	28.85

* Computed on the basis of data obtained from the *Annual Reports of the Comptroller of the Currency.*

In 1932 national banks administered 94,135 individual trusts, which were about equally divided between living and court trusts, and 10,153 corporate trusts. The worth of the individual trust business amounted to over four and a half billion dollars, while the aggregate value of the bond issues, for which the banks acted as trustees, was nearly nine and a half billions. Although in 1932 national banks administered only 572 insurance trusts, the number of such trusts not yet operative was 17,824. Both the number and the value of insurance-trust accounts handled by national banks have been growing very rapidly even during the depression years. They represent potential trust business, as only a very small part of the total number, as well as aggregate value, of the insurance trust accounts is being administered at present, the bulk is held under trust agreement and is not yet operative. The number of various trusts administered and the

TABLE 32

NUMBER OF TRUSTS ADMINISTERED BY NATIONAL BANKS FOR YEARS ENDING JUNE 30

	INDIVIDUAL TRUSTS			CORPORATE TRUSTS	INSURANCE	
	Living	Court	Total		Being Administered	Not Yet Operative
1929	—	—	66,776	9,212	271	9,505
1930	—	—	79,912	11,511	396	13,543
1931	45,484	46,958	92,442	10,545	554	17,656
1932	45,374	48,761	94,135	10,153	572	17,824

VALUE OF TRUSTS ADMINISTERED BY NATIONAL BANKS FOR YEARS ENDING JUNE 30*

(In thousands of dollars)

	INDIVIDUAL TRUSTS	BOND ISSUES OUTSTANDING WITH BANKS ACTING AS TRUSTEES	INSURANCE TRUSTS ADMINISTERED	INSURANCE POLICIES HELD UNDER TRUST AGREEMENTS—NOT YET OPERATIVE
1929	4,237,649	7,370,154	11,385	375,524
1930	4,473,041	11,803,717	13,495	586,706
1931	5,241,991	10,719,846	21,668	734,831
1932	4,642,065	9,497,247	25,573	732,498

* Compiled from the *Annual Reports of the Comptroller of the Currency.*

dollar values for the four years, 1929-1932, are given in Table 32.

It is seen from the combined balance sheet of the trust departments of national banks presented in Table 33, that most of the trust funds are invested. Banks operating trust departments must derive a considerable profit from the deposit phase of the business, as a substantial amount of the trust assets is deposited in the same banks while comparatively few funds are placed in other banks. On the liability side about three-fourths of the aggregate liabilities of trust departments of national banks are accounted for by private trusts and only about one-fourth by court trusts, although the number of living and court trusts is about equal.

Trust funds handled by national banks were invested in 1932, as we can see from Table 34 to the extent of 37.6 per cent in bonds, 30.9 per cent in stocks, and 16.1 per cent in real estate mortgages. The real-estate investments of the trust departments of national banks form a smaller percentage of total investments than the real-estate loans of the commercial banking departments of the national system comprise of total loans. They are also slightly higher than the combined loans on real estate, and real estate held by the trust companies in the state of Massachusetts. On the other hand, if we compare them to the real-estate investments of a group of large trust companies (the results of an analysis of the investments of a group of trust companies is presented in the next section of this chapter), we find that the national-banking system invested its trust assets in real estate to a slightly less degree than did the trust companies making up our sample.

The fact has already been mentioned that four-fifths of the capital and resources of all national banks are held by institutions that have permits to operate trust departments, while the number of such banks is about one-third of the total number of national banks. Further proof that large national banks handle the bulk of the trust business is provided if we analyze the distribution of trust assets among banks of various sizes. Table 35 shows the average amount of trust business per bank of a certain size, as well as the changes in the average amount of business per trust according to the size of the bank.

Table 35 shows that in the years 1930, 1931, and 1932, the average amount of trust business handled is much greater in the group of banks with a capital of over $500,000 than in banks of smaller size. The same holds true, although to a much less degree, of the average amount of business per trust.

TABLE 33

COMBINED BALANCE SHEET OF TRUST DEPARTMENTS OF NATIONAL BANKS AS OF JUNE 30*

(In thousands of dollars)

YEAR	ASSETS					LIABILITIES					TOTAL RESOURCES
	Invest-ments	Deposits in Savings Banks	Deposits in Other Banks	Deposits in Own Bank	Other Assets	Private Trusts	Private Trusts Income	Court Trusts	Court Trusts Income	Other Liabili-ties	
1929	3,507	9	18	210	494	2,405	19	856	16	942	4,238
1930	3,506	9	16	153	589	3,394	—	1,079	—	—	4,473
1931	4,774	12	9	211	236	3,933	—	1,309	—	—	5,242
1932	4,162	12	7	165	296	3,780	—	1,262	—	—	4,642

* Abstracted from the *Annual Reports of the Comptroller of the Currency.*

TABLE 34

COMBINED INVESTMENT PORTFOLIOS OF TRUST DEPARTMENTS OF NATIONAL BANKS AS OF JUNE 30*

(In thousands of dollars)

	BONDS		REAL ESTATE MORTGAGES		STOCKS		MISCELLANEOUS INVESTMENTS		TOTAL INVESTMENTS	
	Amount	Per Cent of Total	Amount	Per Cent of Total	Amount	Per Cent of Total	Amount	Per Cent of Total	Amount	Per Cent of Total
1931	1,265,609	26.5	675,088	14.1	1,260,471	26.4	1,572,961	33.0	4,774,131	100.0
1932	1,562,954	37.6	671,796	16.1	1,285,289	30.9	641,610	15.4	4,161,649	100.0

* Compiled from the *Annual Reports of the Comptroller of the Currency.*

An even more striking picture is presented by the distribution of the aggregate trust business among banks of various sizes. In 1932 national banks with a capital of over $500,000 were responsible for 83.6 per cent of trust assets of all national banks,

TABLE 35

AVERAGE AMOUNTS OF TRUST BUSINESS OF NATIONAL BANKS BY SIZE OF BANKS; BY BANK, AND TRUST, PER YEARS*

(In thousands of dollars)

BANKS WITH CAPITAL OF	YEARS	INDIVIDUAL TRUST ASSETS		CORPORATE TRUST ASSETS		INSURANCE TRUST ASSETS		INS. POLICIES UNDER TRUST AGREEMENT NOT OPERATIVE	
		Per Bank	*Per Trust*	*Per Bank*	*Per Trust*	*Per Bank*	*Per Trust*	*Per Bank*	*Per Trust*
25,000	1930	13	5	145	72	28	28	—	—
	1931	12	4	65	65	38	38	—	—
	1932	17	6	45	45	34	34	—	—
Over	1930	46	8	94	37	—	—	95	28
25,000 to	1931	52	8	100	48	—	—	81	23
50,000	1932	52	8	85	23	2	2	97	25
Over	1930	116	11	257	54	31	22	72	8
50,000 to	1931	110	10	286	77	18	17	78	9
100,000	1932	123	10	256	62	32	21	84	13
Over	1930	298	13	320	57	36	29	154	33
100,000 to	1931	294	11	342	98	57	47	165	31
200,000	1932	320	11	327	95	43	28	156	31
Over	1930	1,136	27	1,041	151	44	22	359	38
200,000 to	1931	1,275	26	893	130	74	35	410	37
500,000	1932	1,296	25	861	118	105	49	442	37
Over	1930	15,651	83	55,988	1,393	129	39	2,296	48
500,00	1931	17,911	89	52,014	1,346	144	40	2,684	45
	1932	16,171	76	46,939	1,279	157	47	2,769	44
Total	1930	2,630	56	15,349	1,025	88	34	863	43
	1931	2,824	57	13,708	1,017	102	39	962	42
	1932	2,617	49	12,255	935	117	45	995	41

* Compiled from the *Annual Reports of the Comptroller of the Currency.*

for 96.9 per cent of the total volume of bonds outstanding, for which national banks were acting as trustees, and for 67.5 per cent of the volume and 80.1 per cent of the face value of insurance policies held under trust agreements but not yet operative. This indicates that a predominant share of all the individual and corporate trust business that is being handled by national banks is concentrated in the largest banking units. The same aspect is further emphasized by the distribution of trust assets of the national banking system according to the size of the population of the locality in which the banks are placed. From Table 36 it is clearly seen that, in 1932, between one-third and one-half of the aggregate trust assets of the national system were handled by institutions located in cities with a population of over 1,000,000 inhabitants.

TABLE 36

DISTRIBUTION OF THE AGGREGATE AMOUNT OF TRUST BUSINESS HANDLED BY NATIONAL BANKS

(BY SIZE OF POPULATION UNIT IN WHICH THE BANK IS LOCATED, FOR 1932)*

(In thousands of dollars)

PLACES WITH A POPULATION OF	TRUST ASSETS	VOLUME OF INSURANCE ASSETS†	FACE VALUE OF INSURANCE ASSETS†	BOND ISSUES FOR WHICH BANK ACT AS TRUSTEES
Less than 1,000	$ 2,132	$ —	$ 147	$ 102
1,000 to 2,499	12,760	92	958	3,083
2,500 to 4,999	35,598	265	3,166	16,147
5,000 to 9,999	70,288	412	9,993	25,040
10,000 to 24,999	196,325	1,310	33,138	75,322
25,000 to 49,999	246,722	1,582	42,775	77,428
50,000 to 99,999	399,073	6,101	89,862	165,979
100,000 to 249,999	731,616	3,038	137,588	212,797
250,000 to 499,999	656,669	2,438	122,680	331,158
500,000 to 999,999	656,077	4,191	106,236	894,713
1,000,000 or over	1,634,806	6,144	185,956	7,695,477
Total	$4,642,065	$25,573	$732,498	$9,497,247

* Compiled from the *Annual Reports of the Comptroller of the Currency.*
† Policies held under trust agreement—not operative.

The only tendency in the opposite direction is furnished—as may be observed from Tables 35 and 36—by the distribution of insurance assets and especially by that of the face value of insurance policies not yet operative. Although both the average amount of such assets per bank, and the share of the aggregate that can be found in banks with a capital of over $500,000 (or in cities with a population of over 1,000,000 inhabitants) is still larger than for other groups of banks; nevertheless, insurance assets and, especially, the face value of policies under trust agreement but not yet operative are distributed among the banks of various sizes much more evenly than other trust assets. This type of business is more easily handled by a small bank and originates more frequently in a small community than other kinds of fiduciary transactions.

We have already pointed out that the great bulk of insurance-trust assets of national banks is held under trust agreement, being not yet operative. The fact that this type of fiduciary business is growing rapidly and has continued to increase, even during the depression years, has also been mentioned. It may, therefore, fairly be said that insurance-trust business contains certain potentialities for the medium-sized and, probably, even for the small, national bank, and it must be concluded, on the basis of the data so far available, that other types of trust business do not seem to furnish any particular opportunities for the small and medium-sized banking units.

The concentration of most of the fiduciary business in large banks is also owing to the fact that the handling of trust accounts involves a considerable overhead which can be carried only by a large financial unit. The gross earnings derived from the handling of trust accounts are also concentrated in large banks, as we may see from Table 37.

TABLE 37

AVERAGE GROSS EARNINGS OF NATIONAL BANKS OPERATING TRUST DEPARTMENTS*

(By size of banks; by fiscal years)

EARNINGS	CAPITAL OF 25,000	OVER 25,000 to 50,000	OVER 50,000 to 100,000	OVER 100,000 to 200,000	OVER 200,000 to 500,000	OVER 500,000	TOTAL
				PER BANK			
1930	$374	$761	$1,145	$2,012	$5,687	$ 79,559	$14,839
1931	188	596	1,100	2,153	6,024	101,597	18,415
1932	223	573	1,015	1,906	5,631	84,800	15,390
				PER TRUST			
1930	114	90	75	71	122	351	248
1931	39	55	68	66	103	426	278
1932	28	52	58	56	91	339	222

* Compiled from the *Annual Reports of Comptroller of the Currency.*

Obviously, thus, gross earnings from fiduciary transactions reach substantial amounts only in the case of banks with a capital of over $500,000. For the entire national-banking system the earnings derived from the operation of trust departments were comparatively insignificant.

TABLE 38*

	GROSS EARNINGS OF ALL NATIONAL BANKS	GROSS EARNINGS OF TRUST DEPARTMENTS	TRUST EARNINGS AS A PERCENTAGE OF GROSS EARNINGS
	$	$	%
1929	1,424,485	20,583	1.44
1930	1,427,341	22,765	1.59
1931	1,308,764	26,688	2.04
1932	1,090,041	22,366	2.05

* Compiled from the *Annual Reports of the Comptroller of the Currency.*

On the basis of these figures it is clearly true, that large net earnings derived from the operation of trust departments are probably limited to a few large institutions handling very substantial amounts of that type of business.

The fundamental reason for the concentration of fiduciary business in big banks located in the large population centers is found in the nature of our distribution of wealth. On December 31, 1921, there were in the continental United States 40.9 million property owners whose total wealth, if measured in dollars, amounted to $281 billion. Individuals whose wealth was below $10,000 made up 89.27 per cent of the total number, while their wealth amounted to 44.90 per cent of the aggregate. Individuals with a capital of over $25,000 comprised 4.29 per cent of the total owners of wealth, but controlled 50.57 per cent of the volume. Finally, more than one-quarter of the aggregate capital (28.14 per cent) was in the hands of 0.63 per cent of the total number of property owners, whose capital was over $100,000.[6]

A similar type of distribution is found in the estates probated.[7] Out of 43,512 estates probated, the estates under

[6] Figures by Dr. W. I. King of the National Bureau of Economic Research.

[7] The data are taken from a study made by the Federal Trade Commission for the twelve-year period 1912 to 1923 of records of the probate courts in select

$100,000 made up 97.8 per cent of the number, while their total value comprised 49.1 per cent of the aggregate value. The remaining 2.3 per cent of the total number represented 50.9 per cent of the aggregate value. Of the total number of estates 77.5 per cent were under $10,000 with their value equal to only 13.5 per cent of the aggregate; while estates over $250,000 made up 0.3 per cent of the number, but constituted 36.3 per cent of the total value.

Income tax returns show that a very large share of the payments is made in a comparatively few localities. The control of capital is not only in the hands of relatively few individuals, but it is also concentrated geographically. This accounts for the fact, brought out by the data received, that most of the trust business handled by national banks is found in large institutions located in the bigger cities. Although the figures of the Federal Trade Commission do not cover the post-war decade, the concentration movement in the United States has not abated, but has, on the contrary, increased. During the years 1930, 1931, and 1932, for which we have reported the trust activities of national banks, the tendency brought out by the earlier figures on wealth is probably even more marked.

It is difficult for the small bank to engage in trust activities (with the exception of insurance trusts), not only because of the overhead expense involved, but also because the source of the business—wealth, is distributed in a manner favoring the large unit. We may also restate here that while the number of individual trusts handled by national banks is nine times greater than that of corporate trusts, the dollar value of corporate business is twice as large. In so far as corporate wealth is probably concentrated geographically even to a larger extent than individual wealth, we may therefore, conclude on the basis of the above description, that although national banks have made liberal use of the authority to exercise fiduciary powers granted to them by the Federal Reserve Act (by 1932 more than one-third of them had taken out permits to transact trust business), only

counties of various states. Federal Trade Commission, National Wealth and Income, 67th Cong., 4th Sess., Senate Doc. 126.

the large banks have succeeded in building up a substantial trust business.

In drawing any conclusions as to the nature and scope of fiduciary activities of commercial banks from the above analysis, it must be kept in mind, however, that commercial banks chartered by various states have also entered the trust field, and that the information contained in this section is based on data covering only the national banking system, which includes but a portion of all the commercial banks in the country. The total amount of fiduciary business carried by commercial banks is, therefore, undoubtedly much larger, if not twice as large, than the figures given here indicate.

IV. Investment of Trust Funds

We have reviewed so far the development of the trust company as an institution, the work of the banking departments of trust companies and the growth and nature of the fiduciary activities of the national-banking system. In the beginning of this presentation, it was observed that because of inadequacy of existing statistics it is impossible to arrive at an exact figure, either as to the number of institutions engaged in trust work or as to the aggregate dollar amount of fiduciary business for the entire country. According to certain estimates, about 4,500 financial institutions administer around half a million trust accounts, the aggregate value of which is somewhere between thirty and forty billion dollars, or equal to about 10 per cent of the national wealth of the United States. There is no way of determining with any degree of accuracy how this enormous sum is allocated; an idea may be had of the prevailing investment practices of trust companies from sample data available for specific groups of institutions.

In the various states there exists a great diversity of practice as to the investment of trust funds. Some states have prescribed by law the limits for the investment of such funds; others provide that the trustee must exercise the care and prudence of the average man, and still others have said nothing about the character of the investments which can be made by a trustee. In such cases the trustee is required to exercise due diligence and strive for "reasonable diversification," in doing so he must be guided by the principles of "reasonably safe" investment. In states where there are statutory provisions regulating the investment of trust funds, the law has, presumably, the same object in view. We present here the results of the activity of a group of trust companies in order to show to what extent these canons for the handling of fiduciary funds have been effective.

This analysis of investments contained in 184 testamentary trusts is based on figures obtained from eighteen trust companies, ten of which are located in New York City, three in Boston, three in Cleveland, and one each in Chicago and St. Louis; the investigation covered the years 1919 to 1931.

At the time the assets comprising the sample of 184 trust funds were received in trust, their relative diversification was as follows: 16.6 per cent bonds, 45.6 per cent stocks, 27.9 per cent real estate, and 9.9 per cent cash. Table 39 shows what became of these funds after they were reinvested by the trust institutions.

TABLE 39

DISTRIBUTION OF TRUST INVESTMENTS BY CLASSES, BASED ON 184 TRUSTS

(In percentages of total)

CLASS OF INVESTMENT	1920	1925	1930	1931	1919-1931 *Average*
Bonds	23.6	29.2	28.0	32.3	28.0
Preferred Stocks	8.1	7.4	7.0	4.1	7.0
Common Stocks	34.7	31.5	34.1	34.7	33.5
Real Estate Obligations	15.6	18.7	24.9	25.9	18.9
Real Estate	17.3	12.3	4.3	2.4	11.2
Miscellaneous	.7	.9	1.7	.6	1.4
Total	100.0	100.0	100.0	100.0	100.0

As thus observed from the column of this table giving the average percentages for the period 1919-1931 the relative distribution of the assets changed very little, outside of the fact that the cash item has disappeared. If the same trust assets are broken up according to the type of securities in which they were invested by the trust companies, the following picture appears:

TABLE 40

DISTRIBUTION OF TRUST INVESTMENTS BASED ON 184 TRUSTS

(In percentages of total)

TYPE OF INVESTMENT	1920	1925	1930	1931	1919-1931 *Average*
United States Bonds	4.1	3.8	1.5	1.6	3.1
State & Municipal Bonds	6.3	10.3	11.1	14.2	9.3
Railroad Bonds	8.6	7.8	5.0	5.4	7.5
Utility Bonds	2.7	4.1	7.3	7.3	4.5
Industrial Bonds	1.4	2.1	2.5	3.2	2.1
Foreign Bonds	.5	.9	.6	.6	.7
Railroad Preferred Stock	2.8	2.1	1.3	.5	2.0
Utilities Preferred Stock	.7	.9	1.5	.6	.8
Industrial Preferred Stock	4.6	4.4	4.2	3.0	4.2
Railroad Common Stock	9.9	6.5	2.3	1.7	6.1
Utility Common Stock	8.0	4.1	3.4	3.8	5.1
Industrial Common Stock	12.3	17.1	23.3	24.4	18.0
Bank and Finance Stock	4.5	3.8	5.1	4.8	4.3
Land Bank Bonds	—	2.4	3.2	2.2	1.8
Real Estate Obligations	15.6	16.3	21.7	23.7	16.9
Real Estate	17.3	12.3	4.3	2.4	11.0
Miscellaneous	.7	.9	1.7	.6	2.6
Total	100.0	100.0	100.0	100.0	100.0

From the above distribution of trust assets it is clear that during the post-war era United States bonds and all railroad securities decreased in importance as an investment for trust funds, but public utility securities, state and municipal bonds, and real estate obligations began to absorb a larger share of trust assets. During the period 1919 to 1931, the aggregate of the principal of the trust funds studied increased nearly 28 per cent. The gains in principal arising largely from the sale of stocks and real estate, were reinvested in real estate and bonds; this accounts for the greater share of trust funds invested in these two types of assets.

If we break up the same trust assets according to the field of activity in which the funds were placed, the distribution is afforded.

From Table 41 not much change appears to have taken place in the group of government securities. United States bonds declined, but state and municipal tax-exempt securities increased, while the share of foreign government securities was insignificant (as we may see from Table 40); as a result government obligations remained relatively stable. The importance of railroad securities declined very considerably, as was also the case in the investment portfolios of commercial banks.[8] Public utilities seem to show a tendency to take the place formerly occupied by railroads. The industrial group, consisting of miscellaneous issues, is larger than either railroads or utilities and real estate commitments and constitute the largest single item, which, incidentally, is also the case in the investments of life insurance companies as well as of savings banks.

TABLE 41

DISTRIBUTION OF TRUST INVESTMENTS BASED ON 184 TRUSTS BY FIELD

(In percentages of total)

	1920	1925	1930	1931	1919-1931 *Average*
Government	10.9	15.2	12.6	15.8	13.8
Railroad	21.3	16.4	8.6	7.6	15.6
Utility	11.4	9.1	12.2	11.7	10.4
Industrial	18.3	23.6	30.0	30.6	24.3
Real Estate	32.9	31.0	29.2	28.3	30.1
Finance	4.5	3.8	5.1	4.8	4.3
Miscellaneous	.7	.9	2.3	1.2	1.5
Total	100.0	100.0	100.0	100.0	100.0

The choice of investments also varies according to the size of the trust. Table 42 presents the distribution of investments for the years 1920 and 1930 arranged by classes of trusts.

Table 42 fairly demonstrates that from 1920 to 1930, in the smaller trust accounts, the portion of assets invested in bonds decreased, while in the larger accounts the bond holdings grew relatively to the total. The small trusts steadily invest a greater portion of their assets in preferred stocks all through the period, while the holdings of common stock grow larger with the increase of the size of the trust. Real-estate obligations are the largest single item in the small trusts accounts and occupy a definitely less important position in the large trust funds, while

[8] This fact is treated in detail in Part IV of this book devoted to Bank Portfolios.

TABLE 42

DISTRIBUTION OF INVESTMENTS ACCORDING TO CLASSES OF TRUSTS, GROUPED BY SIZES, 1920 AND 1930

(In percentages of total)

CLASS OF INVESTMENT	0 to 25,000		25,000 to 75,000		75,000 to 200,000		200,000 to 500,000		500,000 to 1,000,000		1,000,000 or over	
	1920	1930	1920	1930	1920	1930	1920	1930	1920	1930	1920	1930
Bonds	30.5	16.2	24.3	23.6	33.8	24.3	27.0	20.5	30.4	34.2	18.9	30.1
Preferred Stock	9.0	13.2	13.8	14.1	8.9	8.1	7.7	6.7	5.0	5.0	5.6	6.2
Common Stocks	26.8	23.8	21.4	12.5	20.0	22.4	35.9	37.6	28.4	29.2	40.2	38.2
Real Estate Obligations	27.3	44.5	31.0	41.0	26.5	37.1	20.3	23.8	.7	6.5	11.3	20.1
Real Estate	5.1	1.2	9.3	4.3	9.1	4.1	4.8	3.0	34.9	19.6	23.1	3.2
Miscellaneous	1.3	1.1	.2	4.5	1.7	4.0	4.3	8.4	.6	5.5	.9	2.2
Total	100.0	100.0	100.0	100.0	100.0	100.0	100.0	100.0	100.0	100.0	100.0	100.0

just the reverse takes place in the case of real estate owned. In the small accounts the tendency to invest a larger portion of the assets in real-estate obligations has increased from 1920 to 1930, while the larger trust funds have, during the same period, decreased the relative size of their ownership of real estate.

Distributing now the trust assets comprising this sample by field of activity, as well as by size of trust account, we obtain the following distribution for the years 1920 and 1930.

Table 43 shows that trust assets are apportioned among the various fields with less variety, owing to size of trusts, than is found in the similar distribution by classes of investments. Only in the case of real estate do we find that in 1930 the small accounts have greater holdings than the large ones. Otherwise, the same tendencies which have been already brought out in Table 40: namely, the decline of railroad securities and of government securities, and the increase in utilities, industrial issues and real-estate holdings, are characteristic. Investments in "governments" which were fairly steady for the entire sample show a decrease for all trusts except the account of over one million dollars.

Before taking up the reasons for these shifts and the significance of the changes that the investment of the trust funds have undergone in the post-war period, inquiry is needed as to quality of the investments, the distribution of which has just been presented. The securities which enter into our sample have been graded on the basis of rates that prevailed during the period from 1928 to 1931, so that the distributions obtained refer to dates prior to the drastic decline in the security market during 1932. Table 44 shows the securities in which the trust assets of our sample were invested, distributed according to the rating given to them in the Fitch Bond and Stock Records.

In inspecting the above distribution it is seen that the railroad bonds present a better picture than utility bonds, and that the industrial group has a large percentage (26.6 per cent) of unrated securities. The rating of the composite fund of all bonds is very high if compared to common and preferred stock, as slightly over 90 per cent of all the bonds fall into grade A or higher, but the reader should always recall that the grading was done prior to 1932.

The quality of preferred stocks is decidedly lower than that of bonds, as only 37.1 per cent fall into grade A or higher. In the case of industrial preferred stocks, slightly over 70 per cent of the total is below the A grade and 22.2 per cent of the utilities are unrated.

Common stocks which exceeded both bonds and real estate in volume get a rate of A or higher for 41 per cent of the total. The worst showing is made by industrial common stocks where 57.2 per cent were either lower than BB grade, or unrated; and less than one per cent qualified for the AAA grade.

The combined investment in all types of securities (exclusive of real estate, real-estate obligations and miscellaneous items) presents the following picture when graded:

RATING	PERCENTAGE OF TOTAL STOCKS AND BONDS %
AAA	26.5
AA	15.6
A	10.3
BBB	16.1
BB	4.8
Lower	13.1
Unrated	13.6
Total	100.0

As common stocks constitute more than one-half of the grand total of stocks and bonds, the average quality was lowered by their record and especially by that of industrial common stocks, while the favorable showing must be attributed to the high average quality of bonds.

It is the duty of the trustee not only to conserve the principal of the trust, but also to provide earnings from the investment of the principal. Table 45 shows the average earning from the trust accounts making up our sample. (Data could not be obtained for all of the 184 trusts; therefore, only 178 accounts are included.)

TABLE 43

DISTRIBUTION OF INVESTMENTS ACCORDING TO FIELDS IN TRUSTS, GROUPED BY SIZES, 1920 AND 1930

(In percentages of total)

FIELD	0 to 25,000		25,000 to 75,000		75,000 to 200,000		200,000 to 500,000		500,000 to 1,000,000		1,000,000 or over	
	1920	1930	1920	1930	1920	1930	1920	1930	1920	1930	1920	1930
Government	10.5	3.6	16.5	5.1	14.5	4.2	12.2	6.8	6.5	5.1	8.4	19.0
Railroad	20.8	8.2	11.7	14.3	14.6	14.0	22.2	10.5	39.6	13.3	21.1	5.8
Utility	14.6	16.0	10.9	18.2	7.2	13.3	13.3	18.3	6.9	26.3	12.4	7.2
Industrial	17.4	23.0	19.9	17.8	17.2	19.5	19.3	29.6	9.4	13.7	18.2	35.4
Real Estate	33.6	42.7	42.3	43.8	35.5	41.3	25.1	26.8	35.6	26.1	34.4	24.9
Miscellaneous	3.2	6.5	—	.8	7.0	7.7	7.9	8.0	2.0	15.5	5.4	7.7
Total	100.0	100.0	100.0	100.0	100.0	100.0	100.0	100.0	100.0	100.0	100.0	100.0

TABLE 44

INVESTMENT QUALITY OF BONDS, PREFERRED AND COMMON STOCKS FOR LAST YEAR OF THE TRUSTS, BASED ON 184 TRUSTS

	AAA %	AA %	A %	BBB %	BB %	LOWER %	UNGRADED %	TOTAL %
All Bonds	63.0	17.8	9.8	4.1	0.3	0.3	4.7	100.0
All Preferred Stocks	19.1	4.4	13.6	43.0	5.7	3.2	11.0	100.0
All Common Stocks	14.9	17.5	8.6	14.3	6.5	20.5	17.6	100.0
U. S. Government Bonds	100.0	0.0	0.0	0.0	0.0	0.0	0.0	100.0
State and Municipal Bonds	80.0	11.0	4.9	1.0	0.2	0.3	2.6	100.0
Railroads:								
Bonds	78.5	11.1	6.0	1.9	0.4	0.7	1.4	100.0
Preferred Stocks	30.7	5.7	23.6	10.7	16.6	2.7	10.7	100.0
Common Stocks	11.4	49.9	14.2	3.7	10.7	5.7	4.4	100.0
Utilities:								
Bonds	39.0	26.9	19.9	10.1	0.2	0.4	3.6	100.0
Preferred Stocks	12.6	8.1	22.5	15.9	9.3	9.4	22.2	100.0
Common Stocks	24.6	7.0	32.9	25.6	2.7	1.2	6.0	100.0
Industriais:								
Bonds	29.7	18.5	16.1	8.9	0.0	0.2	26.6	100.0
Preferred Stocks	16.6	3.4	9.4	57.0	1.7	2.5	9.3	100.0
Common Stocks	0.9	12.5	4.8	17.4	7.2	31.1	26.1	100.0
Financial:								
Common Stocks	83.3	6.6	3.0	4.9	0.0	0.0	2.2	100.0

TABLE 45

INCOME RETURNS OF 178 TRUSTS AS AN AGGREGATE AND CLASSIFIED ACCORDING TO SIZE, FOR 1920-1931

SIZE OF TRUSTS	NUMBER OF TRUSTS	AVERAGE PERCENTAGE EARNED ON INVESTMENT (GROSS)
\$0–\$25,000	30	5.5
25,000–75,000	48	6.1
75,000–200,000	41	5.5
200,000–500,000	37	5.6
500,000–1,000,000	8	6.7
1,000,000 and over	14	6.6
Total	178	5.8

These returns were figured on the basis of the book value of the investments. In case the market value could have been taken, the percentages would have been lower during the prosperity period and higher in the initial stages of the depression when the market values declined more rapidly than the returns. An appraisal has already been given of the quality of the investment values on which the principal of the trust assets was invested. This was done on the basis of rates based on 1928-1931 standards. Table 46 presents the rate of current returns based on the market values in 1930 and the first part of 1931.

TABLE 46

CURRENT RETURN ON MARKET VALUE OF BONDS, PREFERRED AND COMMON STOCKS, BY FIELDS, FOR THE END OF THE TRUSTS, BASED ON 184 TRUSTS

FIELD	BONDS	PREFERRED STOCK	COMMON STOCK
	%	%	%
Railroad	5.47	6.29	6.10
Public Utility	5.50	6.30	6.08
Industrial	6.17	7.10	6.64
United States Government	4.01	—	—
State and Municipal	4.74	—	—
Bank and Insurance	—	—	5.33
Composite Average	5.23	6.70	6.60

As may be observed from Table 46 income from securities was higher during the first years of the depression than for the entire post-war period. The composite return for bonds and stocks for the period 1920-1931 was 5.8 per cent; while on the basis of 1930 and early 1931 values it amounted to 6.15 per cent. But if this tabulation be compared with Table 44 giving the grades of the securities, we notice that the highest returns are found among the groups that made the most unsatisfactory showing when rated according to the quality of the securities. This holds true of industrial stocks both common and preferred, as well as of bonds. The investment of trust funds may be approached from another angle by analysis of the composition of trust portfolios, not in a select group of institutions as we have done so far, but in a certain geographic locality. The sample that has just been presented was based on eighteen trust companies located in large financial centers; the table below covers all the fiduciary assets in the trust companies, both large and small, located in the state of Massachusetts.

From Table 47 first of all, may be seen that the composition of the assets is entirely different both from that of national banks as well as from that of the banking departments of trust companies. Loans comprise only a very small part of total trust assets and consist nearly entirely of advances on real estate. More than 80 per cent of the assets are invested in stocks and bonds, while those two items are approximately equal all through the post-war period. During the depression years the total investments in stocks increased relative to all assets, while bonds declined; but this falling off of bonds was smaller than the relative increase in stocks.

Comparison of the above tabulation with Table 39 giving the distribution of investments by classes in the trust companies located in five large cities, thus shows that in the case of aggregate trust assets in the State of Massachusetts (exclusive of national banks having trust departments) the share of total trust assets invested both in bonds and especially in real estate is smaller than in the eighteen large trust companies we have just reviewed. In Massachusetts a slightly greater percentage of total trust assets is invested in government, state, and municipal bonds. while corporate bonds play a noticeably more important part

TABLE 47

PERCENTAGE DISTRIBUTION OF AGGREGATE TRUST ASSETS IN MASSACHUSETTS TRUST COMPANIES*

YEAR	GOVERNMENT, STATE AND MUNICIPAL BONDS	OTHER BONDS	ALL BONDS	ALL STOCKS	LOANS ON REAL ESTATE	OTHER LOANS	ALL LOANS	REAL ESTATE OWNED	MISCEL- LANEOUS ASSETS	CASH IN BANKS
	%	%	%	%	%	%	%	%	%	%
1919	16.0	17.9	33.9	40.2	15.2	0.9	16.1	6.0	1.2	2.6
1920	19.0	18.7	37.6	38.6	13.0	1.3	14.2	5.7	1.8	2.1
1921	19.7	19.3	39.0	40.8	10.7	0.7	11.4	5.9	0.9	2.0
1922	20.0	20.7	40.7	39.5	9.4	0.7	10.1	5.3	1.6	2.9
1923	18.8	21.4	40.3	41.4	9.3	0.7	10.0	4.9	0.7	2.7
1924	17.6	22.4	40.0	40.8	9.9	0.6	10.5	5.0	0.6	3.1
1925	16.2	23.7	40.0	39.6	11.0	0.9	11.8	5.1	0.6	3.0
1926	15.1	24.6	39.7	39.5	11.5	0.9	12.4	5.0	0.6	2.9
1927	13.4	26.9	40.4	39.0	11.1	0.6	11.7	4.6	0.4	3.9
1928	12.4	29.1	41.5	39.4	9.7	0.6	10.3	4.5	0.4	4.0
1929	11.3	28.9	40.2	43.0	8.2	0.5	8.7	4.5	0.4	3.2
1930	10.0	28.4	38.5	46.0	7.0	0.4	7.4	4.6	0.5	3.1
1931	9.6	28.9	38.5	47.1	6.4	0.3	6.7	4.6	0.5	2.6

* Computed on the basis of data obtained from the *Annual Reports of the Commissioner of Banks of the State of Massachusetts*. Percentages do not add exactly to 100.0.

than in the case of the sample of large trust companies analyzed. Stocks are about equal (around 40.0 per cent of the total) in both cases. The marked difference appears in the extent of real-estate commitments. The Massachusetts trust companies diverted a much smaller portion of their assets into the real-estate field than the eighteen large institutions already reviewed, and kept up the pre-war practice of investing heavily in bonds.

In so far as the evaluation of both the principal and the earnings of the trust assets included in the sample is based on standards established prior to 1932, it is not possible to judge to what extent both the principal and the earnings suffered from the depression. At the end of 1933, readjustment due to the depression can not be considered as completed; therefore, the question of how well fiduciary assets and earnings withstand a major economic recession has to be left unanswered.

But the analysis of investments made by the eighteen trust companies studied in the sample warrants the conclusion that they were not widely different from those made by the average run of investors during the same years. Whether the trust companies were guided by the principles of "reasonably safe" investment, and exercised "reasonable diversification" in following the path taken by the average run of investors in the post-war era, is a debatable point, to which no answer can be given without passing judgment on the reasonableness of the course of economic activity during this period. This being, however, outside the scope of this inquiry, there need only be pointed out the following conclusion: popular opinion credits the institutional investor with the possession of superior judgment, owing to the facilities at his disposal, the scope of his operations and his greater experience. The factual presentation just completed indicates that the institutional investor with all these qualifications, if and when possessed, had placed during the post-war decade the assets entrusted to him in approximately the same fashion as the so-called average man whose judgment was supposed to be inferior. It must be noted, however, in fairness to the institutional investor, that not all of the accounts analyzed were discretionary trusts and that in many cases the hands of the institutional trustee were tied by the will of the testator.

The data on the distribution of investments of 184 trusts that are thus presented indicates during the post-war period that state and municipal bonds, all real estate commitments, utility issues, common stocks, and all industrial securities have grown in importance as an investment for trust funds, while railroad securities and United States bonds have declined. These tendencies coincide with the notions, prevalent at that time among the business community, as to what constitutes a safe investment.

It is hardly necessary to do more than recall the arguments advanced prior to the depression in favor of common stocks as an investment. These pleas were undoubtedly responsible for the increase of holdings of common stocks in trust accounts of large size shown in Table 42. The funded debt of public utilities increased after the war. The debt of the electric industry rose from 1.1 billion dollars, in 1912, to 5.8 billions in 1931, and the long term debt of the telephone industry increased during the same period by 250 per cent.[9] The bonded indebtedness of industrial corporations increased from 3.7 billions in 1913, to 10.5 billions in 1932.[10] The gross funded debt of states and municipalities rose from 4.8 billions, in 1914, to 16.6 billions in 1931.[11] The bonds of states and municipalities are tax exempt and were therefore especially attractive to trustees; the major portion of government bonds held consisted of these securities as one may see from Table 40. After the World War commercial banks went into the field of real-estate financing (this is treated in greater detail in Part IV of this book dealing with bank portfolios), and the total amount of real-estate loans and real estate held by all banking institutions is estimated as having increased from 2.9 billion dollars, in 1913, to 9.1 billions in 1931.[12] At the same time the funded debt of the railroads rose from 11.2 billions, in 1913, to 14.3 billions in 1931.[13] Owing to the provisions of the law of 1920 and the pending consolidation

[9] *The Internal Debt of the United States,* ed. by Evans Clark, 1933, Chap. V, by John Bauer.
[10] *Ibid.,* Chap. VI, by Gardiner Means.
[11] *Ibid.,* Chap. IX, by Wylie Kilpatrick.
[12] *Ibid.,* Chap. III, by Victoria Pederson.
[13] *Ibid.,* Chap. IV, by Wilfred Eldred.

of railroads, railroad securities as a whole lost their attractiveness to the average investor. United States government bonds having tax exempt privileges were absorbed by individual investors of very large means (which is reflected in trust accounts of over $1,000,000) and by commercial banks—a new development since the war. (This phase also is covered in Part IV dealing with the bank portfolios.)

The rapid increase in the funded debt of public utilities, state and municipal governments, industrial corporations, and of urban real estate, directed the funds of the community into these fields, and made the securities floated by these industries more prevalent as an investment among the public as well as the banks. The institutional trustee appears to have followed along the path taken by the rest of the investors. Railroad securities declined in importance, and United States government bonds found a new market. The average investor diverted his attention from these issues and so did the institutional trustee.

Summary

We may summarize this discussion of the status of fiduciary banking by restating: first, that the intermingling of banking functions has gone so far that trust companies must be considered as engaged in commercial banking business, and national and state commercial institutions with trust departments as institutional trustees; second, that the inadequacy of existing statistical data prevents presentation of any complete picture of the scope of fiduciary banking in the United States.

During the period studied—1900 to 1932—there took place a very substantial increase in the banking resources of trust companies, while the number of trust companies grew at a much slower rate. Trust companies are largely concentrated in certain sections of the country; with the large trust institutions located primarily in the industrial East. The average trust company is a larger institution than the average commercial banking unit. The commercial-banking business of trust companies is very similar to that of national banks and especially to that of commercial banks located in large financial centers.

Although only about one-third of the total number of national banks have taken out permits to exercise fiduciary powers, this number includes approximately four-fifths of the aggregate capitalization and total resources of the national system.

A very large share of all the trust business is found in the larger banks, as measured by the size of the capital stock. The only exception is furnished by the insurance trust assets, which are spread out more evenly among banks of various sizes. We also find that most of the trust business, especially in the case of bond issues for which national banks act as trustees, is found in banks located in cities with a population of more than 1,000,000 inhabitants.

The overhead expense involved in operating a trust department, the concentration of the bulk of the wealth of the country in the hands of a comparatively small group of individuals, and the geographic concentration of the control of this wealth, all account for the fact that it is difficult for a small bank to build up a trust business, and that most of it finds its way into the larger banking units. The insurance trust assets, a very large portion of which are not yet operative, are distributed more evenly and represent one branch of fiduciary business which holds future possibilities for the small bank.

In analyzing the use to which trust funds are put, it is clear that the institutional trustee invested the assets entrusted to him during the post-war era approximately along the same lines as did other investors. The tendency to follow the trend of the times appears to be stronger in the case of the large trust accounts as compared with those of smaller size. The large trust institutions also show a tendency to deviate more from the prewar standards for the investment of fiduciary assets than can be observed from the sample containing trust companies of various sizes. The poorest results in the investment of trust funds are shown in the case of all industrial issues and common stocks, or along the lines which were most popular in the post-war decade.

CHAPTER XII

SAVINGS BANKING[1]

A little over a century ago the mutual savings bank first made its appearance in the United States. In the older eastern states, with a wage-earning class unable to lay out its own funds and a wealthy class not bent solely on business enterprise for individual gain, this institution supplied a distinct need. Elsewhere, however, more opportunity for investment existed, and the individual tended to employ directly such funds as he had saved. With the passage of time the mutual banks grew in number and in influence, and came to constitute practically the sole repository for savings in the country. Geographically, however, they remained restricted—a twofold result of the frontier and of the uncertainties induced by the Civil War.

In the later years of the 19th century, a radical change in the situation began to make itself felt. As the newer sections became more settled, and as they accumulated surplus funds, these funds found their way, not into newly-established mutual banks, but instead into already existing so-called commercial banks. Such stock savings banks as were formed, in many cases, differed from state banks only in name, and received checking as well as savings accounts. To an increasing extent the commercial banks received deposits—whether evidenced by passbook entry or by certificate—upon which they paid interest, and which were subject to notice of withdrawal or matured on a fixed date. Bankers recognized the tendency, and at various con-

[1] The material contained in the following chapter was presented in substance as a part of the *Report on the Banking Inquiry of 1925-26*. The preparation of the work was then in charge of Dr. W. H. Steiner. In its present form (pp. 243-79) the statistics of the inquiry of 1925-26 have been brought down to date, and corresponding changes made in the text-interpretation of them. Additional material, descriptive of trends in savings and time deposits subsequent to 1926, has been added by the staff. In the latter part of the chapter the effect of the Banking Act of 1933 upon the savings and time-deposit movement has been discussed. The last part of the chapter dealing with Building and Loan Associations represents the work of Mr. J. A. Griswold.

ventions of their state associations discussed the desirability of such business. Practical experience must have answered almost unanimously in the affirmative, for, especially with the opening of the new century, the number of banks receiving such deposits grew by leaps and bounds. National banks, not specifically authorized nor prohibited to receive such deposits, did not lag behind state banks and trust companies. Nor did these stock institutions confine themselves to nonmutual territory; instead, they also invaded the older mutual states and competed more or less openly and actively with the mutual banks. The increasingly rapid growth of their time deposits is depicted in Table 48:[2]

TABLE 48

SUMMARY OF TIME[3] DEPOSITS AND DEPOSITORS

DEPOSITS IN CLASSIFIED BANKS
(INCLUDING TIME CERTIFICATES AND POSTAL SAVINGS)
(In millions of dollars)

YEAR	MUTUAL SAVINGS	"STATE"	TRUST COMPANIES	PRIVATE	NATIONAL
1910	a	a	a	a	$1,014,229
1911	$ 3,458,961	$2,009,143	$ 963,840	$51,053	1,480,112
1912	3,608,882	2,147,412	1,056,095	55,998	1,535,986
1913	3,811,713	2,302,143	1,016,555	49,131	1,368,803
1914	3,910,499	2,244,755	1,061,531	41,352	1,453,838
1915	3,944,568	2,339,662	1,164,348	37,356	1,321,486
1916	4,102,481	2,581,711	1,021,347	37,977	1,715,792
1917	4,339,044	3,426,364	899,706	37,822	2,172,666
1918	4,381,910	3,852,961	919,969	43,939	2,336,071
1919	4,731,739	4,392,317	1,105,942	34,088	2,776,307
1920	5,058,282	5,395,937	1,225,606	46,016	3,462,800
1921	5,568,340	5,583,910	1,634,525	46,677	3,677,211
1922	5,817,699	6,104,752	1,525,431	56,757	4,074,281
1923	6,273,151	6,456,649	2,252,203	58,194	4,686,337
1924	6,693,247	6,789,872	2,501,244	46,365	5,158,006
1925	7,152,258	7,253,437	2,870,389	47,702	5,810,266
1926	7,525,189	7,674,880	3,270,494	47,899	6,177,730
1927	8,039,784	7,382,147	3,530,954	49,725	7,088,297
1928	8,668,090	7,597,977	4,080,324	16,797	8,049,773
1929	8,903,557	7,369,512	4,022,735	33,440	7,888,567
1930	9,205,580	6,803,672	4,349,057	23,546	8,096,776
1931	10,034,022	5,985,274	4,115,826	27,413	8,044,709
1932	10,039,958	4,259,494	3,005,439	17,997	6,958,458

a—Included in Total

[2] *Savings Deposits and Depositories;* compiled and published by Savings Division—American Bankers Association.

[3] Called "savings" by American Bankers Association.

TABLE 48 *(Continued)*

CLASSIFICATION OF DEPOSITS—ALL BANKS
(In millions of dollars)

YEAR	TOTAL SAVINGS DEPOSITS	TOTAL INDIVIDUAL DEPOSITS	REL. SAVINGS TO TOTAL IND. DEP.	PER INHAB. SAVINGS DEP.	PER INHAB. TOTAL IND. DEP.	TOTAL NUMBER SAVINGS DEPOSITORS
1910	$ 6,835,494	$14,675,681	.47	$ 74	$159	16,372,057
1911	7,963,109	15,604,453	.51	85	167	17,210,969
1912	8,404,373	16,741,589	.50	88	176	12,605,260
1913	8,548,345	18,122,480	.47	89	187	11,295,931
1914	8,711,975	18,890,595	.46	89	192	11,385,734
1915	8,807,420	18,674,451	.47	90	187	16,124,786
1916	9,459,308	22,064,607	.43	94	218	10,482,832
1917	10,875,602	22,831,023	.47	106	223	11,826,773
1918	11,534,850	24,518,440	.47	111	236	10,632,938
1919	13,040,393	28,449,491	.46	124	271	18,221,453
1920	15,188,641	32,360,748	.47	144	303	22,415,148
1921	16,500,663	34,232,612	.48	153	317	27,792,948
1922	17,578,920	36,336,247	.48	161	332	30,544,738
1923	19,726,534	40,491,308	.49	178	366	35,878,758
1924	21,188,734	41,063,769	.51	185	366	38,741,634
1925	23,134,052	45,463,928	.51	204	399	43,850,127
1926	24,696,192	47,472,118	.52	211	405	46,762,240
1927	26,090,907	49,106,235	.53	220	414	48,354,784
1928	28,412,961	51,199,264	.56	237	427	53,188,348
1929	28,217,811	50,788,861	.56	235	422	52,764,127
1930	28,478,631	50,543,056	.56	232	411	52,729,432
1931	28,207,244	47,863,555	.59	227	385	51,399,446
1932	24,281,346	39,306,214	.62	194	315	44,352,106

The foregoing tabular presentation should be contrasted with the figures showing aggregate deposits of all kinds in various types of banks. They are presented, as compiled from the *Annual Reports of the Comptroller of the Currency* and differ slightly from those presented in Table 48, owing chiefly to the fact that they are taken as of different dates. This Table 49 may be contrasted with the figures for time deposits already supplied, and with Table 50 showing the percentage distribution of total deposits among different classes of banks.

The fact that certain national banks entered the field as independent banks, instead of by means of affiliated state-chartered institutions which really represented one department of their business, should be borne in mind in considering these statistics.

TABLE 49

TOTAL DEPOSITS (EXCLUSIVE OF DUE TO BANKS)*

(By type of banks, by years, in millions of dollars)

YEARS	ALL BANKS	NATIONAL	ALL BANKS OTHER THAN NATIONAL	STATE COMMERCIAL	LOAN AND TRUST COMPANIES	STOCK SAVINGS	MUTUAL SAVINGS	PRIVATE
1909	14,109	4,897	9,212	2,468	2,837	569	3,145	193
1910	15,359	5,357	10,002	2,730	3,076	710	3,361	125
1911	15,960	5,528	10,432	2,779	3,298	752	3,461	142
1912	17,087	5,886	11,201	2,921	3,675	843	3,609	153
1913	17,554	6,023	11,531	3,084	3,576	958	3,770	143
1914	18,655	6,378	12,277	3,235	3,957	1,023	3,916	146
1915	19,248	6,613	12,635	3,284	4,217	1,049	3,951	134
1916	22,913	8,164	14,749	4,304	5,207	903	4,188	147
1917	26,529	9,746	16,783	5,397	5,805	996	4,423	162
1918	28,994	11,219	17,775	6,125	5,984	1,050	4,422	194
1919	33,778	12,940	20,838	9,016	5,702	1,152	4,751	217
1920	38,006	14,311	23,695	10,893	6,094	1,351	5,187	170
1921	35,849	12,991	22,858	10,850	5,856	443	5,575	134
1922	37,876	13,819	24,057	10,185	6,541	1,406	5,779	146
1923	40,631	14,489	26,142	11,222	6,883	1,616	6,289	132
1924	43,771	15,527	28,244	11,846	7,832	1,752	6,693	121
1925	47,612	17,023	30,589	12,796	8,594	1,925	7,148	126
1926	49,726	17,743	31,983	13,266	8,985	2,022	7,578	132
1927	52,446	18,918	33,528	13,137	10,528	1,663	8,077	123
1928	54,332	19,901	34,431	12,843	11,242	1,562	8,673	111
1929	54,281	19,422	34,859	12,937	11,355	1,456	9,003	108
1930	55,510	20,589	34,921	11,738	12,495	1,392	9,216	80
1931	52,036	19,452	32,584	10,019	11,267	1,204	10,035	59
1932	42,178	15,661	26,517	6,776	8,685	977	10,039	40

* Data for 1909 from the *Report of National Monetary Commission;* all other figures from the *Annual Reports of the Comptroller of the Currency*

TABLE 50

PERCENTAGE DISTRIBUTION OF TOTAL DEPOSITS*
(EXCLUSIVE OF DUE TO BANKS)

YEARS	NATIONAL	OTHER THAN NATIONAL	STATE COMMERCIAL	LOAN AND TRUST COMPANIES	STOCK SAVINGS	MUTUAL SAVINGS	PRIVATE
1909	34.7	65.3	17.5	20.1	4.0	22.3	1.4
1910	34.9	65.1	17.8	20.0	4.6	21.9	.8
1911	34.6	65.4	17.4	20.7	4.7	21.7	.9
1912	34.4	65.6	17.1	21.5	4.9	21.1	.9
1913	34.3	65.7	17.6	20.4	5.5	21.5	.8
1914	34.2	65.8	17.3	21.2	5.5	21.0	.8
1915	34.4	65.6	17.1	21.9	5.4	20.5	.7
1916	35.6	64.4	18.8	22.7	3.9	18.3	.6
1917	36.7	63.3	20.3	21.9	3.8	16.7	.6
1918	38.7	61.3	21.1	20.6	3.6	15.3	.7
1919	38.3	61.7	26.7	16.9	3.4	14.1	.6
1920	37.7	62.3	28.7	16.0	3.6	13.6	.4
1921	36.2	63.8	30.3	16.3	1.2	15.6	.4
1922	36.5	63.5	26.9	17.3	3.7	15.3	.4
1923	35.7	64.3	27.6	16.9	4.0	15.5	.3
1924	35.5	64.5	27.1	17.9	4.0	15.3	.3
1925	35.8	64.2	26.9	18.0	4.0	15.0	.3
1926	35.7	64.3	26.7	18.1	4.1	15.2	.3
1927	36.1	63.9	25.0	20.1	3.2	15.4	.2
1928	36.6	63.4	23.6	20.7	2.9	16.0	.2
1929	35.8	64.2	23.8	20.9	2.7	16.6	.2
1930	37.1	62.9	21.1	22.5	2.5	16.6	.2
1931	37.4	62.6	19.3	21.7	2.3	19.3	.1
1932	37.1	62.9	16.1	20.6	2.3	23.8	.1

* The addition of the percentages for the five types of state banks differs in some instances by 0.1 from the percentage for all banks other than national. Computed from figures given in Table 49.

THE GROWTH OF SPECIAL LEGISLATION

Striking and peculiarly significant for the present purpose is the fact that, with rare exception, no special recognition was given nor special treatment accorded these time deposits in non-mutual banks. But few states had legislated to bring them under control more or less similar to that exercised over mutual savings bank funds, while the national banks were not required to make any difference between their treatment of them and their demand deposits; in fact, the National Bank Act and the amendments made to it, from time to time, entirely ignored the existence of time as distinct from demand deposits. This was typical also of most state laws.

Such was the situation prevailing when the panic of 1907 occurred. Failure of various institutions at that time brought peculiar hardships to time depositors and raised in various minds the query whether special protection should not be granted them—granted, not as a favor, but as a right to which such depositors were entitled. It is a curious fact, incidentally, that in almost every state in which special measures calling for protection of an advanced sort were enacted a prominent bank failure served to drive home the lesson and to arouse public opinion. The result was that several states passed laws calling for segregation of savings deposits for the benefit of savings depositors, together with investment of such funds in a manner akin to that prescribed for mutual savings banks in the eastern states. Connecticut passed such a law in 1907, Massachusetts and Rhode Island followed suit in 1908, and California and Texas in 1909. The California law went furthest of all, providing complete departmentalization. Thus five states were added to New Hampshire, the pioneer, which already had legislated in 1891, and to Michigan, which had provided prescribed investment in 1893, added segregation in 1899, and instituted a penalty for violation of the act in 1909.[4]

Vermont, it may be noted, required all banks to invest their funds in securities of a savings-bank nature, although it required no segregation of assets. Moreover, interest was displayed in other states. For example, Idaho provided in 1905 for savings departments with separate books and prescribed investments, but evidently not complete segregation; while in 1911 the New York Superintendent consulted bankers in his state in an effort to devise a plan, but went out of office before any results could be achieved.

This wave of state legislation found a counterpart in the attention given the matter in the case of the national banks. The

[4] Barnett, "State Banks and Trust Companies Since the Passage of the National Bank Act," *Publications of the National Monetary Commission,* 1911, pp. 21-22. The Michigan and New Hampshire laws, it is stated, have been sustained by the highest courts.

action of the National Association of Supervisors of State Banks, in going on record in 1908 and 1909 as favoring segregation and prescribed investment for state chartered institutions, was paralleled by that of the Comptroller of the Currency, who favored enactment of such legislation for national banks. The Savings Bank Section of the American Bankers Association also interested itself actively in the problem, of which it made a detailed survey (as did also the Association's law committee), and in 1912 provided for a standing committee of five on segregation. The Federal legislative committee of the Association presented a plan to the National Monetary Commission in 1908 calling for both devices to be applied to national banks. A bill along these lines was introduced in the House of Representatives in 1909. Incidentally, much of the enthusiasm displayed in various quarters appeared to be due to a feeling that such legislation would serve to "head off" the agitation for Federal guaranty of bank deposits in national banks, and for the establishment of a postal-savings system. That bankers, however, were by no means a unit in the endorsement of the proposals is shown by the criticism directed against them (usually, it appears, by country bankers) at the conventions of the various state bankers' associations held in these years. Further evidence of the divided attitude of the national banks is seen in the replies to the Comptroller's inquiry of October 9, 1911, addressed to all national banks, as to the desirability of an amendment authorizing the establishment of savings departments and limiting their investments.[5]

He received replies from 6,813 national banks, 3,502, or 51 per cent, of which received savings deposits. Their replies dealing with various aspects of the general question were tabulated as follows:

The number of national banks favoring an amendment to the law allowing banks to invest a certain percentage of their deposits in real estate loans is 81 per cent, or	5,543
Of this number, an average of 25 per cent of all deposits was favored by	4,928

[5] *Annual Report of the Comptroller of the Currency*, 1911, pp. 28, 216.

The number of banks not favoring such an amendment is 17 per cent, or	1,186
The number of national banks favoring an amendment to the law specifically authorizing the establishment of savings departments in national banks is 68 per cent, or	4,682
The number of banks not favoring such an amendment is 29 per cent, or	1,979
The number of national banks favoring restricting real estate loans to a certain percentage of their savings deposits is 59 per cent, or	4,034
Of this number, an average of 40 per cent is favored by 54 per cent, or	3,692
The number of banks not favoring this restriction is 30 per cent, or	2,044
The number of national banks favoring the segregation of savings deposits and restriction of their investment is 35 per cent, or	2,241
The number of banks not favoring this restriction is 54 per cent, or	3,495

Similar evidence was afforded by the report of the Law Committee of the American Bankers Association to the Executive Council upon the question of special investment for savings deposits, made at Briarcliff, May 7, 1912. More than one-fourth of the membership replied, 3,119 institutions in all, of which 1,571 were national banks and 1,548 state-chartered institutions. The responses to pertinent questions may be presented as follows:

		Yes	*No*
Do you feel that when a bank retains the right to defer payments for savings deposits, it is under any obligation to set aside for them a corresponding amount of assets?	National	766	769
	State	809	699
		1,575	1,468
Do you feel that there is any obligation to invest savings deposits differently from commercial and other deposits because			

they represent all or nearly all the capital of the depositor, or because the savings depositors, as a class, are unable to invest their money themselves?	National	665	883
	State	723	785
		1,388	1,668
If so, should legislation prescribe the classes of loans and investments in which savings deposits should be invested?	National	642	701
	State	715	659
		1,357	1,360
Do you believe that the further adoption of the principles of segregation and special investment of savings deposits under the conditions above is advisable and practicable?	National	694	797
	State	753	692
		1,447	1,489

It was stated that the New England and the Pacific Coast answers were distinctly favorable; with New York, New Jersey, and Pennsylvania opposed, the South slightly opposed, and the Middle West and the Rocky Mountain states evenly divided.

THE PERIOD SINCE 1913

With the passage of the Federal Reserve Act in 1913, the agitation slumbered for a time. Evidently the problem was either regarded as "settled" or as overshadowed by other more important developments which were in process of working themselves out. The Federal Reserve Act itself, as passed by the House, in section 27 provided separate assignment of capital as well as segregation and permitted the Federal Reserve Board to regulate the conduct of the savings department and to prescribe its investments, although an earlier form had described carefully the permitted bonds and mortgages. American Bankers Association interests, at a conference in Chicago on August 22 and 23, 1913, called by its currency commission, opposed the provision, as did a conference of country bankers held in Boston,

October 6, and bankers generally in their testimony at the Senate hearings. The section did not appear in the Act as finally passed, but provision for restricted and limited real-estate loans was retained in section 24, and in 1916 was broadened to include city as well as farm land. For the time being, this legislation was apparently regarded as satisfactory. The various repeated recommendations of Comptroller Williams—that deposits be limited in relation to capital and surplus, that rates of interest be limited, and that deposits in small sums be guaranteed—must be regarded merely as individual views.

In the succeeding years, the matter once more raised its head. The tremendous growth of time deposits during the war and post-war periods—stimulated by wartime sales of Liberty bonds and active bank solicitation—attracted much attention, while the large number of bank failures, both national and state, which began in 1921 caused severe loss to time depositors. At the same time, during the post-war period more and more emphasis was placed upon "protecting" the small saver, by means of blue-sky laws and otherwise, against fraudulent or unduly hazardous securities. From several angles, segregation and prescribed investment have been urged. First may be mentioned several measures introduced in Congress affecting national banks in the keeping of their time deposits. The 1921 hearings on the Calder bill (S. 4721, 66th Congress, third session), while designed to aid homebuilding rather than to consider the situation of time depositors, served to elicit some expression of bankers' opinions. In opposing it, General Counsel Paton of the American Bankers Association stated that "There does not appear to be any demand for this bill on the part of the national banks, nor on the part of the depositors of the national banks"; H. H. McKee, Chairman of the executive committee of the Association's national-bank section, stated, however, that "There does not seem to be any objection to the principle of segregation of savings from commercial deposits, nor does there seem to be any particular objection to the amendment of the Federal Reserve Act that would allow a greater amount to be loaned on real estate." Bankers' opinions submitted by him show, on the whole, opposition to one or more features of the plan. Again, at the 1924 hearing on H. R. 6855, 68th Congress, first session, J. S. Drum stated: "Of course, it is futile to suggest a scheme of departmental banking in the national banking system at this time, particularly as a requirement. If it were optional, that would be one thing." The analysis, however, made in 1925 by General Counsel Wyatt of the Federal Reserve Board of S. 3316 and H. R. 887, 68th Congress, second session, favored savings departments with segregated assets if real-estate-loan powers were to be extended.

Discussion has taken place also in several other directions. The savings-bank section of the American Bankers Association considered the problem briefly at its 1919, 1920, and 1921 conventions, the national bank section at its 1921 convention, and the National Association of Mutual Savings Banks at its 1922 conference, but apparently all let the matter rest. Again, in 1921-23 the bankers in the state of Washington considered segregation, but it is said, overwhelmingly opposed it. Later still, several articles were issued by California banking interests, active in the discussion fifteen years earlier, urging resort to these measures. Again, from time to time the more progressive states have revised their banking codes, and "departmentalization" has usually made a strong appeal on such occasions; but, on the whole, there was a distinct apathy in sharp contrast to the active discussion in the years following 1907. Mutual savings bankers, in general, favored the remedial legislation, some of them actively, most, perhaps, rather passively; national bankers were as strongly divided as they were in the two 1911 surveys cited, with the country bankers strongly opposed to disturbing the *status quo*.

The Deposit-Reserve Problem

Deposit developments during the past few years have brought to the front a phase of the problem of caring for funds that had previously not made its appearance. For many years past the question of reserves against deposits has been conspicuous and the question has been raised whether existing reserves were adequate. The requirements of the National Bank Act which were in force in 1913, at the time of the adoption of the Federal

Reserve Act, are well known. Roughly speaking, they called for a division of the country between three groups, or classes, of banks—the first comprising the so-called central reserve city banks; the second, the reserve city banks; and the third, the country banks. In the central reserve city banks, reserves were 25 per cent in cash against demand deposits. In the reserve city banks they were 25 per cent of which half might be in cash and the other half balances in other banks. In the country banks they were 15 per cent, of which 6 per cent must be in cash in vault and the rest might be balances in other banks.

Change of Reserve Requirements under Federal Reserve Act

The Federal Reserve Act changed the reserve requirements by cutting the central bank reserves to 18, the reserve city reserves to 15, and the country bank reserves to 12 per cent. A further change in 1917 cut these reserves to 13, 10, and 7 per cent respectively, and provided that the reserves should be carried entirely as balances with the reserve banks, which themselves were required to carry 35 per cent in immediate funds as a reserve against outstanding deposits, and 40 per cent as a reserve against outstanding notes. The theory upon which these reductions were made was that central banking, being a more economical method of handling bank funds, could safely be relied upon to preserve equilibrium with a much smaller actual balance than could be the case under the former diffused reserve system. The final change was made under the influence of war, with the tacit understanding that the member banks themselves would find it necessary to carry an estimated 5 per cent additional in their own vaults which probably would be in the form of Federal Reserve notes. This expectation proved to be warranted in a general way, although many banks, especially those close to the Reserve institutions, found it practical to cut their vault reserves below 5 per cent. In order to gain a clear idea of the transformation thus brought about, the following tables, showing the total reserves have been compiled:[6]

[6] Recent proposals for modifying the reserve position of deposits, including time deposits, have been discussed in Part III, Chap. VI, of the present volume.

TABLE 51

RESERVE POSITION OF THE NATIONAL BANKING SYSTEM ON OR AROUND JUNE 30, 1909-1932*

(*In millions of dollars*)

YEARS	NUMBER OF BANKS	NET DEPOSITS	RESERVE REQUIRED	RESERVE HELD	RATIO OF RESERVES HELD TO NET DEPOSITS†
		$	$	$	
1909	6,926	6,075	1,243	1,359	22.37
1910	7,145	6,196	1,248	1,315	21.22
1911	7,277	6,689	1,356	1,478	22.10
1912	7,372	7,050	1,423	1,505	21.35
1913	7,473	7,125	1,420	1,493	20.95
1914	7,525	7,495	1,505	1,546	20.63
1915	7,605	7,283	1,062	1,840	25.26
1916	7,579	8,702	1,275	2,076	23.86
1917	7,604	10,084	1,468	2,310	22.91
1918	7,705	10,128	977	1,132	11.17
1919	7,785	11,576	1,108	1,211	10.46
1920	8,030	12,728	1,205	1,247	9.80
1921	8,154	11,017	1,038	1,042	9.46
1922	8,249	11,817	1,124	1,153	9.76
1923	8,241	12,186	1,130	1,145	9.39
1924	8,085	12,801	1,204	1,200	9.38
1925	8,072	13,775	1,289	1,329	9.65
1926	7,978	14,286	1,338	1,383	9.68
1927	7,796	14,704	1,379	1,409	9.58
1928	7,691	20,326	1,420	1,456	7.16
1929	7,536	19,510	1,320	1,347	6.90
1930	7,252	20,087	1,376	1,354	6.74
1931	6,805	19,743	1,361	1,423	7.21
1932	6,150	17,303	1,185	1,143	6.61

* *Annual Reports of the Comptroller of the Currency.*

† After 1927 the ratios published by the Comptroller are based on reserves required. The above ratios for 1928 to 1932 are computed on the basis of reserves held and net deposits figures.

GROWTH OF TIME DEPOSITS

The general growth of time deposits in the various classes of institutions, mutual savings banks, trust companies, and national banks already has been noted. From the figures of the American Bankers Association given in Table 48, it is evident that national banks have shown the greatest relative increase, and mutual savings banks the least, with the state banks and trust companies intermediate between the other two. In part, it is true, this may be owing to the fact that the last-mentioned group includes stock savings banks which early placed considerable emphasis upon time deposits, whereas national banks did not; but, when the figures for the last decade or two are compared, the national-bank record still stands out. During the sixteen-year period, 1910-1925, time deposits in national banks increased almost sevenfold, while those of state banks and trust companies increased only slightly over half as much in dollar amounts. If the eleven-year period, 1915-1925, be taken instead, a threefold increase on the part of the national banks is to be contrasted with a twofold increase for the other group. The six years, 1920-25, show a 110 per cent increase for the national banks and an 85 per cent increase for the state-chartered institutions, while the years 1931-1932 show similar results. From 1923 to 1924, the national banks showed about a 10 per cent increase, and from 1924 to 1925 they showed about a 12 per cent gain, in the face of increases for the other group of 7 and 9 per cent respectively. Between 1925 and 1931, another six-year period witnessed a 33⅓ per cent advance for the national banks and only in 1932 did the depression at last force a recession.

When amounts of time deposits now held are considered, however, the picture is changed. The state banks and trust companies today hold about 30 per cent of total time deposits, the mutual savings banks 40 and the national banks about 28 per cent. Fifteen to twenty years ago the mutual institutions held first place, but their slower rate of growth, owing in part to restricted territory and severely restricted branch facilities, forced them into second place, their old position of leadership being regained after the panic of 1929. To what extent the situation may be changed in future, it is difficult to say. National banks have demonstrated great capacity for expansion of their time deposit business, but their state-chartered rivals have the decided advantage of an early start, and it must not be forgotten that time deposits today, as well as twenty years ago, despite the tremendous war and post-war expansion, much exceed demand deposits.

The figures cited, applying only to the country as a whole,

TABLE 52

TIME* DEPOSITS IN VARIOUS CLASSES OF BANKING INSTITUTIONS, 1912, 1925, 1927, AND 1932, BY SECTIONS

(000,000 omitted)

	NEW ENGLAND	EASTERN	SOUTHERN	MIDDLE WESTERN	WESTERN	PACIFIC	UNITED STATES
1912							
Mutual Savings Banks	$1,421	$ 2,039	$ 1	$ 94	$—	$ 53	$ 3,609
State Banks & Trust Cos.†	168	764	285	1,411	152	423	3,203
National Banks	70	492	193	547	146	87	1,536
Total‡	1,660	3,305	481	2,091	303	564	8,404
1925							
Mutual Savings Banks	2,593	4,279	—	169	—	111	7,152
State Banks & Trust Cos.†	633	2,748	943	3,884	451	1,464	10,124
National Banks	519	2,236	818	1,445	373	419	5,810
Total‡	3,750	9,290	762	508	830	1,994	23,134
1927							
Mutual Savings Banks	2,889	4,843	—	182	—	126	8,040
State Banks & Trust Cos.†	756	3,296	948	4,277	379	1,255	10,913
National Banks	637	2,655	966	1,603	380	847	7,088
Total‡	4,291	10,810	1,915	6,081	766	2,228	26,091
1932							
Mutual Savings Banks	3,318	6,376	—	202	—	144	10,040
State Banks & Trust Cos.†	590	2,582	608	2,536	172	767	7,265
National Banks	613	2,468	763	1,592	356	1,166	6,958
Total‡	4,522	11,434	1,370	4,341	528	2,086	24,281

* Called "Savings" by the American Bankers Association.

† Includes stock savings banks.

‡ Includes a small amount in private banks, not shown separately here.

suggest the desirability of more detailed analysis. Such a survey, in fact, is essential in order to provide an adequate background for later discussion. For this present purpose figures of the Comptroller of the Currency are used, chiefly in the form tabulated by the savings-bank division of the American Bankers Association. The figures for the years after 1912 display much greater accuracy than those for earlier years (national-bank figures date back only to 1908, and were at first incomplete), while the later period is the one to which principal interest attaches.

Despite the rapid growth of time deposits in the nonmutual institutions, the center of attention in the problem tends to shift but slightly from the northeastern sections of the country. This is evident in Table 52, which depicts the situation in 1912, 1925, 1927 and 1932, by sections and by types of institutions.

The above figures show less than the average increase (over 1912) for the country as a whole in the New England, Western, Middle Western, and Eastern states; more than the average in the Southern and Pacific states. The result is that, whereas, in 1912, New England and the Eastern states held 59 per cent of the country's time deposits, in 1925 they held 66 2/3 per cent. At the same time, it must be mentioned that the national banks have shown remarkable increase in their time deposits in the New England and the Eastern States, as well as on the Pacific Coast—much more, in fact, than in the case of the state banks and trust companies. As a result, in 1932 the national banks had 44 per cent of the time deposits in these two groups of states, as compared with only 36 per cent in 1912, when their holdings in these states were relatively small. The state banks and trust companies showed a larger relative increase, their percentage held in these two groups of states rising from 29 to 44 per cent.

This general analysis is borne out when the change during the period in the relative proportion of time deposits to total individual deposits is compared. For this purpose, both actual figures and percentages should be considered, and they are given in Table 53.

In Table 53 is to be noted the slight percentual falling off in the Middle Western states followed by recovery, in the face of

TABLE 53

TIME* DEPOSITS AND TOTAL INDIVIDUAL DEPOSITS IN ALL BANKS 1912, 1925, 1927, AND 1932, BY SECTIONS

(000,000 omitted)

	NEW ENGLAND	EASTERN	SOUTHERN	MIDDLE WESTERN	WESTERN	PACIFIC	UNITED STATES
1912							
Time deposits	$1,660	$ 3,305	$ 481	$ 2091	$ 303	$ 564	$ 8,404
Total Individual Deposits	2,460	6,914	1,366	4,046	778	1,177	16,741
Percentage of time to individual	67%	47%	35%	52%	39%	47%	50%
1925							
Time deposits	3,750	9,290	1,762	5,508	830	1,994	23,134
Total Individual Deposits	5,180	19,125	4,250	11,164	1,940	3,426	45,085
Percentage of time to individual	72%	49%	41%	49%	43%	58%	51%
1927							
Time deposits	4,291	10,810	1,915	6,081	766	2,228	26,091
Total Individual Deposits	6,012	21,657	4,456	11,519	1,793	3,669	49,106
Percentage of time to individual	72%	50%	43%	53%	43%	61%	53%
1932							
Time Deposits	4,522	11,434	1,370	4,341	528	2,086	24,281
Total Individual Deposits	5,702	19,069	2,809	7,638	1,056	3,032	39,306
Percentage of time to individual	79%	60%	49%	57%	50%	69%	62%

* Called "Savings" by the American Bankers Association.

the increases elsewhere; and likewise, the slight change in the relative ranking of the sections. Confirmatory evidence is afforded when analysis is made of the number of states in which the amount outstanding on certificates exceeded the amount outstanding in deposit accounts. In 1912 this was true of 22 of the 49 states (including the District of Columbia); in 1925, however, only of 9, and in 1932 of 4. All of the nine Western states were represented, in 1912; in 1925, however, only 7 of them, and in 1932 there remained the two Dakotas, Nebraska, and Kansas. New England states were highest on all dates; Eastern states, third or fourth on all occasions; Southern states remain the lowest on all occasions; Middle Western states fall from second to third; Western states remain in next to last position on all occasions; and the Pacific states rise from third to second place.

Incidentally, it should be noted that there has been a change in the form of time deposits during the period in question. The time certificate of deposit, it is true, shows an absolute increase in amount for the country as a whole, and for all six sections except the Eastern states; yet when compared with the great increase in deposit accounts, it has clearly lost ground, and very greatly, too. In 1912, 22.8 per cent of the total amount of time deposits in the country was represented by certificates; in 1925 only 13.1 per cent, and in 1932 the percentage declined to 9.30 per cent. In the later year, however, the stronghold of the certificate—the Western states—still showed it predominant over the account, but to a relatively lesser extent than at the earlier date. This is clearly brought out in Table 54.

New York as an example.—In the discussion heretofore undertaken, an attempt has been made to deal with the time deposits of the country, largely from the standpoint of liability in its different forms, and to trace the gradual development of this liability during the past twenty years or more. The contemporary problem of time and savings deposits is somewhat different from that which existed in former years, and grows out of the fact that during the past five years the policies of investment of former times have been put to a severe test, with results which, in many cases, have turned out to be very unsatisfactory. At the

TABLE 54

CLASSES OF TIME DEPOSITS IN ALL BANKS, 1912, 1925 AND 1932 BY SECTIONS

(000,000 omitted)

GROUPS OF STATES	1912		1925		1932	
	DEPOSITS IN SAVINGS ACCOUNTS	CERTIFICATE OF DEPOSIT 30 DAYS AND OVER	DEPOSITS IN SAVINGS ACCOUNTS	CERTIFICATE OF DEPOSIT 30 DAYS AND OVER	DEPOSITS EVIDENCED BY SAVINGS PASS BOOKS	TIME CERTIFICATES OF DEPOSIT
New England	$1,616	$ 44	$ 3,635	$ 106	$ 4,348	$ 107
Eastern	2,856	449	8,912	338	10,239	312
Southern	264	217	1,249	508	870	374
Mid-Western	1,202	889	4,081	1,408	2,944	998
Western	68	236	254	564	214	217
Pacific	479	85	1,872	108	1,879	93
United States	6,486	1,919	20,004	3,032	20,494	2,101

present moment the problem of the average savings institution is found in the necessity of keeping its funds invested in such a way as to permit liquidation under fair conditions, preferably upon demand, and the experience of the past five years is regarded as affording as many warnings of policies to be avoided, as it has examples of precedents to be followed. The following survey[7] of what has taken place in the management of New York savings banks between the years 1927-33 illustrates the complex character of the problems to which we have thus referred.

The discussion may be made concrete by considering the record of mutual savings banks in New York State since 1927. Table 55 presents summary statements of their condition at the close of each year. Three periods may be distinguished:

1. 1927-29. An increase in deposits occurred until the spring of 1929, when, for some six months prior to the stock market crash, deposits declined, and they were less at the close of 1929 than a year before.* The savings banks sought by active advertising and by raising the rate paid to depositors to offset the lure of common stocks and the competition for savings by other institutions. Some New York City banks increased their rate to 4½ per cent, in place of four per cent. They were enabled to do this because of high yields on new investments, although this very fact caused the market value of their existing holdings to decline. Reflecting this condition, surplus (figuring investments at market value) actually declined between the 1927 and 1928, and between the 1928 and 1929 statements. Bond investments, worth $23,000,000 more in 1927 than they cost, depreciated, until they were worth $56,000,000 less than cost in 1929. In the investment policy pursued, a tendency was manifest to increase real estate loans, both absolutely and relatively, and to decrease bond investments. In other words, all

[7] The accompanying survey of the years 1927-1933 was prepared by Dr. W. H. Steiner, during the early months of 1933, supplementing his earlier studies as embodied in the *Report on the Banking Inquiry of 1925-26*. This survey has been published in *Money and Banking*, by William Howard Steiner, Chap. XVII, "Savings Banking," pp. 442-45.

* [Footnote by Steiner.] W. J. Carson, *Savings and Employee Savings Plans in Philadelphia* (Philadelphia, 1932), p. 86, observes that general business change is reflected far less in withdrawals than in receipts.

the increased deposits and some of the funds from old bond investments went into mortgage loans. Especially marked was the decline in holdings of United States governments; this, coupled with the decline in cash and bankers' acceptances, reflected a decline in relative liquidity.

2. 1930-31. During this period, conditions changed. Deposits grew by leaps and bounds, reflecting low commercial rates and the closing of two commercial banking institutions in New York City with large thrift accounts. The result was to add to genuine savers patrons whose prospective abode with the bank appeared but temporary. This plethora of funds, some of them undesirable in nature, caused the savings banks to reduce rates and to limit the size of accounts. The 4½ per cent rate in New York City was abandoned in the autumn of 1930, and less than a year later leading institutions further reduced the rate to 3½ per cent—the lowest since 1919—which other banks subsequently adopted. A number limited initial deposits.†

During these two years, difficult investment conditions obtained. General money rates were low; bond prices showed little stability and tended to decline; and real estate conditions were bad. In 1931, badly impaired rail earnings affected legal rail-bond prices very adversely; the European collapse in the middle of that year, and peak American bank failures added to the unsettlement in the securities markets. The Superintendent of Banks adopted an arbitrary basis of evaluating savings-bank security holdings. In 1930, new money went apparently roughly equally (in absolute amounts) into real estate loans, bonds, and deposits in other banks. The result was, of course, a relative decrease in the proportion of mortgage loans, and an increase in the other two. Thus liquidity improved, although the new bond money apparently went to a greater extent into rails than into utilities. In 1931, the new money went far more heavily into bonds than into mortgage loans, which again showed a relative decrease. But bond purchases centered on United States governments and utilities, rails and municipals showing a relative decline. But the 1931 bond figures must be used with caution; an arbitrary basis of evaluation probably under-

† [Footnote by Steiner.] Incidentally, the situation of the regular patron of the savings bank was rather ironical. Prior to 1929, he had helped pay the cost of inducing additional patronage, and later he paid again in a reduced rate when others gave it their patronage.

TABLE 55

CONDITION OF NEW YORK SAVINGS BANKS, DEC. 31, 1927-32

(000 omitted)

	1927	1928	1929	1930	1931	1932
Bonds and mortgages	$2,893,059	$3,133,511	$3,235,422	$3,356,665	$3,534,144	$3,529,042
Bond investments*	1,545,908	1,538,734	1,403,099	1,538,734	1,904,642	1,829,426
Promissory notes	18,643	29,121	18,973	11,412	5,590	4,348
Bankers' acceptances	10,956	7,645	7,034		3,470	
Banking houses and lots	55,868	61,312	68,069	73,596	79,859	83,591
Other real estate	1,503	2,342	8,629	15,131	26,422	75,548
Cash on deposit in banks and trust companies	131,773	109,675	115,811	199,734	194,874	242,757
Cash on hand	17,103	19,004	19,754	25,374	27,201	27,546
Total collectible interest	54,870	59,131	61,716	67,365	75,724	82,156
Other assets	1,124	3,651	1,362	1,867	2,214	2,676
Total Assets	$4,730,806	$4,964,126	$4,939,869	$5,428,469	$5,854,140	$5,897,089
Amount due depositors	$4,168,129	$4,411,126	$4,391,284	$4,796,224	$5,261,866	$5,316,775
Other liabilities	13,281	3,384	4,833	3,442	3,925	15,708
Surplus†	559,396	549,617	543,753	628,803	588,349	564,607
Total Liabilities	$4,730,806	$4,964,126	$4,939,869	$5,428,469	$5,854,140	$5,897,089
* Estimated market value; original cost	$1,522,735	$1,562,803	$1,459,464	$1,686,682	$2,001,038	$2,035,316

TABLE 55 *(Continued)*

Percentage distribution of principal assets (estimated market value‡)

	1927	1928	1929	1930	1931	1932
Bonds and mortgages	61.1	63.1	65.5	61.8	60.4	59.8
Bond investments:						
United States	8.0	6.7	4.6	4.4	6.0	6.5
Municipals	12.2	11.5	10.5	10.6	10.2	9.9
Rails	12.3	11.7	11.8	13.5	12.6	11.5
Public utilities		0.8	1.2	2.1	3.6	3.2
Land bank bonds	0.1	0.1	0.1	0.1	0.1	0.1
Port of N. Y. authority		0.1	0.1	0.1	0.2	0.2
Promissory notes	0.4	0.6	0.4	0.2	0.1	0.1
Cash and bankers' acceptances	3.4	2.7	2.9	4.1	3.9	4.6

† Estimated market value.

‡ Securities may be shown in four ways: par value, original cost, investment value (premium or discount amortized to maturity) and estimated market. The second and fourth are important for our present purpose, although the 1931 and 1932 figures above reflect the use of special methods of valuation.

states their total amount, as well as possibly misleads for the different categories. Yet even if this be the case, and bonds are included at artificially high figures, bond depreciation below cost had mounted in 1931 to $96,000,000 from the $56,000,000 of 1929, although 1930 had showed $148,000,000. Surplus, too, declined sharply, and stood at only 11 per cent of deposits in 1931, as compared with 12 per cent in 1928 and 1929, and 13 per cent in 1927, although it had again reached 13 per cent in 1930.‡

3. 1932-33. The economic collapse of 1931 and long continued depression were reflected in a loss of savings deposits, beginning in the fourth quarter. The net result was an increase of only $55,000,000 in deposits during 1932. During the year the banks further reduced the rate paid to depositors, reaching three per cent early in 1933. Certain banks again restricted the amount they would receive from any one depositor.

Despite the growth in total resources, both real estate loans and bond investments declined. All classes of bonds shared in the decline, with the exception of those issued by the United States and by New York State. In fact, bond depreciation mounted, reaching the record figure of $206,000,000, and surplus declined further to about 10.6 per cent of deposits. Difficulty with real estate loans is shown in the reduction in interest rates paid depositors in order to extend necessary assistance to borrowers who because of decreased earnings, experienced difficulty in meeting fixed charges on mortgaged property. It is reflected in the fact that other holdings of real estate other than banking house almost trebled during the year and equaled 1.3 per cent of assets. Yet in the face of this, the banks further increased their investment in banking houses, to 1.4 per cent of assets—a continued growth since 1927 which greatly exceeded the growth of deposits. On the other hand, the banks increased their cash holdings considerably to 4.6 per cent of deposits, thus substantially increasing their liquidity. This was the sole favorable factor shown in the investment results for the year.

In March, 1933, the bank holiday occurred, just prior to which several New York City savings banks had faced sub-

‡ [Footnote by Steiner.] How it did this in face of a deposit increase of $405,000,000 and the record security depreciation, is an unexplained mystery.

stantial withdrawals. When the suspension was lifted, the State Banking Department limited withdrawals, at first to $25 per week and then to $250, thus limiting pressure from depositors.

Present Situation of National Banks

A somewhat more thorough survey of certain features of the national bank statistics may now be made. The Comptroller of the Currency published two classes of data: in one part of his report, he classified national bank deposits into demand and time, with subclasses under each head; in another part, he gave separate information as to their "savings deposits." In response to an inquiry, Deputy Comptroller Fowler advised under date of August 17, 1925:

> The figures . . . represent deposits reported by national banks . . . as savings deposits in a special schedule called for on the report of condition blank for that date. The amount of these deposits ordinarily would be comparable with the amount shown under the heading of other time deposits. . . . The figures reported by national banks in this schedule are accepted as submitted, and in some instances include time certificates or other time deposits, which accounts for the discrepancy between the two amounts.

The Savings Bank Division of the American Bankers Association, it may be noted, prepares its figures from the time-deposit data, thus including all the time certificates of deposit.

Be that as it may, the Comptroller has for certain years prepared such figures for "savings deposits" as well as time deposits, and the increasing interest of national banks in the problem may thus be traced somewhat more closely from them than would otherwise be possible. Between 1912 and 1925 the number of national banks receiving "savings" deposits almost doubled, while the amount increased until it was over six times as great and was held by more than five times as many depositors. Part of the increase, it must not be forgotten, arises from the shift, during the period, from the use of certificates to deposit accounts. In 1925, 4,558 of the banks maintained separate savings departments, while they paid an average interest rate of 3.64 per cent to their depositors. The increase is shown in Table 56.

TABLE 56

SAVINGS DEPOSITS IN NATIONAL BANKS, 1912, 1925, AND 1932

	1912	1925	1932
Number of National Banks	7,372	8,070	6,150
Number reporting savings deposits	3,220	6,377	——
Number of savings depositors	2,600,610	11,867,948	14,149,732
Amount of savings deposits (000 omitted)	$719,640	$4,558,899	$6,199,120
Per cent of savings to total individual deposits	12.35	27.87	43.27

The increase is found in all sections. Because of the shift, just mentioned, from the use of certificates to deposit accounts, especially in the Western sections, the figures of "savings" deposits as distinct from time deposits unduly exaggerate the growth in those sections. They are of interest, however, and are accordingly set forth in Table 57, as prepared by the Comptroller, for the years 1913, 1923 and 1932. The remarkable increases shown in the percentage of total individual deposits are owing to the rapid increase of the accounts in states where previously little used, as well as to substantial further progress in other states.

A more detailed analysis of the present situation is now in order. Particularly does the query arise, what is the relative importance of the savings or time deposits in the larger city as distinct from the country banks? Despite the relatively large number of central reserve city and reserve city banks receiving savings deposits, the 1924 figures show that the time deposits of central reserve city banks are only about one-eighth their demand deposits, and of other reserve city banks only about one-third, although the time deposits of country banks are almost equal to their demand deposits. To take another method of analysis, less than 6 per cent of the time deposits of national banks are in institutions located in central reserve cities, somewhat more than 20 per cent in reserve city banks, and the remainder in country banks. In other words, the time deposit problem is, then, in large measure at least, a country-bank problem. This is shown clearly in Table 58.

This table throws further light upon the special interest

TABLE 57: SAVINGS DEPOSITS IN NATIONAL BANKS, 1913, 1923, AND 1932 BY SECTIONS

GROUP OF STATES	NUMBER OF NATIONAL BANKS	NUMBER REPORTING SAVINGS DEPOSITS	AMT. OF SAVINGS DEPOSITS (000 omitted)	PERCENTAGE OF TOTAL INDIVIDUAL DEPOSITS		
				Average	Lowest State	Highest State
			1913			
New England	453	145	$ 60,195	11.91	4.90	52.44
Eastern	1,653	1,120	373,545	17.57	4.87	31.36
Southern	1,505	550	107,697	15.15	4.46	44.41
Mid-Western	2,063	999	211,675	13.24	2.48	34.13
Western	1,280	338	21,744	4.96	1.38	11.51
Pacific	513	260	49,484	11.05	0.46	19.81
United States	7,473	3,416	824,777	14.15		
			1923			
New England	401	269	$ 355,750	29.57	22.64	64.78
Eastern	1,736	1,559	1,468,891	27.27	17.58	44.54
Southern	1,695	1,012	533,818	28.50	14.76	54.04
Mid-Western	2,223	1,790	847,586	24.85	16.03	37.79
Western	1,573	933	157,621	15.00	6.42	31.66
Pacific	608	517	281,289	25.27	20.17	37.12
United States	8,241	6,083	3,645,648	25.96		
			1932			
New England	350	—	$ 487,185	35.21	27.68	76.24
Eastern	1,623	—	1,983,838	34.39	22.15	58.21
Southern	1,265	—	511,524	29.56	20.56	44.50
Mid-Western	1,526	—	1,047,220	31.07	14.28	52.01
Western	983	—	165,781	19.20	11.96	35.57
Pacific	398	—	995,076	46.20	20.62	51.56
United States	6,150*	—	5,202,948†	34.22		

* Includes 4 national banks in Alaska and 1 in Hawaii. † Includes $12,324,000 for 5 banks in Possessions.

of national banks in the northeastern section in the problem. Only in the Eastern states do time deposits of country banks greatly exceed their demand deposits; in the Middle Western group, the excess is slight, and in the four remaining groups, the demand considerably exceeds the time deposits. In the Eastern group, too, the number of banks reporting savings deposits is relatively largest; but this does not mean that elsewhere country banks have no interest in the problem; the large majority of the banks report savings deposits, and their time deposits in no case represent a small item.

Nature of the Deposits

It will be noted that in the historical discussion above, reference has been made both to time deposits and to savings deposits. This was, in fact, done consciously. One of the stock objections raised, during the years after 1907 by those opposed to special protection for savings deposits, was that the term "savings deposits" embraced a number of different ideas, hence was not capable of precise definition. Yet those who discuss the treatment of time deposits held by "commercial" banks usually refer to such deposits as "savings." In their minds, they ally these deposits with those held by the mutual savings banks created a century ago to safeguard "the results of the accumulations of the provident poor." Accordingly the clue, in their opinion, to a proper treatment of these deposits held by commercial banks is to be found in the treatment accorded deposits in mutual savings banks, if the depositor is to be afforded the protection which he deserves and to which he is regarded as entitled. This view, it has already been noted, was opposed by over half the bankers approached by the Law Committee of the American Bankers Association in 1911. Likewise, most of the national and state bankers that responded to questions of the Senate Committee, in 1931, emphatically disagreed. Their answer to the question "do you believe it is desirable that time depositors receive special protection of some sort or other not accorded to demand depositors?" unqualifiedly was in the negative. In fact, this was true of twenty-one out of the twenty-eight general banker

TABLE 58

DEMAND, TIME, AND SAVINGS DEPOSITS IN NATIONAL BANKS, JUNE 30, 1932, BY CLASSES OF BANKS AND SECTIONS

(In thousands of dollars)

	NUMBER OF NATIONAL BANKS	NUMBER OF SAVINGS DEPOSITORS	AMOUNT OF SAVINGS DEPOSITS $	AMOUNT OF TIME DEPOSITS $	AMOUNT OF DEMAND DEPOSITS $
Central Reserve Cities	18	765,329	170,139	384,993	2,038,990
Reserve Cities	239	5,093,401	1,990,750	2,786,676	2,987,029
Country Banks*	5,893	8,291,002	3,042,059	4,093,971	2,914,634
New England	344	915,228	395,092	442,796	321,339
Eastern	1,556	3,603,534	1,598,508	1,841,056	940,473
Southern	1,213	970,539	312,714	512,792	548,528
Mid-Western	1,457	1,975,505	499,606	849,937	633,333
Western	947	351,962	78,869	231,449	280,075
Pacific	371	421,628	144,946	200,187	176,565
United States†	6,150	14,149,732	5,202,948	7,265,640	7,940,653

* Country Banks total and United States total include five national banks—1 in Hawaii and 4 in Alaska—that are not given in this table. These 5 banks have 52,606 savings depositories, $12,324,000 in savings deposits, $15,754,000 in time deposits and $14,321,000 in demand deposits.

† Only deposits evidenced by savings pass books.

replies, as well as of most of the interviews. Such bankers as gave further explanation of their position tended to feel that the interest received by the time depositor was ample reward, and one went so far as to hold specifically that it included an insurance premium against possible greater risk of loss.

Yet the problem or task is by no means so simple as either of these extreme positions assumes. There are strong grounds for feeling that time deposits in commercial banks today partake of an intermediate character—that they are between the orthodox interest-bearing savings deposits of the mutual savings banks in years gone by, and the older non-interest-bearing checking accounts of the commercial banks, and contain an admixture of both. True, part of the great increase in time deposits of commercial banks must undoubtedly be explained as owing to increased saving. Coupled with this is the increasing pressure upon distributors of more or less worthless securities to curtail their activities, and the aggressive attitude of banks as a whole in soliciting "savings" deposits by offering convenient facilities and by vigorous advertising campaigns. Moreover, if the increase in time deposits is compared with the increased cost of living and general level of prices, it will be found that the increase in real purchasing power saved has not been phenomenal. It has been absolutely necessary to save more to buy as much.

Intermediate Character of Time Deposits

Competent opinion is of the view that, in part, the great growth of time deposits already noted reflects a change in form rather than in substance. Some of these deposits, in other words, represent less active deposits of a commercial nature, instead of, perhaps, more active deposits of an essentially savings nature. Some deposits are placed in the time, rather than in the demand, category, at the depositor's instance, perhaps, because he wishes the higher interest return that banks can pay thereon, and with the bank's acquiescence, because it has a lowered reserve requirement under the Federal Reserve Act—3 per cent now, instead of 13, 10, and 7 per cent, as might otherwise be the case. In member banks, time deposits are the only ones on which interest will be allowed; hence, time deposits will tend to be maximized; but city banks often solicit more actively, although they perhaps have held down the volume of time deposits somewhat by increasing tendency toward allowing interest on average daily balances in checking accounts. In the large city bank, both savings deposits and time deposits of the intermediate stamp, may perhaps, more readily be distinguished. Many such banks have compound interest departments in which they receive largely the funds of small savers; but they receive also other time deposits, in many cases in the commercial department. The latter represent special funds set aside for a definite purpose or for emergencies. They reflect in considerable measure the rapid accumulation of working capital—the result, in part, of heavy post-war funding of short-term loans, in part, of recent developments in industrial methods, such as hand-to-mouth buying and improved transportation facilities. But, even in such banks, a certain number of demand depositors undoubtedly use the compound interest department for capital accumulations, which are drawn after dividend dates as occasion for investment arises, and some of these deposits are trust funds. Other depositors, again, tend to use savings accounts as semicommercial accounts, making frequent deposits and withdrawals. That a considerable part of time deposits is of a nature different from the old-style savings deposits, is seen by the fact that about half of the general bankers favoring special protection wish to limit it to savings as distinct from other time deposits.

"Semicommercial" Facilities

The call for semicommercial facilities is seen in the growth of so-called "special savings accounts" received by certain institutions. Started in Southern California some years ago, the thought of permitting a limited checking privilege against accounts on which the bank reserves the right to require notice of withdrawal, but on which it allows a higher rate of interest, has spread to other sections of the country. In fact, in the Comptroller's 1911 survey, 810 out of the 6,812 national banks stated that they permitted checking against their savings accounts.

They were distributed as follows: Northeast, 23; Eastern states, 303; Southern states, 211; Middle Western states, 183; Western states, 74; and Pacific states, 16. An outline survey made in 1925 for the National Association of Mutual Savings Banks shows the following results, reported chiefly by Federal Reserve authorities:

Boston district—15 smaller Massachusetts trust companies mentioned (see Commissioner's annual report, data on time deposits in commercial department); also a few of the smaller country national banks believed to be carrying them.

Philadelphia district—6 small trust companies mentioned.

Chicago district—several institutions, with a recent modification in the "combination checking-savings account" of one bank.

Cleveland, Richmond, Atlanta, Minneapolis, Kansas City, and Dallas districts—no record of such accounts.

Dallas district—no record of such accounts, but a few banks allow savings accounts to be combined with checking accounts in determining minimum balance required to exempt from service charge.

Later Inquiries Confirm These Results

Even the analysis just made—indicating that in many banks time deposits are of a hybrid or twofold character—cannot be applied too rigidly to all parts of the country. In some sections, the nonsavings characteristic even seems predominant. Thus the Chairman of the Federal Reserve Bank of Kansas City states: "The great bulk of time deposits in banks of this District consists of more or less temporarily idle funds deposited on time certificate or under agreement to give notice prior to withdrawal." The use of time certificates to attract outside funds in the Northwestern banks is well known.

Analysis of Activity of Accounts

The analysis which has been made, indicating that time deposits are in considerable measure of an intermediate character, is borne out by the statistics available in several Northeastern mutual savings bank states which publish separate figures for the savings as distinct from the commercial departments of other institutions.[8] Study of certain Massachusetts data, taken from the Bank Commissioner's annual reports for the years ending October 31, 1920, 1924 and 1931, shows the following with respect to amounts deposited and withdrawn (000,000 omitted):

TABLE 59

VELOCITY OF MASSACHUSETTS SAVINGS DEPOSITS

(In millions of dollars)

	SAVINGS BANK			SAVINGS DEPARTMENTS OF TRUST COMPANIES		
	1920	1924	1931	1920	1924	1931
Average deposits held during year	$1,160	$1,477	$2,132	$ 132	$ 141	$ 202
Amount deposited during year	318	345	372	127	84	85
Amount withdrawn during year	275	324	414	101	75	97

Figures for number of transactions, instead of amounts involved, are as follows (000 omitted):

	1920	1924	1931	1920	1924	1931
Number of accounts open at close of year	2,593	2,786	2,924	470	402	458
Number of deposits made during year	4,766	4,972	4,220	1,600	1,080	1,007
Number of withdrawals made during year	2,076	2,752	3,724	711	646	868

When amounts are considered, evidently, deposits in savings departments are over twice as active as accounts in savings banks. When the number of transactions are analyzed, the savings bank depositor makes on the average less than two deposits a year, and less than one withdrawal, while the savings-department depositor makes over two and one-half deposits a year and one and one-half withdrawals. While these Massachusetts figures are by no means ideal in view of the trust-company situation in that state several years ago, Connecticut figures show a similar tendency. Inquiry of bankers leads to the belief that the difference has an actual basis in the facts stated in the preceding section

[8] *Savings Bank Journal,* Oct., 1925, and later issues.

and is not merely because a depositor in a savings department may carry also a checking account in the same institution, and hence visit the bank more frequently.

Not only is this difference between savings banks and savings departments found, but apparently fashions in savings themselves have changed. Emphasis today is placed, not upon provision for old age, but upon saving for a particular and immediate purpose—home ownership, travel, etc. Massachusetts mutual savings bank figures over the years show distinctly greater activity with the passage of time, especially since the war.[9] This is evident from Table 60.

Effect on the Problem

In short, many of the time deposits held by "commercial" banks have a commercial, and not a savings tinge, and cannot be identified with the latter group. If this is the case, the query arises, should these time deposits be treated on exactly the same basis as savings deposits in mutual savings banks? It must be borne in mind, however, that a large part is in the nature of savings, and it is better to give too much protection than too little. An average cannot well be struck; if care were not taken, the result would be merely to arrive at a type too low for the savings group, yet too high or rigid for the other group, hence typical of neither, nor satisfactory to them.

This does not mean that such deposits should be treated along exactly the same lines as were originally laid down for mutual savings banks. It has been shown that the latter's deposits are today much more active than heretofore. In view of this fact, should they obey strictly the old investment maxims formulated once more in 1907 by Andrew Mills, President of the Dry Dock Savings Institution of New York, which were as follows?

First: Security, as absolute as human judgment can determine.
Second: The first being assured, then the security yielding the highest income.
Third: Availability, so that in case of necessity the security can be disposed of without needless sacrifice.

[9] *Savings Bank Journal,* Oct. 1925, and later issues.

These canons of safety, liquidity, and yield, especially the third, must be interpreted to apply rather to the general investments of the institution as a whole than to each individual security it holds; but, when so interpreted, do the canons not lose much

TABLE 60

DEPOSITS IN MASSACHUSETTS MUTUAL SAVINGS BANKS

AMOUNTS *(000,000 omitted)*

	On deposit Oct. 31	Deposited during year	Withdrawn during year
1931	$2,159	$372	$414
1930	2,105	386	415
1929	2,036	385	419
1928	1,977	418	368
1927	1,842	395	343
1926	1,710	361	344
1925	1,618	369	341
1924	1,520	345	324
1920	1,207	318	275
1910	771	140	140
1900	540	93	90
1890	354	72	65
1881	230	40	40

NUMBERS *(000 omitted)*

	Accounts open Oct. 31	Opened during year	Closed during year	Deposits during year	Withdrawals during year
1931	2,924	294	315	4,221	3,724
1930	2,945	203	307	4,586	3,485
1929	2,949	314	294	4,888	3,225
1928	2,929	316	303	4,970	3,189
1927	2,916	330	287	5,105	2,966
1926	2,874	331	284	5,108	2,885
1925	2,827	329	287	4,996	2,852
1924	2,786	337	298	4,972	2,752
1920	2,593	356	290	4,766	2,976
1910	2,101	285	225	2,425	1,715
1900	1,535	—	—	1,771	1,328
1890	1,084	—	—	1,061	726
1881	674	—	—	616	420

of their force, and does the problem not require a rational approach rather than the sentimental one so often given to it? On the other hand, however, does it not call, and just as strongly, for some measure of protection to the time depositor, instead of no special distinction at all, as is now so often the case? The problem, in other words, becomes this: how much protection, and what kind? And the answer depends, in considerable measure at least, upon the three other aspects or features already mentioned—the effect upon the individual institution, the service to the community, and the relation to the banking system. The protective aspect cannot be divorced from them, nor can it alone be made decisive.

Tendency to Self-Investing

Nor is this conclusion as to treatment to be accorded time deposits vitiated by the tendency which some bankers believe is now manifest toward greater direct investment by the saver himself, instead of mere deposit in a bank which invests, so to speak, on his behalf. They profess to see considerable diversion of funds hitherto finding their way into the bank as time deposits, into (1) purchase of real-estate mortgages and bonds, and (2) purchase of lots in real-estate developments, as well as (3) purchase of various articles for the home on the installment plan. Added to this is the fact that a booming stock market always attracts widespread participation by the small speculator led on by the lure of large profits.

Time vs. Demand Deposits

This discussion, it will be observed, assumes that time and savings deposits cannot be completely distinguished. This was one of the stock objections early made to special protection, although then made from a purely objective point of view. Savings deposits were regarded as incapable of precise definition, embracing the thoughts of requirements of notice of withdrawal by the depositor, presentation of pass-book, or other evidence of obligation at time of withdrawal, and payment of interest on the deposit. The present subjective approach intensifies the difficulty of making a rigid distinction. Restriction of the use of the word "savings" results merely in creation of competing "thrift" departments, while limitation of the amount to the credit of one depositor is of but limited efficacy. Provision for time deposits—perhaps on certificate—in the commercial department, alongside of savings deposits in the savings department, does not necessarily keep the latter "pure"; and, while this is often urged as a solution, if care be not taken, the result may even be to make the savings department provision a dead letter, as practically obtains in Texas today. Most savers, in such cases, may be without any protection whatsoever, despite the apparent intent of the law. Everything considered, better too much included than too little. Hence a provision along present California or present Massachusetts lines would seem best. Such a requirement would permit the banks to receive time deposits in their commercial departments, but would avoid the other extreme found in Texas.

New phase of problem.—A new phase of the entire savings- and time-deposit problem has come to the front as the result of the adoption of the Banking Act of 1933.[10]

This Act, as elsewhere explained, had been undertaken partly as a result of the feeling that the numerous bank failures of preceding years had inflicted upon the depositor—particularly upon the time depositor—a very serious and unmerited hardship. This hardship was found in the fact that so large a proportion of persons had had their funds "tied up," or rendered unavailable, as a result of the numerous bank failures and, in spite of all that had been said with regard to the protection of individual savings, had, nevertheless, found themselves, if anything, worse off than the demand depositor; inasmuch as the latter had been able, in many cases, to protect himself by reason of superior knowledge of events, through the hasty withdrawal of his funds from banks which were recognized as being in difficult straits. Owing to difficulties of treatment, elsewhere recognized (see Part I already referred to), the Senate Banking Committee which originated the Glass bill, afterward the Banking Act of 1933, had determined to limit itself to a few important changes, as follows:

1. Establishment of a liquidating corporation, whose duty it should be to take over the assets of failed or closed banks, pay for them in available funds immediately transferred to the de-

[10] See detailed account of Banking Act of 1933 in Part I.

positors, and then proceed to liquidate the assets for the purpose of reimbursement.

2. Increase of reserves held against time and savings deposits up to an amount equal to reserves required against demand deposits in any given bank.

3. Segregation of the assets of banks in such a way as to give to savings and time deposits a first lien upon assets in which their deposits had been invested.

These proposals, after long and difficult discussion and negotiation, underwent great changes as follows:

1. In place of the liquidating corporation, provision was made for a depositors' insurance corporation, whose function it should be to guarantee the depositor and indemnify him under specified conditions and at specified dates.

2. The provision for an increase of reserve against savings and time deposits was dropped.

3. The provisions calling for segregation of assets held behind savings and time deposits were, likewise, dropped.

These changes in effect, amounted to the substitution of a blanket provision of guarantee (both for time and for demand deposits), in place of the program of protection designed to care for the interests of the small saver and of the time depositor.

Thus enacted, it has been supposed by many persons that the Banking Act of 1933 practically revolutionized the entire deposit problem and rendered a great deal of the discussions of time deposits obsolete. This, however, is an erroneous assumption. It remains to be seen how banks will be affected by the necessity imposed upon them in the new law of regularly paying into the hands of a quasi-public corporation the amounts levied upon them for the purpose of making good deficiencies owing to the failure of banks. It is a proposal, which, as we have seen elsewhere, has never been successful in American experience among the states, and may turn out to be as unsuccessful in Federal experience as it has in state. The actual outcome remains to be ascertained, but, in the meanwhile, we may confidently expect that no matter what transformations in banking structure may grow out of the guaranty-of-deposit plan, success in carrying the burden imposed by bank failures will depend entirely upon the adoption of a sound policy in the application of funds left on deposit.

In order to prevent losses from becoming excessive—so excessive as to break down the guarantee fund, even greater care and foresight than has been devoted to the subject in times past, will be essential, in order to prevent banks, *a*) from incurring heavy depreciation of assets, such as took place between 1929 and 1933, and, *b*) from becoming so extensively frozen as to be unable to realize upon assets presumed to be sufficiently liquid to permit their holders to meet such savings-deposit claims as might be presented to them for cashing. It can hardly be too strongly insisted that observance of these requirements must be more strict than ever if the banking system is to enjoy even a nominal measure of success, in complying with the terms of the new "guarantee" section of the Banking Act of 1933.

Although permitted under the new law, to become members of the Federal Reserve system, many mutual savings banks are indisposed to join, for their own protection, by reason of certain requirements. This fact obviously strengthens the opinion entertained by many, that existing banks are likely to encounter great difficulty in successfully complying with the guarantee project. Be this as it may, their chances of success in so complying must obviously be dependent upon the faithful observance of the lessons of past experience. No guarantee will serve to protect a whole system of banks from the consequences of general mistakes committed by the members at large, and the responsibilities involved in safeguarding the funds of banks subject to such a guarantee may easily result in a tendency to restrict rather than to accentuate the growth of time deposits, which has been so outstanding a feature of recent years. It is evident that our experience in this field has not yet been sufficient to furnish conclusive evidence regarding a desirable course of action, and in these circumstances, the guaranty-of-deposits project must continue for some time to come to be merely an experimental effort to reassure public opinion, the success of which will depend entirely upon the observance of canons which, if strictly followed, would render such expedient unnecessary.

Building and loan associations and the savings problem.—In any phase of the treatment of savings deposits, in dealing with the question of time and savings deposits, it has been assumed throughout that such deposits were to include only recognized liabilities on the books of regularly organized banks. Of recent years, however, there has appeared, to complicate the whole savings question, a new phase of the use of funds for investment, particularly the use of funds in small amounts, or in the hands of small savers. This problem is presented in its most acute form in connection with the experience of building and loan associations. These associations were originally organized as enterprises designed to facilitate the coöperative building and ownership of houses. Coöperative groups were formed consisting of persons of somewhat similar means, whose regular payments into the treasury of the association constituted the funds from which advances were made to those members who desired to use them in construction, or where the supply of funds was inadequate to meet the demand of those who were willing to pay most, by way of premium for the award of the funds. The movement, in this shape, soon lost its early connections and gradually developed into a system of real-estate investment in that form; although not, perhaps, as fully entitled to hearty support and approbation as was the building and loan association in its original aspect, it nevertheless represented a desirable way of applying savings in connection with the development of real estate.

Building and loan associations, however, soon began to compete actively with one another for support and this competition frequently led to bidding for funds in which an effort was made to induce savers and owners of savings to shift their funds from one direction to another, usually as the result of an offer of high interest. From this beginning, it was easy for the movement to develop into a process of competition which took effect through extending to the saver or owner of funds other inducements, such as the return of his money practically when desired, and the like. From this it was easy to reach a position in which the building and loan association held itself out as practically a savings bank, receiving the funds on deposit, paying interest on them, and normally undertaking to return the "deposit" upon request.

"Savings" Business of Associations

Such building and loan associations frequently issued to their customers small account books, closely resembling in appearance the deposit books issued by savings banks, and not infrequently described as "savings bank" books or "deposit" books. Such books usually contained a printed proviso, or agreement, often required by the law of the state in which the association was organized, stating that the recipient of the book was a stockholder in the association, not a depositor with it; his claim, therefore, being for shares of stock and such dividends as might be declared thereon, while an effort to realize cash at any time could be permitted only to the extent that the association was in a position to obtain cash through new subscriptions to stock or through in-payments upon its mortgages or other assets. To these provisions the customer usually paid no attention. Indeed, he frequently did not know of their existence, but regarded himself as a "depositor" and viewed the building and loan association as a savings institution.

Unforeseen results of this state of things have been revealed from time to time and, perhaps, never so clearly as has been the case since the panic of 1929 and the shrinkage of real-estate values which followed it. The effect of this shrinkage has been to render many real-estate mortgages uncollectible, while the property underlying such mortgages has shrunk in value by enormous percentages. The result has been the collapse of many building and loan associations, and the development of unsound and insolvent conditions among them has been such as to parallel in some states the existence of similar conditions among the banks. Restoration of sound deposit banking, and particularly of sound savings-bank management and time-deposit banking will probably necessitate in the future a general reform of the building and loan situation.

In this discussion, therefore, it has been thought best to devote some detailed attention to the status of building and loan associations with a view to ascertaining the precise position of these organizations.[11]

Building and Loan Associations in the East North Central States

Since 1890 the building and loan association has been of ever increasing importance as a savings institution in the United States. The total assets of all associations in 1893 amounted to $528,825,885; in 1930 the total was $8,824,119,159. During this period the number of associations increased from 5,838 to 11,767, and the membership multiplied eightfold, increasing from 1,745,725 to 12,336,754.[12]

A building and loan association may be defined as "a mutual financial institution usually operated under articles of incorporation issued by the state and composed of members who thus associate themselves together for mutual benefit and financial aid."[13] The Commissioner of Internal Revenue stated in 1921 that any association entitled to tax exemption under Federal law must have two characteristics: It must be mutual, and it must be operated so that substantially all of its business would be confined to making loans to bona fide shareholders.[14]

These definitions, however, do not explain fully the nature of the building and loan association. Such an association, besides being a mutual organization which makes loans to bona fide shareholders, makes loans to its members generally on real-estate security. The borrower, at the time the loan is granted, buys an equivalent amount of stock on which dues are payable weekly or monthly. When the stock matures the loan is automatically cancelled and the borrower is relieved of his obligation. In most states the associations are allowed also to make straight mortgage loans of small amount. In many states, associations may invest their surplus funds in bonds, but the amount so placed is usually small.

[11] The study of building and loan associations has been prepared by Mr. J. A. Griswold.

[12] U. S. Building and Loan League, Secretary's report, *U. S. Building and Loan Annals*, 1930.

[13] *Cyclopedia of Building and Loan Associations* (5th ed., 1923), p. 9.

[14] Revenue Act of 1921, Article 515.

In view of the great increase in assets it would appear that building and loan associations are becoming increasingly popular as depositories for savings. This is evidenced more strongly in some sections of the country than in others. The Middle Atlantic states and the East North Central group head the list in number of associations as well as in assets and membership. Here we are particularly concerned with the East North Central States.

Growth of Associations in the Midwest

The growth of associations in the states of Illinois, Michigan, and Wisconsin has been phenomenal. The greatest increase in assets occurred in Ohio. In 1891 the assets of all associations in the state of Ohio amounted to over $50,000,000, while in 1930 the total stood at more than $1,000,000,000. Illinois associations experienced a somewhat similar growth increasing their total assets from $81,760,000, in 1891, to $470,000,000 in 1930. Although the early growth in Wisconsin was slow, the assets increased about $287,000,000 during the period from 1891 to 1930. Michigan, as contrasted with her sister states of this group, has shown herself not so well adapted to associations. The assets of Michigan associations grew from $11,584,000, in 1891, to $165,269,560 in 1930.

This growth of building and loan associations gives rise to two questions. The association is a mutual savings institution that loans money to its own stockholders on comparatively long-time real-estate security. Since the growth of these organizations has been marked, particularly in the states of the North Central group, it seems logical to conclude that an ever increasing amount of the savings of these states has been invested in loans on real estate. The question then arises: To what extent have the savings of the North Central states been placed in building and loan associations?

In order to arrive at the relationship between savings placed with building and loan associations and with other institutions, it was necessary to consider two factors. The first was the amount of savings paid into the associations. These payments took three forms: installments on running stock, the money paid for prepaid and paid-up stock, and straight deposits with the associations, permitted in some states. In arriving at the desired figures the items were taken from the consolidated balance sheet, published each year by the auditors of the respective states, and added.

TABLE 61

OHIO, 1908-1931

(Amounts in millions of dollars)

YEAR	SAVINGS IN BUILDING & LOANS ASSNS.	SAVINGS DEPOSITS IN BANKS	SAVINGS IN BLDG. & LOAN ASSNS. AS A PERCENTAGE OF TOTAL SAVINGS
	$	$	%
1908	114	173	39.8
1909	120	294	29.1
1910	130	317	29.2
1911	164	327	31.5
1912	181	340	37.0
1913	196	221	46.9
1914	197	421	31.9
1915	204	450	31.1
1916	236	585	28.6
1917	275	682	28.7
1918	315	677	31.8
1919	339	731	31.7
1920	406	790	33.1
1921	468	813	38.1
1922	496	826	37.5
1923	567	968	36.9
1924	637	1,044	37.8
1925	735	1,120	39.6
1926	805	1,145	41.4
1927	922	1,219	43.0
1928	1,113	1,256	51.5
1929	1,155	1,303	46.9
1930	1,107	1,283	46.3
1931	1,015	1,075	48.6

The second factor to be considered is the total amount of savings in the community. The figures for the various states were arrived at by combining the data on savings from all reporting institutions which received savings deposits. This figure was considered to represent approximately the total savings of the community. Of course this total does not include invest-

TABLE 62

WISCONSIN, 1899-1931

(Amounts in millions of dollars)

YEAR	SAVINGS IN BUILDING & LOAN ASSNS.	SAVINGS DEPOSITS IN BANKS	SAVINGS IN BLDG. & LOAN ASSNS. AS A PERCENTAGE OF TOTAL SAVINGS
	$	$	%
1899	3	33	8.5
1900	3	36	7.7
1901	3	51	5.5
1902	3	58	4.6
1903	3	35	7.9
1904	3	39	7.4
1905	4	43	9.9
1906	3	64	5.0
1907	4	74	4.6
1908	3	88	3.5
1909	4	101	3.6
1910	4	132	3.0
1911	5	133	3.7
1912	6	126	4.3
1913	7	134	4.9
1914	10	172	5.6
1915	11	179	5.9
1916	15	214	6.6
1917	17	235	6.9
1918	22	226	9.0
1919	27	273	8.8
1920	36	370	8.8
1921	46	326	12.0
1922	59	351	14.3
1923	83	395	17.5
1924	105	411	20.9
1925	133	356	27.2
1926	162	366	30.6
1927	195	498	28.2
1928	227	493	31.5
1929	256	485	34.5
1930	272	459	37.2
1931	258	311	45.6

ments in stocks, bonds or insurance policies; but in so far as we are interested in discovering the relationship between savings deposits in banks and in building and loan associations, it was not deemed necessary to include these other types of investment. What is sought is to trace the relationship that exists

TABLE 63

ILLINOIS, 1899-1931

(Amounts in millions of dollars)

YEAR	SAVINGS IN BUILDING & LOAN ASSNS.	SAVINGS DEPOSITS IN BANKS	SAVINGS IN BLDG. & LOAN ASSNS. AS A PERCENTAGE OF TOTAL SAVINGS
	$	$	%
1899	39	47	45.3
1900	34	71	32.5
1901	32	103	23.7
1902	30	104	22.5
1903	30	151	16.4
1904	32	177	15.1
1905	31	213	12.2
1906	35	228	13.8
1907	28	219	11.0
1908	41	222	15.6
1909	44	275	13.8
1910	48	308	14.7
1911	52	349	13.0
1912	56	380	12.6
1913	62	320	16.2
1914	68	440	13.4
1915	74	432	14.6
1916	79	373	17.4
1917	87	436	16.6
1918	91	625	12.7
1919	97	685	12.5
1920	103	801	11.3
1921	133	877	13.2
1922	154	906	13.6
1923	176	1,035	14.5
1924	210	1,126	15.6
1925	247	1,252	16.4
1926	272	1,280	18.6
1927	301	1,211	19.9
1928	327	1,593	17.0
1929	349	1,359	20.9
1930	366	1,302	21.8
1931	358	1,031	25.7

between the savings deposited with various institutions. This is done by computing the percentage of the total savings comprised in the deposits in building and loan associations.

In the State of Ohio there has been a steady increase in both the amount and the percentage of savings placed with the build-

TABLE 64

MICHIGAN, 1896-1931

(Amounts in millions of dollars)

YEAR	SAVINGS IN BUILDING & LOAN ASSNS.	SAVINGS DEPOSITS IN BANKS	SAVINGS IN BLDG. & LOAN ASSNS. AS A PERCENTAGE OF TOTAL SAVINGS
	$	$	%
1896	9	49	16.0
1897	9	56	14.3
1898	9	64	12.4
1899	9	75	10.2
1900	8	82	9.1
1901	9	86	9.0
1902	8	106	7.2
1903	—	100	—
1904	—	111	—
1905	11	125	8.1
1906	12	134	7.9
1907	13	137	8.5
1908	13	151	8.1
1909	14	170	7.9
1910	16	191	7.6
1911	18	—	—
1912	19	212	8.4
1913	20	224	8.3
1914	24	297	7.5
1915	24	378	5.9
1916	—	491	—
1917	31	—	—
1918	34	623	5.1
1919	38	544	6.5
1920	47	646	7.7
1921	54	613	8.4
1922	59	769	7.0
1923	61	742	7.6
1924	80	673	10.6
1925	96	701	12.0
1926	113	658	10.7
1927	127	800	13.0
1928	143	—	—
1929	161	1,015	13.7
1930	167	1,024	14.0
1931	165	944	14.9

ing and loan associations. In 1908, the first year for which savings figures are available in the auditor's reports, 39.8 per cent of the savings, or $114,000,000, were in the hands of the building and loan associations. The lowest point was reached in 1916 when the percentage fell to 28.6 per cent. From that date there has been a fairly steady gain by the building and loan associations, so that by 1931 they held 48.6 per cent of the total savings deposits in the state.

In the State of Wisconsin, building and loan associations had a small beginning. In the first report of 1899, associations held only $3,000,000, or 8.5 per cent of the total savings in the state. In 1910 this percentage fell as low as 3.0 per cent, but the absolute amount had increased to slightly over $4,000,000 dollars. After 1918, there was a remarkable growth, as a result of which, in 1931, we find 45.6 per cent of the total savings in building and loan associations.

The first comparable data for Illinois appear in 1899. In that year, 45.3 per cent, or $39,000,000, of the savings were in the building and loan associations, while savings in banks amounted to $47,000,000. Contrary to the experience of the other states, the percentage of savings held by building and loan associations declined relative to total savings. In 1920 the associations held only 11.3 per cent of the savings, or $103,000,000. After that year the percentage began to increase and in 1931, the associations held $358,000,000, or 25.7 per cent of the total savings.

The first comparable figures for total savings and deposits in building and loan associations in Michigan appeared in 1896. In that year building and loan associations held 16 per cent of the total savings. By 1931 the amount had grown to $165,000,000, but in relation to total savings, this sum represented only 15 per cent. It seems fair to conclude that building and loan associations do not play a very important rôle in Michigan.

From the foregoing data it may be concluded that building and loan associations as institutions for saving are increasing in importance in the East North Central states. The greatest growth has taken place in Ohio, where the associations are allowed to receive ordinary savings deposits on the same terms as banks. In Wisconsin, the growth has been at an accelerated rate since 1923, whereas before that year the associations were of little importance. Illinois shows some growth of dollar amounts, but the associations carry a smaller percentage of total savings. Since 1920, however, the amount of savings that they have taken in has increased steadily. The building and loan associations in Michigan have grown in recent years, but as yet, they are of little importance as savings institutions.

State Laws and Investment

As has been said, the building and loan associations have grown tremendously in the last few years. This means that an ever increasing amount of the country's savings has been used for purposes of real-estate development. Thus, the expansion of real-estate development has been encouraged by the building and loan associations. In far too many cases the associations have been the tools of selfish real-estate interests, although on the whole, most associations are guided by well-meaning officials.

One situation that makes for this expansion of real-estate development is the laxness and lack of uniformity of the various state laws. The nature of the building and loan associations makes it imperative to have an outlet for the funds which are paid in; the states have endeavored to regulate the forms which these loans shall take. The majority of states allow loans to be made on first mortgages, while a few allow second mortgages as well. In addition, the courts have held that these loans need not be confined to members, but may be made to non-members.[15] All states allow loans on personal security to the stockholders up to the value of the shares held. In only three states may loans be made on personal property. In one state, loans may be made on any security in accordance with the by-laws.

Under the limits set by state laws, the associations offer three different types of loans for the convenience of their borrowers: (1) The commonest type is the loan made on subscription to shares of stock in the association. This loan is paid off on the amortization principle, the dividends and weekly payments of the borrower being applied to this end. (2) Straight loans are

[15] Ackley vs. Peoples Savings Association of Toledo (293 Fed. Rep. 392).

often made where such a practice is lawful. In this case loans are made without stock subscription. (3) The split loan is partially a straight loan and partially one on stock subscription, so arranged as conveniently to meet the requirements of the borrower.

Easy Incorporation

Besides these lax laws regarding the types of loans that may be made by associations, the multiplication of associations is encouraged by easy incorporation. In thirteen states three persons may organize a building and loan association; five organizers are required in eleven states, and in the others the number varies from three to ten. Since the basic idea of a building and loan association is coöperative credit, it would seem that the states which allow associations to be formed with so few organizers are defeating the purpose of the whole movement by placing the associations on a commercial plane. In the original associations, a much larger number of organizers was required in order to insure operation on a coöperative basis.

State laws are also different in many other particulars. The qualification of directors ranges all the way from the requirement of one share of stock to leaving the decision "up to" the by-laws of the association; and, as was pointed out above, although the associations are expected to lend their funds under one of the regular building and loan plans, in practically all states excess funds may be used for straight loans. In addition, the problem of contingent reserves has not been studied with sufficient care by those responsible for the regulation of the associations. Most states require the building up of reserves, but the amount required is often inadequate. On the whole the state laws are very unsatisfactory and really encourage the organization and growth of building and loan associations without setting any limits to expansion.

In many cases building and loan associations, in order to make themselves as accessible to the borrower as possible, employ a "conveyancer," whose duty it is to obtain borrowers for the association, for which he receives a commission. In many cases the conveyancer is a real-estate dealer, in which case it is to his interest to arrange for a loan in order to complete his real-estate transaction. In some associations the conveyancer extended highly unsatisfactory loans, thus weakening the association and at the same time drawing more of the funds of the community into real-estate development.

Overappraisal

In many instances the property is appraised too high. "The whole subject of appraisal is of such fundamental importance in building and loan work that the fortunes of an association may rise or fall with changes in appraisal policy."[16] Many of the larger associations engage disinterested experts to appraise the property. These appraisals usually are arrived at scientifically, for the reputation of the individual or firm depends on their use of good judgment. Many of the smaller associations cannot afford such service and rely on the judgment of their own member to whom they pay a small fee. In answer to inquiries, several officers of smaller associations merely stated that they "used their own heads" in arriving at the value of a piece of property. In case the appraisal was outside the community, they usually consulted the local banker. The most common method used was the comparative method in which the property is appraised according to the most recent sales in the community. This method may be satisfactory when business is active, but in a period when sales are few and far between, or the value of real estate is dropping rapidly, it obviously leads to overvaluation.

In addition to making high appraisals, associations often loan too much on the property, that is, too large a percentage of the appraised value. The average association usually loans between 40 and 50 per cent of the appraised value, while in some cases loans as high as 70 and 80 per cent have been made. The policy of loaning over 50 per cent of the appraised value is, of course, rash and fortunately is not the common practice.

Besides the eagerness—and the laxity—in extending loans,

[16] Clark, H. F., and Chase, F. A., *Elements of Building and Loan Associations* (Macmillan, 1925), p. 230.

there is still another way in which these associations tend to foster real-estate development. This is by attempts to get loanable funds. The best way to get such funds is through advertising. Most of the building and loan associations use the "by-word-of-mouth" method, wherein the directors endeavor to make as many contacts as possible. Newspapers get their share of advertising, direct solicitation through the mail is also very popular, and radio advertising has been used in many cases. In these publicity campaigns three points generally are stressed: dividends, safety, and availability of funds.

Dividends are paid to stockholders whether they are borrowers or not. Most of the profits are distributed in this manner, except those reserved for expenses and for the contingent fund. In many advertisements these dividends are compared either directly or indirectly to the rate of interest paid on savings by banks. As far back as 1852 there were complaints about this type of advertising. One New York association advertised: "These associations are destined to take the place of savings institutions; for whilst the latter pay 4-5% interest, building and loan associations pay 15-20% interest."[17] Today the claim of high dividends is still made, although the records of the convention of the United States Building and Loan League indicate that two per cent above the bank rate is all that can be promised.[18] At present associations generally advertise a return of from five to six per cent on investments.

Depositors vs Stockholders

A second point that building and loan associations stress to their customers is "safety for savings." Whether intentionally or not, the purchaser of shares of stock is led to believe that he is placing his money in an institution similar to, and somewhat better than, a savings bank. "Sell your association to young and old, rich and poor. Explain that there are no preferred shareholders and that no amount is too large or too small and that

[17] A Citizen, *Building Associations, Their Deceptive Character and Ruinous Tendency Explained* (J. Perry, New York, 1852), p. 27.

[18] U. S. League of Building and Loan Associations, *Annual Proceedings*, 1931, p. 233.

all are welcome. Show that we have the best security in the world, even better than the banks, for we have moral security as well as first-mortgage bonds and mortgages on improved real estate."[19]

The fact that the investor is a stockholder in a corporation is not stressed by many associations. Many investors do not understand that they are merely shareholders and not depositors. The idea is either consciously or unconsciously hidden by the advertising of associations that use such mottoes as "Safety for Savings," or "Lend don't Spend."[20] It must be said, however, in defense of many building and loan men that they have not lost sight of the fact that investors are shareholders. "The rights of the stockholders and the individual members must be safeguarded."[21] Also, "Savings and loan associations are created for the stockholders."[22] There are many other similar statements throughout the various volumes of *Annual Proceedings* of the different associations.

Third, many associations advertise the liquidity of funds placed with them. As an example of this practice the following quotation from a question-and-answer pamphlet may be cited:

Question—Can I withdraw my money from a building and loan association?

Answer—Money may be withdrawn from a building and loan association as it can from a bank with interest graduated according to the time that it has been deposited.[23]

Such advertising misleads the public into believing that associations can meet withdrawals at any time; however, such is not the case. One executive frankly states: "One cannot say to the depositor, 'Your money will be instantly at hand.' I am the president of an institution that had securities amounting to millions of dollars, that was refusing further loans amounting to millions of dollars, and yet in six months found itself unable

[19] New York State Building and Loan League, *Annual Proceedings*, 1921, p. 63.
[20] United States Building and Loan League, *Annual Proceedings*, 1931, p. 240.
[21] *Ibid.*, p. 346.
[22] *Ibid.*, 1914, p. 106.
[23] Reigel, Robert, and Doubman, J. R., *The Building and Loan Association* (John Wiley, 1927), p. 52.

to meet its withdrawal notices."[24] Still another prominent building and loan official says: "Do not expect a building and loan association to pay on demand, for a building and loan association is not a banking institution."[25] It is clear that it is not the opinion of all building and loan officials that money can be withdrawn at will from the association.

Some General Conclusions

1. The growth of building and loan associations may be attributed to two factors: *a*) the laxity of state laws regulating the organization and operation of the associations; and, *b*) the activities of the associations themselves in attracting both borrowing and nonborrowing stockholders.

2. Both the state authorities and the building and loan officials seem to have forgotten the original purpose of such associations, in that they started as coöperative ventures. Instead of being composed of groups interested in local real-estate development, building and loan associations have become commercial ventures, operated mainly for profit. The local interest and the idea of coöperative credit to aid in home building have too often disappeared.

3. In order to remedy this situation it will be necessary for the several states to regulate building and loan associations more closely. The principles underlying any such legislation should be to return them to their original purpose of providing local coöperative credit in order to facilitate the building of homes. This would require close supervision of incorporation as well as of the loan policy after incorporation. The purpose, on the whole, should be to change the present trend of building and loan associations from becoming something similar to banking institutions and return them to the path from which they have wandered so widely. In some cases they may best be allowed to convert into savings institutions subject to the stricter requirements necessarily applicable in such a case.

[24] U. S. Building and Loan Association League, *Annual Proceedings*, 1931, p. 190.

[25] *Ibid.*, p. 233.

CHAPTER XIII

BANK FAILURES[1]

The failure of more than 11,125 banks in the United States, involving more than $5,200,000,000 deposits from the end of 1920 to March 1, 1933, has marked this phase of American banking as one of outstanding importance. This represents approximately 36 per cent of all banks in operation on June 30, 1921, or 14.5 per cent of the total deposits of all banks on that date. There is scarcely a section of the entire country which was not directly or indirectly affected by this epidemic of bank failures. The number of failures fluctuated from year to year, the largest being 1931 when almost 2,300 banks were closed, or an average of slightly more than six banks per day for each day of the year—truly an astounding record. Furthermore, the failures during 1931 represented more than 10 per cent of all banks in operation on June 30, 1931, and about 3.25 per cent of the total deposits of all active banks on the same date.

The effects and results following in the wake of this long stream of bank failures have been, and are still, so far-reaching in their significance and influence upon the course of banking legislation and practice in this country that the bank failure movement warrants a rather extensive and careful statistical study of the type and location of the banks which have been most susceptible of failure. Have large banks been more or less likely to fail than small banks? Have banks located in the larger cities, regardless of the size of the individual bank, been more likely to get into difficulties than banks located in the smaller cities and towns? Have member banks been more successful than nonmembers? Have national banks proved to be any

[1] This chapter was prepared by John M. Chapman. The text is based very largely upon the data collected by the Federal Reserve Board and the Report of the Federal Reserve Committee on Branch, Group and Chain Banking, on *Bank Suspensions in the United States* and the *Report on Branch Banking in the United States*. Special acknowledgment is made for the data prepared by the Federal Reserve Committee.

sounder than banks operating under state laws? With this general statement, let us now outline the scope and extent of bank failures since 1920.

Scope and Extent of Bank Failures

Despite the fact that there were fluctuations in the number of bank failures from year to year, there was a tendency for the banking situation to become more and more involved with an increase in the number of failures from 1920 to the end of 1931. During the year 1932 there was a marked decrease over that of 1931 but the number was still greater than for any other one year except 1931. In the first two months of 1933 the failures were very heavy, resulting in the closing of 389 banks, or at the rate of 2,334 for the year as a whole. In considering the total number of banks in operation with the number of failures, the later years of this period were very unfavorable as compared with the earlier years for the reason that there was a much larger number of small banks in the earlier years; hence, the risk of the potential number of bank closings should have been greater. The total number of banks closed, the number reopened, the total deposits of closed banks and reopened banks, and the percentage relationship of failed banks to total banks in operation, are presented in Table 65.

The total deposits of the failed banks are given in Table 65, as well as the total deposits of all banks reopened for each year. It should be observed that the number reopened in any given year may, and usually would, involve certain banks which had failed in an earlier year or years. During the period covered by Table 65 there were 11,130 banks closed and 1,413 reopened. The deposits of the reopened banks amounted to $768,000,000 for the period which represented, on an average, more than 14.7 per cent of the grand total of all deposits involved in failed banks in the United States. Statistics do not indicate the number of banks which were reopened and which failed again at a later date. The number in this class is generally considered by banking supervisors to be quite substantial, so that the volume of deposits of failed banks that reopened and closed again, is much smaller

TABLE 65

BANKS SUSPENDED AND REOPENED

(Dollar amounts in millions of dollars)

YEAR	TOTAL NUMBER OF BANKS IN OPERATION IN THE U.S.	NUMBER FAILED BANKS	FAILED BANKS AS PER CENT OF ALL BANKS IN OPERATION	DEPOSITS OF ALL BANKS IN OPERATION IN THE U.S.	DEPOSITS OF FAILED BANKS		BANKS REOPENED		
					Amount	Per cent of All Banks in U.S.	No.	Amt.	Per cent of All Failed Banks
1921	30,812	501	1.63	$35,849	$ 196	.55	60	$ 17	8.67
1922	30,389	354	1.16	37,876	111	.29	65	36	32.43
1923	30,178	648	2.15	40,631	189	.47	37	12	6.35
1924	29,348	776	2.64	43,771	213	.49	94	22	10.33
1925	28,241	612	2.17	47,612	173	.36	62	17	9.83
1926	28,146	956	3.40	49,726	272	.55	149	61	22.43
1927	27,061	662	2.45	52,446	194	.37	95	36	18.56
1928	26,213	491	1.87	54,332	139	.26	39	16	11.51
1929	25,330	642	2.53	54,281	235	.43	58	26	11.06
1930	24,079	1,345	5.59	55,510	865	1.56	147	62	7.17
1931	22,071	2,298	10.41	52,036	1,692	3.25	276	158	9.34
1932	19,163	1,456	7.60	42,178	716	1.70	290	276	38.54
1933*		389			208		41	29	
Total		11,130			5,203		1,413	768	

* Includes only the preliminary data for the first two months of the year, January and February. See *Federal Reserve Bulletin*, March, 1933, p. 144.

than the amount given in Table 65, hence misleading in this respect.

It is impossible to determine the total loss to depositors and stockholders of failed banks. From the data presented, some indication of the actual loss of funds on deposit is given but such data do not take into account the greater loss to the community, perhaps, in the tying up of funds which are not available for use for a long period of time. Some of the results of freezing assets in this way appear in the slowing down of business activity and the curtailment of income for a large number in the community. The losses suffered in this connection are more depressing than the direct loss which the depositor has to undergo as a result of losing a certain per cent of his total deposits at the time of failure. Approximately 75 per cent (not including preferred creditors, offsets, etc.) of deposits at the time of closing are realized by the depositors,[2] but these deposits are liquidated slowly over a long period of time, in many cases resulting in almost nothing for the depositors.

Size of Failed Banks

A study of the data covering the failed banks reveals some interesting results regarding the size of the banks which have failed in this country during the period 1921-1931, inclusive. These data should be viewed from different angles in order to determine if the large banks are any better prepared to ward off failure than the small banks. First, if the banks be classified according to the amount of capital, it will be readily seen that the small banks fail in much larger number than the larger banks. This condition is more fully shown in Table 66.

Table 66 shows that 5,337 banks with a capital of $25,000, or less, failed out of a total of 9,285 bank failures during the

[2] "... The average percentage of all dividends paid on the aggregate of secured and unsecured claims proved against the 1,086 receiverships that have been finally closed, but not including the 109 restored to solvency which paid 100 per cent, was 67.19 per cent. If payments to secured and preferred creditors, offsets, and other disbursements, as indicated above, were included with the dividends paid in this calculation, the total disbursements to creditors would amount to $414,701,237 or 77.06 per cent of claims proved." The *Annual Report of the Comptroller of Currency*, 1932, p. 14. These calculations however take no account of many obvious sources of loss, such as unpaid interest on claims.

TABLE 66

BANK SUSPENSIONS CLASSIFIED ACCORDING TO CAPITAL STOCK*

BANKS HAVING STOCK OF	1921	1922	1923	1924	1925	1926	1927	1928	1929	1930	1931
Less than $25,000	194	117	295	319	234	384	247	191	223	466	548
$25,000	104	85	151	191	135	230	165	106	143	296	513
25,000–$ 49,000	31	39	49	55	46	100	60	38	67	140	220
50,000– 99,000	78	53	91	130	133	164	122	94	120	221	457
100,000– 199,000	47	24	32	61	43	46	47	46	58	131	285
200,000– 999,000	12	15	16	15	18	16	13	11	19	70	227
1,000,000 and over	4†	..	..	..	..	..	..	..	5‡	11§	32
Not Available	31	21	14	5	3	16	8	5	7	10	16
Total	501	354	648	776	612	956	662	491	642	1,345	2,298

* *Annual Report of the Federal Reserve Board,* 1931, p. 127.
† Includes one bank with a capital of $1,309,000.
‡ Includes one bank with a capital of $1,225,000.
§ Includes one bank each with capital of $1,218,000, $1,750,000, $2,500,000, $4,000,000, $4,877,000, and $25,250,000.

period 1921-1931. The position of the smaller bank is made more emphatic if all failed banks having a capital of less than $50,000 be included in this group. From this point of view it is certainly clear that a larger per cent of all failed banks consist of banks having a capital of less than $50,000, of which a very large proportion consists of banks with a capital of $25,000 or less.

A classification of failed banks according to total volume of loans and investments gives essentially the same results as those reached on the capital-classification basis. More than 80 per cent of the failed banks had total loans and investments of $500,000 or less, while 59 per cent had total loans and investments of $250,000 or less. Almost 40 per cent of all failed banks had total loans and investments of $150,000 or less. The distribution of the failed banks based upon this classification is shown in Table 67.

Size of the Town or City

A large percentage of all failed banks were located in the smaller towns and cities. Data compiled by the Federal Reserve Board show that approximately 75 per cent of all failed banks were situated at the time of failure in towns of 2,500 or less; 13 per cent were located in towns or cities having a population of 10,000 or less. The situation is clearly indicated in Table 68.

Similar results were indicated by the Federal Reserve Committee in its study of the location of failed banks. According to data compiled by that Committee covering national and state banks, nearly 75 per cent of all failed banks were located in towns with a population of 2,500 or less, and nearly 88 per cent in towns of 10,000 or less. The details of this classification presented in Table 69 follow:

Geographic Distribution of Failed Banks

A study[8] of failed banks shows that a large per cent of all national and state bank failures occurred in agricultural states.

[8] Report of the Federal Reserve Committee on Branch, Group and Chain Banking on *Bank Suspensions in the United States*, 1892-1931, pp. 24-26.

TABLE 67

BANK SUSPENSIONS DURING 1921-1931, BY SIZE OF LOANS AND INVESTMENTS*

SIZE GROUP LOANS AND INVESTMENTS (000 OMITTED)	NATIONAL BANKS		STATE BANKS		NATIONAL AND STATE BANKS	
	Number	Per cent of total	Number	Per cent of total	Number	Per cent of total
Under $150	154	11.5	3,350	44.2	3,504	39.3
150–250	253	18.9	1,501	19.8	1,754	19.7
250–500	413	30.9	1,478	19.5	1,891	21.2
500–750	170	12.7	481	6.3	651	7.3
750–1,000	89	6.7	248	3.3	337	3.8
1,000–2,000	157	11.8	285	3.8	442	5.0
2,000–5,000	74	5.5	158	2.1	232	2.6
5,000–10,000	20	1.5	47	0.6	67	0.7
10,000–50,000	5	0.4	31	0.4	36	0.4
50,000 and over	1	0.1	1	0.01	2	0.02
Total	1,336	100.0	7,580	100.0	8,916	100.0

* Report of Federal Reserve Committee on Branch, Group and Chain Banking, 1932, on *Bank Suspensions in the United States, 1892-1931*, p. 51.

TABLE 68

BANK SUSPENSIONS BY SIZE OF TOWN OR CITY*

PLACES WITH POPULATION OF	1921	1922	1923	1924	1925	1926	1927	1928	1929	1930	1931
Less than 500	181	120	331	335	226	372	266	207	240	442	666
500 to 1,000	99	75	104	158	130	204	142	93	128	278	402
1,000 to 1,500	47	23	58	71	67	115	61	48	77	128	202
1,500 to 2,500	39	44	55	75	56	88	65	52	63	137	225
2,500 to 5,000	33	30	35	55	60	79	53	33	35	119	214
5,000 to 10,000	32	18	24	28	32	30	22	18	35	60	140
10,000 to 25,000	21	12	14	22	18	22	30	17	24	57	134
25,000 and over	49	32	27	32	23	46	23	23	40	124	315
Total	501	354	648	776	612	956	662	491	642	1,345	2,298

* *Annual Report of the Federal Reserve Board,* 1931, p. 127.

TABLE 69

BANK SUSPENSIONS DURING 1921-1931 BY SIZE OF TOWN*

POPULATION OF TOWN	NATIONAL BANKS		STATE BANKS		NATIONAL AND STATE BANKS	
	Number of suspensions	Per cent of total suspensions	Number of suspensions	Per cent of total suspensions	Number of suspensions	Per cent of total suspensions
Under 500	171	12.8	2,982	39.3	3,153	35.4
500–1,000	255	19.1	1,476	19.5	1,731	19.4
1,000–2,500	408	30.6	1,348	17.8	1,756	19.7
2,500–5,000	202	15.1	568	7.5	770	8.6
5,000–10,000	118	8.8	309	4.1	427	4.8
10,000–25,000	92	6.9	297	3.9	389	4.4
25,000–50,000	36	2.7	112	1.5	148	1.6
50,000–100,000	19	1.4	130	1.7	149	1.7
100,000 and over	35	2.6	358	4.7	393	4.4
Total	1,336	100.0	7,580	100.0	8,916	100.0

* Report of Federal Reserve Committee on Branch, Group and Chain Banking, 1932, on *Bank Suspensions in the United States, 1892-1931*, p. 73.

These failures were fairly highly concentrated in what are known generally as Western Grain States. About 41 per cent of all bank failures reported for the period 1921-1929 were found among the banks in this area. The data prepared by the Federal Reserve Committee showed also that, if certain other agricultural states were included in the above group, the total would be about 70 per cent of all bank failures in this country. In this connection the report states:[4]

> During the nine years 1921-1929, 70 per cent of the suspensions occurred in twelve agricultural States, including the seven Western Grain States listed above, and Georgia, South Carolina, Montana, Oklahoma, and Texas. During 1930 and 1931 suspensions increased in the industrial districts, but they did not decline in the agricultural regions. While only 40 per cent of the total during 1930 and 1931 occurred in these twelve agricultural States, the actual number of suspensions therein was greater in 1931 than during any previous year.

The distribution of bank failures on a geographical basis is more fully shown in Table 70.

If bank failures be considered from the point of view of size, the relative position of each geographical section varies considerably from that prevailing when considered from point of view of numbers only. Based upon total loans and investments, the North Central States showed a larger percentage than any other division in the United States for the period 1921-1931. Of the total loans and investments of all failed banks reported by the Federal Reserve Committee more than 62 per cent represented banks located in the Middle Atlantic (20 per cent), North Central (21.9 per cent) and Western grain (20.7 per cent) states. Distribution of loans and investments of failed banks classified on a geographical basis is more fully shown in Table 71.

There was a tendency for larger banks to fail during the latter part of this period of bank failures. The movement had spread to the Eastern States including New York, Pennsylvania, and Massachusetts where larger banks were closed. The situa-

[4] Report of the Federal Reserve Committee on Branch, Group and Chain Banking on *Bank Suspensions in the United States*, 1892-1931, p. 26.

TABLE 70

BANK SUSPENSIONS DURING 1921-1931, BY GEOGRAPHIC DIVISIONS*

GEOGRAPHIC DIVISION†	NATIONAL BANKS		STATE BANKS		NATIONAL AND STATE BANKS	
	Number	Per cent of total	Number	Per cent of total	Number	Per cent of total
New England	10	0.7	39	0.5	49	0.5
Middle Atlantic	114	8.5	194	2.6	308	3.5
North Central	163	12.2	1,049	13.8	1,212	13.6
Southern Mountain	57	4.3	370	4.9	427	4.8
Southeastern	152	11.4	1,323	17.5	1,475	16.6
Southwestern	195	14.6	779	10.3	974	10.9
Western Grain	430	32.2	3,228	42.6	3,658	41.0
Rocky Mountain	159	11.9	458	6.0	617	6.9
Pacific Coast	56	4.2	140	1.8	196	2.2
United States	1,336	100.0	7,580	100.0	8,916	100.0

* Report of Federal Reserve Committee on Branch, Group and Chain Banking, 1932, on *Bank Suspensions in the United States, 1892-1931*, p. 26.

† New England: Maine, New Hampshire, Vermont, Massachusetts, Rhode Island, Connecticut.
Middle Atlantic: New York, New Jersey, Delaware, Pennsylvania, Maryland, District of Columbia.
North Central: Michigan, Wisconsin, Illinois, Indiana, Ohio.
Southern Mountain: West Virginia, Virginia, Kentucky, Tennessee.
Southeastern: North Carolina, South Carolina, Georgia, Florida, Alabama, Mississippi.
Southwestern: Louisiana, Texas, Arkansas, Oklahoma.
Western Grain: Minnesota, North Dakota, South Dakota, Iowa, Nebraska, Missouri, Kansas.
Rocky Mountain: Montana, Idaho, Wyoming, Colorado, New Mexico, Arizona, Utah, Nevada.
Pacific Coast: Washington, Oregon, California.

TABLE 71

LOANS AND INVESTMENTS OF BANKS SUSPENDING DURING 1921-1931, BY GEOGRAPHIC DIVISIONS*

GEOGRAPHIC DIVISION	NATIONAL BANKS		STATE BANKS		NATIONAL AND STATE BANKS	
	Loans and Investments *(000 omitted)*	Per cent of total	Loans and Investments *(000 omitted)*	Per cent of total	Loans and Investments *(000 omitted)*	Per cent of total
New England	$ 50,136	4.4	$ 124,475	3.5	$ 174,611	3.7
Middle Atlantic	211,491	18.5	732,410	20.5	943,901	20.0
North Central	178,574	15.6	852,657	23.9	1,031,231	21.9
Southern Mountain	103,175	9.0	170,066	4.8	273,241	5.8
Southeastern	145,613	12.7	499,274	14.0	644,887	13.7
Southwestern	116,256	10.1	211,193	5.9	327,449	7.0
Western Grain	203,302	17.7	774,998	21.7	978,300	20.7
Rocky Mountain	86,812	7.6	126,528	3.5	213,340	4.5
Pacific Coast	50,848	4.4	78,514	2.2	129,362	2.7
United States	$1,146,207	100.0	$3,570,115	100.0	$4,716,322	100.0

* Report of Federal Reserve Committee on Branch, Group and Chain Banking, 1932, on *Bank Suspensions in the United States, 1892-1931*, p. 41.

tion[5] was described by the Federal Reserve Committee as follows:

The banks suspending during 1930-1931 were of larger average size than those suspending during the preceding nine years. Although the number of suspensions during the two years was only about two-thirds as large as during the previous nine years, the loans and investments were about 62 per cent greater. There is also a striking contrast in the geographic distribution of the loans and investments of banks suspending during the two periods. During the earlier period roughly 60 per cent of the total loans and investments of suspending banks were in the Western Grain and Southeastern sections; while during the later period 60 per cent of the total were in the Middle Atlantic and North Central States.

TABLE 72

NATIONAL AND STATE BANK SUSPENSIONS, 1921-1932*

	NATIONAL BANKS		STATE BANKS	
YEAR	Number	Gross Deposits (000 omitted)	Number	Gross Deposits (000 omitted)
1921	52	$ 20,777	409	$ 142,522
1922	49	20,197	294	69,077
1923	90	34,244	533	112,103
1924	122	64,890	616	137,533
1925	118	55,574	461	104,330
1926	123	43,998	801	206,436
1927	91	45,547	545	149,445
1928	57	36,483	422	102,917
1929	64	41,614	564	181,317
1930	161	170,446	1,131	651,388
1931	409	439,171	1,804	1,229,904
1932	276	214,150	1,140	484,232
Total	1,612	$1,187,091	8,720	$3,571,204

* Report of Federal Reserve Committee on Branch, Group and Chain Banking, 1932, on *Bank Suspensions in the United States*, 1892-1931, p. 12.

A large percentage of all bank failures in the United States during 1921 to 1932, inclusive, were not members of the Federal Reserve system. Of the total number of failures which amounted to 10,332 according to report of the Reserve Committee on Branch, Group and Chain Banking, 1,612 were national banks and 418 were member state banks and trust companies, leaving the remainder, 8,302, as nonmember banks and trust companies. The total deposits of member banks amounted

[5] Report of the Federal Reserve Committee on Branch, Group and Chain Banking on *Bank Suspensions in the United States*, 1892-1931, pp. 41-42.

TABLE 73

SUSPENSIONS OF BANKS WITH BRANCHES, 1921-1931*

YEAR	NUMBER OF SUSPENSIONS	PER CENT OF TOTAL	NUMBER OF BRANCHES: In Head-Office City	NUMBER OF BRANCHES: Outside Head-Office City	NUMBER OF BRANCHES: Total	PER CENT OF TOTAL	LOANS AND INVESTMENTS (000 omitted)	PER CENT OF TOTAL
1921	6	3.4	3	3	6	1.3	$ 33,911	3.2
1922	2	1.1		2	2	0.4	1,921	0.2
1923	4	2.2		6	6	1.3	2,629	0.2
1924	4	2.2		5	5	1.0	1,867	0.2
1925	2	1.1	1	1	2	0.4	2,652	0.3
1926	11	6.1		33	33	7.0	11,724	1.1
1927	3	1.7		7	7	1.5	2,226	0.2
1928	3	1.7		7	7	1.5	2,843	0.3
1929	10	5.6	7	11	18	3.8	23,213	2.2
1930	40	22.4	109	38	147	31.0	434,074	41.1
1931	94	52.5	166	75	241	50.8	538,947	51.0
Total	179	100.0	286	188	474	100.0	$1,056,007	100.0

* Report of the Reserve Committee on Branch, Group and Chain Banking, 1932, on *Branch Banking in the United States*, p. 231.

TABLE 74

SUSPENSIONS OF STATE AND NATIONAL BANKS WITH BRANCHES, 1921-1931*

YEAR	STATE BANKS					NATIONAL BANKS				
	NUMBER OF SUSPENSIONS	NUMBER OF BRANCHES			LOANS AND INVESTMENTS (000 omitted)	NUMBER OF SUSPENSIONS	NUMBER OF BRANCHES			LOANS AND INVESTMENTS (000 omitted)
		In Head-Office City	Outside Head-Office City	Total			In Head-Office City	Outside Head-Office City	Total	
1921	6	3	3	6	$ 33,911					
1922	2		2	2	1,921					
1923	4		6	6	2,629					
1924	4		5	5	1,867					
1925	2	1	1	2	2,652					
1926	11		33	33	11,724					
1927	3		7	7	2,226					
1928	3		7	7	2,843					
1929	10	7	11	18	23,213					
1930	38	107	38	145	383,407	2	2		2	$ 50,667
1931	85	144	74	218	483,564	9	22	1	23	55,383
Total	168	262	187	449	$949,957	11	24	1	25	$106,050

* Report of the Reserve Committee on Branch, Group, and Chain Banking, 1932, on *Branch Banking in the United States*, p. 232.

to $1,867,267, as compared with $2,891,018 for all nonmember banks, showing that the member banks which failed were much larger than the nonmember banks. The failure situation as regards member and nonmember banks is shown in Table 72.

Branch Bank Failures

The most complete and reliable data on the failure of banks operating branches seem to be the figures of the Reserve Committee on Branch, Group and Chain Banking. The results of that

TABLE 75

SUSPENSIONS OF BANKS WITH BRANCHES, 1921-31, AND ACTIVE BANKS WITH BRANCHES, DECEMBER 31, 1931, IN IMPORTANT BRANCH-BANKING STATES*

STATE†	ACTIVE BANKS WITH BRANCHES DECEMBER 31, 1931		SUSPENSIONS OF BANKS WITH BRANCHES, 1921-1931	
	Number of Banks	Number of Branches	Number of Banks	Number of Branches
California	50	801	5	15
Maryland	27	108	4	17
Louisiana	39	98	12	18
North Carolina	23	84	24	40
South Carolina	11	77	9	24
Maine	19	73	3	5
Virginia	30	57	6	7
Tennessee	25	58	4	5
Total	224	1,356	67	131

* Report of the Federal Reserve Committee on Branch, Group and Chain Banking, 1932, on *Branch Banking in the United States,* p. 232.

† Only those states are given in which a substantial number of branches have been in operation outside the city of the head-office for several years, although the number of branches shown includes both those inside and outside the city of the head office of the bank.

study show that 179 banks with branches failed during the years 1921-1931, inclusive. Total loans and investments for these 179 banks amounted to more than $1,056,000. The details of the number and distribution of branch bank failures are presented in Table 73.

Attention is called to the large concentration of failures during the years 1930 and 1931 which was similar to the conditions prevailing among the group and chain bank organizations.

A larger number of state banks operating branches failed than of national banks operating branches. This cannot be taken as a reflection upon state banks, for the reason that the number of state banks operating branches was much larger than in the case of national banks. A comparison of national and state branch-bank failures is given in Table 74.

The states in which the largest number of banks operating branches failed are presented in Table 75.

TABLE 76

SUSPENSIONS OF GROUP AND CHAIN BANKS DURING 1921-1931 BY GEOGRAPHIC EDIVISIONS*

GEOGRAPHIC DIVISION	NUMBER OF SYSTEMS†	SUSPENDED BANKS			
		Number	Per cent of Total	Loans and investments (000 omitted)	Per cent of Total
New England	1	10	1.8	$ 61,934	11.9
Middle Atlantic	7	15	2.7	89,004	17.1
North Central	12	48	8.7	83,626	16.1
Southern Mountain	2	5	.9	85,293	16.4
Southeastern	14	167	30.3	89,359	17.2
Southwestern	12	103	18.7	44,553	8.6
Western Grain	59	168	30.5	45,804	8.8
Rocky Mountain	8	28	5.1	17,534	3.4
Pacific Coast	5	7	1.3	2,589	.5
United States	120	551	100.0	$519,696	100.0

* Report of Federal Reserve Committee on Branch, Group and Chain Banking, 1932, on *Banking Groups and Chains*, p. 148.

† Systems in which one or more banks failed.

More than 550 banks owned and controlled by chain and group managements failed during the period 1921-1931. Based upon a geographical distribution, a large per cent of these banks were located in the agricultural areas, namely Western grain states (30.5 per cent), the Southeastern states (30.3 per cent), and the Southwestern states (18.7 per cent), or 79.5 per cent of all chain and group bank failures. The extent and distribution of failures in these two classes are shown in Tables 76 and 77.

Based upon size, the results are about the same as those shown for all banks in the United States, namely, the small banks made up a large percentage of all failed banks. By reference to Table 77 it will be seen that 36 per cent of all failed group and chain banks had total loans and investments of less than $150,000 and that 72 per cent had total loans and investments of $500,000 or less. This result again emphasizes the point already made,

TABLE 77

SUSPENSIONS OF GROUP AND CHAIN BANKS DURING 1921-1931 BY SIZE OF LOANS AND INVESTMENTS*

SIZE GROUP LOANS AND INVESTMENTS	SUSPENDED BANKS Number	Per cent of total	Loans and investments (*000 omitted*)	Per cent of total
Under $150,000	198	36.0	$ 17,735	3.4
150,000–250,000	108	19.6	20,515	3.9
250,000–500,000	91	16.5	32,522	6.3
500,000–750,000	38	6.9	23,000	4.4
750,000–1,000,000	30	5.5	25,653	4.9
1,000,000–2,000,000	42	7.6	58,887	11.3
2,000,000–5,000,000	26	4.7	78,689	15.2
5,000,000–10,000,000	9	1.6	64,712	12.5
10,000,000–50,000,000	9	1.6	197,983	38.1
50,000,000 and over	—	—	—	—
Total	551	100.0	$519,696	100.0

* Report of Federal Reserve Committee on Branch, Group and Chain Banking, 1932, on *Banking Groups and Chains*, p. 155.

that the smaller banks and in this country have shown a greater tendency to failure than have the larger banks.

The failures of group and chain banks were concentrated fairly heavily in the years 1930 and 1931. During the nine year period, 1921-1929, 314 banks, or 57 per cent of the total, failed, while in the two year period 1930-31 there were 237 failures, or 43 per cent of the total of 551 banks. In this connection the Report of the Reserve Committee states:[6]

[6] Report of the Federal Reserve Committee on Branch, Group and Chain Banking on *Banking Groups and Chains*, p. 152.

During 1921-1929, 80.2 per cent of the suspensions were among banks with loans and investments under $500,000, while in the years 1930 and 1931 the proportion in this size class was 61.2 per cent. The distribution of loans and investments among the size classes during the two periods is even more striking. In the early period banks larger than $5,000,000 accounted for 13.8 per cent of the loans and investments of group and chain suspensions, compared with 63.4 per cent in the years 1930-1931. This change in the size of suspended group and chain banks is similar to that shown for all suspended banks.

Conclusions

1. There were 11,130 bank failures involving over $5,200,000,000 deposits in the United States from January 1, 1921 to March 1, 1933. The largest number for any one year was 2,298 in 1931 which was more than 10.4 per cent of all banks in operation on June 30 of that year.

2. During the period from January 1, 1921 to March 1, 1933, more than 1,410 failed banks involving about $768,000,000 deposits, were reopened.

3. A large percentage of all banks that failed from 1921 to 1931, inclusive, had capital of $25,000 or less. There was a noticeable increase in the number of larger banks that failed during 1930 and 1931. This would seem to indicate that the larger banks were able to stand up longer under a period of depression than the smaller banks, since the bank failure epidemic had been in process for several years prior to the beginning of the depression in 1929.

4. Approximately 75 per cent of all failed banks, during the period 1921-1931, were located at the time of failure in towns of 2,500 or less.

5. About 70 per cent of all bank failures during the period 1921-1929 occurred in twelve agricultural states, of which 41 per cent consisted of banks situated in seven Western grain states.

6. According to the study of the Reserve Committee on Branch, Group and Chain Banking, 179 banks operating 474 branches failed. These banks had, at the time of failure, over

$1,056,000,000 loans and investments, of which more than $970,000,000 was held by branch banks which closed during 1930 and 1931.

7. More than 550 group and chain banks, with total loans and investments of slightly more than $519,600,000, failed during the period 1921-1929.

CHAPTER XIV

GEOGRAPHICAL DISTRIBUTION OF BANKING FACILITIES IN THE UNITED STATES IN 1933[1]

This section is devoted, not to bank failures, but rather, to an analysis of one of the problems created by the bank failures of the past decade or two. It undertakes to determine the geographical distribution, not of bank mortality in the United States, but of the facilities that the closings, both endemic and epidemic, since 1920 have left available in a dozen states chosen as fairly representative. It further makes an effort in a few selected areas to relate, at least in a rough way, the distribution of these facilities to the presumed needs of the communities.

This is an aspect of the current banking problem that, to date, has not had the attention it deserves. For this neglect there are probably a number of reasons. One of them presumably is that a complete exposition of the facts upon which final conclusions may be based would be exceedingly difficult and very costly. Obviously mere lists of failures, statistics of deposits and assets involved in such suspensions, or even geographical study of failures carried forward in no greater geographical detail than is usual, throw but scant light on the problem here envisaged. A state or a section of the country with an unnecessarily large number of banks—as many parts of the country unquestionably had in 1920—might lose a substantial percentage of its banks without leaving the population acutely in want of banking facilities of the ordinary variety, provided, of course, the institutions remaining were satisfactorily distributed and adequately capitalized. The tragedy of bank failures in such a case would be found chiefly, if not solely, in the inconvenience and loss inflicted upon depositors and stockholders, with the consequent disruption of normal industrial, agricultural, and commercial business.

On the other hand a relatively small ratio of failures, if con-

[1] Prepared by F. W. Jones.

centrated in one area, or in a series of smaller areas, could easily result in robbing whole communities of banking facilities altogether. We shall find as we proceed that the failures of the past ten or fifteen years took practically all banks from very considerable territories in several of the states. This was because of the fact that failures were not evenly distributed, taking a given percentage of banks from each community, but were so distributed as to remove all the banks from certain towns and sometimes all the banks from all the towns in substantial areas within certain states, notably in Montana and South Carolina. Maps have been prepared showing the locations of towns in which failures occurred. These give certain presumptive evidence of lack of remaining facilities. But obviously the extent to which any given number of failures have denuded sections of all banking facilities, depends upon the number of banks in the section before the failures occurred.

Obviously the adequacy of remaining banking facilities cannot be fully measured by merely indicating the location of open banks at the present time. There are wide areas in most of the states that never have had a bank, and where there is not, and never has been, sufficient business to support a bank or even a branch of a bank in a neighboring town or village. There are unquestionably many communities that, at some time during the past decade or two, enjoyed for a time a bank in their midst which they could not then and cannot now support. It is equally certain that other sections having a sufficient number of banks are nonetheless without adequate banking facilities by reason of the smallness and the weakness of existing institutions.

With modern roads and means of transportation it is highly probable that, in some more thickly settled districts, there are still an unnecessarily large number of banks. On the whole these communities would be much better served if there were fewer towns with banks, and if those banks were stronger and more serviceable than the existing institutions.

A complete inquiry into this whole phase of the present banking situation would obviously necessitate an elaborate analysis of the industrial, agricultural, and commercial life of the individual communities of the nation, a careful study of transportation and transit facilities of localities, and a full knowledge of the real condition of banks now in operation in such communities. It is a field of inquiry that urgently calls for much more study than it has had at any time, and of course for much fuller analysis than the resources of this inquiry permit. In connection, first, with the problem of licensing banks that were closed under the Presidential order of March 6, 1933, and, more recently, as a result of the necessity of certifying the banks of the country for deposit insurance under the provisions of the Banking Act of 1933, the national banking authorities (and in some degree at least the state banking authorities throughout the country) have at length thought it worth while to know just what the real condition of each of the institutions under their respective jurisdictions is. A very substantial body of information on the subject has, therefore, come into existence. For obvious reasons, however, it is not made available to the general public. In what follows use is made of such information on this subject as is available and could be compiled with the resources at hand.

The states that have been chosen for detailed study are: California, Montana, North Dakota, South Dakota, Minnesota, North Carolina, South Carolina, Georgia, Alabama, Pennsylvania, Massachusetts, and Michigan. California was chosen as more or less representative of the west coast, and also because, as is well known, it has for many years past been the state in which branch banking has made the most progress. The group in the near Northwest was selected because, in that general part of the country, bank failures have been particularly conspicuous. Somewhat the same reason governed the choice of the states of the Southeast. Pennsylvania and Massachusetts seem fairly representative of the eastern industrial states, one of them having suffered heavy bank mortality in certain sections, while in the other failures have not been relatively so great. Michigan is, of course, the state in which the most spectacular developments occurred during and after the banking crises early in 1933.

The course of procedure in general has been to compare the geographical distribution of banks in 1920 with that of 1932, and that existing subsequent to the relicensing of most of the banks after the banking holiday of 1933. It is, of course, not assumed that an ideal situation existed in 1920; on the contrary it is quite certain that in some instances at least, particularly in the agricultural regions of the Northwest and Southeast, more banks had sprung into existence than these populations were able to support, or than there was any economic justification for. It is likewise necessary to bear carefully in mind the fact that, during the thirteen years between 1920 and 1933, economic and other changes have taken place which necessitate caution in drawing conclusions from such comparisons.

Some general idea of the situation as it now exists can be obtained from a comparison of the number of banks in operation in May, 1933 with the number in operation in 1920. Table 78 makes such a comparison state by state, and also in addition shows the number in operation on June 30, 1932. The figures for the two earlier years are taken from the Reports of the Comptroller of Currency, and the 1933 data are the result of an actual count of the banks reported in operation by the respective Federal Reserve banks. In all cases the figures include all types of banks, national, state, trust companies, savings banks, and private banks under state supervision. It will be observed that, in nine of the twelve states, the number of banks was reduced by more than one half between 1920 and 1933, and that in two states the number was reduced to less than one-quarter of the number operating at the earlier date. The figures must, however, be read with the understanding that in several states there was a considerable growth of branch banking during the years in question, and that Reports of the Comptroller of the Currency give the number of independently operating institutions. Thus it is to be carefully noted that while only 275 banks are reported in operation in California in 1933 as compared with 704 in 1920, there were in addition a large number of branches doing business in the latter year. It is plain of course that a good many banks in this state, at one time operating independently, by 1933 were operating as branches of other banks. Adding the two figures (the one for independent banks and the other for branches) we get a total of 675 for 1933 which is nearly as large as that for 1920. As noted in the table somewhat the same factors were at work, to an important extent, in the states of North and South Carolina. It is likewise to be assumed that, in 1920, an unnecessarily large number of banks were in existence in most of these states. This, probably, was most pronouncedly true in those towns and villages that in the earlier year had several banks in each. The disappearance of a substantial number of these institutions, either by failures or by mergers, whatever the results in respect of inconvenience and loss to depositors and others, was, in many cases, doubtless effected without depriving local communities of banking facilities since the banks remaining are reasonably strong institutions, able to provide the needed services to the communities in question.

TABLE 78

NUMBER OF BANKS IN OPERATION UNDER NATIONAL AND STATE SUPERVISION IN THE STATES LISTED

	JUNE 30, 1920	JUNE 30, 1932	MAY 1933
California	704	363	275*
Montana	431	151	133
North Dakota	898	237	219
South Dakota	694	257	215
Minnesota	1,502	840	646
Alabama	350	243	217
Georgia	734	312	281
South Carolina	456	124	113†
North Carolina	623	257	275‡
Pennsylvania	1,498	1,260	1,048
Michigan	694	581	256
Massachusetts	453	416	308

* In addition there were 400 branches in operation in the state.
† In addition there were 25 branches in operation in the state.
‡ In addition there were 64 branches in operation in the state.

In any event a more enlightening picture, from the point of view of this study, is obtained by comparison of the number of points in each state at which banking facilities were available at the two dates. Table 79 presents these facts, and in addition carries a column showing the same data for 1932. Wide variations are shown in the results, a good many of which are startling. With the exceptions of California (where the number of places at which banking facilities were available in 1920 is larger by four than in 1933), and of Massachusetts and Pennsylvania, the change is dramatic in every instance. As a matter of fact, when the striking economic development of California, during

TABLE 79

NUMBER OF BANKING TOWNS IN THE STATES LISTED*

	1920	1932	1933
California	394	435	390
Montana	250	120	106
North Dakota	541	231	193
South Dakota	417	224	188
Minnesota	841	645	477
Alabama	232	183	160
Georgia	451	277	217
South Carolina	236	121	109
North Carolina	370	276	241
Pennsylvania	689	739	624
Michigan	590	499	193
Massachusetts	170	189	131

* The figures in the table above were obtained (for the years 1920 and 1932) by actual count of the number of towns reported as having one or more banks, by the March number of Polk's Bankers Encyclopedia. The 1933 figures are the result of actual count of towns having licensed banks as reported by the respective Federal Reserve banks at about the middle of May, 1933. The exact date varies somewhat depending upon the date of the latest reports obtainable at the time that the work of compiling the figures was completed.

the past dozen years, is taken into consideration, the question is raised whether that state either had not gone to extremes in covering its area with banks in 1920, or whether there is a shortage, geographically speaking, at the present time. The great growth in transportation facilities during these years may have, and probably has, wrought a substantial change in the extent to which it is necessary to distribute banking facilities throughout the smaller towns and villages of the state.

The changes in Pennsylvania and Massachusetts are especially interesting in certain particulars. In both states the decline came entirely as a result of the crisis ending in the banking holiday in March, 1933. Both states had more banking towns in 1932 than in 1920. In 1932 there were 739 banking towns in Pennsylvania compared with 689 in 1920. Massachusetts, in 1932, had 189 such towns as compared with 170 in 1920.

In the near Northwest and the Southeast there can be no question, from the face of the figures, that startlingly drastic situations have arisen. Banking towns in the four states in the Northwest have diminished by substantially more than fifty per cent taking the area as a whole. Montana, for example, in 1933 had only 106 such towns as compared with 250 in 1920; North Dakota had 193 against 541; South Dakota, 188 against 417; and Minnesota, 477 against 841. In some instances, as later analysis will show, the changes that have occurred in these states, during the past 13 years, have simply taken all banks from large and relatively important local areas—particularly in the state of Montana.

Developments in the Southeast, though not quite so drastic, have been drastic enough, as the figures disclose. South Carolina, for example, in 1933 had 109 banking towns as compared with 236 in 1920, while Georgia, with 217 in 1933 against 451 in 1920, has been hit about as hard. Alabama with 160 such towns against 232, and North Carolina, 241 against 370, have escaped with somewhat less drastic damage. In this area, too, as will be evident upon study of the maps, there are several substantial districts that emerged almost without banking facilities. Owing to limitations of space only a few of the maps so prepared are reproduced at the end of this chapter on pp. 333-348.

We turn next to the task of obtaining, so far as possible, an idea of the geographical distribution of remaining banks within each of these states. For this purpose a series of maps has been prepared, three for each of the states under examination. On these maps a dot has been placed at the approximate location of each town or locality where, at the date represented by the map, at least one bank was in operation. The resulting picture in each case then is that of an array of towns, cities, and villages where banking facilities were available at the specified date. To express the same thing in more technical language each is a map of the state in question showing "banking towns."

The work on these maps was begun in 1932 and was planned to cover two dates—early 1920 and early 1932.[2] As the work progressed, however, banks continued to fail in large numbers, the movement finally culminating in the bank holiday early in March, 1933. It was, therefore, thought essential to prepare a similar map in each case showing the situation at as late a date in 1933 as possible. By use of the reports of the several Federal Reserve banks, it proved possible to prepare another set of maps, one for each state, as of May, 1933. The exact date varied somewhat from Reserve district to Reserve district in accordance with the date for which information was available, but the difference is slight and is not believed to affect the results in any important degree.

Comparison state by state of the maps for each of the three dates reveals a number of very interesting facts. It shows at once of course the truth that the reduction in the number of "banking towns" followed different courses in different states so far as chronological sequence is concerned. In the Northwest for example the thinning out of the dots occurred in a very striking way between 1920 and 1932. Somewhat the same is true of the states in the Southeast. To a less extent it is true in Michigan. In such states as Montana, South Carolina, and Georgia, it is clear that as long ago as a year before the banking holiday very substantial bankless areas had developed. On the other hand, in the industrial Northeast, specifically in Massachusetts and Pennsylvania, there were substantially more banking towns in 1932 than in 1920. This is likewise rather dramatically true of the state of California. Such is the case in these latter states despite the fact that in all of them a substantial number of bank failures had occurred during 1931.

But after all, the important comparison for the purposes here in hand is that between 1920 and 1933, since this is not a study

[2] The exact dates are those represented by the compilations appearing in *Polk's Bankers Encyclopedia,* March, 1920 and March, 1932 (published by Polk's Encyclopedia Company, Detroit and New York). From these manuals the data for the maps were procured. (The base maps employed were Rand McNally's.)

of the history of bank failures, or, for that matter, a study of bank failures at all, but rather as already indicated, a study of the geographical adequacy of remaining banks. If then we concentrate our attention upon the 1933 maps in comparison with those for 1920, we find again a very substantial variation from state to state in the results of the loss of always substantial numbers of banks during the thirteen-year period. In Massachusetts and Pennsylvania in the East, and California in the Far West, there are even yet no bankless areas if we may take 1920 as having an adequate geographical distribution of banking facilities. Massachusetts shows only a few relatively small areas not as well situated, so far as having some sort of bank available, as in 1920. In both Pennsylvania and California banking facilities of one sort or another are more widely, and as evenly, distributed in 1933 as in 1920. Certainly in California, and probably in Pennsylvania, this is hardly an entirely fair comparison. The economic development of California in the past 13 years has been very large. Doubtless there are many more communities in the state now than in the earlier year that need, and can support, at least branch banks. The same is in some degree true of Pennsylvania. On the other hand, the large-scale extension of road systems and improvements, and the much wider ownership and use of automobiles, as well as the installation of motor bus lines, tends to make it less needful to have the banking facilities available so closely spread over the area of the states in question. But however these aspects of the case may be, a comparison of the situation in this respect in 1933 with that of 1920 indicates that the failures during the intervening period, including those that came along at the time of the banking holiday, have left but few people in these three states dwelling or doing business at points more distant from banks than in 1920 and probably not substantially more disadvantageously situated in this regard than at any time in their history.

The problem for the most part in these states, apart from that of making good the damage that has been done by bank closings, is primarily that of restoring banks now in operation to health and real strength and, where needed, that of enlarging and improving their facilities. In addition, of course, it is probably true that the continued existence of a good many banks is not to be taken for granted, but must be rendered certain by recapitalization, reorganization, reform of practices and in a great many instances by change in the personnel of management.

A vastly different situation is found in certain of the other states specifically under study here. In these states there appear substantial areas that have been deprived of banking facilities of any sort, in some instances embracing communities plainly capable of supporting banks, or at least branches of banks located elsewhere, and where the absence of banking facilities undeniably constitutes a hardship upon the populations there situated. In others the territory embraced is sufficiently large and important at least to raise a presumption of such conditions —if not a certainty. These states include South Carolina, Georgia, Montana, Michigan, and South Dakota.

The developments in Montana are worthy of special analysis. The drastic nature of the changes that have occurred in this state is revealed by a glance at the two maps (Charts VII and VIII) here presented. The true nature of the situation existing at the present time may be obtained from brief analysis of the recent economic history of the state.

On June 30, 1914, there were about 285 banks of all sorts in Montana, with capital, surplus, and undivided profits of $21,657,000. At the corresponding date in 1920 the state reported 431 such institutions with capital, surplus, and undivided profits of $32,760,000. On June 30, 1932, the state had 151 banking institutions of all sorts, with capital and surplus of $16,515,000. In May 1933 there were 133 banks in operation of which 6 were under "restrictions." The number of banking towns, respectively, were 1920—250, 1932—120, and 1933—106. It is evident that bank facilities available in Montana are substantially less extensive than they were in 1914. It will, moreover, be observed that bank failures in Montana were most frequent not in the past year or two but prior to the depression of 1929. The 431 banks of the state in 1920 had been reduced to less than 240 by the early months of 1926, and the number was reduced below 200 before the Wall Street crash of 1929.

The significance of these facts and of the resulting situation existing in Montana today will be better understood if they are related to the recent economic history of the state. During the twenty years or more prior to 1920 the population of Montana was growing with rather unusual rapidity. This was particularly true of those sections of the state where banks became so much more numerous between 1914 and 1920, and where, since the latter date, so many have disappeared. Curiously enough the period from 1920 to 1930 was marked on the one hand by a cessation of growth in population, and on the other by an exceptionally rapid growth in an economic sense. Although the banking history of the past two decades has, so far as this state is concerned, been written in sections devoted in large part to agriculture, it is worth noting first of all that the mineral production of the state showed at least a normal growth, the value of such products being $73,630,824 for 1919 and $93,842,135 for 1929. But still more interesting is the growth in agriculture. The value of all farm crops and live stock products in 1929 was $122,000,000, as compared with $94,800,000 ten years earlier. Such figures as these, in view of the very large price decline in the interim, are impressive. The growth of the state as a producer of spring wheat is particularly noteworthy. A state of secondary importance ten years ago in respect of this crop, Montana for several years now has been outranked only by North Dakota in its annual production of this grain. A good general idea of the economic history of the state for the past two decades is afforded by Table 80.

A glance at the maps reveals that the most startling changes have occurred in three fairly well defined areas or sections of the state. First, there is a band of territory running from Hill, Liberty, and Toole counties in the north to Carbon and Yellowstone counties in the south in which banking towns were numerous in 1920, and in which there are relatively few left now. Second, there is an area in the northeast corner of the state in which the banking history of the dozen years under consideration is closely similar to that in the central district. Third, a much smaller territory in the southwestern corner of the state embracing Gallatin, Madison, and Park counties is worthy of special attention for the same reasons.

We shall turn our attention first to the central area. This is primarily a spring wheat territory. A very substantial portion of the wheat grown in the whole state is harvested in this district. It is important, too, as a wool producing area, and cattle raising and dairying have now reached the stage where they must be termed major industries. Poultry raising has attained some local importance in several of the counties, and, in a few localities, important quantities of potatoes and sundry crop seeds are produced for the market. The sixteen counties comprising this area threshed more than 20,000,000 bushels of wheat in 1929, or about one-half of the state's output, and clipped more than 9,300,000 pounds of wool, or nearly one-third of the output of the whole state. Cream sold as butter fat amounted to more than one-third of the total for the state. Only in one or two instances is there a mineral production of much consequence in this belt. In Judith Basin county a very large increase in the output of lead brought the mineral-products value for the county up $1,770,000 in 1929. Cascade county usually reports appreciable mineral products, seldom in excess of half

TABLE 80

ANNUAL PRODUCTION OF CERTAIN FARM AND OTHER PRODUCTS IN THE STATE OF MONTANA 1909-1929

	1909	1919	1929
Wheat (bus.)	6,251,945	7,799,647	40,558,049
Flaxseed (bus).	447,484	325,838	1,177,086
Oats (bus.)	13,805,735	2,583,908	4,809,018
Barley (bus.)	753,268	346,972	3,798,109
Eggs (dozens)	5,950,015	11,858,042	15,428,608
All farm crops (value) and live stock products	$41,600,000	$94,800,000	$122,000,000
All mineral products (value)		76,630,824	93,840,000

a million dollars in value for any year. In this area there were 104 banking towns in 1920; in March, 1932, 42 of them still had banks. In May, 1933 there were 37 towns with banking facilities.

Turning now to the second section in the Northeast, that has suffered most severely, we find a spring-wheat area par excellence. There is no mineral production of consequence, and less attention is paid to sheep raising, dairying, and beef production. Although a much smaller territory than the central section already described, embracing only five counties, it threshed more than 7,500,000 bushels of wheat in 1929. The loss of banking towns in this area has been less severe than is the case with the central section of the state; but the change is drastic. It had 35 banking towns in 1920; it had 18 in March, 1932, and 15 in May, 1933. The third section selected for study (the counties of Gallatin, Madison, and Park) is somewhat more varied as to its economic characteristics. Madison county reported a production of metals from its mines, in 1929, valued at $342,305, which was below the production for the previous year. Park county as late as 1925 produced metals, largely from gold-arsenic ores, to the value of $294,248, but in recent years has not had much production, the value of such output in 1929 being only $18,595—chiefly silver and lead. Gallatin is in large part, particularly in the more northerly section where most of the banks were located, a spring wheat producing county. There 1,345,327 bushels of wheat were threshed in 1929. The three counties together reported seven banking towns in 1932, and 18 such towns in 1920. In May, 1933, it had 7 banking towns.

With these facts before us what are we to say as to the adequacy of existing banking facilities, or rather as to the availability of banking facilities, geographically speaking, to local communities in these three areas? At the very outset it may be observed that, in several instances, it is clear that, for all practical purposes, substantial localities and considerable groups of the population are today without banking facilities at all. Take the instance of Liberty county in the extreme north center of the central area already indicated. Here is a county with a population of over 2,000 people which produced more than three-quarters of a million bushels of wheat in 1929, and which was about proportionately important in sheep-raising and in the cattle growing and dairying industries. It had in May, 1933 no bank at all. That is, moreover, not the full story. Hill county on the east had only one banking town, and that is situated on the farther edge of this broad county. Toole county to the west had only two banking towns left, and they, likewise, are clear across on the farther edge from Liberty county farmers. To the south the story is about the same. The many farmers in this section were from 25 to 50 miles from a town in which a bank is open for business. Liberty county, or the territory that is now Liberty county, had, in 1920, three banking towns, Toole, 6, and Hill, 9. Golden Valley county, in the southeastern section of the area, presents about the same picture as that just outlined in the case of Liberty county. There are others. Fergus county, an enormous county in almost the exact center of the state, had ten banking towns in 1920, and has only two left now. It boasts a wheat production, in 1929, of more than two and three-quarter million bushels, and a proportionately substantial output of other crops such as wool and dairy products. It has a population of 16,531. The geographical center of the county is nearly as far from a banking town of any sort as is the case in Liberty county. Several other communities in the same general area present situations almost, but not quite, as striking as those thus specifically cited. In the other two areas selected for special study situations as unfortunate as these thus painted are not the rule, but in a number of instances it is evident enough that local residents were, practically speaking, without the services of a bank in May 1933. Of course it is to be remembered at all times, that the data here presented do not in any way reveal the facts as to the ability of the banks that are left to meet the legitimate needs of their respective communities. Many of them are small institutions with very meager resources, and, one often suspects, without knowing, that they are in no position to lend in more than rather moderate sums. But this aspect of the case is another, and a long story that cannot be presented at this time.

A few of the towns now having banks still have more than one such institution when there appears no good warrant for the duplication of facilities. For the most part however this superfluity of banks has disappeared from the picture.

There are areas in South Carolina that equally merit special attention. One of the most interesting of these is found in a stretch of territory beginning in about the center of the state and running in a southeasterly direction to the coast, and along the coast to the northern boundary of the state. It includes Berkeley, Calhoun, Clarendon, Dorchester, Fairfield, Georgetown, Horry, Lexington, Marion, Newberry, Orangeburg, Richland, Sumter, and Williamsburg counties. These counties, in 1929, produced more than 187,000 of the state's 836,000 bales of cotton. The value of their manufactured products in that year amounted to something more than $58,000,000. In 1920 they had 68 banking towns; in 1932, 34 towns were left; while in May 1933, only 23 still had banks.

Not the least interesting section of this area is that surrounding the city of Columbia near the boundary line between Richland and Lexington counties. To the south only a short distance, Calhoun county begins. The population of Richland county was about 87,700 in 1930 of which 51,600 lived in Columbia. Lexington to the south and west had 36,500 population, and Calhoun to the south and east had 16,700. This section, as is well known, enjoyed a marked growth in textile manufacturing during the ten years from 1919 to 1929. The value of manufactures in Richland county, in 1929, amounted to $21,550,000. Lexington reported nearly $5,000,000 worth of manufactures in 1929, while Calhoun, a much smaller county, only a part of which fell within the area here specially under consideration, reported more than $400,000 worth of manufactures. The area of these counties, in square miles, is: Richland, 765; Lexington, 743; and Calhoun, 391. Richland produced 8,000 bales of cotton in 1929, Lexington 12,800, and Calhoun 18,000.

Columbia is a center from which railroad lines run in all directions through Richland county, yet this county, even in 1920, had only two banking towns. It has lost one of them, the county boasting no banks in May 1933 outside of Columbia itself. Lexington, particularly in the more westerly sections distant from Columbia, which was well supplied with banking towns in 1920 (having 8 in all), had two in 1933. Calhoun has done better. Out of three in 1920, it had two in 1933. There is, however, a very substantial area around Columbia without banking facilities at all in 1933 except to the degree that it is feasible for the residents of this section to do their banking in Columbia, which would require in many instances a very considerable journey. Whether and to what extent the towns and villages in this territory could support banks, or strong branches of Columbia banks, only first-hand observation and study could ascertain. It is further to be observed that the city of Columbia, so far as reported by the Reserve Bank of Richmond up to and including May 24, had no member bank in operation.

Williamsburg county in the eastern section of the state is another interesting case. It is a large county with an area of 882 square miles. It had 7 banking towns in 1920, and had only one left in 1933. Berkeley to the south of it, with an area of 1,203 square miles had three in 1920 and had one in 1933. Georgetown to the east, with an area of 828 square miles, has lost one of its two banking towns. Williamsburg county in 1929 produced 13,300 bales of cotton, and boasted a population of 34,900. Berkeley with a population of 22,200 produced manufactured goods valued at nearly $1,500,000 in 1929 and produced nearly 3,000 bales of cotton. Georgetown county had a population of 21,700 and produced manufactured goods valued at about $2,700,000.

DISTRIBUTION OF BANKING FACILITIES IN
SEVEN STATES IN THE YEARS 1920 AND 1933

(Each "banking town" is marked by
a dot on the map of the states)

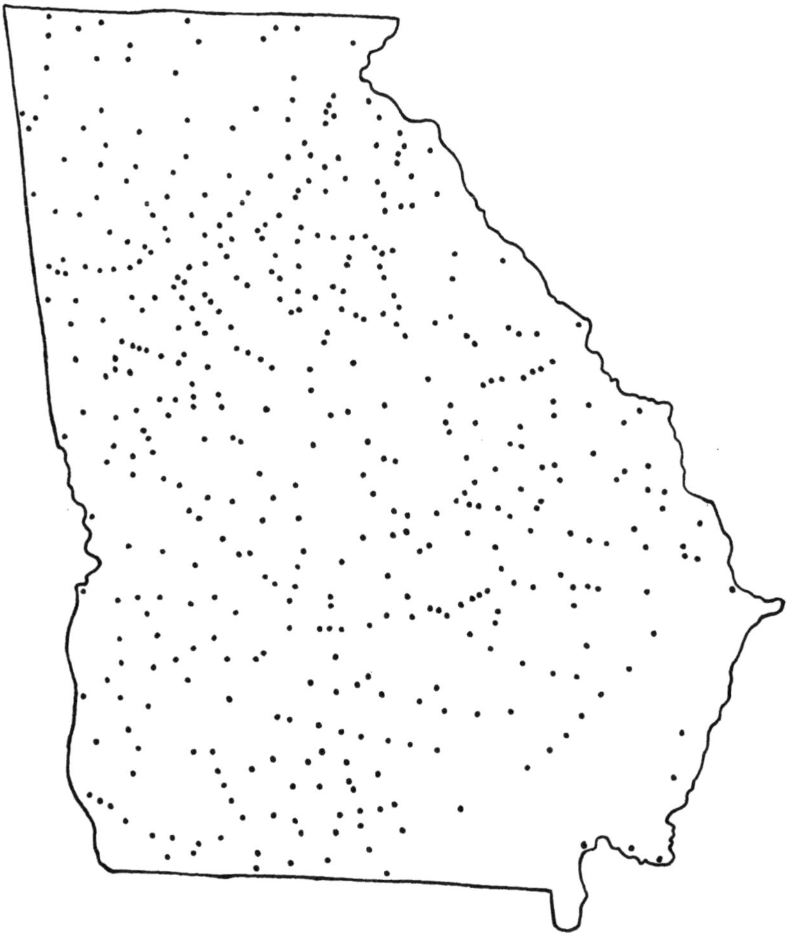

CHART I. GEORGIA, 1920

CHART II. GEORGIA, 1933

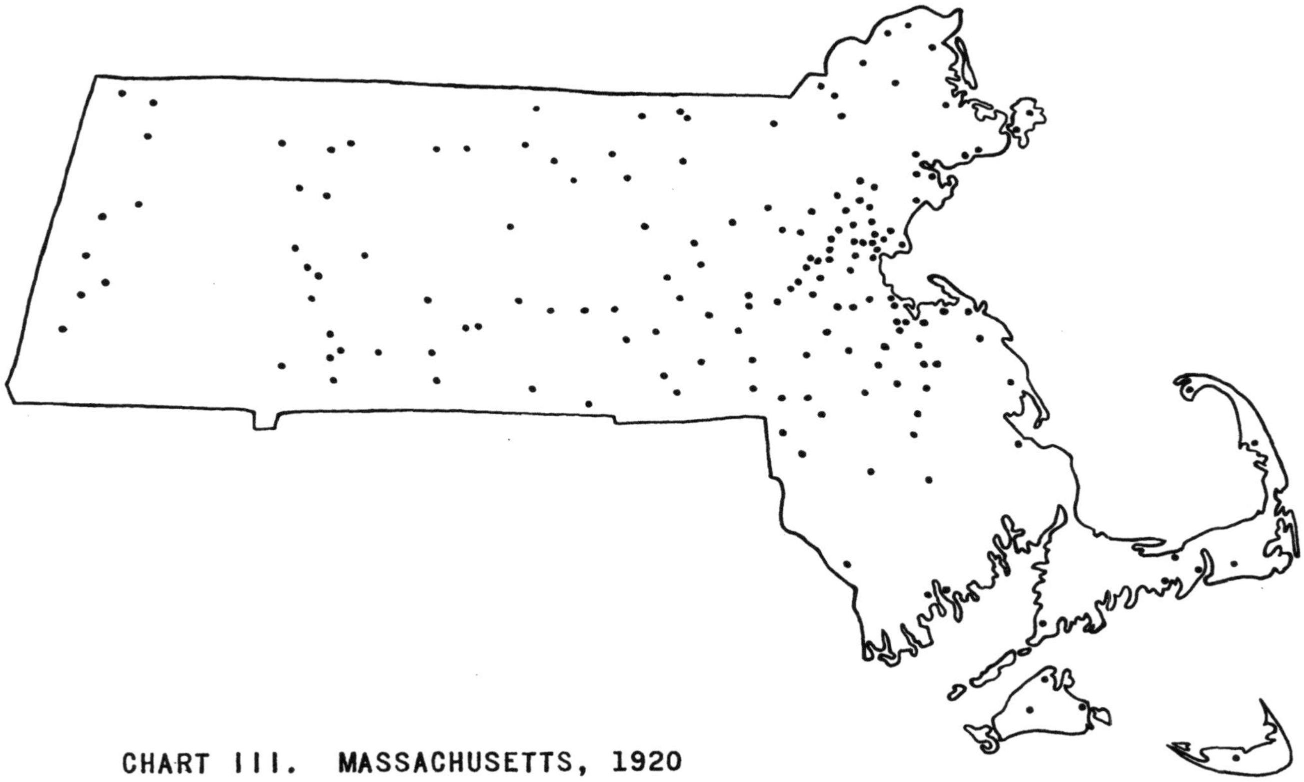

CHART III. MASSACHUSETTS, 1920

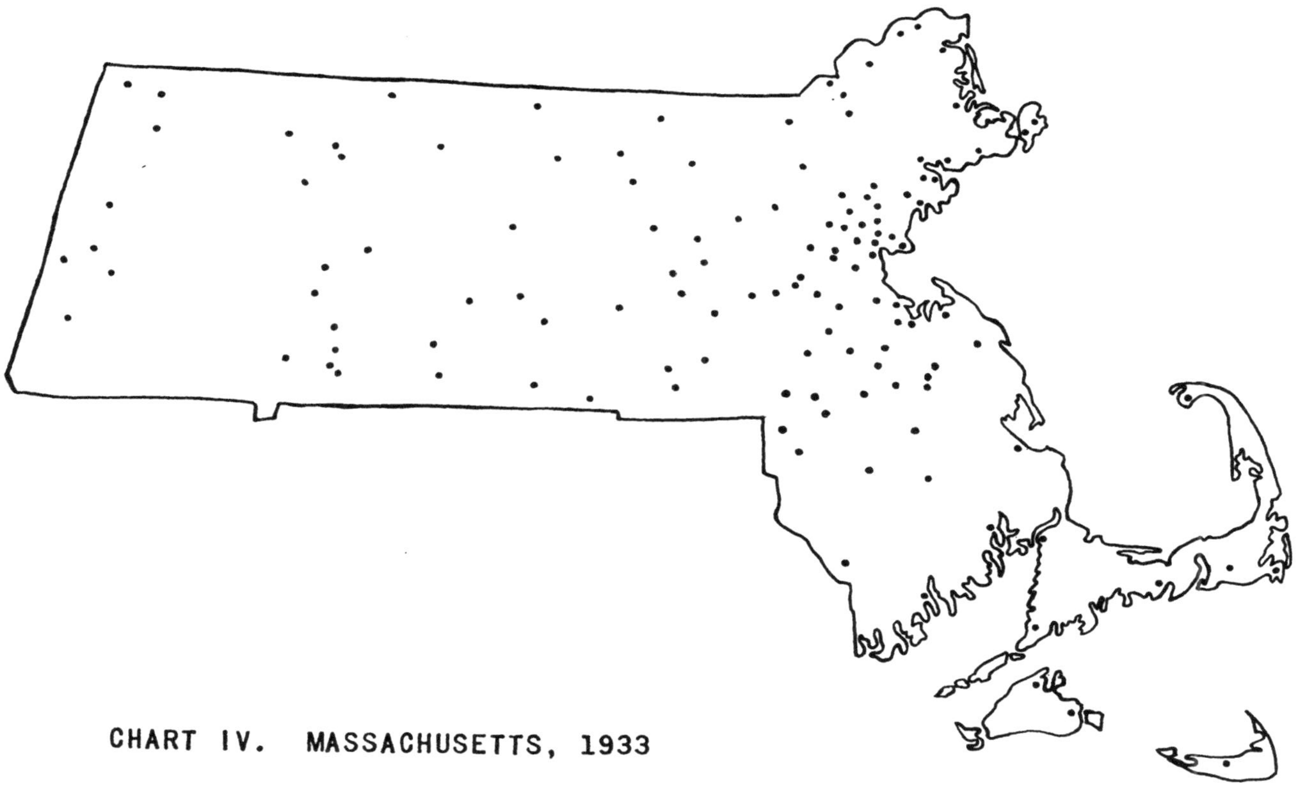

CHART IV. MASSACHUSETTS, 1933

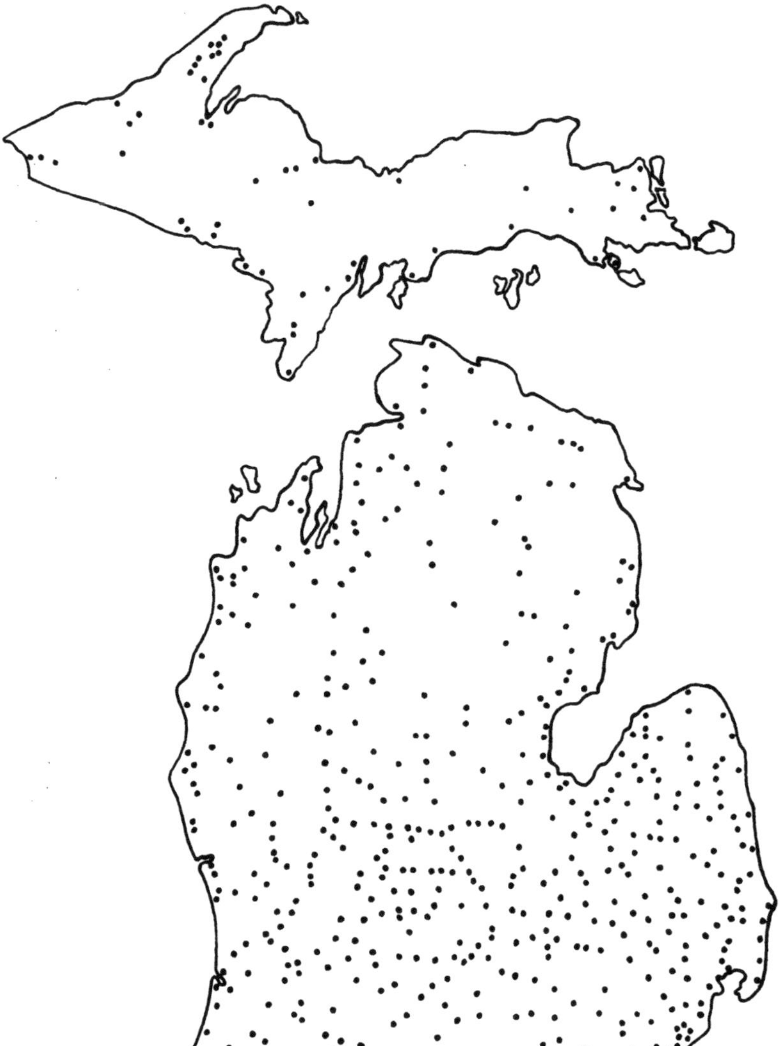

CHART V. MICHIGAN, 1920

CHART VI. MICHIGAN, 1933

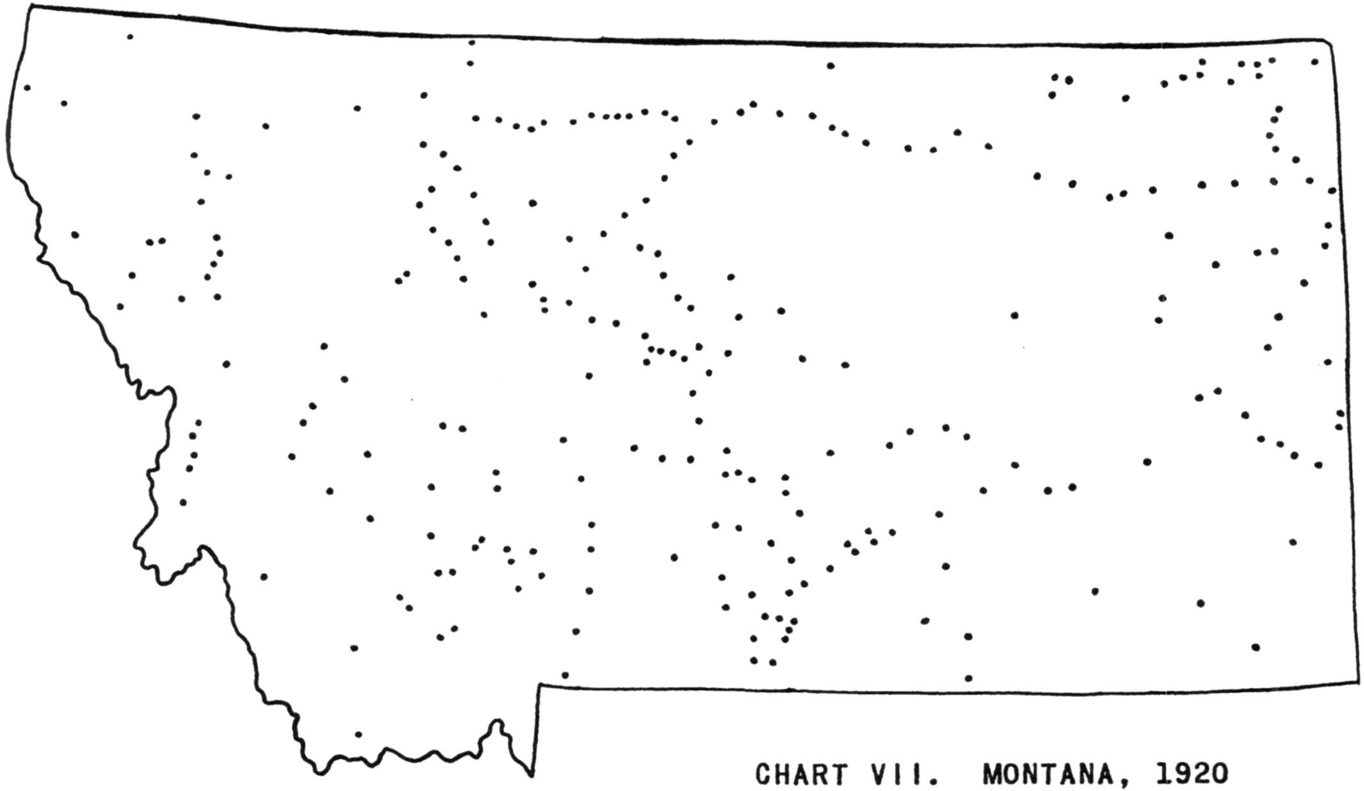

CHART VII. MONTANA, 1920

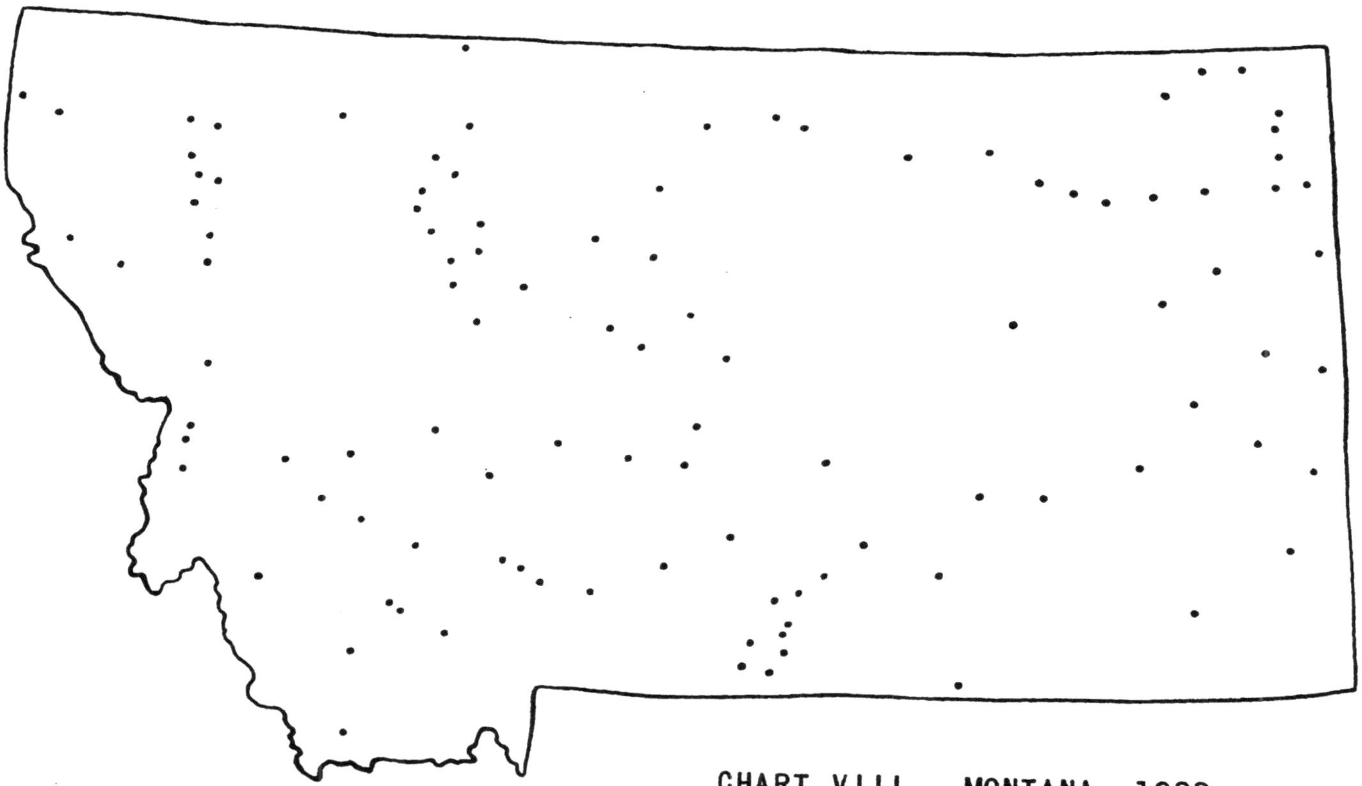

CHART VIII. MONTANA, 1933

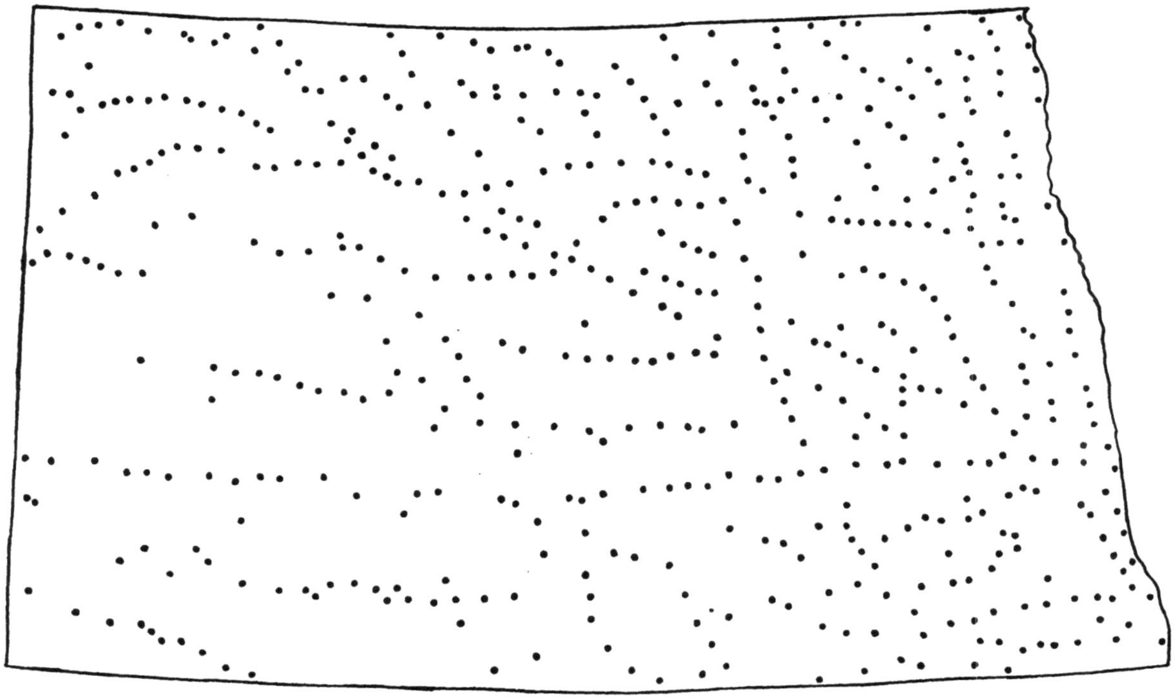

CHART IX. NORTH DAKOTA, 1920

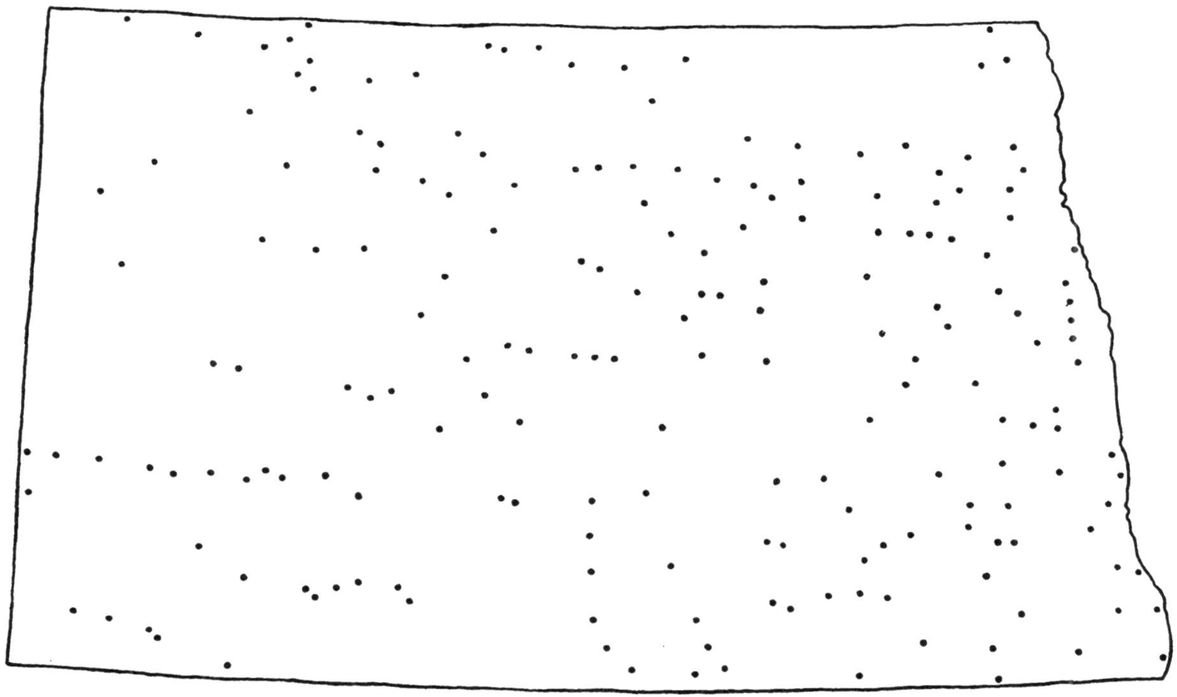

CHART X. NORTH DAKOTA, 1933

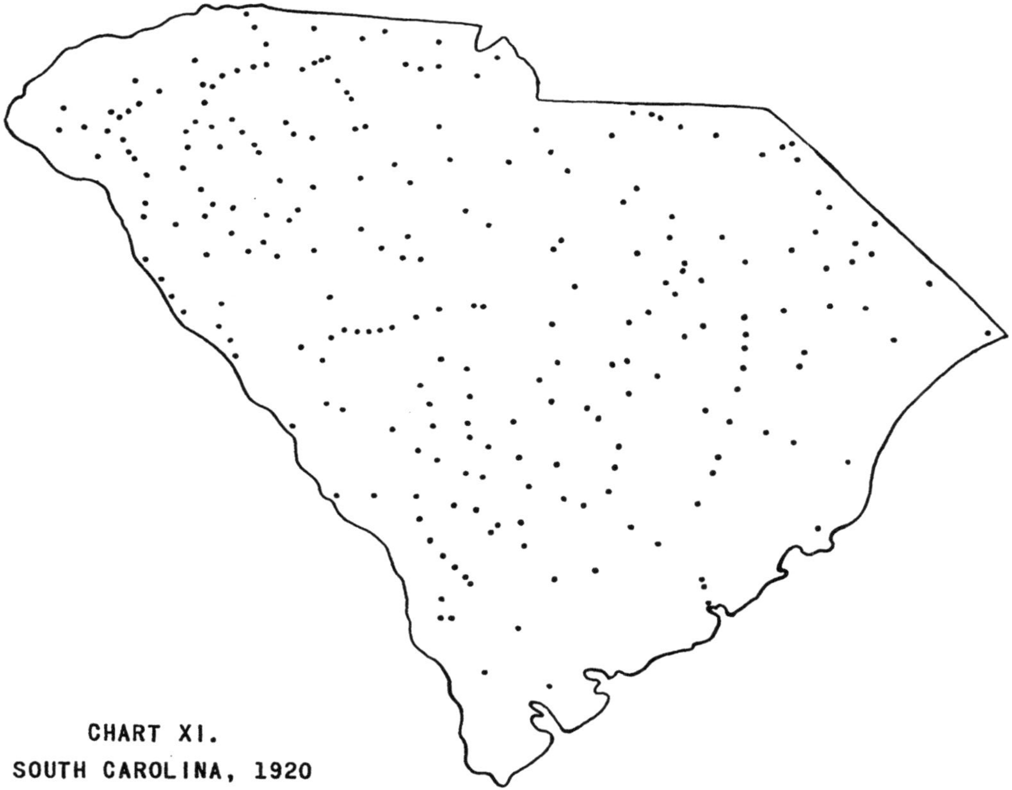

CHART XI.
SOUTH CAROLINA, 1920

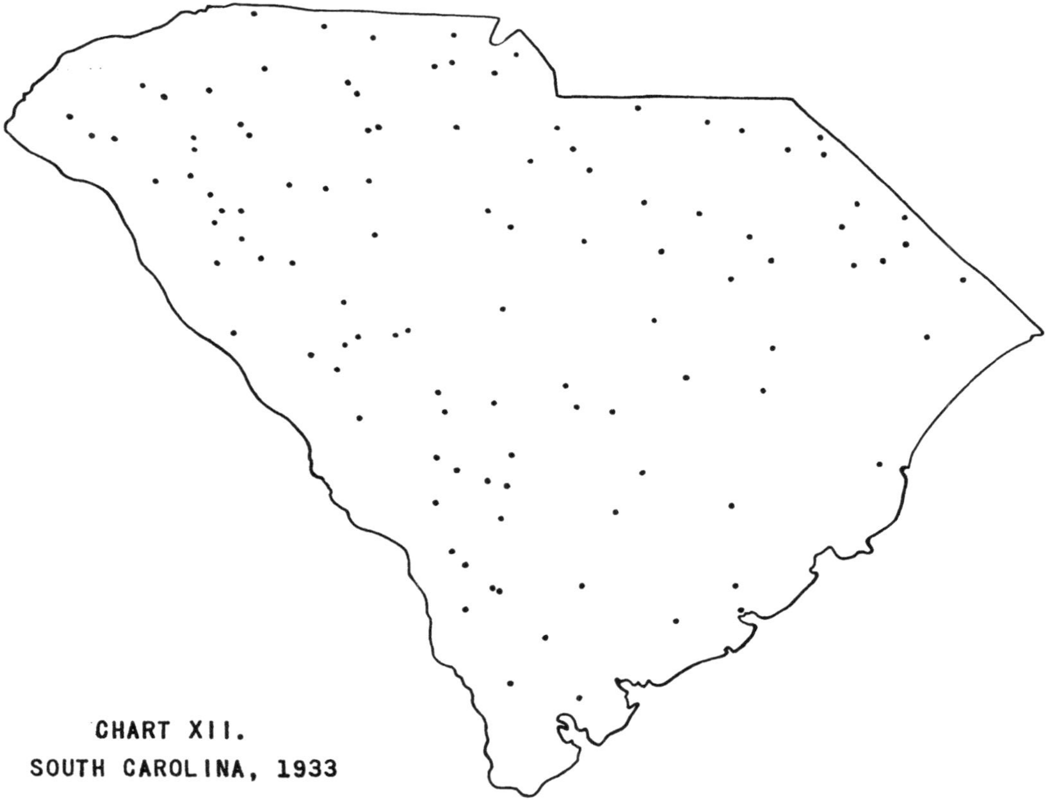

CHART XII.
SOUTH CAROLINA, 1933

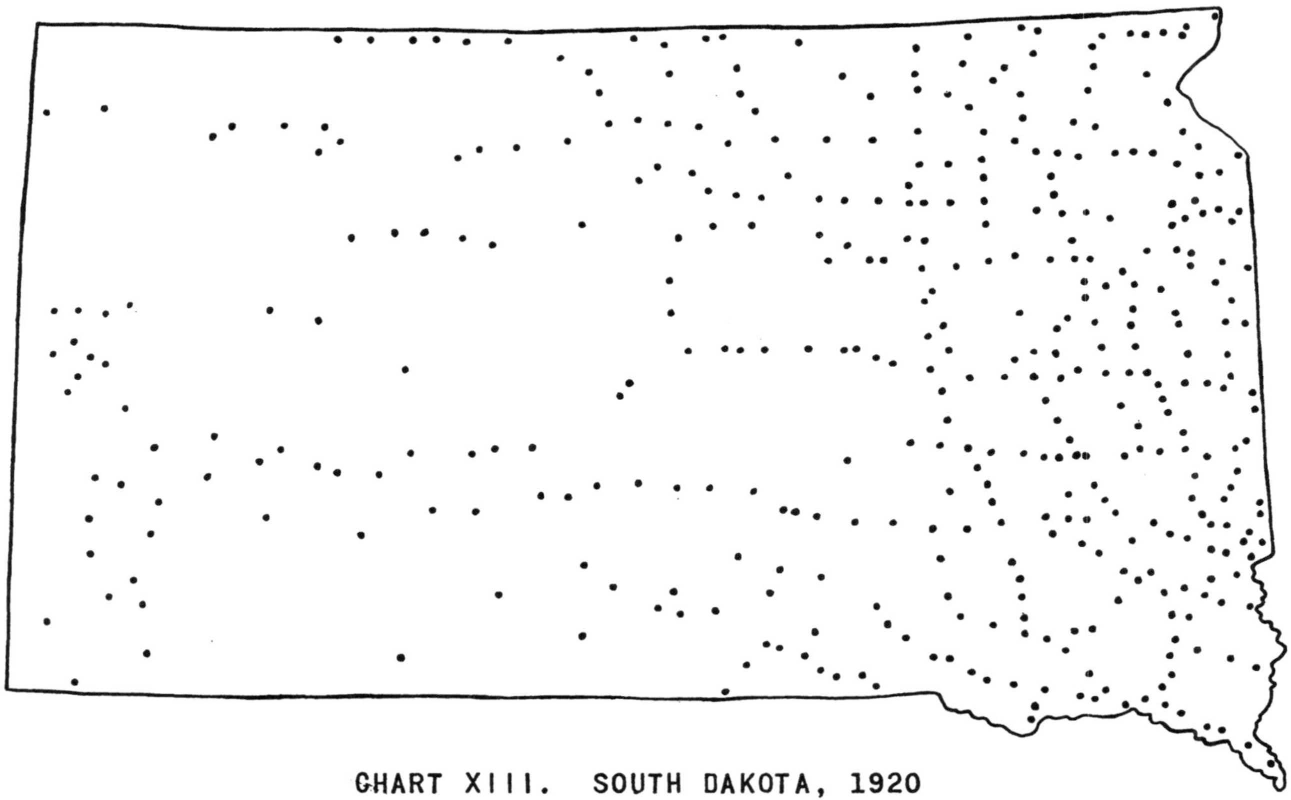

CHART XIII. SOUTH DAKOTA, 1920

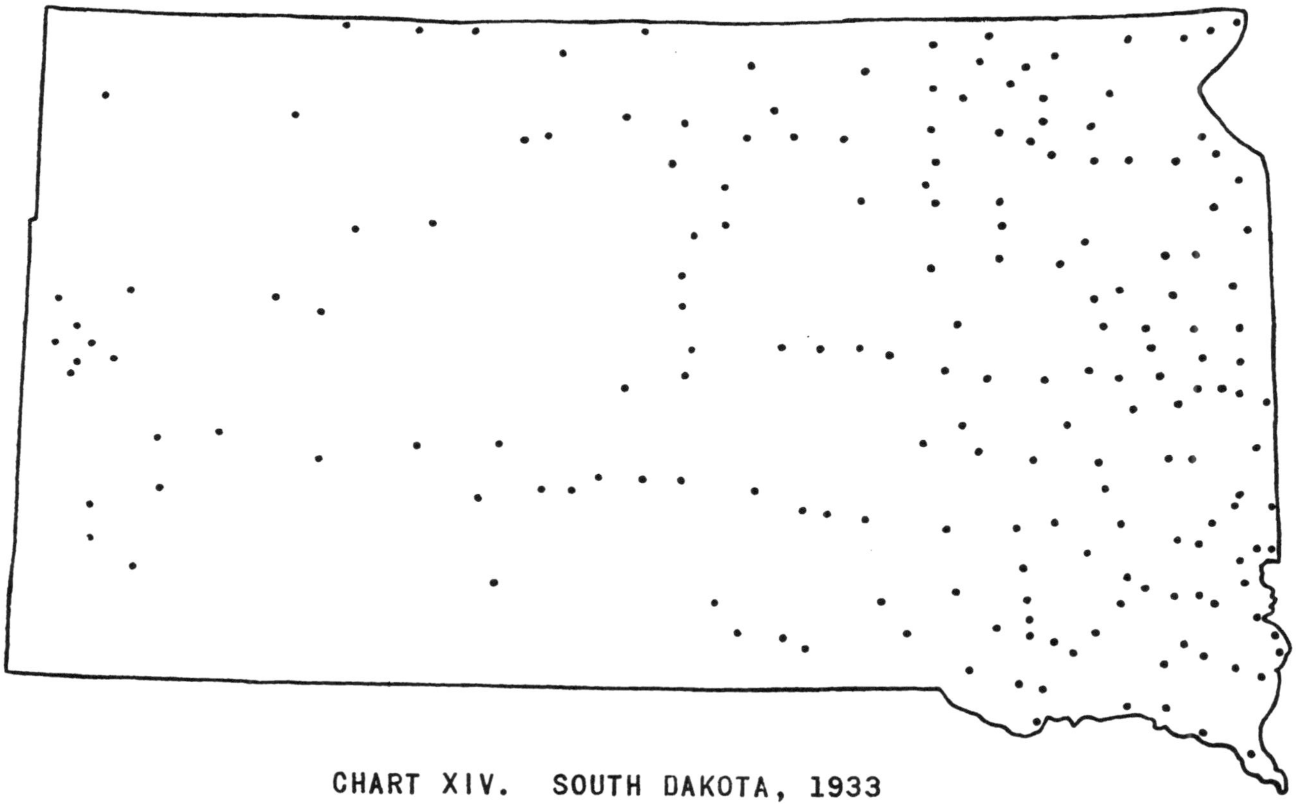

CHART XIV. SOUTH DAKOTA, 1933

PART III

CONTROL

CHAPTER XV

BANK MERGERS AND CONSOLIDATIONS

Introduction

The foregoing chapters outline the present position of banking in the United States. Processes by which existing conditions were attained and the present position of the system have been reviewed; the development of various types of financial institutions surveyed; the bank-failure situation sketched. This survey has been purely descriptive—a consideration and analysis of the factors which have led to the gradual evolution of the present banking structure. By the side of this change in structure, there has, however, proceeded a parallel change in control. Indeed, we may seriously question whether the changes that have taken place in the structural position of banking in the United States could have been expected to occur—certainly not in any such form or sequence—had there not been important and far-reaching alterations in the management and control of the banks from a corporate standpoint.

Perhaps in no department of American financial and industrial life has the change of control been so remarkable as has been the case in connection with the corporate organization of the banks of the country. The tendencies which have been at work in this connection may be qualified broadly under a few heads, as follows:

1. The drift toward the establishment of a branch-banking system with branch offices whose assets and liabilities constituted a part of the combined balance sheet of the parent bank.

2. The parallel drift toward a holding-company type of organization in which a single corporate entity became the actual owner of a series of corporately organized banking units.

3. As a phase or coördinate element in the foregoing trend, the parallel development of what is called "chain banking," wherein control or domination is exercised by one or more

large stockholders who retain in their own hands the dominating voice in a series of banking institutions.

4. The establishment of an intimate connection between the commercial and investment banking situations through the organization of so-called "affiliates," corporately organized enterprises, devoted to the performance of various functions which were judged to be outside of the charter powers of the parent banks.

5. The tendency to unite banking institutions by the means of mergers, or consolidations, with a view to bringing about the organization of institutions of very large size and with widespread affiliations, resulting in the control of other banks, usually through the correspondent system.

These alterations in corporate control have been rendered more significant and important by reason of various modifications that have taken place in the relationship between the banks themselves and the reserve institutions. It has been natural that as the development of the country proceeded, there should be an alteration in point of view with regard to the necessity and amount of banking reserves that were to be carried. It would have been well if this alteration had been produced, as for example, in Canada, through the self-conscious action of the community in periodically revising its banking laws. It has not taken place, however, in that way at all, but as the result of changes in practice and technique, reinterpretation of the constituent banking legislation of the country, and it must be added, in some cases, through disregard or violation of these fundamental banking laws. The following chapters are intended to review the alterations in control which have thus taken place, and to set forth as compactly as possible the changes that have thus developed in the administration and oversight of the banking system as such. No such sketch would be complete unless it also included a survey of the influence or oversight exerted by the government over the banks. This influence has been produced in two ways; through the fact that the government was itself a very large customer or a depositor in the various banks of the country, and again, through the long process of examination and administrative correction. It has, therefore, been thought desirable to add a brief chapter dealing with the subject of public deposits to conclude the section, with an additional chapter relating to some of the pending questions of examination which present themselves most urgently at the present moment.

CONCENTRATION MOVEMENT[1]

A phase of the changing banking situation which has received much attention during recent years is the growth and extent of the merger or consolidation movement among commercial institutions. Certain phases of the movement have an important bearing upon general organization. Changes which have occurred from a legal point of view since 1900 have made it easier and less costly to effect bank consolidations. The causes working toward concentration have been such as to result in a more definite tendency of the movement, and to indicate that the culmination of so large a number of mergers is the result of banking changes made necessary by general trends in the banking system over a long period of years. Some of these factors were the chartering of a large number of small banks, inefficient bank management, and the creation of far too many banks in certain communities.

Despite the general recognition among bankers, business men, and economists that concentration has grown apace in recent years, it is doubtful if the public fully realizes the extent and importance of the movement. It is not new, nor is it limited to any particular country or type of banking. It pervades practically all classes of business enterprise. We are here essentially interested with this development as it relates to the general field of banking. In this field the movement has attained its greatest growth in England, France, and Germany. There the banking business has gradually passed, over a period of time, into the hands of a few large financial institutions. Concentration has manifested itself in larger and fewer banks. The decline of numbers has been accompanied by an increase in most countries in the number of branches or banking offices. The process of bring-

[1] The remainder of this chapter has been written by John M. Chapman.

ing institutions together in foreign countries has been commonly referred to as the *amalgamation* movement. In the United States it is generally known as the bank merger or consolidation movement.

The concentration movement includes such phases of banking as chain and group banking (in the United States), branch banking ,the development of larger unit banks, bank mergers and control through interlocking directorates. This chapter, however, is intended to present some of the legal aspects of the case as well as the scope and extent, and results of bank mergers and consolidations. Other aspects of the concentration movement have been dealt with, at least in part, in other sections of this study. We shall outline only the more salient features of this important development in banking.

Legal Obstacles

The late appearance of bank mergers in large numbers in the United States as compared with England and other European countries may be explained by a number of factors. Among the most important were legal difficulties, the extensive development of unit banking, the opposition to any form of branch banking, and the almost unlimited opportunities for all who care to enter the banking business. Banking competition had not, until recently, reached a point where the banker was unable, generally speaking, to secure or develop sufficient business to make his bank fairly profitable.

The process of effecting bank mergers and consolidations has been made more difficult by the existence of state and national banks which are administered under different sets of laws enacted, in turn, by different legislative bodies. The obstacles growing out of this dual system were modified considerably by two acts of Congress: the Consolidation Act of November 7, 1918, and the McFadden-Pepper Act of 1927. The latter granted national banks the right to merge or consolidate with state banks on the same terms and conditions essentially as those required for the consolidation of two or more national banks. Yet, it is, perhaps even now, slightly more convenient for two national banks to merge than for a state bank and a national bank. Certainly in the former case only one supervising authority must be consulted, while in the latter, two or more may be involved.

Prior to the passage of the Consolidation Act of November 7, 1918, a national bank could not consolidate with another national or state bank until one or both had gone into voluntary liquidation; in which case it was possible for the continuing bank to buy the assets of the liquidating bank. In other cases, both banks went into voluntary liquidation, whereupon a new bank was organized which, in turn, bought the assets of the liquidating banks. The Act of 1918 permitted two or more national banks to consolidate directly without the liquidation of either. This law, however, made no provision for the merging of state and national banks. In order to avoid the liquidating process some national banks were converted into state banks before the merger in order to permit the consolidation directly under state laws. The reverse was true in connection with the absorption of state banks by national banks after the enactment of the legislation in 1918. The McFadden Amendment of 1927 provided that national banks could consolidate directly with state banks. This latter law greatly simplified the process of merging banking institutions.

The different state banking laws have varied and do vary considerably, one from another, regarding methods and procedure for effecting bank mergers and consolidations. In the main, however, such combinations could be effected easily when all participating banks were being operated under a single state jurisdiction. It was an unusual occurrence when a state bank in one state was merged with, or absorbed by, a state bank located in another state. The same was true of the union of national banks. In general, then, it may be said that no special legal problems were involved so far as state bank mergers were concerned.

In a few states, where a guaranty deposit law was in operation, there has been a tendency for state bankers to shift from the state to the national system in order to free themselves from the liabilities imposed by such a guaranty law. This condition was marked in the state of Oklahoma during the period when the compulsory guaranty law was effective. The results were conclusive as shown by the number of state banks which entered the national system either by merger or conversion. The number of national banks that left the national system to become state banks was small, comparatively. The general breakdown of these various "protective laws" has, of course, largely removed this from the list of causes for the shifting of banks from state to national system or national to state system, except in so far as early experience with the guaranty fund still exerts an influence on the state bankers.

Prohibitive branch-banking laws in several states have had a tremendous effect, indirectly, upon the merger movement. There is usually no incentive for a bank to absorb another bank situated at a distance from the absorbing bank unless the absorbed institution may be continued as a branch. In such circumstances all that the absorbing bank could do would be to provide an orderly method for the liquidation of the absorbed bank with the possibility that it might secure some of the old accounts of the liquidating bank. Such transfer of business is not likely if there are other banks situated in the same community as the bank that is absorbed. Even if such a process be used there is present the danger that the absorbing bank may, in the circumstances, drive a "hard bargain," leaving less for the depositors and stockholders than they are entitled to.

The effects or results of prohibitive branch banking legislation are clearly demonstrated by comparison of the conditions in the branch-banking states with those in states where branch-banking is not permitted in any form. They are especially noticeable in those states which allow state-wide branches, and to a lesser extent in states in which branches are operated on a more restricted basis. A comparison of merger developments in the states of California and Missouri illustrates this point admirably. In the former there has been a large number of mergers many of which have been sponsored by the Bank of America

National Trust and Savings Association,[2] or its affiliates. A larger number of the banks absorbed by this institution later became branches. In Missouri, with few exceptions, the banks involved were small and located in the same town or city as the absorbing bank. Doubtless there would have been a different type of merger in Missouri had banks there been allowed to operate branches. Branch-banking restrictions in this country limit the field and opportunities for bank mergers greatly as compared with the conditions in Germany and France where banks may establish branches where they please.

Scope and Extent of Bank Mergers

Deductions or conclusions regarding the consolidation movement should be based upon the number of mergers together with the volume of assets involved in relation to the number of banks in operation and their total resources. In this phase of our discussion we are particularly interested in the tendencies and scope of the merger movement in the United States in recent years. The growth of this movement since 1920 is especially marked and shows a distinct tendency toward a concentration of banking power and resources in the hands of fewer and fewer institutions. The number of mergers has been greatly accelerated since the beginning of the depression in 1929.

The importance of the merger development can not be satisfactorily measured by taking the total number of such combinations. Such data are both interesting and instructive but inadequate to portray the situation. The volume of resources in relation to the total resources of all banks in operation in the United States is a much better guide. Regardless of the relative merits of these two tests it is important to understand that whichever be applied, the results are striking. In 1929 there were more than 550 mergers involving more than 1,000 banks with total resources or more than $20,000,000,000, or more than 27 per cent of the total resources of all banks in the United States at that time. Since then the number of mergers has in-

[2] Formerly the Bank of Italy.

creased while the total volume of banking resources involved has declined sharply. The volume is still large and gives evidence of a continuation of the movement until such time as the total number of banks will be so decreased as to make a decline in the number of mergers a foregone conclusion. Such a decline in number may, in fact probably will, mean that the percentage volume of banking resources of all banks participating directly in the merger movement will increase both relatively and in the

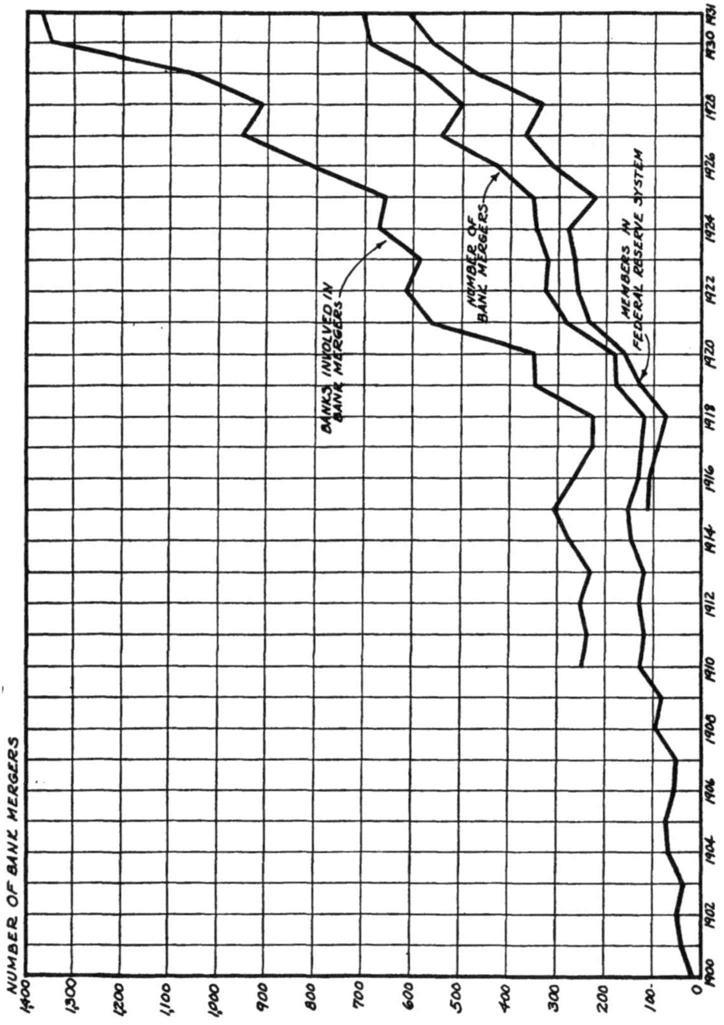

CHART XV. NUMBER OF BANK MERGERS AND CONSOLIDATIONS

aggregate in comparison with all banks in operation in the United States.

In Table 81, page 360, and Chart XV, it appears that the number of mergers increased from 1925 to 1931, year by year, with the exception of a slight decline in 1928 as compared with 1927. The volume of total resources of banks participating in mergers increased rapidly from 1925 to 1930, but registered a heavy drop during the two depression years, 1930 and 1931. In other words, the number of mergers increased during the so-called prosperous years, as well as during the lean years; whereas, the resources of participating banks dropped during the depression. The "average size" of the banks involved in 1930 and 1931 was much smaller than during the earlier years.

Reasons for mergers during the two periods were different in many cases. The larger banks did not expand through mergers and consolidations, to any great extent, after 1929. Smaller banks were being absorbed in order to relieve "banks in distress" or to relieve an "over-banked" condition. Among the various causes for bank mergers and consolidations outlined in the following section of this chapter, that of preventing bank failures has become much more important since the beginning of the depression in 1929. The desire to secure branches and trust business has declined in importance. This is an extremely interesting and an important feature of the depression period of bank mergers. The factors at work in 1929 especially, were the desire to secure size, power, and prestige—in some sections ambition to get a larger number of branches was predominant.

In Table 81 are presented statistics to show the growth and extent of bank mergers and consolidations throughout the period 1919 to 1931, inclusive.

The number of banks involved was slightly less than twice the number of mergers. This does not mean that there were invariably two banks involved in each merger. Although this was generally the case, there were many instances in which one bank was taken over by two, three, or more banks. On the other hand there were a large number of mergers in which one bank absorbed during one year several small banks. That was notably

TABLE 81

DATA FOR ALL BANKS INVOLVED IN BANK MERGERS AND CONSOLIDATIONS, AND FOR ALL BANKS IN OPERATION IN THE UNITED STATES

(All dollar amounts in millions of dollars)

DATA OF BANKS PARTICIPATING IN BANK MERGERS AND CONSOLIDATIONS, 1919 TO 1931

YEAR	NUMBER OF MERGERS	TOTAL NUMBER BANKS INVOLVED	TOTAL NUMBER BANKS ABSORBED	DISTRIBUTION OF ABSORBED BANKS				NUMBER BANKS MEMBER FEDERAL RESERVE SYSTEM	TOTAL CAPITAL FUNDS	TOTAL RE-SOURCES
				National Banks by National Banks	State Banks by National Banks	State Banks by State Banks	National Banks by State Banks			
1919	178	345	178	32	19	101	26	134	261	1,862
1920	181	349	183	29	30	88	36	164	295	3,060
1921	281	559	292	38	50	159	45	222	409	3,798
1922	337	616	340	49	53	182	56	259	399	3,266
1923	325	584	325	47	41	172	65	261	524	4,354
1924	350	668	352	56	60	174	62	277	340	3,318
1925	352	657	356	41	46	214	55	227	376	3,606
1926	429	814	429	70	57	243	59	310	739	6,974
1927	543	955	544	69	95	286	94	362	801	7,403
1928	501	916	507	71	88	277	71	338	874	7,455
1929	571	1,060	575	96	108	261	110	474	2,420	20,053
1930	699	1,346	698	130	135	322	111	564	1,695	11,598
1931	706	1,363	719	164	107	320	128	612	1,465	10,729

TABLE 81 (*Continued*)

DATA FOR ALL BANKS INVOLVED IN BANK MERGERS AND CONSOLIDATIONS, AND FOR ALL BANKS IN OPERATION IN THE UNITED STATES

(*All dollar amounts in millions of dollars*)

DATA OF ALL BANKS IN THE UNITED STATES, 1919 TO 1932

YEAR	TOTAL NUMBER BANKS	National Banks	All State Banks	Member Federal Reserve System	TOTAL CAPITAL FUNDS	TOTAL RESOURCES
1919	29,123	7,785	21,338	8,822	5,445	47,615
1920	30,139	8,030	22,109	9,399	6,089	53,079
1921	30,812	8,154	22,658	9,745	6,357	49,671
1922	30,389	8,249	22,140	9,892	6,575	50,425
1923	30,178	8,241	21,937	9,856	6,806	54,035
1924	29,348	8,085	21,263	9,650	7,053	57,145
1925	28,841	8,072	20,769	9,538	7,350	62,057
1926	28,146	7,978	20,168	9,375	7,808	64,893
1927	27,061	7,796	19,265	9,099	8,272	68,133
1928	26,213	7,691	18,522	8,929	8,897	71,574
1929	25,330	7,536	17,794	8,707	9,506	72,173
1930	24,079	7,252	16,827	8,315	10,013	74,020
1931	22,071	6,805	15,266	7,782	9,473	70,209
1932	19,163	6,150	13,013	6,980	8,093	57,245

the case with the Bank of Italy in 1927, just before the provisions of the McFadden-Pepper Act became effective. The results of such mergers are clearly indicated in Table 81 which shows that the number of banks engaged, or participating in, the mergers was not double the number of mergers reported. There was a considerable increase in the number of members of the Federal Reserve system affected by mergers.

Much of the data given in Table 81 are presented in chart form. This chart will assist those who are interested in the consolidation movement to get a clearer picture of the changes taking place in this connection during the past 13 years. Table 81 and Chart XV present a very complete picture of the whole movement.

A review of Chart XV brings out some significant points relative to the consolidation of banks. The decline in the total number of banks in operation in the United States was not accompanied by a falling off in the number of bank mergers and consolidations. In fact the reverse was true. No doubt one of the primary causes for the decline in the number of banking institutions was found in the bank merger movement itself. As evidence of the accuracy of this conclusion it is interesting to observe that during the period 1921 to 1931 more than 5,490 banks were absorbed.

Table 82, page 363, shows generally the relative importance of state and national banking systems as regards the tendency of banks to shift from one system to another. By far the larger number of banks involved in mergers belonged to the state systems. State banks absorbed more banks than did national. The number of state banks absorbed by national banks was approximately equal to the number of national banks absorbed by state banks. In some years one, and in some years the other, was the larger. Percentage Table 82 showing the distribution of absorbed banks according to their membership in a state, or in the national system, illustrates this point clearly. Relatively speaking, there has been a decline in the number of national banks absorbed by other national banks, with a corresponding increase in the number of state banks absorbed by national banks and, the number of national banks absorbed by state banks.

Metropolitan Bank Mergers

The most widely heralded bank consolidations have been those which took place in the large metropolitan cities and which involved the larger commercial banks and trust com-

TABLE 82

PERCENTAGE DISTRIBUTION OF BANK MERGERS AND CONSOLIDATIONS SHOWING THE NUMBER OF BANKS ABSORBED BY STATE AND NATIONAL BANKS

(Each class expressed as a percentage of total)

YEAR	TOTAL NUMBER BANKS ABSORBED	NATIONAL BANKS ABSORBED BY NATIONAL BANKS	STATE BANKS ABSORBED BY NATIONAL BANKS	STATE BANKS ABSORBED BY STATE BANKS	NATIONAL BANKS ABSORBED BY STATE BANKS
1910	128	25.0	10.2	54.6	10.2
1911	119	21.0	15.1	55.5	8.4
1912	128	30.5	10.2	52.3	7.0
1913	118	13.6	8.5	66.1	11.8
1914	143	20.3	16.8	53.1	9.8
1915	154	21.4	15.6	48.7	14.3
1916	134	26.8	11.2	46.3	15.7
1917	123	21.1	12.2	50.5	16.3
1918	125	12.8	16.0	58.4	12.8
1919	178	17.9	10.6	56.9	14.6
1920	183	15.8	16.4	48.1	19.7
1921	292	13.0	17.2	54.4	15.4
1922	340	14.4	15.6	53.5	16.5
1923	325	14.5	12.6	52.9	20.0
1924	352	14.2	17.1	49.4	17.3
1925	356	11.5	12.9	60.1	15.5
1926	429	16.3	13.3	56.6	13.8
1927	544	12.7	17.4	52.6	17.3
1928	507	14.0	17.4	54.6	14.0
1929	575	16.7	18.8	45.4	19.1
1930	698	18.6	19.4	46.1	15.9
1931	719	22.8	14.9	44.5	17.8

panies. Mergers involving the largest volume of banking resources and attracting the widest public attention have been sponsored by banks in New York City, Boston, Chicago, Los

Angeles, San Francisco, Detroit, and Philadelphia. Other cities have also witnessed the building up of huge financial institutions through consolidations. The largest merger on record occurred in New York in May, 1930, and involved the Chase National Bank, the Equitable Trust Company, and the Interstate Trust Company. As a result of the union of these three banks, the Chase became the largest bank, not only in the United States, but in the world. By a series of many mergers, running over a period of years and including both state and national banks, the Bank of Italy, now the Bank of America, National Trust and Savings Association, San Francisco, became the largest branch-banking institution in this country which operated branches on a state-wide basis.

The almost sudden development of these enormous financial institutions in the United States was largely because of the many mergers consummated in the larger cities. Without resort to this method of growth, many years would have been necessary to permit these banks to reach anything like their present size. The existence, therefore, of these large aggregations must be ascribed to the merger movement.

The size of the banks involved and the publicity given to consolidations have lessened the degree of interest in the much larger number of small bank combinations which occurred in different parts of the country. In fact many of these smaller bank mergers have been only stepping stones to larger mergers, as is seen from the circumstance that, in many cases, several small banks were absorbed, or brought together and later absorbed, by a large bank. This process has been especially marked in California, where the Bank of Italy, its affiliates and successors, have secured a very large number of branches in different parts of the state. It is, of course, true that the process was much more extensively used there than elsewhere, but would have been more extensively employed had the National Bank Act and the Federal Reserve system not prohibited national banks and state member banks from establishing branches on a state-wide basis. Similar results have been attained, perhaps not consciously, in New York and Detroit.

Reasons for Bank Mergers

Once it is realized that there have been many bank mergers and consolidations among our banking institutions during the past two decades, and especially during the last decade, it is natural to make inquiry into the causes and effects of this development in our banking system. Our first question is naturally, "What has caused this movement?" Second, "What are the results to our banking and economic system?" It is interesting, of course, to know the type of bank involved and the number of the mergers, but, fundamentally and finally, we are anxious to ascertain the results to be derived or enjoyed from such a wide and important development in the field of banking. Let us now consider the causes for these mergers, leaving for a later part of this discussion a consideration of the effects.

There is no one cause for bank mergers and consolidations in the United States. The causes differ in different parts of the country as well as in the same community. The underlying factors vary also from year to year. Causes and factors at work in one state may be entirely lacking or absent in another state. In some states there are certain forces at work to bring about an almost continuous stream of consolidations, whereas, in certain other states the mergers come sporadically, and the cause for one merger has nothing in common with the cause or causes of another merger in the same or adjoining city or county. In some states the banking officials take a special interest in effecting mergers for one cause or another, while, at the same time, there is very little interest in the subject on the part of the state or federal banking authorities in other sections of the country.

No attempt will be made to list or discuss the causes for bank mergers and consolidations in the order of their importance. This would be useless, for it is a well-known fact that the principal cause in one community may be a minor cause, if one at all, in another community. Let us now discuss these causes in the following order.

1. *Bank failures.*—One of the outstanding factors in the consolidation movement has been bank failures. In an effort to avoid bank failures, many bankers and stockholders have made

serious attempts to have their bank taken over by a stronger institution. In some cases two or more banks may be in difficulties and a reorganization is effected and the banking resources are pooled with the idea that a crisis may be avoided for each of the banks involved. In not a few cases, as already indicated, the banking officials have urged banks to unite in order to prevent a failure. The number of bank mergers effected each year during the last decade in this country, as a result of the unhealthy banking institutions, has been large. This cause has been exceedingly important in several southern and mid-western states. It may properly be regarded as one of the few most powerful forces at work in this country to bring about bank consolidations.

2. *Branch banking.*—Branch banking has been, perhaps, the most effective cause in the State of California and, to a lesser degree, in New York City. The *de novo* rule of the state banking department in California made it difficult for the large banks in San Francisco and Los Angeles to extend their branches in many communities where other banks were in operation. By buying out or absorbing these smaller banks, branches may be established; hence the close relationship between the merger and branch-banking movements in that state. The relationship has been close in other branch banking states but not to the same degree, perhaps, as in California.

3. *Trust business.*—The keen competition among bankers for commercial banking business and the comparatively undeveloped trust field induced not a few banks to enter the trust business. The nature of trust work is such that it requires considerable time in order to develop a large volume of this business from the "ground up." Many bankers found a short cut by uniting with, or absorbing, a smaller trust company which had a sizeable volume of business already on its books. It may be safely concluded, therefore, that trust business has had a very important bearing upon the growth of bank mergers and consolidations. This factor has been of considerable importance in the consolidation movement and is likely to continue to be so in the near future.

4. *Size and prestige.*—Not a few bankers seek to control and operate the largest bank in the community. Other bankers strive to be among the "leaders." To maintain their stride, it is frequently difficult to develop sufficient new business. One way to avoid this difficulty and, at the same time, to increase the volume of business, is to take over a bank already in existence. At one stroke, so to speak, the absorbing bank increases its size in a very effective manner. Often months and years would be required to secure as much new business as is obtained by one merger. In like manner some bankers seek to be the president or chairman of the largest bank in their own city. This desire for position and power impels them to consummate one or more bank mergers in order to out-strip their competitors. These two factors either jointly, or separately, have been quite effective forces in this concentration movement.

5. *Over-banked communities.*—In not a few communities in certain parts of the country there were too many banks in comparison with the volume of banking business to be done. Under such conditions the banks engaged or tended to engage in rather severe and costly competition. The overhead expenses were too great for the potential returns, especially if the banks stuck closely to sound banking business. Many banks operating under these unfavorable circumstances undertook to meet their expenses by investing in speculative loans and securities because of the higher yields which were promised. In due course these practices and policies put the banks into a position of having to write off heavy losses which they were in no financial position to do. As this continued, and as other banks failed to earn a substantial income, there was a real demand for a reduction in the number of banking institutions. Under conditions such as these it becomes fairly easy to induce bankers to consider merging their bank, or banks with others, in order to make them more successful and to reduce or eliminate the danger of further losses or failure, or both. This factor has been an important one in certain sections or parts of the West and Northwest.

6. *Enlarged banking facilities.*—The growing size of the business unit has placed not a few bankers in a position where

they were unable to provide the kind of banking services needed by their customers. In order to keep themselves in line or in a position in which they could finance such concerns the bankers have taken steps in many instances to enlarge their banks so as to be able to make the larger loans which were demanded. In other cases customers became interested in foreign credits which, in turn, required a different type of financing. Bankers, in order to supply such facilities, undertook to merge or absorb other banks, and thus place themselves in a position where they could undertake this type of financing. This has been advanced by bankers as the "cause" for mergers, whereas mere size or prestige was the true underlying factor causing the consolidations

Effects of Bank Mergers

The merger and consolidation movement which has attained such importance in recent years in this country had, several years ago, reached a rather advanced stage in many leading foreign countries, as for example, England, France, and Germany. The movement in this country has been closely related to other fundamental changes taking place in our banking system as a whole. The merger movement is a part of the concentration movement and as such has played a very important rôle in the changes which have been taking place in the general field of banking during recent years; especially has this relationship been marked since 1924. The individual mergers and consolidations have been, for the most part, a means to an end, such as the prevention of bank failures, increase in size, the securing of branches, etc. The results of this development are closely tied in with the causes of mergers.

The results of bank mergers and consolidations may be conveniently summarized as follows:

1. The large number of such combinations has greatly reduced the number of banking institutions in this country. It has reduced the number of banks in many communities without causing, in most cases, any reduction in the necessary banking facilities of the community. The total number of banks declined from 30,812, in 1921, to 19,163 in 1932, one of the major factors of which has been bank mergers. Since other factors have been

important in this decline, it must not be assumed that this is the only cause, or even the most important one.

2. There has been a decline in the number of members in the Federal Reserve system. This decline in membership has been the result primarily of some four factors: (*a*) bank failures, (*b*) bank mergers, (*c*) voluntary withdrawals from the system, and (*d*) the decline in the total number of national banks which has been, in turn, very largely due to the causes *a, b,* and *c.*

3. This movement has been accompanied by a strong tendency toward larger banking unts. It is true, of course, that most banks have shrunk in total resources since 1929, regardless of mergers and consolidations. It is, nevertheless, true that these banks are still larger in most cases than they would be had they not absorbed other banks in recent months or years. The further the movement goes the larger will be the "average size" of the American bank.

4. Many bank failures have been permanently avoided by means of a bank merger, or mergers. Many others have been temporarily "saved" by being absorbed. Data are not available to show what proportion of these absorbed banks have later been involved in a bank failure by reason of the unhealthy condition of the absorbing institution. In some states the loss in this way has been substantial. After making due allowance for such losses, it still holds true that many banks in the aggregate have avoided the onus and losses of bank failure which could not have been avoided by any means other than that of a bank merger.

5. As already outlined under the head of causes for bank mergers, branch banking has been an outstanding factor. An expansion of branches has been an important result in California, New York, Michigan, and, to a lesser extent, in several other states which permit branch banking in one form or another. It has not been possible to compile statistics to show the exact number of branches obtained through bank mergers. Attempts have been made to secure such information, but the difficulties of securing the number of branches for each bank just before and just after the merger have been too great. Moreover, a merger may result in a temporary increase in branches,

only to be followed later on by a loss of some of the additional offices by reason of a duplication of banking offices in a given community or certain section of the city. It should be further added that plans are often formulated, in effecting one merger, which contemplate the extension of branches later. Such facts and conditions can not be ascertained by merely enumerating the number and location of the mergers and consolidations. It is fair to assert, therefore, that there is an important relationship between the growth of bank mergers and the development of branch banking. This relationship will be greatly accelerated in the future should there be a liberalization of our branch-banking laws, either state or national or both.

6. Another interesting result of bank mergers has been to increase the capital funds in many cases. It should be added that an increase here is, by no means, a foregone conclusion. In far too many cases there is a drastic decline in the amount of capital funds reported. As a whole, the amount of capital funds reported over several years has shown a decline after the merger as compared with the amounts reported for the several banks prior to the merger or mergers. What has been accomplished in many such cases, however, has been the writing down of the stated capital to a figure more nearly in harmony with the capital actually possessed by the banks. This has been an important result. To the extent that this "write down" has been attained, mergers and consolidations have performed a very useful function in assisting in improving the banking situation.

7. The lending power of many individual banking institutions has been considerably augmented and, to a certain extent, the same applies to the banking system as a whole. The legal limits on loans would not be increased, of course, unless the total capital and surplus was expanded. This is true for the well known reason that the restrictions on loans (to individual borrowers) are based upon the capital and surplus of the lending bank. The lending power would be increased from an economic point of view since the bank would be able to get along on less cash reserves and balances in other banks aside from their legal reserve requirements. This would be possible for the same reason that a banking system which is well coördinated operates

with a smaller reserve than one which is loosely knit together. This point is illustrated by the reduction in reserve requirements under the Federal Reserve system as compared with those required under the old national banking system.

Aside from the total amount which could be loaned to one borrower, the bank, thus enlarged, would be able to make larger loans to individuals and to finance business concerns which they were unable to do before there had been an expansion in the capital and resources of the bank. The larger the lending power, the greater would be the possibilities for diversification in the portfolio, which is a desirable feature in sound banking practice. The larger the institution the better able will it be to finance international trade and commerce. Such a bank will be in a more favorable position to establish and maintain foreign banking connections and branches abroad. The question of the lending power of the banking community is a very important phase of the merger and consolidation developments as well as of the larger field of banking concentration in general.

Conclusions

Some problems involved in bank mergers and consolidations, as well as statistics showing the scope and extent of this development, have been stated in the preceding pages. The most important causes for the growth of this movement were included. It now appears necessary to summarize the more salient features of merger movement.

1. There have been more than 5,450 mergers and consolidations in the United States since 1918. The importance of the movement is more fully shown by the total volume of resources of banks involved in these changes. This has varied greatly from year to year, but in 1929 it amounted to more than $20,000,000,000, while in 1931 it had declined to $6,500,000,000.

2. One of the results of these consolidations has been that of reducing the number of banking institutions. During this period over 10,230 banks were involved in mergers with a total loss in the number of banks of more than 5,490.

3. The consolidation movement is itself a part of the concentration movement taking place in our banking system which

is widespread in its scope, and effects and includes the increasing size of the unit bank, chain and group banking, and branch banking.

4. Bank mergers have been used in many instances with success to prevent failures. So far as the method was used honestly, with proper adjustments in capital structure and the writing down of worthless or doubtless assets, it has been most helpful. Where these precautions were not taken, the results were not generally satisfactory, and in many such instances the continuing bank had to be closed at a later date.

5. The prohibition of branch banking in many states and the limited restrictions in other states have prevented the use of the merger process in adjusting the banking situation in a great many communities in the past. There is no particular reason why the stockholders of one bank should take over another bank unless there is a possibility of securing some permanent business, either directly or indirectly, from consolidation. In some cases banks have acted in the capacity of liquidators for banks which could not be absorbed and continued as branches. The extent to which this may be relied upon is small in comparison with the size and number of banks needing assistance.

6. Some of the legal obstacles which have prevented the absorption of national banks by national banks, or state banks by national banks, have been removed by the Consolidation Act of 1918 and the McFadden Act of 1927. The former permitted national banks to consolidate directly while the latter act permitted the absorption of state banks without either bank going into voluntary liquidation.

7. Some of the largest and most far-reaching mergers have occurred in the large cities and have been referred to as metropolitan bank mergers. Branch banking and trust business have been outstanding as causes for mergers of this type.

The principal causes for bank mergers have been to prevent bank failures, to secure trust business, to obtain branches, to enable the bank to provide broader services for their customers, to relieve an over-banked condition and, in some cases, to enable the officers and directors to satisfy their personal wishes to have the largest, or one of the largest, banks in the community.

CHAPTER XVI

CHAIN AND GROUP BANKING[1]

I. Chain Banking

Two other phases of the bank concentration movement in this country which have attracted wide attention are chain and group banking. These subjects are regarded as one, by some writers, while others treat them as being essentially different. We prefer the latter method for certain reasons, despite the fact that practically all important statistical data covering them have been jointly compiled. Chain banking is much older, historically speaking, dating back at least to the early nineties, whereas group banking as we know it today has had its principal growth since the end of 1926. Prior to 1927, as a matter of fact, the term group banking was very seldom used. Let us now consider the differences between these two types of banking.

"Chain banking" is generally used to designate that type of banking control and ownership in which an individual, or a group of individuals, own and control the majority stock of two or more banks. "Group banking," on the other hand, refers to that type of banking control and ownership in which the stock of the banks owned and controlled is in the hands of some holding company, the stock of which is held by a number of individual shareholders. In many cases there is a metropolitan bank around which clusters a number of smaller institutions. This latter type is sometimes referred to as "holding company banking." Such companies have often been small and did not sell their stock as widely as is the present practice. At first, such stock was closely held for the most part and there was no essential difference between it and chain banking, except that individuals

[1] By John M. Chapman. For a fuller and more complete discussion of this subject the reader is referred to Chapter XVIII in *Concentration of Banking* by the author. A very complete statistical study is that prepared under the general direction of the Federal Reserve Committee on Branch, Group and Chain Banking, on *Branch Groups and Chains*, 1932.

lessened their liability by reason of having the stock of the banks owned by the holding company.

The reasons underlying the organization of a chain of banks varied somewhat but in the main it was a "case of profits or income." These profits or income were derived in different ways. Some instances are known in which the stockholders were interested in building up a chain with the distinct purpose of selling out for a profit. In other cases the owners hoped to improve the management and increase the earning power of the banks thus owned, hence secure larger dividends. Larger salaries served as the motive in at least a number of instances, while in other cases the owners sought control of the banks in order to make loans or advances to themselves, the proceeds from such loans being used in the various kinds of business in which the stockholders might be interested. In far too many cases, such loans were used for undesirable and speculative purposes with the final result that they were never repaid and the banks failed leaving the depositors stranded. It was this latter type of transaction and use of power that has done most to discredit the chain type of banking.

Methods used in building up chains.—Different methods were used in bringing together or building up chain systems. A very common method was the purchase by large stockholders of one bank of controlling interests in other banks, paying cash for such stock. This was, of course, the simplest and, perhaps, the most desirable way. Another method frequently used, in some parts of the country, was that in which the shareholders of one bank pledged their own stock and secured bank loans, the proceeds of which were used to buy up the controlling interest in the stock of another financial institution. The stock of the second bank was frequently used as collateral for still another loan which, in turn, provided funds to buy still another bank. This practice was repeated till the individual or individuals controlled several banks. The small amount of capital invested in this way by such individuals gave rise to the term "building up chains on a shoestring." This method is essentially vicious and has generally resulted in heavy losses to the depositors for the reason that the individual who adopted such methods was not generally very scrupulous in operating the banks once control was attained.

A third method, followed in some instances, was used in certain sections of the South where the promoters or organizers merely agreed to provide certain financial services for a stated fee. Ownership was not necessary under this type of relationship. A contract between the parties was all that was needed. Such contracts varied in maturity, some running for five years. Services rendered by the fiscal agent in this case included the handling of short-term funds, investments, arrangements for excess loans of certain customers, and the making of arrangements for outside loans to the bank when necessary.

The organization of new banks was still another method employed at times. The group or individual simply went into a community and organized a bank, putting up a considerable amount of capital funds and securing the remainder locally. In this way the bank was under control from the very beginning. Another method of securing control is the use of interlocking directorates. The practice of this method in connection with chain banking and to an even greater extent among banks finally gave rise to considerable feeling against interlocking directorates. That ultimately resulted in the passage of a law in 1914 designed in part to prevent this type of control, especially among the larger and more powerful banking institutions.

Extent of chain banking.—Chain banking has been, and still is, rather widely scattered throughout this country. It has been more highly concentrated in the Northwest and Southeast, but it has existed in many states. It is impossible to give any exact data of a current nature, about chain banking, which do not include group banking as well. Emphasis has been placed in recent discussions on group banking rather than chain banking. Definite statistical data were not compiled officially for chain banking until after the appearance of group banking during and following 1927. If one were to specify certain specific states where chain banking has been most extensively developed, he would undoubtedly name Minnesota and Georgia. Yet, certain other states have had a considerable development at one time or another. Such states would include Arkansas, Illinois, North and South Dakota, Iowa, and California. "Chains" are not limited to states which prohibit branch banking, though prohibitory branch banking laws have no doubt been very influential in many cases in encouraging them.

In 1925 a rather extensive research was made to determine the scope and extent of this class of banking control, but the results were by no means complete or satisfactory. Yet, considerable light was thrown on the subject by reason of the evidence thus assembled. The summary table of the data thus collected is reproduced here:

STATE	NO. CHAINS	NUMBER OF BANKS National	State	Total
Arkansas	2	7	17	24
Arizona	4	1	14	15
California	20	43	23	66
Colorado	Two or three reported—banks failed			
Florida	1	5	49	54
Georgia	2		163	163
Idaho	18	36	37	73
Illinois	3		18	18
Iowa	8	21	24	45
Massachusetts	1 Reported for an earlier date in Boston			
Minnesota	5		103	103
Mississippi	2	1	16	17
Missouri	1	3	3	6
Montana	Some reported, the number not given			
Nebraska	2	2	9	11
Nevada	1	2	7	9
New Jersey	6	11	15	26
New Mexico	2	2	6	8
New York	10	23	12	35
North Dakota	Some reported, the number not given			
Oklahoma	6	22	23	45
Oregon	6	7	15	22
Pennsylvania	2	3	13	16
South Dakota	1		6	6
Texas	2	5	23	28
Utah	9	21	31	52
Washington	16	32	37	69
Wisconsin	2		14	14
Wyoming	1	5	3	8
Totals	133	252	681	933

The number of chains has undoubtedly declined since 1925. During the years 1924-1925 certain small chains failed in some states, among them Iowa, Colorado, and Illinois. The Witham Chain went down in 1926 involving many banks located in the states of Georgia and Florida. From that time to the present day chain banking as such has been in bad repute. The bad showing during those earlier years made it much easier to turn to group banking in 1927 and later. The interest in chain banking declined after 1927, and today does not hold a very important place when considered as distinct from group banking, although there are many such organizations in existence at the present time. Chain banking suffered another severe shock when the A. B. Banks chain failed in Arkansas in the latter part of 1930. The connection between that and the Caldwell & Co. chain of Nashville, Tennessee, assisted in carrying this influence and effects to the states of Tennessee and Kentucky, involving the Bancokentucky Corporation which owned and controlled a group of banks some of which were in Cincinnati and others in Louisville, Kentucky. Perhaps the union of these two organizations was one of the reasons for the downfall of the chain in Arkansas.

Data will be presented in the section on Group Banking to show the status of these two classes of organizations or types of banking. About all that need now be said regarding its scope and extent is that there are no definite signs of growth, while there are, as already noted, certain indications that chain banking is declining and that the feeling against it is so marked that we are not likely to have a renewed interest in the subject in this country.

The size of the individual chain organizations in this country has varied very greatly from time to time. In the earlier days the number of banks, as well as the amount of banking resources involved, was small. A few chains brought together a rather large number, the largest being, perhaps, the Witham chain which had approximately 175 banks in 1922.[2] The A. B. Banks chain had a large number of banks, but was much smaller than the

[2] *Annual Report, Federal Reserve Board*, 1922, p. 6.

Witham chain. Certainly the banking resources were much smaller than those now owned and controlled by a number of group organizations. In fact one of the important distinctions to be noted between chain and group banking is found in the volume of resources owned. For this reason the group organizations have replaced the chain system as a method of securing control over a number of banks.

Branch banking versus chain banking.—The laws against branch banking in this country running over a long period of time in many states have played a very important rôle in the development of chain banking. The failure of existing banks in communities where banking services were needed, served to induce certain managements to establish a new bank, or to buy out the controlling interest of banks already in operation, in a given community. In many cases if the shareholders of a given bank, or its management, had been able to establish branches in certain locations, that method would have been employed, with the result that we would have had much less chain banking and more branch banking.

One of the arguments against chain banking as compared with branch banking is found in the degree of reliability or responsibility of the management and stockholders. In a branch banking system the head office and each branch is liable for the obligations of each and every other branch including the head office. This places greater responsibility on the officers and directors of the so-called head office of the organization. In a chain system each branch has a separate charter and, while the stockholders are liable in each case, they are jointly liable. If one bank fails in a chain it is apt to injure the other members to a certain extent, but the depositor can not hold any stockholders liable except those of his own bank. It follows, therefore, that greater responsibility is imposed upon the officers, directors, and shareholders in branch banking than in chain banking.

Another point in favor of branch banking is that greater publicity is given to the ownership and management of each branch than that awarded the ownership and control of chain banks. In the latter, the real owners are not well known to the depositors. Frequently the stock of the banks involved in a chain is purchased or secured secretly in order that the depositors of the bank may not know that the bank is largely owned and controlled by individuals outside the community altogether. This is undesirable and sometimes leads to abuses which prove in the end to be very costly. It is much better to have the real ownership publicly known.

Supervision and regulation.—It is difficult to get complete and adequate supervision of a chain of banks—particularly if these institutions are partly state and partly national banks. There is a divided supervision, and it is not easy for the state authorities to ascertain the true status of the national banks and vice versa. The problem of examination and supervision is made more difficult in many cases by reason of the fact that some of the banks are located in one state while other banks are operating in other states—sometimes at considerable distance. This complicates the supervision to such an extent that in the past managements of some chains have transferred worthless or doubtful assets from one bank to another to avoid having to "write off" the loss. Such a practice, where followed, generally leads to failure in the end. Sometimes this practice might be checked earlier with less loss to the depositors and the community, if a more concentrated type of examination and supervision was possible. This is a serious, practical problem. The failure risk militated very greatly against chain banking as carried on in the United States.

Conclusions regarding chain banking.—It is now possible to draw certain conclusions from this brief study of chain banking in the United States. The more important facts to be kept in mind by the student interested in current banking may be briefly summarized as follows:

1. The available data dealing with chain banking are very scarce and unsatisfactory. For the most part, the information we have is tied up closely with the data covering group banking and for all practical purposes it is not possible to separate the one from the other. Our discussion has been, therefore, largely nonstatistical even though it would be most helpful if we were able to know the exact extent of this type of banking at the present time.

2. Chain banking in the United States dates back to 1890 or earlier. It appeared about that time to a limited extent in the Northwest around Minneapolis and in the states of North and South Dakota and Montana. Another important development took place in Georgia. From 1900 to 1924 or 1925 there was considerable growth, but since the latter date it has assumed or occupied a less important place in American banking. It is on the decline at the present time.

3. Chain banking has not been regarded as successful in this country. This failure has been in some cases, probably owing to the character of the management, while in others it resulted from dishonesty. The chains have not been for the most part very strong financially, hence unable to stand a very severe strain during periods of depression. There is nothing inherently dangerous in chain banking. If we could assume capable and honest management, there is no reason why such organizations should not render good banking service to the communities, and substantial profits in the form of dividends to shareholders.

4. There are certain difficulties encountered in public supervision and regulation of chain banking. The fact that chains frequently include both state and national banks, located at times in widely separated states, makes the task of examining these banks difficult.

5. Chain banking does not possess any advantages not possessed by a well organized system of branch banking. On the other hand, it has sundry advantages generally admitted for branch banking and in addition it possesses certain disadvantages. It lacks the direct responsibility maintained under branch systems and does not lend itself to publicity.

6. If chains are to be permitted they should be regulated by national laws subjecting them either to the supervision of the Federal Reserve Board or the Federal Trade Commission. Unless this or some other desirable means is found and applied, it would be better to prohibit such organization as far as possible.

7. Chain banking has had its greatest development in those states which have in the past prohibited branch banking, but it has not been restricted to such states.

8. Chains are usually the result of bringing a number of small state banks together through common stock ownership by certain individuals. The amount of available capital has been so limited in the past that it has not been found feasible to include large banks. It may then be said to be "a small bank proposition" or undertaking. In this respect it differs markedly, as we shall see later, from group banking where many large banks have been included in groups of banks.

The future of chain banking in this country is unsettled, but one is justified in saying that it is not likely to expand to any marked extent. There is very little interest in the method today as such, while public sentiment is unfriendly, generally speaking. It may be assumed, therefore, that it has passed its zenith and will, in the future, continue to decline with an expansion of branch banking which now seems certain.

II. Group Banking

From the end of 1926 to about the end of 1930, there was an important development in the scope and extent of group banking. This growth, substantial in the aggregate, was very significant when compared with the changes in the banking system of the country as a whole, as will be more fully realized by a study of the data collected by the Federal Reserve Committee on Branch, Group and Chain Banking, presented in a later part of this chapter. Three studies have been made in recent years of the growth and extent of group banking. The first was made by Andrew Price, President of the Marine Bancorporation, Seattle. This study, while interesting and important, has been surpassed by two other studies—that made by the Economic Policy Committee of the American Bankers Association, and another by the Reserve Committee referred to above. We shall consider only the last two.

Report on group and chain banking, American Bankers Association.[3]—The growth of group banking and the widespread

[3] This section is a summary of the *Study of Group and Chain Banking,* by the Economic Policy Commission of the American Bankers Association, New York, Oct. 14, 1929, of which commission R. S. Hecht was chairman.

interest developed therein during the year 1929 were instrumental in inducing the Economic Policy Commission of the American Bankers Association to make a rather extensive study on the scope and development of both group and chain banking. A report was published in October, 1929, preceding the reports of the Federal Reserve Board, although in many respects not so complete and satisfactory. In the study made by this commission, group and chain banking were treated as one, although there were recognized certain differences as regards the methods of control. Upon the basis of the type of ownership, these groups were classified as follows:

1. Groups or organizations in which a particular bank is the controlling element. In this class there were reported to be 78 chains or groups, involving 406 banks with total resources of approximately $6,473,000,000.

2. Groups or chains in which a nonbanking holding company, not subsidiary to any particular bank, was the dominant element in the control of the institutions. There were reported 28 chains in this group, involving 380 banks with total resources of about $5,335,000,000.

3. Groups and chains in which the dominant control was exercised by an individual or group of individuals acting for themselves. In this class there were reported 166 chains, involving 1,071 banks with total resources of approximately $1,468,000,000.

The results of this very interesting and timely report of the Economic Policy Commission are most succinctly stated by quoting two paragraphs from the report in which the study was summarized as follows:

> These three classes represent a total of 273 chains involving 1,858 banks and over $13,275,000,000 in aggregate resources. Some of these chain systems comprise 50 to 100 banks each. If there are now approximately 25,000 banks in the country with resources of $72,000,000,000, these figures indicate that almost 7-1/2 per cent of our banks and over 18 per cent of our banking resources are enmeshed in the great web of chain banking that now covers almost every part of the country.

Of one class or another chain head offices appear in our figures in all but nine of the forty-eight states and the District of Columbia; and as to these our information is chiefly negative, and we cannot say positively whether there is chain banking going on there or not.[4]

The movement included all but nine states. The largest number of chains or groups reported for any state was 34 for Minnesota. These 34 organizations had 435 banks (also the largest number of banks controlled by groups in one state) with total resources of about $995,350,000. New York State had 17 chains or groups involving 117 banks with total resources of $4,206,790,000, or approximately 31 per cent of the total resources of all banks in the country owned or controlled by group or chain organizations.

Results shown by the study of the Economic Policy Commission are, moreover, similar to those of the Federal Reserve Board covering group and chain banking for the same period, although the Board's study did not appear until some time later. The Economic Policy Commission reported that 7.5 per cent of all banks were involved as compared with 7.7 per cent by the Board. The Board took as a measure of growth the total loans and investments, while the Commission used total resources. In 1929 the Board reported that chains and groups controlled 19.5 per cent of the total loans and investments of all banks, whereas the Economic Policy Commission's report indicated that these organizations had about 18 per cent of the total resources of all banks in operation at that time.

The work or study of the Economic Policy Commission performed a great service, in showing the extent of the movement at a time when our information was far from complete, but it rendered a greater service in calling attention again to fundamental changes which had been going on in our banking system during recent years. Work of the Federal Reserve Board in compiling data on these types of banking rendered it unnecessary for the commission to continue collecting data.

The Federal Reserve system.—Of the two studies that of the Reserve Committee is more complete and up-to-date. The

[4] *Ibid.*, pp. 381-82.

Board, in 1930, classified groups and chains under the following heads:

1. Instances where control is exercised by a holding corporation, which has usually been formed by interests connected with one or more of the principal banks belonging to the system.

2. Instances where control is exercised by the principal bank of the system, either through direct ownership of stock by the bank, or through ownership of directors of the bank.

3. Instances of ownership of controlling or substantial interests in a number of banks by individual, family or group of individuals.

Since the data given in the Report of the Federal Reserve Board are less complete and up-to-date than those of the Reserve Committee, it does not seem desirable to present the statistical data thus prepared. The study made no attempt to classify the data according to whether they represented chain or group organizations.

Chain and group organizations exist in practically all sections of the country. Measured in terms of the number of banks which were members of groups, the greatest concentration occurred in the Western Grain States while the Middle Atlantic States ranked second. If measured by total loans and investment, it will be found that the Middle Atlantic states rank first, the North Central states second, and the Pacific Coast states third. The extent of group and chain banking for the years 1929 to 1931 is shown in Table 83 which classifies the groups and chains by geographical regions and shows the amount of loans and discounts, held by banks located in each region.

The number of banks owned by groups and chains amounted to 2,229 on June 30, 1930, which was the largest number reported at any one time by the Reserve Committee study. If the banks owned by these organizations be grouped according to membership in the Reserve system, it will be seen that the largest number were nonmember state banks, while national banks ranked second and state member banks third. If, however, total loans and investments be taken as the measure of importance, national banks are the most important—amounting to more than 50 per cent of the total loans and investments for group and

TABLE 83

NUMBER OF GROUPS AND CHAINS CLASSIFIED ACCORDING TO GEOGRAPHICAL REGION AND THE AMOUNT OF LOANS AND INVESTMENTS, JUNE 30, 1929 TO DECEMBER 31, 1931*

(Amounts in millions of dollars)

	1929				1930				1931			
	JUNE 30		DEC. 31		JUNE 30		DEC. 31		JUNE 30		DEC. 31	
	No. of Grps.	Lns. & Inv.	No. of Grps.	Lns. & Inv.	No. of Grps.	Lns. & Inv.	No. of Grps.	Lns. & Inv.	No. of Grps.	Lns. & Inv.	No. of Grps.	Lns. & Inv.
New England	7	$ 763	10	$ 1,087	11	$ 1,267	12	$ 1,235	12	$ 1,208	11	$1,030
Middle Atlantic	48	3,236	54	3,784	56	4,083	55	3,533	53	5,332	43	2,774
North Central	40	1,745	42	2,682	44	2,839	42	2,810	35	2,545	33	2,138
Southern Mountain	5	154	7	270	6	303	5	184	5	185	4	153
South Eastern	23	382	24	406	23	433	24	429	21	421	21	399
South Western	41	294	39	336	38	315	37	276	38	346	35	253
Western Grain	109	850	107	1,013	100	986	96	985	96	983	84	900
Rocky Mountain	22	223	21	266	20	260	19	249	19	236	17	215
Pacific	26	2,122	28	2,251	25	2,280	26	2,155	26	2,099	25	1,779
United States	321	9,768	332	12,093	327	12,766	316	11,856	305	13,355	273	9,643

* Report of the Federal Reserve Committee on Branch, Group and Chain Banking, 1932, on *Banking Groups and Chains.*

chain banks during the period as a whole. Total loans and investments for all banks owned by these organizations amounted to $13,355,000 on June 30, 1931, of which the national banks owned or held $8,099,000, or 60.6 per cent. The data covering these points are more fully presented in Table 84.

A comparison of the total loans and investments of all banks owned and controlled by groups and chains with the total loans and investments of all banks in the United States, shows that there was a marked growth comparatively in the loans and investments of group and chain banks. The total loans and investments of all banks in the United States, and of all banks owned by group and chain organizations declined considerably, but the decline was much less proportionately (as well as in the aggregate) than for all banks in the United States. On June 30, 1929, the banks involved by these group and chain systems amounted to 19.5 per cent of total loans and investments of all banks in the United States, whereas, on June 30, 1931, the percentage had risen to 30.6 per cent. Similar results, though less marked, took place between the total loans and investments of all national banks and the national banks owned and controlled by group and chain systems.

The number of banks owned by chain and group organizations varies considerably. The Federal Reserve Board study showed that a large number of these organizations owned and supervised comparatively few banking institutions. The following table shows the results of the Board's study in this connection in 1930:[5]

NUMBER OF BANKS	NUMBER OF SYSTEMS
3 banks	64
4	56
5	39
6 to 9 banks	86
10 to 19 banks	32
20 or more	10
Total	287

According to the report of the Federal Reserve Board on December 31, 1929, 119 banks owned by group or chain organi-

[5] *Federal Reserve Bulletin*, April, 1930, pp. 153-54.

TABLE 84

NUMBER OF BANKS OWNED BY GROUPS AND CHAIN SYSTEMS SHOWING THE DISTRIBUTION OF LOANS AND INVESTMENTS ACCORDING TO THE CLASS OF BANKS*

	NO. OF BANKS				LOANS & INVESTMENTS *(000,000 omitted)*				
	All Bks.	Natl. Bks.	State Mem.	Nonmem. State	All Bks.	Natl. Bks.	State Mem.	Nonmem. State	No. Groups
June 30, 1929	1,921	715	106	1,100	$ 9,768	$5,012	$3,008	$1,748	321
Dec. 31, 1929	2,165	854	124	1,187	12,093	6,336	3,786	1,971	332
June 30, 1930	2,229	886	126	1,217	12,766	6,765	3,876	2,125	325
Dec. 31, 1930	2,154	872	121	1,161	11,856	6,649	3,390	1,817	316
June 30, 1931	2,071	863	116	1,092	13,355	8,099	3,543	1,713	305
Dec. 31, 1931	1,886	805	98	983	9,642	5,818	2,398	1,426	273

* Report of the Federal Reserve Committee on Branch, Group and Chain Banking, 1932, on *Banking Groups and Chains*.

zations were operating 1,415 branches, or about 40 per cent of all branches in operation at that time. On the same date the banks operating branches had total loans and investments of $11,177,000,000, of which $6,264,000,000, or over 50 per cent, was held by banks which were owned by some group or chain. On December 31, 1931, there were 1,886 banks owned by groups and chains, and, of this list of banks, 121 were operating branches. All banks operating branches in the United States on December 31, 1931, had 3,375 branches,[6] of which the 121 chain and group members had 1,320, or approximately 39 per cent of all branches in the United States. On the same date all banks operating branches had $22,263,000,000 total loans and investments, of which the 121 banks owned $9,643,000, or about 43 per cent of the total loans and investments of all branch banks in the country.[7]

A more complete picture of the growth of branches among those banks which are members of chains and groups on December 31, 1931, is shown in the following table:

TABLE 85

BANKS OPERATING BRANCHES IN GROUPS AND CHAINS

	NUMBER			TOTAL LOANS & INVESTMENTS
	Banks	Banks Operating Branches	Branches	*(000,000 omitted)*
34 leading groups	674	63	898	$ 927
63 other groups	304	33	321	2,415
176 Chains	908	25	101	6,301
273	1,886	121	1,320	$9,643

Reasons for growth of group banking.—The rapidly declining interest in chain banking and the opposition to branch banking were important factors in the growth of group banking

[6] Report of the Federal Reserve Committee on Branch, Group and Chain Banking, on *Banking Groups and Chains.*

[7] Chapman, John M., Concentration of Banking (New York, Columbia University Press, 1934), p. 199; Report of the Federal Reserve Committee on Branch, Group and Chain Banking, 1932, on *Banking Groups and Chains,* pp. 78-79, and Tables X, XI, XII (Appendix).

in the United States during the last years of the bull market—the years 1927 to 1929 inclusive. The failure of a number of chains, especially the Witham chain in Georgia, and the failures in Minnesota and Iowa did much to bring chain banking into disfavor in many parts of the country. Group banking was advanced by some bankers as a new type of banking, and was claimed by them to be superior to branch banking as it existed in foreign countries. There are a number of factors or causes underlying the rapid expansion of this type of banking among which the following are the most important:

1. *Branch banking prohibited in a number of states.*—The banking laws in a number of states prohibited branch banking in any form; a limited number of states permitted branches to be operated on a state-wide basis, while a somewhat larger number allowed state banks to operate branches in the city or county of the parent bank. In practically all cases such banks could not operate branches outside the boundaries of the state in which the parent bank was located. The national bank act did not permit national banks to operate branches outside the city of the head office except in a few minor cases and such branches were further restricted to the states which permitted state banks to operate branches. Branches being denied banks the management of which wanted or needed to extend their services to adjoining communities or to other sections of the same city found this impossible in many cases, and in all cases if the new territory was located outside the state. Group banking offered a way out. It was used in many instances with what seemed to be quite satisfactory results. Well-known examples of such concerns or groups so organized were the Transamerica Corporation, the Marine Midland Corporation of New York and the Northwest Bancorporation of Minneapolis.

2. *Reputation of chain banks.*—Reference has already been made to the fact that chain banking had fallen into disrepute as a result of the heavy losses caused by the failure and mismanagement of a number of chains in different parts of the country. This set-back suffered by chain banking during the years 1925 and 1926, was further emphasized by the failure of

Caldwell & Co., Nashville, and A. B. Banks's chain of banks with headquarters in Little Rock, Arkansas in 1930. Group banking offered something new; hence, there arose a wide interest in it.

3. *Opportunities for making profits.*—There were two or three ways by which promoters hoped to make substantial profits by organizing or bringing together a group of banks. First, if the banks could be placed under better management many of them promised larger dividends and salaries to the persons concerned. These returns would come to the promoters or organizers as officers and stockholders of the holding company. Second, there were many opportunities for buying bank shares and reselling to holding companies for higher prices, thus realizing substantial profits out of the transaction. Third, through the organization and distribution of the shares of the holding company itself there were attractive possibilities for a wide margin of profits to the promoters.

4. *Threatened loss of correspondent business.*—Officers and directors of a few of the larger metropolitan banks which had enjoyed many correspondent accounts, feared a loss of some of this business to the holding companies or group concerns. Many other accounts of this kind were threatened if the group banking movement spread rapidly. In order to offset this threatened loss of accounts, some of the metropolitan banks and others interested in them, decided to enter the field of group banking and, in this way, through holding companies or security affiliates, bought up a controlling interest in banks which were regarded as being desirable institutions. This method offered the larger institutions two kinds of profits or returns—one, the income from the operations of the banks obtained; second, the continued correspondent business of such institutions plus any additional business which might be developed as a result of the closer connection thus formed.

5. *Preparation for branch banking.*—The managements of a few holding companies believed that a change of sentiment in favor of branch banking was taking place. When that sentiment crystallized there would be, it was believed, a decided rush

on the part of certain banking institutions to establish and operate branches in strategic locations. In order to be prepared for such a contingency, certain groups were organized with this plan specifically in mind. Others felt that there would be a drift in the course of time toward branch banking which they favored. In the meantime, branches could not be formed or established. For them group banking offered a temporary alternative. The group could be organized and the banks purchased and controlled or managed until the branch banking laws were amended; then entrance to the branch banking field could be accomplished easily and quickly. During the interim there was an opportunity to make substantial profits and income. A number of group managers frankly admitted their intention to shift to branch banking as soon as they were legally permitted to do so.

6. *Conclusions regarding group banking.*—The advocates of group banking have advanced many reasons why this type of banking should be developed as compared with either chain or branch banking. It is desirable to summarize very briefly the major points in this discussion, as follows:

1. There does not appear to be any marked advantage in a group system that could not be attained by branch banking. Of the two, branch banking is the more desirable from a social point of view for the reason that a greater degree of responsibility may be placed upon the management and the branches may be more successfully examined and supervised. There is less expense attached to the operation of a branch than to an individual bank under the group system. Capital requirements may be more accurately adjusted to the needs of the community under branch banking, thus rendering the cost of banking service less. In a group system banks will be operated only in localities where profits may be made, and since the cost of operating a bank is greater than of a branch, there are likely to be more branches established under branch systems than unit banks under group systems. If this be true, branch banking will provide more banking offices which will reach a larger number of individuals or communities. These are important differences

which should be taken into consideration when judging branch and group banking. It is believed that most group bankers recognize and admit these points, hence are willing to convert their groups into branch systems as soon as legal restrictions have been removed.

2. The size of the group system makes it possible to carry on a trust business which is not possible under a unit system in many cases, especially the smaller unit banks.

3. Group banking has certain advantages in comparison with unit banking which may be summarized as follows:

a) A larger and more carefully trained staff of employees
b) Larger lines of credit to the business community
c) More extensive credit and bond departments
d) A more satisfactory diversification of both loans and investments
e) A great economy in the handling of both the actual and secondary reserves of banks
f) Economies in overhead expenses

4. It is easier and more economical at times to raise capital for extending banking facilities. The stock of the holding company may be listed on the exchanges and in that way bank shares may be made more desirable from an investor's point of view.

5. Groups have frequently been organized in the past purely for the purpose of marking up the price of bank shares with the idea of selling out for a profit. Such a practice endangers the banking system and is to be deplored at all times.

6. There are certain difficulties in supervising and regulating group-banking systems. This difficulty becomes accentuated when the membership of the group is divided between the national and state systems, as well as between different states and subject to different jurisdictions.

7. The double liability of the bank shareholders is partly circumvented through the holding company form of ownership. This lessens to an extent the protection of depositors since the holding company assets may consist almost, if not entirely, of shares of banks which are themselves involved in the loss if such failure occurs.

8. Weak or inefficient management is dangerous and is likely to lead to failure. Losses sustained in such cases are more severe than if the banks were being operated under the unit system since if one member of a group becomes affected it, in turn, reacts against other members which may bring about a failure of all banks belonging to the group. Even though the loss is one of degree, nevertheless, it must be taken into consideration in attempting to appraise the advantages and disadvantages of the group system of banking.

CHAPTER XVII

BRANCH BANKING[1]

Branch banking has grown very greatly in economic significance during the past two decades. Long before the beginning of the present depression branch banking had made considerable progress and had become a subject of great importance to the banking community as a whole, regardless of the fact that many states still prohibited it in any form whatever. Shortly after the opening of the depression, the extension of branch banking was urged by many as a banking reform greatly needed and likely to aid in giving us a banking system better able to cope with the business situation as it then existed. In short, there has recently been a rapid and wide expansion of public interest in the subject.

Before discussing or outlining the present scope of this development, it seems desirable to indicate the relationship between branch banking and certain other developments in the field of banking.

To understand recent branch banking tendencies, it is necessary to consider the relationship of the branch system to other parts of the general field and especially to certain recent developments of a special type in banking. The growth of branch banking is a part of a much larger movement, taking place not only here, but in practically all leading countries. This larger and broader trend has already been designated and is known as the concentration movement in banking.[2] The failure of the unit system consisting of a large number of small independent banks explains in part the changes taking place not only in the structure of American banking but also the sentiment favoring branch banking in some form. These changes are re-

[1] Written by John M. Chapman.

[2] The term "concentration movement," as used here, includes branch, group, and chain banking, bank mergers, and the trend to an increasing size of unit banks. See also the chapter on Bank Mergers and Consolidations, pp. 353-54 for a similar use of the term.

sulting in fewer but larger banking institutions with the control of the banking business in fewer hands. Such a concentration may be good or bad, depending upon the way in which the power is used by those having the management and control of the larger banking institutions thus developed.

The connection of branch banking with chain and group banking, and bank mergers and consolidations is exceedingly close. These phases of banking are treated in separate chapters of this study, but it may be helpful to point out at this stage of our discussion that there are reasons for believing that the legal status of branch banking has had much to do in shaping the development of chain and group banking in the United States. The prohibition of branch banking to national banks and to many state banks and trust companies has led to the use of these two methods for bringing banks under a centralized control.[3]

Likewise, the merger movement has been conducive to the extension of branches, and has been itself limited by the laws against branch banking in several states. In some branch banking states, and even in those states limiting branches to the city or county of the parent bank, bankers will not consider seriously the question of absorbing other banks located at a distance unless there is a possibility of retaining the banking business of the community. The restrictions against branch banking in many cases make this impossible, hence one phase of the relationship between bank mergers and branch making. In certain branch banking states, however, the desire to secure new branches has been directly responsible for many mergers, both with banks located in the city of the parent bank, as well as in other parts of the state. This phase of the movement has been especially marked in the State of California and to a less degree, perhaps, in New York, Ohio, and Michigan.

THE UNIT BANKING SYSTEM

Our unit banking system (which dates back to the very beginning of banking in this country), has had a long and check-

[3] For a fuller treatment of chain and group banking see Chapter XVI.

ered history. Prior to the enactment of the National Bank Act in 1863 there had been, at times, a mixture of unit and branch banking. In some states the unit system prevailed, while in others branch banking predominated. Branch systems, in states like Ohio and Indiana, proved to be quite successful, while in certain southern states results were not so satisfactory. In a few cases, the branch banks which were organized fell under inefficient or dishonest management, or political influence, with the general effect that such banks had sooner or later to be closed. The slow and unsatisfactory character of our transportation system made it extremely difficult to supervise and operate branch offices situated at a distance from the parent bank.

The advent of the National system in 1863 and the Amendment made by the Revenue Act of 1865, imposing a tax upon the state banks' issues, together with the Civil War, gave a clear field to unit banking for more than half a century. During this long period, the vicissitudes of changing economic conditions supplied first a fairly satisfactory system and then a system in which the number of bank failures and losses to depositors and stockholders was large. At no time was the system fully satisfactory. Banking reform has always been extremely difficult to secure and has generally come only after a period of unfavorable banking in which the losses were heavy, or in which the banking system failed to provide the type of banking service actually needed by the business community.

Many of the weaknesses of the unit system lingered and, in not a few cases, were cumulative to such a degree that sooner or later there was certain to be a breakdown. This breakdown came shortly after the close of the World War. Beginning with 1921, weak spots began to appear in the West and South, with the result that there were many bank failures. This period of failures has continued down to the present time, the climax having been reached with the bank holiday of March 6, 1933. The number of banks declined from more than 30,000, in 1921, to less than 15,000 at the present time.

Losses to the stockholders were exceedingly great both in actual dividends and in original investment in bank stock, as well as in the payments required under the double liability provision in bank shares. In many cases where dividends had been paid they had not been earned, hence came out of the capital funds of the bank. The loss to the depositors and community was tremendous for the reason that large amounts were never paid, while the depositors had to do without the funds they finally received, for many months, or even in some cases, years. The effect was to "tie up" the short-term working capital of the community or communities, and thus to reduce the volume of business and employment in the sections of the country affected. In these ways total losses became appalling.

Another result of considerable magnitude was the changing of the distribution of banking offices and facilities. In many cities and counties all the banks failed leaving such communities without any local office at which to do banking business. Hundreds of communities, formerly accustomed to one or more banks, now had none. This situation caused great inconvenience to all classes in the locality. One of the worst features of the situation is found in the fact that there seems to be at present little, if any, possibility of reëstablishing independent banks in such localities.

Recent developments and tendencies in branch banking have a close relationship to the whole subject of bank failures and suspensions. The failure of thousands of banks in this country during the past ten or twelve years has gone far toward breaking down opposition to branch banking. The heavy losses and the tying up of depositors' funds have brought home to many the fact that the system of unit banks is far from perfect. It has taken a number of years to bring about this change in public opinion. It developed slowly prior to the economic depression, but since 1929 the movement has spread much more rapidly, so that today there is a strong feeling in favor of branch banking which did not exist a few years ago.

Without the long list of failures, it is doubtful if this wide change in favor of some type of branch banking would have occurred. The closing of the small banks has left many communities without local banking facilities. The realization by many business men that these unit banks are gone and are not likely to reappear in the form of reorganized banks, or as new banks, has led to a feeling that outside larger institutions should be allowed to establish branches in such communities, in order to restore some local banking facilities. There are literally hundreds of small towns and cities without such accommodations. Good reason thus exists for the extension of branch banking in some form, even though we believe that there are many localities in which banks formerly existed which must do without them and even without branches in the future. If we are to continue the existence of the old unit system the public, in general, must realize that there will be fewer banks and that these banks must be located in the larger towns and cities, at a considerable distance from many smaller towns. To continue the present unit system means that less, not more, banking service will be provided for the business community. Many such communities are without the volume of business necessary to enable a bank to operate successfully there. A small branch could be operated in many of these small towns, but independent banks with separate capital are out of the question. Even if sufficient capital could here be raised to meet the legal requirements, the question of getting a sufficient volume and variety of business to make the bank safe over a period of years would still remain. There seems to be no conclusion other than to reduce the number of banking offices and to curtail the facilities for the country at large, or else to adopt branch banking on a rather extensive scale.

Legal Status of Branch Banking

The legal status of branch banking varies widely today from state to state. In no two branch banking states are the laws permitting the establishment and operation of branches identical. In some respects the laws of certain states are similar. For example, a number of states restrict the operation of branches by state banks and trust companies to the city of the parent bank, while a limited number permit the operation of branches on a state-wide basis. The laws regulating or prohibiting branch banking have changed many times during the last few decades. Thus, the state of Georgia permitted the establishment of branches on a state-wide basis before the failure of the "Witham Chain" of banks in 1926. This latter failure involved a few banks operating branches. The Witham debacle was instrumental in bringing about a reaction against "multiple" banking—so strong that the state banking law providing for the operation of branches on a state-wide basis was repealed and banks were prohibited from establishing further branches. The law of Georgia was later modified so as to permit branches within the city of the parent bank. Situations similar to the one just discussed have developed in New Jersey, Wisconsin, and Indiana. The geographical unit was not the same in these states although the principles involved in all were similar.

The two most common bases for the operation of branches by banks in the United States are : (1) the city of the parent bank, and (2) a state-wide basis. An intermediate step between these is found in Maine where banks may operate branches within the county, and any adjoining county of head office, or in Tennessee and Ohio, where branches are limited to the county of the parent institution.

In certain states, of recent years, there has been a marked, or, at least noticeable, change in the status of branch banking. Indiana and Wisconsin which in former years had permitted branches but had enacted laws against them, have recently passed laws allowing banks to operate branches under restricted conditions within the county of the parent bank. The states of Iowa, Montana, Washington, Idaho, and South Carolina have enacted legislation providing for the extension of branch banking on a limited basis. Opinion favorable to branch banking has, at times, been noticeable in certain other states, even though no favorable laws have been enacted. Illustrations of a like tendency have been found in Illinois and Oklahoma while there has been some evidence of a growing recognition of branch banking in West Virginia and Minnesota.

The National Bank Act prohibited, in 1865, the establishment of branches by national banks. State banks and trust companies were authorized to convert into the national system and to retain any branches in operation at the time of conversion, but were not allowed to establish new branches. There has been some doubt in the mind of banking students regarding the full force of the statement. Some have held rather to the idea that national banks could with the approval of the Comptroller of the Currency have established branches. Be that as it may, it is a fact that the Office of the Comptroller opposed branch banking for a long period of time and was upheld in this attitude by the Attorney General of the United States. The most well-known opinion in this connection was that handed down by Attorney-General Wickersham in 1911, in which he held that the national bank act did not authorize national banks to operate branches.

A slight modification was made by the Consolidation Act of 1918 which permitted national banks absorbing other banks with branches to retain the branches in existence at the time of the consolidation. A much more important change came in 1922, when Comptroller of the Currency Crissinger authorized national banks to establish and operate teller windows or additional offices for the purpose of receiving deposits or checks (not to make loans) provided these offices were located within the corporate limits of the city of the parent bank. Such offices were not regarded by him as "branches." This was a very important step in the development of branch banking in this country.

The next step in the national system came with the passage of the McFadden Act in 1927, which permitted national banks to establish and operate branches in the city of the parent bank, provided the state banking laws permited state banks and trust companies to operate branches in such states. Any national bank which had had a branch in existence for a period of twenty-five years, either with or without official sanction, was to be granted the permission to continue such office as a branch of the bank. There was a very considerable expansion in the number of branches by national banks after the passage of the McFadden Act.

The last step in this field came with the enactment of the Glass-Steagall Act of June 16, 1933, which gave national banks the same rights to establish and operate branches that were enjoyed by state banks and trust companies in those states where the national banks were located. This means state-wide branches for the national banks located in the states which permit state-wide branch banking for state banks. There is a difference between the status of state and national banks in that there is a higher capital requirement for national banks before they are permitted to establish branches outside the city of the parent institution.

Scope and Extent of Branch Banking

The branch-banking area in the United States is restricted in comparison with the scope and extent of banking in general. In some particular areas branch banking is rather highly developed. On a state-wide basis, that is true of certain parts of the state of California. It is especially true of certain cities like New York, Detroit, Cleveland, and Philadelphia, notwithstanding the continuance of a considerable number of non-branch banking institutions in these cities. The scope and extent of branches for the country as a whole is limited both in the number of banks operating branches and the number of branches. The movement presents a more formidable appearance if the total banking resources of banks operating branches be compared with the total of all banks in operation.

In 1919 there were 476 banks operating 1,082 branches, of which 18 banks were national, 446 were state banks and trust companies and 12 were mutual savings banks. At the same time the branches were divided as follows: 52 by the national system, 1,005 by state banks and trust companies and 25 by mutual savings banks. Of the 1,082 branches operated at that time 631 were located within the city of the parent bank while the remainder, 451, were located outside the city limits of the parent institution. The total resources of all banks operating branches in 1919 amounted to $7,695,000,000, or 16.2 per cent of the resources of all banks in operation in the United States.

From 1919 there was a gradual increase in the number of

banks operating branches till 1928 at which time there were 844. Since then the number has declined to 747 as of the end of 1932. During the same period the number of branches increased to 3,307 (the maximum number of branches was reached in 1929 with a total of 3,603). There were 3,290 branches at the end of 1932, which was a decline of 8.6 per cent from the high of 1929. The total resources of banks operating branches increased yearly until 1929 when they amounted to $33,269,000,000 or 46.1 per cent of the resources of all banks in operation in this country. This percentage declined to 41.1 per cent in 1931. Measured in terms of total resources, this represents a very remarkable increase. The great size of the resources involved, however, is owing to a considerable extent to the fact that many of the very largest banks in the metropolitan cities operate one or more branches. It can not be taken, therefore, to mean that the territory served by banks operating branches represent any considerable portion of the country geographically.

Relatively the greatest increase in branches took place among banks operating under national charters. In 1919 the resources of national banks operating branches amounted to 7.93 per cent of the resources of all banks operating branches, whereas in 1931 they represented 37.00 per cent. Mutual Savings banks operating branches increased from 1.89 per cent of the total in 1919 to 15.30 per cent in 1931. During the same period state banks and trust companies declined from 90.17 per cent of the total to 47.69 in 1931. This change of relationship was the result of the rapid growth in the national banks and mutual savings banks relatively and did not represent a decline in the aggregate volume of resources of state banks and trust companies. As a mater of fact the total resources of this latter group actually increased annually until 1930. During both 1930 and 1931 there were decreases. The resources for national banks operating branches did not decline until 1931 and mutual savings bank resources showed an increase for each year over the preceding throughout the period 1919 to 1931, inclusive.

A more complete picture of the growth in the number of

TABLE 86

NUMBER OF BRANCHES IN OPERATION CLASSIFIED ACCORDING TO TYPE OF BANKING INSTITUTION, 1919-1932

YEAR	ALL BANKS IN THE UNITED STATES					NATIONAL BANKS					STATE BANKS & TRUST COS.					MUTUAL SAVINGS BANKS				
	Banks		Branches			Banks		Branches			Banks		Branches			Banks		Branches		
	No.	Mem. F.R.	To-tal	In	Out	No.	Mem. F.R.	To-tal	In	Out	No.	Mem. F.R.	To-tal	In	Out	No.	Mem. F.R.	To-tal	In	Out
1919	476	134	1082	631	451	18	18	52	30	22	446	116	1005	581	424	12	—	25	20	5
1920	524	176	1239	745	494	21	21	63	41	22	488	155	1148	681	467	15	—	28	23	5
1921	535	194	1366	849	517	24	24	74	52	22	495	170	1263	774	489	16	—	29	23	6
1922	608	246	1715	1112	603	56	56	140	119	21	532	190	1538	965	573	20	—	37	28	9
1923	673	275	2044	1346	698	90	90	203	181	22	553	185	1792	1125	667	30	—	49	40	9
1924	716	296	2299	1545	754	108	108	249	227	22	566	188	1985	1266	719	42	—	65	52	13
1925	784	335	2586	1788	798	144	144	363	343	20	591	191	2149	1386	763	49	—	74	59	15
1926	787	334	2796	1962	834	143	143	425	396	29	590	191	2291	1500	791	54	—	80	66	14
1927	833	352	3149	2166	983	165	165	922	575	347	605	187	2137	1516	621	63	—	90	75	15
1928	844	352	3307	2271	1036	162	162	948	607	341	615	190	2262	1584	678	67	—	97	80	17
1929	816	337	3603	2491	1112	160	160	1071	716	355	584	177	2425	1684	741	72	—	107	91	16
1930	799	330	3567	2451	1116	168	168	1113	713	400	557	162	2346	1646	700	74	—	108	92	16
1931	737	296	3375	2293	1082	157	157	1274	886	388	505	139	1989	1311	678	75	—	112	96	16
1932	747		3290	2220	1070	157	157	1205	825	380	515		1961	1286	675	75	—	124	109	15

TABLE 87

STATISTICS OF BANKS OPERATING BRANCHES CLASSIFIED ACCORDING TO TYPE OF BANKING INSTITUTION, 1919-1931

(Amounts in millions of dollars)

YEAR	ALL BANKS OPERATING BRANCHES IN THE UNITED STATES				NATIONAL BANKS			
	Number Banks	Loans & Discounts	Invest-ments	Resources	Number Banks	Loans & Discounts	Invest-ments	Resources
1919	476	$ 3,967	$ 1,812	$ 7,695	18	$ 353	$ 100	$ 610
1920	524	5,123	2,168	9,592	21	698	104	1,100
1921	535	5,473	2,431	10,266	24	1,186	198	1,919
1922	608	5,802	3,302	12,619	56	1,775	492	3,157
1923	673	7,740	3,598	14,966	90	2,263	733	3,839
1924	716	9,063	5,009	17,878	108	2,813	944	4,960
1925	784	10,589	5,841	21,165	144	3,569	1,166	6,705
1926	787	11,569	6,312	22,947	143	3,970	1,243	6,984
1927	833	14,505	7,979	27,153	165	5,474	1,914	9,339
1928	844	15,232	8,409	32,030	162	6,163	2,155	11,818
1929	816	16,501	8,230	33,269	160	6,101	1,758	11,338
1930	799	14,962	9,376	33,229	168	6,362	2,192	12,159
1931	737	12,185	10,078	28,877	157	5,559	2,417	10,686

TABLE 87 (*Continued*)

STATISTICS OF BANKS OPERATING BRANCHES CLASSIFIED ACCORDING TO TYPE OF BANKING INSTITUTION, 1919-1931

(*Amounts in millions of dollars*)

YEAR	STATE BANKS AND TRUST COMPANIES				MUTUAL SAVINGS BANKS			
	Number Banks	Loans & Discounts	Invest-ments	Resources	Number Banks	Loans & Discounts	Invest-ments	Resources
1919	446	$ 3,569	$1,621	$ 6,939	12	$ 45	$ 91	$ 146
1920	488	4,369	1,652	7,985	15	56	412	507
1921	495	4,225	1,794	7,822	16	61	438	525
1922	532	3,965	2,358	8,899	20	62	452	564
1923	553	5,404	2,099	10,217	30	73	767	910
1924	566	6,123	2,952	11,576	42	128	1,114	1,342
1925	591	6,847	3,041	12,547	49	172	1,635	1,913
1926	590	7,379	3,192	13,669	54	221	1,877	2,294
1927	605	8,765	3,648	14,896	63	265	2,417	2,918
1928	615	8,772	3,600	16,890	67	296	2,653	3,323
1929	584	10,019	3,630	18,398	72	380	2,842	3,533
1930	557	8,233	4,103	16,948	74	367	3,081	4,122
1931	505	6,252	4,096	13,772	75	373	3,565	4,419

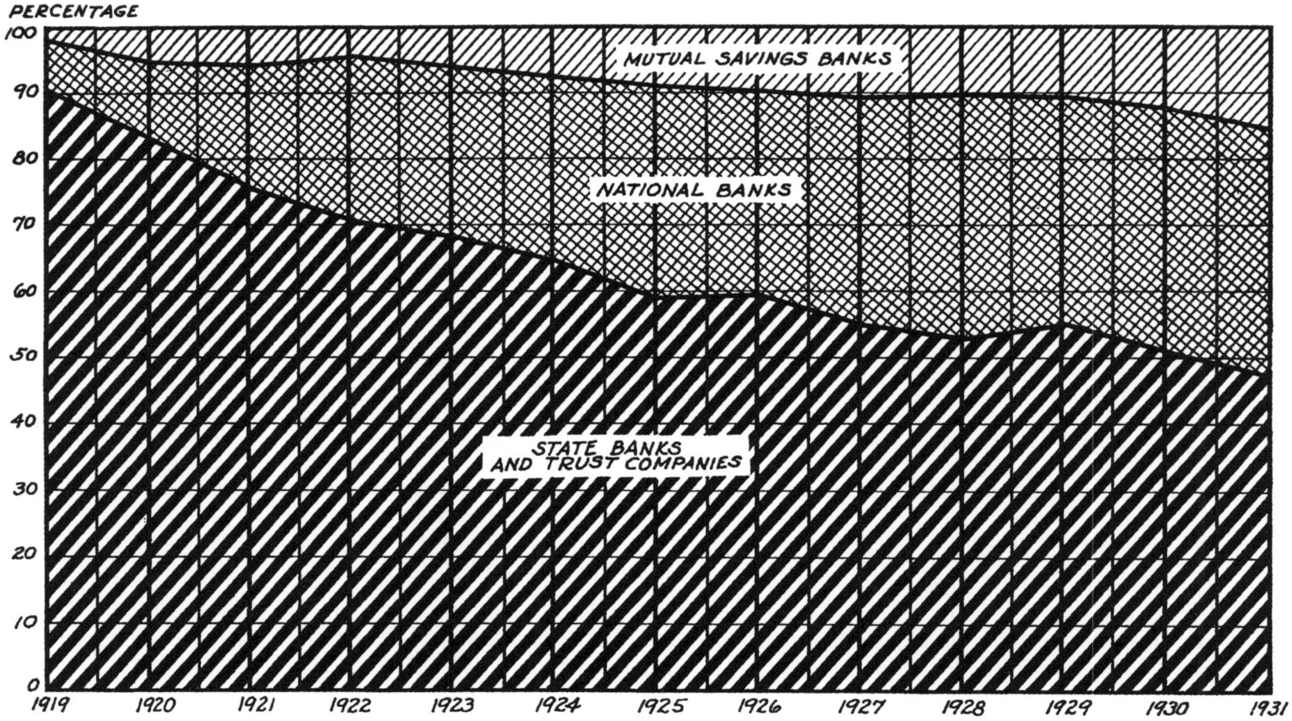

CHART XVI. PERCENTAGE DISTRIBUTION OF RESOURCES OF ALL BANKS OPERATING BRANCHES IN THE UNITED STATES, CLASSIFIED ACCORDING TO TYPE OF BANK

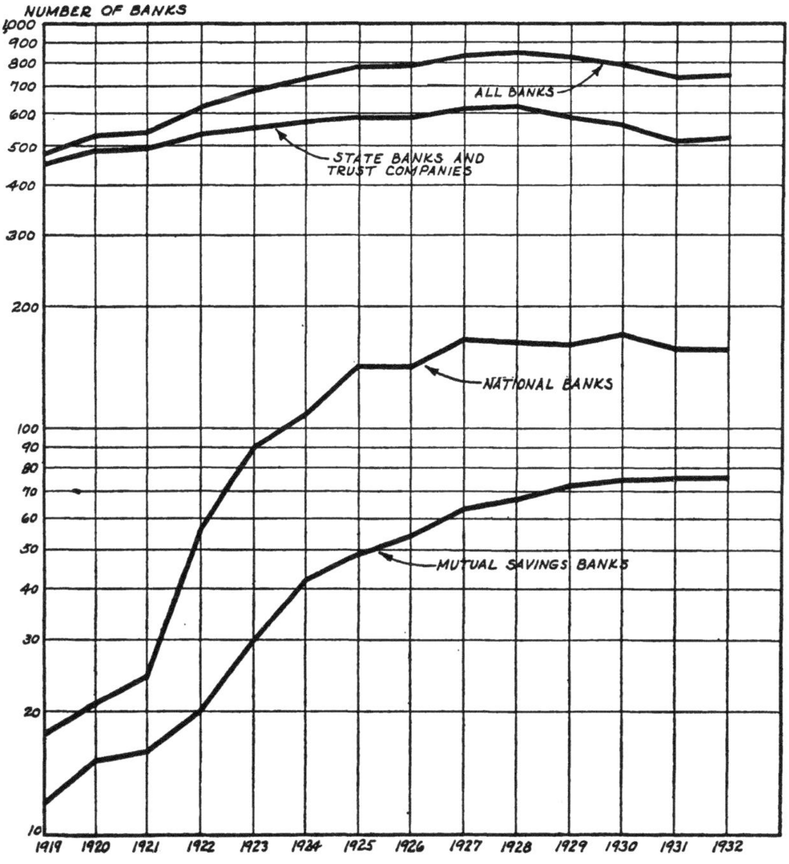

CHART XVII. TOTAL NUMBER OF BANKS OPERATING BRANCHES IN THE UNITED STATES banks operating branches, together with the number of branches is given in Table 86 and Chart XVI which set forth some of the more salient features of the branch banking development in comparison with similar data for all banks in operation in the United States during the period 1919 to 1932, inclusive.

The data outlined in the preceding pages regarding the volume of loans and discounts and total resources of banks operating branches is set forth in Table 87 and Chart XVII which give the data for the period 1919 to 1931, inclusive, classified according to the type of bank operating branches. Table 86 in conjunction with Tables 87, and 88 give sufficient data to enable the student of banking to understand the growth and development of the branch banking movement in the United States during the period under study.

Chart XVIII presents a very interesting picture of the percentage relationship of national banks, state banks, and trust companies operating branches according to the total resources of each type of bank.[4]

Mutual Savings Banks

The relationship of mutual savings banks to branch banking, or the extent to which mutual savings banks have entered the branch-banking business has been neglected or omitted in most of the recent discussions of this subject. It is, of course, less than the growth of branches among the national or state institutions, but the growth has attained imports sufficient to warrant some consideration of it. Mutual savings banks as a group are limited to a small region of the country and in certain of the states where mutual savings banks are operated, branch banking is either prohibited or the development is small. The bulk of such savings bank business is found in the states of Massachusetts, New York, and Pennsylvania. It is also in these three states that practically all of the branches of mutual savings banks are found. A limited number (very small indeed) of branches of mutual savings banks are found in the states of Rhode Island, New Jersey, Delaware, Maryland, and California.

[4] Chart XVIII is based upon Table 89 in this Chapter.

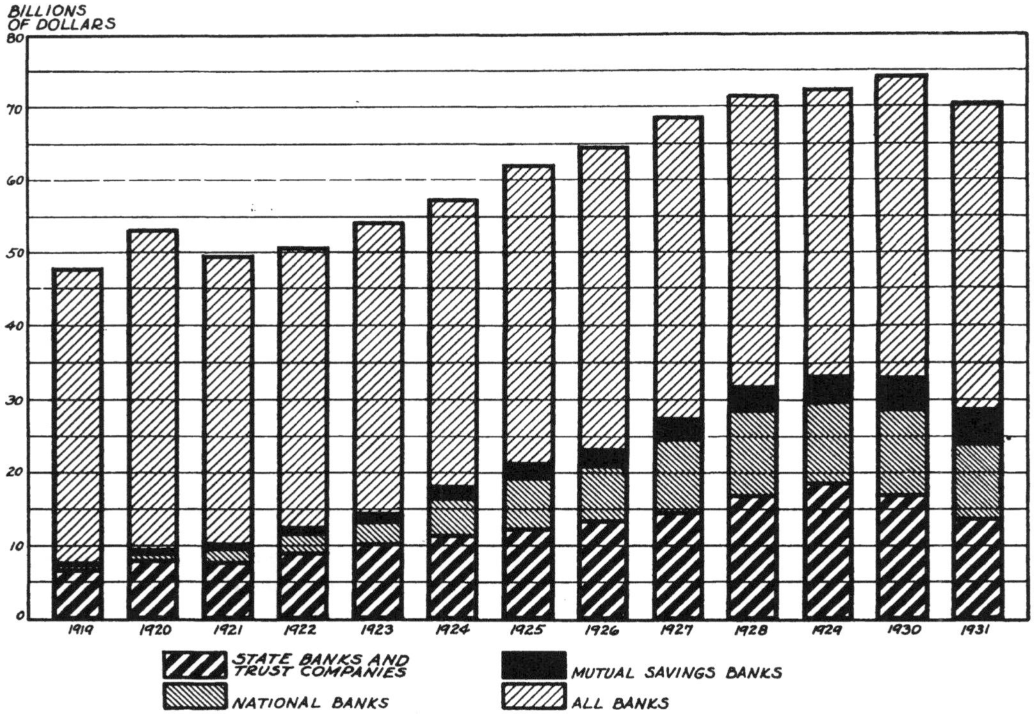

CHART XVIII. RESOURCES OF (1) ALL BANKS OPERATING BRANCHES; (2) STATE BANKS AND TRUST COMPANIES; (3) NATIONAL BANKS; AND (4) MUTUAL SAVINGS BANKS

TABLE 88

STATISTICS OF BANKS OPERATING BRANCHES CLASSIFIED ACCORDING TO TYPE OF BANKING INSTITUTION, 1919-1931

(Amounts in millions of dollars)

YEAR	ALL BANKS OPERATING BRANCHES IN THE UNITED STATES				BANKS OPERATING BRANCHES ON STATE-WIDE BASIS			
	Number Banks	Loans & Discounts	Invest-ments	Resources	Number Banks	Loans & Discounts	Invest-ments	Resources
1919	476	$ 3,967	$ 1,812	$ 7,695	199	$ 682	$ 278	$1,224
1920	524	5,123	2,168	9,592	214	916	325	1,527
1921	535	5,473	2,431	10,266	213	969	363	1,600
1922	608	5,802	3,302	12,619	250	1,274	507	2,301
1923	673	7,740	3,598	14,966	281	1,779	585	2,900
1924	716	9,063	5,009	17,878	285	2,011	678	3,348
1925	784	10,589	5,841	21,165	277	2,274	832	3,837
1926	787	11,569	6,312	22,947	260	2,543	929	4,241
1927	833	14,505	7,979	27,153	228	2,730	1,065	4,244
1928	844	15,232	8,409	32,030	222	2,572	1,242	4,561
1929	816	16,501	8,230	33,269	210	2,903	1,115	5,049
1930	799	14,962	9,377	33,228	209	2,693	1,251	4,968
1931	737	12,185	10,078	28,878	191	2,324	1,355	4,447

TABLE 88 (*Continued*)

STATISTICS OF BANKS OPERATING BRANCHES CLASSIFIED ACCORDING TO TYPE OF BANKING INSTITUTION, 1919-1931

(*Amounts in millions of dollars*)

YEAR	BANKS OPERATING BRANCHES ON RESTRICTED BASIS				BANKS OPERATING BRANCHES IN STATES PROHIBITING FURTHER EXTENSION OF BRANCHES			
	Number Banks	Loans & Discounts	Invest-ments	Resources	Number Banks	Loans & Discounts	Invest-ments	Resources
1919	230	$ 3,110	$1,423	$ 6,098	47	$174	$110	$373
1920	264	4,016	1,738	7,681	46	191	105	384
1921	278	4,337	1,957	8,309	44	166	111	457
1922	310	4,246	2,623	9,726	48	282	172	592
1923	348	5,664	2,820	11,415	44	297	194	651
1924	387	6,733	4,109	13,800	44	319	223	730
1925	467	7,991	4,782	16,612	40	324	227	715
1926	499	8,801	5,291	18,269	28	226	92	436
1927	558	11,407	6,775	22,214	47	367	139	695
1928	579	12,211	7,000	26,639	43	449	167	830
1929	579	12,234	7,002	27,557	27	364	113	663
1930	577	12,111	8,041	27,923	13	157	85	337
1931	535	9,716	8,635	24,122	11	145	88	309

The field for mutual savings branch banking is narrow. The mutual savings bank usually has small accounts, hence the necessity that there be a larger potential number of such accounts.

TABLE 89

A TABLE SHOWING WHAT PERCENTAGE EACH OF THE FOLLOWING ITEMS OF EACH TYPE OF BANKS OPERATING BRANCHES IS OF THE SAME ITEMS OF ALL BANKS OPERATING IN THE UNITED STATES, 1919-1931

ALL NATIONAL BANKS OPERATING BRANCHES

YEAR	No. Banks	Mem. Fed. Res.	Loan and Disc.	In-vest-ments	Re-sources
1919	3.78	13.43	8.89	5.52	7.93
1920	4.00	11.93	13.62	4.78	11.47
1921	4.48	12.37	21.67	8.15	18.69
1922	9.21	22.76	30.58	14.90	25.01
1923	13.37	32.72	29.23	20.36	25.65
1924	15.08	36.48	31.03	18.84	27.74
1925	18.36	42.98	33.70	19.96	31.67
1926	18.17	42.81	34.31	19.69	30.43
1927	19.78	46.74	37.37	23.87	34.11
1928	19.19	46.02	40.46	25.63	36.89
1929	19.60	47.47	36.97	21.36	34.07
1930	21.03	50.91	42.52	23.38	36.59
1931	21.30	53.04	45.62	23.98	37.00

ALL STATE BANKS AND TRUST COMPANIES OPERATING BRANCHES

YEAR	No. Banks	Mem. Fed. Res.	Loan and Disc.	In-vest-ments	Re-sources
1919	93.69	86.56	89.96	89.45	90.17
1920	93.12	88.06	85.28	76.19	83.24
1921	92.52	87.62	77.20	73.80	76.18
1922	87.50	77.23	68.33	71.41	70.51
1923	82.16	67.27	69.82	58.32	68.26
1924	79.05	63.51	67.55	58.92	64.75
1925	75.38	57.01	64.66	52.05	59.28
1926	74.96	57.18	63.78	50.56	59.56
1927	72.66	53.25	60.81	45.96	55.23
1928	72.86	53.97	57.59	42.80	52.73
1929	71.56	52.52	60.71	44.10	55.30
1930	69.71	49.09	55.02	43.76	51.00
1931	68.52	46.96	51.31	40.64	47.69

TABLE 89 *(Continued)*

ALL MUTUAL SAVINGS BANKS
OPERATING BRANCHES

YEAR	No. Banks	Mem. Fed. Res.	Loan and Disc.	In-vest-ments	Re-sources
1919	2.52	—	1.13	5.02	1.89
1920	2.86	—	1.08	19.01	5.28
1921	2.99	—	1.12	18.04	5.11
1922	3.28	—	1.07	13.67	4.46
1923	4.45	—	.94	21.30	6.08
1924	5.86	—	1.40	22.23	7.50
1925	6.25	—	1.62	27.98	9.04
1926	6.86	—	1.90	29.73	10.00
1927	7.55	—	1.81	30.15	10.65
1928	7.93	—	1.94	31.55	10.37
1929	8.82	—	2.30	34.53	10.61
1930	9.26	—	2.45	32.86	12.40
1931	10.18	—	3.07	35.38	15.30

The mutual savings bank can, therefore, operate successfully only in the larger cities. Correspondingly, the branches of mutual savings banks must be located in cities and towns with population larger than required for branches of commercial banks and trust companies. It is unlikely that there will ever be a wide development of this type of branch banking. Yet, it seems perfectly clear that there are opportunity and good reason for a continuation of the growth of branches by mutual savings banks for some time to come.

The very nature of the savings bank business—the fact that the funds are not loaned as a general practice to those who have the deposits, places the mutual savings bank outside certain criticism directed against the branches of commercial banks, namely that the institutions are local and that branch banking would mean the use of the facilities for business concerns or market operations outside the community itself. The funds of mutual savings banks may be, and usually are, loaned to another group. The depositor of the mutual savings bank would not, therefore, be interested in this objection to branch banking. There are certain economies in this type of branch. Overhead would be reduced, the services of the bank could be extended to many communities which are unable to support a mutual savings bank on its own account. There could, likewise, be considerable economies made in the handling of the reserves of the bank and its branches. There is, therefore, a recognized but limited field for this type of branch banking.

Argument for Branch Banking

The advocates of branch banking set forth at considerable length all the advantages of that system as compared with the unit plan of organization. It is interesting to observe, however, that some arguments are used against branch banking by the advocates of unit banking, while the same are advanced by others in favor of branches. Without attempting to exhaust the claims for branch banking, let us now enumerate briefly those points or arguments generally used to illustrate the advantages of such a system.

1. *Mobility of bank credit.*—Banks with branches may more easily and cheaply transfer funds from one community to another. This is merely a process of transferring funds from the head office to the branches or vice versa. The unit bank must use the so-called correspondent for this purpose, with the result that the funds are likely to be transferred to the market centers and used there; whereas in the case of a branch system the funds may be transferred to another community and used for financing commercial business. This argument is especially emphasized by bankers in California and other sections where one-crop regions are to be found. Funds used for commercial purposes may be employed in one community at one time, and then, when no longer needed, be sent to another location through the medium of the head office.

2. *Diversification of loans and investments.*—Banks with branches have a larger volume of funds generally than would be held by unit banks in the same community, hence are in a position to get a greater diversification of their portfolios which would add much to the safety of banking in general and to the depositors of the individual bank in particular. This diversification may be obtained in two ways: (1) The branch system would have its branches in several different communities and hence

secure a variety of business which would provide a large element of diversification. (2) The bank with branches generally has a larger body of funds which would permit it to spread its investments over a larger number of industries as well as a larger number of borrowers. Regardless of the way in which diversification may be obtained, it is usually considered one of the principal arguments in behalf of this type of banking.

3. *Availability of bank credits.*—It is usually maintained by anti-branch bankers that loans are not as easily obtained under a branch as under a unit system. This contention rests upon the assumption that the borrower of the branch institutions will be farther removed from the officers and directors who direct the lending of the bank, hence, less likely to secure the funds than he would if he were doing business with a unit bank. This may or may not be the case, depending upon the particular set of bank officers and the amount of funds actually needed by the borrower at a given time. If the borrower is a large one, he will be more likely, except in the case of large banks, to secure the volume of funds needed than in the case of a smaller unit bank. As a matter of fact this argument may be applied to either side of the controversy depending upon the administration of the bank and its various offices.

4. *Convenience of access.*—The bank with branches is in a position to perform more services than the unit bank. It will be able to locate its offices in smaller localities, hence provide a larger number of places at which the customer may do business. This would bring the bank closer to the business man than would be possible in many cases where the unit banking system was being used.

It is further claimed by those opposed to branch banking that the officers and directors of the bank would have less interest in a community where the branch was located than would the officers and directors of a unit bank located in the same place. This would, it is argued, increase the difficulties in obtaining the needed accommodation. The two main questions at issue are: *a*) is the relationship less personal, and *b*) will the branch managements be less flexible and more rigid in their requirements, thus tending to limit or restrict the extension of bank credit? The answer to the first is positive. It may be assumed that the relationship is less personal. On the other hand it is doubtful if the requirements will be any more rigid. The management of the branch will not be so likely to lend funds on a purely personal basis which will in the end act as much in favor of the borrowing community as it will to the bank itself.

5. *Safety of funds.*—One of the basic questions to be decided in any banking system is that of the safety of the depositors. Neither branch banking nor unit banking is inherently safe; either may be speculative and dangerous. In this respect, a great deal depends upon the type and character of the management. There are features of branch banking which tend to favor the branch system. The larger institutions are in a position to secure and hold expert management. They are, moreover, in a position to do more careful credit work and to diversify more properly their portfolios.

It is true that our unit system has crumbled very badly during the last depression; hence, can not be regarded as satisfactory. Banks operating branches have been closed and still others have been placed in the hands of conservators since the banking holiday in March, 1933. Viewed from a failure standpoint, our branch systems are not safe but the two authorities are not on a par during the present difficulties. Our branch banks have been restricted and undeveloped so that we have not as yet had a branch system in this country that is comparable to that of Canada, England, or of certain other commercial and industrial countries.

6. *Interest rates.*—It is the general claim of branch banking managers that the adoption and operation of branch banking has tended to make interest rates more uniform throughout a country and at the same time to reduce them. There is a tendency for the interest rates in the more highly developed sections where they are lowest to be passed over to the branches and communities where the interest rates have in the past been higher. The results in this country are too limited to permit us to prove either side of the question from American experience.

Our branch bankers in California contend, however, that interest rates have declined in that state since the introduction of branch banking.

Arguments against branch banking have been partly indicated in the discussion of the advantages of branch banking. In addition to those thus set forth, it is, perhaps, desirable at this point to outline the disadvantages of branch banking as viewed by the proponents of the unit system. These various factors are as follows:

1. *Branch banking tends toward monopoly.*—It is asserted that an extension of branches by banks would reduce the number of banks greatly and so would, in the end, lead to a monopoly in the field of banking. These large banks would drive out the small bank and thus be in a position to dictate the terms upon which credit would be extended and to whom it should go. Those who were not in "favor" at the bank would not be able to secure credit when needed. On the other hand the interest rates would be increased, making the cost of credit much higher.

2. *Examination and supervision.*—Those who oppose branch banking argue that it would be impossible properly to examine banks with a large number of branches. It would not be easy to maintain an examination staff sufficiently large to make a simultaneous examination of the bank and all of its branches. The matter would be further complicated by reason of the dual system of chartering and supervising banks in this country. State banks as well as national banks might elect to operate branches in two or more states which would complicate the matter of supervising and regulating such banking business.

It is, of course, contended by branch bankers that it is not necessary to examine all the branches at one time. Just as satisfactory results would be obtained if the examination was started at the head office and then carried to each of the several branches as time might permit.

3. *Drainage of funds into New York and other financial centers.*—According to the anti-branch bankers, a branch-banking system would operate to the advantage of the large metropoli-

tan centers and to the disadvantage of the smaller communities. It is said that the management of the branch system would send inferior men to manage the branches and, then, rather than take the risk of lending the funds in the community, the branch manager would simply transfer the funds to the large financial centers and leave the small towns and cities without funds.

The other side of this argument is found in the fact that a bank can not rob a community of its funds and expect to continue to receive them. If the branch is successful it must both receive deposits and make loans. Both are necessary so that there is no sound reason for expecting a branch-banking system to adopt any such methods in practice. On the other hand it has been pointed out that the correspondent system, which is based upon the unit bank, has worked to do just what the opponents of branch banking say that branches would do. There can be little doubt that where a correspondent system exists there will be some tendency for the banks in the interior to send their excess funds to their correspondent to invest for them. Where this is done, it will as a matter of course, greatly augment the volume of funds passing into the money market centers, where they will be used.

5. *Lack of personal interest.*—There is some fear that an adoption of branch banking would imply lessening of direct attention on the part of the banker in many smaller communities. His support would thus be drawn to the larger communities, leaving the smaller ones lacking the new funds to develop business. This argument has some foundation, but it is true that the same charge can be and has been successfully made against the selfish and incompetent management of many small banks in this country in the past.

The success of the manager would seem to be measured by the success of the branch which would certainly be accomplished best by developing all the business there possible. The manager would serve his own interest best by developing all the business in his community. In this way he would be more likely to be promoted than by transferring funds to some other place, leaving his own community undeveloped because of a scarcity of funds.

6. *Loss of taxes.*—There has been some loss of taxes in communities where the unit bank has been superseded by a branch. The amount of real-estate and building investment has been greatly reduced; hence, a decline in the amount received by the local community in taxes. This is certainly true so far as the general property taxes are concerned.

The Prospect

Without attempting to forecast the future development of branch banking, it may be pointed out that certain changes in our banking system must sooner or later lead to rather extensive growth or expansion of branch banking. These forces which are at work to make necessary a development of branch banking (regardless of the specific cause or causes for each of the changes at the present time) are the rapidly declining number of unit banks, leaving many communities without any local banking facilities; the merger and consolidation movement which is constantly reducing the number of banks; the enactment of some very recent legislation which must reduce still further in the course of time the number of banking offices throughout the country; the efforts on the part of many individuals, firms and corporations to do business with banks which are able to provide the larger services needed, and which can not be supplied often by the smaller banks, would seem to justify recent tendencies in branch banking legislation.

Several states have in the past few years modified their banking laws, either to permit branch banking in a limited form, as for example, Indiana and Iowa, or to broaden the territory in which branches may be operated. In this second category are found the states of Wisconsin, Ohio, and New Jersey. During the past years a few states have enacted new laws which permit branch banking on a wider scale, as for example, Washington, Idaho, and South Dakota. In still other states considerable attention has been given to the subject in one form or another. In this last group may be placed the states of Illinois and Oklahoma. The changes in these several states have not been such as to indicate a sweeping drift to branch banking, but they do indicate a slow but definite tendency in that direction.

When we consider the national situation, there is present the same general tendency. This tendency has been manifested in the past by the rulings of the Comptroller of the Currency in 1922, and the passage of the McFadden Act in 1927. Under this ruling and the Act of 1927 there has come into the national-banking system a considerable number of branches. Of greater importance is the more recent Act of Congress, the Banking Act of 1933. This Act, while it gives, on the surface, only limited rights to national banks which are intended to put the national banks on a basis with state banks and trust companies, contains certain features which will in the course of time require that branch banking be given further consideration and which will be likely to lead to further liberalization of the national laws regarding branch banking. It is the indirect effect of this bill that will in the long run probably lead to a further extension of branch banking, rather than the direct provisions of the present law giving national banks the right to operate branches in their states on the same terms as have been, or are to be, granted by state laws or authorities in the future to state banks and trust companies. What are the indirect provisions of the Act which may lead to a reconsideration of branch banking and to its more extensive development in the future?

The Guaranty Deposit provisions of the Banking Act of 1933 are such that it would seem that practically all banks, both large and small, will be forced for one reason or another to become members of the corporation, which will guarantee the deposits of these several banks. To become members of the guaranty fund system involves membership in the Federal Reserve system within a given period of time. To become a member of the Federal Reserve system, means that banks must have a capital of not less than $25,000. It is a well-known fact that there are literally hundreds of banks in this country which do not have sufficient capital to qualify. Many of these banks could under certain circumstances increase their capital and readjust their portfolios so as to be accepted as members of the Federal Reserve system. It is equally well known that there are a large number of such banks that cannot do so under conditions which will be likely to be successful in the end. Such banks will find it most difficult, if not entirely impossible, to retain their small volume of business when it is recognized that they are outside the pale of the guaranty system.

Since these banks will not be able to continue, there doubtless will follow the introduction of this new guaranty system a substantial decline in the number of banking institutions in this country. What will become of the banking business of those communities which have lost their small unit banks? Much of it will go to nearby larger cities and banks. The changing of the banking facilities in this way will no doubt lead in the near future to a reconsideration of the whole question of branch banking and will, in the end, bring about a more liberal policy toward branch banking; for, without branch banking, these smaller communities can not have the type of banking facilities they so long enjoyed.

There are still other provisions which will in the end operate toward a further extension of branch banking. The increase to $50,000 of the minimum capital requirement for national banks in the future will also tend to make branches desirable, whereas in the early days a small unit bank might have been organized to provide the banking facilities. The general tendency in several states to increase the minimum capital requirements for state banks and trust companies will react in the same way toward an expansion of branch banking.

The separation of the security affiliates and the provisions of the Act regarding the control and operation of banks under what is commonly referred to as chain and group banking, also will tend to induce the stockholders who have brought these organizations together to give their support, as many already are doing, to the modification of state and national bank laws leading to an expansion of branch banking. The opposition to branch banking will decline very rapidly with these changes in the structure of banking.

There is likewise a growing sentiment in this country in

favor of what is generally referred to as *unified banking.* This implies the abandonment of state banks and the extension of the national system to such a degree that there will be a banking system operated under one authority—the complete abolishment, in the course of time, of our dual banking system. If such a system is developed, and certainly the Banking Act of 1933 tends in that direction with its more or less forced guaranty system, it will be followed by a certain growth of branch banking.

To summarize what has been said regarding the future growth of tendencies of branch banking as a result of the Banking Act of 1933, it would seem that the direct changes in the Act relative to the extension of national branch banking and the other indirect changes would, in the course of time, lead us to a national system of branch banking. Such a policy need not authorize the establishment and operation of branches by banks on a nation-wide basis, but it would mean that branch banking on some larger geographical unit would be necessary. This new and larger unit might, and probably should be—at least for a considerable number of years—the Federal Reserve district.

Conclusions

1. The number of banks operating branches increased from 476, in 1919, to 747 in 1932. The largest number operating branches in any one year was 844 in 1928. During the same period the number of branches increased from 1,082, in 1919, to 3,290 at the close of 1932. The largest number reported for any year was 3,603 in 1929. These data show a decline, therefore, of 8.6 per cent in the number of branches in 1932 as compared with 1929.

The total resources of all banks operating branches in 1919 amounted to $7,695,000,000, or 16.2 per cent of the total resources of all banks in operation in the United States. In 1931 the total resources of all banks operating branches amounted to $28,877,000,000, or 41.1 per cent of the resources of all banks in the United States. In 1929 the total resources of all banks operating branches amounted to $33,269,000,000, or 46.1 per cent of the resources of all banks in the United States.

2. The relative position of the various classes measured in total resources has changed considerably. In 1919 national banks had 7.93 per cent of all banks operating branches, state banks and trust companies 90.17 per cent, and mutual savings banks 1.89 per cent; whereas, in 1931 these percentages had changed to 37.00, 47.69, and 15.30 for national banks, state banks and trust companies, and mutual savings banks, respectively.

3. The branch banking movement is, and has been, very closely related to other banking changes—such as bank failures, bank mergers and consolidations, chain and group banking, and the inability of the small unit banks to show sufficient earnings to satisfy their stockholders.

4. The laws, both state and national, have been undergoing gradual modification in favor of a wider extension of branch banking in this country. This is especially true as regards the more recent years, 1927 to date. This change is clearly shown in the changes in the national bank act and the laws of several states, as for example, Indiana, Iowa, Washington, Idaho, and others, where branch banking has been authorized under certain conditions.

5. The failure of the unit system, together with the large number of bank failures—including some large banks and many small ones—during the past ten or twelve years, has greatly increased the interest in branch banking and may be said to have been largely instrumental in bringing about a change or changes in state banking laws permitting a wider operation of branches. There can be no doubt that the failure of these banks has had a most important effect upon the status of branch banking, and will lead, in the end, to a much greater expansion of branches in this country.

6. The passage of the Banking Act in June, 1933, will mean greater interest in branch banking than is at present contemplated by the advocates of this measure itself. The provisions of this Act will, through its guaranty fund and capital, and membership requirements, act to force a very considerable reduction in the number of banks which will, most likely, be followed in

the course of time by a growth of branches in many states. The number in the national system may increase at a very rapid pace, once the guaranty fund corporation is put into operation. The direct widening of the powers of national banks by this Act plus the indirect influences make it one of the most important branch banking acts ever enacted by Congress.

7. The advantages of branch banking may be summarized as follows:

a) Greater mobility of bank credit
b) Greater diversification of loans and discounts
c) Makes bank credit more available
d) Greater convenience of access
e) Safety of funds
f) Lower interest rates

8. The disadvantages of branch banking, acording to the anti-branch bankers, may be summarized as follows:

a) Branch banking is "un-American"
b) Branch banking tends toward monopoly in banking
c) Greater difficulties in bank examination and supervision
d) Drainage of funds from local centers to the large metropolitan districts
e) Decline of the personal element in banking
f) Loss in local taxes

CHAPTER XVIII

THE AFFILIATE SYSTEM[1]

As previously noted, one of the outstanding developments of the decade preceding the panic of 1929, was the growth of a system of associated companies owned by banks, or, through a legal subterfuge, by their stockholders. The position of these affiliates has already been sketched in its relationship to the banks themselves in Part II, Chapter X above (Commercial, Investment and Other Types of Banking). With the general position of the affiliate thus clearly marked out, the factors which gave rise to its existence need no further elaboration and may be taken for granted in the following discussion. It is necessary only, therefore, to indicate in this chapter the functions of the security affiliate and the general results of the operation of such affiliates as established by direct inquiry on the part of the Senate Banking Committee.

Before presenting the conclusions arrived at in the investigation of security affiliates it seems desirable, owing to the fact that there has heretofore been practically no authentic source of information concerning their dealings, to indicate exactly what is the source of the data employed in this chapter. The Senate Banking Committee did not consider that there was any necessity for attempting a complete census of the security affiliates of the country, or for gaining more than a select representative number of such security affiliates. Understanding that the total number of active affiliates was in the neighborhood of 150 (eliminating, of course, all those which had to do with real estate and nonsecurity operations), the Committee addressed to each of this select group, including it was believed, practically all of the larger affiliates of the country, a questionnaire as follows:

[1] The substance of this chapter was prepared by Dr. Jules I. Bogen, Professor of Finance, New York University, formerly a member of the Banking Seminar, and Associate Adviser to the Senate Banking Committee during the preparation of the Banking Act of 1933.

No. 2. Questionnaire on Security Affiliates (to Banks)

Little information is now available on the condition of security affiliates of commercial banks. In view of the important rôle and large resources of such organizations, a clear picture of their condition and relations with parent banks is desirable.

1. List names and addresses of all affiliates of your bank which deal in or hold securities, with capital and surplus of each:

NAME OF AFFILIATE	ADDRESS	CAPITAL	SURPLUS
....	....	....	....
....	....	....	....
....	....	....	....
....	....	....	....
....	....	....	....

2. How was the capital and surplus of each security affiliate provided? ....
....
....

3. What was the maximum indebtedness of each security affiliate to your bank and affiliated institutions in 1929? .... in 1930? ....

4. What was the average amount of such indebtedness in 1929?
....
................................; in 1930? ....
....

5. What proportion of such indebtedness was secured? ....

6. What proportion of such indebtedness was secured by stock collateral? ....
....

7. How is identity of ownership of your bank and security affiliates assured? ....
....

8. What was the total amount of securities bought by you from all your security affiliates under repurchase agreements in each of the past four years? ....
....

9. What was the maximum amount of such repurchase agree-

ments from all your security affiliates outstanding at any one time in each year? ....

....

10. Append income accounts of security affiliates for 1928, 1929, and any portion of 1930 available.

11. Append balance sheets of security affiliates at end of 1928, 1929, and latest date in 1930 available.

12. Append full portfolio of security affiliates at close of 1928, 1929, and latest date in 1930 available, with original cost and present market values indicated.

13. What was the aggregate amount of syndicate and other participations of your security affiliates during each of the past four years? ....

....

14. Describe the nature of the five largest participations of this sort in 1929. ....

....

....

Analysis of the portfolios of the typical group of security affiliates which responded to these inquiries shows that operations of the affiliates included several distinct functions, often exercised individually but frequently in combination as already outlined in Part II, Chapter X above cited. Among the functions thus classified, several stand out as deserving of special analysis at this point. The following from Part VII, Hearings of Senate Banking Committee, 1931, is timely.

An analysis of the portfolios of a typical group of security affiliates indicates that the business of retailing securities seldom involves a large measure of risk. The security inventory carried in this connection, while it may include a relatively large number of individual issues, seldom ties up more than a moderate fraction of the resources of the affiliate; and the rate of turnover, even in comparatively inactive periods in the security business, constitutes an additional source of protection for the security company against being tied up with any large volume of securities that can not be marketed without serious loss.

On the other hand, the wholesale underwriting of securities does tend at times to leave the security affiliates with big unsold commitments that, in times of rapidly declining prices, may result in large losses of at least a temporary nature. At the end of 1930, for example, several of the larger security affiliates still had commitments amounting to several millions of dollars in each case in Bethlehem Steel Corporation common stock, an issue of 800,000 shares of common stock of which company they had underwritten in the fall of 1929. It so happened that the stock offering of this company to its shareholders, underwritten by these security companies, called for payment at the end of October, 1929, coincident with the stock-market panic of that year. Shareholders apparently took little of this stock, so that it was left very largely in the hands of the underwriting bankers. The offering price to the stockholders of the company was $110 per share, from which a commission of several points was allowed the underwriters. In at least two major cases the underwriting commitments taken over were not disposed of to any extent by the end of 1930, and meanwhile the market price of the stock declined by more than 60 per cent from the quotation at which the underwriters acquired the issue.

The portfolios of some of the security affiliates indicate that the profits of years of operations can be more than wiped out through two or three unprofitable commitments of this kind, at least on the basis of quotations prevailing during a depression period.

Activities of a bank's security affiliate as a holding or finance company or an investment trust are also fraught with the danger of large losses during a deflation period. Bank affiliates of this kind show a much greater tendency to operate with borrowed funds than do organizations of this type which are independent of banks; the reason being that the identity of control and management which prevails between the bank and its affiliate tends to encourage reliance upon the lending facilities of the former.

When the affiliate acts as a receptacle for slow or doubtful assets of the bank, its existence is of apparent aid in maintaining the liquidity of the parent institution, especially where the capital of the affiliate is provided by stockholders and not by the bank itself. However, when it becomes necessary to help finance the affiliate through loans from the bank, there is no real benefit to the bank from its operations, since the bank itself then advances the funds to hold these doubtful assets. Furthermore, such transfer of doubtful assets to an affiliated corporation, by giving the bank an appearance of liquidity which is greater than the facts of the case warrant, may encourage assumption of other commitments that might not be desirable in the light of losses already indicated in the portfolio of the affiliate. In fact the mere existence of an affiliate which might be made the receptacle for unwise loans and investments when needed tends to reduce the degree of caution exercised by bank managements, there is reason to believe.

Activities of affiliates in supporting a bank's own stock or in holding real estate have both been the source of substantial loss in individual cases. Taken as a whole, however, it would appear that the security affiliates of the banks studied in connection with the committee's questionnaire ordinarily engaged in such activities to a moderate extent only. It is well to remember, however, that it was precisely this type of activity, and especially that first mentioned, which brought on the disastrous collapse of the Bank of United States in New York in 1930, and contributed to several large bank failures elsewhere. The bank-merger movement of the last few years has at times resulted in specially large commitments in a bank's own stock, as efforts are made to advance the price of the stock of a bank in order to make it more attractive in an exchange for shares of another institution. Also, certain mergers have involved commitments by the absorbing institution that shares of the bank being absorbed would be purchased by the security affiliate of the former if desired, and such arrangements have at times resulted in the affiliate acquiring quite large blocks of the bank's shares.

1. *Analysis of typical security affiliates.*—The period of security-market deflation which began in October, 1929, created an unfavorable situation for the security affiliates of the banks. The usual sources of income from originating and distributing securities tended to dry up, while sharp declines occurred in the market values of these issues which were already held in their portfolios. Summaries of the situations faced by several such organizations as indicated by replies to questionnaire No. 2 on security affiliates are presented in the following cases:

Bank 1: The chief security affiliate of this bank had some 500 individual holdings. Nearly one-half of the total stated value of the security holdings consisted of two issues, representing all of the capital stock of two other affiliates. Each of these, on the basis of market prices of their own holdings, had net asset values far below the sums at which they were carried on the books of the chief affiliate. This would not allow for the substantial good will of these two subsidiary affiliates, however, since they were more than mere investment companies.

Aside from these two subsidiaries, there were several blocks of shares with a cost of $1,000,000 or more in the portfolio of the chief affiliate of this bank, and in the majority of such cases substantial depreciation in market price had taken place by the end of 1930.

Bank 2: The security affiliate of this bank divides its holdings into two groups—trading accounts and inactive accounts. The trading accounts include about 350 bond issues, mostly small amounts apparently purchased or held in connection with a retail security distribution business. About 75 stock issues are also held in trading accounts, of which two only are of substantial size. One of these latter is the stock of an industrial which had been underwritten in connection with an offering to its shareholders, and the second is the stock of the bank itself. These two holdings together showed a depreciation of 25 per cent from cost on December 31, 1930, and at the values then prevailing constituted 15 per cent of the total stock and bond holdings of the affiliate. In the inactive account, there was one very large holding without a market, and nine others with an aggregate cost of approximately $31,000,000 and a stated market value at the end of 1930 of about 35 per cent less.

The inactive accounts, which were apparently operated as an investment-trust-holding company, constituted the larger portion of the portfolio of this security affiliate.

Bank 3: The security affiliate of this bank appeared to operate in large measure as an investment trust dedicated to the principle of long-pull investment. At the end of 1928 its holdings showed an appreciation in market value of more than 100 per cent over cost. At the end of 1929 the appreciation shown was little above 50 per cent. At the end of 1930 such appreciation had dwindled to about 15 per cent, and by the middle of 1931, assuming no substantial changes in the portfolio during the first six months of the year, market value and cost were nearly the same. However, the reported income of this company was quite large in each year, averaging about 50 per cent on its capital, and indicating that its wholesale underwriting and other operations were consistently profitable.

Bank 4: The security affiliate of this bank carries its security holdings in two chief account groups—syndicate, joint, and carrying accounts; and secondly, merchandise accounts. Municipal and general holdings are shown separately for each account group. At the end of 1930, after deducting the reserve account set up from earnings, the aggregate market value of its security holdings was stated to have been less than 5 per cent below the book value.

This security affiliate had only one really large commitment, a block of shares in a large industrial whose offering to stockholders it had underwritten. At the end of 1930 this one holding had depreciated by considerably more than 50 per cent in market price.

Bank 5: The security affiliate of this bank restricts its activities very largely to the distribution of high-grade securities. Its commitments in industrial issues are moderate in size for the most part. The books are kept on a market-value basis, reflecting both appreciation and depreciation, and owing to apparent care with which the inventory of securities is kept down, it was able to end the year 1930 with a profit of more than $1,000,000 after all adjustments to market.

Bank 6: This institution reported two affiliates, a security company and an investment trust, the latter being controlled by the former. The security company, which owned some $20,000,000 of stocks and bonds at the end of 1930, had a diversified bond list and a shorter list of stocks, on several of the latter of which severe shrinkages in market value had occurred. Thus, on five stock holdings which together had a cost equal to about 70 per cent of the total original cost of the security portfolio, a decline of more than 50 per cent in market value had taken place by the end of 1930. The security affiliate also reported a substantial indebtedness to the investment trust affiliate, and on the basis of market prices prevailing at the end of 1930 the market value of the holdings of the security affiliate had declined so far as apparently to eliminate its capital and paid-in surplus on this basis of computation.

Bank 7: The security affiliate of this bank had done a large business in wholesaling, as well as retailing, securities. It held some 300 separate issues. As of the end of 1930 the stock accounts showed a depreciation of almost 50 per cent from cost, the bond accounts more than 20 per cent, and substantial paper losses were also indicated on unclosed syndicate accounts. In this instance also, if securities be taken at market value, the elimination of the capital and surplus of the affiliate would be indicated.

Among the banks outside of New York City, which possessed security affiliates of substantial size, the following references to special cases may prove of interest:

Bank 8: This is a large Eastern bank which possesses an affiliate doing both a security and an acceptance business. The security holdings amount to more than $40,000,000 and fall into two main classes—investments and inventory accounts, the latter being destined for early sale. The investments account for about 30 per cent of the total, and to a substantial degree consist of holdings in affiliated financial institutions. The inventory accounts consist of several hundred different issues, for the most part of very high grade. Taking the portfolio as a whole, the depreciation suffered by the end of 1930 was much below the average for such companies.

Bank 9: About 20 per cent of the securities held by the affiliate of this bank, located in Chicago, consisted of small blocks of bonds, apparently in process of distribution. The balance consisted of stocks, and of the latter more than one-half was a block of 1,000,000 shares of the common stock of an investment trust affiliated with the bank. The second largest holding, amounting to nearly 20 per cent of the total investment list, was the common stock of the bank itself. In other words, about two-thirds of the total security holdings of the affiliate as carried on the books consisted of but two issues, on the larger of which there was a depreciation of about 70 per cent by the middle of 1931, while on the stock of the bank itself, the smaller of the two, a depreciation of about 65 per cent had taken place.

Bank 10: The great bulk of the portfolio of the affiliate of this bank which operates in the West, consists of stocks of affiliated financial organizations and bonds of an affiliated mortgage company. A holding company which controls the bank also has a diversified list of security holdings which is made public.

Bank 11: About two-thirds of the portfolio of the security affiliate of this bank consists of one item—capital stock of the bank itself. However, the affiliate has virtually no loans payable, its own capital funds being almost exclusively used by it in its operations. The second largest item in the portfolio is the stock of a real estate company. The two items together constitute nearly 90 per cent of the total.

2. *Results of security affiliate operations.*—The financial results of the operation of security affiliates during the period following the stock market collapse of 1929 were on the whole unfavorable. Losses of any substantial size were not reported in every case, the chief exceptions being those organizations which restricted themselves to the distribution of high-grade bonds.

The determination of the earning power of security affiliates in any one year, as in the case of all companies whose assets consist chiefly of securities held for investment, is complicated by variations in the market values of stock and bond holdings. Several affiliates reported large earnings in 1930, but at the same time suffered severe shrinkage in the quoted market values of their portfolios. During 1931 such shrinkage was largely extended in most cases.

As a rough indication of the results of operations of security affiliates during 1930, the following data are presented. Lack of quoted markets on many items in the security portfolios of certain of the affiliates makes the determination of the extent of portfolio shrinkage a practical impossibility in certain cases. Reported earnings, as shown below, have also been reduced in many cases by specified adjustments of various kinds.

It will be seen from the above computation that with two exceptions none of the security affiliates included in the list avoided a

TABLE 90

RESULTS OF OPERATION OF SECURITY AFFILIATES, 1930

BANK	REPORTED EARNINGS	APPROXIMATE DECLINE IN MARKET VALUE OF PORTFOLIO FOR YEAR	BANK	REPORTED EARNINGS	APPROXIMATE DECLINE IN MARKET VALUE OF PORTFOLIO FOR YEAR
No. 1	$6,989,628	[1] $12,500,000	No. 8	$ 133,593	$ 4,000,000
No. 2	2,380,691	[1] 12,500,000	No. 9	2,018,956	10,000,000
No. 3	5,032,968	29,562,330	No. 10	2,289,011	2,500,000
No. 4	1,249,517	4,608,835	No. 11	369,127	1,500,000
No. 5	1,067,922	([2])	No. 12	224,210	1,200,000
No. 6	3,099,902	13,235,000	No. 13	133,874	45,239
No. 7	44,569	851,000	No. 14	10,944	950,000

[1] Several large holdings having no markets not included in computation.
[2] Books kept on market-value basis. [The footnotes are in the original.]

net loss for the year, if declines in the quoted values of holdings be allowed for, and in some cases the losses as thus defined reached quite substantial proportions, especially if probable values of issues without quoted markets be considered.

3. *Syndicate participations.*—In view of the fact that syndicate participations in connection with the origination and wholesaling of securities are subject to a special degree of risk during periods of declining security prices, because of the relatively large commitments involved, the banks addressed by the subcommittee were asked to state the aggregate amount of syndicate and other participations of security affiliates during each of the past four years, as well as maximum participations of this kind. The replies for the year 1930 were as follows:

TABLE 91

SYNDICATE PARTICIPATIONS OF SECURITY AFFILIATES, 1930

BANK	AGGREGATE PARTICIPATIONS	MAXIMUM PARTICIPATIONS	BANK	AGGREGATE PARTICIPATIONS	MAXIMUM PARTICIPATIONS
No. 1	$417,052,855	$33,987,105	No. 9	$ 2,026,410	$ 800,000
No. 2	583,193,357	20,000,000	No. 10	111,495,933	8,000,000
No. 3	38,424,627	34,353,911	No. 11	17,189,520	4,852,000
No. 4	452,979,000	18,300,000	No. 12	19,000,000	1,100,000
No. 5	150,602,750	[1] 15,000,000	No. 13	[2] 201,244,694	([3])
No. 6	260,867,029	15,000,000	No. 14	19,348,400	3,151,250
No. 7	102,547,000	12,900,000	No. 15	5,050,000	2,541,500
No. 8	10,855,000	[1] 3,750,000			

[1] Applies to 1929. [2] Retail sales only. [3] Not available.

The replies to this questionnaire indicate that security affiliates follow the practice of assuming syndicate commitments which amount in the aggregate to many times their capital and surplus, and that individual commitments of this kind may amount to from 25 to more than 100 per cent of such capital and surplus in certain cases.

One security affiliate further indicates the nature of its 1930 participation in detail as follows:

1. Underwriting	$ 27,175,442
2. Original terms	314,692,574
3. Purchase group	0
4. Banking group	76,464,590
5. Selling syndicate	164,860,751
Total	$583,193,357

In this computation, duplications exist because of the fact that selling and banking group participation in many cases cover the same issues as those purchased on "original terms" from the Government or corporation which puts out the offering in the first instance. Another large security affiliate reports its participations over the past four years as follows:

YEAR	PURCHASE GROUP	SPECIAL AND BANKING GROUPS	UNDERWRITING SYNDICATES
1927	$222,170,964	$145,877,500	$ 7,165,400
1928	178,856,915	108,163,450	49,072,147
1929	133,644,668	142,672,804	87,297,021
1930	134,369,000	122,909,000	36,609,000

YEAR	SELLING SYNDICATES	JOINT ACCOUNTS	SELLING GROUPS
1927	$34,510,000	$48,444,146	$163,866.900
1928	27,618,000	36,704,490	106,899,100
1929	11,385,000	38,089,000	99,851,321
1930	23,894,000	34,365,000	100,842,000

The banks addressed were also asked to list the five largest syndicate or group operations in which their security affiliates participated during 1929. Replies to this question indicate the varied nature of these major commitments. Thus one bank reports the five largest participations of its affiliate, together amounting to $75,963,695, as follows:

1. Market stabilizing account formed during the crisis of 1929.
2. Texas Corporation 5 per cent convertible bonds.
3. International Hydroelectric, 6/1944.
4. Canadian International Paper, 6/1949.
5. City of Chicago Board of Education 6 per cent tax anticipation notes.

The affiliate of another large Eastern institution reported that its five largest participations in 1929 amounted to $94,194,165. They were as follows:

1. Bethlehem Steel Corporation (28 per cent interest in original underwriting group to underwrite sale of 795,000 shares to stockholders).
2. Bethlehem Steel Corporation (28 per cent interest in original underwriting group to underwrite sale of 600,000 shares to stockholders).
3. American Cyanamid Co. (underwriting entire issue of 808,359½ shares of common B stock).
4. Texas Corporation (20 per cent interest in purchase group on $100,000,000 5 per cent debenture issue).
5. P. Lorillard Co. (underwriting entire issue of 545,024 shares of common stock).

The security affiliate of another large bank reported the following five as its largest participations for 1929:

1. New York Central short-term revenue bills	$16,750,000
2. Offering of shares of an affiliated investment trust	15,000,000
3. Offering of shares of an oil holding company	11,695,000
4. Republic of Cuba serial 5½ per cent certificates	8,001,000
5. Richfield Oil 6's	6,250,000
Total	57,696,000

4. *Relations of security affiliates to banks.*—From the viewpoint of banking regulation, the operations of the security affiliates can be of interest only in so far as they affect the activities and soundness of the banks with which they are affiliated. Basically, there can be no objection to the stockholders of a bank engaging in any other business they prefer with their own funds. However, if such activities tend to affect directly the position and soundness of the bank itself, they then become of prime importance in the regulation of banking.

Reasoning a priori, a number of ways in which the operations of a security affiliate can affect the position of the parent bank may be distinguished. These may be summarized as follows:

(1) The security affiliate may borrow money from the parent bank. This relationship, which is very prevalent, is discussed more fully in the following section.

(2) The affiliate may sell securities to the bank or another of its affiliates under repurchase agreements, or vice versa.

(3) The bank is closely connected in the public mind with its affiliates, and should the latter suffer large losses it is practically unthinkable that they would be allowed to fail. Instead, the bank would normally support it by additional loans or other aid, thus becoming more deeply involved itself. The knowledge that the affiliate has suffered large losses may in itself be sufficient to cause unfavorable rumors, however unjustified, to spread about the bank.

(4) The bank, to relieve the affiliate of excess holdings, may purchase securities from it. In one case of a large New York institution, for example, two blocks of foreign bonds, aggregating approximately $5,000,000, which were included in the portfolio of the affiliate as of the end of 1929 were given in the list of five largest holdings of the parent bank at the end of 1930.

(5) The bank may lend much more freely to customers on issues sponsored by the security affiliate, in order to facilitate their distribution, than it would otherwise do. Also, it may prove more difficult to insist upon the maintenance of adequate margins on these security loans than on other such advances, in view of the fact that customers are encouraged to make the loans by the bank's own affiliate.

(6) The good will of the bank with its depositors may be adversely affected to a serious degree when the latter suffer substantial losses on security issues purchased from the affiliate. Because of the

tendency of the selling organization of the affiliate to consider the bank's depositors as its preferred list of sales prospects, this condition may become an important handicap to a bank during a major period of security market deflation.

(7) Operations by the affiliate in the market for the bank's own stock may cause undesirably wide fluctuations in the latter. Also, efforts made in some cases to push the sale of the bank's stock through the affiliate to depositors of the institution hurt the position of the bank when its shares suffer a major market decline subsequently.

(8) Wide variations in the net asset value, earning power, and dividend-paying ability of security affiliates tend to make bank stock price fluctuations much greater than would otherwise be the case.

(9) The existence of the affiliates may induce the bank to make unwise commitments, in the knowledge that in case of need they can be shifted to the affiliates, and thus be removed from the bank's condition statement.

(10) Knowing its access to the resources of the bank in case of need, security affiliates in their turn may tend to assume various commitments less cautiously than do private investment banking houses.

(11) In the case of a trust company or a bank with a trust department, the possession of a security affiliate may adversely affect the independence with which fiduciary activities are exercised.

In actual practice, the operations of a number of security affiliates have affected the parent institutions to a greater or lesser degree in several of the ways outlined above. The most direct manner in which the affiliate may impair the liquidity of the bank is through the first mentioned method of borrowing.

5. *Bank loans to security affiliates.*—In the first part of this report on security loans, some data was presented on the extent to which banks make advances to their affiliates. In its questionnaire covering the operation of the affiliates the subcommittee asked a list of banks addressed to state the maximum loans outstanding at any one time to affiliates during the years 1929 and 1930, as well as the average indebtedness of these organizations to the parent banks in those years. The proportion of such indebtedness which was secured by collateral was also asked. The answers to these questions are tabulated herewith.

Loan lines of banks to affiliates are at times not covered, in whole

TABLE 92

LOANS BY PARENT BANKS TO SECURITY AFFILIATES, 1929 AND 1930

BANK	MAXIMUM INDEBTEDNESS OF AFFILIATES TO BANKS DURING YEAR		AVERAGE INDEBTEDNESS OF AFFILIATES TO BANKS		PERCENTAGE OF INDEBTEDNESS SECURED	
	1929	1930	1929	1930	1929	1930
No. 1	$16,294,284	[1] $54,839,881	$ 1,802,335	$28,813,049	100	57
No. 2	36,757,742	34,487,742	4,636,573	14,545,779	32	47
No. 3	25,020,000	24,970,000	10,715,000	14,493,000	100	100
No. 4	16,500,000	23,700,000	691,000	326,000	—	—
No. 5	19,172,276	25,504,967	12,022,500	10,387,663	100	100
No. 6	10,500,000	5,500,000	174,151	735,137	100	100
No. 7	7,100,000	6,550,000	2,662,400	3,916,500	100	100
No. 8 [2]	20,570,000	18,970,000	14,574,300	14,946,600	100	100
No. 9	2,134,000	13,878,000	30,000	4,417,000	—	87
No. 10	2,800,000	4,120,000	1,483,333	3,174,583	100	—
No. 11	21,000,000	21,000,000	12,000,000	17,000,000	100	100
No. 12	—	600,000	—	25,000	—	—

[1] Of which $44,241,523 were loans to the chief security affiliate from the parent and affiliated banks.
[2] Most of this indebtedness was from the security affiliate to the investment trust affiliate.

TABLE 93

REPURCHASE AGREEMENTS OF PARENT BANKS WITH SECURITY AFFILIATES, 1929 AND 1930

BANK	TOTAL REPURCHASE AGREEMENTS WITH AFFILIATES		MAXIMUM REPURCHASE AGREEMENTS WITH AFFILIATES		REMARKS
	1929	1930	1929	1930	
No. 1	$ 2,441,251	$ 39,689,064	$ 701,833	$23,002,210	Tax-exempt municipals.
No. 2	57,488,371	116,310,018	23,542,809	24,172,888	From syndicates of which affiliate was manager.
No. 6	391,623	363,048	391,623	363,048	
No. 7	92,938,685	—	16,116,910	—	Mainly governments and municipals.
No. 8	—	9,656,000	—	2,870,000	
No. 9	425,000	2,974,000	425,000	2,974,000	

or in part, by specific collateral, as seen from the last two columns of Table 92. Where loans exceed 10 per cent of the bank's capital and surplus, legal restrictions are avoided by having such excess secured by United States Government bonds, by having more than one affiliate, and, thirdly, by the use of the repurchase agreement.

The banks addressed were asked also to state the total amount of securities purchased by them from their security affiliates under repurchase agreements over a period of years. The use of this contractual device involves, of course, a further close tie between the bank and its affiliate.

The replies of those banks which reported making such agreements with affiliates, with numerical designations corresponding to the preceding table, are given in Table 93.

The relative extent to which security affiliates operate with borrowed capital, including loans from sources other than the parent bank, is indicated in the following table (repurchase agreements not included):

TABLE 94

SOURCES OF FUNDS OF SECURITY AFFILIATES, END OF 1930

BANK	CAPITAL AND BORROWED FUNDS OF AFFILIATE	CAPITAL AND SURPLUS: PERCENTAGE OF TOTAL	BORROWED FUNDS: PERCENTAGE OF TOTAL
No. 1	$137,414,000	79	21
No. 2	93,467,000	76	24
No. 3	61,370,000	36	64
No. 4	34,341,000	83	17
No. 5	17,792,000	39	61
No. 6	23,291,000	76	24
No. 7	35,015,000	66	34
No. 8	23,140,000	38	62
No. 9	60,939,000	43	57
No. 10	41,440,000	53	47
No. 11	6,955,000	96	4
Total, 11 banks	$535,164,000	64	36

If all of the above security affiliates had written down their security holdings to market values by charges against surplus, or capital if necessary, the proportion of loan to own capital would have been very much larger than shown above.

The loan relationship as it exists between the bank and its affiliate differs from that prevailing with the general run of the bank's customers in an essential respect. When dealing with its affiliate, the bank is really dealing with itself, in view of the identity of ownership and management that is established. As a result, there tends to be a breaking down of those limitations on the extension of credit which the bank sets up in other cases to guard against the making of excessive or poorly-secured loans.

6. *Dividends of affiliates.*—Concrete evidence of the manner in which a change in security market conditions affects the position of security affiliates is furnished by the dividend policies of such organizations during the period 1929-1931. Where stock of the affiliate is held in trust for shareholders of the bank, or where shares of the two institutions are printed on the same certificate, each declares dividends separately, payable to the same list of shareholders. In most, but not all, of such cases, announcement is made of the dividend paid by each institution. In other instances the aggregate amount of the dividend is announced publicly, rather than the amount contributed by each institution.

Where the affiliate is a direct subsidiary of the bank, with the latter owning its shares outright, dividends declared by it are paid directly to the bank. In such cases, it is not usual for publicity to be given the amount of the dividend.

The following banks announced changes in rate of dividends paid on shares of affiliates during 1931:

TABLE 95

DIVIDENDS PAID ON NEW YORK BANK STOCKS, 1931

BANK	ANNUAL DIVIDEND RATE, BEGINNING OF 1931			ANNUAL DIVIDEND RATE MIDDLE OF 1931, ALL PAID BY BANK
	Paid by Bank	Paid by Affiliate	Total	
Chase National Bank	$ 3.00	$ 1.00	$ 4.00	$ 4.00
First National Bank	20.00	80.00	100.00	100.00
Bank of America	4.00	.50	4.50	2.00

In addition, several affiliates of trust companies made reductions or omissions of dividends previously paid directly to parent banks, both in 1930 and 1931.

7. *Regulation of security affiliates.*—The first extended reference

to security affiliates of banks by a regulatory authority is found in the Report of the Comptroller of the Currency for 1920. Mindful of the effects on such organizations of the security market deflation of that year, the comptroller made the following statement:

"SECURITIES COMPANIES" AS ADJUNCTS TO NATIONAL BANKS OFTEN A MENACE

Some 'securities companies' operating in close connection with, and often officered by, the same men who manage the national banks with which they are allied, have become instruments of speculation and headquarters for promotions of all kinds of financial schemes. Many of the flotations promoted by the 'securities corporations' which are operated as adjuncts to national banks have proven disastrous to their subscribers, and have in some instances reflected seriously not only upon the credit and the standing of the 'securities companies' by which they are sponsored, but also in some cases have damaged the credit and reputation of national banks with which the 'securities companies' are allied.

It has been established clearly by decisions of the United States Supreme Court that a national bank can not, except as authorized by the Federal reserve act, hold the stock of other national banks or the stock of other corporations; but these adjunct or auxiliary companies whose stockholders are identical with the stockholders of the national banks with which they are connected by various ties and devices frequently deal actively in stocks, and they also sometimes acquire the ownership or control of other banks, National and State, through their stock purchases.

In times of rising prices and active speculation some of these auxiliary corporations have made large profits through their ventures and syndicate operations, but their losses in other periods have been heavy, and they have become an element of increasing peril to the banks with which they are associated. The business of legitimate banking is entirely separate and distinct from the kind of business conducted by many of the 'securities corporations,' and it would be difficult, if not impossible, for the same set of officers to conduct safely, soundly, and successfully the conservative business of the national bank and at the same time direct and manage the speculative ventures and promotions of the ancillary institutions. These varying institutions demand a different kind of ability and experience on the part of those who manage them, and the two types of business when combined with one management are likely to be operated to the advantage of neither.

A national bank lends not only its own capital, but the money of its depositors, and in doing this is not expected to tie up its funds in long-time and unliquid loans in doubtful ventures. The 'securities companies' theoretically invest and speculate with their own funds—that is to say, the funds supplied by their own stockholders—not with the funds of depositors; but as a matter of fact, experience shows that 'securities companies' often draw and absorb large sums of money from the allied national banks, and sometimes also borrow heavily from other national banks which operate other 'securities companies,' and so on, in an endless chain of reciprocal borrowing and mutual lending for the accommodation of speculative cliques.

These ancillary companies are being used with increasing frequency for promotion of speculation and for dealing in bonds and stocks, often those of new and unseasoned issues, and which are attended with improper hazard risk, and as a means of enabling banks to do, indirectly through their instrumentality, things which they can neither safely nor lawfully do directly.[1]

This forceful statement of the situation was without effect at the time, although later the comptroller sought, and in many cases secured, permission to examine security affiliates as part of the examination of banks. However, he did not demand this as of right, and in some instances such permission was refused as not coming within his province.

In New York State, where most of the large security affiliates are to be found, sentiment on the subject was aroused among bankers, as well as the general public, by the effects of the stock market deflation in 1929-30, and later by the collapse of the Bank of United States, with its 59 different affiliates. The superintendent of banks was given legal authority in 1930 to examine bank affiliates by an act of the State legislature.

[1] *Report of the Comptroller of the Currency*, 1920, pp. 55-56. [The footnote is in the original.]

CHAPTER XIX

RESERVES[1]

The question of required reserves for banks has been, historically speaking, one of the leading controversial issues in American banking for generations past. The National Bank Act itself centered largely around the reserve question, and subsequent legislation has been more or less directed toward the regulation of bank reserves, either with an eye to the protection of the depositor, maintenance of liquidity, or some combination of these factors in practice. The Federal Reserve Act itself, as the name denotes, was an effort to deal with the reserve question more carefully and fully than had been possible in past times and to institute a new system of protecting deposits of banks and preventing them from being unduly subject to speculative infringement. In spite of all this legislation and constant discussion of the subject, the issue involved in the whole question of reserves has remained urgent and today stands in the forefront of American banking discussion.

The term "reserve" as currently employed is ordinarily taken to mean the actual cash which a bank has at its disposal for use in meeting the demand claims of its depositors. However, only a little discussion of the word is needed to see that in practice the term "cash reserve" is nearly meaningless, since for many years it has been made to include deposits in other banks—in other words, credit. Thus the term reserve has come to mean, in practice, not merely cash on hand, but demand claims upon solvent banking institutions or, in a word, the demand credit available to the order of any given institution.

It is evident that the amount of the demand credit thus available at any given time depends upon the power of the institution to liquidate its other assets; that is to say, to convert them into demand credit. Such liquidation may be effected by

[1] Prepared by H. Parker Willis with the assistance of Arthur Rosenstein and other members of the staff.

the process of requiring borrowers to pay; and of discounting only paper that may reasonably be regarded as cashable at maturity. From another point of view, banks are often regarded as in a liquid condition when they are able to build up their reserves by actually selling assets; and hence the growth of the school of thought which regards the portfolio of a bank as appropriately consisting, to some extent, of salable securities. The reserve question is thus an auxiliary to, or corollary of, the problem of liquidity or liquidating power.

Two theories regarding bank reserve have been widely entertained for many years past. The first, or British point of view, starts with the assumption that the bank reserve is best determined as the result of experience and represents the judgment of the banker, or in many cases, the average judgment of the banking community, with regard to the proportion of assets which should be kept in demand form in order to meet and settle the liabilities that are likely to require payment. The other point of view lays down the principle that such experience shows in about what proportion such liquidation, or cash, is likely to be asked for, and that the bank ought to be required to maintain at least a minimum percentage of demand credit (reserve) as compared with demand liability; hence the requirement generally in American banking law for many years past, and recognized from the first in the National Banking Act, of a "fixed reserve," and, as a corollary to it, the notion of "surplus" reserves. The adoption of the Reserve Act, as already incidentally mentioned, reflected the development of a definite point of view on this subject and the determination to retain it in practice. Although, during the early stages of the discussion of the Reserve Act, there were proposals to eliminate the reserve requirements, so far as applied to Reserve banks themselves, the departure from accepted theory thus indicated was too great at the time; and, accordingly, the Act retained the idea of a fixed reserve, to be exacted from Reserve banks as well as from their members. The original Reserve Act thus enforced upon the Reserve banks themselves the maintenance of 40 per cent of their outstanding notes in gold, and 35 per cent of their outstanding deposits in legal money, while member banks were required, according to location, to maintain reserves of 18 per cent in central reserve cities, 15 per cent in reserve cities, and 12 per cent in country banks. These reserve requirements were later modified to 13, 10, and 7 per cent for the three classes of members; and, whereas, the original Reserve Act permitted the division of required reserves between the vaults of the Reserve institutions and those of the members, the final (present) form of the law recognized as reserve only balances on the books of the Reserve banks themselves. This prescription of the law has now maintained itself without change for about fifteen years, but the fact that, at various times, the percentages of required reserve have been evidently ill-adapted to the needs of the banks themselves or of the community at large has set on foot agitation for a change in these requirements or for their abolition.

As things stand, the United States, whose inhabitants are inclined for the most part to rely largely upon paper currency as a hand to hand circulating medium, and in normal times are indisposed to hoarding, may, with a degree of justice, regard this entire stock of specie as representing a real bankable reserve. As a matter of fact, in recent years, the actual cash reserves of all reserve banks have hovered around three billion dollars while the "till" or vault money of members, averaging usually 4 or 5 per cent of their outstanding deposits, has consisted largely of the notes of Federal Reserve banks. The actual specie in the Federal Reserve banks has naturally been not far from two-thirds of the entire supply of the country, the remainder of this specie supply being diffused throughout the population in the form of small holdings, or held in the Treasury as a constituent element in the trust funds there retained to protect gold certificates and other obligations for which the government had assumed responsibility. This great amount of gold in Reserve banks has been the object of an immense amount of complaint and theorizing. Many persons have been inclined to speak of it as "sterile" or as having been "sterilized," and a large number have been disposed to think of it as constituting a "dead" fund of no particular service upon which a larger volume of credit ought to be built up. These reflections have been made, it would seem, without a sufficient amount of consideration or thought, inasmuch as it has been evident to more careful observers that the funds of cash thus constituted were, in actual fact, the basis of support for the entire outstanding body of deposits of the member banks and thus constituted only a small percentage, frequently varying from 5 to 7 per cent, of the entire outstanding body of the credit which might conceivably become a draft upon them.

From another point of view, also, criticism has been active. The fact that in normal times the funds carried in Reserve banks were "unproductive," so that the banking community was obliged to "lose interest" upon the deposits that were thus maintained with reserve banks, has made members of the Federal Reserve system restive, and has rendered reserve bankers themselves desirous of bringing about a condition in which they could rely upon a greater amount of contentment among members. In order to obtain the later objective, they have fallen into the habit of undertaking to keep the surplus balances of members (above the minimum required reserve) invested in bankers' acceptances or in government obligations, and they have thus, in a certain sense, guaranteed to members an interest return upon the amounts by which their actual available funds exceeded the minimum reserve, which they were required to carry.

A still further refinement upon, and modification of, the reserve régime has resulted from the habit of member banks of trading among themselves in what are currently called "federal funds." These federal funds are merely the surplus or excess balances owned by members and carried by them upon the books of Federal Reserve banks above the amounts required by law to be maintained thereon. The practice of dealing in such balances, and actually disposing of them to banks which are "short" of reserve, has relieved the latter of any necessity of rediscounting, and has, thereby, brought it about that the banks of the community were never possessed of surplus reserves, but were always practically upon the margin actually set by law. Any excess of funds that they might stand possessed of was speedily invested in bankers' acceptances or government obligations, or were sold by those who possessed such excess to those who were "short," the latter then receiving a transfer on the books of Federal Reserve banks.

As a result of these various interpretations and manipulations, the actual maintenance of reserves has come to be very largely formal in the United States, and has been deprived in a great measure of real vitality. Bankers have been, moreover, constantly on the alert to see how they could obtain the modification and lightening of reserve requirements, and in the search for such a method they have generally come to the conclusion that they might best concentrate their efforts on converting their outstanding deposit liabilities technically into that form of deposits which bore the smallest reserve requirements —namely, the time deposit. The decade 1920-30 thus saw a tremendous increase in the time deposits which, although partly the result of natural changes in banking conditions, was also in no small degree the outgrowth of effort on the part of the banks themselves to induce customers to shift their funds into the time-deposit form, or of the effort of customers to induce banks to apply their deposits on a time classification, often, it may well be believed, with the understanding that they would be converted back into demand deposits when, if, and as, the customer's convenience required it.

In these circumstances it is not strange that the ingenuity of bankers—among others, of reserve bankers—has been quite definitely devoted from time to time to the task of getting a modification of reserve requirements and of the terms of their application. As we have seen, the first form that this effort took was found in the undertaking, continued up to the present day, to invest the funds of deposit banks in income-producing securities of "eligible" variety, and, conversely, to convert these funds back into reserves when and as desired. And this comparatively obvious effort at modifying the reserve situation soon developed into a proposal of widespread character to exempt banks from all, or at least a part, of the existing reserve requirements, upon condition that they should undertake to hold a specified proportion of their portfolios of assets in a form which would insure early convertibility. Thus, during the first half of the decade 1920-30, it was frequently recommended to the reserve authorities that, in lieu of insisting upon a 13 per cent reserve for city banks, the government should require merely the holding of a specified portfolio of bankers' acceptances and government securities, which thus would be made eligible for discount at Reserve banks. This was practically the notion of investing surplus reserves in such a way as to earn interest for their owners, which had already been put into practical operation by the management of sundry reserve banks.

It was not long before the proposals thus made received the assent of reserve bankers in a more official form, and a committee of reserve agents, or chairmen, of Reserve banks which held meetings during 1924 and 1925 was inclined to urge that all existing reserve requirements be abandoned and in lieu of them the portfolio requirements already indicated should be substituted. Many objections were, of course, seen with respect to any such step, the most obvious being that in such circumstances it would be difficult for the Reserve banks to maintain liquidity at all; and that while the duty of such maintenance had, in fact, already rested upon them, the new proposal would in effect make it practically impossible for them to discharge their duty, since it would put them into a position which was almost untenable so far as the actual maintenance of liquidity was concerned.

The pressure for relaxation of reserve requirements, however, continued, and was especially urgent with those institutions which had very large stock market commitments and which found the reserve requirements particularly onerous at times when the market was active, and when they were experiencing direct demand from their customers for large loans on stock exchange collateral. The outcome of all these factors was the setting up of a committee in Washington whose mission it was to make a full study of the reserve question, and to report its findings as soon as the work could be brought to an end. This committee represented the Reserve system as a whole and it was supposed that the results of its studies would clarify the entire situation.

Meanwhile, the Federal Reserve system had been under sharp attack, particularly because of its unwarranted stock exchange activities, with the result that Senate Resolution No. 71, adopted in July, 1930, had made its appearance. This resolution called for a thorough investigation of the national and Federal Reserve systems and for the careful shaping of a piece of legislation designed to correct such evils as were found to exist. The outgrowth of the resolution, as elsewhere seen, was the so-called Glass bill, introduced in January, 1932. One of its leading provisions was found in an attempt to rectify the reserve condition by restoring the reserve against time deposits to an equality with the reserve against other deposits. Whereas, the required percentage of reserve to be held against time deposits was 3 per cent in all classes of banks, the Glass bill now undertook to raise it to 7 per cent in country banks; 10 in reserve city and 13 in central reserve city banks.

By taking this step, the Senate committee, after a careful investigation, felt that bankers would be compelled to discontinue the practice of erroneously classifying deposits as "time" when in fact they were "demand." At the same time the tendency to build up, in member banks, very large "lines" of time deposits, which had to be "invested" in such a way as to return a profit equal to the interest paid on such deposits—and something over for the bankers' own profit in the matter—would also tend to be brought under control.

The Federal Reserve Board, recognizing that the Glass measure was likely soon to be introduced, hastened to present to the banking committee and through it to the country at large, in December, 1931, the results of the study to which reference has already been made; and thus the issue as to actual reserve requirements was definitely joined in a public way.

The outcome of the studies of the Federal Reserve Committee already described had led it to a conclusion very different from that which was represented by existing law. In line with the criticisms upon reserve practice which had been urged by many banks in past years, the committee admitted the unsatisfactoriness of fixed reserve requirements, but the evil resulting from it, according to their opinion, was not found in the effect of a positive fixation of reserves, but in their lack of adaptability to actual requirements. According to their opinion, the modification which was chiefly needed was to be found in a better adjustment of the reserve which would give greater flexibility, and thus would permit the adaptation of bank resources to the meeting of actual deposit demand. Accordingly the Committee had eventually decided upon two major ideas or premises, as follows:

1. The notion of fixed federal reserves is desirable at least in the United States or under American conditions.

2. Such fixed reserves should be determined in amount by the activity or rate of turnover of the deposit accounts and not by their mere aggregate or face total.

It was the view of the Committee that a deposit of $1,000 with a "turnover"—that is to say, paid, reconstituted, and then repaid—three times during the course of 30 days, should be protected by a reserve vastly different from that which would be required if this $1,000 deposit were left idle and not drawn upon at all during the thirty days, or perhaps drawn on and reconstituted once to the extent of say $500.

In working out this notion of reserves in proportion to the velocity of use or redemption of bank deposits, the commission found itself aided by the fact that the Reserve system was already obtaining and issuing each week data designed to show the "debits to individual account" in the several banks of the system. These data were obtained from reports made to the Federal Reserve Board by 141 clearing houses situated at different points throughout the United States, and indicated the amount of checks drawn and actually charged to deposit accounts during the report period in question.

In support of the proposal to give up the idea of reserves computed as percentages of fixed amounts of deposits, and to substitute reserves computed as percentages of deposit turnover, the committee which had the matter in charge found itself compelled to take the view that large reserves were needed where deposit accounts were steadily most active.

The proposal in question was embodied by the Senate Banking and Currency Committee in one of the drafts of the so-called Glass bill, or Banking Act of 1933. It evidently obviated any necessity for raising the required reserve against time deposits since it made the distinction between demand and time deposits obsolete, basing as it did their protection, or "required reserve," upon the difference in their rates of turnover. Accordingly, by the spring of 1932 a definite issue was sharply drawn between the proposal to increase the time deposit reserves and the proposal to substitute a reserve based upon velocity of turnover and without any distinction between the maturity of the deposits which were to be protected. The controversy and difference of opinion eventually compelled the dropping of both proposals out of the Glass bill, which eventually came to adoption on June 16, 1933 without any change in legal reserve requirements. This, however, was obviously a shirking of an urgent issue; and the question accordingly remains active whether to alter existing reserves and, if so, whether to raise or otherwise change the percentages for time or demand deposits or both; or whether, on the other hand, to substitute the idea of a reserve based upon velocity of use. Immediate urgency of this question has, it is true, been set aside by reason of the fact that after the bank holiday a complete suspension of specie redemption for bank paper throughout the United States was ordered by President Roosevelt, and immediately took effect. Since, however, we cannot suppose that this condition of suspension will be a permanent situation, it seems clear that the reserve problem, as already stated, must inevitably recur in urgent form. Attention has, therefore, been devoted to it in the present discussion for the purpose of reaching certain conclusions, and of setting them before the reader as clearly as may be possible.

TABLE 96

RATIO OF REQUIRED RESERVES TO NET DEMAND AND TIME DEPOSITS FOR THE ENTIRE MEMBERSHIP OF THE FEDERAL RESERVE SYSTEM*

ABSTRACTED FROM CALL REPORTS: (By number)	ALL MEMBER BANKS	NEW YORK CITY BANKS	CHICAGO BANKS	CENTRAL RESERVE CITY BANKS	OTHER RESERVE CITY BANKS	COUNTRY BANKS
34 Dec. 31, 1926	7.4	11.6	10.4	11.3	7.2	5.0
35 Mar. 23, 1927	7.3	11.5	10.4	11.3	7.1	5.0
36 June 30, 1927	7.4	11.5	10.3	11.3	7.1	4.9
37 Oct. 10, 1927	7.3	11.4	10.3	11.2	7.1	5.0
38 Dec. 31, 1927	7.4	11.5	10.1	11.2	7.1	5.0
39 Feb. 28, 1928	7.3	11.3	10.0	11.1	7.1	4.9
40 June 10, 1928	7.2	11.3	9.7	10.9	7.0	4.9
41 Oct. 3, 1928	7.1	11.1	9.8	10.9	7.0	4.9
42 Dec. 31, 1928	7.3	11.3	9.8	11.0	7.0	4.9
43 Mar. 27, 1929	7.2	11.1	10.3	11.0	6.9	4.9
44 June 29, 1929	7.2	11.3	10.2	11.1	6.9	4.8
45 Oct. 4, 1929	7.2	11.0	10.2	10.9	7.0	4.9
46 Dec. 31, 1929	7.4	11.3	10.4	11.1	6.9	4.9
47 Mar. 27, 1930	7.2	10.9	10.3	10.8	6.8	4.8
48 June 30, 1930	7.2	11.0	10.1	10.8	6.8	4.8
49 Sept. 24, 1930	7.2	11.0	9.8	10.7	6.8	4.8
50 Dec. 31, 1930	7.3	11.3	10.1	11.1	6.8	4.8
51 Mar. 25, 1931	7.2	11.3	9.9	11.0	6.7	4.8
52 June 30, 1931	7.2	11.3	10.0	11.0	6.7	4.8
53 Sept. 29, 1931	7.3	11.4	10.1	11.2	6.7	4.7
54 Dec. 31, 1931	7.4	11.7	10.3	11.4	6.7	4.7
55 June 30, 1932	7.3	11.7	10.0	11.4	6.7	4.7
56 Sept. 30, 1932	7.4	11.6	10.2	11.4	6.6	4.7
57 Dec. 31, 1932	7.5	11.7	10.4	11.5	6.7	4.7

* Ratios for the entire Federal Reserve system are not available prior to *Call Report No. 34,* Dec. 31, 1926.

PRESENT RESERVE POSITION

It is now time to state the arguments on proposed reserve reform practically and fully.

In Table 96 has been computed the ratio of required reserve to net demand and time deposits, over a series of recent years, the figures being based upon the returns made at the time of the regular call reports, 1926 to 1932, inclusive. From these

TABLE 97

RATIO OF RESERVES HELD WITH FEDERAL RESERVE TO NET DEPOSITS OF MEMBER BANKS—OTHER THAN NATIONAL (STATE BANKS AND TRUST COMPANIES)*

ABSTRACTED FROM CALL REPORTS: (By number)	ALL BANKS	NEW YORK CITY BANKS	CAGO CHI-BANKS	CEN-TRAL RESERVE CITY† BANKS	OTHER RESERVE CITY BANKS‡	COUN-TRY BANKS
9 June 30, 1919	10.8	13.1	11.1	12.8	10.0	7.1
10 Nov. 17, 1919	10.4	12.6	12.7	12.6	9.5	6.9
11 Dec. 31, 1919	10.4	12.3	13.5	12.5	10.0	6.7
12 May 4, 1920	10.5	12.5	12.9	12.6	10.3	6.9
13 June 30, 1920	10.1	12.0	12.4	12.1	10.0	6.6
14 Dec. 29, 1920	10.4	12.6	12.8	12.7	9.9	7.2
15 Apr. 28, 1921	10.3	12.4	13.2	12.6	9.9	7.1
16 June 30, 1921	10.4	12.6	12.7	12.6	9.8	7.2
17 Dec. 31, 1921	10.8	13.0	13.0	13.5	10.2	7.1
18 Mar. 10, 1922	10.6	13.3	13.2	13.2	9.8	7.2
19 June 30, 1922	10.8	14.1	13.5	14.0	9.6	6.9
20 Dec. 29, 1922	10.8	14.0	13.1	13.9	10.0	7.3
21 June 30, 1923	10.6	14.0	12.5	13.7	9.5	7.0
22 Sept. 14, 1923	10.4	13.3	13.2	13.3	9.8	7.1
23 Dec. 31, 1923	10.2	13.0	12.5	12.9	9.5	7.0
24 Mar. 31, 1924	10.5	13.5	12.9	13.4	9.7	7.1
25 June 30, 1924	10.4	13.2	12.3	13.1	9.7	7.1
26 Oct. 10, 1924	10.4	12.8	12.6	12.9	10.0	7.0
27 Dec. 31, 1924	10.3	12.8	12.9	12.8	9.5	7.0
28 Apr. 6, 1925	10.5	12.9	12.8	12.8	10.1	7.1
29 June 30, 1925	10.5	13.1	12.3	13.0	10.0	7.0
30 Sept. 28, 1925	10.2	12.2	14.0	12.6	9.7	7.3
31 Dec. 31, 1925	10.1	12.7	11.9	12.6	9.7	6.5
32 Apr. 12, 1926	10.2	12.3	12.5	12.3	10.0	7.1
33 June 30, 1926	10.0	12.3	13.0	12.4	9.6	6.9

* Source: *Call Reports,* U. S. Federal Reserve Board.

† From June 30, 1919 to June 30, 1922, St. Louis was included in Central Reserve City Banks.

‡ From Dec. 29, 1922 to June 30, 1926, St. Louis is included in Other Reserve City Banks.

it appears that the actual ratio of required reserves held, stated as a percentage of net demand and time deposits has usually been in the case of country banks slightly below 5 per cent; while in those banks that have maintained highest percentages of reserves it has been rare that more than 11.5 per cent was maintained. The state of affairs has been more striking in the case of all member banks and among those the member state banks and trust companies of the Federal Reserve system, as will be seen by the compilation afforded in Table 98. This merely amounts to saying that existing conditions in law and the necessities of banking have resulted in a stronger percentage of reserves for state member institutions. Experience, moreover, has shown that these percentages of reserve were largely inadequate in those institutions which were carrying a large volume of time deposits.

"Effect" of Proposed Increase

Let us now note what the change proposed in the original draft of the Glass bill (and often proposed elsewhere) would mean. The proposed alteration meant merely the placing of time and demand deposits upon the same reserve requirement basis, and evidently would have amounted to advancing the average reserve in the case of country banks to 7 per cent as compared with (as we have seen) about 5 per cent during the period in question—or an enlargement of some 40 per cent. In the same way it would have meant an advance at central reserve city banks from around a mean of about 11 per cent or slightly higher to about 13 per cent—or an advance of nearly 2 points. Stated percentually this would have been an increase in actual existing reserves of some 20 to 25 per cent of their real current amount. In the other reserve city banks the advance would have been from about 7 per cent to about 10 per cent, or in other words, would have been an increase of something like three-sevenths, or something over 40 per cent.

It was often contended during the hearings on the Glass bill that any such increases as these would have resulted in bankrupting many institutions, or would at least have driven them out of the Federal Reserve system or compelled them to resort to what is called "drastic liquidation." Without passing upon such a question at this point it may be sufficient to say that in all events the change proposed would have necessitated a readjustment of the structure of credit to a considerable degree, and if this change were to be supplied through rediscount of eligible paper, it would have necessitated the putting of a considerably greater amount of the indebtedness of the business of the country into eligible paper form.

By way of contrast with this suggestion we may now note the proposal of the committee of the Federal Reserve system to which reference has already been made. The Committee summarized its proposed plan in part as follows:[2]

Summary of Committee Recommendations

In accordance with its terms of reference, the committee has examined the operation of present legal requirements governing the reserves held by member banks and submits herewith definite rec-State and National, which are members of the Federal reserve system.

Defects of Present Reserve Requirements

In the opinion of the committee, our present system of legal requirements for member bank reserves has never functioned effectively since its inception in 1914. It has not operated to relate the expansion of member bank credit to the needs of trade and industry, nor has it adequately reflected changes in the volume and activity of member bank credit. Furthermore, the committee also finds that present requirements for reserves are inequitable and unfair as between individual member banks and groups of member banks and do not adequately take into account genuine differences in the character of banking in which a member bank may be engaged.

The committee takes the position that it is no longer the primary function of legal reserve requirements to assure or preserve the liquidity of the individual member bank. The maintenance of liquidity is necessarily the responsibility of bank management and is achieved by the individual bank when an adequate proportion of its portfolio consists of assets that can be readily converted into cash. Since the establishment of the Federal reserve system, the liquidity of an individual bank is more adequately safeguarded by the presence of the Federal reserve banks, which were organized for the purpose, among others, of increasing the liquidity of member banks by providing for the rediscount of their eligible paper, than by the possession of legal reserves. The two main functions of legal requirements for member bank reserves under our present banking struc-

[2] Report of the Committee on Bank Reserves of the Federal Reserve System on *Member Bank Reserves* (Washington, D.C., 1931), pp. 5-6.

ture are, first, to operate in the direction of sound credit conditions by exerting an influence on changes in the volume of bank credit, and, secondly, to provide the Federal reserve banks with sufficient resources to enable them to pursue an effective banking and credit policy. Since the volume of member bank credit needed to meet the legitimate needs of trade and industry depends on the rate at which credit is being used as well as on its aggregate amount, it is essential for the exercise of a sound control that legal requirements differentiate in operation between highly active deposits and deposits of a less active character. Requirements for reserves should also be equitable in their incidence, simple in administration, and, so far as possible, not susceptible of abuse.

Similar principles underlie present reserve law, which in requiring lower reserves against time deposits than against demand deposits, and lower reserves against the demand deposits of country banks than against the demand deposits of reserve and central reserve city banks may have been expected to impose higher reserves on more active deposits than on less active deposits. Notwithstanding the fact, however, that existing requirements would appear to be so arranged as to make reserve requirements vary with the volume and activity of deposits, experience shows that since 1914 and especially since 1922 the proportion of primary reserves held by member banks has steadily declined in relation to the volume of member bank deposits and to their activity.

This outcome has been the result of defects in the definition of reserves, in the method of determining liabilities against which reserves must be carried, and in the classification of banks and of deposits for reserve purposes. The exclusion of vault cash from required reserves of member banks in 1917 has been followed by a reduction in the vault cash holdings of some city banks to a minimum; the rule that amounts due from banks may be deducted only from amounts due to banks has tended to decrease reserves in times of business activity and to increase reserves in times of depression, and the establishment of a low reserve against time deposits in 1914 has facilitated the growth of bank credit without a corresponding growth in reserves. Even if these particular defects in the present system of reserves had not existed, however, the rapid increase in the turnover of demand deposits which has occurred in recent years would still have tended to prevent reserve requirements from increasing in proportion to the growth in the effective use of credit by the customers of member banks.

Proposals of the committee.—Before deciding to recommend fundamental changes looking toward the establishment of a new basis for calculating required reserves, the committee made every effort to frame provisions designed to correct the existing situation through modifications in the classification of cities for reserve purposes and in the classification of deposits subject to reserve, including a more stringent definition of time deposits. As these proposals were studied, however, it became more and more evident that they would not be effective and that an entirely new approach to the reserve problem was necessary.

The committee proposes, consequently, to abolish completely the classification of deposits into time and demand deposits, and the classification of member banks according to their location, into central reserve city banks, reserve city banks, and country banks. Instead, the committee recommends that all member banks and all deposits be treated alike for reserve purposes, and that the formula used in calculating reserve requirements take into account directly, instead of indirectly as in the existing law, the activity as well as the volume of the deposits held by each individual member bank, without regard to the location of the bank or the terms of withdrawal, on which the deposits are technically held. To accomplish this, the committee proposes that each member bank be required to hold a reserve equivalent to (a) 5 per cent of its total net deposits, plus (b) 50 per cent of the average daily withdrawals actually made from all of its deposit accounts. These withdrawals, which are shown by debit entries on the books of member banks, are the only real test of the activity of a deposit account and furnish the only basis by which that activity can be equitably and effectively reflected in requirements for reserves. Under this proposal, therefore, each deposit will carry a total reserve based on its activity as well as on its amount. A totally inactive deposit will carry a total reserve of only 5 per cent, while a deposit balance which is checked out on the average once a week will carry a total reserve equivalent to 12 per cent of its amount. For the average member bank the total reserve under the proposed formula will be equivalent to about 8 per cent of its deposits. To prevent this formula from imposing too great a burden in extreme cases, the recommendations of the committee also provide that in no case shall the aggregate reserve required of a bank exceed 15 per cent of its gross deposits.

The committee proposes to include in legal reserves, in addition to the funds which member banks have on deposit with their Federal reserve bank, their vault cash, with certain limitations, as both classes of funds contribute to the strength of the reserve banks and have a direct effect on the reserve system's control of changes in member bank credit. It proposes also to place country member banks on a parity with city banks with respect to deductions from deposit accounts by permitting banks in calculating net deposits subject to reserve to deduct balances due from member banks and items in process of collection from total deposits instead of from balances due to banks alone, as is the practice at present.

Volume of reserves.—The committee feels that the existing volume of reserves is sufficient at the present time to provide the reserve banks with the funds they require to perform their functions. Its proposals, consequently, do not contemplate a change in the total amount of reserves. They are intended rather to change the nature of fluctuations in the volume of reserves and to iron out inequitable features in their distribution among the member banks.

Criticism of the proposed plan of the Federal Reserve system evidently implies some considerations of fundamental problems of banking credit. Perhaps the most serious attack upon the proposal was that furnished by the Chase National Bank in the Chase Economic Bulletin (April 1932) in which the whole subject was surveyed. The Chase National Bank analysis made substantially the following points in opposing the scheme recommended:

(1) Activity of account is not a sound criterion for bank reserves. Irregularity is much more significant.

(2) The new plan would increase the tension of the money market at the year-end settlements.

(3) The proposed plan would not restrict excessive expansion of bank credit when excess reserves appear.

These statements were all accompanied by more or less detailed arguments and statistical analysis.

In judging of them it is desirable to make a brief examination of our own and for that purpose the following tables have been computed, designed to show present and proposed reserves likely to be required under the new plan. The results thus obtained have been graphically presented in Chart XIX:[3]

[3] Prepared by Arthur Rosenstein and Irving Kahn with statistical aid of staff.

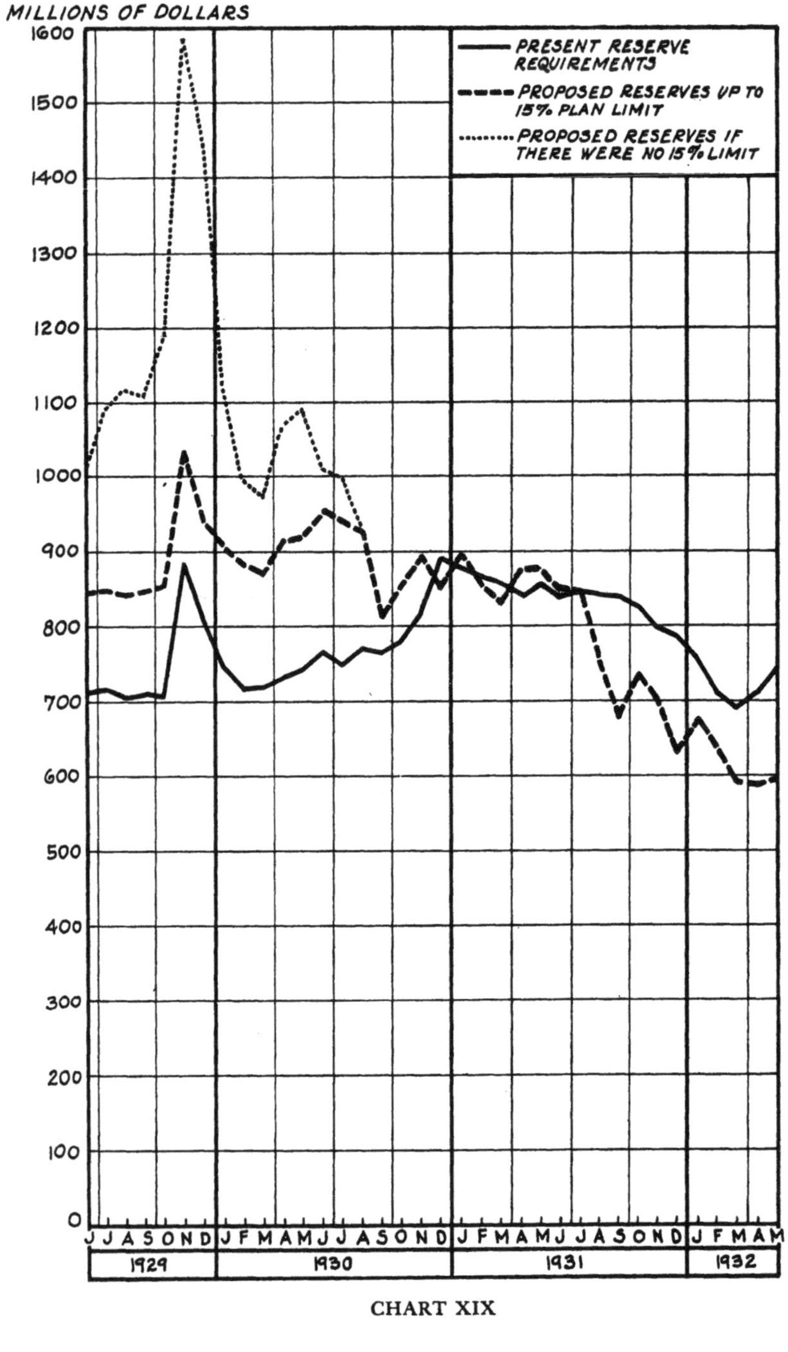

MILLIONS OF DOLLARS
1600
1500
1400
1300
1200
1100
1000
900
800
700
600
500
400
300
200
100
0
PRESENT RESERVE REQUIREMENTS
PROPOSED RESERVES UP TO 15% PLAN LIMIT
PROPOSED RESERVES IF THERE WERE NO 15% LIMIT
J J A S O N D J F M A M J J A S O N D J F M A M J J A S O N D J F M A M
1929
1930
1931
1932

CHART XIX

The study which has just been made would seem to furnish ground for several conclusions, certainly tentative—but probably well founded. The chief of them may be stated as follows:

1. Careful study of the data upon which the proposed computations of reserves in terms of velocity of circulation of credit are to be made does not furnish convincing evidence of their soundness. The statistics are incomplete, unsatisfactory and varying in validity. They have afforded an interesting index of business activity, although one which has, in many instances, proven itself unreliable. In order to employ these data as a basis for prescribing the reserve holdings of the banks of the country it would be necessary to go very much further and to develop the statistics upon a definitely standardized basis, and in such a way as to confine their inaccuracies within well-recognized limits. To state this point briefly, the analysis of debits to individual accounts is not usually a feasible basis for use in reserve computation.

2. Even assuming that perfectly unquestionable standardized figures of debits to individual accounts were in hand, the question whether they would furnish a satisfactory basis for computation of reserves is still open to discussion. On the surface it would seem that the activity of an account is a much better test of the necessity of reserve requirement behind it than is its mere aggregate amount; and in this connection it must be freely admitted that the practice of treating all "demand" deposits as requiring a like amount of reserve, while all "time" deposits are disposed of in the same way, is obviously the roughest approximation to soundness. However, the point raised by the Chase National Bank in the statement that irregularity of account is, if anything, a more important criterion of bank reserves than its activity, unquestionably must be duly considered and given its due weight.

3. The negative fact that in a time of excess or surplus reserves the principal alleged merit of the proposed plan—its power to restrict the expansion of bank credit—would disappear, must likewise be allowed due weight in any effort to choose between two types of reserve computation.

TABLE 98: CALCULATIONS OF PRESENT RESERVES AND PROPOSED RESERVES REQUIRED UNDER THE FEDERAL RESERVE BOARD PLAN: FOR NEW YORK CITY CLEARING HOUSE BANKS

(Amounts in millions of dollars)

	NET DEMAND DE-POSITS*	TIME DE-POSITS*	NET DEMAND TIME & GOVT. DEPOSITS (COLS. 1, 2 & GOV. DEP.)†	VAULT CASH†	13% OF NET DEMAND DE-POSITS (COL. 1)	3% OF TIME DE-POSITS (COL. 2)	50% OF DAILY AVGE. DEBITS‡	5% OF THE SUM OF NET DEMAND, TIME & GOV. DEP. (COL. 3)	PRES-ENT RE-QUIRED RESERVES (COLS. 4 5 & 6)	PRO-POSED RESERVES UP TO 15% PLAN LIMIT	PROPOSED RESERVES IF PLAN HAD NOT 15% UPPER LIMIT (COLS. 7 & 8)
1929											
June 12	4873	753	5646	56	633	23	895	282	712	846	1177
July 10	4930	692	5660	55	641	21	910	283	717	849	1193
Aug. 14	4814	772	5597	56	626	23	935	280	705	840	1215
Sept. 11	4847	820	5667	54	630	25	925	283	709	849	1208
Oct. 9	4786	860	5706	56	622	26	1003	285	704	855	1288
Nov. 13	6012	855	6863	77	782	26	1242	344	885	1032	1586
Dec. 11	5450	830	6282	72	709	25	1131	314	806	942	1445
1930											
Jan. 15	5120	905	6033	51	666	27	813	302	744	906	1115
Feb. 12	4934	858	5794	49	641	26	707	290	716	882	997
Mar. 12	4945	927	5872	48	643	28	683	294	719	870	977
Apr. 9	5028	996	6085	47	654	30	764	304	731	912	1068
May 14	5118	989	6125	46	665	30	779	306	741	918	1085
June 11	5300	1034	6341	49	689	31	693	317	769	951	1010
July 9	5186	1058	6289	45	674	32	683	314	751	942	997
Aug. 13	5336	1064	6415	44	694	32	605	321	770	926	
Sept. 10	5297	1177	6374	46	687	32	493	319	765	812	
Oct. 8	5396	1099	6531	45	701	33	530	327	779	857	
Nov. 12	5630	1116	6755	51	732	33	558	338	816	896	
Dec. 10	5961	1225	7186	79	775	37	493	359	891	852	

TABLE 98 (*Continued*)

	Net demand deposits*	Time deposits*	Net demand time & govt. deposits (Cols. 1, 2 & gov. dep.)†	Vault cash†	13% of net demand deposits (Col. 1)	3% of time deposits (Col. 2)	50% of daily avge. debits‡	5% of the sum of net demand, time & gov. dep. (Col. 3)	Present required reserves (Cols. 4 5 & 6)	Proposed reserves up to 15% plan limit	Proposed reserves if plan had not 15% upper limit (Cols. 7 & 8)
1931											
Jan. 14	6012	1157	7189	62	782	35	538	359	879	897	
Feb. 11	5953	1206	7173	54	774	36	500	359	864	859	
Mar. 11	6001	1181	7182	44	780	35	473	359	859	832	
Apr. 8	5855	1192	7145	43	761	36	518	357	840	875	
May 13	5949	1249	7228	48	773	37	515	361	858	876	
June 10	5843	1198	7043	45	760	36	501	352	841	853	
July 8	5896	1162	7153	44	766	35	484	358	845	842	
Aug. 12	5784	1109	6920	55	752	33	412	346	840	758	
Sept. 9	5780	1078	6858	55	751	32	336	343	839	679	
Oct. 14	5638	1022	6747	65	733	31	397	337	828	734	
Nov. 11	5505	890	6422	53	716	27	388	321	795	709	
Dec. 9	5431	822	6254	51	706	25	316	313	782	629	
1932											
Jan. 13	5233	763	6120	51	679	23	368	306	753	674	
Feb. 10	4898	739	5856	50	637	22	346	293	709	639	
Mar. 9	4818	740	5656	42	626	22	307	283	690	590	
Apr. 13	4986	739	5854	40	648	22	296	293	710	589	
May 11	5229	758	6124	40	680	23	289	306	743	595	

* As reported by all members of the New York Clearing House.
† As reported weekly by the Federal Reserve Board for reporting member banks in N. Y. City.
‡ As reported to the Federal Reserve Board by members of the New York Clearing House.

4. The foregoing factors indicate clearly, therefore, that whatever may be worked out in the future, the present projects for reserve computation as based upon activity or turnover of deposit account are inadequate and will not answer the purpose. Even those who devised the plan suggested by the Federal Reserve Board were not willing to abide by their own conclusion since they found it necessary to provide that their plan, when in effect, could never be held to require a reserve in excess of 15 per centum of outstanding liabilities. The reason for this qualification is easily seen from the chart on page 460 already furnished which shows that under some circumstances the new plan would have exacted a tremendously heavy reserve protection. This, in effect, was put forward as one of its major merits; yet those who urged it evidently did not insist upon an actual trial in practice. Moreover, if the danger of requiring a very heavy reserve must be guarded against in this way, it would seem that prudence would require the application of a restriction to the effect that the actual reserves must never be allowed to fall below a specified limit. In fact the proposal does establish such a limit at 5 per cent; but the figure thus named, if to be regarded as a real limitation, is far from being sufficient. Wisdom would require, therefore, that, if under any such plan reserves should actually fall below present requirements, the operation of the new plan should be suspended and the existing reserve requirements should again come into force. The effect of any such provision would be merely to give the new plan an experimental test within the limits of 15 per cent maximum and 7, 10, and 13 per cent minimum, as at present.

All these considerations may be summed up in the statement that the reserve situation has not yet been satisfactorily thought out or brought to a definite conclusion; and that it remains, therefore, as an open issue in current monetary and banking theory, and particularly in the banking policy of the United States.

The Banking Act of 1933 (Glass bill) failed, as we have seen, to make any change in the reserve situation, thus testifying to the belief on the part of its framers that the discussion had not been carried to a sufficiently advanced point to warrant confidence in the conclusions currently put forward. As long as that situation exists, there will be little warrant for the view that any cut and dried scheme of changes in reserve method can be successfully applied. Meanwhile, however, it will continue to be true that existing reserves, as demonstrated by past practical experience, are inadequate. One of the important lessons demonstrated by the collapse of 1932-1933 was the inadequacy of the Federal Reserve system to withstand the strain caused by the redemption of time deposits—or for that matter the effort to secure payment of demand deposits in terms of currency. Reserve banks were not in a position to meet the redemption in favor of their member banks, even when the latter were amply supplied with satisfactory quantities of eligible paper.

The conclusion is inevitable that in any process of returning to sound banking conditions and in restoring convertibility on the part of American currency, it will be needful to determine the safe proportion of reserves to be required of the member banks of the country. As things stand today, with paper currency of the nation irredeemable, it still remains true that the member bank must regard it as a fundamental problem of operation to determine how large a credit balance it ought to carry on the books of the Federal Reserve bank of its district. This ascertainment of the amount of demand credit that ought to be carried in the portfolio of the ordinary bank as compared with the amount of its demand liabilities which it may at any time be summoned to meet, is obviously one of the most urgent and serious questions of practice that any bank is likely to be called upon to solve. Experience thus far has shown, as we have seen, that as regards the so-called time deposits of the country, the protection afforded by the present volume of demand credit is insufficient. It will remain, therefore, to be determined in the future what must be done to bring about a better state of affairs as regards this demand credit. The indications are clearly to the effect that it should be enlarged; but these indications are based upon a state of things which involves the position of a given kind of portfolio. If that portfolio could be altered and the investments of the bank rendered more liquid, the situation would be different. It would seem a fair statement that banking reform legislation must, in the future, be directed either to the requirement of a different kind of portfolio on the part of members or a larger amount of liquid credit for such reserves as they regularly carry on the books of the reserve bank to which the member belongs. Either plan implies a restriction of the freedom of credit granting which, during the "boom" period after 1925, was so conspicuous an element in American banking. In its final analysis, therefore, this whole question settles down into a judgment with reference to the degree of freedom with which extensions of bank credit may be made.

CHAPTER XX

PUBLIC DEPOSITS[1]

The problem of handling the public money has for a long time been one of the principal issues in American banking. It was the basis of lengthy controversy which centered around the Second Bank of the United States, and it was one of the major sources of dissatisfaction with the State banking régime which succeeded the termination of the charter of the Second Bank of the United States. It was the immediate reason for the establishment of the independent treasury system of the United States and, in turn, it lay at the root of the action, taken early in the Civil War, suspending the independent treasury act from further operation. Ever since the close of the Civil War the relationship between the government and the national banks has been close; and, when the evils of the independent treasury system had become so marked as to constitute an important reason for banking reform, at the time of the adoption of the Federal Reserve Act, the plan for the establishment of Federal Reserve banks was so framed, from the outset, as to afford as one of its major services—a means of caring for the public deposits.

In a later chapter of the present study the principal questions which have arisen in connection with the holding of public funds, as the result of deficit financing and other difficulties of similar sort, have been reviewed with considerable detail. In the present chapter, however, it is desired only to analyze the deposit situation as descriptive of an important phase of government influence over banking, and as a factor which necessarily will play an increasingly important part so long as the expenditures of the government, not merely for current operation but for the construction of public works, continue to grow, as has been true within recent years.

[1] By H. Parker Willis; statistics compiled by V. D. Kazakévich and Hervé Schwedersky.

Distribution of Public Deposits

The use of the term "public deposits" frequently confines itself to the Federal government, but it should be noted that federal deposits, although large in amount, are by no means the only, or even the most troublesome, type of these deposits with which the banks have to deal. Generally speaking, public deposits may be classified as federal, state, municipal, and "other"; the latter term including, in many commonwealths, deposits made by the fiscal officers of other grades of government; while, again, in some states, they include the deposits placed in the banks by special administrative agencies which are authorized to make use of the banking service on their own initiative and responsibility.

The first approach to the problem of public deposits should, accordingly, be made through a survey of the actual volume and character of the deposits of the various grades of government, both in ordinary banks and in Federal Reserve banks. Unfortunately the data available do not permit of a complete survey of public deposits for the national, state, and municipal governments, so classified. Data for United States government deposits, on the other hand, are available in fairly complete form, and attention in this investigation has, therefore, been primarily devoted to the analysis and classification of data relating to federal deposits.

Public Deposits in Their Relationship to Banking Conditions

The following table is designed to show the aggregate amount of United States Government deposits in banks during the past decade, arranged by groups of states. It will be observed that there has been a considerable breadth of variation during the decade in the amount of deposits actually carried at the date selected, and that of recent years there has been an increasing tendency toward the placement of the bulk of the deposits in the Eastern states of the Alantic Seaboard, which means, primarily, in New York, renewing a situation that had been emphatically developed during the years immediately after the World War.

TABLE 99

UNITED STATES GOVERNMENT DEPOSITS*
BY GROUPS OF STATES—BY YEARS†

(In thousands of dollars)

YEAR	NEW ENG-LAND	MIDDLE ATLAN-TIC	EAST NORTH CENTRAL	WEST NORTH CENTRAL	SOUTH ATLAN-TIC	EAST SOUTH CENTRAL	WEST SOUTH CENTRAL	MOUN-TAIN	PACIF-IC	POS-SES-SIONS	TOTAL
1921	$30,260	$265,865	$42,681	$15,004	$12,491	$3,090	$8,283	$1,736	$7,118	$3,702	$390,230
1922	14,577	47,689	20,115	11,091	9,199	2,925	6,440	1,777	12,781	2,293	128,887
1923	35,764	80,876	41,313	18,074	18,326	5,142	13,207	1,460	22,655	1,622	238,439
1924	23,217	49,995	26,349	8,625	13,111	2,617	10,440	1,703	13,504	2,741	152,302
1925	9,864	46,975	33,404	9,893	15,354	2,963	10,284	1,523	14,594	2,366	147,220
1926	31,943	70,935	27,105	13,763	18,017	3,286	10,667	1,679	8,547	1,885	187,827
1927	26,790	71,592	19,191	11,576	17,340	5,237	13,589	1,144	25,407	2,158	194,024
1928	26,344	70,242	20,254	11,527	14,964	5,511	21,155	1,587	49,253	1,979	222,816
1929	22,462	105,068	33,863	15,228	27,114	6,936	25,257	1,567	45,841	2,776	286,112
1930	27,058	86,707	17,450	6,925	23,837	6,307	17,989	1,327	24,457	1,665	213,722
1931	33,837	198,524	83,939	16,990	48,572	7,028	28,666	1,943	27,169	1,521	448,189
1932	23,012	195,088	64,358	23,013	33,261	9,359	40,703	2,278	31,734	1,519	424,325

* Compiled on the basis of information abstracted from *Annual Reports of the Comptroller of the Currency*.
† Similar data not obtainable prior to 1921.

TABLE 100

UNITED STATES GOVERNMENT DEPOSITS EXPRESSED AS A PERCENTAGE OF DEMAND AND TOTAL DEPOSITS*

ON OR ABOUT JUNE 30 OF EVERY YEAR	NATIONAL BANKS		STATE (COMM.) BANKS		LOANS & TRUST COMPANIES		STOCK, MUTUAL & PRIVATE BANKS		ALL BANKS IN THE U. S.	
	Per cent of demand	Per cent of total	Per cent of demand	Per cent of total	Per cent of demand	Per cent of total	Per cent of demand	Per cent of total	Per cent of demand	Per cent of total
1916	0.61	0.48	—	—	—	—	—	—	—	—
1917	1.79	1.36	—	—	—	—	—	—	—	—
1918	11.23	9.25	—	—	—	—	—	—	—	—
1919	4.98	4.38	—	—	—	—	—	—	—	—
1920	1.65	1.23	—	—	—	—	—	—	—	—
1921	2.67	1.91	0.60	0.37	2.40	1.72	0.05	0.004	1.89	1.09
1922	1.06	0.75	0.12	0.08	0.28	0.21	0.35	0.05	0.58	0.34
1923	1.96	1.33	0.23	0.15	0.48	0.36	1.62	0.06	1.05	0.59
1924	1.19	0.79	0.10	0.07	0.28	0.21	0.81	0.05	0.62	0.35
1925	0.97	0.64	0.20	0.13	0.23	0.18	2.64	0.07	0.55	0.31
1926	1.25	0.81	0.14	0.08	0.55	0.37	—	—	0.74	0.38
1927	1.21	0.74	0.07	0.04	0.68	0.46	0.19	0.01	0.74	0.37
1928	1.60	0.93	0.12	0.06	0.39	0.26	0.12	0.003	0.86	0.41
1929	2.06	1.18	0.11	0.06	0.60	0.39	1.67	0.06	1.12	0.53
1930	1.45	0.84	0.07	0.04	0.42	0.28	1.58	0.03	0.82	0.39
1931	2.16	1.21	1.82	0.86	1.73	1.09	2.53	0.03	1.96	0.86
1932	2.54	1.36	2.53	1.20	2.23	1.47	2.55	0.02	2.44	1.01

* Computed on the basis of data abstracted from *Annual Reports of the Comptroller of the Currency*.

We shall attempt presently to examine more in detail whether this geographical concentration of deposits does or does not correspond generally to the distribution of bank resources. For the moment it is necessary only to note this tendency to concentration, and also to call attention to the considerable variations which from time to time occur, both in aggregate amount and percentually in the distribution of deposits geographically.

It is desirable to form a definite opinion regarding the extent of government business as contrasted with the deposit business of other customers at banks. Illustration of the situation is afforded by Table 100 which shows government deposits expressed as percentages of demand and of total deposits for each class of banks. This showing indicates that government deposits for the year 1932 were not far from 2.44 per cent of all demand deposits for all banks; while national banks held practically the average amount, their per cent being 2.54, and state banks about the same, 2.53; savings and private banks had 2.55, and loan and trust companies were slightly lower with 2.23. The percentages of greatest deposits, although showing a larger variation, did not vary sufficiently far from the average to afford any very striking inferences. A few years of wide variation from averages must be explained by temporary and special factors affecting government finance. This is undoubtedly true of the year 1918 when the national banks held 11.23 per cent of demand deposits in the form of government funds.

To furnish a more accurate idea of the distribution of the deposit business by classes of banks, a segregation has been effected as between national and state banks, loan and trust companies, savings and private banks, and finally a grouping of deposits in all banks of the United States. The results thus attained will be more clearly understood by a study of Table 101, in which the figures have been set forth on a percentage basis. It will be noted that during the decade the relative amounts carried by the different groups of banks have varied considerably; the tendency soon after the World War being to mass the deposits in large banks wherever situated, so that loan and trust companies both have numerically had more than a quarter of all. A decade has witnessed a slight increase in the deposits held in loan and trust companies, but a substantial decrease in the amount held in national banks and a corresponding increase in the amounts carried by state commercial banks of all sizes.

The geographical distribution of government deposits is, perhaps, a leading factor of interest in the public deposits problem, inasmuch as the chief source of disturbance in banking, resulting from the movement of public funds, has been found in the artificial redistribution of such funds, sometimes caused by the political placement of them. A careful study has been made, therefore, of the figures furnished by the Comptroller of the Currency, by states. The results of this study are presented in Table 102, which is designed to show the changes, over the decade in question, in the percentages of public funds carried in the banks of the several states. A striking result of this computation is the continuously large and sometimes preponderant per cent of public deposits that are carried in New York. The

TABLE 101

PERCENTAGE DISTRIBUTION OF UNITED STATES GOVERNMENT DEPOSITS AMONG VARIOUS TYPES OF BANKS*

ON OR ABOUT JUNE 30 OF EVERY YEAR	NATIONAL BANKS	STATE (COMM.) BANKS	LOAN AND TRUST COMPANIES	STOCK, MUTUAL SAVINGS AND PRIVATE BANKS	ALL BANKS IN THE UNITED STATES
	%	%	%	%	%
1921	63.82	10.26	25.87	0.06	100.1
1922	80.21	6.00	10.71	3.09	100.1
1923	80.58	7.00	10.45	1.97	100.0
1924	80.97	5.18	11.02	2.83	100.0
1925	73.43	11.50	10.69	4.38	100.0
1926	76.93	5.48	17.58	—	99.9
1927	72.08	2.62	25.01	0.29	100.0
1928	83.44	3.53	12.88	0.15	100.0
1929	79.77	2.55	15.43	2.25	100.0
1930	80.46	2.00	16.23	1.32	100.1
1931	52.48	19.23	27.44	0.85	100.0
1932	50.27	19.11	29.99	0.64	100.1

* Computed on the basis of data abstracted from *Annual Reports of the Comptroller of the Currency.*

TABLE 102

PERCENTAGE DISTRIBUTION AMONG THE STATES OF THE UNITED STATES GOVERNMENT DEPOSITS CONTRASTED WITH A PERCENTAGE DISTRIBUTION OF TOTAL RESOURCES OF ALL BANKS

UNITED STATES GOVERNMENT DEPOSITS FOR EACH STATE EXPRESSED AS A PERCENTAGE OF THE ENTIRE AMOUNT OF UNITED STATES GOVERNMENT DEPOSITS FOR EVERY YEAR. TOTAL BANKING RESOURCES FOR EACH STATE EXPRESSED AS A PERCENTAGE OF THE TOTAL RESOURCES OF ALL BANKS IN THE UNITED STATES FOR EACH YEAR.

(Computed on the basis of data abstracted from Annual Reports of the Comptroller of the Currency)

	1921		1922		1923		1924	
	U. S. Dep.	Total Res.	U. S. Dep.	Total Res.	U. S. Dep.	Total Res.	U. S. Dep.	Total Res.
	%	%	%	%	%	%	%	%
Alabama	.11	.51	.48	.48	.34	.53	.50	.53
Arizona	.06	.18	.14	.17	.06	.15	.08	.14
Arkansas	.11	.48	.22	.44	.19	.47	.17	.44
California	1.44	4.95	8.60	5.19	8.27	5.57	7.39	5.53
Colorado	.20	.68	.55	.66	.20	.66	.52	.62
Connecticut	.86	1.75	.74	1.74	.91	1.79	.73	1.82
Delaware	.14	.20	.44	.20	.45	.20	.47	.22
Dist. of Col.	.77	.44	.62	.46	.92	.46	1.06	.45
Florida	.20	.45	.43	.48	.52	.54	.33	.61
Georgia	.22	.91	.91	.83	1.04	.85	1.13	.80
Idaho	.01	.25	.07	.21	.05	.18	.09	.17
Illinois	3.30	6.86	5.47	6.92	4.64	7.04	4.80	7.09
Indiana	.60	1.88	.94	1.83	1.42	1.88	1.08	1.80
Iowa	.16	2.33	.81	2.23	1.22	2.18	.62	2.00
Kansas	.47	1.11	.89	1.06	.75	.99	.69	.87
Kentucky	.46	.91	1.20	.91	1.01	.98	.51	.91
Louisiana	.11	.87	.26	.85	.85	.85	.90	.82
Maine	.10	.74	.20	.74	.17	.73	.14	.71
Maryland	.82	1.39	1.37	1.42	2.81	1.39	2.96	1.37
Massachusetts	5.63	6.22	9.47	6.39	12.95	6.48	13.85	6.37
Michigan	1.90	2.80	2.82	2.81	5.76	2.92	2.93	2.99
Minnesota	1.56	2.23	3.90	2.14	2.36	2.11	2.60	1.97
Mississippi	.06	.44	.23	.40	.29	.42	.21	.41
Missouri	1.39	2.83	2.09	2.74	2.62	2.76	1.04	2.61
Montana	.06	.42	.12	.39	.09	.35	.11	.26
Nebraska	.10	1.06	.44	1.06	.33	1.03	.32	.94
Nevada	.03	.08	.07	.08	.04	.07	.06	.07
New Hampshire	.15	.45	.22	.46	.25	.47	.14	.46
New Jersey	1.87	2.94	1.97	3.07	3.64	3.25	3.42	3.34
New Mexico	.05	.14	.29	.13	.10	.11	.13	.07
New York	50.01	25.34	19.80	26.28	15.52	24.79	10.23	26.47
North Carolina	.13	.81	.34	.81	.32	.82	.39	.80
North Dakota	.05	.45	.10	.44	.07	.41	.09	.33
Ohio	4.09	4.75	5.09	4.64	4.23	4.80	7.04	4.77

TABLE 102 *(Continued)*

	1921		1922		1923		1924	
	U. S. Dep.	Total Res.	U. S. Dep.	Total Res.	U. S. Dep.	Total Res.	U. S. Dep.	Total Res.
	%	%	%	%	%	%	%	%
Oklahoma	.45	1.00	1.04	.95	1.55	.89	2.17	.76
Oregon	.04	.58	.21	.56	.14	.57	.18	.54
Pennsylvania	16.25	9.44	15.23	9.24	14.75	9.70	19.17	9.67
Rhode Island	.98	.80	.64	.83	.68	.84	.32	.84
South Carolina	.18	.59	.51	.53	.28	.51	.41	.49
South Dakota	.11	.56	.37	.57	.22	.54	.30	.39
Tennessee	.17	.90	.35	.83	.51	.89	.50	.85
Texas	1.44	2.17	3.47	2.08	2.95	1.97	3.61	2.00
Utah	.01	.30	.04	.28	.02	.28	.02	.27
Vermont	.03	.39	.04	.39	.04	.40	.07	.40
Virginia	.59	1.17	2.16	1.10	1.09	1.12	1.51	1.10
Washington	.34	.85	1.11	.82	1.08	.84	1.31	.86
West Virginia	.16	.81	.35	.78	.25	.82	.35	.77
Wisconsin	1.05	1.76	1.29	1.65	1.28	1.71	1.46	1.66
Wyoming	.03	.18	.11	.16	.07	.17	.12	.14
Tot. for Poss.	.95	.64	1.78	.55	.68	.50	1.80	.51
All United States	100.00	99.99	99.99	99.98	99.98	99.98	100.03	100.01

	1925		1926		1927		1928	
	U. S. Dep.	Total Res.	U. S. Dep.	Total Res.	U. S. Dep.	Total Res.	U. S. Dep.	Total Res.
	%	%	%	%	%	%	%	%
Alabama	.88	.51	.62	.52	1.19	.51	1.23	.52
Arizona	.08	.13	.05	.12	.06	.12	.05	.14
Arkansas	.23	.44	.26	.44	.14	.39	.22	.38
California	7.99	5.58	1.29	5.71	11.58	5.63	20.16	5.62
Colorado	.45	.59	.39	.53	.13	.50	.21	.49
Connecticut	.49	1.80	.64	1.89	1.01	1.94	.67	2.00
Delaware	.35	.21	.36	.21	.04	.22	.04	.23
Dist. of Col.	2.24	.46	1.71	.47	1.79	.46	1.47	.46
Florida	.69	1.06	.71	1.10	.56	.83	.87	.68
Georgia	1.43	.77	1.77	.75	2.32	.68	1.20	.67
Idaho	.09	.15	.06	.15	.06	.14	.15	.15
Illinois	3.31	7.06	2.35	6.96	3.14	6.78	1.28	6.84
Indiana	1.20	1.74	1.19	1.84	.88	1.76	.88	1.71
Iowa	.75	1.83	.43	1.67	1.00	1.50	.54	1.42
Kansas	.87	.89	.73	.84	.55	.79	.80	.76
Kentucky	.40	.88	.34	.87	.41	.87	.25	.89
Louisiana	.70	.80	1.10	.82	.61	.78	1.11	.75
Maine	.17	.67	.16	.69	.10	.68	.11	.67
Maryland	2.65	1.39	2.89	1.38	1.55	1.38	.65	1.35
Massachusetts	5.34	6.39	15.54	6.50	12.10	7.21	10.36	7.35
Michigan	7.34	3.19	4.47	3.30	2.90	3.33	3.47	3.36

TABLE 102 *(Continued)*

	1925		1926		1927		1928	
	U. S. Dep.	Total Res.	U. S. Dep.	Total Res.	U. S. Dep.	Total Res.	U. S. Dep.	Total Res.
	%	%	%	%	%	%	%	%
Minnesota	2.33	1.90	2.32	1.78	2.13	1.66	1.91	1.61
Mississippi	.25	.40	.24	.43	.15	.41	.20	.40
Missouri	2.03	2.57	3.01	2.49	1.53	2.35	1.37	2.26
Montana	.16	.26	.18	.25	.16	.25	.15	.27
Nebraska	.36	.94	.36	.87	.30	.79	.23	.76
Nevada	.06	.07	.05	.07	.05	.07	.04	.07
New Hampshire	.27	.44	.24	.45	.22	.45	.33	.45
New Jersey	3.52	3.49	3.17	3.68	5.51	3.84	3.70	3.93
New Mexico	.09	.06	.07	.06	.06	.06	.05	.07
New York	8.16	26.82	11.86	26.77	7.77	27.73	16.55	28.00
North Carolina	.41	.77	.38	.78	.74	.74	.52	.73
North Dakota	.14	.32	.07	.29	.09	.24	.07	.23
Ohio	9.21	4.68	5.60	4.71	2.14	4.75	2.37	4.72
Oklahoma	.71	.80	.69	.79	.70	.77	.47	.74
Oregon	.20	.52	.18	.52	.14	.48	.12	.47
Pennsylvania	20.23	9.60	22.74	9.63	23.62	9.56	11.28	9.55
Rhode Island	.35	.82	.37	.82	.33	.84	.23	.82
South Carolina	.48	.44	.42	.39	.52	.34	.58	.34
South Dakota	.23	.35	.40	.30	.36	.23	.25	.25
Tennessee	.48	.81	.55	.81	.95	.77	.80	.77
Texas	5.34	2.03	3.62	1.97	5.55	1.93	7.70	1.97
Utah	.02	.26	.01	.26	.02	.26	.01	.26
Vermont	.07	.39	.06	.39	.05	.38	.12	.39
Virginia	1.62	1.03	1.08	1.02	1.20	.99	1.18	.96
Washington	1.72	.78	3.08	.79	1.38	.76	1.82	.77
West Virginia	.55	.70	.27	.69	.23	.66	.20	.62
Wisconsin	1.64	1.61	.83	1.65	.83	1.62	1.09	1.59
Wyoming	.08	.11	.07	.10	.05	.10	.06	.10
Tot. for Poss.	1.61	.48	1.00	.47	1.11	.45	.89	.48
All United States	99.97	99.99	99.98	99.99	100.01	99.98	100.01	100.02

	1929		1930		1931		1932	
	U. S. Dep.	Total Res.	U. S. Dep.	Total Res.	U. S. Dep.	Total Res.	U. S. Dep.	Total Res.
	%	%	%	%	%	%	%	%
Alabama	1.14	.52	1.81	.45	.79	.42	1.07	.41
Arizona	.07	.15	.06	.13	.03	.12	.08	.10
Arkansas	.19	.37	.13	.34	.08	.27	.06	.25
California	14.10	5.78	10.03	5.72	4.72	5.76	5.56	6.12
Colorado	.17	.48	.12	.46	.19	.47	.29	.47
Connecticut	1.30	2.07	1.52	2.05	1.02	2.15	.64	2.31
Delaware	.02	.26	.03	.26	.13	.28	.20	.32
Dist. of Col.	1.30	.46	1.01	.44	.43	.48	.36	.56

TABLE 102 *(Continued)*

	1929		1930		1931		1932	
	U. S. Dep.	Total Res.	U. S. Dep.	Total Res.	U. S. Dep.	Total Res.	U. S. Dep.	Total Res.
	%	%	%	%	%	%	%	%
Florida	.78	.58	1.89	.41	1.41	.39	1.20	.42
Georgia	2.65	.63	2.82	.59	2.22	.58	1.13	.59
Idaho	.03	.14	.05	.14	.03	.13	.03	.12
Illinois	4.39	6.82	2.42	6.60	8.72	6.02	7.10	5.16
Indiana	1.10	1.71	.64	1.59	.70	1.48	.48	1.47
Iowa	.69	1.41	.24	1.30	.31	1.24	.43	1.03
Kansas	.70	.75	.53	.68	.44	.65	.47	.65
Kentucky	.41	.95	.41	.87	.27	.76	.35	.77
Louisiana	1.24	.77	.90	.71	2.26	.73	4.14	.76
Maine	.11	.66	.10	.64	.17	.68	.12	.77
Maryland	1.98	1.38	2.73	1.36	3.21	1.43	2.21	1.55
Massachusetts	5.98	6.64	10.59	6.65	5.92	6.92	3.99	7.34
Michigan	2.16	3.47	1.27	3.23	3.45	3.12	1.90	2.92
Minnesota	1.74	1.56	.64	1.51	.58	1.56	.75	1.58
Mississippi	.25	.38	.19	.36	.11	.27	.15	.28
Missouri	1.53	2.06	1.34	2.06	2.16	2.04	2.82	2.06
Montana	.15	.26	.17	.24	.07	.22	.03	.22
Nebraska	.38	.71	.18	.61	.13	.60	.44	.52
Nevada	.03	.07	.05	.07	.02	.07	.03	.07
New Hampshire	.19	.46	.15	.44	.11	.46	.07	.54
New Jersey	3.46	3.97	3.64	3.78	2.51	3.90	2.28	4.09
New Mexico	.05	.07	.06	.07	.03	0.7	.03	.06
New York	13.99	28.83	15.68	31.47	30.66	32.01	33.20	32.06
North Carolina	.64	.69	.33	.61	.88	.52	1.09	.46
North Dakota	.06	.20	.06	.17	.03	.16	.03	.16
Ohio	2.67	4.59	2.72	4.59	4.98	4.35	4.32	4.14
Oklahoma	.28	.75	.57	.70	.22	.62	.26	.62
Oregon	.13	.45	.08	.44	.13	.44	.24	.42
Pennsylvania	19.27	9.57	21.25	9.41	11.12	9.81	10.50	9.69
Rhode Island	.22	.81	.26	.81	.29	.87	.57	.95
South Carolina	.88	.31	.77	.28	1.30	.25	.68	.21
South Dakota	.21	.25	.25	.23	.15	.20	.48	.18
Tennessee	.62	.80	.54	.78	.41	.68	.63	.70
Texas	7.12	2.00	6.82	1.84	3.83	1.80	5.13	1.78
Utah	.01	.27	.02	.26	.04	.26	.03	.23
Vermont	.05	.40	.04	.37	.02	.38	.03	.43
Virginia	1.02	.93	1.36	.90	1.06	.89	.81	.95
Washington	1.80	.79	1.33	.79	1.21	.81	1.68	.75
West Virginia	.19	.61	.21	.56	.20	.53	.15	.52
Wisconsin	1.52	1.59	1.11	1.50	.87	1.55	1.36	1.57
Wyoming	.03	.10	.09	.10	.02	.10	.02	.10
Tot. for Poss.	.97	.51	.78	.43	.34	.51	.36	.57
All United States	99.97	99.99	99.99	100.00	99.98	100.01	99.98	100.00

figures, however, show that the percentage carried in New York banks runs closely parallel much of the time to the percentage of total banking resources carried by banks in the larger centers.

In New York the figures cited indicate that only in the immediate post-war years did public deposits tend to accumulate in New York to a greater extent than was warranted by the relative importance of the deposits of the local banks. While there are some tendencies toward a concentration of funds, the distribution effected among the several states is, for the most part, reasonably proportional to the distribution of actual aggregate banking resources among the several states.

Table 103 shows the distribution of current government holdings between Federal Reserve banks and depository banks from 1916 to 1932. There was a tendency throughout the period to reduce the volume of funds actually carried in Federal Reserve banks except in periods of acute difficulty or crisis, and to increase the amount carried in national and member banks and special depositories. From the period of the World War onward there has been a tendency to keep the amounts in Federal Reserve institutions down to a figure well below 10 per cent of the aggregate total available in all classes of depositories.

Since foreign and insular depositories and deposits in the Treasury of the Philippine Islands are usually of small importance, they are of no special interest for the present purpose. Deposits in national and member bank depositories are fairly constant and represent, to a large extent, special deposits designed to cover the needs of paymasters, post offices, Federal courts, and the like. These deposits have been gradually reduced, do not fluctuate appreciably, and have but little influence on the banking structure of the country. Government expenditures and current financing are dealt with through the Federal Reserve banks and the accounts carried by special depositories. The importance of the total monthly turnover of government funds from the standpoint of current banking is not generally understood. In studying these figures one should also remember that as things have gone during the past decade, the government usually spends borrowed money and uses its income chiefly to retire maturing short-term debt—a plan which formed the basis of government financing during the periods of surplus revenue but has had to be decidedly modified since the appearance of deficit conditions.

TABLE 103

PUBLIC MONEYS HELD BY DEPOSITORY BANKS*

(In thousands of dollars)

AS OF JUNE 30TH OF EVERY YEAR	FEDERAL RESERVE BANKS	FEDERAL LAND BANKS	NAT'L AND MEMBER BANK DEPOSITORIES	PHILIPPINE TREASURY AND INSULAR DEPOSITS	FOREIGN DEPOSITORIES	SPECIAL DEPOSITORIES	TOTAL	NATIONAL AND SPECIAL DEPOSITORIES
1916	$113,481	$ —	$61,211	$3,968	$ —	$ —	$ 178,560	$ 61,211
1917	305,744	—	52,598	2,081	—	714,841	1,075,264	767,439
1918	29,369	430	53,748	6,827	7,831	1,473,727	1,571,932	1,527,475
1919	105,457	500	54,574	8,376	24,641	905,397	1,098,945	959,971
1920	44,393	5,950	24,211	1,893	8,609	273,335	358,391	297,546
1921	79,813	—	21,210	8,057	54,046	393,289	556,415	414,499
1922	33,092	—	24,002	4,418	1,233	146,477	209,222	170,479
1923	33,681	—	26,154	2,541	817	297,833	361,026	323,987
1924	43,250	1,000	25,383	2,194	380	162,092	234,299	187,475
1925	25,434	—	27,310	2,399	258	150,716	206,117	178,026
1926	10,719	—	26,684	2,175	154	202,729	242,461	229,413
1927	30,656	—	25,381	1,935	512	198,607	257,091	223,988
1928	23,648	—	24,349	2,032	372	245,731	296,132	270,080
1929	35,891	—	25,799	1,205	1,600	356,842	421,337	382,641
1930	26,524	—	24,268	1,829	1,612	296,624	350,857	320,892
1931	46,573	—	27,009	838	2,060	413,125	489,605	440,134
1932	3,758	—	24,466	1,915	785	405,648	436,572	430,114

* Abstracted from the "Report of the Division of Deposits," as given in the *Annual Reports of the Secretary of the Treasury.*

The appointment of Federal Reserve banks as fiscal agents meant, in effect, that the proceeds of tax payments were collected by the Reserve system and resulted in a decrease of member bank balances with Reserve banks, while government expenditures, taking the form of checks payable at the Reserve banks, resulted in increased balances of member banks with the Reserve system. As the balances of member banks with the Reserve institutions also represented their legal reserves, the fluctuations in such balances became a factor of great importance in the analysis of banking conditions. It was in order to minimize such fluctuations and to distribute government funds at points where they were most needed that the present system of depositories was developed. By it a bank was able to offset large tax payments through subscriptions to government bonds, the proceeds being retained on deposit so that the banks themselves were able to effect a rough distribution of government funds in accordance with their position.

Government balances held by banks throughout the country and resulting from sales of bonds are later called in only if and as needed, and are transferred to the credit of the government with the Reserve banks; the balances in such banks thus constitute the immediate drawing account upon which the Treasury relies for payments of its expenses. Transfers to it are made by calls through which a percentage of a given issue of bonds or other forms of indebtedness is required to be paid in by the depository banks to the Reserve banks. They are made in chronological order and cover all special depositories alike. The only exception made to this plan of regularly calling in proceeds of government loans, in rotation in the order in which floated, has been afforded by the so-called "Baby Bond Issue" or "Anti-hoarding Bond" flotation put out in March, 1932.

It will be seen from what has been said that the fluctuations of government deposits as between banks result from the action of the banks themselves; hence, do not represent a determined policy on the part of the government. The shifting of such deposits actually represents changes in credit conditions, excess reserves, and the like, among the various groups of banks and are especially interesting for that reason. The analysis that has been made of government deposits illustrates the reason why the Treasury has been disposed to handle its borrowings by means of short-term debt issues which may be purchased, in the form of certificates and notes, by the banks and held by them as liquid resources in order to enable them to obtain and hold government deposits in the proportions that they think necessary. It seems fairly to be inferred from the facts, that the amounts of such short-term debt would naturally increase materially during periods of heavy government borrowing.

There is, however, nothing in what has been stated to show what the desirable aggregate amount of such short-term debt should be, or what is its proper relationship to deficit conditions —an inquiry which will be presented in some detail in the last section (Part VI) of the present study. The study also indicates the great and increasing power of the Treasury Department as a factor in the money market. Inasmuch as the Treasury is a very large holder of claims upon the banks, the department can, when it wishes, by transferring its balances to the Reserve banks and thus reducing the reserve accounts of member banks with the reserve institutions, exercise a very severe pressure upon the banks for the purpose of controlling their speculative tendencies in the direction of loans to brokers, and the like. In the same way it is entirely possible for the Treasury, reversely, to stimulate an easy money situation by allowing its balances with Reserve banks to run down while at the same time the reserve accounts of the depository members are maintained, and they are thus provided with funds which they may use in other phases of their financing.

There is one aspect of this relationship of the Treasury to the banks which has not thus far been mentioned, but which deserves at least casual treatment. This is the Postal Savings situation which was provided for by an act of Congress in 1910. The deposits of the system were of little or no importance until the year 1930, when the increasing number of bank failures led to a loss of confidence on the part of the public in the banks. This was reflected in the form of a tremendous increase in Postal

Savings deposits in the years following 1929—eventually reaching a peak of more than a billion dollars. These represented withdrawals of funds which had been left on deposit in the banks, but which, ordinarily under the circumstances would probably have been hoarded. They were now transferred to the keeping of the government in the belief that this was the safer disposition of them.

The government, after receiving the funds on deposit, transferred them to the extent of about 90 per cent back to the banks throughout the country so that the operation of the system was really tantamount to a government guarantee of such deposits. The adoption of a general government blanket guarantee in the Banking Act June 16, 1933 has changed the situation and may result in a gradual backflow of Postal Savings deposits to the banks, by depositors who reason that since they are guaranteed by the government in any case, they will be as well protected in the form of direct bank deposits as in the form of Postal Savings deposits. At all events the Postal Savings problem adds an element of considerable complication to the situation which would not exist without it.

Control of Public Deposits

Public deposits differ from those of the individual business man and corporation in the irregularity of their receipt and disbursement. In those cases in which a government receives its income largely from duties such as customs, the income-receiving periods may be very strongly marked. Conversely, in those cases in which the government has important annual disbursements, the period of outgo of disbursements for expenditures, likewise, will be marked. It is not always possible to dictate this seasonal quality in the accounts of governments whose income is composite—derived from various sources which yield their incomes at balanced periods so arranged as to provide for a steady flow of revenue into the Treasury. Usually, however, a fairly well-marked seasonal quality is to be noted in the deposits of the government, partly because of this fact and partly because the payments made by governments are seldom, to any considerable extent, in the form of currency, so that as a rule they are effected through the transfer of credit.

It has been for many years customary in the United States to exempt the banks from the necessity of carrying reserves against the deposits of the federal government. Such exemption has added a superficial attractiveness to government deposit accounts, while the seasonality of the government's need enables it to refrain from drawing upon a large fraction of its accounts, thereby resulting in a classification of them as "active" and "inactive." This has had the effect of adding to the desire of the banks to obtain such funds.

The deposits of states and municipalities have not, of course, been exempt from reserve requirements, the banks usually finding it necessary to treat these deposits the same as if they had been made by individuals or corporations. They have, however, exhibited the same quality of irregularity in their turnover, and in many cases have been practically time deposits held for designated periods, with the result that it was possible for the various governments to ask for and obtain a status as preferred creditors through the segregation of special portions of the bank assets. Such segregation was generally insisted upon by the United States prior to the organization of the Federal Reserve system, it being then the custom to demand of the national banks in which the funds of the governments were placed, the deposit in trust first of national bonds, and later of satisfactory state, municipal and other bonds, designated for this purpose by the authorities of the Treasury Department. The establishment of the Federal Reserve system naturally changed this condition of affairs and was intended to eliminate the practice of requiring security against deposits, the government being authorized to place its funds in the Federal Reserve banks as its fiscal agent and, of course, without any specific protection.

Conditions during the War, and the immense growth of the funds belonging to the government were thought to necessitate a change in this particular, and eventually a system was installed whereby the Federal Reserve banks left upon deposit with members, funds growing out of the purchase of bonds or other evidences of national indebtedness. The consequences of this innovation were expected to come to an end with the close of the War, but the suddenness of the end of the struggle necessitated continuation for some months of large advances to the Allied nations, while the heavy taxation of the War was likewise continued for a time.

The advent of President Harding, and the policies of the current Treasury administration, which actually abandoned the older policy of forcing the debt of the government out of the banks, opened a period of continuous deficit financiering in which advances from banks were constantly asked, on the ground that it was desirable to have a substantial proportion of public indebtedness carried as short-term debt. It was thus requisite to ask the banks, almost continuously, to become buyers of government obligations, and thus to maintain the connection which had been established between the Treasury and depository institutions. This situation has continued down to the present time with, under existing conditions, an enormous government deficit each year ($1,780,000,000 for the fiscal year ending June 30, 1933) which seems likely to continue for a good while to come.

State and Municipal Control of Deposits

In viewing the problem of state and municipal control of public deposits, a situation of considerably greater difficulty is necessarily encountered, owing to the fact that the systems of supervision and control necessarily vary from state to state, so that it is not possible to lay down general dogmatic statements which are applicable to all or nearly all indifferently. Generally speaking, we may recognize the following different types of relationship between the states and the local grades of government on the one hand and the banks on the other:

1. Ordinary straight deposits in banks upon the same terms as any other depositor.
2. Ordinary straight deposits in banks, but with satisfactory bond or other protection given by the fiscal officer, who then uses his own judgment where to deposit and is personally responsible for the deposit.
3. Direct deposit in banks, but with special segregation of

collateral to protect the deposit—the so-called "secured" deposit.

4. Time deposits made direct in bank, but with the special protection or security accorded to savings bank funds, and subject, of course, to the same conditions relating to withdrawal which apply in the case of savings banks.

While it is not possible, as already stated, to furnish exact specifications as to the relative extent of these different plans, it may be stated generally that the bulk of non-Federal government deposits are probably carried either as straight open accounts protected by the personal bond of the fiscal officer in charge of them, or as secured deposits protected by segregation of assets, and, in a great many cases, intended to be left with the banks on a time basis pending the date when they will be called for in the construction of some public works or for similar purposes. This method is frequently employed in connection with the proceeds of a bond issue which has been placed in advance of the exact date when the funds must be disbursed, so that provision must be made for caring for the balances during the interval between realization and disbursement.

Theory of Direction of Public Deposits[2]

In reaching any conclusion with respect to the possible changes that might be introduced for the betterment of the deposits situation as we have just set it forth, it is necessary to consider some of the major theoretical aspects of government borrowing at banks.

Inasmuch as the government derives its revenue from citizens whose business is likely to be seasonal and whose incomes are correspondingly irregular, its own income is not likely to be stable. Experience shows that in the United States there are well-marked taxpaying periods when returns are much higher than at others, so that as a result the government has months of excess revenue and others of deficit. This would be true even in years when there was a "balanced budget," *i.e.,* when the year's income is equal to the year's outgo, or roughly so.

[2] Willis, Chapman, and Robey, *Contemporary Banking* (Harper Brothers, New York, 1933), Chapter 43, pp. 755-56; 763-64.

There is, therefore, the same reason why the government should need the aid of banks as there is why individuals should likewise need to borrow. This necessity was in former times much more evident than at present, because, in a time when income was derived largely from consumption, taxable revenues were usually steadier, while at periods when income was low in total amount it tended to be a much smaller fraction of total community income and, hence, less liable to reflect the fluctuations of the latter. Direct taxation on incomes, dependent upon customs receipts, and other characteristic features of modern public finance have brought with them a decidedly greater "seasonality" than formerly.

Unbalanced Budgets

This situation does not last for more than a short period when a public budget is balanced annually. As has been shown by various writers, however, the requirement of an annual budget balance is more or less artificial, the main requirements of sound finance being that there shall be a balancing of income and outgo at reasonably short periods which may be considerably longer than a year. The longer they are, of course, the greater the time during which it becomes necessary for the government to fall back upon borrowing as a means of meeting its obligations, inasmuch as the latter usually recur in relatively regular amounts on a monthly or semimonthly basis, or when seasonal, as in the case of interest, may nevertheless be distributed at such intervals as to "spread out" the obligations throughout the year. Generally speaking, therefore, extension of their duration within the time in which a budget balance is effected means greater and longer dependence upon borrowing.

If the period during which the budget is out of balance continues for a good while, the government may fairly be said to be on a deficit basis; and in that case its borrowing becomes recurring and habitual with no indication of a definite nature when a reduction will take place. Such a government must meet its obligations through the steady increase of its debt; and this means that as it enlarges its obligations at banks its only means of settling them is found in borrowing elsewhere—usually from its own citizens who are asked to purchase long-term bonds and thus to furnish the means of settling with the banks which have advanced the funds needed for short-term requirements. In this case the bank borrowing of the government is effected for the purpose of carrying it over not from periods of short to periods of full revenue, but from periods of short revenue to periods when funding takes place through the issue of long-term securities which are sold to the general public.

Theory of Public Bank Borrowing

The theory of public bank borrowing is now sufficiently clear. It is the same as that of any kind of sane and careful borrowing at banks. The difference in technique which renders the problem difficult to deal with is found in the fact that the government itself is not a commercial undertaking and is not subject to exactly the same methods of test that apply to other borrowers. It is, however, subject to exactly the same methods of judgment based upon duration and purpose of borrowing that apply in the case of such other borrowers. Applying these tests to government paper, just as to other obligations, it shortly appears that banks—including the central bank of a nation—are warranted in absorbing government obligations in proportion as they have long or slow paper whose turnover is such as to permit a satisfactory period of waiting when it is necessary to realize through resorting to the open market. So far the current portfolio is concerned with the amount of government advances which depend strictly upon the volume of taxation, and so should not exceed the amount that can be liquidated within a reasonably brief fiscal period (whether a "year" or not is a secondary matter), just as is true in the case of a commercial establishment.

The total of the government's bank borrowing power is measured by its short-term taxing power; and the total of its long-term borrowing power must be tested by the willingness of the public to purchase its long-term obligations. The rate of government borrowing should correspond to the prevailing rate in the market and should be dependent upon this rate rather than to make market rates depend on the public. Loans to individuals on government collateral should be based upon the same terms and conditions that would control if there were no such collateral. The collateral is then used merely for safety's sake and not for the sake of reducing the rate or obtaining larger amounts than would otherwise have been made available; least of all for the purpose of borrowing to carry out plans or projects which otherwise would not have been sanctioned by the banker. These conclusions, as already stated, are those which result from the application of ideal standards of lending and borrowing and should be examined in the light of actual practical experience, based upon the lessons learned by banks in actually making their advances from time to time in response to government need.

Program of Changes

In dealing with the situation thus described from the standpoint of future policy, it is necessary to inquire what actual changes should be introduced into existing methods. These may now be considered in order; but before thus dealing with them, it is necessary to observe the fact that the Banking Act of 1933 has, by reason of its guaranty of deposits provision, introduced a distinctly new situation which changes the actual proposals that would otherwise be made for the strengthening of existing government deposit methods. Under the Act in question (Banking Act of June 16, 1933), provision is made for a mutual or joint guarantee of deposits fund to be subscribed by the different member banks of the Federal Reserve system. In so far as such guarantee is provided as against bank deposits, it is evident that the argument, whatever weight may have been given to it for the requirements of special security behind public deposits, is very largely weakened. It would be impossible in any case for a government to protect its deposits to a point where they were safer than the general average of the entire deposit liabilities of the nation.

The whole theory of requiring special security against bank deposits rests upon the assumption that such deposits are subject to more than average risk. When this risk is reduced to a point where it is no greater than average for the entire deposits for the banks of the nation, the argument in favor of insurance against it vanishes. There was always the strongest of arguments against the idea of special protection of government deposits, but in view of the alteration in national law, repetition of it is hardly worth while. It will still remain true, however, that, even under the new law, a local government may deposit its funds in nonmember banks that do not enjoy the protection of the new guarantee of deposits. In such cases the problem here contemplated will be a special and local one; but this after all will be only a minor phase of the general problem, since it is not to be expected that any considerable proportion of the public funds of the country will thus be placed in the weaker banks. It is, therefore, reasonable to lay down as the first requirements of a sound public deposit policy in the future that:

1. The practice of requiring security against public deposits should be abandoned both by governments of every grade and by Federal Reserve banks, with the possible exception of special cases involving nonmember institutions in which local funds may be placed for local reasons. A corollary from this conclusion is easily drawn and recognizes essentially the same general set of conditions which support the first conclusion already mentioned. This is that;

2. The usual reserve protection should be exacted behind public deposits in either case, whether held by Federal Reserve banks on behalf of the national government or by member banks, or by state institutions which receive them direct from local governments.

Protected by reserves like other deposits and subject to the same kind of treatment as others, we may ask whether there are additional special phases of deposit policy that need to be applied in the case of public funds, either initially or as a modification of existing conditions. The answer to this question must be based in part at least upon the fiscal practices and policies of the government. Where a substantial amount of borrowing is to be undertaken it is desirable to carry this borrowing in the form of long-term bonds which were sold as largely as may be to actual investors who were then expected to retain them as a source of income. This leads to the further conclusion;

3. The balances carried by governments in banks should be, to as small an extent as possible, the proceeds of bank borrowing, representatives of such borrowing taking the form of long-term bonds suitable for sale to investors. Growing out of this effort to keep the funds in the government from assuming a form which tends to enlarge the deposit liabilities of the banks through borrowing, we must, furthermore infer;

4. Where current financing has been carried out on the basis

of short-term notes which are held by the banks, it is desirable to leave the proceeds thereof on deposit with the banks until transferred to others, and, as already noted, to carry such deposits in the form of unsecured claims, or demand liabilities, on the books of the banks.

Inasmuch as a great many of the existing banks have proven to be weak or untrustworthy, there would seem to be a very distinct reason for amending the Federal Reserve Act in such a way as to permit state, municipal and other governmental agencies to deposit direct in Federal Reserve banks, thus constituting these banks the fiscal agents of such governments, as they are now for the government of the United States. This is in fact what is done in foreign countries where the government is centralized so that its banking operations include not only transactions of the "central" but also those of the "provincial" and other local governments. It is to be expected that in such an event the Federal Reserve banks would maintain with banks chartered under state authority—whether members or not—the same kind of redeposit relations that they now maintain with their own members, and upon terms which, presumably, would afford as much protection and safety to the owners of the funds as is now enjoyed by governmental depositors under existing conditions.

CHAPTER XXI

BANK EXAMINATIONS[1]

In the first chapter of Part III attention was called to the fact that changing methods of control of the banking system had been partly brought about and partly caused by changing relationships between the state and the banks. The system of oversight, or examination, has been named as one of the major ways in which such a relationship is established. In this chapter it is intended to discuss some of the basic problems and conditions relative to bank examinations.

There is little necessity of attempting to detail the technique[2] of bank examination. This technique has assumed a stereotyped form and is well known. The methods pursued by state bank examination staffs follow substantially along the same lines that have been developed by the office of the Comptroller of the Currency on behalf of the Federal Government, and have, during recent years, been modified or altered only in minor particulars.

It is not now with the technique of examination, therefore, but chiefly with the purpose of studying the point of view that we observe in oversight, that the student of contemporary banking conditions is fundamentally concerned.

Two phases of banking suggest themselves at the very outset of such a study as having a close relationship to the entire problem of governmental oversight. One of these is the question of failures; the other the problem of investments. Much has already been said of failures, but principally from the point of view suggested by the statistics relating to the subject. It is now desirable, first of all, to consider the bank failures in connection with bank examinations.

[1] By H. Parker Willis. Special use has been made of the data compiled by the Federal Reserve Committee on Branch, Group and Chain Banking.

[2] The technique of bank examination has been fully discussed and the forms relating to it reproduced in Willis and Steiner, *Federal Reserve Banking Practice*, Chap. XXVI.

Responsibility for Bank Failures

What are the causes of bank failures? In years past there has been a tendency to answer this question in a more or less conventional way through the use of the familiar official expressions of "bad banking," "dishonesty," "unwise judgment," or "speculation." These captions have little or no meaning, but such meaning as they have is developed only in relation to individual cases of failure or suspension. They evidently do not have much significance when they are used in connection with the problem of failure on a large scale or tendency of an entire system to suspend. Thus, for example, the suspension of the banks in Germany and in England in 1931 probably could not have been averted by any system of administrative bank examination, and it may be doubted whether such a system could have averted the bank holidays which culminated in the United States in a national holiday from and after March 4, 1933. These phenomena of mass bank failure are evidently not of a nature which can be obviated or reduced through the application of corrective measures to individual banks. They are cases which raise the question of general policy, and in which the discussion needs to take into account the broader aspects of management and supervision.

Abstractly stated, it ought to be possible to prevent any bank from ever failing if its management is not only honest but prudent and careful. Abstractly stated on the other side, however, is the fact that the failure of any bank will be unavoidable if the depositors of such a bank insist upon subjecting it to the necessity of complete liquidation through what is called a "run," or simultaneous presentation of liabilities for any purpose whatever. It is desirable, therefore, to recognize at the outset, that completely successful administration of a banking system calls for collaboration on the part of the public (customers of the bank) and the administrative authorities. Working together with the banking management itself, these elements should be able to prevent bank failures, except under unusual conditions. The question whether in those unusual cases where bank failures do occur, the responsibility for loss should be borne by all of the banks in the community, is one that has been widely under discussion for many years past. No attempt will be made to deal with it here.

The legislation incorporated into the Banking Act of 1933 implied an acceptance of the notion that the general community of banks is responsible for the doings of each and every member of that community, and that in the event of actual failure the responsibility must rest upon the shoulders of the other institutions jointly. It is worth observing that a somewhat similar point of view has, in effect, been adopted by such countries as Great Britain, Canada, and others, inasmuch as in those countries the other banks usually unite to absorb the assets and liabilities of an institution which is on the verge of failure. The assumption of this responsibility may be, in some measure, due to the pressure of public opinion and the growth of the general idea that banking is a public service occupation, but it is also due in no small degree to the recognition by the bankers of the fact that the failure of one institution is a bad thing for those remaining, and that a sound position in banking can be maintained only by preventing the growth and development of failures.

Blame for Receivership

While thus recognizing the bank-failure problem as one of those broad issues in American banking which have come more and more of recent years to be recognized as having a social or community aspect, our present system of bank examination was undoubtedly conceived upon different lines, and based upon the thought that it is possible, through frequent and careful survey of a bank's business and through audits of its accounts, to prevent it from getting into an embarrassed condition. This method of procedure, as we have seen, would probably never suffice to check an epidemic of bank failures such as that which has already developed in the United States in recent years. It would, however, in many instances suffice to anticipate and check the gradual deterioration of bank assets if signs of danger were recognized at an early stage of their existence and were immediately met by the application of known remedies whose introduction was strongly insisted upon as a condition of the continued existence of the bank. Accordingly, students of bank examination and examination methods in the United States have been more and more inclined of late to place major emphasis upon individual cases, and to judge the success or failure of bank examinations by the date and positiveness with which examination staffs have made their judgments effective in cases where unsoundness or bad practice had been detected. We must, undoubtedly, judge the efficiency of our bank examination system, both federal and state, by the degree in which it has been able to detect blunders or malpractice and to bring about their correction before they had done serious harm.

Ground for Unsoundness

The fact that in a good many cases in recent years it has been obvious that the banking authorities have not been either firm or stringent in their application of criticism to unsound banking methods has been widely realized. Notorious bank failures —such as that of the Bank of the United States, the Bank of Kentucky, and others—have impressed the facts upon the public, largely because of the circumstance that, in such cases, the details of mismanagement had been definitely ascertained and had been emphasized in a striking way through legal or other procedures which had made them common property. The doubts in the minds of many persons have centered around the question whether the laxity and inefficiency exhibited in these outstanding cases was or was not generally characteristic, or whether it was rather to be taken as an exceptional case; and it was in order to answer this query that the Committee of Federal Reserve system, in its review to which reference has already been made,[3] has wisely devoted itself to the actual study of case histories in instances where failure had taken place, the object being to ascertain how far these selected cases furnished general warrant for conclusions regarding the efficiency or inefficiency of supervision.

The Committee of Federal Reserve system studied 225 cases

[3] For description of this study, see Preface.

of bank suspensions, taking the histories from actual examiners' reports. Of these banks 120 were institutions which suspended during 1921-1930, but later a list of 105 other banks suspending in 1931 was added. These banks were distributed among seven Federal Reserve districts in fairly equal proportions and in such a way as to make the sample as thoroughly representative as possible. The banks so chosen were distributed according to size in such a way as to obtain representative conditions, the majority of them being found in places of population between 500 and 10,000 persons, although a few banks in the smaller villages and the larger cities were also included. Of the banks in question, by far the greater number had deposits between $150,000 and $1,000,000. The 1931 study included, as already stated, 105 banks; the same principles of distribution by size, by community, and by characteristics were pursued.

Three types of information concerning these selected banks were filed. The first consisted of excerpts from bank examiners' criticisms over a period of years of bank suspensions. These were collected for suspended banks only. The second type consisted of statistical material taken from balance sheets of examiners' reports and earnings and dividend reports. The third type of data—collected only for the banks which closed in 1931—related to bond and security holdings. In analyzing the situation of these banks, statistical approach was made to the subject by the use of balance sheet ratios. To do this the several ratios of each class of banks for given periods were assembled and median ratios were found.

Proceeding to the study of bank failures in relation to bank examinations from this point of view, the Committee in question, first of all found that a review of bank failures studied from the evolutionary standpoint was simply a history of deterioration of assets and that this deterioration was in most cases the result of a process developing over a period of years. According to the reports of bank examiners, questionable assets of suspended banks had in almost every case assumed relatively large proportions, when compared with the capital and surplus of these banks, a good while before failure occurred. Heavy borrowings were characteristic for a considerable period prior to suspension of most of these banks, and in a substantial number of cases had given rise to criticism of banking authorities because of such continuous borrowings. It was found also, that in the 225 cases studied, the ratio of loans to officers, directors, and allied interests, was distinctly higher, as compared to capital and surplus, than was the case in a similar group of banks that did not suspend. The typical bank in the group which is thus subjected to study was found to have advanced (prior to failure), to officers, directors, and allied interests, an amount roughly equivalent to one-third of the capital and surplus.

Along with these factors tending to bring about steady deterioration of assets, and refusal to pay attention to the criticisms of examiners based upon unwise or poor application of the banks' funds, it was found that examiners' reports constantly criticized officials in a majority of cases because of lax and careless lending policies, often accompanied by doubtful practice. Many of the practices had to do with real estate mortgages and general loans to farmers, often made without specific security and often protected in an insufficient way by taking of junior mortgages on farms. Loans that could not be paid in the ordinary course of business at maturity were constantly renewed, while various methods for the evasion of the limits fixed by law upon the loan lines of the banks were common, and so found to be an important element in bringing about the collapse or failure.

From this point of view then it appears that case histories of failed banks appear to confirm the opinion, rightly entertained in times past, that the difficulties leading to failure had never been definitely corrected, but had been allowed to continue from year to year with nothing more than an admonitory letter. The findings of the Federal Reserve Committee, in the case of these 225 institutions, thus reflect most seriously upon the present management of examinations, and this reflection is borne out by information derived from other sources which points in many cases to the presence of political influences as a means of protecting or maintaining banks in the continued pursuit of practices for which they had been criticized. Of course, this is a severe indictment, not only of the present examination system as it has existed, but of its potentialities, since it is only by a stretch of the imagination that any assurance can be acquired of a very greatly improved banking-examination system at any time in the early future.

It is a known fact that within recent years large banks, which were being hardpressed by members of an examination force with urgent recommendations that they should improve their practice, have been able to enlist on their side the support of highly placed officials of the government who have expressed a wish that no action should be taken, designed to correct the conditions complained of. Striking testimony to the same effect was furnished by an ex-officer of the Department of Justice who, in recent testimony before a special Senate investigating committee convened in New York during late June 1933 for the purpose of studying the conditions relating to the failure of the Harriman National Bank, asserted that false entries and misrepresentations of banking conditions on the books were characteristic of very many banks at the moment he was furnishing this evidence. There is much corroborative testimony to a similar effect, and from it all the conclusion seems to be inevitable that the vigor and determination with which bank supervision has been carried on is too low.[4]

In concluding this survey of the relationship of bank supervision to bank failure, it is worth while to reproduce from the study of the Federal Reserve Committee, already described, the following tables and data designed to furnish the major facts with regard to the 225 banks, whose cases, historically, were carefully studied.

Table 104 shows the comparative histories of the active banks and suspended banks used in this study, as measured in terms of ratios of non-liquidity.

The typical active bank never allowed its fixed and questionable assets to rise above 68 per cent of capital and surplus,

[4] Striking testimony of like sort is afforded by words of the Hon. James Couzens before the investigating Committee in Detroit, Mich., Aug. 21, 1933.

and during good years, such as 1920 and 1929, the active banks' ratios were less than 50 per cent. To state the policy of active banks in another way, they always kept their total of criticized and fixed assets well below their stockholders' investment in the bank.

TABLE 104

FIXED AND QUESTIONABLE ASSETS PER $100 OF CAPITAL AND SURPLUS

DATE	SUSPENDED BANKS: 120 Banks Suspending in 1920-1930 *(median)*	SUSPENDED BANKS: 105 Banks Suspending in 1931 *(median)*	33 SELECTED ACTIVE BANKS* *(median)*
1920—1st half	$ 30	$ 23	$11
1920—2d half	46		23
1921—1st half	78	38	37
1921—2d half	110		34
1922—1st half	141	47	50
1922—2d half	155		48
1923—1st half	148	61	50
1923—2d half	164		68
1924—1st half	168	79	66
1924—2d half	156		60
1925—1st half	183	92	52
1925—2d half	169		68
1926—1st half	189	95	51
1926—2d half	198		43
1927—1st half	202	114	38
1927—2d half	203		38
1928—1st half	213	129	44
1928—2d half	242		45
1929—1st half	252	157	37
1929—2d half	191	153	40
1930—1st half	296	176	30
1930—2d half		208	38
1931—1st half		236	

* Banks still in operation when these data were compiled. They were selected from communities which had had failures.

Banks which later suspended followed a very different course. In 1920 their ratios of non-liquidity were not materially worse than the ratios of the active banks. This was partly because of the favorable agricultural situation. From 1920 on, however, the amount of fixed and questionable assets of suspended banks rose steadily until the typical banks showed ratios much above 100 per cent. This means that the banks which later failed had criticized and fixed assets much larger than their capital and surplus for an extended period before they closed. In some cases the undesirable assets amounted to several times capital and surplus.

TABLE 105

FIXED AND QUESTIONABLE ASSETS PER $100 OF CAPITAL AND SURPLUS

DATE	BANKS SUSPENDING IN										
	1921	1922	1923	1924	1925	1926	1927	1928	1929	1930	1931
1921—1st half	$ 10	$ 42	$ 51	$ 28	$ 12	$ 51	$ 23	$ 51	$ 9	$ 17	$ 23
1920—2d half	6	74	58	50	28	86	38	77	12	16	
1921—1st half	180	149	62	94	61	99	155	86	40	66	38
1921—2d half	164	218	106	137	108	139	227	96	59	71	
1922—1st half		273	154	156	130	266	107	162	139	65	47
1922—2d half		292	200	145	176	303	125	155	172	107	
1923—1st half			252	177	155	141	141	189	114	142	61
1923—2d half			280	230	196	151	229	163	112	108	
1924—1st half				297	204	189	322	141	85	110	79
1924—2d half					207	225	238	146	85	133	
1925—1st half					352	230	331	153	113	125	92
1925—2d half						206	271	150	107	132	
1926—1st half						218	321	209	121	120	95
1926—2d half							430	224	129	154	
1927—1st half							447	240	151	174	114
1927—2d half								292	211	167	
1928—1st half								299	248	176	129
1928—2d half								343	260	223	
1929—1st half									257	243	157
1929—2d half										199	153
1930—1st half										296	176
1930—2d half											208
1931—1st half											236

An analysis of the ratios of nonliquidity of suspended banks divided into groups according to the year of failure shows that a similar development occurred among banks failing in each year from 1921 to 1930, inclusive. The ratios of typical banks in all groups were small in 1920, but deteriorated rapidly as the banks approached failure. Banks which closed in 1927 had the worst ratios according to median experience.

An analysis of the ratios of nonliquidity of the banks, which failed in 1931, by economic areas shows that banks in the large cities and in selected communities made far more favorable showing than banks in the other groups. A part of this better comparative showing was no doubt caused by the fact that the larger portion of their weak assets was in the form of bonds. The examiners in setting up criticized assets merely include the depreciation on bonds, and recently have omitted entirely the depreciation on the higher grades of bonds, whereas they include the total book value of other weak assets in the criticizable total. This explains in some measure why the fixed and questionable assets of banks in the two farming groups, where bond investments were small, reached higher levels. Banks in suburban and smaller industrial cities which were adversely affected by the collapse of the city real estate boom, found their ratios of nonliquidity rising materially as city real estate loans began to be added to the criticized assets beginning in 1926.

TABLE 106

FIXED AND QUESTIONABLE ASSETS PER $100 OF CAPITAL AND SURPLUS IN SELECTED BANKS SUSPENDING IN 1931

DATE	MEDIAN OR TYPICAL BANK IN				
	Cities of over 100,000 population (*16 banks*)	Other Industrial and suburban cities (*16 banks*)	Mining communities (*8 banks*)	North-eastern farming region (*10 banks*)	Other farming regions (*55 banks*)
1920	$ 11	$ 35	$ 42	$ 9	$ 22
1921	39	11	26	41	67
1922	28	26	22	24	73
1923	28	45	39	21	107
1924	36	36	43	80	114
1925	68	74	57	91	144
1926	46	62	41	106	159
1927	54	94	60	157	155
1928	55	90	58	172	183
1929—1st half	60	108	81	224	181
1929—2d half	107	165	97	199	188
1930—1st half	123	181	122	200	187
1930—2d half	168	211	153	196	220
1931—1st half	175	270	177	233	260

Loans to Officers, Directors, Relatives, and Their Interests

A study of the histories of representative active banks and banks which closed shows a wide difference in the amounts loaned to officers, directors, and related interests. The figures are given in Table 107.

TABLE 107

LOANS TO OFFICERS, DIRECTORS, AND THEIR INTERESTS PER $100 OF CAPITAL AND SURPLUS

	SUSPENDED BANKS		
DATE	120 banks suspending in 1920-1930 *(median)*	105 banks suspending in 1931 *(median)*	33 selected active banks *(median)*
1920—1st half	$30	$26	$19
1920—2d half	30		15
1921—1st half	31	29	25
1921—2d half	33		21
1922—1st half	30	33	19
1922—2d half	34		23
1923—1st half	36	31	15
1923—2d half	36		22
1924—1st half	32	33	12
1924—2d half	30		18
1925—1st half	30	38	16
1925—2d half	33		15
1926—1st half	34	36	18
1926—2d half	31		22
1927—1st half	34	39	22
1927—2d half	30		19
1928—1st half	32		12
1928—2d half	36	35	16
1929—1st half	30	38	10
1929—2d half	34	39	9
1930—1st half	33	38	6
1930—2d half		38	7
1931—1st half		39	

For active banks the general trend of these loans was downward, especially after 1927. For the banks suspending in 1931, however, the trend was upward, and just prior to failure the loans to officers, directors, etc., amounted to nearly 40 per cent of capital and surplus.

It is evident that the typical active bank reduced loans to the management when circumstances were favorable, whereas in many of the banks which later suspended the management increased their borrowings as the years passed, in spite of the fact that the condition of these banks was growing worse.

The median histories of the suspended banks, grouped according to the year of failure, were very similar to the composite for all the suspended banks as shown in the above table. Loans to officers, directors, and their interests were larger relative to capital and surplus than in the active banks, and these loans were not reduced as a rule during the years covered by the study.

TABLE 108

LOANS TO OFFICERS, DIRECTORS, AND THEIR INTERESTS PER $100 OF CAPITAL AND SURPLUS IN SELECTED BANKS SUSPENDING IN 1931

DATE	MEDIAN OR TYPICAL BANK IN				
	Cities of over 100,000 population (*16 banks*)	Other industrial and suburban cities (*16 banks*)	Mining communities (*8 banks*)	North-eastern farming region (*10 banks*)	Other farming regions (*55 banks*)
1920	$46	$37	$27	$24	$20
1921	52	53	33	36	21
1922	49	54	38	33	20
1923	51	60	29	42	21
1924	52	58	36	35	20
1925	50	65	45	40	26
1926	49	58	40	36	25
1927	60	49	46	35	27
1928	59	56	50	36	25
1929—1st half	60	56	53	39	29
1929—2d half	59	54	45	37	28
1930—1st half	53	66	46	34	29
1930—2d half	58	62	38	33	32
1931—1st half	60	53	32	34	32

A closer analysis of the 1931 bank failures shows that suspended banks in each of the economic regions habitually loaned larger amounts to their officers, directors, and related interests than the typical active bank. The heaviest lenders to these interests were the banks in large cities and in other industrial and suburban cities.

Control of Investment Policy

As has elsewhere been pointed out in the course of this study, the investments of banks have, within recent years, come to occupy a position of importance far superior to that of former times. The question has arisen in many minds whether the individual unit banks are sufficiently capable of exercising sound judgment with respect to the character of the investments that they are permitted to buy with banks funds, and whether, therefore, a much closer degree of supervision over these investments may not be necessary. It is the expressed opinion of one of the abler state superintendents of banking that unwise bond investments have been the primary cause of bank failures within the past two or three years in his district. When these questions are asked, however, they must be followed by another, namely, whether and if so, how far the superintendents of banks and the bank examination staffs generally are in a position to give wise and sound advice with respect to the direction of bank investments. Obviously if they are in such position that they are able at an early date to detect unsoundness in the use of the banks' funds in this connection, it may be possible in future years to reorganize our bank-examination system to an extent which will render it possible to check unsound use of bank funds in the purchase of bonds and other securities.

With a view to testing this matter, the Federal Reserve Committee, whose results have already been quoted, in connection with the use of bank funds and direct loans, have made an equally careful study of the securities situation in the same banks already referred to. It turns out that only one bank of the 1921-1930 group of suspensions which were selected for study had been criticized by examiners because of its investments. In fact most of the banks in that group had only negligible amounts of bonds. Among the 105 banks selected for study in 1931, however, a number had large bond accounts and serious trouble had arisen from efforts to make their investments yield too high a return. This effort had resulted in bond speculation, trading out the high-grade issues into low-grade issues during periods of rising bond prices and the purchase of undesirable bonds for the sake of high return. Nearly one-third of these banks were criticized by examiners more or less severely for their investments, and a number of others held bonds of poor quality. Bond depreciation was the primary cause of failure in six of the 105 suspensions, and an important contributing cause in 4 other cases. Such studies as have been made of the failures of 1932 also show that bond depreciation was a much larger factor as a cause of failure in that year than in 1931.

In endeavoring to obtain a fair basis of comparison for bond portfolios of the banks which were under investigation, the Federal Reserve Committee made use of a so-called bond-quality index, computed in such a way as to afford an arithmetical estimate of the relative desirability of the bond holdings of the several banks. The purpose of such indexes is indicated by the fact that if all the bonds chosen by the banks in question had been of I-a, or I-b grade, the index of quality would have been 100 per cent. The studies of the Federal Reserve Committee on this subject are lengthy and can be reproduced only in part, but the following excerpt from the study in question furnishes a general view of the situation developed as a result of the study:

The banks that failed in 1931 and were covered by this study fell far short of a satisfactory record in the matter of bond investments. Only 18 of the 105 banks had bond quality indexes over 90 per cent at the last examination before suspension, and only 30 had bond quality indexes over 80 per cent. Their records at earlier dates were not much better. Only 26 had bond quality indexes over 90 per cent one year prior to their last examination, and only 27 had bond quality indexes over 90 per cent two years prior to their last examination. On the other hand, 35 of these banks had bond quality indexes of 50 per cent or lower at the time of their last examination. This would indicate that their average bond holdings rated II-b or worse. One year before their last examination 27 of the banks used in this study had bond quality indexes of 50 per cent or lower, and two years before their last examination 17 had bond quality indexes of this very unsatisfactory character.

Unsatisfactory as the above figures show the bond buying habits of these banks to have been, they do not give an adequate picture of the holdings of those banks which were heavy bond buyers. In the list of 105 bank failures were a group of 49 banks whose bond holdings were small or negligible. Banks with very small bond holdings frequently hold nothing but United States Government bonds or high-grade municipal bonds, which are held for special purposes such as collateral for borrowed money or collateral for public deposits. Some of these banks hold nothing but United States Government bonds simply because they do not pretend to know anything about other bonds and wisely prefer to place the small amount of their investment funds in Government securities whose soundness is beyond question. Other banks hold United States Government bonds to improve the appearance of their balance sheets.

TABLE 109

BOND QUALITY INDEXES OF BANKS HAVING LESS THAN 15 PER CENT OF DEPOSITS IN MARKETABLE SECURITIES IN 1929

BOND QUALITY INDEX	NUMBER OF BANKS: Last examination before suspension	One year earlier	Two years earlier
95.1–100	12	12	12
90.1–95	3	6	5
85.1–90	5	2	5
80.1–85	0	2	2
75.1–80	4	3	5
70.1–75	1	4	2
65.1–70	4	1	2
60.1–65	1	4	2
55.1–60	2	0	3
50.1–55	1	2	0
45.1–50	0	3	1
40.1–45	5	2	1
35.1–40	1	0	0
30.1–35	0	0	0
25.1–30	0	0	0
20.1–25	1	0	0
15.1–20	0	0	1
10.1–15	0	0	1
5.1–10	1	0	0
.1 –5	0	1	1
0.	6	5	3
No securities	2	2	3
Total	49	49	49

For purposes of more intensive study the banks used in this survey were divided into two groups—those having marketable securities (at market prices and excluding circulation bonds and miscellaneous items) amounting to less than 15 per cent of their deposits in 1929, and those having marketable securities amounting to 15 per cent or more of their deposits in 1929. The dividing point between large securities portfolios and small ones was arbitrarily fixed at 15 per cent of deposits, without undertaking to take a position on the proper quantity of marketable bonds for a bank to own.

In Table 109 is shown the distribution of the banks in the first group (those with small bond accounts) according to the quality indexes of their bonds. The quality index distribution is given for three dates: the last examination before suspension, one year earlier, and two years earlier. It will be noted that 12 of these banks with small bond accounts had bond quality indexes ranging from 95.1 to 100 per cent. Most of these banks had few bonds other than United States Government securities. Two of the banks had no securities at the last examination before suspension. The remainder of the banks in this group had bond quality indexes ranging all the way from 95 to zero, showing that there was a great disparity among these banks in the grades of bonds held.

For the banks having larger bond accounts, that is, marketable bonds amounting to 15 per cent or more of deposits in 1929, the record of bond buying practices is even less satisfactory than in the group of banks with small bond accounts, as illustrated in Table 110. Only 3 out of 56 banks in this group had bond quality indexes above 90 per cent at the last examination before suspension, and only 10 had bond quality indexes above 90 per cent two years earlier. The remainder of the banks owned bonds whose average quality ranged from zero to 90 per cent, and in a large proportion of these banks the quality indexes were below 50 per cent.

A study of the relative qualities of the bond accounts of banks in various economic subdivisions of the country indicates that the bond accounts of banks in the farming communities were of better grade than those of banks in the cities and mining communities. One explanation of this fact is that the bond accounts of banks in the farming communities were usually a smaller percentage of deposits than in the case of the city banks, and consequently, it was probably true that government bonds constituted a larger percentage of the total bond holdings of rural banks than of city banks. It is customary for most banks to have a "backlog" of United States Government bonds and then, if circumstances permit, to invest other available funds in general market securities. A second factor accounting for part of the better bond quality indexes of banks in the farming country is that those banks are large recipients of public deposits of minor government subdivisions. The government officials require collateral or surety bonds for these deposits and generally designate high-grade municipal and other securities for this purpose. Unfortunately, it is impossible to isolate pledged securities for special analysis. A third reason, which appears to have accounted for some of the unfavorable comparison between the bond habits of city banks and country banks, is the fact that the city banks were more exposed to speculative influences, and this speculative sentiment pervaded their bond policies.

TABLE 110

BOND QUALITY INDEXES OF BANKS HAVING 15 PER CENT OR MORE OF DEPOSITS IN MARKETABLE SECURITIES IN 1929

BOND QUALITY INDEX	NUMBER OF BANKS		
	Last examination before suspension	One year earlier	Two years earlier
95.1–100	1	4	4
90.1–95	2	4	6
85.1–90	4	3	2
80.1–85	3	3	8
75.1–80	1	7	5
70.1–75	9	5	6
65.1–70	5	8	6
60.1–65	4	5	7
55.1–60	5	2	5
50.1–55	3	0	1
45.1–50	3	6	3
40.1–45	4	5	2
35.1–40	3	1	1
30.1–35	5	2	0
25.1–30	1	0	0
20.1–25	1	0	0
15.1–20	1	0	0
10.1–15	0	0	0
5.1–10	0	0	0
.1– 5	0	0	0
0	1	0	0
Total	56	55*	56

* One bond list not furnished to the Committee.

Using the bond-quality indexes two years prior to failure as the best test of the bond-buying habits of the banks with the larger bond accounts, it was found that 7 out of 28 banks in farming communities had bond-quality indexes above 90 per cent, whereas only 1 bank out of 11 in the large cities had a bond-quality index above 90 per cent, and only 2 out of 10 banks in the smaller industrial and suburban cities had bond-quality indexes of this grade. No banks in the mining communities had indexes above 90 per cent.

Securities Depreciation.—With the available material this study attempts to show the total amount of depreciation in the securities accounts of the banks which failed and the classes of banks suffering most heavily from securities depreciation. Two methods have been used to measure the depreciation in the security accounts of

TABLE 111

SECURITIES DEPRECIATION PER $100 OF LOANS AND INVESTMENTS

(Securities do not include circulation bonds)

DEPRECIATION	NUMBER OF BANKS: Two years before last examination	Last examination
Appreciation	7	15
$0	21	14
0.1– 1	56	26
1.1– 2	7	11
2.1– 3	7	10
3.1– 4	3	2
4.1– 5	1	6
5.1– 6	1	3
6.1– 7	1	3
7.1– 8	0	5
8.1– 9	1	1
9.1–10	0	0
10.1–15	0	5
15.1–20	0	2
20.1–25	0	0
25.1–30	0	1
30.1–35	0	1
Total	105	105

the sample banks. The first was to compare the amount of depreciation with loans and investments and with capital funds. The second method was to compare securities depreciation with the book value of the securities owned.

The securities whose depreciation was compared with loans and investments and with capital funds were the total bonds and securities of each bank, excluding circulation bonds. Circulation bonds usually sell at a premium, and their price fluctuations are subject to influences quite different from those affecting other securities.

Depreciation on securities, as shown in Table 111, was not large relative to loans and investments, even at the last examination of the sample banks. All but 9 of the banks had depreciation in their securities accounts of less than 10 per cent of loans and investments at their last examination. Of the 9 banks with depreciation of more than 10 per cent of loans and investments, only 4 had depreciation of over 15 per cent of loans and investments, and only 2 had depreciation of more than 25 per cent of loans and investments. Two years before their last examinations none of the sample banks had depreciation in their securities accounts of more than 10 per cent of loans and investments.

Securities depreciation is compared with capital funds in Table 112. Capital funds include the capital stock, surplus, undivided profits, and sundry reserves of the failed banks.

The second method of measuring securities depreciation was to compare the depreciation with the value at which the securities were carried on the books of each bank. The investments used in this comparison are those used in constructing the bond quality indexes. United States Government bonds held by these banks as collateral for national bank notes, and miscellaneous items, such as foreclosures, claims, judgments, tax certificates, etc., were omitted from this tabulation. The miscellaneous items excluded from the total investments were usually a very small part of the total investment account, but there were a few exceptions. In 4 of the 105 failed banks used in the 1931 study, all or the greater part of the bonds and securities (excluding circulation bonds) consisted of these miscellaneous items.

At the time of their last examination before suspension, the 105 banks owned securities (excluding circulation bonds and $430,000 of miscellaneous items) with a book value of $69,753,972. The market value, however, was only $59,779,938, resulting in a depreciation of $9,974,034, or 14.3 per cent. One year earlier the book value of the securities of these banks was slightly higher and the depreciation amounted to only 7.3 per cent. Two years earlier the book value of the securities of these banks was about $2,000,000 higher than in 1931 and the depreciation was only 3.8 per cent.

Another sample.—In order to get another sample of the banking situation as viewed from the standpoint of examination, we have devoted some attention to the studies of failed banks in the state of New York during the period 1929-1932 inclusive. The results there obtained have been summarized more at length under the general discussion of failures, where it was shown that in the opinion of the banking authorities of the state of New York, the three major causes of failure may be said to have consisted of: (1) unsatisfactory bond investments, (2) loans to officers and directors, and (3) operations in real estate. Nothing was there said of the question how far the ob-

TABLE 112

SECURITIES DEPRECIATION PER $100 OF CAPITAL FUNDS

(Securities do not include circulation bonds)

DEPRECIATION	NUMBER OF BANKS: Two years before last examination	Last examination
Appreciation	8	15
$ 0	21	14
0.1– 10	58	33
10.1– 20	7	14
20.1– 30	5	4
30.1– 40	6	3
40.1– 50	0	5
50.1– 60	0	4
60.1– 70	0	4
70.1– 80	0	1
80.1– 90	0	0
90.1–100	0	2
100.1–110	0	1
110.1–120	0	0
120.1–130	0	2
130.1–140	0	0
140.1–150	0	1
150.1–160	0	1
160.1–170	0	0
170.1–180	0	1
Total	105	105

jectionable dealings of the banks had or had not been actually open to criticism by the superintendent of banks and his staff of examiners, and, accordingly, a few general comments upon it are worth while at this point.

The investigation shows that in the case of practically every such bank the institution had been open to criticism for a long time before it actually came to the point of failure, and with such criticism reflected practically the same elements that were found to exist in the case of studies of the Federal Reserve Committee. The failure was, in short, in practically every instance the outcome of a long period of disregard of the criticisms that had been offered from time to time when examination of the bank's condition had revealed situations that called for improvement.

Senate Committee's Inquiry into Examinations

The Senate Banking Committee, very early in its inquiry, determined to devote some special attention to the status of bank examinations and with this in mind it addressed certain questions to the examination authorities of various grades. The result of these inquiries threw a bright light upon the present examination status, particularly with those phases of it which have to do with security portfolios. We can not do better than to reproduce here the essential features of the examination system as thus discussed by the inquiry.[5]

Examination of Security Loans and Investments

There are three kinds of examinations to which commercial banks may be subjected. The first, which applies to all banks, is the examination prescribed by Federal or State statute. In the case of national banks, this is carried out by the Comptroller of the Currency, while for State institutions the respective State departments of banking perform this function.

A second kind of examination is that made by the Federal Reserve banks of their member institutions. Such examination is less formal, and usually much less complete, than in the case of the examinations prescribed by statute for the legally constituted authorities already referred to. This is a natural consequence of the fact that the Federal Reserve examination is designed in the main to determine the soundness of rediscounts or advances secured by United States Government bonds made by the reserve bank to its members, as well as the soundness of the member institutions in relation to the activities of the Federal Reserve bank as collecting agent for out-of-town checks.

The Federal Reserve Bank of Chicago describes its practices in

[5] *Hearings before Subcommittee on Banking and Currency, United States Senate,* 71 Cong. 3d Sess., S. Res. 71, Part VII, pp. 1069-1080, as cited in Willis, Chapman, and Robey, *Contemporary Banking* (Harper Brothers, New York, 1933), pp. 406-7.

the examination of member banks, which appear to be typical for the system, as follows:

"Supervision of national banks rests with the Comptroller of the Currency, and of State banks with the State banking departments. Copies of the reports of examination of all national banks are filed with us by the comptroller's representatives, and copies of reports of examinations of all member State banks by the respective State banking departments, five States being represented. All reports are carefully analyzed by agent's department, and a complete report made thereon in each case, with its own classifications and conclusions.

Our field work in actual examinations is confined to a limited number of State banks, principally the smaller institutions. A special examination is made for our own account of all State banks applying for membership. In addition, we are in contact with all member banks in the district through frequent calls by men in our bank relations department, from whom we get much valuable information as to management of banks and general conditions.

A third kind of examination is that carried out by a limited number of local clearing houses. Originally designed to protect the members of a clearing house from losses they might incur from the failure of a member, whose checks they might freely receive for deposit and immediate credit, such examinations have in some cases become quite comprehensive. In the case of the New York Clearing House, for example, the examination of members has become so thorough, and insistence upon compliance with recommendations made is so great, that such examination is now regarded as considerably more significant than that of the statutory authorities, while the examination by the Federal Reserve bank in that district has tended to become more and more perfunctory, reliance being placed upon the other examining agencies for the most part by the reserve bank. The fact that no bank belonging to the New York Clearing House has ever been closed because of insolvency is attributed in part to the effectiveness of its system of examination.

The increased importance of security loans, investments, and security affiliates in the operations of commercial banks has made these items loom larger in recent years in any comprehensive examination of the condition of individual banks. The subcommittee addressed a questionnaire to bank examiners of the three classes mentioned to determine their practices with regard to loans and investments.

Present Status and Problems of Examination

The general situation with reference to examination may now be advantageously summed up—partly on the basis of the inquiries already reviewed, including particularly those of the Senate Committee on Banking and of the Federal Reserve Bank Committee of Inquiry in its study of case histories. Reviewing the situation as thus set forth, we seem to be warranted in stating the following general conclusions:

1. The bank examination system of the United States at the present time, no matter how or by whom carried on, has not resulted in preventing bank failures or embarrassments as is amply proven by the immense and unprecedented record of bank failures occurring during recent years.

2. This record of bank failures does not depend upon conditions in the "country" for its support, since as a matter of fact, serious embarrassments of large banks, to say nothing of striking cases of malfeasance in office or actual dishonesty which were not detected—certainly not corrected, by the work of the examination staffs—have been recognized within recent years. Conspicuous examples of this sort have been furnished by the notorious cases of the Bank of the United States and the Harriman Bank of New York, the Bank of Kentucky in Louisville, Ky., and many others, some of them perhaps only less striking than the ones which have just been mentioned.

3. Bank examinations are apparently most successful in their bearing upon ordinary "straight" loans on commercial paper, and are less successful in their relationship to investment paper, bonds, and similar securities. This latter weakness is apparently due to inexperience and lack of information in the judgment of bonds by examination staffs, and partly to the fact that most bank-examination staffs have been in the habit of judging bonds on the basis of their marketability rather than by applying to them the same tests that would ordinarily be applied to commercial paper in the effort to ascertain the degree of its goodness.

4. Analysis seems to show that within the limits thus indicated the faults of bank examinations are found largely in an

unwillingness on the part of the examiners to insist upon the observance of their findings, and a readiness on their part to acquiesce in the wishes or dictates of outside interests or, perhaps, to withhold positive action in the belief that by so doing they may succeed in alleviating or smoothing over dangerous conditions which would otherwise develop into more widespread financial troubles.

5. Of the various kinds of bank examination the most successful is probably that which has been applied by the banks to one another through self-examination; and now that a bank deposit guarantee has been enacted into law, it would seem likely that self-examination by the banks through joint action, analogous to that heretofore initiated by clearing houses, would be likely to furnish the best solution of the examination problem.

6. Outstanding examples of direct political interference and favoritism in which examiners failed to enforce laws and regulations, and even to exact the observance of the principles of common honesty, have been developed by recent legislative inquiries. The conclusion strongly to be enforced as the result of such disclosures is the absolute necessity for eliminating political interference with bank examiners or with bank administration. This action probably emphasizes the conclusion already set forth, that the effective examination of the future will be one conducted by the banks themselves.

7. The question whether Federal Reserve banks may or may not be used as the medium through which bank examination shall be carried on, is one which has been under discussion for a good many years. It was originally supposed that the Reserve banks would be ideal agencies through which to conduct mutual supervision of banks over one another's affairs designed to bring about a sounder condition of bank portfolio. Experience has not confirmed this anticipation, due to the fact that the Reserve banks have apparently been unwilling to act vigorously in the examination of their members; partly because of a feeling on their part that their members are already subject to very exacting requirements at the hands of state and national

examiners, and partly because of the fact that they have been so largely controlled by important banking interests which have had their own purposes to serve. Future success in making the Federal Reserve Banks an effective agency in the management of examinations must be largely dependent upon the extent to which it is possible to strengthen and improve the directorates of Federal Reserve Banks.

8. Under the new system of banking called into existence by the Banking Act of 1933, and particularly in view of the necessities and obligations which will grow out of the provision for guarantee of bank deposits, it will be quite essential to do two things: (*a*) to detect early, and before it becomes rooted, any evidence of unsoundness in portfolio or method of operation of banks; (*b*) to apply to such conditions, when detected, unhesitating remedies in order that they may not be permitted to assume a confirmed or rooted appearance.

The examination system is thus simultaneously placed on trial before the country because of its failure to correct disastrously bad conditions which have led to an unprecedented epidemic of failures and partly because of the initiation of a new system of mutual responsibility, whose success will depend entirely upon early knowledge (and correction) of dangerous tendencies. These problems would be much simpler in a highly concentrated branch-banking system in which each large bank was familiar with the condition of its various branches, while the few such large banks in existence maintained fairly careful supervision of one another. The Banking Act of 1933 has continued the small banking system and has again endeavored to protect it.

From any point of view, it is likely that a system of rather wide diffusion will continue for a long time to be characteristic of banking in the United States. In such circumstances, closer reliance upon examination would seem to be essential, and this must imply immediate improvement and strengthening of the examination system in such a way as to enable it to produce its best results.

PART IV

BANK PORTFOLIOS

CHAPTER XXII

BANK PORTFOLIOS AND BANK OPERATIONS

INTRODUCTION

We have surveyed the principal facts relating to the structure and to the changing character of the control of the banking system of the United States. It is now necessary to devote our attention to the internal condition of the banks, and to note with some care the general direction that has been taken by the asset holdings of the banks in constituting their portfolios. It is at this point that the banking situation establishes its closest relationship to the condition of business. Were it true that banking methods and banking portfolios continued approximately identical, regardless of changing conditions of structure and of corporate control, it would be unnecessary to do more than lay down the general principles of bank operation, which should give rise to a sound portfolio or asset position on the part of the banks.

The fact is, however, that fundamental changes in structure and size, such as those we have been reviewing, and, still more important, basic alterations of corporate control, tend to produce fundamental changes in the type of the portfolio held by the banks, while the changing character of the portfolio, itself, in turn, brings about alterations in structure and management. In many ways, the analysis of bank portfolios thus becomes the central, or crucial, element in correctly estimating the position of banking at any given time. It is moreover true that careful portfolio analysis materially assists in forming a correct idea of major changes that are in progress in business generally. It is, accordingly, necessary to devote, as already stated, analytical attention to the problem of which we have spoken.

In approaching the subject of bank portfolios and investments, it is desirable, first of all, to outline in general terms the basic ideas fundamental to bank operation, and particularly to bank operation in the United States, in order that standards of judgment available for the criticism of the statistical showing made by actual bank portfolios at any given time may be in hand.

The bank is, of course, an institution whose purpose may be stated as follows:[1]

Determination of Quantity of Credit

(1) The business of the bank is that of judging and determining credit, and of exchanging such credit for its own in various forms of the latter:

(2) in carrying on this business, the bank undertakes to maintain its credit upon a basis convertible into that of other institutions, normally into money either upon time or at demand, and usually at demand;

(3) its ability to continue such convertibility depends upon the character of the assets it holds, and upon the rate at which it is likely to be asked to make the conversion;

(4) the latter rate depends essentially upon the kind of credit it has placed in circulation, and upon the "turnover" or rate of presentation which the business customs and habits of the community call for. Bank operation is fundamentally a process of exchanging credit against credit, as has just been pointed out, but it is also a process of determining how much credit can be kept outstanding and of fixing the amount exchanged or assumed at a level which will allow this maintenance of exchangeability.

One of the basic problems of the bank thus seems to settle down into a determination of the conditions under which redemption or conversion is likely to be asked, and the making of provision for meeting it. Such provision may consist in the getting of the new counterclaims that have been spoken of above, or it may consist in the provision of arrangements for converting assets into funds when and as needed, or it may consist in arrangements for the quicker cancellation of such claims.

Every banker has to decide in his own mind what his institution is capable of doing in the granting or establishment of new credit —or, to put the matter practically, he is called upon to determine, as skillfully and successfully as may be, what total "line of credit" he is able or authorized to put into circulation, or use, and to keep

[1] This extract was taken from Chapter XVI, *Contemporary Banking*, by Willis, Chapman, and Robey, pp. 285, 286 and 292 to 298.

redeemed or convertible into immediate funds. A mistake in such calculation is likely to result in the presentation to the bank for redemption, of claims at a rate in excess of what it can arrange to meet, or else the presentation to it at the clearing house or through collections from other places of claims larger than it can arrange to settle through compensation by the presentation to others of claims on themselves which it has received.

Practically the bank must, therefore, have a steady flow of "new business," or what is ordinarily called "deposits"—increases of credit on its own books against other banks, or else it must content itself with the ascertainment of the point of equilibrium at which its business is likely to take care of itself—its claim on others balancing their claims upon it, so that it is satisfied not to increase the size of its total credit lines, but to remain in a stable position with an approximately stable volume of business and of exchanges. In some institutions growth comes as the result of advertising, solicitation and general effort to obtain new accounts; in others, simply as the result of a slowly growing reputation for honesty and reliability; in still others, merely as the result of the steady growth of the community and of its resources which tends to place more and more credit claims with the banks as population and business increase.

Investments

At an earlier point reference has been made to the concept of bank investments, it being then suggested that these holdings represent the use given to the surplus funds of the bank for which no profitable employment has been found in the course of the regular extension of credits represented by "deposits." It is necessary at this point to indicate how these investments fit with the conception of bank management that has been presented in the accompanying pages. In so doing we must, moreover, recognize the fact that the banker, in practical life, feels two inducements tending to lead him to put his funds into the investment form. One is the fact that there is a surplus of funds for which there is no immediate call on the part of the bank's direct-credit customers, who wish to have the institution serve them through the familiar channels already indicated—those of exchanging their own credit for the bank's credit forms. The other is the fact that often, due to lack of accurate adjustment between the money and investment markets, there appears to be an advantage in interest rates on the side of the investment as against the rate to be earned on bank paper.

Here the familiar principle that no increase of income is likely to be secured without a corresponding increase of risk stands out as conspicuously as usual and suggests that, even in cases where there is large return to be had through the entering of the investment market—as, for instance, by the making of call loans when rates are very high—the policy is one that must be carefully considered. The rates are placed high in order to induce funds to move out of the one market and into the other, and the result may be a curtailment of the credit resources available at the banks in order to take advantage of what looks like an opportunity to reap a harvest of larger income. If foresighted, the banker will in such cases guide himself not primarily by the rate to be earned, but by the probable effect on his own business for the future. He may have customers whose need for aid in connection with their investment commitments is serious, and who will be helped more by direct purchases on his part or by collateral loans intended to enable them to carry investments already bought or spoken for than they will by the conservation of his resources for the support of the usual bank credit operations. On the other hand, such assistance to them may involve far too great a hazard or far too great a drain upon his own resources. This is a problem which calls for great care in adjustment of the holdings or commitments in long-term or investment credit to the holdings of current short-term paper, and presents one of the issues that are always to the fore in practical management of the banking business.

"Portfolio" Concept

The thought that there is a logical, or wise, or "scientific" adjustment of bank assets which shall give a due place to quick paper, another to slower or longer maturities, and a proper position to investments, proportioning all in such a way as to get the maximum yield, with maximum safety and at the same time with maximum practical service to the customer, is the root of the conception of bank "portfolios." The term is ordinarily used as meaning merely the entire list of assets carried by the institution, but its appropriate application is broader and indicates the policy pursued in the making up of the lists of assets.

A bank portfolio, in other words, is not merely a collection of assets but a grouping that has been made with an eye to the logical and serviceable arrangement to which reference has been made above; it is a collection of assets arranged or chosen on banking principles. Thus an excellent portfolio means not, as often interpreted, a safe, or peculiarly sound or liquid, group of assets, but a holding that has been arranged with an eye to the best interests of the bank, all things considered. The portfolio may thus be thought of as the embodiment of banking principle, in practical operation. The proper development of the portfolio may thus be spoken of as the chief object of the work of the banker.

What is called "diversification" is frequently mentioned as an element in the formation of the portfolio, but it is questionable whether this concept has any place there. It is an investment banking idea, and the thought that the commercial bank is warranted in its placement of funds in taking risks that are more or less offset by averaging them (which is the notion at the bottom of the diversification idea) seems to lack a sound basis in the theory of banking. The principles already indicated in connection with portfolio make-up take their rise from a radically different conception—that of credit analysis combined with analysis of the actual position of the bank itself.

In developing portfolios on these lines, reference is frequently made to the time element, and there is often an assumption that the making up of a portfolio is largely a matter of adjusting maturities. Thus, if deposits are classed as time and demand, it is often suggested that the banker's portfolio should provide for demand claims upon others or for paper that can be realized practically at will, while it should likewise provide for time investments or long-term paper corresponding to the time deposits, thus affording opportunity to the bank to make use of its time funds in a profitable fashion, as it may be able to do to good advantage if it be free of the necessity of purchasing only narrowly limited types of short-term paper. This, however, rests upon a misconception of the nature of credit.

Time Element in Credit

This misconception grows out of the familiar and erroneous thought already referred to, that the bank lends something—usually described as "money." If it lends—then, of course, it lends for a certain time either stated or later determined, as in call and demand loans, since time is the essence of a loan. Thinking of banking as a process of exchanging credit of one type for credit of another, it is at once seen that considerable modification of this view is needful. The bank's credit contract, as we have seen, is a contract of guaranty rather than a time contract. It is quite true that the guaranty is to last for a definite time, and for that only, but that is merely a convenient way of limiting the liability of the bank. As a matter of fact, time does not necessarily enter into the relationship between banker and borrower at all. The bank is concerned with present, not future, values, and when it discounts a piece of paper or takes a note from a customer it estimates the real present worth and ability of the borrower to pay, and it bases its action thereon.

The time of the loan presumably corresponds to the period required by the borrower to bring to the consumer the goods which are in process of exchange. The loan is not a transfer of capital to be employed for a certain time and then recovered and returned to the bank. It is a guaranty to the world at large that, for a given period, the bank will stand ready to give to anyone who may be entitled to it the actual economic value in terms of general purchasing power represented by the economic processes going forward under the direction of the customer. The bank does not usually lend on an indefinite contract, though a considerable proportion of loans at some banks are frequently made on demand, as, e.g., in 1929, but it wishes to know the term for which its liability is to extend. Its task then consists in adjusting these contracts of customers' liability (or what we call loans) to its contracts of bank liability (customarily termed deposits).

In thinking of this principle, it will be found easier to grasp its general bearings if we remember that, whereas bank loans are constantly being paid off and canceled, the general body of bank deposits goes on increasing, while the body of bank paper held likewise usually increases from year to year. There is no such "payment" as is ordinarily imagined in connection with banking, and in the nature of the case cannot be, since the values with which banking deals are continuously engaged in bank operations and cannot be withdrawn without destroying the structure of business. The bare fact that, whereas total outstanding deposits on the books of the banks of the United States are usually between $40,000,000,000 and $60,000,000,000, the total supply of coin of every kind in the hands of the inhabitants is not over $5,000,000,000 at the utmost enforces this view of the situation.

Payment of bank credit is merely a release of the contract of mutual liability made between banker and customer whenever a loan is negotiated. The portfolio, therefore, is not an adjustment of periods within which a loan will be repaid, but is an adjustment of contracts of liability or liquidating power; and the banker, in making up his portfolio, finds the problems presented to him those which have to do with the real nature of the transactions underlying the advances he makes. If they relate to the exchange of goods, he is warranted in undertaking to guarantee them; whereas, if they grow out of the production of goods or ownership of capital, he is warranted in such an undertaking only to the extent that he has in his hands funds which are not to be employed by their holders in current operations at all—but which are definitely set aside as a fund from which income is to be realized by the process of production. The portfolio judgment of the banker is thus seen to be a judgment resting upon information as to the kind and character of the operations or transactions in which the borrower is engaged, not of the time for which he wants a "loan" of "money."

Liquidity Concept

The idea of liquidity as the practical test of sound bank credit is directly in opposition to that of what has been called "shiftability," and is likewise opposed to the view that banking operations are loans made for a definite time and hence susceptible to arrangement on the footing of maturity. It represents the view that in every transaction some one must make a decision which determines the uses to be made of funds employed in such transactions. It further assumes that in every operation there is fairly definite possibility of converting its resources into direct consumption credit. The bank has, to be sure, this power of conversion and has, as we shall see, various rules of credit test currently applied for that purpose.

Liquidity, in other words, is the power inherent in production and consumption operations to obtain titles to actual current wealth, as distinct from what may be produced in the future or may be derived from later employment of productive capital in the turning out of goods that will be wanted by actual users at a later date. This conversion power in business operations is what the banker has to measure, and should afford the limit of current bank credit at any given moment. It is true, of course, that banks often extend credits or make loans upon security that confessedly represents production goods, or in some cases deficits in operating expenses, backed or made good by nothing more substantial than titles to productive capital that may or may not be profitably operated at some time in the future.

In such cases the extension of credit is merely an undertaking to maintain convertibility of credit into immediate funds which can be made good only to the extent that the bank itself is in possession of unused purchasing power belonging to its depositors and not being at the time applied by them. If and when they call for this buying power, the bank will find itself unable to continue the extension of credit on long-term or "frozen" assets and will be under the necessity of effecting conversion. This it can do only by obtaining a transfer of purchasing power from some other bank or by inducing the central bank to carry through in its favor a somewhat similar operation.

"Shiftability," as already seen, implies the continued existence somewhere of a market for long-term securities which stands ready to effect their conversion upon demand of the holder. This market must itself draw its conversion power from the same general fund already described, and if that fund be already in use to its full extent, the market will disappear—not because the securities are worthless, or even possibly reduced in value, but because there is no surplus of free or available current funds that may be employed in buying or advancing funds upon them in the shape of loans.

Summary and Review of Conflicting Ideas

To summarize the discussion thus offered, we may say that bank operation is essentially a process whereby those who have free purchasing power are induced to place it at the disposal of those who are temporarily out of possession of it, and that the bank finds its sphere of operations limited by the total amount of such power in existence and transferable. The bank is thus not able to "create" credit, as is often supposed, but must confine itself to the recognition of its existence followed, when desired, by a process of guaranty. This latter process results in the establishment of bank deposits (or the issue of notes) or the extension of some other form of credit in favor of customers.

Customers may then employ the purchasing power thus placed in their hands or they may not. The rate at which they do so employ it is the "turnover" of deposits and measures the rate at which the banker is likely to be called upon to make good his guaranty. His problem is that of arranging his holdings of paper or other assets in a way that will permit him at all times to meet probable demands of this sort and to be ready to meet increased calls whose presentation had not been anticipated. His investments represent such margin or portion of his control of wealth as is quite certainly not to be called for conversion, and which he, therefore, may place in the field of productive capital. His eventual measure of soundness is found in the liquidity of his holdings, which means their correspondence to current wealth not yet specialized as productive capital.

"Shiftability" fails as a test because it depends upon the maintenance of a market which itself depends for its existence upon the readiness of banks and other holders of current wealth to effect conversion when required.

Other Phases of Bank Portfolios and Bank Operation[2]

A great deal of the discussion of banking in the United States, indeed in all countries, relates to matters which have presented themselves in connection with current operating problems. Differences of opinion or questions of judgment have arisen and the result has been that when loss occurred there was a tendency to place the responsibility for such loss upon matters of policy or to take the view that a different method of operation would have avoided disaster or sacrifice. Ordinarily these differences of opinion relate to individual problems of selection in connection with paper or securities or advances of various kinds. From time to time, however, issues of a more general nature present themselves, and there is question at such times about the broader aspects of policy or with reference to the choice of one view as against another of banking management.

In the United States within the past fifteen years, since the close of the World War, a broad issue of banking policy of this sort has presented itself. Difference of opinion has arisen regarding the policy properly to be pursued by banks in the general application of their resources. The tremendous losses followed by the write-down of assets that has been necessitated since 1929, and the further writing down that is already seen to be necessary, has convinced many that policies adopted after the close of the World War were erroneous. Out of this has grown the strong feeling in many quarters that more strict control over banking policies ought to be applied and that such control

[2] The remainder of this chapter is written by H. Parker Willis.

might well be enforced as a result of new legislation designed to specify with greater care the character of the assets to be acquired by banking institutions. Thus, the "portfolio" of the bank—the uses to be made of its funds—has come to be the central point of a sharply disputed public issue.

There is certainly ample warrant for the discussion of bank portfolios that has originated as a result of a hazardous condition of the banks. The enormous numbers of bank failures that have taken place within the past ten years or more, and the vast amount of bank assets which were held "immobilized" as a result of the closing of many institutions, and inability to bring the process of liquidation to a close, have inflicted immense suffering upon large numbers of depositors.

A study of the portfolios of American banks during the fifteen years since the close of the World War shows great transformations in their composition; and a review of them since the year 1915 shows almost a revolution. These changes have occurred as a result of corresponding alterations in the kinds of loans the banks were making, which means in the kind of business which they were, generally speaking, transacting. The general direction of change has been away from so-called short-term advances and in the direction of long-term, by which is ordinarily meant that instead of discounting paper made originally for 30, 60, or 90 days, for the financing of business, banks have, on the whole, been inclined to make loans either on demand without definite maturity or, where the maturity was definite, subject to renewal agreements or understandings so that in fact they were "frozen" and could not be liquidated without the sale of the assets (collateral) held behind them, or by which they were protected.

The changes so brought about reflect some important alterations, both of technique and of theory in connection with American banking. From the technical standpoint they reflect the fact that in a majority of cases the loan is not made for so-called "capital purposes" with the intention on the part of the borrower to keep the funds for use in his business, paying them off when, if, and as, necessary, by obtaining a loan of equal amount in some other quarter. In such a case the loan, although technically payable at an early maturity, is actually not so payable but represents a claim upon business of some kind which may be transferred to another holder so long as the business itself continues prosperous or at least able to meet its obligations. The fact that in many banks a large part of the portfolio consists of obligations of this sort is frequently spoken of as an indication of "bad banking." Whatever may be thought on that point the more important aspect of the situation is that the notion represents a great change in the type of banking, or the canons of banking and, thus, is a circumstance which is of considerably greater importance in any long term consideration of the facts in the case.

The circumstance that for many years past banking legislation, both in England and the United States, has preferred loans or short term, and has assumed that bankers of the community would invariably stick to investments with early maturity, has colored our entire banking law and is based upon a conception of banking now more than a century old. This conception of banking calls for the maintenance of what is called "liquidity," and presupposes that the portfolio of the bank will invariably consist of such assets as may be easily realized upon; with the result that their proceeds can, upon short notice, be brought back into the possession of the bank for use in making immediate payments to depositors upon demand. The National Bank Act and most state banking laws have been framed upon the assumption that it was desirable to constitute bank portfolios in this way, and the Federal Reserve Act expressly limits the maturities of the paper which is to be rediscounted for members in such a way as to keep the portfolio very short-term in character. Much of the National Bank Act, as indeed all state bank legislation, centers, in so far as it relates to bank operations, upon means of insuring this early maturity and guaranteeing prompt convertibility and capacity to realize with a view to enabling the bank presumably to protect itself against sudden drafts upon it originating with depositors.

As has already been stated the conception that has come to prevail in recent years has been based upon a definite premise and in not a few instances has sought chiefly to insure what is called "convertibility of assets." Its object—to insure the making of loans by banks on the basis of the paper of business men—ought rather to make sure that such loans were made upon paper that was most salable in the open market. It is easy to see toward what ultimate object this latter type of legislation has been steadily tending. Whenever it became desirable to borrow from a bank for the purpose of financing a business, the question usually raised by classical writers relative to the liquidity of the paper—meaning, thereby, the capacity of the borrower to settle his note out of his current obligations—became practically obsolete. The real question was not whether the business enterprise in which the funds were being used was able to meet its obligations out of current income, but was whether this enterprise could probably succeed in transferring the loan elsewhere.

It is evident that under these circumstances the canons of banking tended to shift very frequently from their older position and to assume an entirely new orientation. If, for example, a given bank had been in the habit of devoting itself largely to the study of its customers' financial statements, with a view to seeing how the business of such customers was shaping itself, and whether in all probability it was likely to turn out profitable; it now recognized the necessity of shifting its ground and of asking primarily, not whether the concern could easily settle, but whether the bank would be able to find a ready sale for the obligations of the enterprise. Bank credit analysis, in short, has tended to be superseded by the study of the stock market and of the conditions of stock-market development and soundness.

This change in character of the situation was recognized by the Federal Reserve Board as early as 1926. The annual report for that year noted the character of the situation, remarking that,

> The growth in investments and loans on securities, which was characteristic of the two years preceding 1926, was in line with the general trend of banking developments in other recent years. Since the middle of 1915 loans and investments of all the banks in the country have increased by over $30,000,000,000, and about one-third of this increase or about $10,000,000,000, was in the banks' holdings

of investments. These holdings constituted 30 per cent of total loans and investments in the middle of 1926, compared with 27 per cent 11 years earlier. At national banks, which constitute the larger part of the system's membership, there has also been a marked tendency in recent years to use an increasing proportion of their resources in long-term investments. Between the end of June, 1915, and the end of June, 1926, investments of national banks increased from $2,068,000,000 to $5,842,000,000 and their proportion of the banks' total loans and investments from 24 per cent to 30 per cent. At the same time loans on securities also increased rapidly, and loans on real estate rose from $150,000,000 to $725,000,000, while other loans, though they also increased in absolute amount, declined relatively from 56 per cent to 45 per cent of the banks' total loans and investments.

This increased use of bank funds in longer term enterprises, which has continued for a number of years, has been particularly pronounced in the recent five-year period of growth of bank credit beginning in the spring of 1922. Table 113 shows the composition of the earning assets of reporting member banks in leading cities in the spring of 1922 and at the end of 1926.

During this period of nearly five years the proportion of loans and investments of member banks in leading cities that was in securities and in loans on securities increased from 49 to 57 per cent. The largest growth, both absolutely and relatively, was in security loans, which increased by about 66 per cent during the period.

The change thus noted in 1926 was again observed in succeeding years and was particularly a subject of comment in 1929. It has been, likewise, the subject of frequent commentary in other quarters, and, generally speaking, is now a very widely accepted fact in the banking situation. Precisely how far this tendency has gone however, and the direction that it has taken, is much less clear. The following pages have been written with a view to giving the results of some statistical and other inquiry into this matter, and thus of furnishing the basis for a definite judgment as to the extent or degree in which real changes of a permanent nature have taken place in the banking portfolios of the United States.

One other phase of the situation deserves further attention,

TABLE 113

REPORTING MEMBER BANKS IN LEADING CITIES

(In millions of dollars)

					PER CENT OF TOTAL			
	TOTAL LOANS AND INVEST-MENTS	LOANS ON SECURI-TIES	ALL OTHER LOANS	IN-VEST-MENTS	Loans on Securi-ties	All Other Loans	In-vest-ments	Loans on Securities plus in-vestments
March 8, 1922	14,527	3,530	7,366	3,631	24.3	50.7	25.0	49.3
December 29, 1926	20,110	5,852	8,717	5,541	29.1	43.3	27.6	56.7
Percentage of increase	38.4	65.8	18.3	52.8	—	—	—	—

in a preliminary way. It requires but little study of the banking laws of the United States, whether state or national, to make clear the fact that most of the regulation and the control that had been exerted over banks had been exerted for the purpose of insuring a conservative or "safe" handling of so-called short-term or "liquid" paper. From the date of the adoption of the National Bank Act in 1863, straight on down to the present time, the long succession of laws relating to banking has devoted itself chiefly and fundamentally to the protection of all short term loans and the guaranteeing of liquidity. This, in part, is to be ascribed to the fact that the older theories of banking in Great Britain, and later in the United States, unquestioningly accepted the view that a sound bank was one whose portfolio was liquid, so that legislation which aimed at soundness necessarily aimed incidentally at liquidity. In part, however, the fact that our banking legislation took this almost exclusive trend, was owing to the fact that two generations ago the number of publicly traded securities was still small with relatively few actually listed upon stock exchanges, and only a moderately larger number possessing a recognized standard of quality which would fit them, even from the most liberal standpoint, for purchase by banking institutions. The great advance in the number of securities, both listed and otherwise available, and to some extent the improvement of the art of studying and analyzing their worth, have naturally coöperated very powerfully in making such issues available for purchase by banks as elements in their portfolios.

These various factors operating together have, however, tended unmistakably toward the broadening of the scope of bank holdings of securities. It must, nevertheless, be added with regret that the steady growth of such security holdings has in few cases resulted in a corresponding increase in the care and efficiency of the judgment exercised by bankers in the selection of the constituent elements in their portfolio. They have been disposed to accept the representations of security salesmen, or at times to depend upon the statements made to them by their city correspondents, or, in other cases, to be influenced too greatly by rates of interest paid by the bonds or other investment forms which they purchased. Whatever may be thought of the idea of making up the bank portfolio upon the basis of salability or convertibility of assets rather than that of liquidity, the fact remains that even in the most favorable light, the theory has been subjected to a very severe trial under hostile conditions, owing to the carelessness and unsoundness with which new issues have been offered during the past ten or fifteen years in the United States, as well as to the undiscriminating and hasty character of the purchases that have been made by bank buyers who apparently had no hesitancy in absorbing issues of doubtful quality which, in many cases, they would hardly have recommended to their customers for individual holdings.

However, the discussion of bank portfolios, from the contemporary standpoint, is less concerned with theory than with actual technique. Let it be granted that in future, much more largely than in the past, so-called commercial banks will become buyers of securities and, especially, of long-term bonds. However, the problem will still persist whether the existing portfolios are wisely made up even from the standpoint of those who wish to see bank funds engaged in investment issues, and whether the present holdings of the banks are of such a nature as to call absolutely for improvement. If the latter should be the conclusion actually reached, the question will remain whether the write-off on the securities now held is likely to be so serious as to inflict further and, perhaps, unsupportable suffering upon the banks themselves; or whether it may be expected that, as a result of industrial improvement, there will be a gradual gain in the character of the holdings and in the extent of their convertibility into cash.

On these points it is desirable to seek light. The Banking Act of 1933 ("Glass bill"), was undoubtedly conceived by its framers as a step toward more careful restriction and control of the use of bank funds in the development of an investment portfolio; and, while the measure was emasculated during its later stages so that much of the control which had been originally attempted was limited, it remains true, nevertheless, that the measure is more strongly restrictive in this connection than any that has yet been adopted. It is not, however, so restrictive as the actual practice of the better financial institutions of the moment; and regardless of legislation, therefore, the problem will remain, how far, and in what direction, control is most wisely to be exerted by law or regulations over the practice of banks in the building up of their investment portfolios. Abstractly, it would seem that there could be little reasonable objection to the application of the same measures of control in connection with investments which had been found beneficial and desirable in connection with commercial paper in years past. Even this generalization, however, will undoubtedly be combated by many, for there has long been on foot a movement to bring about the opening of bank portfolios to speculative and long-term paper, and especially to speculative paper that has behind it collateral security in the shape of bonds or stocks.

There thus emerges, as a basic issue in the contemporary study of banking, the fundamental question of bank regulation in connection with portfolios—the control that is to be exerted by the community, and by bankers in particular, upon the use of banking funds in buying bonds or stocks, and in lending thereon. This issue comes to an acute point in connection with the new legislation contained in the Glass measure (Banking Act of 1933), relating to the guarantee of deposits. A careful study of the general situation which that Act contemplates drives us irresistibly to the conclusion that, if carried practically into effect, it must result in making the banks of the country jointly responsible, generally speaking, for one another's assets—a condition which naturally renders the character and composition of those assets a matter of utmost importance from the immediate standpoint of profit and loss. For the future, therefore, the portfolio question assumes practical form in its presentation of the problem whether the banks themselves shall be expected to carry the risk or danger involved in the financing of industry through the purchase and holding of securities; and whether in view of their guaranteeing of one another's assets (the same thing, reversely, as the guaranteeing of deposits) they must not protect themselves by prescribing, at least in a negative way, the make-up of these assets.

In answering these questions it is desirable to know first of all, exactly what has taken place in the portfolio situation of American banks, and then to examine more carefully the present position of the portfolio, and the probable changes that may be expected to occur in it during coming years as a result of outside factors.

CHAPTER XXIII

INVESTMENT OPERATIONS OF COMMERCIAL BANKS[1]

Before the World War, national banks held United States Government bonds principally to secure national bank notes in circulation. In 1914 all member banks held $2,079,000,000 in bonds, of which $760,000,000 were United States Government issues, held primarily for circulation purposes, and $1,319,000,000 of other securities. During the War, as is well known, the banks greatly expanded their holdings of Government bonds, so that at the end of the War their holdings of Governments greatly exceeded their other security investments.

In the period from 1921 to 1931 there was a further expansion of bank security holdings, the security investments of all banks increasing from $8,405,814,000 to $13,671,629,000, divided as to years and as to member and non-member banks, as follows:

TABLE 114

SECURITY INVESTMENTS OF BANKS*

(In millions of dollars)

YEAR	NATIONAL BANKS	STATE MEMBER BANKS	STATE NON-MEMBER BANKS	TOTAL
1921	4,025	1,977	2,404	8,406
1922	4,563	2,454	2,162	9,179
1923	5,070	2,687	2,324	10,081
1924	5,142	2,821	2,645	10,608
1925	5,730	3,133	2,720	11,583
1926	5,842	3,281	2,746	11,869
1927	6,393	3,425	3,465	13,283
1928	7,147	3,411	3,805	14,563
1929	6,657	3,395	3,112	13,164
1930	6,888	3,554	3,229	13,671

* Source: *Annual Reports of Comptroller of the Currency.*

It is thus indicated that the greatest increase in security investments was by the State member banks, which showed a rise

[1] Prepared by A. Wilfred May.

of 80% in the period. The increase by national banks was 71% and by State nonmember banks 34%. From 1922-1931 security investments by all banks increased 60.2%, while commercial loans[2] decreased 17.0%.

Neither the original national bank act, itself, nor the banking statutes of this country before 1863-1864, permitted investments in securities by commercial banks. Under an opinion of the Comptroller of the Currency, however, national banks did purchase bonds for investment without additional legislative authorization under section 5136 of the Revised Statutes, permitting them to discount and negotiate promissory notes, drafts, bills of exchange, and other evidences of debts. Bond investments for national banks were given specific recognition in the McFadden Act of 1927, which provided that

> the business of buying and selling investment securities shall hereafter be limited to buying and selling without recourse marketable obligations evidencing indebtedness—in the form of bonds, notes, or debentures, commonly known as investment securities, under such further definition of the term "investment securities" as may by regulation be prescribed by the Comptroller of the Currency.

Thus, bonds may be purchased by national banks if their marketability is approved by the Comptroller of the Currency. Although the Comptroller has stated that his decisions regarding marketability would be governed by three factors, namely: (1) sufficient size of entire issue to make marketability possible, (2) provisions for such public distribution as to insure marketability at intrinsic values, and (3) a bank or trust company acting as an independent trustee for the issue. In practice, there have been almost no restrictions against any public or quasi-public issue of bonds.

State banks have engaged in the purchase of securities on even a broader scale, as state laws often permit banks, and especially trust companies, to purchase common stocks as well. State laws regarding such purchases have been summarized for

[2] Loans other than security and real-estate loans are designated as commercial. A source of potential danger has been the relation of security investments to liquid capital assets: As of September 30, 1932, all national banks held securities totalling 7.5 billions against capital surplus and profits of 3 billions, a ratio of 2.5–1. Source, *Annual Reports of the Comptroller of the Currency*.

the House Committee on Banking and Currency; this summary can be found in a report of that Committee.[3]

The extremely "liberal" attitude of our laws, state and national, with respect to the purchase of securities by both banks and trust companies, or rather the absence of sufficiently thorough and satisfactory regulation developed along the lines that have already been worked out in connection with the control of commercial paper, makes it of special importance to note, through the examination of satisfactory samples, the use that has actually been made by representative banks, of the power they thus possess of directing their assets into specified channels. While in recent years, as has elsewhere been noted, the banks in many parts iof the country have been disposed to place a part of their funds in the hands of so-called "affiliates," whose portfolio holdings were thus, not strictly speaking, a part of the property of the bank, it has remained true that these affiliate holdings were none the less actually directed by the same general oversight and control which prevailed in the case of the bank itself; while the fact that the stock of the affiliate was invariably closely associated with the stock of the parent bank by some one of several plans, makes the portfolios of these affiliates, from the present standpoint of trend in the use of bank funds a part, to all intents and purposes, of the bank's own holdings; although not so classified in the statistics already given which relate merely to the technicial position of the banks themselves.

In the absence of general statistical summaries of affiliate holdings it is, therefore, desirable to consider sample cases, involving: *(a)* the portfolio position of banks that have failed; *(b)* the portfolio position of banks that have continued open, and whose holdings are still in possession of the parent corporation; and *(c)* banks that have continued open, but have transferred a portion of their securities holdings and business to affiliates.

Sample of Closed Bank Portfolio

Records of liquidation of all New York State banks closed since 1929, have been compiled in the following tabulation,

[3] Branch, Chain and Group Banking, Hearings before Committee on Banking and Currency, H. of R., 71st Cong., 2d Sess., 1930, Vol. I, pp. 595-97.

showing total assets, the security portfolios at cost at time of closing, the portion of the portfolio at cost which had been sold up to December, 1932, the losses realized on these sales, and these losses figured as a percentage of cost:

TABLE 115

STATE BANKS LIQUIDATED—NEW YORK STATE

(In thousands of dollars)

BANKS DESIGNATED BY NUMBER	TOTAL ASSETS	SECURITIES PORTFOLIO	SECURITY PORTFOLIO EXPRESSED AS A PERCENTAGE OF TOTAL ASSETS	SECURITIES SOLD ON CLOSING‡	LOSS ON SALES	LOSS ON SALES EXPRESSED AS A PERCENTAGE OF COST AT CLOSING§
	$	$	%	$	$	%
No. 1.	10,420	1,174	11.27	1,124	219	19.48
No. 2.	2,151	1,064	49.47	1,042	435	41.75
No. 3.	3,564	1,158	32.49	1,132	758	66.96
No. 4.	915	194	21.20	194	115	59.28
No. 5.*	13,620	5,980	43.91	5,475	1,385	25.30
No. 6.	2,728	1,353	49.60	1,267	446	35.20
No. 7.†	820	288	35.12	277	127	45.85
No. 8.	237,863	23,690	9.96	11,668	4,425	37.92
No. 9.	2,938	1,833	62.39	1,453	610	41.98
No. 10.	331	225	67.98	220	148	67.27
No. 11.	2,646	797	30.12	782	280	35.81
No. 12.	1,967	673	34.21	666	254	38.14
No. 13.	2,632	624	23.71	616	317	51.46
No. 14.	650	262	40.31	256	123	48.05
No. 15.	1,614	751	46.53	739	373	50.47
No. 16.	15,248	6,255	41.02	3,190	1,594	49.97
No. 17.	272	88	32.35	88	32	36.36
No. 18.	8,724	1,586	18.18	1,585	236	14.89
No. 19.	1,682	667	39.66	633	328	51.82

* Figures are up to time institution was taken over by another bank.
† (Excl. Affiliates.)
‡ Figures represent cost.
§ Represents average percentage.

The realized figure of 37 per cent below cost for these bonds will no doubt seem low to many. It must, moreover, be realized that this liquidation was carried on under disadvantageous conditions. There was a drastic general liquidation on all security markets; there was hoarding and a seepage of deposits in almost

TABLE 115 *(Continued)*

BANKS DESIGNATED BY NUMBER	TOTAL ASSETS	SECURITIES PORTFOLIO	SECURITY PORTFOLIO EXPRESSED AS A PERCENTAGE OF TOTAL ASSETS	SECURITIES SOLD ON CLOSING‡	LOSS ON SALES	LOSS ON SALES EXPRESSED AS A PERCENTAGE OF COST AT CLOSING§
No. 20.	822	704	85.64	12	10	83.33
No. 21.	130	51	42.50	45	7	15.55
No. 22.	1,569	377	24.03	344	157	45.64
No. 23.	4,840	2,535	52.38	2,327	1,043	44.82
No. 24.	2,317	1,532	66.12	1,514	236	15.59
No. 25.	974	196	20.12	151	68	45.03
No. 26.	1,572	519	33.02	519	284	54.72
No. 27.	1,188	556	46.80	552	176	31.88
No. 28.	1,698	482	28.39	448	196	43.75
No. 29.	923	217	23.51	183	71	38.80
No. 30.	297	72	24.24	72	33	45.83
No. 31.	1,213	971	80.05	952	379	39.81
No. 32.	3,911	479	12.25	419	183	43.68
No. 33.	2,147	705	32.83	679	278	40.95
No. 34.	359	82	22.84	77	36	46.75
Totals	$334,332	58,140	37.00§	40,701	15,362	37.49

all banks so that the usual sources of absorption of bonds and securities were greatly curtailed, and banks all over the country were thus selling out on a declining market. On the other hand it should be acknowledged that, there being no exchange for sales of, or quotations on commercial loans, it is, of course, impossible to tell the actual realizable value of the commercial loans of these banks during the period in question.

Perhaps the most severe criticism to be offered upon the policies of these banks in connection with their securities holdings is furnished by the fact that they evidently were prone to treat these securities practically as a secondary reserve which could be availed of at any time. The question whether they were or were not subject to greater loss, or were or were not more or less marketable than the commercial loans of the banks is a secondary issue. The important thing in the whole situation is that the securities so held were a major source of difficulty, primarily because they had provided a basis for the belief that they possessed unique qualities as a means of guarding against danger and this belief proved to be erroneous.

Portfolios of Selected "Going" Banks

The study of portfolios held by occasional going banking concerns does not, however, furnish greater reassurance than the facts disclosed by the sample of failed bank asset positions already furnished.

We have noted the ever-increasing amounts of government securities held by our banks since 1909, as well as the increasing

TABLE 116

DISTRIBUTION OF INVESTMENTS

TYPE OF SECURITY	CENTRAL RESERVE CITIES % OF TOTAL		OTHER RESERVE CITIES % OF TOTAL		COUNTRY BANKS % OF TOTAL	
	1921	1930	1921	1930	1921	1930
	%	%	%	%	%	%
United States Govt. Bonds	52	56	53	52	48	28
State, County & Municipal Bonds	10	5	11	13	9	12
Railroad & Public Utility Bonds	15	16	13	13	19	29
Other Bonds Stocks	23	23	23	22	24	33

amount of bonds outside the government group since 1921 in relation to the security portfolio. This tendency toward less marketable and more insecure investments is especially observable in the case of the smaller banks, as is illustrated by Table 116, showing the percentage distribution of investments, by groups of member banks, as of 1921 and 1930.[4]

Also to be noted in the case of the smaller banks is their tendency to have securities portfolios which are inordinately large in relation to their liquid capital—a potential source of danger. The composite bond account of a great number of country banks compiled by Messrs. Ostrolenk and Massie,[5] in 1932,

[4] Member bank *Call Reports,* Federal Reserve Board.

[5] *How Banks Buy Bonds* (Harpers, 1933).

showed that the total amount of their liquid capital was $1,577,096,000, while the bond portfolios of the five largest banks in the New York Clearing House were only 1.1 times the liquid capital funds. Portfolios of a number of banks were collected by a subcommittee of the Committee on Banking and Currency of the United States Senate in 1931.

One tendency noted in these portfolios is the practice of investing in convertible bonds or "bonds" with common-stock purchase warrants attached. These issues almost invariably were never secured by a mortgage and were bonds in name only, being often debenture obligations of chain store, public-utility holding, or investment trust companies. The conversion or warrant provisions afforded the banks the speculative proclivities which legislative prohibitions against common stocks denied them. Below is a list of some banks with their holdings of this type of issue, expressed as a percentage of their total bond portfolio:

BANK	STATE IN WHICH LOCATED	PERCENTAGE IN CONV. OR OPTION ISSUES
"1"	New York	3.91
"3"	New York	4.09
"4"	New York	7.96
"5"	Ohio	13.00
"6"	Ohio	11.00
"15"	New York	14.89
"18"	New York	15.00

Going into the actual detail of issues held, it is found that owing to their poor security, they were a source of great relative loss to the banks. Bank "1" held the following issues of this class, among others:[6]

Chicago, Rock Island & Pacific 4½/1960	Cost $2,481,250
F. and W. Grand-Silver Stores 6/1940	2,395,312
Atchison, Topeka & Santa Fe 4½/1948	2,184,380
Chicago and Northwestern 4¾/1949	2,015,277
General Theatre Equipment 6/1940	1,422,006
Metropolitan Stores 6/1940	958,125
Baltimore and Ohio 4½/1960	847,968
American International 5½/1949	797,820
Texas Corporation 5/1944	622,989
Southern Pacific 4½/1969	479,131

[6] *Hearings before U. S. Senate Subcommittee on Banking and Currency,* under S. Res. 71.

Four of these issues, Grand-Silver, Metropolitan Stores, Rock Island and General Theatre are obligations of corporations which have since gone into receivership; General Theatre Equipment is currently quoted at $1, and all the others, with the exception of the Atchison issue, have suffered very severe declines.

An examination of the portfolios of affiliates discloses that with the exception of railroad obligations, they held very few convertible or option-warrant issues, for the obvious reason that they are permitted to hold common stocks, which they had in great number. One affiliate, that of an Illinois bank, reported, however, that in 1929 it participated in syndicates extensively involving such issues, as follows:

$100,000,000 The Texas Corp. conv. s. f. 5% Debs. of '44.
72,335,000 Chicago & Northwestern Ry. Co. 4¾ Conv. Gold Bonds of '49.
65,166,000 Southern Pacific Co. 40 yr. 4½% Gold Bonds with warrants, of '69.

Figured at recent market prices, these issues showed a combined shrinkage of $95,611,000.

Another tendency of security investment, and especially on the part of the larger banks, is to neglect wide diversification, and to concentrate a larger percentage of its assets in a few individual issues than it would in *indivdual commercial loans.* Following is a list of the percentage of their investments in an individual issue (outside of U. S. Governments) by certain large banks:[7]

BANK	PERCENTAGE OF TOTAL IN LARGEST INDIVIDUAL HOLDING	PERCENTAGE OF TOTAL IN 10 LARGEST HOLDINGS
"8"	16	41
"13"	16	78
"16"	73	84
"14"	29	76
"3"	13	90

And we also find among bank holdings a very large proportion of the whole of a single issue. A New York City bank, for instance, in 1930, held $2,800,000 St. Louis-Southwestern 4's, which constituted 56% of the entire issue, amounting to $5,000,000. In 1931 the price of the issue declined to 60, at which price a loss of $1,116,500 on this investment was indicated.

[7] *Hearings before the U. S. Senate Subcommittee on Banking and Currency,* under S. Res. 71.

Some other New York City banks held the following individual issues in the various indicated large amounts:[8]

Southern Ry. Co. Genl. 4s	4,099,333
Mo. Pacific Conv. 5½s/49	3,000,000
Deutsche Std. Works 6/30-39	2,700,000
Florida East Coast 5/74	2,335,000
National Hotel of Cuba	1,808,365
Argentine 5's/31	9,375,000
Middle West Utilities (various)	3,938,000
Fox Film Corp. 6/31	2,880,000
Simmons Co. 5/44	1,845,000
Republic of Cuba 5½/31	5,333,333
Province of Santa Fe, Argentina 6's	995,000
Province of Cordova	1,980,000

And following are the ten largest issues held by a single New York City bank. Here there is both lack of diversification as well as of marketability:

Concord Estate Corporation 6/33 (Entire issue held by this one bank)	4,620,000
Associated Gas & Electric 5/32	4,066,655
New York City 4/30	3,121,943
Stern Bros. 6/1947	2,432,000
Benenson City Terminal Corp. 6½/33	2,431,570
Gotham National Bldg. 6/41	1,850,000
Warner Pictures 6/39	1,215,225
500 Fifth Ave. Corp. 6½/49	1,034,038
Elks Bldg., Bklyn., Lodge No. 22	879,131
Bklyn. Manhattan Transit 6/68	482,644
Total	22,133,206

The affiliates have been more guilty than have the banks, of tying up an inordinate amount of their invested funds in some particular issues. Thus, as of December 31, 1930, the affiliate of a New York bank had a total bond portfolio of $9,487,918, of which $6,750,000 in all was in a single issue—Empire State, Inc., 7's. This is a junior mortgage, subject to $31,500,000 prior mortgages on the Empire State Building. An affiliate of another New York City bank held among its bonds $829,000 McKesson & Robbins (a drug company) 5½s, and among its stocks 318,368 shares of Chatham Phenix Allied Stock, 30,944 shares Chatham Phenix Bank, 15,000 shares Shepard Stores, 23,324 shares Spiegel, May, Stern common, and 12,434 shares of Zonite Products common.

[8] *Report to Stockholders,* of Feb. 7, 1933.

An affiliate of a national bank of California had an industrial bond portfolio of $18,342,167, of which $17,160,377 consisted of "Bancitaly 5% Mortgage" due 1948 (its "market" value as of May, 1932, had shrunk to $10,192,256). Another affiliate, for some reason, became greatly interested in the Atlantic Coast Fisheries Co. As of November 30, 1930, it held 23,261 shares of common stock of this company at a total cost of $1,090,679; 17,000 shares being purchased at $60 per share. At the present writing the stock is selling at 75 cents per share giving a value of $17,445 to their holdings, and indicating a loss of $1,073,234 or 98 per cent on the investment, if it is still held. The Atlantic Coast Fisheries constituted a large part of their assets, being their largest individual holding, except the stock of the affiliate's parent bank. The noteworthy feature is not the decline in market value, but that so large a portion of the institution's assets should have been tied up in one company of this character. This is a bank outside of New York City.

The Senate Subcommittee inquired as to the proportion of investments that could be considered readily marketable. Table 117, page 545, shows the proportion of security investments listed on the New York and other exchanges, for a number of banks. A very irregular record is presented, the percentage of unlisted security issues ranging from 0 to 89 per cent.

Affiliate Holdings

While some reference has been made in the foregoing discussion to the actual holdings of security affiliates, no effort has been made to differentiate them distinctly from the parent banks up to this point.

The situation of the affiliates has been fully studied by the Senate Banking and Currency Committee, and its principal findings have been set forth in Part VII on the Hearings of 1932. It is sufficient to say at this point that the tendencies already noted in connection with the banks' own holdings of securities are found to be greatly intensified in the case of those holdings which they are undertaking to carry for their own account in the security affiliates. Perhaps the most striking feature of bank-

TABLE 117

SECURITIES HELD BY BANKS

BANK	PERCENTAGE LISTED ON NEW YORK STOCK EXCHANGE	PERCENTAGE LISTED ON OTHER EXCHANGES	PERCENTAGE UNLISTED
By no.	%	%	%
1	61	2	37
2	73	5	22
3	77	2	21
4	90	4	6
5	42	6	52
6	80	—	20
7	83	2	15
8	45	1	54
9	83	7	10
10	51	23	26
11	66	19	21
12	75	13	12
13	85	3	12
14	69	8	23
15	83	4	13
16	60	10	30
17	50	13	37
18	65	—	35
19	75	5	20
20	22	1	37
21	76	5	19
22	26	9	65
23	70	30	—
24	83	1	16
25	50	35	15
26	30	—	70
27	74	—	26
28	70	30	—
29	46	—	54
30	50	12	38
31	73	6	21
32	25	1	74
33	9	2	89
34	76	6	18
35	42	7	51
36	18	1	81
37	95	5	—
38	81	15	4

ing management in this connection is found in the fact that, although the purchases made by the larger institutions are likely to be superior in average quality to those of country banks even when held for affiliate account, the larger institutions—particularly through their affiliates—tend to become encumbered with an excessive amount of single issues, thereby concentrating their risks to an undue extent.

Some Conclusions

In closing the present chapter it seems desirable to state a few very general conclusions which would seem to be warranted by the facts that we have just set forth. They are as follows:

1. The position of the asset holdings of American banks of all classes has been rapidly changing during the past fifteen years.

2. The general trend of this change has been in the direction of what is called "illiquid"—that is to say, it has been away from the so-called self-liquidating paper formerly regarded as the best form of bank holdings, and it has been toward holdings composed of securities and long-term loans of various kinds.

3. This change in composition has been generally affecting all banks, but it has been most serious in connection with the national banks, because it was this group of institutions which formerly constituted a nucleus of liquidity for the nation as a whole.

4. The supervision of banks provided for in the National Bank Act and in the earlier state banking laws related chiefly to the holdings of commercial paper, and loans made by the bank for the financing of so-called liquid transactions.

5. It was only at a considerably later date that the banks began to buy heavily of bonds and other long-term securities; and when they did so, they found themselves but little hampered by legal limitations or by the orders of banking supervisors.

6. The typical bank portfolio since the close of the War has undergone a radical transformation, because of the fact that the increasing practice on the part of industrial enterprises of financing themselves through the agency of the securities market has tended strongly to put bank funds primarily into securities and less and less (relatively speaking) into "paper." This change has already been emphatically noted and commented upon by the Federal Reserve Board.

7. In thus transforming that part of its portfolio which consists of bonds and other securities, the average bank has displayed almost entire disregard of the principles of investment. The result has been the development of extremely unsatisfactory bond portfolios in the banks—so unsatisfactory that various banking superintendents have of late classified unsatisfactory bond holdings as a primary cause of failure.

8. Most of the bonds held by banks have thus far been judged or criticised by superintendents on the basis of their market value, as shown by current trading in the securities market. This has, sometimes, given to such bonds an unwarrantedly high apparent worth, and at other times has seemed to depress them to an unwarrantedly low figure.

9. New principles of supervision and control of the banking portfolio are called for. Recent legislation (Banking Act of 1933) takes some very moderate steps toward regulation, but this is insufficient to produce much result.

10. A clearing up of frozen portfolios throughout the country will be necessary before we can expect that the banking system of the nation will be restored to efficiency, and before it can be felt that either the securities markets or the banks occupy a reasonably strong or satisfactory position.

CHAPTER XXIV

THE BALANCE SHEET SITUATION[1]

An investigation of changes in the portfolios of the American banking system must overcome the difficulty of obtaining not only adequate information but also data that would be comparable over a period of years. In 1909 the National Monetary Commission made a thorough survey of the entire banking system and produced a summary balance sheet for all banks in the United States as of the close of business on April 28, 1909. The part of this balance sheet covering loans and investments is presented on pages 550 and 551 with a similar statement by the Comptroller pertaining to loans and investments of all banks in the United States as of the close of business on June 30, 1932. Contrasting the two statements it is difficult to find any one item—among the subclasses of the main groups—which can be considered comparable.

It is apparently impossible to assemble on the basis of published records alone an adequate set of annual balance sheets for the entire banking system, which would be reasonably comparable and would cover a sufficient number of years to make a comparison of the pre-war period with the more recent developments feasible. We have to choose, therefore, some part of the banking system for which more exact information is available, and regard this part as a representative sample of the whole system. The most complete published statistics are to be found on national banks, which are also fairly representative of commercial banking in general. In this instance, the analysis of the bank portfolio is confined to the national banking system.

The figures of loans and investments of National Banks are taken from the *Annual Reports of the Comptroller of the Currency*. The Comptroller of the Currency subdivides the loans of National Banks into demand and time loans, as well as secured

[1] Written by V. D. Kazakévich; J. Torpats, and G. Wittmann assisted in compiling the statistics.

and unsecured loans. For the purposes of this analysis it seemed more important to trace the relationship between secured and unsecured loans rather than the demand or time phase. Therefore, the latter classification was eliminated and all the figures grouped according to whether they represented secured or unsecured loans, and by types of security. It became apparent, as soon as the figures were tabulated, that the increase in absolute figures is over a period of years so great that in order to compare the composition of loans or investments for one year with that of another, it is essential to work out the relative distribution inside each year and contrast percentages of totals instead of actual figures. This procedure is followed all through the discussion.

Having thus indicated the nature of the portfolio statistics for the banks of the country in the aggregate, let us now turn to a consideration of the actual facts with respect to the position of a definite group of institutions. As already stated, among the various groups of banks, the one which unquestionably affords the most complete data with respect to portfolio composition is the national banking system. It has, therefore, been sought to present here, as compactly as possible, the changes in the portfolios of National Banks *a)* as to loans; *b)* as to investments; and *c)* as to the relationship between loans and investments.

LOANS OF NATIONAL BANKS

An analysis of loans of national banks should show the changes in the relation between secured and unsecured loans, and also trace, in so far as data are available, the fluctuations in the composition of secured loans according to the type of collateral. In order to accomplish the first purpose the figures on loans of national banks were abstracted from the Reports of the Comptroller of the Currency and arranged in two categories—loans secured by various collateral and endorsed paper or loans on one or more name individual or firm paper without other security.[2]

From 1900 to 1928 both secured and unsecured loans for the

[2] Such a classification can be extended over the period from 1900 to 1928; it is impossible to bring it up to date, as beginning with 1929, the figures published by the Comptroller are not comparable with earlier years.

THE LOAN AND INVESTMENT PORTFOLIO OF ALL BANKS IN THE UNITED STATES COMPARING THE YEARS 1909 AND 1932

APRIL 28, 1909*

(In thousands of dollars)

1. Loans & Discounts	
a) On demand, unsecured by collateral	$ 660,426
b) On demand, secured by collateral	1,939,635
c) On time, with two or more names, unsecured by collateral	2,539,966
d) On time, single-name paper unsecured by collateral	1,351,782
e) On time, secured by collateral	2,036,358
f) Secured by real estate, mtgs., or other liens on realty	1,127,276
g) Not classified	269,373
Total Loans and Discounts	9,924,816
2. Overdrafts:	
a) Secured	29,435
b) Unsecured	40,264
Total Overdrafts	69,699

* Source: *Annual Report of the Comptroller of the Currency* 1909: summary of the special reports obtained for and compiled by the National Monetary Commission from 22,491 banks of the United States and island possessions (including national, state, savings, and private banks and loan and trust companies) showing their condition at the close of business on April 28, 1909.

JUNE 30, 1932†

(In thousands of dollars)

Loans & Discounts (including rediscounts):	
Real estate loans, mtgs., deeds of trust, and other liens on real estate:	
On farm land	$ 507,876
On other real estate	9,433,768
Loans secured by United States Government and other bonds, stocks and securities (exclusive of loans to banks)	6,011,057
Loans to Banks	489,763
Commercial paper bought in open market; acceptances payable in United States; and notes, bills, and acceptances payable in foreign countries	638,710
All other loans	10,993,466
Total Loans and Discounts	28,074,640

† Source: *Annual Report of the Comptroller of the Currency* 1932: summary of reports of condition of all reporting banks in the United States (19,163 banks) and possessions, at the close of business June 30, 1932.

THE LOAN AND INVESTMENT PORTFOLIO OF ALL BANKS IN THE UNITED STATES COMPARING THE YEARS 1909 AND 1932 *(Continued)*

APRIL 28, 1909 (*In thousands of dollars*)		JUNE 30, 1932 (*In thousands of dollars*)	
3. Bonds, Securities, etc. (including premiums thereon):		Overdrafts	15,213
1. Domestic securities:		Investments:	
a) U. S. bonds	792,788	U. S. Govt. securities	6,455,583
b) State, county, & municipal bonds	1,091,541	State, county, municipal bonds	2,801,750
c) Railroad bonds	1,560,006	Railroad and other public service corporation bonds	4,276,059
d) Bonds of other public service corps. (including street and interurban railway bonds)	466,527	Stock of Federal Reserve banks and other corporations	735,266
e) Other bonds	379,647	Foreign govt. bonds and other foreign securities	580,780
f) Stocks	280,227	Other bonds, notes, warrants, etc.	3,373,803
Total Domestic Securities	4,570,736	Total Investments	18,223,241
2. Foreign Securities:		Total Loans and Investments	46,313,094
a) Government bonds	24,637	Total Assets	57,245,131
b) Other securities	19,069		
Total Foreign Securities	43,706		
Total Bonds, Securities, etc.	4,614,442		
Total Loans and Investments	14,608,957		
Total Assets	21,095,054		

TABLE 118

CHANGES IN THE VOLUME OF VARIOUS TYPES OF LOANS OF NATIONAL BANKS*

(In millions of dollars)

TYPE OF LOANS	ALL NATIONAL BANKS		NEW YORK CITY BANKS		ALL OTHER CITY BANKS		COUNTRY BANKS	
	Beginning of period	End of period	Beginning of period	End of period	Beginning of period	End of period	Beginning of period	End of period
Loans secured by personal property; 1915 and 1928	$ 883	$1,476	$113	$ 187	$ 334	$ 624	$ 436	$ 665
Loans secured by stocks and bonds; 1915 and 1932	1,751	3,379	606	812	580	1,411	565	1,156
Loans on real estate; 1915 and 1932	151	1,617	9	15	35	793	107	809
On farm land; 1921 and 1932	159	300	†	†	11	101	148	198
On other real estate; 1921 and 1932	120	1,317	1	14	28	692	91	611
Total secured loans 1900 and 1928	1,103	7,876	384	1,571	396	3,293	323	3,022
Total unsecured loans; 1900 and 1928	1,583	7,098	185	1,111	520	2,496	878	3,491
Loans secured by United States government obligations; 1923 and 1932	234	93	37	33	98	35	99	25
Amount eligible for rediscount and rediscounted with the Federal Reserve; 1923 and 1932	3,564	1,650	466	224	1,376	610	1,722	816

* Compiled on the basis of data abstracted from the *Annual Reports of the Comptroller of the Currency.*

† Less than $500,000.

entire national system show a very decided growth (see Table 118); secured loans increased seven-fold and unsecured loans about five-fold. The relative importance of the two groups of loans also changed; secured loans grew at the expense of non-collateraled advances. In 1900 only 41.1 per cent of all loans of national banks were secured and 58.9 per cent unsecured; by 1928 the situation reversed itself; secured loans rose to 52.0 per cent of the total while unsecured advances declined to 46.9 per cent.

This shift is even more clearly marked in the case of the country bank group. In 1900 slightly over one-fourth (26.9 per cent) of all the loans made by country banks were secured and nearly three-fourths (73.1 per cent) unsecured. By 1928 secured loans increased to 46.3 per cent, while unsecured loans fell off to only slightly over one-half of all loans.

The composition of loans of city banks outside of New York does not show so definite a trend in the same direction. Up to 1927 unsecured loans comprised more than half of all loans; between the years 1908 and 1914 they rose to over 60 per cent; in this period they were higher than in the years immediately following 1900. Only from 1924 on, do secured loans in city banks outside of New York show again a tendency to increase, reaching 56.4 per cent in 1928.

New York City national banks seem to have generally preferred secured loans to indorsed paper. Exceptions are found in 1918, 1920 and 1921 when unsecured loans rose to 49.6, 59.2 and 58.5 per cent of all loans. The general trend in New York City national banks tends to reverse that of the entire system and the country banks.

The change in the relationship of secured to unsecured loans, shown in Table 119, may be summarized as follows: in the national-banking system during the period from 1900 to 1928 about 10 per cent of all loans have been shifted from the unsecured to the secured category; in country banks a similar shift of about 20 per cent of the total loans from indorsed paper to secured advances took place during the same period; in all city banks outside of New York City there is no pronounced prefer-

TABLE 119: UNSECURED VERSUS SECURED LOANS OF NATIONAL BANKS, EXPRESSED AS A PERCENTAGE OF TOTAL LOANS 1900-1928*

YEARS	ALL NATIONAL BANKS		NEW YORK CITY BANKS		ALL OTHER CITY BANKS		COUNTRY BANKS	
	Unsecured	Secured	Unsecured	Secured	Unsecured	Secured	Unsecured	Secured
	%	%	%	%	%	%	%	%
1900	58.9	41.1	32.5	67.5	56.8	43.2	73.1	26.9
1901	58.5	41.5	34.5	65.5	55.0	45.0	72.0	28.0
1902	58.9	41.1	34.7	65.3	55.1	44.8	71.2	28.8
1903	60.6	39.4	38.0	62.0	58.5	41.4	70.5	29.5
1904	59.2	40.8	33.3	66.7	59.8	40.2	71.1	28.9
1905	59.9	40.2	32.6	67.4	59.8	40.2	71.7	28.3
1906	61.7	38.2	37.0	63.0	60.3	39.7	70.9	29.1
1907	63.6	36.4	43.2	56.8	61.4	38.6	71.2	28.8
1908	59.6	40.4	31.5	68.5	59.8	40.2	70.6	29.4
1909	60.7	39.3	34.2	65.8	60.0	40.0	71.1	28.9
1910	62.8	37.2	40.9	59.1	60.9	39.4	71.2	28.8
1911	63.1	36.9	42.5	57.5	61.3	38.7	71.1	28.9
1912	62.9	37.1	42.6	57.4	60.8	39.2	70.8	29.2
1913	63.5	36.5	43.0	57.0	60.7	38.8	70.6	29.4
1914	62.5	37.5	40.9	59.1	61.7	38.3	70.1	29.9
1915	58.2	41.8	40.9	59.1	57.1	42.9	65.6	34.4
1916	57.6	42.4	39.0	61.0	58.5	41.3	65.9	34.1
1917†	58.7	40.0	44.1	51.9	59.5	39.7	65.3	34.5
1918	58.4	39.7	49.6	44.9	57.2	41.3	64.2	35.4
1919	53.1	45.0	40.8	55.0	50.5	47.3	62.2	37.5
1920	61.1	37.7	59.2	38.8	58.6	40.1	64.2	35.1
1921	60.3	38.2	58.5	40.2	57.9	41.4	63.1	35.9
1922	57.6	41.4	47.6	49.1	56.1	43.3	62.6	37.2
1923	58.5	40.9	49.8	48.7	57.2	42.1	62.2	37.5
1924	57.3	41.7	45.5	50.4	56.7	42.6	61.9	38.0
1925	54.1	44.6	41.6	53.6	52.0	47.1	60.1	39.7
1926	53.1	43.8	43.7	54.4	50.4	49.0	58.4	41.5
1927	49.8	49.4	39.8	57.3	46.4	53.0	56.5	43.1
1928	46.9	52.0	39.9	56.4	42.8	56.4	53.5	46.3

* Table computed on the basis of data abstracted from the *Annual Reports of the Comptroller of the Currency*.

† From 1917 the percentages do not equal 100 owing to the inclusion in Total Loans of miscellaneous acceptance credit items.

ence for secured loans until about 1924, in New York City national banks' secured loans seem to be equally high throughout the period covered, outside of a tendency to decline in relation to total loans during depression years. We must point out here that in country banks secured loans were slightly higher in the early years of the century than in the period from 1909 to 1914; the same holds true of city banks outside of New York City and even to a larger extent of New York City national banks.

TABLE 120

LOANS OF NATIONAL BANKS SECURED BY PERSONAL SECURITY, MERCHANDISE, WAREHOUSE RECEIPTS, EXPRESSED AS A PERCENTAGE OF TOTAL LOANS, 1915-1928*

YEARS	ALL NATIONAL BANKS	NEW YORK CITY BANKS	ALL OTHER CITY BANKS	COUNTRY BANKS
	%	%	%	%
1915	13.3	9.2	14.1	13.6
1916	11.5	6.8	12.7	12.8
1917	12.0	7.0	13.1	13.5
1918	12.4	6.8	13.8	14.2
1919	12.1	8.2	12.5	13.9
1920	13.1	10.1	14.1	13.6
1921	13.9	12.9	14.7	13.5
1922	12.3	7.5	13.4	13.3
1923	11.7	7.4	12.5	12.5
1924	11.3	6.3	12.4	12.2
1925	10.8	5.9	12.2	11.4
1926	10.9	6.6	12.3	11.3
1927	9.9	5.7	10.9	10.7
1928	9.7	6.7	10.7	10.2

* Table based on data abstracted from the *Annual Reports of the Comptroller of the Currency*.

In order to allocate the cause for this shift from indorsed paper to advances on collateral, we must determine which types of collateral loans account for the growth in total secured loans. Due to lack of comparable data we cannot account for the prewar tendencies, but beginning with 1915 we are able to break up total secured loans into three sub-groups: loans secured by personal property and merchandise; loans secured by stocks and bonds; and loans on real estate.

The figures for loans secured by personal property and merchandise, presented in Table 120, were available only for the years 1915 to 1928; since 1929 the Comptroller includes this sub-group of secured loans in "All Other Loans." Although for all national banks during these years loans secured by personal property and merchandise nearly doubled in dollar amounts relative to total loans, they steadily declined in importance. For

TABLE 121

LOANS OF NATIONAL BANKS SECURED BY STOCKS AND BONDS EXPRESSED AS A PERCENTAGE OF TOTAL LOANS, 1915-1932*

YEARS	ALL NATIONAL BANKS	NEW YORK CITY BANKS	ALL OTHER CITY BANKS	COUNTRY BANKS
	%	%	%	%
1915	26.3	49.2	26.2	17.6
1916	28.5	54.1	27.4	17.5
1917	26.0	44.9	25.7	17.0
1918	25.4	38.0	26.7	17.5
1919	31.2	46.8	34.1	20.2
1920	22.9	28.6	25.3	18.0
1921	22.5	27.2	25.7	18.1
1922	25.9	41.5	28.4	17.8
1923	25.2	41.1	27.6	18.3
1924	25.9	43.9	28.2	18.0
1925	28.9	47.6	32.8	19.3
1926	30.1	47.6	34.4	20.5
1927	31.8	51.5	29.2	21.9
1928	33.8	49.4	36.9	24.3
1929	34.6†	55.5†	35.6†	26.1†
1930	37.8	61.1	39.1	26.3
1931	35.4	53.6	35.8	26.8
1932	32.9	51.8	33.3	25.8

* Table based on data abstracted from the *Annual Reports of the Comptroller of Currency.*

† This figure does not include loans on securities made to banks and to trust companies.

the entire national system they dropped from 13.3 per cent of all loans in 1915, to 9.7 per cent in 1928; in New York City the decline for the same period was from 9.2 per cent to 6.7 per cent; in all city banks outside of New York City they fell from 14.1 per cent to 10.7 per cent; and in country banks, the decrease in the same years was from 13.6 per cent to 10.2 per cent; so that as a component part of the loan portfolio, advances on personal and merchandise collateral were steadily declining in importance during the fourteen years from 1915 to 1928. Only in New York City, in 1920 and 1921, did loans on personal property and merchandise show an increase, partially offsetting a heavy deflation of loans secured by stocks and bonds. The counterbalancing effect of this rise was not sufficient, however, to check the drop in all secured loans for New York City national banks during these two years. The general shift from indorsed paper toward secured loans did, therefore, take place in the national banking system in spite of a relative decline of one type of secured loans, namely, loans based on personal property and merchandise.

Data for the second sub-group of secured loans—advances on stocks and bonds—are available from 1915 to 1932 as shown in Table 121 above. For all national banks these loans nearly doubled as we may see from Table 118. Relative to the entire loan portfolio they rose from about one-quarter (26.3 per cent) of all loans, in 1915, to approximately one-third (32.9 per cent) for 1932. In city banks outside of New York City, loans on stocks and bonds rose from 26.2 per cent of all loans, in 1915, to 33.3 per cent in 1932; in country banks, this growth was even more marked during the same period, such loans increasing from 17.6 per cent to 25.8 per cent of all loans. Only in New York City did national banks' loans secured by stocks and bonds tend to comprise approximately one-half of all loans.

Throughout the national system loans on stocks and bonds fell off relatively to total loans in the depression years 1920 and 1921, and again in 1931 and 1932. In New York City such loans declined from 46.8 per cent of all loans, in 1919, to 28.6 and 27.2 per cent in 1920 and 1921. Security loans reached their all-time peak in 1930, when, in New York City national banks, they amounted to 61.1 per cent of all loans. The only exception is furnished by country banks, where security loans continued to rise through 1931.

It should be pointed out here that loans secured by United States Government obligations form not only an insignificant part of all loans, but have also been steadily on the decrease. In

1923, the first year for which such data are available, they form only 2 per cent of all loans for the entire national system, declining to 0.9 per cent by 1932. The same drop is present in the case of city banks outside of New York and country banks. The only exception is found in New York City where loans secured by United States Government obligations declined from 2.5 per cent in 1924 to 0.8 per cent in 1929, and rose again to 2.5 per cent of all loans in 1931.

Data for the third sub-group of secured loans—advances on real estate—are also available from 1915 to 1932.[3] For all national banks, loans on real estate increased more than ten-fold (see Table 118); and, relative to all loans, they rose from 2.3 per cent to 15.7 per cent. An even greater increase took place in city banks outside of New York City where real-estate loans went up from 1.6 per cent of all loans in 1915 to 18.7 per cent in 1932. In country banks they rose from 3.3 per cent to 18.1 per cent. Only in New York City national banks did all real-estate loans amount through the same period to less than 1 per cent of the loan portfolio.

From 1921 to 1932 total real-estate loans of national banks can be broken up into loans on farm land and loans on other real estate. During this period loans on farm land only, almost doubled for the entire national system. In city banks outside of New York City they rose from 0.3 per cent to 2.4 per cent of all loans; in country banks the increase was from 2.7 per cent to 4.4 per cent; in New York City national banks' farm-land loans were comparatively insignificant, they did not exceed 0.1 per cent of all loans during the years 1921 to 1932.

The increase in real-estate loans can, therefore, in no way be attributed to the growth of loaning on farm lands, but is owing to an expansion of loans secured by so-called other real estate. In the case of all national banks, of city banks outside of New York City, and of country banks, loans on other real estate increased from between one and two per cent of all loans for the three groups, in 1921, to 12.8 per cent, 16.3 per cent, and 13.6

[3] The figures on which this discussion of real-estate loans is based are given in Chap. XXV, Tables 133-38.

per cent, respectively, in 1932. The growth of total real-estate loans in national banks to about one-fifth of the entire loan portfolio in 1932 is a direct result, even in the case of country banks, of the expansion of city and suburban real-estate financing. As measured only by the figures on loans, New York City national banks seem to have kept out of the real-estate field altogether. The data on loans, however, can not be regarded as representing all real-estate commitments of national banks, as real-estate bonds are held in investment portfolios under the caption of "Bonds of Other Corporations," and the security affiliates of banks, especially of large urban banks, are often heavily involved in real-estate transactions.

This analysis of the changes in the composition of the loan portfolio of national banks shows that, from 1915 to 1932, the definite shift from indorsed paper toward secured loans was because of the growth on loans secured by stocks and bonds, and the branching out of commercial national banks into the field of city real-estate financing. Loans on indorsed paper, namely, commercial paper with one or more individual or firm names without other security—a traditional form of American commercial credit—had been steadily declining in importance. Advances on the basis of merchandise collateral had been also losing ground steadily. At the same time combined loans on securities and real estate—not a commercial banking function at all from the point of view of orthodox banking theory—had by 1932 risen to nearly one-half of all loans.

At this point we must recall that, prior to 1915, a very substantial part of all loans of national banks consisted of secured advances; this holds true of city banks outside of New York City, and especially of New York City national banks where secured loans were exceptionally high. Since it is impossible to break up the figures for total secured loans prior to 1915 into loans on personal property and merchandise, on stocks and bonds, and on real estate, it is difficult to say whether the tendency to have a large part of all loans secured by what is really investment collateral is a recent development or an inherent trait of commercial banking in the United States, as represented by the national system. If most of total secured loans of national banks consisted prior to the War, of loans on personal property and merchandise, then a greater portion of their loan portfolios could have been composed of advances based on commercial assets. If, on the other hand, this was not so, and loans on personal property and merchandise formed as small a part of all loans prior to 1915 as they did after that year, then we are bound to conclude that, even before the War, national banks, and especially city banks, were heavily involved in loans that were not liquid from the orthodox banking point of view. In spite of the fact that in 1915, the first full year in which the Federal Reserve was in operation, around one-third of all loans of national banks were secured by investment collateral, the lack of information for previous years prevents us from making the statement that such has been the usual practice of urban commercial banks, as represented by national banks located in cities. But, whatever the prevailing practise may have been prior to the Federal Reserve era, for which we have no comparable information, it is clear, from the figures available since 1915, that commercial national banks tend in a constantly increasing proportion to make loans on the basis of non-commercial assets.

The tendency of the national-banking system to lose its commercial character can be further illustrated by the decline in assets eligible for rediscounting shown in Table 122.

According to the original idea the Federal Reserve should be a commercial central bank, with its members deriving one of their main advantages from participating in the system through the use of rediscount privileges. In 1923, the first year for which such information is available, only one-third of all the loans of national banks were rediscounted or eligible for rediscount with the Federal Reserve. By 1932 the total amount rediscounted or eligible for rediscount declined to 16 per cent of all loans for the entire system, to 14.3 per cent for New York City, to 14.4 per cent for other city banks, and to 18.2 per cent for country banks; so that only from one-sixth to one-fifth of all loans of commercial banks were or could be rediscounted.

In concluding this analysis of the composition of the loan

portfolio of national banks, we must point out that even the very way in which the office of the Comptroller has changed the method of presenting the data on loans, indicates that increased emphasis is put on the institutional connection of a loan and less stress is laid on the nature of the underlying transaction. At first, in 1900 and the years immediately following, loans were subdivided into demand and time, and secured and unsecured. Beginning with 1915 secured loans are given in greater detail,

TABLE 122

LOANS OF NATIONAL BANKS ELIGIBLE FOR REDISCOUNT OR REDISCOUNTED WITH THE FEDERAL RESERVE BANKS, EXPRESSED AS A PERCENTAGE OF TOTAL LOANS, 1923-1932*

YEARS	ALL NATIONAL BANKS	NEW YORK CITY BANKS	ALL OTHER CITY BANKS	COUNTRY BANKS
	%	%	%	%
1923	30.2	25.5	32.1	30.2
1924	29.6	26.9	30.5	29.9
1925	26.9	21.0	27.0	28.9
1926	26.1	19.7	26.3	28.2
1927	24.1	20.4	23.0	26.4
1928	21.6	16.6	19.8	25.3
1929	20.1	14.8	19.8	22.3
1930	18.3	10.9	18.5	21.3
1931	16.4	9.5	16.0	19.8
1932	16.0	14.3	14.4	18.2

* Table based on data abstracted from the *Annual Reports of the Comptroller of the Currency.*

but still sub-classified into demand and time. In 1918 there appears a group of acceptance credits which may be either secured or unsecured, either demand or time. In 1923 a sub-group—that is not included in the total—of loans secured by United States Government obligations is introduced; in 1923 a similar sub-group is started for the total amount eligible for rediscount or rediscounted with the Federal Reserve. Finally, in 1929, the entire demand and time classification is abandoned, and indorsed paper and loans on personal property and merchandise—demand as well as time—are grouped together under the caption of "All Other Loans."

In the years following 1900 the demand and time qualification was, apparently, considered the most important one. Since 1915 another point of view gradually makes itself felt, and some loans begin to be classified according to what we may call institutional characteristics instead of qualitative ones. After 1928 the traditional time and demand subdivision of loans is practically discontinued, and, from 1929 on, the entire loan portfolio is classified according to the kind of security pledged, or the institutional connection or dependence of the particular type of credit. Such a change in the method of presenting information is extremely significant, as it indicates that the growing preference of national banks to loan on investment collateral has been gradually changing the point of view of the office of the Comptroller; so that now, the supervisory authorities arrange the information on loans of national banks from the standpoint of the intrinsic nature of the underlying assets, rather than the duration of the transaction on which the loan is made, as was the practice prior to the War.

Investments of National Banks

Changes in the composition of the security portfolios of national banks may now be noted. As in the case of the preceding section on loans, we deal with four parallel sets of figures covering the entire national banking system, New York City banks, city banks outside of New York City, and country banks. Total investments of national banks have been subdivided into the three following categories, and are treated in the order indicated; bonds and notes of domestic corporations, foreign bonds, and United States government securities.

From Table 123 it appears that domestic securities (the first category) held by the national-banking system, grew more than four-fold in the period from 1909 to 1932. Relative to total investments, as shown by Table 124, these holdings varied but slightly; from 52.8 per cent, in 1909, to 48.6 per cent in 1932. In the years immediately following 1909 this category formed about one-half of total investments; during the period of heavy government financing at the time of the World War and the depression that followed, it fell off to one-third of the entire se-

TABLE 123

GROWTH OF VARIOUS TYPES OF INVESTMENTS IN NATIONAL BANKS, 1909 AND 1932*

(In millions of dollars)

TYPE OF INVESTMENT	ALL NATIONAL BANKS		NEW YORK CITY BANKS		ALL OTHER CITY BANKS		COUNTRY BANKS	
	1909	1932	1909	1932	1909	1932	1909	1932
State, county and municipal bonds	156	1,031	20	113	42	428	94	490
Railroad bonds	343	653	90	132	79	142	174	379
Other public service bonds	152	684	18	51	40	126	94	507
All other bonds	171	686	34	59	52	195	85	432
Stocks (incl. Fed. Res. bk. stk.)	34	205	4	44	12	88	18	73
Collateral trust and other corp. notes	†	118	†	26	†	54	†	38
Municipal warrants, claims, etc.	22	121	1	4	6	43	15	74
Total domestic securities	878	3,499	167	429	232	1,076	479	1,994
Foreign government bonds	13	168	4	32	2	34	7	102
Other foreign securities	8	177	4	17	1	50	3	110
Total securities excl. of U. S. bonds	898	3,844	175	478	235	1,160	488	2,206
U. S. Government securities	746	3,353	61	690	216	1,472	469	1,191
All securities held	1,662	7,196	238	1,168	460	2,632	964	3,396

* Data abstracted from *Annual Reports of the Comptroller of the Currency*. Because of rounding out of figures and the omission of minor miscellaneous items, both the 1909 and the 1932 data do not add exactly to their totals.

† Unavailable for 1909.

curity portfolio. In the post-war decade domestic securities held by the national system were again equal to about one-half of total investments; but during the depression years 1931 and 1932 they declined once more relative to the aggregate.

TABLE 124

DOMESTIC SECURITIES EXCLUSIVE OF U. S. GOVERNMENT BONDS HELD BY NATIONAL BANKS, EXPRESSED AS A PERCENTAGE OF TOTAL INVESTMENTS, 1909-1932*

YEARS	ALL NATIONAL BANKS	NEW YORK CITY BANKS	ALL OTHER CITY BANKS	COUNTRY BANKS
	%	%	%	%
1909	52.8	70.3	50.3	49.7
1910	52.0	70.9	48.3	49.6
1911	54.9	75.7	51.7	51.0
1912	55.4	76.2	53.5	51.9
1913	54.1	71.1	51.8	51.7
1914	54.1	72.6	49.7	52.7
1915	59.8	75.4	58.3	57.4
1916	62.2	74.9	62.0	59.3
1917	55.7	53.0	54.8	56.9
1918	39.3	29.6	38.3	43.5
1919	32.2	28.6	28.0	35.7
1920	40.1	36.2	37.9	41.9
1921	44.8	40.5	44.1	46.0
1922	44.4	34.8	39.5	49.9
1923	42.0	27.2	35.7	49.1
1924	46.6	34.3	38.8	53.8
1925	49.4	38.9	42.1	56.2
1926	51.4	39.2	44.7	58.1
1927	52.7	39.6	45.2	60.5
1928	51.9	34.0	44.6	61.5
1929	50.5	34.4	40.9	59.5
1930	52.4	36.0	43.8	62.3
1931	51.4	34.7	43.9	62.9
1932	48.6	36.7	40.9	58.7

* Table based on data abstracted from the *Annual Reports of the Comptroller of the Currency*.

In country banks the holdings of domestic securities also decreased relative to all securities owned in the years 1918 to 1921 and regained their former position of about one-half of the entire investment portfolio in the post-war decade. In New York City national banks this type of investment amounted, prior to 1917, to about three-fourths of all bonds, declined in importance during the War, and since that time comprises only about one-third of all investments. A similar tendency, although not so pronounced, is found in the case of city banks outside of New York where domestic securities equal, since the War, about 40 per cent of total investments.

In order to allocate the cause for these changes, we must look into the changes that took place in the composition of the domestic securities group. The following types of securities are included in this category:

1. State, county, and municipal bonds
2. Railroad bonds
3. Other public service corporations
4. All other bonds
5. Stock of Federal Reserve banks
6. Stock of other corporations
7. Collateral trust and other corporate notes
8. Municipal warrants
9. All other municipal notes, including judgments, etc.

The amount of state, county, and municipal bonds purchased by the entire national system has increased very substantially since 1909 (see Table 123) . Relative to all investments, as shown by Table 125, these holdings grew in the years 1915, 1916, and 1917, and also in the post-war decade as well as during 1931 and 1932. This tendency is especially marked in the case of country banks; it is less pronounced in city banks outside of New York and is entirely absent in New York City national banks.

From 1909 to 1932 holdings of railroad securities nearly doubled (see Table 123), while Table 125 shows that relative to the entire security portfolio they declined from 20.6 per cent to 9.1 per cent. Within the same period—a similar decline took place—in city banks outside of New York City, from 17.1 per cent to 5.4 per cent, and in country banks from 18 per cent to 11.2 per cent. The same tendency is especially pronounced in the case of New York City national banks; in 1909 railroad bonds comprised 37.9 per cent of all their bond holdings as against only 11.3 per cent in 1932. So that, while prior to the War, national banks banks invested heavily in railroad bonds, in the post-war period railroad securities have occupied a much less important position, especially in the case of urban national banks.

From Table 125 it is also noted that bonds of other public service corporations amounted to about 10 per cent of all bonds owned by the national system prior to 1918; they declined in relative importance in the years 1918-1922 to around 6 per cent, and rose again to 10.1 per cent in 1927. In New York City national banks, and city banks outside of New York City this post-war rise in relation to the aggregate did not take place; in both cases the percentage of the total bond portfolio represented by the holdings of other public service corporations was approximately one-half after the War of what it was prior to 1917. On the other hand, in case of country banks, investment in these bonds made up 16.8 per cent of all investments in 1931, while the pre-war peak was 12.3 per cent. As with the railroad bonds, securities of other public service corporations lost in the post-war period their relative importance in urban national banks, although they still comprised about one-sixth of all the bonds held in country banks.

All other bonds representing miscellaneous securities amounted in the case of the entire national system (see Table 125) to about 10 per cent of the aggregate securities held in the periods 1909-1917 and 1923-1931. In the years of heavy war financing and in depressions this group tends to decrease in importance. In country banks other bonds held comprised 18.3 per cent of total bonds in 1928 after declining to 6.7 per cent in 1919; and in 1932 they again fell off, this time to 12.7 per cent of the investment portfolio. In New York City national banks all other bonds equaled more than 14 per cent of all security holdings from 1909 to 1914, but did not regain their former importance after the war-time decline. But, in city banks outside of New York City, the trend was similar to the one for the country as a whole. Evidently this type of investment tends to decline in periods of depression in all groups of national banks; in the post-war period it is definitely losing out in New York City national banks and gaining in country banks.

For the entire national system, stock in Federal Reserve banks about doubled in amount (from $54,200,000 in 1916 to $90,417,000 in 1932), while on a relative basis it fell off from 2.6 per cent to 1.3 per cent of all investments. As a percentage of the entire investment portfolio, Federal Reserve banks stock was losing in importance in all groups of national banks. Holdings of miscellaneous stocks are also quite insignificant, although for all groups of national banks they comprise a slightly higher percentage of all investments in the years 1909 to 1914. Collateral trust and other corporate notes declined for the national system from 3.6 per cent of all investments, in 1918, to 1.6 per cent in 1932. It is evident that all groups of national banks tend to hold fewer stocks.

Municipal warrants held by the national system oscillated around 2 per cent of all investments in the period from 1909 to 1917; since that time they were declining in importance. Only in city banks outside of New York City municipal warrants showed a slight increase in 1930 and 1931. Other forms of municipal short-term indebtedness such as judgments, show in 1929-1932 a tendency to rise in country banks, but do not rise beyond one per cent of all investments.

From this analysis of the holdings of domestic securities by national banks based on the data presented in Table 125, we may draw the following conclusions: In the case of the entire national-banking system about one-half of the investment portfolio is composed of bonds and notes of domestic corporations. Prior to the War even a larger portion of the total security holdings of banks located in cities was composed of domestic securities, since the War this type of investment has fallen off in importance in urban banks, and especially so in New York City. In the war period national banks purchased foreign securities and United States government obligations, and decreased very substantially their ownership of domestic corporate securities. The same applies to the first post-war depression of 1920 and 1921, when, as compared to the pre-war period all groups of national banks held much fewer domestic securities. The same deflation of this type of investment took place in the depression

TABLE 125

FOUR TYPES OF BONDS HELD BY NATIONAL BANKS EXPRESSED AS PERCENTAGES OF TOTAL INVESTMENTS*

YEARS	STATE, COUNTY AND MUNICIPAL BONDS				RAILROAD BONDS			
	All National Banks	New York City Banks	All Other City Banks	Country Banks	All National Banks	New York City Banks	All Other City Banks	Country Banks
	%	%	%	%	%	%	%	%
1909	9.4	8.3	9.1	9.7	20.6	37.9	17.1	18.0
1910	9.1	3.8	9.2	10.3	17.9	35.4	12.4	16.6
1911	9.2	3.3	10.4	10.2	20.2	43.2	14.4	16.9
1912	9.6	6.6	9.4	10.4	19.0	41.3	14.6	16.3
1913	9.2	3.7	9.5	10.2	18.1	38.3	14.2	15.9
1914	9.1	4.3	8.2	10.5	17.7	38.0	14.1	15.5
1915	11.8	7.6	11.6	12.8	18.3	37.8	15.7	15.6
1916	11.8	8.5	12.9	12.2	19.9	39.8	17.2	16.4
1917	11.1	5.5	12.4	12.0	16.4	23.5	14.7	15.4
1918	8.1	4.5	8.3	9.3	10.3	12.0	8.7	10.5
1919	6.4	4.5	6.5	6.9	8.2	10.9	6.1	8.6
1920	8.1	4.9	9.2	8.4	9.9	13.6	7.9	10.0
1921	9.8	9.1	11.7	9.2	10.1	11.9	7.9	10.5
1922	9.1	6.1	9.8	9.7	10.7	11.4	7.2	12.1
1923	7.9	4.5	7.9	8.9	9.9	9.9	6.0	11.9
1924	9.8	9.2	9.4	10.2	11.2	11.3	6.9	13.1
1925	10.4	10.3	10.4	10.4	11.8	11.9	8.1	13.6
1926	11.1	8.4	12.1	11.3	10.8	11.4	7.3	12.4
1927	11.6	9.1	13.2	11.4	10.3	10.5	7.2	11.9
1928	11.8	7.2	13.9	11.7	9.5	8.0	7.3	11.4
1929	11.4	5.4	12.8	11.8	8.9	11.0	5.4	10.5
1930	11.5	5.1	13.3	12.3	9.6	11.6	6.1	11.1
1931	13.0	5.6	15.3	13.7	9.4	11.3	5.8	11.5
1932	14.3	9.7	16.3	14.4	9.1	11.3	5.4	11.2

* Table compiled on the basis of data abstracted from the *Annual Reports of the Comptroller of the Currency.*

TABLE 125 *(Continued)*

FOUR TYPES OF BONDS HELD BY NATIONAL BANKS EXPRESSED AS PERCENTAGES OF TOTAL INVESTMENTS*

YEARS	OTHER PUBLIC SERVICE CORPORATION BONDS				MISCELLANEOUS BONDS			
	All National Banks	New York City Banks	All Other City Banks	Country Banks	All National Banks	New York City Banks	All Other City Banks	Country Banks
	%	%	%	%	%	%	%	%
1909	9.1	7.7	8.7	9.7	10.3	14.2	11.3	8.8
1910	10.0	10.6	9.9	9.9	10.6	17.3	10.9	9.1
1911	10.2	8.8	10.4	10.5	11.1	17.3	11.0	9.6
1912	10.5	9.9	9.9	10.8	12.0	15.8	13.6	10.5
1913	10.4	10.4	9.7	10.7	11.6	15.5	11.7	10.7
1914	11.3	12.8	11.0	11.2	11.8	15.8	11.5	11.2
1915	10.7	8.4	10.7	11.1	11.9	14.4	12.5	11.1
1916	11.7	8.9	11.7	12.3	12.8	14.5	13.2	12.3
1917	10.4	6.4	9.1	12.0	12.7	15.0	12.6	12.2
1918	6.8	2.8	5.4	8.9	6.9	4.7	6.9	7.7
1919	5.5	2.5	3.7	7.4	6.1	5.0	5.5	6.7
1920	6.8	3.1	5.4	8.3	7.4	7.3	6.6	7.8
1921	6.9	3.5	5.2	8.3	8.8	6.5	7.8	9.6
1922	7.0	2.9	4.8	9.3	9.3	6.1	7.4	11.2
1923	6.7	1.9	3.9	9.3	10.3	5.9	8.3	12.4
1924	7.7	2.6	4.5	10.7	11.2	6.5	9.5	13.4
1925	8.6	3.3	5.2	12.0	12.2	7.9	10.0	14.6
1926	9.3	3.2	5.7	12.9	13.2	9.1	10.5	15.7
1927	10.1	3.4	6.6	14.0	14.2	9.2	10.7	17.6
1928	10.4	3.4	6.2	15.0	14.4	8.0	11.1	18.3
1929	10.4	3.8	5.3	14.9	13.2	6.0	10.1	16.6
1930	11.4	4.3	6.7	16.2	12.9	7.5	9.1	16.9
1931	10.8	4.4	5.9	16.8	11.6	6.5	9.1	15.2
1932	9.5	4.3	4.8	14.9	9.5	5.1	7.4	12.7

of 1930-1932, but on a lesser scale than in the crisis of the early twenties, and with the difference that the holdings of state, county, and municipal bonds increased rather than declined.

At present there is a marked difference in the extent to which New York City national banks, city banks outside of New York City, and country banks invest in stocks and bonds of domestic corporations. In New York City national banks, domestic securities declined from 70.3 per cent of the entire investment portfolio, in 1909, to 36.7 per cent in 1932, owing to the fact that state, county, and municipal bonds, railroad bonds, securities of public service corporations and miscellaneous bonds, never regained their former importance after the war-time drop and the post-war depression.

In city banks outside of New York City the decrease in domestic securities held was about 10 per cent of the entire bond portfolio (50.3 per cent, in 1909, to 40.9 per cent in 1932) owing to the drop in the holdings of railroad and public-service corporation bonds. The offsetting influence was the rapid increase in state, county, and municipal bonds, and the comparatively slight decline in the holdings of miscellaneous bonds.

In country banks the relative importance of domestic securities increased as compared with the pre-war years (49.7 per cent, in 1909, to 58.7 per cent in 1932.) This is because of the fact that railroad and public-service bonds rose after the depression of 1921 to about the same percentage of total investments as before the War, and the holdings of state, county, and municipal bonds and miscellaneous securities increased relative to the total in the post-war period.

The second category into which was subdivided the security portfolio of national banks consists of various foreign bonds. Foreign government bonds were of minor importance as a bank investment prior to the War. They rose to 10 per cent of all investments in 1917 for the entire national system, to 21.4 per cent in New York City national banks, to 9.7 per cent in city banks outside of New York City, and 7.1 per cent in country banks. After the close of the War the holdings of foreign government bonds declined very rapidly, and, during the post-war era, in not one of the groups of national banks did they exceed 5 per cent of all investments. Foreign bonds other than governments did not show any exceptional rise during the War. After the War this type of investment showed a slight trend upwards so far as relative importance goes; and, although it does not exceed in any group of national banks 5 per cent of all investment, it is about equal to bonds of foreign governments.

We have shown that for the entire national-banking system about one-half of all investments consisted in recent years of domestic issues and that bonds of foreign governments and corporations comprised not more than 10 per cent of total investments. The rest of the investments, or around 40 per cent of the aggregate, are United States government obligations.

We observe from Table 126 that in the entire national-banking system the United States government securities held amounted to around one-half of all investments in 1900; this percentage gradually declined so that in 1916 government bonds owned were equal to slightly less than one-third of all bonds. In the war years national banks purchased great quantities of government bonds; in 1919 such obligations comprised 62.8 per cent of the entire bond portfolio. This expansion of investment in government bonds took place at the expense of the holdings of domestic securities, which declined in these years from one-half to about one-third of the aggregate investments. In the post-war decade the government bonds owned by the national system fell off to around forty per cent of all securities; but, because of renewed heavy financing on the part of the Federal Government in the present depression, they rose again to 46.6 per cent in 1932.

A somewhat similar tendency can be observed for the first two decades of the century in New York City national banks and in city banks outside of New York City. In both of these groups of national banks the holdings of government bonds comprised around one-half of the investments in 1900, and declined steadily up to the time of heavy war financing. In New York City national banks this decline was especially pronounced. From 1906 on, government bonds amounted to less than one-third of all

TABLE 126

UNITED STATES GOVERNMENT BONDS HELD BY NATIONAL BANKS EXPRESSED AS A PERCENTAGE OF TOTAL INVESTMENTS, 1900-1932*

YEARS	ALL NATIONAL BANKS	NEW YORK CITY BANKS	ALL OTHER CITY BANKS	COUNTRY BANKS
	%	%	%	%
1900	53.3	47.0	50.1	57.0
1901	50.3	44.7	48.1	53.3
1902	48.8	46.3	46.4	50.7
1903	49.8	41.5	49.1	53.1
1904	48.1	34.6	48.4	52.3
1905	45.7	32.0	45.4	50.0
1906	48.3	30.2	49.2	52.5
1907	46.8	26.1	49.7	50.9
1908	46.1	27.0	47.0	50.7
1909	44.9	25.5	46.8	48.7
1910	46.5	26.4	49.4	49.5
1911	43.4	22.0	46.1	47.7
1912	42.1	21.9	43.6	45.7
1913	41.9	22.5	42.9	45.3
1914	41.3	22.0	43.5	43.9
1915	37.9	17.8	40.0	41.0
1916	31.1	11.5	30.8	35.8
1917	31.8	23.6	32.9	33.5
1918	53.5	60.3	55.0	50.2
1919	62.8	64.9	67.7	59.4
1920	54.2	55.8	57.8	52.2
1921	50.2	54.1	52.4	48.4
1922	50.1	62.0	56.7	43.1
1923	53.1	69.6	61.3	44.7
1924	48.3	61.3	57.7	40.0
1925	44.3	56.0	52.2	36.8
1926	42.3	56.9	49.9	34.3
1927	40.6	56.0	50.0	31.1
1928	40.5	60.0	50.0	28.9
1929	42.1	59.4	54.8	30.9
1930	40.0	57.6	51.2	28.1
1931	42.4	58.9	52.3	29.0
1932	46.6	59.1	55.9	35.1

* Table based on data abstracted from the *Annual Reports of the Comptroller of the Currency.*

bonds and fell off to 11.5 per cent of the entire security portfolio in 1916. After the period of heavy governmental financing was over, the holdings of United States securities by urban banks did not decline to the same extent as was the case in the national-banking system as a whole. In New York City national banks government bonds continued to comprise around 60 per cent of all investments; in city banks outside of New York City they make up around one-half of all bonds owned.

In country national banks the pre-war decline in government bonds owned was much less marked than in urban national banks; up to 1915 this type of investment comprised more than 40 per cent of all bond holdings. After the war country banks decreased their investments in government bonds to about one-third of their aggregate investments, and began placing their funds once more in securities of domestic corporations.

We can thus conclude, from the data presented in Table 126, that before the War United States government bonds were losing their importance as an investment for national banks, especially in the case of city national banks. In the war period all groups of national banks increased their government-bond portfolio and decreased their holdings of domestic corporate securities. In the post-war decade city national banks continued to hold one-half, or more, of their total investments in government obligations, while country banks deflated their government-bond portfolios and reverted to the original practice of purchasing corporate securities.

National banks have to hold United States government obligations in order to secure their outstanding national-bank notes and they may also purchase such securities as an investment for their surplus funds. At the beginning of the century a considerable amount of government bonds was held for purely investment purposes by all groups of national banks. In 1900 in the entire national system 15.8 per cent of all investments consisted of government bonds owned exclusive of bonds held to secure circulation. Since 1900 that amount was steadily declining owing to the fact that the federal debt was being rapidly amortized, and there were fewer government bonds available for purchase; so that in 1916 only 1.7 per cent of the aggregate investments of the national system were placed in government obligations that were not held as a cover for national-bank notes. At the same time the percentage of all investments comprised by government bonds, held to secure circulation, remained fairly stationary during the years 1900 to 1914.

Since the War the amount of national-bank notes outstanding has been declining, and the bonds pledged to secure these notes also declined so that, by 1932, they equaled less than ten per cent of the entire bond portfolio. But throughout the post-war period the government bonds held as an investment continued to comprise more than one-third of all the bonds owned by the national-banking system. This change in the purpose for which the national-banking system purchases obligations of the federal government is demonstrated by Table 127.

The post-war tendency of national banks to invest a considerable part of their secondary reserves in governmental obligations can be attributed to the following cause. In 1916 the Federal Reserve Act was amended, and member banks were permitted to discount their own direct notes secured by United States government obligations. In 1917 the Act was further amended, the reserve requirements were cut, and banks were required to carry all legal reserves as balances with the Federal Reserve banks. For many years banks were accustomed to keep a part of the reserve funds in their own vaults. The law of 1917 deprived them of this right, but the amendment of 1916 made it possible for national banks to convert their holdings of government bonds into other forms of credit through the use of the rediscount privilege. National banks therefore, simply continued the practice acquired in the era of heavy war financing and went on holding large quantities of federal securities.

This new investment practice brought about a definite change in the idea underlying the investment policy of national banks and of American commercial banking in general. Investments of a commercial bank must—according to the orthodox theory of commercial banking—constitute its secondary reserve and must be composed of a variety of securities that are easily marketable. The placing of one-third or more of all investments in a single type of security—government bonds—creates a definite dependence on the one market for these bonds that is always open to the bank, namely the Federal Reserve. This has not only brought about an investment dependence of commercial-national banks on the Reserve banks which were originally

TABLE 127

UNITED STATES GOVERNMENT BONDS HELD TO SECURE CIRCULATION AND AS AN INVESTMENT EXPRESSED AS A PERCENTAGE OF INVESTMENTS, 1900-1932*

YEAR	U. S. GOVERNMENT BONDS HELD TO SECURE CIRCULATION	U. S. GOVERNMENT BONDS HELD AS AN INVESTMENT
	%	%
1900	37.5	15.8
1901	36.5	13.9
1902	33.7	15.1
1903	35.4	14.5
1904	36.2	11.9
1905	38.5	7.1
1906	39.4	8.9
1907	38.6	8.1
1908	39.5	6.6
1909	40.2	4.6
1910	42.4	4.1
1911	39.6	3.8
1912	38.8	3.3
1913	38.7	3.2
1914	38.2	3.0
1915	35.7	2.2
1916	29.4	1.7
1917	23.6	8.2
1918	17.4	36.0
1919	13.7	49.1
1920	16.9	37.3
1921	18.0	32.2
1922	16.1	34.0
1923	14.7	38.4
1924	14.6	33.7
1925	11.6	32.7
1926	11.4	30.9
1927	10.4	30.2
1928	9.3	31.1
1929	10.0	32.1
1930	9.7	30.3
1931	8.7	33.7
1932	9.3	37.3

* Table based on data abstracted from *Annual Reports of the Comptroller of the Currency.*

planned as purely commercial-paper central banks, but it has also given the Reserve banks themselves the investment function of providing a market for government bonds, either through rediscounts or through direct purchases. This post-war practice of national banks to build up large portfolios of United States government obligations does not mean, therefore, merely that the national system follows a new investment policy; a very definite change in the nature of operations of commercial banks, as such, has taken place which, in turn, has been partially responsible for the "switch" in the functions of the central banks into investment channels, that has taken place since the War.

Comparison of Loans and Investments

After having analyzed the composition of both the loans and the investments of national banks, we may compare these two parts of the portfolio with each other. We find that, up to the time of the War, investments made up about one-quarter and loans about three-quarters, of the entire portfolio. In urban national banks investment tended to be slightly below one-fourth, and in rural banks somewhat above one-quarter, of all loans and investments. In the war period in all groups of national-banks investments rose sharply to about one-third of the entire portfolio; but in 1920 and 1921 they fell off to the pre-war proportions. After the depression of the early twenties, investments began to increase in all groups of national banks; in the so-called prosperity period they began to equal once more about one-third of the entire portfolio. With the coming of the present depression investments started to increase at a war-time pace and, by 1932, they comprised more than 40 per cent of the combined loans and investments of the national-banking system. This post-war growth of investments as well as the trend back to 1900 are shown in Table 128, where the total investments are expressed in percentages of the entire portfolio.

The cause of the growth of investments after the War, as well as of their rapid increase in the depression, is found in the policy followed by national banks in respect to the purchase of United States government bonds. In 1932 government bonds owned by the national system equaled 19.2 per cent of combined loans and investments. In the same year one-quarter of the combined loan and security portfolio of New York City national banks was

TABLE 128: RELATIVE IMPORTANCE OF LOANS AND INVESTMENTS OF NATIONAL BANKS, 1900-1932*

YEARS	LOANS AS PERCENTAGES OF LOANS AND INVESTMENTS				INVESTMENTS AS PERCENTAGES OF LOANS AND INVESTMENTS			
	All Natl. Banks	N.Y.C. Banks	All Other City Banks	Country Banks	All Natl. Banks	N.Y.C. Banks	All Other City Banks	Country Banks
1900	77.4%	79.8%	81.0%	73.8%	22.6%	20.2%	19.0%	26.2%
1901	77.0	79.5	80.2	73.7	23.0	20.5	19.8	26.3
1902	77.3	78.0	81.1	74.5	22.7	22.0	18.9	25.5
1903	76.4	76.2	79.8	74.2	23.6	23.8	20.2	25.8
1904	76.3	79.5	79.3	73.0	23.7	20.5	20.7	27.0
1905	76.3	79.0	80.1	72.8	23.7	21.0	19.9	27.2
1906	76.4	78.2	79.9	73.5	23.6	21.8	20.1	26.5
1907	76.4	76.3	80.7	73.8	23.6	23.7	19.3	26.2
1908	74.9	79.2	78.1	71.4	25.1	20.8	21.9	28.6
1909	75.5	79.6	79.2	71.8	24.5	20.4	20.8	28.2
1910	77.2	80.8	80.7	74.0	22.8	19.2	19.3	26.0
1911	75.9	77.0	80.0	72.9	24.1	23.0	20.0	27.1
1912	76.2	80.2	80.0	72.6	23.8	19.8	20.0	27.4
1913	76.4	79.3	80.2	73.3	23.6	20.7	19.8	26.7
1914	76.9	82.7	80.3	73.2	23.1	17.3	19.7	26.8
1915	76.3	82.9	79.4	72.2	23.7	17.1	20.6	27.8
1916	76.6	82.9	80.5	71.3	23.4	17.1	19.5	28.7
1917	75.9	81.4	80.7	70.2	24.1	18.6	19.3	29.8
1918	71.9	74.6	77.0	66.6	28.1	25.4	23.0	33.4
1919	68.5	75.9	72.1	62.5	31.5	24.1	27.9	37.5
1920	76.5	82.0	82.2	69.9	23.5	18.0	17.8	30.1
1921	74.9	80.0	81.7	68.6	25.1	20.0	18.3	31.4
1922	71.1	71.7	76.3	67.5	28.9	28.3	23.7	32.5
1923	70.0	70.2	75.2	66.5	30.0	29.8	24.8	33.5
1924	70.0	70.2	75.5	66.3	30.0	29.8	24.5	33.7
1925	68.9	68.7	74.2	65.3	31.1	31.3	25.8	34.7
1926	69.7	71.5	74.4	65.8	30.3	28.5	25.6	34.2
1927	68.6	71.5	72.9	64.4	31.4	28.5	27.1	35.6
1928	67.9	72.2	71.4	63.6	32.1	27.8	28.6	36.4
1929	69.0	75.6	72.2	64.6	31.0	24.4	27.8	35.4
1930	68.4	73.0	72.0	63.8	31.6	27.0	28.0	36.2
1931	63.2	66.9	64.3	60.7	36.8	33.1	35.7	39.3
1932	58.8	57.3	61.7	56.9	41.2	42.7	38.3	43.1

* Compiled on the basis of data abstracted from the *Annual Reports of the Comptroller of the Currency.*

TABLE 129

UNITED STATES GOVERNMENT SECURITIES HELD EXPRESSED AS A PERCENTAGE OF COMBINED LOANS AND INVESTMENTS*

YEARS	ALL NATIONAL BANKS	NEW YORK CITY BANKS	ALL OTHER CITY BANKS	COUNTRY BANKS
	%	%	%	%
1900	12.1	9.5	9.5	14.9
1901	11.6	9.2	9.5	14.0
1902	11.1	10.2	8.8	12.9
1903	11.8	9.9	9.9	13.7
1904	11.4	7.1	10.0	14.1
1905	10.8	6.7	9.0	13.6
1906	11.4	6.6	9.9	13.9
1907	11.0	6.2	9.6	13.3
1908	11.6	5.6	10.3	14.5
1909	11.0	5.2	9.7	13.8
1910	10.6	5.1	9.5	12.9
1911	10.5	5.1	9.2	12.9
1912	10.0	4.3	8.7	12.5
1913	9.9	4.7	8.5	12.1
1914	9.5	3.8	8.6	11.8
1915	9.0	3.1	8.2	11.4
1916	7.3	2.0	6.0	10.3
1917	7.7	4.4	6.4	10.0
1918	15.0	15.3	12.7	16.7
1919	19.8	15.7	18.9	22.3
1920	12.8	10.1	10.3	15.7
1921	12.6	10.8	9.6	15.2
1922	14.5	17.5	13.4	14.0
1923	16.0	20.7	15.2	15.0
1924	14.5	18.3	14.1	13.5
1925	13.8	17.5	13.5	12.7
1926	12.8	16.2	12.8	11.7
1927	12.8	16.0	13.6	11.1
1928	13.0	16.7	14.3	10.5
1929	13.1	14.5	15.3	11.0
1930	12.6	15.6	14.3	10.2
1931	15.6	19.5	18.7	11.4
1932	19.2	25.2	21.4	15.1

* Computed on the basis of data compiled from the *Annual Reports of the Comptroller of the Currency.*

placed in government bonds; in city banks outside of New York City 21.4 per cent of the aggregate portfolio consisted of government obligations. So that the growth of investments at the expense of loans after the War, and especially in the present depression, must be attributed in the case of urban national banks to the increase of government-bond holdings.

In country banks holdings of government bonds comprised a smaller part of all earning assets in the last ten years than they did prior to the War. At the same time, as has been shown in Table 128, the growth of investments has been especially pronounced in country banks. This was owing to the fact that, although country banks decreased their holdings of government obligations after the War, they increased their purchases of bonds of domestic corporations and of state, municipal, and county issues. As a result investments of country banks increased at the expense of loans even to a larger extent than those of urban national banks; but the expanded investment portfolio of country banks was made up largely of various corporate issues, instead of government bonds, as was the case in city national banks.

If we compare the loans and investments of national banks with their deposit liabilities, we find that a substantial change took place in the relation of loans to deposits, but that the ratio of investments to deposits remained comparatively unaltered. Prior to the War loans were practically equal to total deposits, while investments amounted to about one-third of deposits. Since the War the ratio of loans to deposits has been declining; in the past ten years loans amounted to about three-quarters of total deposits. In the same post-war years investments rose only slightly above one-third of deposits or their pre-war ratio. However, in the depression years a change did take place: in 1932 loans declined further to 65.7 per cent of total deposits, and investments rose to 46.9 per cent of deposits. But during the entire period, from 1900 up to the depression, investments amounted to about one-third of total deposits while loans, which were equal to deposits before and in the war period, declined to about three-fourths of total deposits.

This description may well be closed by indicating the change that has taken place in the years 1915 to 1932 in the relationship of commercial and investment assets of national banks. In investment assets we include all bonds owned, loans secured by

TABLE 130

RELATION OF LOANS AND INVESTMENTS OF NATIONAL BANKS TO TOTAL DEPOSITS, 1900-1932*

YEARS	LOANS AS A PERCENTAGE OF TOTAL DEPOSITS	INVESTMENTS AS A PERCENTAGE OF TOTAL DEPOSITS
	%	%
1900	103.4	31.3
1901	97.9	29.9
1902	100.7	30.0
1903	102.8	32.5
1904	105.8	33.7
1905	101.8	32.6
1906	102.2	31.4
1907	103.5	32.5
1908	102.9	35.3
1909	101.7	33.4
1910	101.9	30.5
1911	101.9	32.3
1912	101.5	32.2
1913	102.3	31.9
1914	101.1	30.0
1915	100.8	31.9
1916	94.1	29.4
1917	92.0	31.4
1918	90.5	35.7
1919	87.6	39.4
1920	98.5	29.6
1921	94.3	31.4
1922	82.7	33.5
1923	89.9	38.6
1924	78.1	33.8
1925	75.5	40.2
1926	77.0	33.6
1927	73.8	34.4
1928	76.3	36.6
1929	76.3	34.9
1930	77.4	34.1
1931	67.8	40.1
1932	65.7	46.9

* Table based on data abstracted from *Annual Reports of the Comptroller of the Currency.*

stocks and bonds, and loans collateraled by real estate; the commercial assets comprise all other loans.

As we see from the accompanying Table 131, in 1915 more than 40 per cent of combined loans and investments of all national banks consisted of investment assets; in New York City national banks such assets comprised 58.5 per cent of the aggregate. In the post-war depression the investment assets fell off, and the commercial side of the portfolio increased, but, in 1922, investment assets resumed their growth and increased steadily through the post-war decade and the present depression for all

TABLE 131

INVESTMENT ASSETS OF NATIONAL BANKS EXPRESSED AS A PERCENTAGE OF ALL EARNING ASSETS*

(Investment assets—bonds owned, loans on stocks and bonds, and loans on real estate. All earning assets—loans and investments combined)

YEARS	ALL NATIONAL BANKS	NEW YORK CITY BANKS	ALL OTHER CITY BANKS	COUNTRY BANKS
	%	%	%	%
1915	45.5	58.5	42.7	42.9
1916	46.8	62.0	42.5	43.4
1917	45.4	55.1	40.8	44.0
1918	48.7	53.8	44.2	47.5
1919	54.0	59.6	53.0	52.3
1920	42.3	41.6	39.1	45.1
1921	43.6	42.8	40.4	46.8
1922	49.6	57.2	46.4	48.6
1923	47.9	58.8	47.0	50.1
1924	51.2	60.8	47.3	50.7
1925	54.5	64.1	51.6	52.2
1926	55.1	62.6	52.9	54.1
1927	58.4	65.4	57.8	56.6
1928	60.8	63.6	61.2	59.3
1929	61.5	66.9	61.0	59.0
1930	64.2	72.0	64.0	61.4
1931	66.8	69.4	67.9	64.8
1932	69.8	72.9	70.5	68.1

* Computed on the bases of data abstracted from the *Annual Reports of the Comptroller of the Currency.*

groups of national banks. The percentage Table 131 likewise shows that by 1932 investment assets of commercial-national banks amounted to about three-quarters of all earning assets, with the commercial side of the portfolio declining to only around one-fourth of the aggregate.

As must be clear from the preceding pages, this expansion of investment assets, at the expense of commercial assets, has been owing to increases in the amount of government securities held by city banks, and miscellaneous bonds held by country banks. In addition national banks acquired the practice of loaning heavily on stocks and bonds and financing city real estate. The growth of these three types of activity, which do not constitute a commercial-banking function according to the older theory of commercial banking, has resulted in bringing down the commercial assets of national banks to only slightly above one-fourth of their total earning assets, or combined loans and investments. This has taken place while the liabilities of national banks continue to consist of demand deposits and time deposits which are to a considerable extent subject to withdrawal upon notice.

The ramifications of this change in the composition of the portfolio of national banks have been briefly indicated in the process of presenting the various shifts in the composition of loans and investments. They are taken up separately and discussed in detail and at greater length in other parts of this book; here we can only restate the conclusions drawn in the course of our descriptive presentation.

SUMMARY

In the thirty years from 1900 to 1932 the traditional form of American commercial credit—endorsed paper—has been declining, and loans on collateral have increased. This tendency is especially strong in country banks, about one-half as pronounced in city national banks, and practically absent in New York City.

The increase in collateral loans at the expense of endorsed paper has been owing, since 1915, to a growth of loans secured by stocks and bonds, as well as by city real estate. During the same years, from 1915 to 1932, loans on personal property and merchandise declined in importance, and loans on farm land were comparatively insignificant.

In the selection of loans national banks show a tendency to shift from self-liquidating transactions to advances based on securities and fixed assets. Since 1915 all loans backed by investment collateral grew from less than one-third to nearly one-half of aggregate loans by 1932.

The use made of Federal Reserve facilities in commercial-banking transactions is decreasing, and the commercial-paper link between the member institutions and the reserve banks is growing weaker. National banks are carrying a constantly smaller percentage of loans that are eligible for rediscount; in 1932 less than one-sixth of all loans of national banks was rediscounted or eligible for rediscount at the reserve banks.

The way in which the office of the Comptroller has changed the presentation of its statistics of loans indicates that banking authorities are gradually placing greater emphasis on the institutional characteristics of a loan rather than on the nature of the underlying transaction.

The nature of published data on national banks is such that it is difficult to make an adequate comparison of the composition of secured loans in the pre-war period with the years following 1915: therefore, it is hard to say to what extent the above tendencies prevailed prior to the War.

Before the War national banks invested heavily in securities of domestic corporations and especially in railroad bonds. In the period of heavy government financing during, and immediately after, the War domestic securities were to a large extent replaced by government bonds.

After the War city national banks continued to carry large amounts of government bonds; railroad bonds and most other domestic securities did not resume their original importance. Country banks, however, deflated their holdings of government obligations and not only resumed but expanded their old practice of holding domestic issues.

The purpose for which national banks purchase government bonds has changed since the close of the War. In the past decade about one-third of all investments of the national system is composed of government bonds that are not held to secure circulation, but as an outright investment.

Since the War the investment part of the portfolio of national banks has been increasing. While before the War investments were equal to about one-fourth of the total portfolio, after the War they rose to one-third of the aggregate and continued to increase even further in the depression. In the depression of 1920 and 1921 investments declined and loans increased relative to the total portfolio; during the present depression the reverse took place.

The post-war growth of investments is owing to increased holding of government bonds in the case of city national banks; in country banks the expansion of investments is owing to extensive purchases of domestic corporate issues and state, county, and municipal bonds.

The ratio between investments and deposits of one to three has undergone few changes from 1900 to 1930, while the ratio of loans to deposits has declined from one to one before the War to three to four after the War.

The portfolio of national banks has definitely lost its commercial character; in 1932 nearly three-fourths of all loans and investments consisted of investment assets and only slightly more than one-fourth was made up of commercial assets. This is owing to the practice of holding greater amounts of bonds and to the expansion of loans based on non-commercial assets, such as stocks and bonds as well as city real estate.

These changes, in the composition of the portfolio of national banks, have brought about an investment dependence of commercial banks upon the Reserve banks, and have also fostered the performance of investment functions by the reserve banks themselves.

CHAPTER XXV

BANKS AND REAL-ESTATE LOANS[1]

The question of bank portfolios and of banking relationship to the securities market furnishes a background for the discussion of various important special situations affecting the use of bank assets. In this, the application of bank funds in the financing of real-estate operations, and in the making of real-estate loans, is probably the most significant.

The older conception of banking, upon which American banking legislation was modeled, did not recognize real-estate lending as a satisfactory form of bank activity. The early years of the national-banking system and the contemporary period under state banking, undoubtedly saw a great deal of real-estate security in the hands of banks. A good deal of it, however, was security that had been taken to protect loans that had been made upon a more or less self-liquidating or current business basis. Other real-estate holdings had been placed in the banks as security for the working out of indebtedness that had been contracted upon some other footing which had developed disappointingly, and hence had to be paid off through the realization of long-term loans when, as, and if possible. The banks tended, however, more and more toward the making, through one excuse or another, of loans directly founded upon real estate, during the twenty years which preceded the adoption of the Federal Reserve Act.

The mutual-savings-bank system of the Eastern states, which had tended to concentrate its loans upon city real-estate security did not spread rapidly into other parts of the country, while any distinct financial organization for the purpose of lending to the farmer was absent. Thus, at the close of the first decade of the twentieth century, the banking system of the United States was fairly open to the charge that it provided wholly inadequate and

[1] A substantial part of this present chapter was prepared by John G. Becker; statistical tables by V. D. Kazakévich.

unsatisfactory methods for the furnishing of capital, either to farm development or city growth and need. In these circumstances, the general movement which produced the Federal Reserve Act, and later the Federal Farm Loan Act of 1916, proposed to itself a relaxation of restricting law which would permit the freer use of bank funds in the development of land and of enterprises connected therewith.

The endeavor to protect the bankers' ability to pay deposits upon demand had for a long time been centered in the provisions which forbade the banker any voluntary investment in real estate, or any investment with real estate as the collateral security.

Section 3137 of the National Banking Act[2] read:

> A National Bank Association may purchase, hold, and convey real estate for the following purpose and no others: 1) that necessary for the immediate transaction of its own business; 2) such as shall be mortgaged to it by way of security for previous debts.

The loophole in the second clause was partially stopped by requiring banks acquiring such real-estate security to dispose of it within five years.[3] The courts, however, interpreting sections 5136 and 5137 of the National Bank Act, held that where violation of the provisions prohibiting holding of real estate did take place, these acts were not of themselves null and void, but were subject only to positive protest by the Federal Government alone. It is a matter of history that many violations did take place and loans were frequently granted to names whose security was implicit largely in their realty holdings.

The demand for permission to employ real estate as a basis of credit became particularly urgent in the case of farm lands. Both public policy and the convenience of the farmer and the banker pleaded the admission of this form of wealth, often the only tangible form in the farmer's possession, as a base for bank credit. Recognition of this plea made its first appearance in the Federal Reserve Act of December 23, 1913. Section 24 of that Act read:[4]

[2] Willis Seaver Paine, *National Banking Laws* (1914).
[3] Nat. Bank vs. Matthews 98 U. S. 621 and Slade vs. Squire 133 App. Div. 666.
[4] Text of Act slightly elided for purpose of clarity at expense of legal formality.

Loans aggregating 25% of capital and surplus or one-third of time deposits permitted on improved and unencumbered farm lands up to 50% of their worth for a period not longer than 5 years.

This entering wedge into the solid wall of prohibition was widened some three years later in the amendments to the Act in a bill passed September 7, 1916.[5] Retaining all the restrictions of the original act as to:

50% of valuation
25% of capital and surplus in aggregate amount, and 1/3 of time deposits

this amendment added to the farm-land maturities of five years, permission to lend on non-farm land for one year, if it were "improved and unencumbered." In both of these permissive enactments the general provisions of Section 5200[6] were wisely retained and, in fact, have not been rescinded in any way to the present day. This section prevents lending to any one interest more than 10 per cent of the capital and surplus in the aggregate at any one time on his own unsecured note.

Central Reserve city banks were not at that time allowed the advantage of investing in real estate, as the lawmakers contemplated their liquidity as a matter of prime importance. The larger banks in Reserve cities and certain others have been conspicuous for refraining from real-estate commitments in spite of later relaxation of the stringent prohibition applied to them in the division of investment.

Further Relaxations of Law

As the post-war period advanced well into the third decade of the century, the increasing scarcity of commercial paper, the convenience of customers and the necessities of the bankers combined to put pressure on Congress for a further relaxation of the real-estate provisions in Sec. 24 of the Reserve Act as amended in 1916. About this time real-estate bonds put in their appearance. These undivided fractional interests in mortgages or less than mortgages gained wide popular vogue through high returns and such advertising propaganda employed in their promotion as "not a dollar of principal or interest ever lost."

[5] *Digest of Rulings of Federal Reserve Board,* 1914-1923 incl., p. 340.
[6] Revised Statutes, Sec. 3200.

Banks in the interior clamored for relaxation of the real-estate strictures in one form or another.

A bill—the McFadden-Pepper bill—was introduced into the Congress. Representative McFadden of Pennsylvania, in an article in the *Bank Director,* for December, 1926, prior to the passage of the bill, wrote as follows, "a one-year loan (on non-farm land) is not as liquid as a loan for a longer period. Moreover, few persons want to borrow for one year." Consequently, the provisions of Sec. 15 in the McFadden-Pepper bill lengthened the maximum maturity of loans on non-farm land from one year to five years, thereby putting non-farm-land mortgages on a parity with farm-land loans in respect to maturity. This increase of the permitted maximum maturity merely recognized legally the non-liquid nature that had already manifested itself in practice, for it had been found necessary previously, through rulings of the Reserve Board and the Comptroller of the Currency, to allow renewals of the one-year loans. And these loans had been formulated so as to contemplate renewal without the necessity of drawing up a new and original set of documents at each renewal.[7]

At hearings on the bill, testimony of its authors on the provisions pertinent to real estate commitments revealed the following:

> The purpose of Sec. 15 is to broaden the powers of banks in granting loans on real estate by increasing the maximum maturity from one to five years. Sec. 2-b is designed to prevent the acquisition of real estate bonds. If the bank makes a loan, it must take the entire obligation covered by the original mortgage.

Prior to this provision in the McFadden-Pepper bill, rulings from Washington had rejected real-estate bonds as being mostly of greater than five-year maturity, although subsequent to their issue banks were permitted to buy them when they had approached to within five years of their due date.

The Act of 1927 also increased the aggregate amount of loans made by a bank on real estate from one-third of the time de-

[7] Cf. descriptive brochure on McFadden-Pepper Act, distributed by Bank of America, 1927.

posits to one-half thereof although still retaining the restriction of to 25 per cent of capital and surplus and the general restrictions on an individual loan to 10 per cent of capital and surplus as provided in Sec. 5200 of the National Banking Act.

A further relaxation of the real estate provisions was the striking out of the word "immediate" from the first clause of Sec. 5137 of the National Banking Act, so that a bank might now hold real estate "necessary for the transaction of its own business," in the future.

So from complete prohibition to very considerable legal latitude in the matter of investing in real-estate loans, the progress of enactment had brought the banks of the Federal Reserve system in the years 1913 to 1927. A boom in real estate comparable to that in bonds and shares of industry took place throughout the later half of the decade of the 'twenties. Beginning in Florida, it gradually extended throughout the whole country. Bank portfolios became farther and farther swollen with real-estate investments. Their increase may be marked on the accompanying chart and tabulation.

The current situation.—It is now desirable to attempt to summarize the data relating to the present real-estate situation as it bears upon the current position of the banks; data for that purpose must be found in the tabulated reports of the state and national systems, but valuable indications are also derived from the general testimony of bankers, investigators, and business men before committees of Congress. The Committee of the Reserve system, whose work has already been frequently referred to, has paid some attention to the presence of real-estate loans in banks, and we shall have occasion to refer to their findings.

A beginning may be made by analyzing generally the situation of the national banks with respect to real-estate lending. The following Table 132 furnishes a survey of the advances made by all banks on real estate during the years 1921 to 1932, inclusive. From this will be noted the general tendencies of growth, and from the percentage figures accompanying Table 132 will be observed the variations in the rate of growth among the different groups.

TABLE 132

REAL-ESTATE LOANS, BY TYPES OF BANKS*

(In millions of dollars)

YEARS	NATIONAL BANKS		STATE COMMERCIAL BANKS		LOAN & TRUST COMPANIES		STOCK SAVINGS BANKS		MUTUAL SAVINGS BANKS		PRIVATE BANKS		ALL BANKS	
		%		%		%		%		%		%		%
1921	$ 280	5.9	$1,485	31.2	$ 488	10.3	$ 24	0.5	$2,460	51.8	$16	0.3	$ 4,753	100.0
1922	371	10.6	1,101	31.4	494	14.1	577	16.4	945	26.9	23	0.6	3,511	100.0
1923	463	9.2	336	6.6	647	12.8	835	16.5	2,766	54.7	7	0.2	5,054	100.0
1924	535	14.3	266	7.1	704	18.9	25	0.7	2,193	58.8	8	0.2	3,731	100.0
1925	637	31.1	318	15.5	699	34.2	37	1.8	350	17.1	6	0.3	2,047	100.0
1926	726	26.4	624	22.7	671	24.4	25	1.0	696	25.3	6	0.2	2,748	100.0
1927	1,062	18.2	1,085	18.6	1,032	17.6	761	13.0	1,898	32.4	12	0.2	5,850	100.0
1928	1,286	20.1	1,242	19.5	1,099	17.2	673	10.6	2,071	32.4	10	0.2	6,381	100.0
1929	1,413	13.6	1,712	16.4	1,399	13.4	566	5.4	5,315	51.0	15	0.2	10,420	100.0
1930	1,473	14.1	1,624	15.5	1,304	12.5	516	4.9	5,518	52.8	11	0.2	10,446	100.0
1931	1,585	15.6	1,462	14.4	1,261	12.4	91	0.9	5,731	56.5	7	0.2	10,137	100.0
1932	1,617	16.2	1,117	11.2	1,240	12.5	68	0.7	5,895	59.3	5	0.1	9,942	100.0

* Tables based on data abstracted from *Annual Reports of the Comptroller of the Currency.*

These figures may now be segregated as between national banks and others for the purpose of seeing how far real-estate lending has actually influenced portfolios of the national banks as distinct from others. Table 133 furnishes a survey of the growth of loans made by national banks on all classes of real estate, grouped as between New York City banks, Reserve and Reserve city banks, and country banks; while the subsequent table classifies the loans on farm land made by national banks as between the different groups:

TABLE 133

TOTAL REAL-ESTATE LOANS OF NATIONAL BANKS, 1915-1932

(In thousands of dollars)

YEARS	ALL NATIONAL BANKS	NEW YORK CITY BANKS	CENT. RES. AND RES. CITY BANKS	COUNTRY BANKS
1915	150,595	8,719	35,014	106,862
1916	160,633	874	29,940	129,819
1917	185,424	767	29,845	154,812
1918	185,117	1,016	29,657	154,444
1919	183,982	725	28,596	154,661
1920	229,829	1,871	31,342	196,616
1921	280,237	1,419	39,808	239,010
1922	371,391	1,759	50,105	319,427
1923	462,757	1,470	82,015	379,251
1924	535,137	4,386	84,827	445,924
1925	636,798	2,508	95,366	538,924
1926	725,452	3,737	111,679	610,036
1927	1,062,529	3,712	387,805	671,008
1928	1,285,915	9,368	516,425	760,122
1929	1,413,005	16,228	586,367	810,410
1930	1,473,001	15,827	618,041	839,133
1931	1,585,423	14,165	728,409	842,849
1932	1,617,281	14,512	793,501	809,268

Interpretation of statistics.—In studying the foregoing figures it needs to be borne in mind that the figures as given in official reports are never up to date, but often lag six months to a year behind actual conditions. In times of slow change this lag may be less harmful in creating erroneous impressions than it is in times of rapid change as at present. Many other sources of error are evident to the statistical analyst, but available returns do not permit of correcting them. A great many loans listed in other categories may eventually have to be classified as real estate advances; since the present difficulty of repayment, more and more titles to land are being delivered to banks. Generally speaking, however, the figures warrant the conclusion that, both absolutely and relatively, the amount of bank funds loaned against real-estate security increased very greatly during the decade 1922-1932, and was particularly instrumental in dimin-

TABLE 134

TOTAL REAL-ESTATE LOANS OF NATIONAL BANKS EXPRESSED AS A PERCENTAGE OF TOTAL LOANS, 1915-1932*

YEARS	ALL NATIONAL BANKS	NEW YORK CITY BANKS	CENT. RES. AND RES. CITY BANKS	COUNTRY BANKS
	%	%	%	%
1915	2.3	0.7	1.6	3.3
1916	2.3	0.1	1.1	3.8
1917	2.1	†	0.9	4.0
1918	1.8	0.1	0.8	3.7
1919	1.7	†	0.7	3.5
1920	1.7	0.1	0.6	3.4
1921	2.3	0.1	0.6	4.4
1922	3.3	0.1	1.3	6.1
1923	3.9	0.1	1.9	6.7
1924	4.5	0.2	2.0	7.7
1925	5.0	0.1	2.1	9.0
1926	5.4	0.2	2.3	9.7
1927	7.6	0.2	7.3	10.7
1928	8.5	0.3	8.8	11.7
1929	9.5	0.7	10.4	12.0
1930	9.9	0.6	10.9	13.1
1931	12.0	0.6	14.4	15.1
1932	15.7	0.9	18.7	18.1

* Table based on data abstracted from the *Annual Reports of the Comptroller of the Currency*.

† Less than 0.1 of one per cent.

ishing the degree of liquidity of the national banks. There are few regions of the country that have been free of excessive real-estate commitments by the banks.

In Table 133 the absolute figures for increases in real-estate loans by all national banks, New York City banks, all other city banks, and country banks, reveal the huge totals attained by the year 1932 that resulted from the gradually lowered legal obstacles and the pressure upon the banks to find suitable employment at profitable terms for their funds. In Table 133 the increase noted in the column for New York City banks shows that their increased real-estate commitments, while nearly doubling from 1915 to 1929, were relatively not so great as either the increases in the same item by all other city banks or the country banks.

Table 134 reveals that this doubling of real-estate commitments on the part of the New York banks was *pari passu* with

TABLE 135

LOANS OF NATIONAL BANKS ON "FARM LAND," 1921-1932

(In thousands of dollars)

YEARS	ALL NATIONAL BANKS	NEW YORK CITY BANKS	CENT. RES. AND RES. CITY BANKS	COUNTRY BANKS
	%	%	%	%
1921	159,836	451	11,291	148,044
1922	209,101	—	17,094	192,007
1923	246,624	118	36,257	210,249
1924	245,162	115	23,940	221,107
1925	255,880	38	23,714	232,128
1926	252,083	16	20,158	231,909
1927	305,213	—	78,103	227,106
1928	325,125	12	94,019	231,094
1929	308,785	40	88,935	219,810
1930	296,970	35	83,327	213,608
1931	304,824	246	97,759	206,819
1932	299,794	458	101,438	197,898

the increase of their total loans, so that relatively there was no increase at all. In Table 134, column 2, it will be noted that in 1915, 0.7 per cent of the total loans of New York City banks were in real estate, and in 1929—although the actual real-estate item had doubled, it still remained but 0.7 per cent of the total. This indicates clearly that the relaxed provisions of the law were not availed of in the case of these metropolitan institutions. And such a conclusion is further confirmed by conversations with branch managers of banks in New York City who united in voicing the unpopularity of real-estate ventures in the central comptroller's offices of their respective institutions.

Proceeding to an inspection of the condition of the "Central

Reserve and Reserve city banks" it becomes apparent that both absolutely and relatively the situation is very different. In 1915 the "Central Reserve and Reserve city" grouping employed but 1.6 per cent of their total loans in real estate ventures. This was about twice the proportion allocated by the New York City banks (0.7 per cent). As the years succeeded 1915, the proportion of total loans allocated to real estate by the Central Reserve and Reserve city banks mounted to 10.4 per cent in 1929 when

TABLE 136

LOANS OF NATIONAL BANKS ON "FARM LAND," EXPRESSED AS A PERCENTAGE OF TOTAL LOANS, 1921-1932*

YEARS	ALL NATIONAL BANKS	NEW YORK CITY BANKS	CENT. RES. AND RES. CITY BANKS	COUNTRY BANKS
	%	%	%	%
1921	1.3	†	0.3	2.7
1922	1.9	–	0.4	3.6
1923	2.1	†	0.8	3.7
1924	2.0	†	0.6	3.8
1925	2.0	†	0.5	3.9
1926	1.9	†	0.4	3.7
1927	2.2	–	1.5	3.6
1928	2.1	†	1.6	3.5
1929	2.1	†	1.6	3.3
1930	2.0	†	1.4	3.3
1931	2.3	†	1.9	3.7
1932	2.9	†	2.4	4.4

* Table based on data abstracted from the *Annual Reports of the Comptroller of the Currency.*

† Less than 0.1 of one per cent.

the New York City ratio (0.7 per cent) remained constant. By 1932 the percentage had increased to 18.7 per cent with the "Central Reserve and the Reserve city" banks. Here then is the concentration of the real estate increases together with that shown by the country banks, whose proportion of real-estate loans had also risen to 18.1 per cent of the total by 1932. It is of significance that in fifteen to seventeen years the proportions of real-estate loans in the "Central Reserve and Reserve cities" should have risen even more than the proportions to the total loans of the country banks. The "Central Reserve and Reserve cities" advanced from 1.6 per cent to 18.7 per cent while in the same period the country banks advanced from 3.3 per cent to 18.1 per cent.

Further significance may be seen in the rapid acceleration of the proportions from 1928 to 1932 in the cases of both Central Reserve and Reserve city banks and country banks. The percentage increase to the total loans rose nearly 8 per cent in those four years. It is thought that this phenomenal rise was largely

TABLE 137

LOANS OF NATIONAL BANKS ON "OTHER REAL ESTATE," 1921-1932

(In thousands of dollars)

YEARS	ALL NATIONAL BANKS	NEW YORK CITY BANKS	CENT. RES. AND RES. CITY BANKS	COUNTRY BANKS
1921	120,040	968	28,517	90,916
1922	162,292	1,759	33,011	127,420
1923	216,113	1,352	45,758	169,002
1924	289,975	4,146	60,887	224,817
1925	380,918	2,470	71,652	306,796
1926	473,369	3,721	91,521	378,127
1927	757,316	3,712	309,702	443,902
1928	960,790	9,356	422,406	529,028
1929	1,104,220	16,188	497,432	590,600
1930	1,176,031	15,792	534,714	625,525
1931	1,280,599	13,919	630,650	636,030
1932	1,317,487	14,054	692,063	611,370

the result of the letting down of the bars to real-estate investment by the McFadden Act, in 1927, to whose provisions reference has already been made. The statistics presented in Table 133 absolve the country banks from sole responsibility for what is often referred to as the "real estate *impasse.*" It shows clearly that the "Central Reserve and Reserve city banks" participated to the extent of $793,500,000 in 1932, nearly as large as the $809,268,000 contribution to the *impasse* by the country banks. In percentage to total loans, both the "Central Reserve and Reserve city banks" and the country banks allocated to real estate approximately 18 per cent of their loanable funds.

Farm Loans

Next in order the subject of farm loans, as a subdivision of the total loans and total real-estate commitments, appears in

Tables 135 and 136. The New York City banks have an almost negligible share in the farm-loan division. In the peak year of 1932 not 0.1 per cent of their total loan portfolio was in farm loans, nor in any previous years did a greater relative amount so appear.

It is observed, as would be naturally expected, that the country banks surpassed the "Central Reserve and Reserve city banks" in farm loan advances. In the year 1932 the comparison is

	COUNTRY BANKS	CENTRAL RESERVE & RESERVE CITY BANKS
Total Amount	$197,898,000	$101,438,000
Percentage of total loans	4.4	2.4

What, perhaps, is not so naturally expected, is the rapid acceleration of farm-loan commitments by the "Central Reserve and Reserve city banks" as compared with the country institutions. From 1921 to 1932 the relative farm loan investment of the country banks nearly doubled—2.7 per cent to 4.4 per cent. In the same time the relative farm-loan investment of the "Central Reserve and Reserve city banks" multiplied almost eightfold—0.3 per cent to 2.4 per cent. This indicates clearly that the "Central Reserve and Reserve city banks" were inaugurating a policy that for them was an innovation, namely substantial advances on farm land, the bulk of which financing, prior to 1921, had been in the hands of the country banks. Whether this new use of bank funds of the cities is wise or otherwise presents one of the few clearly defined questions of the real-estate prob lem. The supposed nearness of the country banks to the farm lands on which they advanced money had always been a factor of safety. The invasion of the farm-land field by the city banks can only be judged fairly as to its benefit, when figures showing the respective loss ratios shall be available.

Other Real Estate

Tables 137 and 138 deal with the problem of "other real estate" than farm land. In the decade of the 'twenties, all national banks multiplied several times the proportion of their total loans devoted to real estate other than farm land. By 1932, all national banks had placed 12.8 per cent of their loan funds in "other real estate." To this increase New York banks did not greatly contribute. In all classifications of real-estate loans and in the total, this section of the banking system showed greatest restraint. At the end of the period under discussion, 1932, the percentage of total loans by New York City banks allocated to "other real estate" was less than one per cent.

TABLE 138

LOANS OF NATIONAL BANKS ON "OTHER REAL ESTATE" EXPRESSED AS A PERCENTAGE OF TOTAL LOANS, 1921-1932*

YEARS	ALL NATIONAL BANKS	NEW YORK CITY BANKS	CENT. RES. AND RES. CITY BANKS	COUNTRY BANKS
	%	%	%	%
1921	0.9	†	0.6	1.7
1922	1.4	0.1	0.8	2.4
1923	1.8	0.1	1.1	3.0
1924	2.4	0.2	1.4	3.9
1925	3.0	0.1	1.6	5.1
1926	3.5	0.2	1.9	6.0
1927	5.4	0.2	5.8	7.1
1928	6.3	0.3	7.2	8.1
1929	7.5	0.7	8.8	8.8
1930	7.9	0.6	9.5	9.8
1931	9.7	0.6	12.4	11.4
1932	12.8	0.9	16.3	13.6

* Table based on data abstracted from the *Annual Reports of the Comptroller of the Currency.*

† Less than 0.1 of one per cent.

The situation found in comparing the Central Reserve and reserve city and the country banks is practically the reverse of the conditions appertaining to the farm-loan position. The Central Reserve and Reserve city banks, in the matter of loans against "other real estate" are both absolutely and relatively ahead of the country banks, not however by great amounts. In 1932 the total of "other real estate" commitments by the Central Reserve and Reserve city banks was but $81,000,000 in excess of the total of similar commitments by country banks; and relative to their respective total loans, only 2.7 per cent greater.

The figures with reference to loans on farm-land contrast

favorably enough in total amount with the total of all real-estate advances and the total of "other real estate" commitment. From these tabular enumerations it would not seem apparent that the farm-loan sums, although greatly increased within the decade, were a great menace to the liquidity of the banking systems either in the country, or in the Central Reserve and Reserve cities; and not at all in New York City, inasmuch as "other land

TABLE 139

REAL-ESTATE LOANS OF NATIONAL BANKS*

(In millions of dollars)

YEARS	REAL ESTATE LOANS	CAPITAL AND SURPLUS	TIME DEPOSITS	REAL ESTATE AS A PERCENTAGE OF CAP. & SURP.	REAL ESTATE AS A PERCENTAGE OF TIME DEP.
1915	151	1,791	1,327	8.4	11.3
1916	161	1,797	1,730	8.9	9.3
1917	185	1,845	2,179	10.0	8.5
1918	185	1,908	2,337	9.7	7.9
1919	184	1,991	2,777	9.2	6.6
1920	230	2,211	3,486	10.4	6.6
1921	280	2,300	3,678	12.2	7.6
1922	371	2,356	4,075	15.8	9.1
1923	463	2,400	4,687	19.3	9.9
1924	535	2,415	5,159	22.2	10.4
1925	637	2,488	5,812	25.6	11.0
1926	725	3,079	6,179	23.5	11.7
1927	1,063	2,731	7,316	38.9	14.5
1928	1,286	3,014	8,297	42.7	15.5
1929	1,413	3,106	8,317	45.5	17.0
1930	1,473	3,335	8,753	44.2	16.8
1931	1,585	3,182	8,580	49.8	18.5
1932	1,617	2,828	7,266	57.2	22.3

* Data for real estate loans, capital and surplus and time deposits abstracted from the *Annual Reports of the Comptroller of the Currency.*

loans" provided the greater part of the increase in total real-estate commitments. The great increase seems to be in the item of "other real estate" affecting both the Central Reserve and Reserve city banks and the country banks. It is in this division of the real-estate portfolio, for banks outside New York City, that some decision must be made. This decision must comprehend both the need for financing and the need of the banks for liquidity; must arbitrate between the conflict of needs if such there be, although it would seem evident that the paramount need were the latter.

The figures in Tables 133-138 dealing with the real estate problem increase both absolutely and relatively, for all national banks, exclusive of those in New York City. The increase and the amounts themselves devoted to farm loans do not constitute as striking a menace as do those devoted to "other real estate." It is probable that the farm financing of America has been achieved through other means.

TABLE 140

RATIO OF REAL ESTATE ITEMS TO CAPITAL FUNDS,*

NEW YORK CITY STATE BANKS

BANK	PERCENTAGE
Bank of New York & Trust	80
Bankers	30
Brooklyn Trust	75
Central Hanover	32
Chemical	17
Corn Exchange	110
Empire	44
Fifth Avenue	49
Fulton	22
Guaranty	6
Irving Trust	33
Kings County	43
Manhattan	70
Manufacturers	119
Marine Midland	12
New York Trust	30
Title Guarantee & Trust	100
United States Trust	31

* Publication of the *New York Evening Post,* Feb. 19, 1933, on data received from the Banking Department of the State of New York.

Real Estate and Time Deposits

Table 139[8] presents the ratio of real-estate commitments on the part of the banks to the total time deposits. The chief interest of this data is that it bears out the arguments made by

[8] Competent observers have expressed doubt as to the correctness of this table. It has been verified with the Comptroller of Currency's reports, but the reader must note that the figures (and conclusions) have been questioned.

proponents of the increasing admission of real estate to bank portfolios on the grounds that the great increase of time deposits, in reality permanent savings of the community, needed and were needed in real-estate financing. For the earlier years 1915 to 1920 the small percentage to time deposit totals reflects the stringent laws, the war conditions, and conservatism of bankers prior to the boom decade of the nineteen twenties. From then on, the mere doubling of the percentage to time deposits scarcely portrays the real growth. For it must also be borne in mind that in this interval time deposits were multiplied four-fold.

Real Estate and Capital Funds

The relation of the real-estate totals to bank capital repeats the familiar pattern of steady ratio rise. Table 139 for all national banks is confirmed by a supplementary report on state institutions in New York City. The business of the latter, of course, necessitates different requirements, but the wide variation of the percentages illustrates the complexity of the problem when a general rule is desired to serve the uses of differing circumstances. This wide variation also bears witness to the various financial policies and degrees of conservatism to be found in comparable institutions.

In Table 139 it appears that by 1932 all national banks had 57 per cent of their capital and surplus devoted to real estate items as opposed to but 8.4 per cent fifteen years previously. This measures the change in the whole conception of a bank, its nature and function. It would also seem to portray with clarity one cause of illiquidity among banks generally.

Geographical Aspects of the Real-Estate Problem

In attempting to assess the geographical aspects of the bank's real-estate problem, the lack of competent comparable statistics has prevented the presentation of adequate tables.[9] From a general inspection of these heterogeneous data, in so far as a general tendency is to be noted, it concerns the Northern Mis-

[9] Such information as is available in the *Annual Report of the Comptroller of the Currency* 1923, p. 496; 1924, p. 600; 1925, p. 632; 1926, p. 598; 1927, p. 774; 1928, p. 712; 1930, p. 748; 1931, p. 1010.

sissippi states,[10] where the advances on farm real estate rise far above the average relation of farm loans to loans on "other real estate." The balance of the Middle Western states remains poised about equally between the farm and urban real-estate commitments. In the Southern states the farm loans fall more nearly to their average relation to the total of real-estate commitments, while in the industrialized East, New England, and the Far West, the farm-loan ratio to "other real estate loans" conforms to the ratio for all national banks.

These findings confirm the early tendency of both the agricultural and "Central Reserve and Reserve city banks" to expand the total amount of their loans to longer and more rigid investments, and the gradual growth of illiquidity in bank portfolios. The regularity with which this tendency was manifest in all regions bears witness to the universality of the trend. One cannot select one state—say Massachusetts—and set it off for favorable contrast with an agricultural state such as Kansas. For the year 1931 it may be noted that in Kansas $5,380,000 was invested in farm loans, against $3,669,000 in "other real estate"; while in Massachusetts for the same year, $1,491,000 was loaned on farm land as contrasted with $97,393,000 on "other real estate." This instance notably exposes the relative disposition of funds in real estate as between the farm and urban land in different localities; but when it is noted that the totals in each state bear the same general ratio to capital funds and deposits, the regularity of the tendency becomes manifest.

Subsequent to 1931, the statistics are not yet available. From impressions published in the daily press, the *Commercial and Financial Chronicle,* etc., it would seem that defaults on farm land and on "other real estate" were in the same proportion. If any differentiation were possible, it would favor the desirability of the average run of farm loans as opposed to "other real estate." This differentiation can be measured only qualitatively so far, in the absence of quantitative statistics on default. The favorable inclination toward the farm-land loans rests on their greater

[10] Comprising Ohio, Indiana, Illinois, Michigan, Wisconsin, Minnesota, Iowa, and Missouri.

diversification, more conservative valuation and on the stable character of the makers of such loans in contradistinction to the same features of "other real estate" commitments.

In what has thus far been said, reference has been made entirely to the banks as going concerns, and the statistics furnished have been statistics of aggregates relating to all of the banks. It is worth while before leaving this subject to consider, briefly, the relation of real-estate loans to bank failures. On this point the most conclusive of recent research information is supplied by the Committee of the Federal Reserve system, which has sketched the real-estate aspect of its inquiries as reflected in 105 cases of bank suspensions in 1931, as follows:

Capital Loans, Loans on Inflated Real Estate Values, and Excessive Loans to Tenants

Errors in policy regarding loans on real estate and loans to farmers were common in the group of closed banks used in this survey. Frequently loans were made without specific security which proved to be undesirably large, and in an effort to secure the loans junior mortgages were taken. This habit was not the subject of general comment by the examiners, but in studying the histories of banks that closed, it was found that the practice was present in exaggerated form in a large number of cases. Many faulty loans on real estate bore evidence that they were made to give a special benefit or profit to officers, directors, or interests close to the management and thus were merely a phase of exploitation of banks by their management.

Capital loans.—Banks frequently make loans which cannot be repaid at maturity in the ordinary course of business transactions, and sometimes several renewals are necessary. It is not the intention here to make a general condemnation of such loans. However, the examiners' comments show that in the group of suspended banks studied capital loans were excessive.

In case 62 the examiner made pertinent comments as to the shortcomings of capital loans. In January, 1920, he wrote:

It is hard in the final analysis to criticize individual loans, but the cumulative character of the large lines and their seeming fixity of amount and continuity of the accommodations do produce a situation of non-liquidity which is not satisfactory to your examiner. . . . Examiner lists large lines and classified interests in order to emphasize the tendency to make what approach, if they are not in fact, capital or partial capital loans, which are necessarily of a non-liquid or, at least, of a not easily liquidating character. Individually considered the various lines possess merit and may be rated good, but taken collectively produce a condition of non-liquidity. This situation is not regarded as satisfactory and is considered to be one which is likely to cause trouble to both borrowers and bank in the event of a recession of deposits requiring liquidation of loans.

These comments were further elaborated in August, 1920, as follows:

The habit of loaning to corporations all that they should borrow, and then to the individual for company's benefit is as unsafe as it is unlawful. It will be noted that practically all excess loans are otherwise criticized.

In case 68 the examiner described typical capital loans. In 1922 he wrote:

Acting as manager for the ---- Stock and Farming Company in the sale and management of large land holdings, he has taken into the bank many top-heavy lines to contract holders, whose equities in their respective lands are consistently small.

In 1923 the succeeding examiner described the capital loans of this bank as follows:

A large proportion of the bank's loans are to tenant farmers, and to individuals who are buying their farms on contracts. Generally, the terms of these contracts are favorable to the holder, but the conditions of recent years have not permitted them to improve their position to any degree, and when consideration is given to the fact that in some cases credits are extended using the equities in these contracts as a basis, the situation cannot be said to be satisfactory.

In case 63 the bad effect of capital loans on a bank was well described by an examiner in 1922.

They have extended unwarranted credit to so great a degree that only through the success of the farmers for several seasons can they hope to bring this battered ship of distorted finance to a harbor of safety. In my opinion, the damage has not been done this year, but in the past, and they now find themselves confronted with the day of reckoning—loaded up with paper which no one can adjust without serious loss. They must, therefore, face the issue of charging out the difference between what their actual securities are worth and the face of the loan. The customers realize their position, and many are quitting with frequent cases of bankruptcy. The serious question here is whether continual nursing of their unwarranted loans will serve any purpose. They have already reached a limit where the farmer cannot pay his interest, let alone make a payment on principal.

In case 33 capital loans were made to finance land speculation outside of the community for nonresident borrowers. The serious effects of this unwise policy were described in 1922 as follows:

The bank's paper is not of the best sort, a large part of it being trading paper growing out of land deals and smaller transactions. Many of these loans have been made to aid land speculation. The bank has been finding it difficult or impossible to effect reduction of its paper, and it will be likely be some months before any material reduction can be brought about.

The seriousness of the situation had become more evident in 1923, and the examiner wrote:

A real menace lies in the large amount of loans that are dependent on the security of lands that are either non-productive or are subject to heavy prior liens. This has come about by a policy formerly pursued of loaning money too freely to outsiders and in furtherance of land speculations. This tendency has been corrected.

By 1925 the examiner found the bank in an alarming condition and commented as follows:

The directors are leaving the management to the president who fails to comprehend the bank's perilous situation. The loans generally are of a poor class, many were made to aid land speculations and in place of improving are growing constantly worse as the land equities in which they are invested are being wiped out. In examiner's opinion, resources classified as doubtful are likely soon to develop entirely bad.

Loans and inflated farm land.—Loans based on farm land values, made at the height of the farm real-estate boom during the war by bankers who did not recognize the temporary nature of high land prices, frequently caused serious trouble. In case 25 the examiner wrote in 1921:

> It appears that practically all paper of this bank classed as doubtful, grew out of land speculation, cattle feeding, and the general slump in all farm products.

By January, 1924, the hopelessly frozen character of these real-estate loans, based on inflated prices, had become evident, and the examiner wrote:

> The aggregate of slow and questionable assets of this bank is unreasonably high, a large per cent of which is dependent on real estate security, and of this a considerable amount can be liquidated only from the sale of the security which is largely farm lands and for which there is practically no market. During the boom period, land in this locality, in some instances, sold as high as $500 per acre and at the present time it would not sell for one half that amount.

In August, 1924, the nature of the frozen real-estate loans was further described in the following words:

> Under the management of the president, loans were made in this bank during the high tide of prosperity without regard for the financial standing of the tenant farmers, and those with heavy encumbrances on their land. As a natural result, the bank is now loaded with a large amount of slow and doubtful assets that are dependent, in a large measure, on the successful sale of real estate.

In case 21 unsound real-estate loans were augmented by loans to finance the raising of pure-bred live stock. In 1923 the examiner wrote:

> This section ran rampant on the subject of high-grade cattle and hogs which, coupled with high land speculation aided and abetted by the present officers of the bank who had no conception of what the future might hold, and instead of calling in loans as they matured chose the policy of borrowing from an outside source, which is an incident thereto, loaded the bank with a most unwieldly mass of frozen assets.

Loans on inflated city real estate.—City bankers made just as glaring errors in loans on urban property as country bankers made in their loans on farms during the various real-estate booms. Comment has already been made on the generally slack lending policy which created a mass of undesirable loans in an oil-boom town. Two other examples are given here of faulty loans on city real estate. In case 120 the president was interested in city real estate and undoubtedly his judgment was colored by his personal interests. The effects of his policies began to appear in 1921 when the examiner wrote as follows:

> Primary cause of present non-liquid condition was loaning by President to investors in local city real estate and the placing of large loans, which could not be handled by this bank, of sheep and cattlemen with city correspondents.

In 1922 the following comment was made:

> This bank is carrying an enormous amount of paper which is dependent upon the sale of real estate for liquidation, largely city property. This condition reflects the management of President who has personally invested heavily in city real estate.

By January, 1923, the situation had become worse, as indicated by the following sentence:

> Many of the bank's loans are so frozen and so dependent on sale of real estate that the bank can almost be classed as a real estate holding company.

The ultimate effect of this policy was described in 1926 as follows:

> It might be able to pay its depositors in full over a long period of time, but with the large number of other real estate now owned, unsalable at almost any price, immovable for the past three to five years, and with but little prospects of moving any material part of it within a reasonable future period, if the present management continues to grant credit as freely and liberally as they have the past five years, the bank is inevitably headed for the rocks.

In case 9 a bank in an entirely different part of the country with a satisfactory record of growth and sound banking lost its sense of values in the Florida boom and was plunged into serious difficulties. Between July, 1925, and January, 1926, the deposits of this bank increased more than one million dollars from $1,936,000 to $2,966,000. Its loans also increased from $1,148,000 to $1,931,000. The increase in deposits and loans and the causes were described by the examiner as follows:

> Deposits since the last examination show healthy increase, but it might be proper to say that a substantial portion should be attributed to an augmented loan account. B. is supported by a rich truck farming section, also some citrus fruit growing. For a long time, the expansion and development of the little city could be justly stated to be the result of a natural growth. However, here recently, like most other places considerable real estate activities have taken place, with resultant greatly enhanced property values. The President considers himself a very conservative banker. However, in this your examiner does not fully agree. I believe he wants to be conservative and, no doubt, is more so than the other local state bankers. The examiner feels, has made criticism, also told President and Cashier that they are too liberal in credit extensions, and once a loan develops weak and slow they are not disposed to push it for collection with the proper vigor they should.

With the collapse of the Florida boom, land values declined sharply and the bank found itself possessed of a large volume of frozen loans to real-estate operators, as well as a large loan to a tourist hotel, which is discussed later under real-estate bonds.

A number of the banks used in the 1931 study were plunged into difficulties either by being operated by real-estate promoters or by being carried away by the enthusiasm of city real-estate booms in their communities. When these booms collapsed, the banks found that they had made undesirable loans based on inflated land values. Many of these loans were thoroughly frozen; some of them were converted into real estate, which, in turn, was frozen; and in a few cases, the real-estate loan mistakes were directly responsible for the suspension of the bank.

The worst case of unsound real-estate loans among the 1931 suspensions was bank 171. This bank was operated by real-estate promoters who placed the greater part of their loanable funds in loans to real-estate dealers, home purchasers, churches, hotels, building contractors, and building and loan associations. To avoid excessive loans to certain parties, this bank even followed the unethical practice of making loans to "straw men," or, in other words, loans to men of no financial worth who were merely acting as agents for other interests so that the names of these interests would not appear on the bank's books.

These considerations must be taken as practically representative of the entire situation throughout the country, since they were selected with a view to representing the character of the loans both geographically and by size of banks.

Apart from these very broad generalizations, a few further conclusions may be warranted, as follows:

1. The data that have been presented do not show trends such as are exhibited by some of the other tabulated matter presented in this study. Some of the most violent fluctuations noted in the figures would apparently be owing to differences in method of keeping records. In view of this aspect of the statistical analysis, conclusions drawn from real-estate-loan figures must be very carefully drawn.

2. Nevertheless, we may say that excessive real-estate lending has unquestionably contributed during the decade 1920 to 1930 to the increasingly unliquid position of American banks, and has been a major factor in bringing about a "tied up" position which has doubtless often contributed to suspensions and failures.

3. This over-investment in real-estate security is exhibited in its most dangerous phases in specified localities or portions of the country in which "booms" have taken place, or at times in the case of individual institutions which were being used to finance and further some promoters' enterprises in the real-estate field.

4. In spite of the fact that national banks, as well as the majority of state institutions, are now allowed to receive what are practically savings deposits and bid fair to continue to engage in this phase of business, the question is seriously to be asked, whether an extensive revision of the current legislation

permitting the making of real-estate loans by banks should not be undertaken, with a view to limiting the amount of loans so made and with the further view to preventing the undue application of bank funds to particular enterprises through one device or another.

The question is one that calls for discussion from a reasonably broad standpoint, in view of the fact already stated that it is the apparent intention of the community to permit commercial banks to continue to receive deposits on time.

Following are some of the suggestions that have been currently made for alteration of the present legal status, with regard to real estate lending.

1. *Complete prohibition of real-estate loans.*—This implies complete prohibition of direct loans as well as of loans collaterally secured by real estate. There are various forms of this suggestion. Some would permit improved real-estate loans, while excluding unimproved and farm lands. The plan also comprehends some measure of relief to those interested in real estate by means of special mortgage banks or a systematic mortgage market.

2. *Mandatory amortization.*—Carefully prepared mandatory amortization of all loans connected with real estate. Opposition to this plan largely devotes itself to the mandatory feature. It is contended that no law can properly fit even a majority of cases for amortization, and that such amortization should be adapted to the particular case by the judgment of the banker.

3. *Tightening restrictions.*—A general tightening of the present restrictions without other changes in method. This plan, of course, varies considerably, and may be said to fit almost any opinion—that of the complete prohibition school to that of the loosest constructionist.

4. *A general reorganization.*—A continuation of the present National Bank and Federal Reserve regulations applied to an all-inclusive banking system. This would tend rather to enlarge than to contract the sphere of freedom of action for the individual banker, while putting him on a basis of legal equality with other local banks.

CHAPTER XXVI

BANKS AND THE SECURITIES MARKET[1]

A review of the general problems of bank operation in relation to investments and portfolios of National banks indicates that there are two major aspects involved in the present banking situation: (1) the extensive modification that has taken place in the character of the holdings of active banks; (2) the divergence from what was formerly considered sound-banking principle, which is exhibited by this change in condition.

It has frequently been shown in former portions of the study, that the changes in bank portfolios which have thus occurred, could not have taken place had there not been another alteration of relationship between the banking system and the public markets for securities. This change of relationship, it should constantly be borne in mind, was not only the outcome but, also, in a way, the cause of the alteration of banking conditions.

It would be a serious mistake, however, to treat this change in the relationship between banking and the securities market as if it were an independent financial phenomenon. It represented merely one phase of an alteration in business organization and in the attitude of the public toward business which has proven fundamentally significant in altering commercial organization and relationships since the close of the World War. The older idea that the banking system owed an obligation to the community which could be fulfilled only by careful supervision and guidance of business enterprises, through the extension or withholding of credit, had long been distasteful to the bolder spirits engaged in business, who desired to emancipate themselves entirely from any sort of financial oversight or direction. Thus, the deep-seated change of relationship between the banks and the securities markets which we are about to trace in

[1] Chapter prepared by A. W. May; statistical data chiefly drawn from original material compiled by Senate Banking Committee, general tables relating thereto being published in Part VII of *Hearings,* 1931, Section I.

detail was developed upon a foundation provided by the underlying industrial conditions, to which reference has already been made.

It has been frequently asserted that the increase in bank deposits held by national and state institutions from slightly below 30 billion dollars, in 1921, to a little less than 50 billion dollars in 1930, or a growth of about 65 per cent, practically compelled the banks to become large participants in the securities market. This, however, as we have just seen, in large measure omits the complete explanation; certainly, it fails to admit the reflex character of the financial industrial situation.

The basic factor which should be studied in connection with the change now under consideration is doubtless furnished by the increasing development of an actual market for securities after the World War. It is not necessary to inquire whether this development was greatly fostered by the Liberty Loan campaigns and the widespread insistence upon public buying—the fact is, that such a market for securities actually sprang up. In this way an avenue was opened through which corporations might find a way to free themselves from control by commercial banks, securing huge amounts of capital through the placement of new capital-security issues directly in the hands of speculators and investors. The totals of new annual security offerings from 1924 to 1929 follow:[2]

1924	$5,097,800,000	1927	$ 7,714,600,000
1925	6,133,200,000	1928	11,848,800,700
1926	6,684,800,000	1929	11,410,100,000

These figures compare with new capital issues of but $1,646,000,000 in 1913, and $1,344,000,000 in 1918.

Thus, many corporations were enabled not only to eliminate entirely their loans from the banks, but to retire large portions of their funded indebtedness. This was done, for example, by the United States Steel Corporation and the Anaconda Copper Company, among many others; an inexpensive way of substituting an equity in profits for debt and of aiding long-term solvency at the expense of the common stockholder. The acquisi-

[2] Standard Statistics Co. *Bulletin*, 1930-31, Base Book.

tion of funds not needed for current commercial transactions is in fact termed, by some, overcapitalization.

Corporations themselves increased their investments in other corporations. According to the figures furnished by the Standard Statistics Company, 442 American corporations had the following amounts invested in cash and securities at the dates named:

(*In millions of dollars*)

	1927	1928	1929	1930	1931	1932
Cash and equivalent	3,135	3,799	3,658	3,645	3,578	3,361
Investments	2,171	2,436	2,971	2,875	2,727	2,792

In connection with the furnishing of this large reservoir of non-banking credit or capital to large corporations, we must bear in mind that industry has been concentrating to an even greater degree in the hands of comparatively few large business units. In the last decade many small independent enterprises were eliminated through failure while others were absorbed through mergers and consolidations. The changed requirements of corporate finance thus reduced the former credit demands of commercial borrowers throughout the country. Another factor reducing the demands for commercial credit was the changed buying habits of the American business man. After the 1919-1920 commodity boom, large inventories proved a source of terrific loss; bearing this lesson in mind thereafter, business men frequently pursued a strict policy of "hand-to-mouth" buying in accordance with their minimum requirements. This obviously reduced the demand for bank credit by commercial business.

Constantly improving corporate financial structures more and more enabled corporations to finance themselves without banking aid. It is estimated[3] that a total of 29.4 per cent of the very large national corporate net income was reinvested by the various enterprises between 1922 and 1927; and even since 1929, although earnings decreased sharply, managers have succeeded in creating balance sheets of great liquidity and independence. A survey covering 729 companies in 30 different industries shows that average quick assets increased from $11,742,000 in 1922 to

[3] *The Modern Corporation and Private Property*, by Berle and Means, p. 42.

$15,449,000 in 1928, while the average bank loan decreased from $929,000 to $582,000.[4]

Likewise there was a great rise in installment financing after 1921. Huge organizations specializing in secured loans to distributors (such as automobile), as well as to consumers, sprang up. One of these concerns, the Commercial Investment Trust Company does, at present, a textile factoring business of over $100,000,000 annually through one of its subsidiaries. The capital of many of these firms—such as the General Motors Acceptance Company, the Commercial Credit Company, and the Commercial Investment Trust Company, has been secured by sales of its own long-term securities to the public.

In addition to the total of $11,410,000,000 of new issues sold to the public in 1929, $4,205,100,000 of preferred and common stocks of seventy-two listed companies were subscribed for by stockholders through "rights" issued by the companies in which they already had an interest.

Money furnished in both of these ways, through new issues and through rights, provided capital for industry that bore no consistent relationship to industry's actual needs. The demand coming from the vast nation-wide army of speculators in the period of common-stock "craze" and the insatiable demand of the public for more and more stock, represented a condition in which "the cart was before the horse," in the sense that speculators' funds were forcing their way into commercial and industrial expansion in direct proportion to stock market requirement rather than in response to the legitimate demands of industry. Moreover, this new trend in the financing of industry through the stock market was dangerous in that it led people to believe in new limitless and permanent sources of national capital wealth. Illustrative of widespread reasoning current at the time, regarding the new method of financing, are the views of the then President of the New York Stock Exchange, Mr. E. H. H. Simmons:[5]

[4] "The Decline of the Commercial Loan," by Lauchlin Currie, *Quarterly Journal of Economics* (Aug., 1931), Vol. XLV.

[5] Before Virginia Bankers Association, 1929.

The flow of capital into our industries upon which our present prosperity depends must not be experimentally operated upon with hacksaws by amateur surgeons. . . . The Stock Exchange enters into the important work of assisting in the financing of our business enterprises. . . . When a bank lends money on securities, it may be assisting the private operations of some speculator in securities. But this is only a superficial aspect of the story. Such brokers' security collateral loans constantly enable American business corporations to distribute larger security issues than otherwise could be distributed, and this results in a vastly increased facility for financing our business corporations. The modern American business corporation cannot in practice wait to sell its shares completely to outright and permanent investors. *For growth and expansion* our business companies need funds in large amounts at one time, *not in small driblets of capital slowly and painfully acquired.*[6] The machinery of the stock market and call loan market enable just this thing. It is after all because we have in our financial system provided superior facilities for *financing American business growth,* that our business enterprises have been continually able to expand and progress. . . . Today our business corporations are more and more avoiding the issuance of bonds, and are resorting to the issue of shares in order to avoid *short-term financing at their banks or with open market commercial paper.* This new trend in corporate financing has resulted in important changes in the business of finance. . . . Similar changes have occurred in commercial banks, where loans on security collateral have increased at a time when holdings of open market commercial paper have greatly diminished and even credit advances of business corporations have frequently remained stationary or have actually declined. . . . Undoubtedly the large American corporations are today in better financial shape than ever before in our history.

In other words, billions of dollars of marginal stock buying with the aid of enormous brokers' loans was considered the sound "new" way of financing industry and a means of normal expansion of plants. As a matter of fact, great over-expansion of long-term plant equipment was caused by the over-supply of credit looking for speculative profits—ready to withdraw at a moment's notice. As Mr. Simmons said further:[7] "The problem was to

[6] Author's italics.
[7] *New Aspects of American Financing,* 1929.

make more good securities available to absorb excess supplies of capital."

Not only was there thus a prevalent misconception of the nature of the non-banking credit that was being extended, but the fact that the banker was being supplanted by the stock speculator eliminated all possibility of scientific credit analysis. It caused ruinous and uneconomic over-expansion in many industries, such as copper production, chain-store organizations, public utility combination, automobile manufacturing, and many others; and also, in the case of foreign financing, prudent credit analysis by conservative bankers was nullified by the uncontrolled desire of the public to purchase any foreign issue with a high-rate coupon.

The foregoing survey indicates to some extent the changed methods of corporate financing that occurred during the decade 1919-1929. Let us note how these changes in corporate financing influenced our banking system to effect a major change in the character of its assets from a predominance of liquid commercial paper to a type of asset based on non-liquid securities. This can be noted quantitatively in statistics relative to portfolios and to loans on securities, and qualitatively by examining the types, character, and methods employed in direct security investment.

Loans on Securities

The great increase in bank credit arising from reduced reserve requirements and Federal Reserve activities creating great excess reserves, coupled with the relatively decreased needs for bank credit by commercial borrowers, already outlined, necessitated new outlets for bank credit. One of these outlets was the bank security loan.

Loans on securities have been a major banking asset only since the World War. Before 1914 the *Annual Reports of the Comptroller of the Currency* classified loans mainly into "demand" and "time." Beginning with 1914, statistics of state banks and trust companies, but not of national banks, distinguished loans secured by stocks and bonds from other secured loans. On June 30, 1914, loans secured by stocks and bonds in state banks, and secured loans other than real-estate loans in national banks, were $1,526,319,186.

During the War the nation's enormous fiscal requirements necessitated the flotation of government bond issues. Much of these issues went into the banks as security for loans. This practice extended to other bonds and to stocks of all descriptions. Security loans in all banks grew from 1921 to 1930, as follows:[8]

CLASS OF BANKS	JUNE 30, 1921	JUNE 30, 1930	PER CENT INCREASE
National Banks	4,361,884,000	5,484,713,000	+ 26
State Banks	1,525,894,000	1,435,529,000	— 6
Trust Companies	1,704,065,000	4,534,946,000	+166
Totals	7,591,843,000	11,455,188,000	+ 50

The record of the increase in security loans in reporting Federal Reserve member banks, classified as secured by United States government bonds and by other stocks and bonds, since 1919, follows:[9]

(In thousands of dollars)

YEAR	LOANS SECURED BY U. S. GOVT. BONDS	SECURED BY OTHER STOCKS AND BONDS	TOTAL SECURITY LOANS
1919	1,020,539	3,300,331	4,320,690
1920	908,722	3,173,823	4,082,545
1921	512,520	3,065,481	3,678,001
1922	290,261	3,774,775	4,065,036
1923	228,365	3,857,662	4,086,027
1924	194,974	4,667,760	4,862,734
1925	170,107	5,759,678	5,929,785
1926	144,075	5,708,092	5,852,167
1927	128,253	6,587,067	6,715,320
1928	106,239	7,023,487	7,129,726
1929	8,304,000		8,304,000
1930	7,814,000		7,814,000

The following figures show the proportion of loans on securities made by the various classes of banks and these classes of banks' proportion of the banking system's total loans and investments on June 30, 1930:[10]

[8] *Annual Reports of the Comptroller of the Currency.*

[9] *Annual Reports of the Federal Reserve Board.*

[10] Abstracted from *Annual Reports of the Comptroller of the Currency.*

(In thousands of dollars)

BANKS	SECURITY LOANS Amount	SECURITY LOANS Per cent of total	TOTAL LOANS AND INVESTMENTS Amount	TOTAL LOANS AND INVESTMENTS Per cent of total
Reporting Member	8,442,000	74	23,099,000	50
Non-reporting Member	1,983,000	17	12,556,000	26
Non-member	1,030,000	9	11,643,000	24
Totals	11,455,000	100	47,298,000	100

Thus we see that the reporting member banks, which possessed only half of the total resources, advanced 74 per cent of the security loans.

The following data shows the increase in security loans by different classifications of banks between 1921 and 1930:[11]

CLASS OF BANKS	1921	1930	INCREASE PER CENT
National	4,361,884,000	5,484,713,000	+26
State Member	2,551,022,000	4,940,640,000	+94
State Non-Member	678,937,000	1,029,835,000	+52
Totals	7,591,843,000	11,455,188,000	+50

The following figures for security loans of member banks in New York, Chicago, Reserve cities, and country banks, show the percentage of the total outstanding security loans related to percentage of resources as of June 29, 1929:[12]

CLASS OF BANKS	AMOUNT	PER CENT OF RESOURCES
New York City Banks	$3,236,150,000	28
Chicago Banks	773,972,000	33
Other Reserve City Banks	3,293,710,000	21
Country Banks	2,455,053,000	15
Totals	$9,758,885,000	21

Apart from quantitative considerations in security loans, it is probably worth while to consider qualitatively the purposes for which these loans are made. Of course, the character of these motives varies with different economic conditions, and even changes within the comparatively short life-phase of a financial boom or depression.

[11] *Annual Reports of the Comptroller of the Currency* and *Federal Reserve Bulletin.*

[12] Data abstracted from *Annual Reports of the Federal Reserve Board.*

The chief motives prompting the desire to borrow from banks on the basis of security collateral may be listed as follows:

1. To earn a profit by securing the difference between the income paid on the security put up as collateral and the rate of accommodation charged by the lending bank. (This purpose was especially dominant in 1925, 1926, and 1927.)

2. To carry securities with the intention of reselling them at a higher price. (Prevalent to an enormous degree from 1927-1929.)

3. The carrying of securities by dealers pending distribution to "investors."

4. The carrying of securities for corporate control or similar "non-value" reasons.

5. For commercial, industrial, or agricultural purposes.

6. For miscellaneous consumption purposes.

In 1931 the subcommittee of the Committee on Banking and Currency of the United States Senate attempted to determine quantitatively the uses to which security loans were being put and sent out a questionnaire to a number of banks asking what proportion of existing loans had been made for direct commercial, industrial, or agricultural use and what proportion for the sole purpose of carrying securities. See Table 141 for a compilation of the replies; figures for each bank are given separately.

Some proportion of these percentages are, of course, a matter of estimate, but the dominating motive of borrowing to carry securities for enhancement in value is so preponderant, that this purpose can be accepted as overwhelming. This is not only the case in New York City and the East, but throughout some of the mid-Western states as well.

In order to judge the proper economic significance of these loans, both the spirit in which they were made, as well as the character of the collateral behind them, must be borne in mind.

At the time of huge Government War Loan issues, a large number of loans were collateraled by Government bonds. They constituted about one-third of all security collateral loans of reporting member banks in 1919, but declined thereafter—only about 1.5 per cent of security loans at the end of 1928 being so

TABLE 141

USES TO WHICH BANK LOANS ARE PUT

LOCATION OF BANK	LOANS ON STOCKS AND BONDS (*In millions of dollars*)	LOANS FOR COMMERCIAL INDUSTRIAL AND AGRICULTURAL PURPOSES AS A PERCENTAGE OF TOTAL LOANS	LOANS FOR SOLE PURPOSE OF CARRYING SECURITIES AS A PERCENTAGE OF TOTAL LOANS
	$	%	%
New York City	823	20	80
"	525	5	95
"	311	40	60
"	231	57.1	42.9
"	217	15.3	84.7
"	138	(no estimate)	50
"	110	2.03	(no estimate)
"	105	7.5	75
"	104	2	98
"	33	10	90
Massachusetts	169	20	66⅔
Rhode Island	28	10	85
New York State	82	9.7	90.3
Ohio	113	(no estimate)	36.4
Ohio	36	0	100
Illinois	548	23	77
"	54	5	95
Michigan	47	0	100
"	7	40	60
Minnesota	28	9.2	84
"	16	25	65
"	11	90	10
Missouri	59	10	90
Nebraska	1	17	83
California	159	30	70
"	91	9.4	80.2
"	32	33	50
Washington	1	26	20

collateraled. The Senate Committee, through its questionnaire, compiled information shown in Table 142 regarding the character and marketability of collateral of security loans, as of early 1931.

Dividing the above figures between New York City and non-New York City institutions, the former had 78 per cent of their loans backed by collateral in listed securities and the latter 54 per cent, a conclusion which bears out our expectations. Average percentage of collateral consisting of stocks is about the same,

TABLE 142

TYPES OF COLLATERAL USED FOR BANK LOANS

LOCATION OF BANK	LOANS ON STOCKS AND BONDS *(In millions of dollars)*	PER CENT OF COLLATERAL BEING STOCKS	PER CENT OF COLLATERAL IN LISTED SECURITIES	PER CENT OF COLLATERAL WITHOUT ACTIVE MARKET
	$	%	%	%
New York City	823	59	63	16
"	525	80	68	3.3
"	311	63	69	3.6
"	310	87	89	3.7
"	231	87	80	2.4
"	217	86	76	15
"	138	80	70	2.5
"	110	86	96	4
"	105	80	70	6
"	104	90	95	3
"	95	90	90	4
"	89	75	71	3.3
"	63	75	86	5
"	33	95	90	1
"	31	90	90	2
"	16	80	95	5
"	15	60	83	5
Total	169	77	73	7.6
Massachusetts	59	90	85	5
"	12	82	75	2
"	28	85	85	5
Rhode Island	82	90	85	10.8
New York	56	—	95	0
Pennsylvania	30	52	70	3.5
"	113	77	64	1
Ohio	548	75	90	10
Illinois	54	50	60	25
"	548	75	90	10
Michigan	47	90	98	10
"	7	89	66	1
Minnesota	28	78	100	0
"	16	90	70	15
"	11	44	58	2
Missouri	59	60	95	1
Nebraska	1	60	95	1
California	91	87	83	10
"	39	100	90	0
"	32	67	85	5
"	21	70	75	7
"	20	70	99	1
Washington	1	38	64	36
Totals	4,740	77	–	9

being 76 per cent for New York and 77 per cent for non-New York.

The method of making the security loan in the last decade is indicative of the change in our banking methods. An applicant was granted credit on a purely mathematical basis—that is, on the sole condition that the market price of his collateral provided a sufficient "margin" above the loan. Almost any of the minor officials of a given bank might merely pick up a newspaper containing the quotations of stocks, satisfy himself as to the quoted "value" of the collateral and the bank's protection, and ask no further questions. The condition of the stock market itself or the economic condition of the industry represented in the collateral were of no matter. It was a free and certainly easy method of pouring out credit at profitable rates—quite similar in method to the procedure employed in brokerage offices. Contrasted with traditional methods of commercial credit control—where a prospective borrower has his request for accommodation considered by a bank official specializing in his industry, who discusses with him the economic justification for the loan, the condition of the business, and the general personal and business financial condition of the borrower—and the difference is striking. The banks liked the security loan because it seemed like a conveniently "liquid" and therefore safe asset. They did not realize that in the 1927-1929 period they were thus directly aiding and abetting the common-stock boom and infecting the whole structure, that the securities were only liquid as long as speculators were willing and able to support the market for them at dizzy heights; that the enormous issues of new securities amounting to fifty billions in five years, and stock prices of 200 times earnings represented a national gambling mania, and that in thus furthering and directly stimulating industrial fluctuations and distorting the price structure, they were conducting themselves in a manner directly contrary to rudimentary banking principles.

THE DEFLATION OF SECURITY LOANS SINCE 1929

A consideration of security and loan liquidation in 1930 and 1931 is, we believe, valuable in illustrating the general financial difficulties and trends of the banking and economic systems. Let us go back to June, 1929, because already in the latter half of that year divergent changes, as between various classes of assets, began to appear. In this period bank loans to brokers and dealers in securities decreased, while other loans on securities showed a net increase. Even in the period from June to the beginning of October, member banks decreased their security loans to brokers and dealers, while loans by others increased to a maximum. After the October common-stock collapse, although brokers' loans from member banks continued their decline, loans made by banks directly to customers on security showed a rapid increase, banks to a great extent shouldering the burden of the enormous security loans which had been initiated and carried by brokers. And it is quite noteworthy that in 1930, when all bank loans and investments were decreasing and commercial loans and all loans other than securities were declining, loans on securities were not reduced at all. In the first three quarters of the year 1931, both security and commercial loans declined, although investments in securities increased. But in the last quarter of 1931 the severest liquidation of the entire three year period occurred. Half of the bank credit liquidation of five billion dollars occurring between 1929 and 1931 took place the last quarter of 1931. This liquidation included a drastic deflation of bank loans on securities. In the year ending December 31, 1932, there was a further drastic liquidation of security loans, their reduction amounting to about one-third of the earlier total. In the same period bank investments in securities increased, this being because of an increase in holdings of Government securities while holdings of other securities declined.[13]

In connection with the course of loan liquidation since 1929, it will be well to consider the question of inadequate margin of collateral protection with which the banks found themselves. The subcommittee of the Senate Committee on Banking and Currency sent out a questionnaire, inquiring "What proportion of your outstanding security loans is secured by stocks and or

[13] The above summary is based upon statistics taken from *Annual Reports of the Federal Reserve Board* and *Annual Reports of the Comptroller of the Currency* for the period in question.

bonds having a market value of less than 100 per cent of the amount of the loan (excluding loans on government bonds)?" Unfortunately, the replies apply only to the end of 1930, before the drastic "real" liquidation had fairly begun, but if we realize the extent of the subsequent decline, the figures are of much interest.

It should be noted that the aggregate of loans really undermargined were larger than indicated, owing to the banks' practice of arranging with customers with impaired collateral to convert their loans partly into unsecured advances, leaving the balance as security loans. As a result of this practice the amount of the "security loan" is reduced to a point where it is adequately protected and the safety of the balance cannot be adequately determined.

Brokers Loans

In considering loans to brokers, we are, of course, discussing a type of loan advanced entirely for the purpose of carrying securities for speculative or quasi-speculative purposes.

Street loans placed by New York City daily reporting banks were first reported in 1917. In October of that year they amounted to $903,000,000, of which $688,000,000 was for the account of the reporting banks, and $214,000,000 for correspondents. The highest point they reached in the "boom" of that period was $1,422,000,000 in October, 1919. Subsequently they dropped nearly 50 per cent to $719,000,000 in August, 1921. When we recall that the speculative movement was considered enormous in the 1919-1920 period, we realize the more clearly the significance of the inflation which occurred a decade later. The enormous increase in brokers' loans in this ten-year period was modified by two factors. First, a great part of the inflation of the earlier period took place in commodities and inventories, commercial paper rates reaching over 8 per cent in 1920. The second factor was the enormous expansion of bank credit pumped into use by the Federal Reserve system. Between April, 1917, and December, 1918, a period when four Liberty Loans and a great deal of short-term Government paper were being financed, when industry was being transformed from a peacetime to a war-time basis, and when we were equipping our army

TABLE 143

BANK SECURITY LOANS UNDERMARGINED

(In millions of dollars)

LOCATION OF BANK	LOANS ON STOCKS & BONDS *(Other than U. S. Govt.)*	PERCENTAGE "UNDERMARGINED"
New York City	$823	9.41
"	525	0
"	311	1.5
"	310	0
"	231	3.8
"	217	3
"	138	1
"	110	.9
"	105	1
"	104	4
"	95	10
"	89	.0
"	63	1
"	49	15
"	33	.3
"	31	1
"	16	3.5
"	15	1.3
Massachusetts	169	7.3
"	59	3.75
"	12	.0
Rhode Island	28	7
New York	82	19
Pennsylvania	56	.0
"	30	6
Ohio	113	.69
"	36	1
Illinois	548	7.5
"	54	1
Michigan	47	3
"	38	16
"	7	23
Minnesota	28	5.5
"	16	12
Missouri	59	5
Minnesota	11	9
Nebraska	1	10
California	159	0
"	91	12
"	31	0
"	32	2
"	21	7
"	20	.5
Washington	1	2

and sending it to France, the necessary concomitant bank expansion amounted to five billions—800 millions in deposits and 7 billions in loans and investments. But although we feared this war-time expansion, the expansion from June 30, 1922 to April 11, 1928 was far greater, though with no necessity therefor. In the latter period loans and investments increased 14.5 billions, and deposits 13.5 billions, or over twice the war-time expansion. This expansion was largely furthered by a Federal Reserve Bank policy of keeping rediscount rates below the market and by engaging in heavy open market purchases of Government securities and by wholesale buying of acceptances at low rates. Thus were created great excess reserves which forced the banks to find new outlets for such excess reserves. The effect of these excessive reserves was additionally intensified by the 1919 reduction in reserve requirements of member banks. Then, too, the banks secured freer access to credit under the 15-day amendment to the Federal Reserve Act—which permits 15-day direct loans on United States bonds, under which the banks secured one billion dollars of credit in 1929.

Senator Glass has estimated:[14] "In a single six months' period in 1929, 10 New York banks were given $750,000,000 of Federal Reserve Credit under the 15-day provision. This money was loaned to brokers for stock-gambling purposes."

The resultant great expansion of credit needed an outlet, and in conformity with popular psychology of the times, the Federal Reserve system was indirectly used to feed the brokers' loan supply. The responsibility of these various inflationary functions of the system for the 1927-1929 security and brokers' loan boom was assigned by Hon. A. C. Miller, member of the Board, in testifying before a subcommittee of the Committee on Banking and Currency on January 23, 1931. The practice of member banks using Federal Reserve credit through section 15 of the Act as a means of building up their reserves to support brokers' loans has also been vouched for by former Governor Harrison of the Board.[15]

[14] In radio speech delivered Nov. 1, 1932.

[15] In testimony before a subcommittee of the Committee on Banking and Currency of the U. S. Senate pursuant to Res. 71.

There was developed a great rise in brokers' loans from $719,000,000, in August 1921, to $9,169,000,000 in October 1929. Beginning January 6, 1926, the figures have been made

TABLE 144

BROKERS' LOANS THROUGH REPORTING MEMBER BANKS IN NEW YORK CITY ACCORDING TO STATEMENT OF WEEKLY REPORTING MEMBER BANKS IN NEW YORK CITY

DATE	FOR OWN ACCOUNT	FOR ACCOUNT OF OUT-OF-TOWN BANKS	FOR ACCOUNT OF OTHERS	TOTAL
Jan. 27, 1926	1,201	1,287	610	3,098
Jan. 26, 1927	865	1,126	741	2,752
Jan. 25, 1928	1,275	1,472	1,041	37,89
Jan. 30, 1929	1,091	1,853	2,615	5,559
Oct. 2, 1929	1,071	1,826	3,907	6,804

public weekly, both as to totals, and as to loans "for own account," "for account of out-of-town banks," and loans "for account of others," the latter group comprising non-banking lenders dealing directly with the New York banks.

The amount of loans actually arising from non-banking lenders is not included in the above figures for loans for the

TABLE 145

BROKERS LOANS FROM OUT-OF-TOWN MEMBER BANKS*

(In millions of dollars)

DATE	LOANS FOR ACCOUNT OF OUT-OF-TOWN BANKS	LOANS TO BROKERS IN NEW YORK CITY BY OUTSIDE MEMBER BANKS	BY OUT-OF-TOWN NONMEMBERS AND OTHERS
Oct. 1928	1,682	805	877
Jan. 1929	1,648	917	731
Oct. 1929	1,826	789	1,037

* *Weekly Brokers' Loan Report,* Federal Reserve Bank of New York, and *Member Bank Call Reports* of the Federal Reserve Board.

"account of others," because a great many non-banking lenders throughout the nation placed their funds through and were included with the funds from out-of-town banks. By comparing the figures of loans for account of out-of-town banks with figures of loans to brokers in New York City by outside member banks, an indication is arrived at as to the extent to which the loans for account of out-of-town banks are for non-banking lenders.

It is thus indicated that at some periods half of the out-of-town funds were actually loaned "for the account of others."

Following is a table showing the figures for total brokers' loans, from all sources in 1928 and 1929:

TABLE 146

BROKERS' LOANS FROM ALL SOURCES, 1928 AND 1929*

(In millions of dollars)

DATE	BY AND THROUGH NEW YORK BANKS: Account of Banks	BY AND THROUGH NEW YORK BANKS: Account of Others	FROM PRIVATE BANKS, BROKERS, ETC. TO N. Y. ST. EX. MEMBERS	TO BROKERS OUTSIDE OF NEW YORK BY OUT-OF-TOWN MEMBER BANKS	TOTAL
Oct. 1928	1,807	2,835	866	805	6,313
Jan. 1929	2,008	3,346	1,071	925	7,350
Oct. 1929	1,860	4,944	1,472	893	9,169

* *Weekly Brokers' Loan Report,* Federal Reserve Bank of New York, *Member Bank Call Report,* Federal Reserve Board and *Monthly Report on Members' Borrowings,* New York Stock Exchange.

In a consideration of brokers' loan history in 1928 and 1929, funds advanced by non-banking members are of primary importance. This class of loan totaled $6,416,000,000 in October, 1929, a figure equivalent to 70 per cent of all brokers' loans. It was the great expansion in these loans that intensified the difficulties of the Federal Reserve authorities when they were successful in curtailing the expansion of loans extended by banks for their own account. This is exemplified by the following figures showing the course of growth of these two classes of loans in the twelve-month period ending in October, 1929:

(In millions of dollars)

SOURCE	OCT. '28	OCT. '29	INCREASE PERCENTAGE
Loans to brokers and dealers by banks	2,749	2,824	3
Loans to brokers and dealers by others	3,701	6,416	73

Loans by banks were practically entirely checked after October, 1928, while loans from other sources were expanding by leaps and bounds. As a matter of fact, the amount of loans made by New York banks was actually greater in January, 1926, than in October, 1929.

The loans of "others" were placed by New York City Clearing House member banks in amounts of not less than $100,000, for which service the banks charged a fee of one-half per cent per annum (the practice was discontinued on November 16, 1931). The actual lenders of these funds were mostly business corporations, investment trusts, individual capitalists, foreign banks, and other foreign interests. In order to approximate the relative importance of these sources, the Senate Banking and Currency subcommittee in 1931 sent out a questionnaire on the subject to the largest New York City banks. Here are the tabulated answers:

*(In millions of dollars)**

BANK	MAX. AMOUNT PLACED 1929	PER CENT FROM BUS. CORP.	PER CENT FROM INV. TRUSTS	PER CENT INDUS.	PER CENT ALL FOREIGN SOURCES
"No. 1"	757	68		11	21
"No. 2"	631	49	16	30	5
"No. 3"	437	56	2	33	3
"No. 4"	360	57	18	23	2
"No. 5"	241	42	7	4	1.1
"No. 6"	153	73	0.1	17	11
"No. 7"	97	63	4	15	1
Totals	2,676	58	8	18	9.5

* *Hearings before a Subcommittee of the Committee on Banking and Currency,* U. S. Senate pur. to S. Res. 71.

Of course, not all funds from miscellaneous lenders were placed through the agency of commercial banks, as private banks and money brokers also performed the function of handling these funds. This factor should be borne in mind in any consideration of the action of brokers' loans in any future security boom. Although there was a widespread popular impression to the contrary, the banks actually assumed no responsibility for the safety of these loans, and it was an open question even as to how far the banks could be held legally responsible for maintenance of adequate collateral behind the loans. However, so far as is known, no losses whatever were suffered by private lenders, despite the drastic deflation of 1929 and thereafter. The commercial banks always had to increase loans for their own account to replace the loans of private lenders when they were withdrawn.

The private lenders thus furthered the lack of responsibility for orderly conditions in the money market. The credit-granting function was placed in the hands of a class of irresponsible lenders attracted to a new field by abnormally high interest rates, who were ready to "run out" on a moment's notice. The action of these lenders in the three-month period, from August, 1929 on, is significant. During the week of August 22, the brokers' loans total rose $133,000,000, but in this period loans of "others" rose $200,000,000, so that the loans by the bank actually decreased by $67,000,000 simultaneously with the increase on the part of non-banking lenders.[16] Similarly, during the week ending October 10, 1929, aggregate brokers' loans decreased $91,000,000, at the same time that the loans of "others" rose $34,000,000.[17] So the reduction in the loans made by banks with their own funds in that week was $125,000,000. But it is the action of these "other lenders" after the so-called "panic week" that is especially noteworthy. From October 23 to 30, total loans fell $1,096,000,000 from $6,634,000,000 to $5,538,000,000.

A remarkable feature is that of this grand total, loans made by the reporting member banks in New York City on their own account actually increased by the huge sum of nearly $1,000,000,000 rising from $1,077,000,000 to $2,069,000,000 or almost 100 per cent. The loans of "others," against which no reserves were maintained, fell during the week by $1,380,000,000 or 33 per cent, while in addition, the loans of out-of-town banks shrank by $707,000,000. So the New York banks had to contend with a calling of loans of $2,087,000,000. The banks being forced to take over so many loans of outsiders, naturally had to

[16] *Federal Reserve Bulletin,* Sept., 1929, p. 605.
[17] *Ibid.,* Nov., 1929, p. 724.

increase their reserve borrowing. Member bank borrowing at New York increased from $107,000,000 to $246,000,000, and at the twelve Reserve banks there was an increase from $796,000,000 to $991,000,000 of borrowing during that week. The Federal Reserve system increased its total bills and securities from $1,337,000,000 to $1,649,000,000, an increase of 23 per cent, during the same period. The outside lenders subsequently continued to call in their loans so that in the period from October 23 to December 1, 1929, these loans were reduced by almost $2,000,000,000, or 50 per cent of their former total.[18] So the "net" aftermath of this situation, under which the speculative boom had been supported and stimulated by these huge sums from miscellaneous lenders, was that when the speculative bubble finally burst, this "credit" pool "blew up" as well, and the commercial-banking system had to take over these loans of the irresponsible "others" and shoulder the onerous credit burden.

It should, therefore, be borne in mind that this type of loan constitutes a potential liability of the banking system. It does not give rise to a corresponding increase in bank deposits. Although these loans do not increase the amount of bank deposits transferred, they actually leave the same effect as new bank loans, because of the increase in the velocity of the deposits. And it should be remembered that by their nature these funds of non-banking lenders are funds which would otherwise be relatively dormant and inactive, so their velocity is increased to an even greater degree than is supposed. Thus, these loans may very dangerously build up a multiple expansion of speculative credit in any period of security inflation.

Effects of these Changes

The foregoing survey outlines the changes that have taken place in the securities market, in so far as relates to American banking, and its connection with the public trading in stocks and bonds. It is worth while to summarize the changes in attitude toward the securities market that have thus taken place before we attempt any actual estimate of the degree of permanence

[18] *Ibid.*, Nov., 1929, p. 724, and Dec., 1929, p. 783.

in banking structure brought about thereby. Briefly stated, we may review our findings as follows:

1. Within the past decade, or more, there has been an immense increase in the proportion of bank portfolios or holdings which consists of actually owned long-term securities.

2. At the same time there has been a tremendous increase in the volume of loans made by so-called commercial banks upon collateral security.

3. The changes elsewhere reviewed in the character of the deposit liabilities of the banks, tending as they have to increase the percentage of deposits with a slow turnover (time deposits), in some measure accounts and furnishes defense for the increase in long-term assets.

4. This change in the maturity of deposits has not been sufficient to account for more than a fraction of the increasing proportion of long-term assets held by the banks of the country.

5. The drift toward long-term assets has been partially brought about by the desire of corporations to relieve themselves of dependence on banks.

6. This corporate effort has been accompanied by the growth of willingness on the part of the public, perhaps to some extent stimulated by the "education" furnished during the World War, to buy and hold stock exchange securities.

7. Corporations have, accordingly, been able to place with the public long-term capital obligations in amounts which have enabled them to settle their obligations on short-term accounts to the banks.

8. The settlement of their obligations to the banks has left them with surpluses of funds which they have either carried as reserves, or have, at times, invested in the securities of other corporations, usually in their own line of business.

9. The banks themselves, recognizing this broadening of the market for securities, have been disposed to depend in their lending almost entirely upon current market quotations for such securities, and have paid relatively little attention to the underlying values.

10. By this means bank credit has practically been placed at

the disposal of the speculative markets without limit upon a basis primarily dependent upon the extent to which the markets would be able to mark up or advance the price of securities.

11. The banks thus became absolutely dependent upon the maintenance of relatively stable quotations for securities in order to secure the stability and convertibility of their portfolios.

12. Hence, in time of sharp recession—as in 1929 and successive years—the banks, instead of having a highly liquid portfolio, found themselves in possession of a portfolio that was almost solidly frozen.

13. Reserve banks have found themselves hampered in giving credit to members under the terms of the Federal Reserve Act, by the circumstance that with some banks so large a percentage of assets had come to consist of securities and non-eligible paper generally.

Consideration of these fundamental and far-reaching changes in the securities markets and in the relation of the banks thereto, presents a problem for the present and future which is of first-class interest. While it is true, as shown by contemporary events, that speculative activity and interest of the community as a whole continues on a high level, a study of the securities situation during the past few years has indicated an increasing difficulty in the flotation of new issues. This difficulty is likely to be emphasized both by international events, including the various moratoria in different countries, by domestic legislation and changes of attitude—including the non-collectibility of mortgages, and the effort to relieve debtors of their obligations; while it has also been increased by the continuous doubt as to the industrial future and the probable degree of independence of business in the management of its own affairs. As a result of these various causes and their interworkings, there is ample ground for question whether, in any very early future, there will be a restoration of conditions of bank lending which developed during the decade 1920-1930. Banks are still ready enough to make securities loans, but certainly upon a much more cautious basis than heretofore; while the volume of new securities has already suffered a severe, perhaps permanent, check. The problem, therefore, of banks of the community is found thus in the development of their lending practice for the future—an important element in which will be their lending practice with regard to security loans, while this, in turn, will be to no small extent determined by their attitude toward securities markets and the relation of these markets to them.

CHAPTER XXVII

INDUSTRIAL CHANGES IN BANKING[1]

The changes in banking structure, control, and portfolios that have been outlined, have, for the most part, been studied without reference to their underlying causes. It has been pointed out that changes in types of control tend to react upon changes in structure, and vice versa, and that the modifications of portfolios, through which the banks of the country have gradually passed, have not been the result of arbitrary decision, but must be regarded as the outcome of long-range, slow-working factors. It is now desirable to sketch rather more closely and particularly some of the allied industrial changes that have been working to bring about the modification of contemporary banking conditions in the United States. They will best be reviewed, first of all, in logical order, thus affording a foundation for subsequent analysis and interpretation.

1. *Changes in transportation.*—It is a matter of common observation that the location of banking offices, and, consequently, the general organization of banking necessarily adapts itself more or less closely to alterations in the distribution of population. The widely diffused unit banking of the United States, developed side by side with the growth of towns and villages in which the business of surrounding territories was centralized. Observation of other newly developed countries, such as Canada, Australia, and South Africa, furnishes interesting parallels and at the same time important contrasts which throw light upon the factors tending to determine the location of banking units. In the other countries named, branch banking has from the beginning of their development been the rule; and the result of freedom in the establishment of branches has been to place branch offices at every point throughout the countries referred to, where it was likely that such a branch office could successfully take root and maintain itself. The limit to the num-

[1] Written by H. Parker Willis.

ber of branches in such cases was furnished by the amount of business locally offered for the maintenance of such branches. So, also, in the United States, the establishment of a bank in a town or village has usually been dependent upon the presence of capital to develop enough business in the locality to permit such a bank to "carry" itself, covering its operating expenses and paying its proportion of the "overhead" of the parent. As in the case of post offices and other bureaus whose number is determined partly by the convenience of the public and partly by the amount of possible business to be obtained for their maintenance, the number of banks in the United States like the number of branches in the branch-banking countries was determined by the practical considerations of the need of the public and their willingness to pay for the accommodation. In these circumstances, as already shown, at an earlier point (Part II, Chapter VIII), the numerical growth of banking in the United States reached a peak point shortly after the close of the World War, with a total of more than 30,000 institutions. This total number had shrunk by March 1, 1933 to about 18,000. That figure must be regarded as probably definitely reduced by several thousand more institutions during the year 1933, depending upon the number of those closed at the time of the banking holiday that must continue closed.[2]

This great shrinkage in the number of independent banking institutions, perhaps, greater than has ever before been registered in any one period of banking history, must be regarded as primarily the result of the fundamental banking changes, whose nature we have discussed elsewhere. Underlying these however, has been a widespread change in the transportation habits of the American people, owing to the general and increasing use of the automobile, both in town and country. The effect of this nation-wide "mobilization" of the population has been three-fold: (1) to destroy the importance of former centers of population, market towns, trading places, etc., by rendering it possible to transfer the business of the average individual to a considerable distance; (2) to make movement between different

[2] More than 2,800 remained closed on Aug. 15, 1933.

parts of the country cheaper and more convenient than ever before and, hence, to alter the marketing and trading habits of the community; (3) to alter the distribution of freight and the methods of shipping established under the older régime.

How profoundly these changes have actually worked upon the banking habits of the community it is difficult to realize through mere description. It must be remembered that the public of the United States is not primarily a note-using or money-employing community, but that its distinct preference is for the check and deposit system. Had the branch-banking system been employed in the United States without let or hindrance, it might well be that the number of banking offices throughout the country would have been as great as, or greater, than the total number of unit banks in the country, and it might well be that such branch offices, economically operated, as they could be, would have been able to maintain their existence in the face of fundamental economic changes which have operated to reduce the total number of banking institutions in existence. It is worthy of note that the number of banking offices in the United States per thousand of population has not been excessive as contrasted with those maintained in other countries—a fact made evident by the investigations carried on during the banking inquiry of 1925-1926, and more lately confirmed by the figures compiled and published by the League of Nations in its memorandum on "Commercial Banks." The fact that a locality or community, in order to maintain a unit bank with the overhead and other expense which necessarily attaches to the existence of any independent institution, must give its patronage fully and exclusively to such a bank, practically meant the extinction of many banks from the time that the development of modern means of transportation resulted in the alterations of movement and of marketing to which reference has already been made.

The present investigation has prepared a set of maps, presented to show by representative states the location of banks, with a view to suggesting pictorially the great alteration that has come over the banking map of the United States during recent years, fundamentally because of the changes in conditions of movement and marketing already referred to.

Mr. R. C. Stephenson, former president of the American Bankers Association, took cognizance of this situation in his testimony before the Senate Investigating Committee, remarking: "The farmer who formerly patronized the small stores in the village, when he got the hard-surfaced roads and found he could get to the larger town within one-quarter of the time it used to take him to drive by horse, began to do his trading in the larger place; and, naturally, going there to trade, he would also take his banking business there." Mr. Stephenson went on in the same testimony to discuss the relationship of such changes in population to bank failures, and to the distribution of business, but the substance of his argument was founded upon the factor already outlined—the change in the conditions of transportation.[3]

2. *Changes in business organization.*—The alterations of banking practice and banking institutions which have just been sketched as growing out of changes in transportation conditions have been paralleled by changes in business organization which have probably had an influence of coördinate importance. Let us note, briefly, what these changes are.

The first, perhaps, in importance has been the tendency to consolidate businesses and to bring about a larger size of business unit. One result of this drift has been, as we shall note presently, the necessity for a larger size of banking unit, but, at this point the feature of the situation to which attention should be directed is the effect of industrial consolidations upon the number and location of the banks. Such effect has probably been two-fold:

a) It has tended to transfer a good deal of banking business away from moderate-sized towns and cities, and even from villages, to headquarters' places to which the fiscal or general offices of the consolidated enterprises have been transferred. The result of such transfer has, of course, been to take away business from the banks of the local communities, among which it was

[3] Hearings, Feb. 16, 1931, pp. 376 ff.

formerly centered and to concentrate it in the hands of the banks at the headquarters' points.

b) It has tended also to change the portfolio of the smaller banks, tending to make them very largely "neighborhood institutions," whose business has consisted chiefly in the receipt of deposits from employees of the various larger business concerns and, perhaps, the making of relatively small loans; their real commercial business having been given up when the transfer of headquarters, already referred to, took place. In this way the smaller banks which formerly had substantial access to good paper, have lost it and could have recovered their business of this type only through the use of a considerable amount of initiative and skill, which they have not displayed. Instead they have been inclined to use their available funds in the purchase of investment securities; and, thus, it sometimes has happened that a small bank that formerly held the paper of a local manufacturing company—or even a small bank that had upon occasion declined to take on the paper of such a company—has found itself becoming the holder of the bonds of the concern, in lieu of short-term notes which it formerly had, or which (in some cases) it had declined to hold.

3. *Developments of new methods of merchandising.*—Closely allied to the influence exerted by consolidations and combinations of capital, is the influence exerted by the introduction of new methods of merchandising. Of these, two have been widely noted in other connections, although their relationship to banking has received but little attention. They are: *a*) the mail-order house, and, *b*) the chain-store organization.

These two factors have been substantially identical in the character of the influence they have exerted upon local banking. In the case of both, an important fact is necessarily the transfer of current funds of the community to other places, and, hence, to tend to starve out the local bank. The country town with a bank or two and a few "stores," a generation ago, expected the bank to hold the funds of the community which were then used by the inhabitants in purchasing goods from the storekeepers who redeposited the funds in the banks. At certain seasons of the year they drew upon the banks for amounts with which to import the goods that were needed by the community; at other seasons they received the proceeds of the sale of crops effected by farmers in the surrounding country or, more continuously, they received the proceeds of sales of locally manufactured articles turned out in the establishments of the place. The result was to make the town or village much more nearly self-supporting than it is today. Under modern conditions the chain store, or the mail-order house, supplies the community with the goods it needs, receiving payment in cash, which is then obtained from the local banks and immediately transferred to some point of accumulation elsewhere. The consequence is, a much more steady outflow of available funds, while the merchandising business of the community tends to dry up and, hence, to cease its activity as a source of deposits in the local institution. In those cases where local banks already find it a matter of some difficulty to develop business in sufficient quantities to warrant them in continuing their operations, such a shift of trade has tended strongly to inflict a final blow, whose effect was to lead to the liquidation of the local bank; or, in other cases, to drive it into operations and transactions for which it was not particularly fitted, so that eventually it was driven to failure.

4. *Changes in manufacturing.*—The changes which have just been reviewed are more or less obvious in their reflex effect upon banking, but there are others whose influence, while more subtle and less evident, are probably equally significant. Conspicuous among these is the tendency on the part of most industries toward the assumption of a much more highly mechanized condition. So much has been said of recent years about this increase in mechanization, and especially with reference to the increasing size of the capital investment required by the average industry as contrasted with the total number of employees, that it is probably unnecessary to submit any detailed data on the subject, the condition being merely stated dogmatically, and the reader left to elaborate his inquiries into the subject as he may choose.[4] The fact of an increasing mechanism of industry, both

[4] The literature on this subject is extensive, but reference may be especially made to a few particularly useful discussions. Included among these are Wagemann, *Economic Rhythm;* Pigon, *Industrial Fluctuations, Economics of Welfare;*

absolutely and in proportion to the number of units of labor employed, being given, the relationship of this fact to current banking conditions still remains to be stated. The first outgrowth of it is evidently a necessity, when providing funds or capital for business, to obtain them in much larger proportion than formerly, upon a long-term basis—i.e., to place a greater proportion of the outstanding liabilities of the enterprise in the form of capital obligations, and a relatively smaller one in the form of bank and other short-term obligations. This drift has both intensified and been intensified by the rapid and efficient development of the modern mechanism of corporation finance and speculative trading. Taken together, the two have resulted in rendering it relatively easy for the business enterprise to obtain access to capital funds of which it stood in need, and this fact has encouraged it to continue the expansion of its mechanization, since, on the whole, the funds so to be used could be more conveniently and, at times, more economically obtained than they could be had from banks under the unit banking system. Such an expansion of capital funds would not have been likely without the changes in industrial technique and methods now well-recognized, and the changes which they have brought about in banking must, therefore, be regarded as having been the outgrowth rather than the cause of the modifications in technical processes so referred to.

Be this as it may, and explain the situation as we choose, it will remain a fact that modern industry, by employing a relatively greater proportion of machinery as compared with working capital, has naturally tended to alter the degree of its dependence upon the commercial banks, and particularly to reduce the extent of its dependence upon the smaller bank; inasmuch as increasing mechanization of capital investment tends strongly toward the aggravation of the drift toward large size in the industrial unit.

5. *Development of public utilities.*—Another factor closely in

---

Schlichter, *Economic Society;* and among the older volumes from which much of the latter discussion of the subject has been drawn, Hobson, *Evolution of Modern Capitalism.*

line with the change in mechanization methods has been the widespread development of public utilities, generally organized upon a state or national scale, and involving the application of large volumes of capital for the installation of such facilities as the furnishing of water, light, electricity, and power. Whereas, formerly, the local consumer supplied his own light through the use of lamps, he now has electric installation; and, whereas, he formerly provided himself with water through some local system, he is now, in many cases, a constituent unit in a large "district" or "area" which has combined forces for the purpose of establishing a town water system. The effect of these changes has been to reduce the amount of local expenditure for the facilities thereby represented and to transfer it (as in the case of the trading already discussed above) to headquarters' places located at a distance; the effect of the rapid spread of public utilities services throughout the country being, thus, to increase the centralization of funds, decrease an important element in local trade, and above all, to bring about the transfer of local balances as rapidly as possible away from the banks in which they were at first deposited.[5]

On the whole the conclusion seems unavoidable that the progressive development of the public utility system, particularly in view of the widespread growth of the holding company for public utilities, has tended very strongly toward the intensification of several other factors already mentioned as working strongly toward the revolutionizing of banking conditions.

6. *Growth of government enterprise.*—A final influence operating upon the structure of the banking system, which must not be neglected, is afforded by the advance in all countries of a system of public interference with industry, either through direct regulation or through the actual intervention of the

[5] It is true that some of the more enlightened and large public utilities have devoted a great deal to investigation and devising of plans for the management of their bank deposits with a view of preventing the sudden and inconvenient withdrawal of funds from the communities in which they originate. One such institution, with a total of some 10,000 such bank accounts, a few years ago developed a general plan for the control of its accounts designed to insure the continued use of the bank funds thereby represented, in the localities in which they were drawn, for a period estimated to be at least as long as their average ordinary life.

Government in the construction of factories and the installation of industries. This drift is clearly seen in sundry foreign countries. Not to mention the transformation of banking which has taken place in Soviet Russia, where the conditions of economic life are still so far removed from those in the United States that no comparison is fruitful, we may note in Germany the rapid spread of direct Government ownership and partial operation in the case of the larger banks. This drift has, in recent years, received an artificial impetus owing to the general banking breakdown of 1931; but the tendency had already been at work for long years past. In other countries similar trends have been noted and in the United States, it is possible to observe at first hand the alterations in banking structure and method which are the outgrowth of extension of Government business, and particularly of Government productive activities. These tendencies have necessarily been the gathering of large amounts of funds, either through taxation or borrowing, or both, for use in financing or paying for the undertakings in which the Government has thought fit to engage—public building construction, road building, harbor works, irrigation, river control, and the like. In all such cases, the tendency is emphatically toward centralization of control, and consequently toward concentration of funds, with the attendant effects upon banking that must necessarily grow out of alterations in the location and volume of banking business thereby produced.

Having thus reviewed what appear to be the major reflex effects upon banking that grow out of industrial changes, with their incidental shifts of population and of capital, it is now desirable to trace, more particularly than heretofore, the precise ways in which these alterations affect and influence banking. Several such ways have already been incidentally mentioned as a necessary feature in the discussion, but it is desirable now to gather up these incidental references, and to combine them into a general statement of the banking trends that must be regarded as incidental to those changes of industry and mechanization already referred to. Such changes may, as in the former case, be presented *seriatim* as follows:

1. *Reduction in the total number of banking offices.*—It is not necessary to elaborate what has been said on this point at previous stages of the discussion, but merely to mention it as a basic factor; adding, however, that this tendency toward reduction, although apparently general in all countries, whether of the unit or branch banking type, is necessarily far more pronounced in the unit banking countries.

2. *Enlargement of the average size of banking loan, and consequently in the average size of bank that can be successful.*—The Federal Reserve system committee investigating the changes in the condition of banking throughout the United States, has found this drift toward the enlargement of the desirable size of the banking unit very pronounced, and similar conclusions have been arrived at in earlier parts of the present study (see page 174.) The increase in size, thereby advanced has naturally been an important factor militating against the success of the smaller banks and tending to increase among them the proportion of failures which has already been noted in some detail (see page 315).

3. *Changes in character of bank portfolios.*—As already shown, owing to the increase in capital for investment as compared with working capital in industry, there has been a change in the relative proportions of commercial paper and securities on the market, with the result that—relatively speaking—the amount of bank capital needed has been reduced or, if not so reduced, has been influenced in the direction of investment in bonds and other long-term securities.

4. *Tendency to reduce liquidity.*—By the side of the change in bank portfolios already referred to, there has, moreover, sprung up a tendency to reduce the liquidity of the banks. It may be suggested that this change in liquidity is identical with the shift already noted from commercial paper to bond investments in the portfolios of the banks, but the condition here had in mind is of a different nature. In addition to bringing about a greater development of the bond side of the bank portfolio, it is also true that the industrial changes referred to have operated pretty strongly to cut the liquidity of the actual holdings of

short-term paper held by the banks. This has been owing to the fact that, under the type of industry which has been steadily developing in the United States, a much larger quantity of unsold or unconsumed goods is currently in existence, needing often to be carried by the use of current loans, while, because of the rapid expansion of organized markets, such holdings of goods are frequently regarded as immediately salable, and hence, bank paper protected by them as collateral, is treated or viewed as "liquid."

5. *Use of banks as agents for other banks.*—The conditions referred to have aided, likewise, in the growth of a system whereby bank funds are "placed" or loaned, in many cases by banks through the medium or agency of other banks. Thus, other banks have usually acted as the medium through which the originating banks, possessed of loanable funds, have supplied such funds for use in the purchase of bankers acceptances, or for loans on call, or for the purchase of bonds and other similar securities. The practice of lending through others, however necessary it may be at times, as a phase of practical management of banking, has inevitably tended to reduce the efficiency of the smaller banks in their judgment of credit, and as lending institutions, with the result that they have become more and more accustomed to acting through intermediaries rather than as originators of credit. This situation has naturally tended to render bank examination considerably more difficult because of the fact that so large a portion of the assets of given banks were dependent upon credit conditions, or were the outgrowth of decisions that had been made in distant places which, therefore, were not subject to the same general criticism and severe analysis on the part of examiners that would have been applied had the matter under investigation had to do with local extensions of accommodation. In this connection, it is worth mentioning that the alterations in banking, already referred to, have operated in many cases to increase the degree of mutual dependence among the banks, so that, for example, failures, or the development of weakness in any region or group of institutions, frequently reflected itself in the form of bad effects upon other institutions, often at a distance.

The survey which has thus been made with respect to industrial changes, and their banking consequences, has set forth some of the major inferences to be drawn from the investigations presented in this volume. What is the significance of this interaction between banking and industry? The question is one that has received too little attention within past years, largely because of the preoccupation of students of banking with the purely financial aspects of the situation. Such preoccupation is natural, but must from time to time, be corrected by taking into account the fact that the only reason for the existence of banking is that of affording service to business and to the population in general. Being an intermediary occupation it renders no service in itself, but its success is found in the extent to which it facilitates the effective exchange of goods, and the conservation of the savings and resources of the community at large. A study of banks in this aspect, however, as the outgrowth of general economic change, naturally raises some serious questions which are destined undoubtedly to play a larger and larger part in future banking legislation and readjustments. It is now desirable, therefore, to inquire what these larger aspects of banking administration are and how they should be dealt with.

In their case, also, it is possible to enumerate certain of the outstanding elements involved in the problem, consecutively:

1. *Responsibility in the banking system.*—From early in its investigation, the Senate Banking Committee received from sundry sources recommendations that it devote attention to the question of reorganizing the entire banking system of the United States in such a way as to bring about a more satisfactory coordination of banking institutions and systems (see page 59). Probably the most influential of these recommendations were those which tended to emphasize the restrictive and disturbing influence of a dual banking system in the United States—i.e. a banking system organized partly under federal law and partly under the laws of the several state governments. It was then suggested by sundry witnesses before the Committee, and in numerous communications which were received by that body that the essential root evil of present conditions in American banking was found in this lack of centralization and concentration

of responsibility; although, at no point, and by no single individual, was the case precisely so stated. It was undoubtedly the opinion of those who devoted themselves to this phase of the question that what should be sought was a closer adaptation or "meshing in" between the business and banking systems of the country. Perhaps the most positive and definite recommendation in this connection was that made by Mr. Owen Young, who, in testifying before the Committee, took the position that:[6]

a) The government of the United States, should in the exercise of its power over the currency system, take to itself the entire authority for the granting of charters to banks to engage in the deposit business; perhaps driving out state institutions already engaged in that business by the use of the taxing power.

b) As an incident to the foregoing change, the state governments be left to charter and supervise institutions to be engaged in fiduciary operations and in this only (trust company business), while

c) Savings deposits be likewise left to the jurisdiction of the states, to be dealt with either by savings banks or by savings deposits in fiduciary institutions.

This proposal was favorably regarded by many observers and had attained considerable theoretical standing. Such approval grows out of the evident evils surrounding the competitive granting of charters by many grades of government in the United States. Behind such superficial difficulties, however, is the fact that with many grades of government-granting charters, the reorganization of banking in such a way as to establish satisfactory relations between the banks and their borrowers while at the same time of conserving the interests of depositors, is a matter of extraordinary difficulty. The complex legislation and regulation incident to the performance of more or less conflicting duties inevitably prevent the attainment of full success in such an undertaking, and the result is a banking system which works irregularly and unsatisfactorily, and probably will always continue to do so, so long as it is organized upon the multipurpose basis which now underlies it.

[6] *Hearings*, Feb. 4, 1931, pp. 353 ff.

This question of the dual banking system of the United States has been fully investigated by the Committee of the Reserve system, already referred to, although that Committee has devoted its attention almost entirely to the competitive aspects of the struggle between the national and state banking systems and has, consequently, concentrated its findings upon such matters as excessive chartering of banks, the undue relaxation of restrictions on banking operations, on problems of dual control and supervision of banks, and the changing aspects of the relationship between state banks and the Federal Reserve system. While such investigations develop in convincing detail the difficulties and faults of the present system of dual control and, by thus showing the lines along which errors have been committed, indirectly suggest the method that might be followed in attaining a better status, they nowhere go to the root of the matter. That root is the question whether an end should or should not be put to this whole present system by the concentration of jurisdiction over commercial loans and deposits; while at the same time the jurisdiction over investment operations is left to local control. The subject is one which calls, undoubtedly, for a much more extended and thoughtful discussion than has as yet been accorded to it, and, probably, also for extensive inquiry into the various phases of technique which would be involved in effecting so drastic a reorganization of the entire basis of banking as is thus spoken of. The Banking Committee itself did not deem the matter one which for the time being fell within its jurisdiction or, at least, one with which it could properly undertake to deal. It, nevertheless, requested the governor of the Federal Reserve Board to secure the preparation of a bill designed to strike at the root of the matter (see Hearings on Senate 4412. April, 1932); and it also obtained the opinion of attorneys to the effect that action designed to bring about concentration of the entire deposit banking system under Federal control would be constitutional (see Hearings on Senate Resolution 71, p. 646). This opinion was substantially concurred in by the attorney of the Federal Reserve Board.

2. *Separation of investment and commercial banking.*—In

much that has been said in preceding pages, emphasis has been placed upon the mixture of function, and consequent difficulties, resulting from the attempt to combine investment and commercial banking. It will be remembered that this was the factor which was found to lie at the root of great changes in portfolios that have occurred in the United States within recent years. It will also be recalled that this mixture of investment and commercial functions has, however unintentionally, been the basis for the numerous and extensive blunders in the investment of bank funds which have so largely contributed to the unforeseen failure record of recent years. It will also have been noted in what has been said that, according to the present point of view, it is not sufficient merely to find fault with the banks for bad judgment in bond investments or for engaging their funds too largely in long-term securities, unless, at the same time, there is afforded some kind of definite guide or set of banking canons which can be relied upon by them in connection with the conduct of their affairs. So long as "a free banking system," with access readily granted to almost any group of men who are able to assemble the necessary capital, is the prevalent system, it will be essential to supply to such independent unit banks, information as to the general principles which they should follow in the use of their funds; yet, as has been seen, the banking laws of the United States, although elaborate and meticulous with regard to commercial paper, have had little or nothing to say with regard to the extent and relative proportions in which investment paper may be absorbed by the banks with the approval of the public authorities. The Banking Act of 1933 attempted to apply what may be called "first aid" in this matter by prohibiting commercial banks from paying interest upon demand deposits, from underwriting securities, and generally from conducting investment-banking operations simultaneously with deposit or commercial-banking business. This prohibition, doubtless wise in the sense of what has already been denominated "first aid" to a difficult situation, should not be regarded as a final answer to the problems that have been raised by the changing of relationships between banking and business such as have just been set forth.

It will continue to be true that, under existing industrial conditions, business and manufacturing establishments will find it necessary to supply themselves with investment capital; and it will, probably, also be true that a widespread ownership of such capital on the part of the public will be found advantageous and desirable, so soon, at least, as current evils in connection with flotation and distribution have been corrected.

In these circumstances the question how far a definite separation between commercial and investment banking is to take place, either along the line indicated in the Banking Act of 1933, or under the terms of some more elaborate and extensive scheme of segregation such as that which has just been outlined above, presents obvious difficulties. The Act of 1933 in no way interferes with the acquirement of very large holdings of bonds by banks, although it attempts to prescribe principles for the distribution of funds among different issues; and there is nothing in the plan put forward by Mr. Young, for example, which apparently would prohibit very large holdings of suitable securities by banks engaged in the deposit business. As is well known the Treasury Department of the United States relies very largely upon the banks, and has placed in them an unprecedentedly large percentage of short-term obligations of the Government. Such a situation, of course, begs the questions arising out of the problem of the use of banking funds in relation to business and leaves it still for consideration.

This question was plainly put by the Senate Banking Committee in the course of its studies to the authorities of the stock exchanges in the form of a query, what percentage of commercial bank funds could, with propriety, be used for loans on securities or for the actual outright purchase of securities. To this there was no answer, save the general statement that the issue was one of great scope and difficulty as to which a positive position could not now be taken.

The provision of the Banking Act of 1933, in assigning to the Federal Reserve Board the duty of fixing from time to time the percentage of loans made upon collateral security, likewise, begs the question, since it presupposes that there is some desirable or well-known proportion or extent in which the funds of deposit banks may be allowed to go into securities; but that the Federal Reserve Board or some other body is possessed of, or can get, information on such a subject which is even not accessible to any employed by others. This latter is not the case, but the problem of adjusting the investment position of the ordinary commercial bank—i.e., of determining to what extent these funds may wisely be used in loans on securities or in the purchase of investments, is one of utmost difficulty.

As we have seen, it is around this question that the problems created by the changing relationship of business and banking, because of alteration of distribution method, are centering. Not only a distinct answer to it, but also the establishment of conditions such as will insure continued solvency and efficiency by banks which have complied with recognized principles in the matter, are, therefore, requisite to the full solution of the question. It is around this matter, as we have already remarked, that much of the difficulty growing out of industrial changes and their reflex effects centers.

3. *Central banking and central bank supervision.*—In this discussion thus far, nothing has been said of current conditions in the United States in connection with central banking. That subject is reserved for a subsequent section of the present volume. It is, however, necessary to make brief reference to the general problems of central banking in connection with this matter of industrial and business relationships, since the management of central banking is necessarily a fundamental factor of utmost importance in the working out of the major problems relating to banking, to which reference has already been made. Here, again, the unit banking question enters as a fundamental problem affecting the whole situation. In foreign countries, where branch banking exists, the irresistible tendency of recent years has been toward concentration and centralized control. Such concentration and centralization have necessarily operated to bring about direction from a relatively small group of man-

agers, whose primary duty has been that of establishing banking policies rather than attending to the complex details of practical bank operation. In the United States, when the Federal Reserve Act was framed, it was attempted to obtain something of the same sort of direction, by giving to a central body, known as the Federal Reserve Board, a powerful directive authority, both over the twelve Federal Reserve banks themselves, and, in important particulars, over the member or commercial banks at large. It was often stated at that time by ill-advised persons that the system so established would render panics, breakdowns, or financial disturbances, practically impossible, and the successful financing of the War appeared to give a sort of superficial warrant to these forecasts. Experience since the War has shown, with greater and greater clarity, what the experience of 1929 to 1933 now makes absolutely evident and generally admitted—that in a widely diffused system of unit banks, there will be no success in times of great business change and pressure, except through the exertion of centralized supervision and control, designed to apply to the banking mechanism those results of general observation and knowledge of conditions which are largely outside of the reach of even the most conscientious of local bankers.

Industrial change, if the banking system is to work well and adapt itself to such change—must be accompained by change of financial policy, generally and wisely applied for the purpose of preventing either undue expansion of liabilities of certain classes or unreasonable conservatism, owing to fear of the consequences of even necessary business enlargement.

The study, therefore, of changing relationships between industry and banking, such as have been set forth in the foregoing chapter, strongly suggests the necessity of accompanying centralized action intended to keep the banking system constantly in line with new conditions. This, as already seen, is accomplished in the various foreign countries through centralization of banking in the hands of the abler financial minds of the community and under the influence of honest codes of banking conduct. In the United States it will be necessary, for a long time to come, under our present banking organization, to dispense with this kind of supervision. In lieu of it, apparently, the best substitute will be furnished by some coöperative organization like the Federal Reserve system, and the development of that system or a successor, in such a way as to supply this necessary element of management, would seem to be, beyond question, an immediate necessity, if satisfactory adaptation is to be assured as between banking and business.

PART V

CENTRAL BANKING

CHAPTER XXVIII

ORIGIN AND PURPOSE OF THE RESERVE BANKING SYSTEM[1]

INTRODUCTION

A general survey of banking conditions in the United States may be made without special reference to central-banking problems, or it may be undertaken with particular reference to the working out of such problems. In the present study the original intent was a description and analysis of general banking conditions without particular reference to their reflex effect upon central banking. The rapid development of banking difficulties in the United States, culminating in the banking holiday of February-March, 1933, has sharply called attention to new aspects of the situation. Developments have now reached a stage in which it is not possible to take account of more than a very few of the broader banking issues without at the same time considering their relation to the Federal Reserve organization. At the same time it has become plain that the Federal Reserve system has been, and is, expected to exercise at the present moment functions and responsibilities regarding the general condition of banking from which in former years it was supposedly free. It has, therefore, been deemed desirable to present brief studies of those phases of Federal Reserve policy which have an important bearing upon contemporary conditions.

Analysis of the Federal Reserve system, like analysis of banking conditions in general may be conducted from any one of several fundamental points of view. The rapid evolution of the system during its 20 years of life affords a panoramic picture of the major problems of central banking which is deserving of the closest possible examination.

Rate management and rate policies of Federal Reserve banks have a significant bearing upon contemporary conditions in

[1] Written by H. Parker Willis.

business and in other banks. Discount and purchase of Treasury obligations and holding of government deposits has shown itself a factor of first class importance in connection with the current problem of the national budget and the financing of the government during a deficit period. The entire question of open market operations and its relation to prices has been raised during recent years, and opens a field of inquiry in the theory of money and credit, as well as in connection with the practical application so reached, which is second to none in importance.

In the present study special analysis was made of rate policies and of open market operations. It is intended to offer in this Part a consolidated account of these phases of study, backed by a general historical sketch of the conditions which have gradually given rise to the present situation. A beginning is first made with a sketch of the origin and purpose of the Reserve banking system. This is followed by an outline review of later variations and amendments; and attention is then seriously turned to the general rate policies, and open market dealings, in the order thus indicated.

Original Ideas of the System

A judgment regarding the present status of the Federal Reserve system and its relationship to current problems in American banking must, as we have seen, be formed as a result of general appreciation of the purposes and achievements of the system during the twenty years of its existence. How far has it carried out the purposes for which it was originally set up? Has it failed in any particular because its original objects were essentially unattainable or unsound? Have its failures, whatever they are, been the result of changing conditions in banking and the appearance of new problems which call for independent solutions not previously thought of? These are the fundamental queries which arise in the mind of the student who views the Reserve banking system as an element in the general banking discussion of the time.

The original ideas of the system have been often stated in contradictory ways, but there need be no doubt about their essential nature. Unquestionably, the first and fundamental notion behind the Reserve Act was that of strengthening the existing banking system, and by so doing, rendering it more responsive to the current needs of business. That this end could be accomplished by massing the reserves of the country in a way not contemplated by the so-called Aldrich or Monetary Commission bill which had preceded it, and by establishing an organization for the continuous headship of the money market, was the underlying notion in the whole enterprise. Although at the start voluntary membership in Reserve banks was esteemed sufficient to provide a nucleus of financial strength, discussion early changed this proposal to a plan of compulsory participation by the national banks and for the contribution of reserve funds by each with a view to the upbuilding of a central reserve fund which could be used for the purpose of discounting the paper of banks that were temporarily in need of relief, and for equalizing the resources, generally speaking, of the member banks. Note issue provisions calling for an issue of currency based upon actual live business paper and, therefore, permitting an expansion of such paper to any extent desired provided that the business transactions which called for it had taken place or been brought into existence, was evidently a natural off-shoot of the Reserve project already referred to, notwithstanding that it has often been presented as the more fundamental or elementary of the underlying ideas of the Reserve measures. Generally speaking, then, we may think of the original Reserve Act as essentially an attempt to make the funds of the community more immediately available for, and responsive to business; attaining this object by a combination of available resources coupled with arrangements to shift credit produced by the Reserve mechanism thus created in such directions as circumstances might from time to time indicate.

What is "Business"

To so much perhaps a good many persons would agree in very general terms; and yet, it might be found, upon closer comparison of ideas, that the agreement so expressed was nominal or apparent rather than real. In order to test the actual acceptance of the conception of the Reserve Act as just outlined it is necessary to inquire, of practically any critic or student of it, his definition or conception of "business." It is not enough to say that the purpose of the Reserve Act was the facilitation or service of business, unless, at the same time, we define the latter term.

By business, the framers of the Federal Reserve Act unquestionably meant business in the older sense of that term, namely, exchange of goods including the movement of goods from producer to consumer and all of the operations ancillary thereto, but excluding both manufacturing and production, dependent upon the use of fixed capital, and speculation—the holding of values, securities, or funds purchased at a specified price with the idea that improvement or change in that price would sooner or later take place. The question is fairly to be asked, whether the use of the term business, in this narrow sense, was or was not permissible; whether, in short, it may not be called as essential to public welfare that the manufacturer or speculator be properly financed as it is that the trader, jobber, middleman or retailer may be thus cared for. The inquiry is, of course, legitimate, but in the present discussion it is largely beside the mark.

The question at issue is not the abstract desirability of these various operations, but is whether certain classes of economic transactions may be best cared for by certain banking methods, and cared for independently of others; or, whether it is more to be desired that banking legislation should attempt to make definite provision for economic transactions of all kinds, and should seek to relate such transactions one to another in some definite way. Be the answer what it may, the fact remains that the original Federal Reserve Act proceeded upon the theory, as in the older banking system of England, that it was desirable to have, as the core of the financial system of the country, an institution devoted primarily to the financing of business in the sense that this term has been above defined—distinct from production, storage, or speculation. Many of the disappointments and failures of the Reserve Act may be directly traced to inability or unwillingness to recognize its essential quality in the structure of the legislation or indisposition to act accordingly, or both.

Position of Speculation

The Reserve Act obviously proceeds upon the assumption that the financing of productive business and creation of productive capital is to be brought about by the action of individual investors in drawing upon funds placed to their credit by banks. That is to say, the action of individual investors in undertaking to segregate from their current holdings or operations portions of wealth which they have been devoting to the upbuilding of productive capital or, in other words, the financing of manufacturing and extractive processes generally is a necessary prerequisite. It further recognizes, of course, that even if we assume that provision has been made in this way for investment, the question of financing speculation still remains open; and that although in early British and American practice there was a manifest intent to make a separation between investment and commercial banking, speculation had been pretty definitely allowed to take place as a more or less welcome guest at the commercial banking table. From early in the history of the Reserve Act, therefore, it was determined to reach an arrangement with the speculative interests, whereby they should be granted the use of such portion of current banking funds as they might reasonably lay claim to. The object in mind was to draw a definite line of division between the business and speculative claims on underlying current funds of the community. This object was eventually attained, as we have already seen (Chapter XIX on Reserves), through the reduction of current reserve requirements far below those that were originally set by law;—the reserve requirements, for example, in central reserve cities being reduced to 13 per cent, and to 10, in reserve cities as compared to an original 25 per cent before the adoption of the Reserve Act. Generally speaking, we may say that with all due allowance made, the Reserve Act turned over for speculative use practically one-half of the previously held fluid funds of the community; while by making only a 13 per cent requirement in cities for the future (barely over 50 per cent of old reserve requirements) it established a similar division in time to come between speculation and business as joint claimants upon the fluid funds of the banks. The expectation was that speculative interests or bankers engaged in financing such interests would be willing, or would find themselves compelled, to discontinue their demands upon the fluid resources of the community when a limit had been reached which corresponded roughly with the volume of resources thus definitely assigned for speculative purposes at the will of the banks under whose custody they had been deposited. The Reserve Act, in other words, recognized the fact that, under American practice, it was to be expected that commercial banks would continue to make loans upon securities and to buy securities, and merely undertook to set aside a specified minimum percentage of reserve funds to be definitely devoted to the exclusive financing of business without reference to the possible requirements of speculative commitments or undertakings beyond that amount.

These purposes are plainly set forth not merely in so many words, but also in the negative requirements and prohibitions which are explicitly stated in the Act. According to it none of the funds of Reserve Banks are to be used for the purpose of carrying or trading in investments or speculative securities, or for the financing of speculation; but the resources of the Reserve banks are to be applied exclusively to the satisfaction of the needs of commerce, industry, and agriculture, in connection with their current requirements.

Flexibility of Requirements

It was the object of the original Federal Reserve Act to frame an underlying banking measure which should be reasonably flexible and which would adapt itself readily to the varying volume of business necessities. With this in mind, the framers of the Act were careful not to confine the activities of the Reserve banks within too narrow limits, but to permit a reasonably broad latitude. Thus, for instance, the Federal Reserve

Board was given power to release all reserve requirements when, and if it saw fit to do so, and the Reserve banks themselves were authorized to disregard the fixed reserve requirements to which they themselves were subjected in protecting the deposit accounts of their member banks with them, simply upon the penalty of a fixed fine appropriate to the amount of Reserve deficiency and intended rather as affording a definite warning signal of danger than as anything in the way of positive restraint upon the expansion of credit. In the same way the Act, although nominally designed to confine its extensions of credit and loans to its own members, nevertheless made definite provision for the purchase, and discounting, of paper belonging to nonmember banks, although it made such operations contingent upon the assent at least of the Federal Reserve Board itself.

Scope of Reserve Operations

It has sometimes been represented that the Reserve system was intended as an essentially parochial banking organization designed to maintain order and supply assistance to the banks of United States, but expressly not intended to render any service to outsiders. Nothing, of course, could be further from the facts in the case. The Federal Reserve Act expressly provided for the creation of foreign branches—a permission which has never yet been availed of in any except the most limited and nominal fashion, such voluntary limitations being based on the assertion that in no circumstances must a central or Reserve bank allow itself to enter upon policies which would be distasteful to other central banks in foreign countries. Be this as it may, the original enactment not only granted permission for the establishment of branches of Reserve banks abroad, but it did so in such language as to render their establishment almost mandatory; while it, furthermore, granted to such branches powers of operation very much broader in their scope than those given to the Reserve banks at home. Under the terms of the Act, there was nothing to prevent the foreign branches of the Reserve bank from dealing directly, and as extensively as they pleased, with individuals, discounting, buying, and selling the same classes of paper which had, by the Act itself, been rendered eligible for rediscount. A full enforcement or application of the Reserve Act would thus have resulted in the creation of a group of foreign branch banks situated in other countries and devoting themselves to the development of the foreign trade of the United States, by discounting and dealing in the paper originating in foreign commerce and representing the business dealings of American citizens and their customers in that branch of enterprise.

It is clear from this survey that most of the restrictive regulations and inhibitions by which the operation of Reserve banks has since become "hedged-about" had certainly no basis in the original intent or meaning of the law itself.

Character of Operations

With a system thus organized, it was evidently to be assumed that the character of its operations would be determined by the amount of actual business transacted, and by the volume of the paper representing such business that might offer itself for discount or rediscount. The successful working of the Reserve system, in short, along the lines which have thus been outlined, was dependent upon the existence and offer of a substantial volume of paper of the kinds described in the Act as "eligible"; this term to be further defined by the Federal Reserve Board according to changing circumstances. From the beginning of the Reserve system, therefore, it was a matter of fundamental importance to know whether or not paper of the desired kind was being regularly developed and brought forward. Clearly if such paper were deficient or if changes were to take place in the method of financing business, such as to shut off or reduce this supply of paper, there would be a corresponding alteration of the underlying bases upon which the Reserve system rested and, accordingly, a lessening in the efficiency and success of its operations. The Federal Reserve Board, therefore, at the outset, endeavored to formulate its definitions of commercial paper in such a way as to admit to the benefits of the system as much of the various kinds of paper representing actual current business as was possible; the thought being to develop ways for judging the "self-liquidating" character of the paper so admitted and to make it possible to discount with the Reserve banks practically any kind of paper that really and in effect represented a "commercial transaction," as against any that was based upon operations in securities.

In consonance with this purpose the Reserve Board very early established regulations admitting to discount not only double-named paper, trade acceptances, but also single-named paper when accompanied by evidence that it represented an actual business transaction or was the medium of borrowing employed by an individual or corporation actually desiring to use the proceeds in the development of current business. This led to the attempt to develop a means of ascertaining whether or not the borrowers were actually "liquid"; hence, the call for accountants' certification with reference to the condition of the business or in the absence of this certification by a discounting bank, that it was convinced of the liquid position of the enterprise. These requirements were in line with the policies pursued by foreign central banks, but they were at variance with the practice of American bankers, and the Reserve Board did not have the courage and persistence to insist upon putting them into practical operation. Accordingly the attempt to apply a definite standard of liquidity, and to limit the discount operations of Reserve banks to paper of demonstrably liquid character was gradually abandoned.

One of the Reserve banks from the very beginning, insisted upon making loans against collateral security, including under that head practically every kind of collateral—not only securities but commodities, real estate, and other evidences of ownership. When called to account for the practice it insisted that the paper which it was discounting was "liquid" and that the "collateral" which it was accepting was intended merely as an additional form of protection to guard against loss. Stated in another way, this amounted to saying that the bank desired to judge the liquidity of the paper merely on the basis of salability and to protect itself against danger of loss arising out of hasty judgment by insisting upon the pledging of evidences of ownership. A similar tendency was manifest in other reserve banks, although not generally so pronounced as was the case at the institution which had initiated the practice.

Eventually the Board determined upon a compromise which resulted in permitting member banks to bring in for rediscount any paper which in their opinion appeared to be liquid, while the Reserve bank itself in discounting such paper sought protection by asking for collateral securities. This collateral practice spread rapidly through the system and in later years it often resulted in the lending by Reserve banks to their members of amounts so large and so heavily protected by collateral that, in case of failure, the Reserve bank was found to have possessed itself of most of the available assets of the institution, or, in other words, it had been given a general prior claim over all other creditors as a means of assuring the reimbursement of the advances it had made during the period of active operation of the bank.

This change in point of view and method of handling the credit situation has continued throughout the whole life of the Federal Reserve system, to become more pronounced; but the early steps which were taken in putting it into effect developed so soon after the adoption of the legislation that the student is warranted in treating the system as, from its very beginning, characterized by the practice of lending on collateral without due ascertainment of the liquid character of the paper upon which these transactions were founded. It was, thus, never in effect a system which adhered strictly to the prudent ideas of its framers, since, from the outset, it seemed to prefer the making of loans upon collateral security.

Effect of War

The practical change in the Reserve system which had thus come about, very shortly after its inception, particularly as the result of indisposition to inquire narrowly into the nature of business transactions of member banks requiring to be financed, was necessarily considerably aggravated by the fact that the system had come into existence just at the opening of the World War. Complete organization of the new banks had, in fact, not been accomplished until several months after the World War had definitely opened, and the first two years of its existence were a period of disturbed and abnormal banking and finance. In the third year of the system (1917) the nation definitely entered the war, and the result was the immediate appearance of a supposed necessity for extensive participation by it in the financing of the struggle. Before the end of 1917 it was plain that "commercial paper" (as the only type of bank loan, recognized by the original act generally speaking), had become obsolete, certainly for the period of the war. Not only were most transactions, in one way or another being conducted with a view to the financing of the operations of the government, but borrowing at the banks had been definitely placed upon a government bond basis, and the bulk of member bank borrowing at Reserve banks tended more and more to be the discounting of obligations collateraled by the government bonds.

This tendency continued to grow, so that at the close of the War, toward the end of 1918, there were few cases, indeed, in which the making of an advance, either by a bank or by a Federal Reserve bank, depended upon the commercial character of the transaction, or was the outgrowth of an operation which was expected to produce funds for its own settlement. Because of the fact that this situation had developed, as we have just noted, within the third year of the life of the new system, and before it had been definitely able to develop any established principles of action, we must regard it as a basic factor in determining the trend and later history of the system. It was, thus, from the beginning a system whose management inclined to the use of collateral loans and was sanctioned and stimulated in so doing by the attitude of the government, which had the right to appoint one-third of the directors in every Federal Reserve bank, while it also named the entire personnel of the supervising authority—the Federal Reserve Board.

Stock Exchange Relationship

We have already noted as one of the basic ideas of the Federal Reserve system, the attempt made by its framers to bring about a separation between speculative loans and those which were regarded as having their origin in business. During the first months of the Federal Reserve system, it undoubtedly seemed as if this particular phase of the policy was likely to be successful. There were several reasons for this appearance of things: the "release of reserves" which had been effected by the Act, provided banks with a very large amount of "excess" or "surplus" reserves which they were at liberty to use and could legally apply, in market operations, being thus amply supplied with funds for the financing of any transactions in which they were likely to need to engage in connection with speculation. On the other hand, the immense purchases of the allied nations in the United States, and the fact that, for a good while after the opening of the War, such purchases were paid for either in actual cash or in immediately salable securities, tended to reduce the need of credit and to put the country into what was for the time being an exceptionally liquid position.

Moreover, the early months of the War were characterized by great uncertainties of a financial nature (bank payments and stock exchange transactions being suspended for a good while, at the opening of the War, in New York and elsewhere), so that the violence of speculation was somewhat mitigated, and corresponding reduction effected in its probable demands upon banks. Shortly after the United States itself entered the war, a sharp curb was applied to stock exchange trading and to the issue of new securities, so that all in all—partly through the fact that a release of reserves had provided for all probable requirements during the early years while circumstances had tended to lessen such requirements—the Federal Reserve system was able to make an apparent compliance with the instructions contained in the Reserve Act, to avoid the financing of speculation. It is to be noted, however, that this compliance was purely artificial and fictitious, the outcome, as already explained, of fortuitous circumstances and in no respect the result of self-conscious acceptance of the general philosophy or theory which underlay the legislation.

It may be fairly stated that not until the close of the War, and the removal of the restraint which had been imposed upon securities issues and speculative operations, did any true test of the character and purpose of the Reserve system become possible. Not until that time was it possible, therefore, to ascertain whether the working of the Reserve system could be carried on along the lines that had been planned by its framers, or whether the resistance of the speculative community would necessitate a revision of the project in practice if not in actual law.

Relations with the Treasury

The Reserve Act had originally contemplated the transference of public deposits and fiscal operations completely from the subtreasuries to the Federal Reserve banks, thereby resulting, it was supposed, in ending the political operation of the subtreasuries, and at the same time eliminating the bad influence upon finance and business which had been exerted by the practice of tying up government funds in large amounts of cash in the subtreasuries. There is no reason to doubt that this part of the project would have worked successfully, but in any study of the Reserve system in its relation to contemporary banking, the student must carefully bear in mind that this phase of the law had not then been put into practical operation. Political influence succeeded in maintaining the subtreasuries in continued existence until the War was well advanced so that during the first three years of the system, the Reserve banks never had the opportunity of developing their services to the Government or of restoring the funds, obtained by the Government through taxation, to commercial use. After the United States entered the War, however, a wholly unforeseen change in the treasury situation necessarily occurred. This was the enormous expansion of the volume of funds advanced by the Reserve banks to the Government. The original Reserve Act had exempted transactions in government securities from the general prohibition of discount for collateral and speculative loans, but this provision has been written at a time when the national Government had outstanding less than one billion dollars of bonds.

It was the opinion of Treasury officials from the time of our entry into the War, that the needs of the Government could not be supplied by means of taxation, and this meant a large recourse to borrowing—the practical result being the succession of Liberty Loans and the activity of the Reserve banks in the financing of these loans upon a large scale. Thus, a radical change was effected in the intended character of the Reserve system. It passed from a plan intended to minimize the influence of government finance upon business to one in which government finance was accepted as a permanent and overruling factor in business, and in which the discounting of the paper growing out of government necessities became a continuous and most important phase of banking operation.

Perhaps it may fairly be said that, taking the whole history of the Reserve system, there was no one factor that was destined so to alter its structure and purpose as this change itself. At all events, in the study of the Reserve system it must be constantly remembered that notwithstanding the desire of the framers of the Act to bring about a condition in which Treasury finance would exert as little influence as possible upon business, the new system was plunged, by the force of events, into a position in which the control over business exerted by the Treasury Department was the outstanding factor in the national credit position. There was thus never a time from the opening of the Reserve banks down to the present where opportunity was given, even for a moment, for experimentation with the original provisions upon their own basis.

Supervision of Member Banks

There is another underlying aspect of the Federal Reserve system in which it is essential to recognize the real character of the basis provided by the Federal Reserve Act for a new banking system. For a good many years before the adoption of the Reserve Act, there had been a widespread and well-founded complaint against the character of the examination systems that were then in force. Both state and national examinations had been unsuccessful in preventing failures and, during the period preceding and following the panics of 1893 and 1907, the unsatisfactory character of the supervision had been very widely noted. The fact that clearing house examinations had been able to accomplish much more satisfactory results than those conducted by the government authorities had been noted by many persons as a rather serious reflection upon the latter, and the years immediately prior to the adoption of the Reserve system had been filled with violations of the national banking laws, and had been characterized by acquiescence on the part of the Federal authorities in such violation.

Accordingly, the Federal Reserve Act accepted as one of its basic notions, an expansion of the clearing house principle of mutual supervision. It entrusted the Federal Reserve banks and Board with the power to examine their own members and looked to them to see to it that sound and satisfactory conditions were maintained throughout the banking system, treating themselves as one of the essential elements in the safe extension of credit by Reserve banks. Had it ever been practicable to carry out this idea we may suppose that the panics of 1920 and 1929 would have been avoidable—certainly the latter. It should, however, be observed in any study of the origin of the Federal Reserve system that this plan of mutual examination and supervision, although implicit in the original Act, was never practically brought into effect. From the very beginning member banks, and particularly the larger of them, expressed a disinclination to add, to what they regarded as the already exacting requirements of the national and state examination systems to which they were respectively subject, a new plan of examination which, they thought, would simply increase the expense and difficulty to which they were subject under laws then in force.

From the outset, therefore, it was the effort of the Federal Reserve banks to attempt to soothe this hostile or irritable feeling on the part of the banks that already considered themselves over-examined, and to reconcile such policy with the evident requirements of the law by various indirect methods. Thus, almost immediately upon the adoption of the Federal Reserve Act, it was demanded, and finally agreed, that national bank examiners should be directed to turn over the results of their examinations to Federal Reserve banks in order that the latter might have them available for use as a basis for credit judgment. This proposal in itself was desirable and gave rise to no bad results whatever, but it was unfortunately given from the outset as a reason for surrender or abandonment of the idea of constant or direct examination of members by Reserve banks.

It is true that in various districts Reserve banks delegated examiners to be present at national or state examinations of members in order that they might be actually informed of results or might obtain items of information that they thought would be useful, yet might not be sufficiently, or perhaps at all, provided for in the regular examination. Such incomplete participation has, of course, never been satisfactory, and it is an undoubted fact that in important cases, Reserve banks themselves have at the instance of their more influential members, allowed themselves to become the medium for representations to the Treasury Department in favor of undue leniency toward banks that were engaging in illegal or undesirable operations. Evidence to this effect was clearly developed during the various Congressional inquiries of 1932-33 and confirms impressions that have long been entertained by qualified men conversant with conditions existing in various of the Federal Reserve districts.

Thus, again, in connection with the project of self-examination and inspection on the part of the banks as a body, it must be confessed that the Federal Reserve system never actually took effect in the form in which it had been planned, but was from the very beginning, as a result largely of weakness or indifference on the part of the Federal Reserve Board, a system animated by purposes different from those originally intended by its framers. In this matter, as in that of relations with the Treasury Department, concerning government finance, the system had from the outset subjected itself to tendencies and conditions which worked toward the conversion of it into a branch or agency of any administration which happened to be in power in Washington at a given moment. That in such circumstances the Reserve system could be expected to exert those restraining influences with respect to unsound or excessive bank credit which had been hoped by the framers of the Act, was evidently out of the question.

Real Character of Reserve System

In closing this background survey of the idea and purposes of the Reserve system in its origin, provided as a basis for the analysis of existing banking conditions as affected by Reserve banking, it is desirable again to emphasize the sharp distinction beween what the Act intended and what the administrators of the Act attempted. This difference, let it be again repeated, was not altogether the outgrowth of wilful or voluntary violation of the principles and ideas embodied in the original Act. In part it was undoubtedly the result of lack of sympathy with these original ideas, but in part it was the outgrowth of an extensive change in economic and political conditions which had come about through the opening of the World War simultaneous with the establishment of the Reserve system and through inevitable change of economic and financial position resulting therefrom. If it be granted that the United States was unavoidably drawn into participation in the World War, a further fact of importance is added to the explanation of the change from the original character of the Reserve system.

It was true, unquestionably, that at the very outset, President Woodrow Wilson committed a blunder of first importance in putting in charge of the Reserve system a group of men, who to the extent of a majority at least, were either out of sympathy with the ideas of the Reserve system or had actually campaigned against it. This action of President Wilson was based upon the supposition, perhaps valid elsewhere but certainly not well-founded in American political life, that a feeling of *noblesse oblige* would compel men who had been given charge of something with which they were not wholly in sympathy, to attempt to vindicate themselves and their records by furnishing as fair and nonpartisan administration of the Act as they could; while, on the other hand, persons who would otherwise have been hostile to the act in practice would be conciliated by the fact that members of their own group were in charge of its administration. Neither of these conceptions proved practicable in operation, for the administrators who began work in charge of the system, speedily showed themselves determined either to obtain radical changes in its composition or else to neutralize and destroy it through refusal to apply its chief ideas in practice, while the system itself never received any support whatever from bankers who had been hostile to it until they were driven into compliance either through legislation or through fear of their own position as affected by war conditions.

This unfavorable attitude on the part of administrators probably would not have had as much effect as it actually had, nor could it have been tolerated to the extent that was actually the case by the President himself and his advisers, had it not been for the really fundamental changes in the whole situation which were coming about as a result of war trade and war finance. A consistent and thorough-going adherence to the ideas of the Federal Reserve Act would obviously have resulted in a way of administration that was very different from the one in fact pursued, while it would also have involved, no doubt, an early recurrence to such of its original notions as could be considered workable as soon as war conditions would allow. The fact that the actual administration of the system was hostile to it in its original form, and that the Administration of the country had no definite conception of its meaning in any case, not only formed a bad combination of circumstances with a view to the successful application of the new law, but practically insured the radical changes in the working of the plan from the very beginning, which we have just outlined.

To recapitulate once more, therefore, a fundamental important idea in this matter—it is plain that the contemporary study of the Federal Reserve system in its relation to banking must make use of a background or historical survey which recognizes not merely the abstract original intent of the Federal Reserve Act and its framers, but the real and genuine modifications introduced into the plan of the measure from its very inception as a result of the circumstances which have just been detailed.

SUMMARY OF CONCLUSIONS

Therefore, we must view the Federal Reserve system as embodying the following definite features virtually from the very outset:

1. Rediscounting theoretically based upon commercial paper, but practically upon collateral security.

2. Theoretical avoidance of investment or speculative operations, but practically the financing of speculation through the use of indirect means.

3. Mutual supervision of banks and strict joint oversight, but actually mere extension of Treasury supervision by taking the Reserve banks into partnership with the existing systems of bank examination.

4. The elimination of the influence of government upon business, but practically the introduction of an extended and powerful influence upon business through the vast enlargement of the operations of the government and the enormous extension of government discounting at Reserve banks.

5. Effectual limitation of the operations of Reserve banks to a very small group in the community, partly by refusing to install the foreign branches for which provision had been made, partly through gradual elimination of a large section of the member banks as rediscounters, partly in other ways, so that the system, instead of being a source of mutual aid, was from the very beginning a medium of highly specialized support and relief for particular groups.

CHAPTER XXIX

LATER VARIATIONS AND AMENDMENTS[1]

The Federal Reserve Act has, however, not depended at all upon interpretation or underhand manipulation for the change which has come about in its character. The measure has been amended in all some 25 times during the 20 years or more since its adoption, and these amendments have, in at least two cases (Acts of 1923 and 1933) been so far-reaching as to amount to revision. Second in importance, but nevertheless of very great significance was the Act of 1927 which provided for basic changes, not in the Federal Reserve Act itself, but in member bank practice, although along lines and of such a nature as to produce an important reflex influence upon the Reserve system. Of the multitudinous other amendments to which reference has been made, two classes may be recognized:

1. Those which effected changes of unsound theoretical base and doubtful efficacy which later became "dead letters" or were actually repealed. Conspicuous in this group were such enactments as the so-called Phelan Law, designed to change the method of fixing the rate of rediscount, later withdrawn, and the so-called Edge Act, designed to provide for the financing of foreign trade, and almost a complete dead letter.

2. Those which altered the workings of some basic element in the system and, although inconspicuous on the surface, really worked a permanent theoretical modification of effectiveness. Conspicuous in this class were the so-called amendments to the note section (1918) and the modification of reserves nominally intended to reduce the severity of the reserve requirement but actually designed to permit the placing of bank notes in reserves.

3. A third general group may be recognized, including a great variety of minor changes, and apparently designed to alter the working of the law in practical administration.

[1] Written by H. Parker Willis.

This is not intended as a legislative history of the Federal Reserve Act, or even as a critique of the process by which its structure and application were changed. No reference, therefore, will be made to most of these amendments, and the classification which has just been offered is intended merely as a brief summary designed to show the immense field that must be covered by any careful or inclusive survey of the situation. The aim in this chapter is to set forth the major changes in the basic structure and conception of the law brought about through legislation, and thus to bring down to date the brief sketch of the origin and purposes of the Federal Reserve Act.

Basis of Discount

We have already observed in the preceding chapter the reasons why the Reserve Act had originally sought to found its operations upon real commercial paper and the factors or circumstances which have rendered it possible to make its intentions practically nugatory. The banking community, however, which had, generally speaking, opposed the Federal Reserve Act, was not content with a merely sympathetic attitude on the part of the Reserve Board towards its ideas and purposes in connection with the basis of discount. It desired to have specific changes brought about and to this end it early obtained (in 1916) the adoption of legislation which definitely recognized the idea of lending on collateral security so foreign to the general practice of central banks throughout the world. The amendment of 1919 definitely gave to the member bank customers of Reserve banks the authority, therefore, to borrow from the Reserve banks upon their own direct notes, placing behind such notes protection in the form of collateral which was itself said to be eligible. As presented to Congress, this idea appeared to mean nothing more than this: Suppose a borrowing bank to be possessed, say of 25 notes received from its customers, all representing liquid banking transactions and all eligible, ranging in amounts say from $100 to $5,000 and aggregating $25,000; the borrowing bank desiring a discount at the Reserve bank would, under the original plan of the Act, have presented each of these notes to its

Reserve bank with its own endorsement upon each, thus receiving an advance of $25,000 minus discount. Under the new plan it would have presented to the Reserve bank a direct note of its own, undertaking to pay $25,000 at maturity, and attaching necessary portions of its own assets (notes of its customers) as collateral.

The difference between the two plans was alleged to be that under the new system the borrowing bank was not obliged to borrow for the entire unexpired maturity of the notes, but could simply borrow up to 15 days, subject to renewal, while in case some of the attached collateral should mature meanwhile, it would merely replace the maturing paper with other of the same kind; or, if it chose, could have the amount of the matured paper charged off against the face of the note. The change was presented as nothing more than a matter of convenience designed to aid the member banks in the transaction of their current business and to avoid "red tape." As such it was sanctioned by Congress.

Almost simultaneously with this amendment the United States became involved in war operations, and under pressure from the Treasury Department the Federal Reserve Board and banks put into effect rates of interest designed to encourage the public and the banks to purchase Liberty bonds upon credit, obtaining the funds that they needed eventually from the Reserve banks. This policy received an immediate and enormous development under the amendment of the Reserve Act already referred to. Since the obligations of the government were rediscountable or purchasable at a Reserve bank, it was at once legal and feasible for the member to borrow direct from the Reserve bank on its own note, with the government securities as collateral, or to borrow upon the notes of its customers themselves, protected by such government obligations as collateral.

Thus, during the war, a steady flow of Reserve bank funds into the market without inquiry or information as to the purposes for which they were intended was assured; and after the close of the war it became the general and prevailing practice of the banks to obtain their funds at Reserve banks not by rediscounting commercial paper, but by borrowing upon their own notes protected by Treasury certificates, Treasury notes or government bonds. Inasmuch as there was no inquiry as to the purpose for which the funds were intended, and inasmuch as the policy of the Treasury had been to place in the hands of the banks enormous quantities of government obligations, a definite and well defined arrangement existed whereby funds could be drawn off from Reserve banks for speculative operations.

The situation opened enormously broad avenues of danger for two reasons: (1) It took from Reserve banks the real control over the volume of speculative credit. (2) It practically used the government obligations as a vehicle or medium for the support of such speculative credit. The Glass bill of 1931, later enacted as the Banking Act of 1933, attempted in one of its sections to correct this situation by providing that any member bank which should borrow at a Reserve bank, and which, during the life of such loan increased its loans to customers upon collateral security, should thereupon be debarred from further access to Federal Reserve credit; while on the other hand, its obligations already incurred to the Reserve bank should immediately become due and payable.

The object of this provision plainly was to cut off the enormous amount of purely speculative credit which was being obtained by the banks upon government securities. No provision in the new Act—out of many which were fiercely contested—incurred so much open as well as underhanded antagonism, as did this one. It was regarded by stock exchange authorities as a direct blow at their communications with Reserve banks and was viewed by the so-called "stock exchange banks" (larger banks of New York and other cities) as having been designed to interfere with their operations in the market. The Reserve Bank of New York was particularly hostile to it, submitting as testimony at the hearings before the Senate Committee, a general letter sanctioned and signed by all the directors, and multitudinous memoranda and other data to the same purport. Investigations made by the Committee showed that, in practice, a proportion so large as to be substantially near to total lending operations of many of the Reserve banks was, at the time, being carried on in this way. In 1930-1931 rediscounted notes represented from 30 to 40 per cent of total bills discounted by the system. To put the matter briefly, these investigations showed that commercial rediscounting was growing obsolete, and that its place had been taken largely by direct borrowing upon collateral security—whose proceeds were pretty generally used in stock market loans.

TABLE 147

NUMBER, TOTAL LOANS, AND ELIGIBLE PAPER OF ALL MEMBER BANKS OF THE FEDERAL RESERVE SYSTEM GROUPED ACCORDING TO THE RATIO OF ELIGIBLE PAPER TO TOTAL LOANS, SEPT. 29, 1931

TOTAL ALL DISTRICTS	NUMBER OF BANKS	TOTAL LOANS (In millions of dollars)	ELIGIBLE PAPER (In millions of dollars)
All member banks	7,599	20,874	2,997
Banks with no eligible paper	424	256	—
Banks with following amounts of eligible paper per $100 of loans			
Under $10	1,485	7,955	433
$10–$20	1,571	7,778	1,027
$20–$30	1,304	3,003	708
$30–$40	964	899	306
$40–$50	769	453	198
$50 and over	1,082	529	325

Decadence of Commercial Paper

The situation sketched in the foregoing paragraph was strongly defended both by Reserve and other bankers, with the statement that transactions under the new provision already prescribed were practically indispensable, owing to the decadence of commercial paper of the older variety. There was undoubtedly some basis for the statement that industrial and other changes tended to alter the amount and particularly the distribution of such paper. (See Part IV, Chapter XXIV). It, however, possessed nothing of the extreme sort that was urged by Reserve bankers. The Senate Banking and Currency Committee, during the discussion of the subject, set on foot an inquiry into the actual amounts of available commercial paper in the banks, and hence, theoretically within reach of the Reserve authorities as a basis for the extension of loans and assistance to their members when, and if, the latter needed it. These investigations may be summed up in Tables 147 and 148 which furnish their own indications but are particularly instructive when segregated by districts.

There was at the time of the study thus summarized, an abundance of commercial paper in the banks of the country for the purpose of continuing the method of obtaining credit ac-

TABLE 148

NUMBER, LOANS AND INVESTMENTS, ELIGIBLE ASSETS* AND BORROWINGS FROM ALL MEMBER BANKS OF THE FEDERAL RESERVE SYSTEM, GROUPED ACCORDING TO RATIO OF ELIGIBLE ASSETS TO LOANS AND INVESTMENTS, SEPT. 29, 1931

TOTAL ALL DISTRICTS	NUMBER OF BANKS	LOANS AND INVESTMENTS	ELIGIBLE ASSETS	BORROWINGS FROM F. R. BANK
		(In millions of dollars)		
All member banks	7,599	33,073	7,934	323
Banks with no eligible assets	91	50	—	—
Banks with following amounts of eligible assets per $100 of loans and investments:				
Under $10	1,567	3,526	222	36
$10–$20	2,115	9,938	1,539	140
$20–$30	1,563	8,894	2,159	80
$30–$40	1,003	7,643	2,568	36
$40–$50	643	2,083	906	15
$50 and over	617	939	540	16

* Represents the total of (1) paper eligible for rediscount at Federal Reserve banks, and (2) U. S. Government securities other than securities pledged against national bank-note circulation.

commodation and expansion which had been originally proposed in the Federal Reserve Act. The change that has come about in the actual application of this method must, accordingly, be regarded as having been the result of choice on the part of borrowers at Reserve banks, aided, perhaps, by preference on the part of Reserve banks themselves, but in either case introducing a completely altered type, both of underlying theory and of procedure into the work of many of the Reserve banks.

Changes of Reserve Position

Scarcely less important in its effect upon the character of the Federal Reserve system, was another fundamental change in its structure brought into existence during the World War, upon the excuse that such action was necessary in order to permit expansion of credit. The early months of experience of the United States in the World War had indicated a tremendous shortage of Government income derived from taxation, and hence, the necessity of financing the war—or so it was supposed—by what was called "inflation." Doubt was expressed by many as to the ability of the Reserve banks to furnish the enormous sums that would be needed, and there was a general undiscriminating desire to enlarge the "basis of credit" as much as possible. In the banking community, particularly in the Reserve system, there had, from the start, been a group of persons who were desirous of securing the recognition of Federal Reserve notes as a part of the vault reserves of member banks, and this group had a strong nucleus in the Federal Reserve Board, with one member particularly positive in his advocacy of the proposal.

In order to permit inflation it was, accordingly, frankly proposed that the Reserve Act be amended in such a way as to grant permission to count Federal Reserve notes as an element in the reserves of member banks. This proposal encountered serious opposition both in Congress from the original sponsors of the Reserve Act, and elsewhere. Eventually a compromise was arranged, whereby the total percentages of reserves were reduced, no vault cash reserve whatever being now required of the member banks; while, in view of that fact, it was no longer necessary to prohibit the counting of Reserve notes as a part of reserve. This merely meant, in other words, that under the alteration of the plan, nothing but balances in Reserve banks were to be counted as reserves, while member banks were left to provide their own cash, or till money, from any source that they chose and, of course, were likely to find Reserve notes the most available and cheapest holding they could get. Thus, it was sought to promote what was called inflation, by cutting away the protection of Reserve credit and at the same time by permitting member banks to increase the amount of Reserve notes outstanding by carrying them in their vaults, thereby reducing correspondingly the speed with which they would be likely to come home for redemption.

The early closing of the War made the release of reserves for the inflation purpose thus contemplated, available for stock market operation instead of for war inflation, and the outcome of this legislation was afforded by the steadily thinning Reserve protection of outstanding bank obligations as well as by the increasingly frozen character of the banking position. These conditions were without warrant in any event, but they seemed the more subject to criticism when we remember that the post-war period was characterized by the enormous importation of gold into the United States, so that the fundamental reserve position of the country might have been vastly improved had the banking authorities so desired. Instead of that, the constant effort to keep reserves down to the legal minimum and to avoid the presence of "surplus reserves" or "excess reserves," simply resulted in making normal quantities of credit available at abnormally low rates of interest to the public at large. It has been the opinion of observers of this situation that these great accretions of gold or reserve funds may be regarded as having furnished the basis for, (1) frenzied stock speculation, and (2) excessive operations in real estate. Whether or not we accept this interpretation, the fact remains that the curtailment of reserve requirements and the granting of permission to hold Federal Reserve notes in bank vaults were unnecessary measures of inflation, which at least granted permission to those who were ready to bring about an excessive expansion to proceed with their projects.

Instead, therefore, of acting as a means of putting the brakes upon over-expansion of credit through insistence upon the holding of an adequate reserve, the changes that have been introduced in the Reserve system have resulted: (1) in cutting down the amount of reserve required, (2) in reducing the liquidity of bank assets and holdings, and (3) in preventing the inward movement of gold from producing the effect that might naturally be expected of it in strengthening the position of the banks. There is, thus, a fundamentally different attitude to be adopted toward the Reserve system as compared with the one which was accepted by the framers of the Federal Reserve Act.

Changes in Status of Notes

Incidental reference has already been made to the alteration in the position of the reserve note which took place when the reserve requirements were modified. This, however, was merely a suggestion of the great change in note policy which was initiated as a result of the war amendments to the act.

The original ideas of the Reserve Law had, as we have already seen, clustered closely around the notion of a "flexible note issue" which should expand and contract in harmony with the needs of business, thereby affording the "flexible" currency which had so long been desired. In order to insure this correspondence between note currency and volume of business—sought because of the belief that currency ought not to issue unless there was work for it to do—the original Federal Reserve Act had provided that no notes should ever issue except upon the presentation to the Chairman of the Federal Reserve Bank of eligible discountable paper. In order to meet the objections of bankers who complained that, when the eligible paper so furnished matured and had to be paid, they were obliged to deposit gold with the Chairman of the Federal Reserve Bank unless it so chanced that the Federal Reserve notes had been paid into the bank and would thus be actually cancelled in a volume corresponding to the lessening of the eligible paper behind them, Congress responded by authorizing the direct deposit of gold with the Chairmen of the Reserve banks in exchange for the issue of new notes.

This second stage of Reserve legislation had, accordingly, recognized the reserve note as either a gold certificate or a representation of liquid commercial transactions. The theory of the required deposit of gold or eligible paper with the Chairmen of the banks had nothing to do with the question of a reserve held behind them and, accordingly, the Reserve bank had been directed in the original Act to hold a 40 per cent reserve for their redemption. Complaint made by various bankers and others soon after the adoption of the Reserve Act that there was thus required a holding of 140 per cent in gold behind every reserve note outstanding was technically true, but without real foundation.

It was evidently a fact that, for example, if a bank started with $100,000 in Federal Reserve notes behind which there was $100,000 in eligible paper, $40,000 was held by the Reserve bank as gold, so that there was thus "tied up" $140,000. The "tie up" was theoretical because the eligible paper so placed in the hands of the Reserve agent or chairman was not lost by the bank but was merely pledged, pending the retirement or redemption of the notes. It was a fact that in case a Reserve bank found it impossible to get in its own notes, its only way of ridding itself of the liabilities involved in its relationship with the chairman would lie in the deposit of gold with the Federal Reserve agent; but it is probable that no such situation ever existed, in practice.

When Congress yielded to the complaints and permitted any gold held by Federal Reserve agents behind notes to be counted as a part of the gold reserve of the bank itself, it created an abstractly absurd situation, but it also practically created a state of things in which the liquid character of the reserve note as a representative of business transactions was largely destroyed. The final step taken in 1932 by the Glass-Steagall Act, wherein Reserve banks were permitted to place government obligations in the hands of Reserve agents instead of gold for the protection of notes, practically put the note currency back upon a bond deposit basis, the situation from which the Reserve Act had sought to emancipate the community and which had constituted the chief public reason for legislation in 1913.

Already the Federal Reserve notes had tended to become very largely a bond secured currency, inasmuch as their issue could be obtained by placing with the Reserve agent any kind of "eligible paper" that had been discounted by the Reserve bank. Since, as we have seen, eligible paper had come to consist, during the years after the war, very largely of obligations of banks protected by Government obligations, the reserve notes were already a Treasury bond secured currency. The legislation of 1932 made them completely so (at the will of any Reserve bank), and wholly destroyed the basis for note currency reform which, as we have seen, had lain at the base of the original legislation.

For the time being none of this detailed history is of very much moment. The action of the Roosevelt Administration in suspending (March, 1933) all further redemption made the entire currency inflexible and irredeemable, and rendered of no immediate significance what there was "behind" Federal Reserve currency, save in the event of decline in the market price of Government bonds. The time will, of course, come when this situation must be ended and when it does, the problem of convertibility of Federal Reserve notes will be found to be directly influenced by the character of the assets that are held and to be held behind the notes. To go back to the older plan of making the notes merely representatives of real transactions will be a matter of utmost difficulty.

Open-Market Operations

The Federal Reserve Act had originally authorized Federal Reserve banks to engage in the direct purchase or discount of two-named paper, when, as, and if such action was believed by Reserve banks to be desirable. The first draft of the Act had extended this permission to single-named paper, but the single-named paper so provided for was omitted in consequence of the protests of banking interests, which feared that the results of such permission would be seen in inroads into their business. During the early months of the life of the Federal Reserve Board –regulation was promulgated permitting Reserve banks to establish an active market in two-named paper, buying, and selling, in trade with individuals, corporations, or partnerships. Later the influence of special interests prevailed and this practice was abruptly cut off, the open-market operations being confined very definitely to purchases of Government paper or to acceptances made by bankers whose names were acceptable to Reserve banks.

Even on this basis, the open-market style of operation never appealed to Reserve bankers until after 1924, when it was seen to be a serviceable means of making funds available to large banks usually disposed to use such funds in the stock market and who had reached practically the limit of their credit-expanding powers. Such a bank having, we may suppose, a capital of $5,000,000 with deposit liabilities five times that amount, or $25,000,000 might gain eventual credit expansion by rediscounting or by accepting paper which was then marketed and was likely eventually to be purchased by the Reserve bank. In these circumstances, after 1924 an impetus was given to the making of acceptance paper, and this impetus was the stronger because of the fact that the Reserve Board had voluntarily withdrawn, in 1922, from the practice of controlling acceptance methods through regulation.

By means of this step, the Reserve Board eventually yielded to the Reserve banks themselves the power of saying what an acceptance really was and the definition became so lax that acceptances gradually but thoroughly assumed a completely frozen condition. Since open-market operations were confined to dealings in government securities and in bankers' acceptances, it was only for a short time after about 1925 that the transactions in Government securities could be considered "liquid" by any stretch of the imagination. When a large government deficit made its appearance, as it did, soon after the panic of 1929, the obligations of the Government, likewise, ceased to be liquid, and thus the open-market clause of the Federal Reserve Act which had originally been inserted as a means of compelling banks to bring their discount policies into harmony with those of the Reserve banks, was transformed into a plan for putting the Reserve banks into the open market for frozen paper representing long-term, semi-speculative transactions either in goods acceptances, or stocks, or 15 day notes of member banks. This was a strange reversal of the plans originally made for the application of a system which would insure convertibility and satisfactory headship of the discount market.

In bringing about this situation much help was had from the

various amendments to the Reserve Act relating to the marketing of acceptances, the relief of them from taxes of varying kinds and the general extension of their holding by financial institutions. In the main, the legislation of Congress on this particular subject has been directly dictated by special interests, very largely because of lack of information on the subject generally prevalent among members.

Purchase of Agricultural and Other Frozen Paper

The efficiency and success of the Reserve system in acting as a financial buffer from the very start, contributed strongly to the desire of bankers and others to secure the aid of the Reserve system in various phases of their own financing and was, also, instrumental in encouraging politicians to seek anew to obtain the modification of the Reserve Act in such a way as to make a home for the frozen and otherwise unmarketable paper to which their projects gave rise. In this respect two schemes attained conspicous success: (1) The Agricultural Credit System and, (2) The Reconstruction Finance Corporation. Congress had in 1916 enacted a Federal Farm Loan Act and in 1923, as a means of placating the farmer had amended this Act by providing for "Intermediate credit banks," whose paper, however, was not altogether likely to be salable. In order to give it a better standing Congress made it eligible under specified conditions to purchase and discount by Federal Reserve Banks. As a matter of fact, the Reserve banks never bought much of it in spite of the pressure exerted upon them, but the menace was present and exists today.

When the Reconstruction Finance Corporation Act was first projected, strong pressure was brought by the Administration to make the debentures authorized in the Act available for discount at Federal Reserve banks. This demand was revised and technically overcome by the "sound money" elements in the Banking and Currency Committee; but an almost equal amount of damage was provided for by the authorization granted in the Act to the Treasury Department to purchase the debentures and pay for them with Treasury obligations which could be discounted with, or sold to, the Reserve banks. In one way or another, thus, provision was made for using the Reserve banks upon occasion as the repositories of frozen credit representatives arising out of agricultural and industrial undertakings. This, in itself, was as great a departure from the original conception of liquid holdings as was the alternative in the acceptance provisions of the law, though it should be added that in practice these provisions never exerted so serious a draft upon the resources of the system as that which was furnished by the use of the acceptance method.

SELF-GOVERNING CHARACTER MODIFIED

Of the many other important modifications which were introduced during the passage of years into the structure of the Reserve system through amendments either of law or of practice, there is at least one which requires further consideration.

This is the method of controlling or governing the system. Originally it had been supposed by the framers of the legislation that the member banks felt a strong desire to manage their own affairs and that they were particularly desirous of escaping from the control of larger banks. The Reserve system, in fact, was often described or suggested as a plan for the purpose of enfranchising the smaller banks of the country by enabling them to introduce a system of self-government and of direct individual responsibility. To this end the principle of having each bank provided with a single vote regardless of its size, so that the smallest bank units were equal in voting capacity to the largest institutions, had been adopted.

It was supposed that, in these circumstances, the smaller member banks would participate actively in election of directors and that they would be careful to insure the choice of candidates who would definitely represent them. With a view to attaining this result the banks were divided into groups according to size, in order to prevent those of the larger capitalization from electing, through influence, men of their own choosing for candidacy to directoral appointments in Federal Reserve banks. Early experience with the elections of directors was disappointing, for it was found that the smaller banks had little or no confidence in their own opinions and were indisposed to devote any time or trouble to the choice and election of directors who would adequately represent them in the Reserve institutions. Although the methods of electing directors were once or twice modified by Congress, being materially simplified and rendered more workable, it cannot be said that Reserve banks have ever had genuinely representative boards of directors or that the smaller banks in most of the communities have ever taken a direct positive interest in securing representation on the boards of Reserve banks by electing men who were conversant with their own problems and in some cases at least were members of their own banking groups.

The Reserve banks have, accordingly, tended to fall under the control of the larger banks, and it has sometimes happened that the smaller bankers chose as directors representing their "group" some one of the numerous bankers who were not members of their group but were officers or directors of larger banks—in certain cases, in spite of a known prejudice on the part of such men against the existence of the smaller institutions.

On the other hand, the Government had assigned to the Federal Reserve Board the task of selecting three members of each Board of Directors (one-third of all) on the theory that this Government practice could then be relied upon to safeguard the interests of the public and to see to it that there was no action on the part of Reserve banks that could in any way be deemed prejudicial to the general welfare, or that tended to discriminate against some and in favor of other financial interests. This large power of choice of directors has never been successfully exercised by the Board and in a good many cases the governing directors so chosen have turned out to be men who represented the larger banking interests, or whose appointment had been effectually recommended or even prescribed by those larger banks. The practice has generally been admitted to be that the boards of directors of Federal Reserve banks, instead of being the result of a careful selection with a view to the representation of all interests, have often become small groups of representatives of special banking interests who were not particularly concerned with the promotion of the general welfare, but who much preferred to direct their activity toward the satisfaction of the demands of various local financial groups.

Summary of Changes

This summary of the changes that had taken place in the Federal Reserve system since its initiation and first organization thus evidently exhibits:

1. A fundamental reversal of purpose and technique in regard to methods and objects of discounting, ideals and purposes of open-market operations, character of Reserve protection, attitude toward the issuance of a liquid currency, maintenance of careful supervision of banking condition and technique, and finally, with regard to actual operations of Government.

2. It is not too much to say that the changes which have thus been effected, partly through legislation and partly through administrative rulings, have brought about a total shift in those phases of Reserve banking which had not already been completely altered by the inevitable changes of condition and of financial necessity which have been discussed in the preceding chapter.

3. So gradually, and on the whole so stealthily—certainly with so little public discussion at any time—have these far-reaching changes been initiated and effected that the average man has paid little heed to them and does not realize that the current discussion of the Federal Reserve situation is necessarily based, not at all upon the original enactment, but upon a piece of legislation which is the result of long-continued and piece-meal modification, extending over a considerable period of years. It is a transformation that completely alters the basis of discussion of current banking aspects of the Reserve system.

CHAPTER XXX

DISCOUNT POLICY[1]

I. Objections and Mechanism

The discount policy of the Federal Reserve banks has been characterized by vacillation and uncertainty of purpose. When account is taken of the additional uncertainty as to the method to be used in controlling the discounting of member banks, an inevitable confusion in banking practice results.

The early years of Federal Reserve operation were years of comparative inactivity in Reserve bank credit. Discount policy, therefore, had little effect upon the lending activities of member and nonmember banks. The participation of the United States in the World War altered the situation. The excessive demands of the government for credit caused the member banks to seek assistance from the Reserve banks in order to extend credit to the purchasers of Liberty bonds. From that time until 1922, the members were dependent upon Reserve bank assistance to enable them to maintain reserves sufficient to cover the deposits which they created. In 1922, since gold imports had relieved member banks from having to rediscount, the Reserve banks established contact with the money market through purchases of securities. On the basis of the Reserve bank credit thus extended, both in 1922 and repeatedly thereafter, commercial banks extended so large a volume of credit that they were forced to borrow in later years in order to support the mass of obligations which they had previously incurred. The credit structure collapsed in November, 1929, and the banks were once again freed of dependence upon the Reserve banks. After that date, they were in the discount market only intermittently. The Reserve banks maintained contact with the market through the use of their open market powers, but these powers were so extensively employed that bank credit continued to be based upon Reserve credit rather than on actual cash.

[1] Written by Caroline Whitney.

Aims of discount policy.—Before determining the aims of discount policy, we must define closely the purpose for which the Federal Reserve banks were organized. Their purpose might have been to serve as emergency institutions supplying credit at times of crisis, either when all banks are in difficulty, or when particular institutions were in sudden need of funds. If the Reserve banks are to serve primarily as emergency institutions, the provision of the excess credit needed by agriculture and industry at certain times of year, when seasonal strains are felt, is of course not precluded. Their purpose may, however, be broader, that is, to aid business and industry at all times by extending credit which banks might otherwise refuse, or which might otherwise be unobtainable. In choosing among these alternatives, the Federal Reserve Board took a middle course. In its *First Annual Report* it made the following statement:

> The function of a reserve bank is not to be identified with either of these extremes, although occasion may arise when either of such courses may be imperative. Its duty plainly is not to await emergencies but by anticipation, to do what it can to prevent them.

Since the Federal Reserve system has chosen to anticipate emergencies, it should at all times exercise control over the volume of credit. It may do this by two means—either through what is called credit policy, or through banking policy.

Credit policy implies control over the volume of credit in use. As the credit in use is credit supplied by commercial banks, and as the powers of the Reserve banks are limited to the determination of the volume of credit supplied by the Reserve banks, effective credit policy presupposes a fixed relationship between these two types of credit. In determining the volume of Reserve-bank credit, the powers of the Reserve banks are also somewhat limited. The volume of Reserve-bank credit, extended through the mechanism of purchase of securities in the open market, is under the direct control of the Reserve banks. But Reserve-bank credit, extended through the purchase or discount of bills, is controlled indirectly by the effect which the rate charged is assumed to have upon the volume bought or discounted. Effective credit policy is, therefore, dependent upon: (1) a unified discount and open market policy, and (2) an inverse relationship between the rates charged by the Reserve banks and the volume of Reserve-bank credit applied for by member banks, bill brokers, security dealers, and others who deal directly with the Reserve banks. Therefore, the financial community may circumvent the policies of the Reserve banks by two means. The first is the extension of varying amounts of credit on the basis of a given amount of Reserve-bank credit. The second is the demand for increasing amounts of Reserve-bank credit at times when Reserve bank rates are high.

Banking policy has to do with the supervision of the distribution of the loans and investments of the member banks themselves. Its effectiveness in preventing an overissue of credit is based upon the principle that credit extended for the purpose of moving goods from producer to consumer, through the ordinary channels of trade, cannot be redundant. Supervision by the Federal Reserve system of a member bank's loan and investment policies could prevent the member bank from borrowing at its Reserve bank to support a portfolio which is overloaded with speculative paper.

The Federal Reserve Board has repudiated banking policy as an aim of the Federal Reserve system, in favor of credit policy. In its *Annual Report* for 1928 it made the following statement:

> Influence exerted by a reserve bank on the loan and investment policy of an individual member bank is ordinarily exercised only over banks that are borrowers from the reserve banks. It is in the nature of banking supervision, and is akin in many respects to the bank examination function of the reserve system. This phase of reserve bank policy may be called banking policy, as distinguished from credit policy, which deals with more general developments of banking in relation to the credit needs of the country. . . . For influencing general credit conditions, however, the Federal reserve system relies on credit policy rather than on banking policy.

This report goes on to state that the principal aims of credit policy are, "the continuous provision of credit at reasonable cost in amounts adequate for the requirements of trade and industry and the safeguarding of our gold reserves."

The technique of discount policy.—The discount policy of the Federal Reserve banks is expressed principally in the rate charged member banks for notes which they discount at Reserve banks. If a member bank finds itself in a position where it has no surplus cash on hand with which to repair any deficiency in its reserves, it may borrow temporarily from its Reserve bank by one of two means. Either it may take the paper representing some of its loans and discounts for customers, and rediscount it at the Reserve bank, or it may borrow on its own note for 15 days, giving as collateral for the loan paper which is eligible for rediscount, or government bonds. The latter method of obtaining accommodation was not included in the provisions of the Federal Reserve Act as enacted into law in 1913, but was added later by the amendment to the Act of September 7, 1916. Since that date it has been availed of to an increasing extent.

The rate charged by the Reserve bank is assumed to be a factor encouraging or discouraging the use of the borrowing privilege. Whether in practice it has done so, will be investigated in a later part of this chapter.

In determining when to change discount rates, and at what level to fix them, the Reserve banks have had to depend upon rules which they themselves discovered through trial and error, for there was no previous experience in the United States with a central bank of discount. It was not known what effect a given change in rate would produce. The Bank of England has long used the discount rate as a method of protecting its gold reserves, and of regulating the activity of the London money market. Increases in rates at the Bank of England had the effect of increasing the cost of credit in London—this credit being, for the most part, bankers' and trade bills bought by London banks for investment—and have driven the surplus bills into the Bank of England. Finding that they could only borrow at the high rate published by the Bank, business men and bankers then become more cautious in their lending, and there was a contraction in the outstanding supply of bills, and the desired restrictive effects were felt.

Coincident with a restriction, high rates of interest attracted investment capital to London and gold flowed into Great Britain. Rate reductions made by the Bank produced the opposite effect. The pressure was normally brought to bear upon the bill brokers and not upon the commercial banks. The bill brokers have but small capital of their own, and borrow constantly to maintain their portfolios of undigested bills. Thus an increase in the rate charged causes them to rush to cover. If the joint stock banks appeared to be in a position to lend to the bill brokers at a rate below that of the Bank, the latter, before raising its rate of discount, frequently sold government securities in the open market in order to deprive the banks of funds to lend to bill brokers. Thus a combination of discount rate and open-market operations gave the Bank of England great strength. The operation of these factors was very effective before the War; but their effect has been considerably weakened by recent developments in the London money market, particularly by the subservience of discount policy to the needs of the Treasury, which has been almost constantly increasing its debt, and by the great increase in international capital movements.

Before the War, the open-market powers of the Bank of England were used for one of two purposes—either to make the discount rate effective or to neutralize gold movements. It has only been in recent years that the Bank has bought or sold securities in order to alter the total amount of its private deposits, which correspond to member bank reserve balances in Federal Reserve banks.

When the Federal Reserve Act was passed, it was hoped that a similar mechanism might be set up in this country. One important difference between the plan laid down in the Federal Reserve Act and the British plan was that Reserve banks were to make their advances directly to member banks, while the Bank of England makes its advances to bill brokers. In addition to the advances which they make to member banks, the Reserve banks lend money to dealers in the kinds of paper which they are empowered to buy by the terms of Section 14 of the Federal Reserve Act. This they do by buying paper from dealers under repurchase agreements. The Reserve banks may also extend credit to member banks and others by buying Government securities and bankers' acceptances, as well as municipal warrants and trade acceptances, in the open market. The funds thus released go to such institutions as may have held the paper before purchase. In purchasing securities and warrants, the Reserve banks decide upon the volume which they intend to purchase, and let the market fix the price. In purchasing bankers' acceptances, on the other hand, the Reserve banks fix the rate of discount to be charged and buy all the paper that is brought to them. But the acceptance-buying policy of the Reserve banks is more like a security-buying policy than the discount policy, because acceptance-buying rates are fixed with a view to providing the Reserve banks with a given volume of paper, and are frequently altered to keep the volume of acceptances held by them within control.

At times when the discount policy of the Reserve banks is being circumvented through too liberal discounting by member banks, the Reserve banks resort to warnings "moral suasion" etc., to prevent certain banks from continuing to discount at their Reserve banks for reasons given at the time. It has been emphasized in the published statements of the Federal Reserve Board that rediscounting is a privilege and not a right, and that an individual Reserve bank may deny any bank the privilege of obtaining funds by this means. Accordingly, at the time of the post-war inflation, Reserve banks warned certain member banks that they were using too large a proportion of the funds of the Reserve banks. In 1920 it was evident that these warnings were not being hearkened to, and Congress passed the amendment to the Federal Reserve Act of April 13, 1920, permitting Reserve banks to charge graduated penalty rates to certain member banks. This privilege was availed of by some southern and western Reserve banks in dealing with banks which were borrowing more than their basic line of credit as determined by the Reserve bank in question. After much complaint, the practice was discontinued; and Congress, by an act passed March 4, 1923, revoked the part of the amendment of April 13, 1920, having to do with graduated discount rates. After this, nothing was heard of "warnings" and "moral suasion" until February 7, 1929, when the Federal Reserve Board wrote to all of the Federal Reserve banks asking them to withhold credit accommodation from member banks which were increasing their loans secured by stocks and bonds. This letter was variously received. Some Reserve banks did not follow the mandate contained in the letter, others did it grudgingly, while still others approved such action. The policy was abandoned after a period of four months.

The Federal Reserve Board has a further tool of control over the volume of credit which is based on Reserve bank accommodation. It may alter from time to time the rules on the nature of eligible paper, thus altering the amount of eligible paper in existence. While Section 13 of the Federal Reserve Act defines the types of paper which shall be eligible for rediscount, the definitions given there are loose, and leave room for interpretation. "Eligible paper" is more exactly defined in the regulations of the Federal Reserve Board. In addition to this, counsel for the Board rules upon the eligibility of specific pieces of paper upon whose eligibility doubt has been cast. Unless there be great pressure brought to bear by member banks to rediscount commercial paper rather than Government bonds, such rulings do not noticeably alter the credit policies of member banks. Individual Reserve banks may not alter the rulings and regulations of the Federal Reserve Board defining eligible paper, but the decision whether paper which is eligible for rediscount is acceptable from a credit standpoint is left in their hands.[2] In addition, they have the right to demand excess collateral to protect rediscounted paper. This power has been used by Reserve banks more to restrain the borrowing of member banks which were not in sound condition, than as a method of restricting the total volume of credit.[3]

[2] *Federal Reserve Bulletin,* 1920, p. 1301.

[3] *Hearings before a Subcommittee of the Committee on Banking and Currency of the United States Senate, 71st Cong., 3d Sess., pursuant to S. Res. 71,* 1931, Part 6, App., p. 712.

Limits to effectiveness of discount policy.—The effectiveness of discount policy depends to some extent upon the ability of the Reserve banks to shape the loan policies of their member banks. It depends more upon the effectiveness of the discount rate to influence market rates of interest and customer rates at banks, rather than on effect of interest upon the volume of funds borrowed.

In exercising the power of altering its discount policy, the Reserve system must avoid certain pitfalls. The first of these is the tendency of banks to substitute borrowed reserves for true reserves. Member banks are not permitted to remain continuously in debt to their Reserve banks. Thus they must have the means of cleaning up their borrowings from time to time. At some times only a few member banks are borrowers; at other times, almost all member banks borrow, but take turns in paying off their loans, only to renew them in a few days' time. In such cases, Reserve bank advances are used to increase the lending powers of member banks—a practice which is contrary to the spirit, if not to the letter, of the law. The system also attempts to avoid the use of its credit as a basis for purely speculative loans.[4]

II. Historical Survey

The history of Federal Reserve discount policy divides itself into six distinct periods during each of which a different policy was pursued. Besides differences in the policy, there were differences between the means used to promote the objectives which the system set about to attain.

First period of Federal Reserve policy, 1914-1917.—The first period covers the time from the organization of the Reserve banks until the entry of the United States into the World War. During these years the discount activities of the Reserve banks were quiescent. Because of the fact that member banks were required to deposit only a very small part of their reserves in the Reserve banks, they were possessed of ample resources to extend credit

[4] *Annual Report of the Federal Reserve Board,* 1923, p. 33. "The exclusion of the use of Federal reserve credit for speculative and investment purposes and its limitation to agricultural, industrial or commercial purposes thus clearly indicates the nature of the tests which are appropriate as guides in the extension of Federal reserve credit."

without borrowing.[5] Furthermore, the slight deposits of reserves in the Reserve banks during the first two years kept the resources of the Reserve banks small. What there was of them was invested for the most part in open-market paper, chiefly municipal warrants and a few bankers' acceptances and trade acceptances. The open-market purchases were made solely with a view to maintaining earnings in the absence of sufficient demand for rediscounts.

Anticipating the time when there would be more demand for rediscounts, the Board set itself to the task of defining paper which should be eligible for rediscount under the provisions of section 13 of the Federal Reserve Act. The Act had merely stated that paper must be covered by the following definition—"notes, drafts and bills of exchange issued or drawn for agricultural, industrial, or commercial purposes or the proceeds of which have been used or are to be used for such purposes." Notes, drafts, or bills "covering merely investments or issued or drawn for the purpose of carrying or trading in stocks, bonds, or other investment securities, except bonds and notes of the Government of the United States" were expressly prohibited. In order to define more closely the nature of paper which would be considered eligible for rediscount, the Board stated in Old Circular No. 13, issued November 10, 1914, that paper, to be eligible, must be liquid in the orthodox sense of the word. In the words of the circular, bills, to be eligible, "should represent in every case some distinct step or stage in the productive or distributive process—the progression of goods from producer to consumer.

[5] Section 19 of the Federal Reserve Act considerably lowered the reserve requirements of member banks below the amount previously required of national banks. Central Reserve city banks were required to hold as reserves 18% of their demand deposits and 5% of their time deposits, of which only 7/18 was to be deposited in the Reserve banks. Banks in Reserve cities were required to hold as reserves 15% of demand deposits and 5% of time deposits. Of these only 3/15 were to be deposited in Federal Reserve banks during the first 12 months and 1/15 at the end of each 6-month period thereafter. Country banks were required to hold 12% of demand deposits and 5% of time deposits of which only 2/12 were to be deposited in the Federal Reserve banks during the first 12 months and 1/12 at the end of each 6-month period thereafter. The old law required that national banks maintain a reserve of 25% for Central Reserve city and Reserve city banks, and of 15% for country banks. Thus deposits freed were 7% for Central Reserve city banks, 10% for Reserve city banks and 3% for country banks as well as a larger percentage of all time deposits.

The more nearly these steps approach the consumer the smaller will be the amount involved in each transaction as represented by the bill, and the more automatically self-liquidating will be its character."[6] In the light of this definition of liquid paper, the eligibility of each note was judged by the use to which the proceeds of the loan were put, irrespective of whether or not the paper was secured. Trade acceptances, bearing on their face a description of the transaction underlying the loan, were given preferential treatment, by being accorded eligibility for purchase as well as for rediscount, and were rediscounted at rates lower than those for other paper. Commodity paper was also rediscounted at lower rates, while discount rates on commercial paper were graduated according to maturity.

In fixing their first discount rates, the Reserve banks placed them somewhat above the open-market rate on commercial paper, though below the rates charged customers for commercial loans at banks. In so doing, they expected to avoid discounting paper for the profit of members.

Judged from the point of view of its future effects, the most important development of Federal Reserve policy during this period, was the amendment to the Federal Reserve Act enacted into law on September 7, 1916. That amendment substantially altered section 13 of the Federal Reserve Act in two respects. In the first place, it created the domestic bankers' acceptance, based on goods shipped or stored in warehouses, and the acceptance drawn by bankers in foreign countries for the purpose of furnishing dollar exchange. In order to prevent the misuse of the acceptance privilege for these purposes, it was provided that domestic acceptances be limited as to maturity—in order to prevent their use to hold goods off the market, and the use of the dollar exchange draft was placed under the regulation of the Federal Reserve Board. In the second place, member banks were empowered to borrow from Federal Reserve banks for periods of 15 days, on their own notes secured by paper eligible for rediscount or by Government bonds. This provision made all government bonds, held in the portfolios of member banks, a part of the potential reserves of members in addition to loans

[6] *Annual Report of the Federal Reserve Board,* 1914, p. 183.

by the banks collateraled by Government bonds. This change was of great significance, because member banks were now enabled to obtain reserves at times when—as it was currently expressed by some—there was no demand on the part of their customers for loans which might yield eligible paper.

Second period of Federal Reserve policy, 1917-1919.—The entry of the United States into the World War initiated the second period of Reserve-bank activity. The constant issues of certificates of indebtedness, and the four issues of Liberty bonds put on the market during the years 1917 and 1918, caused demands on the banks for funds far in excess of their power of expansion based on cash reserves. It became necessary for banks to discount their own notes at their Reserve banks, in order to pay for their allotments of certificates of indebtedness. Since the need of the Government for funds exceeded the cash savings of the people, the banks were encouraged to lend freely to their customers against the purchase of Government bonds, and the customers' notes were equally freely rediscounted by the Reserve banks.

The banking resources of the country were further mobilized by means of the amendment to the Federal Reserve Act, enacted into law on June 21, 1917. This amendment lowered the reserve requirements of member banks to 7, 10, and 13 per cent of demand deposits for country banks, Reserve city banks and Central Reserve city banks respectively, which was about the amount which had already been deposited in the Reserve Banks up to that date, according to the provisions of the original Federal Reserve Act. Reserve requirements against time deposits were lowered to 3 per cent. By this means a certain part of the vault cash of banks and of their deposits in national banks in Reserve cities and in Central Reserve cities was freed from being held in reserve and could be used to make loans to purchasers of Government bonds.

In order to assist the Government to float its issues at low rates of interest, the Reserve banks established preferential rates on rediscounts secured by war paper, attempting to make the discount rates on different types of such paper conform to the rates borne by them. Discount rates on commercial paper were sharply graduated according to maturity, so that member bank 15-day notes were discounted at rates below those ruling on commercial paper, other than that of short duration. At the beginning of the war period, some Reserve banks attempted to maintain discount rates on commercial paper above the market rate charged, though this policy was counteracted by the extensive rediscounts of government bond secured paper at preferential rates. After a while, all efforts in the direction of maintaining discount rates above open market interest rates were abandoned.

As the demand for rediscount accommodation rose, the Reserve banks curtailed their purchases of paper in the open market. Some Reserve banks ceased buying municipal warrants at all; and the total amount of such paper, purchased by the system as a whole, shrank to negligible amounts. All Reserve banks continued to buy some bankers' acceptances, in order to promote their purpose of maintaining a market for them. A small part of the Government issues of certificates of indebtedness were held temporarily by the Reserve banks. The bulk of Reserve-bank earning assets consisted in discounted bills. There was a constant increase in discounts of member bank 15-day notes secured by Government bonds, and in rediscounts of customers' paper so secured. Yet, at Reserve banks in agricultural districts, such as Kansas City and San Francisco, rediscounts of commercial and agricultural paper exceeded discounts of notes secured by Government bonds during most of the war period. This new demand for agricultural loans resulted from the orders of the Government for foodstuffs. The Federal Reserve system at the same time tried to discourage the making of loans by banks for non-essential industries.

Immediately upon the close of the War, the Reserve banks faced the problem of liquidating the credit based on Government securities, and of forcing the securities themselves out of the hands of the banks and into the hands of investors. The individual Reserve banks laid plans for accomplishing this end, to be carried out by raising the rates of discount on paper secured by Government bonds to levels nearer those charged for the rediscount of commercial paper. But this program was delayed by the Treasury until after the flotation of the Victory Loan in April and May, 1919. The Victory Loan was only slowly digested, and there were issues of certificates of indebtedness by the Treasury throughout the year. The Reserve banks continued to keep rates of discount on paper secured by certificates of in-indebtedness at the same level as the rates borne by these certificates. The war-time credit policies of the Reserve system continued throughout most of the year 1919.

In spite of the policy of continuing to accommodate the Government, the rediscounts of commercial and agricultural paper were an increasing portion of Reserve-bank advances during the year 1919.

The post-war period of liquidation of the government debt, 1920-1922.—The events of this period, particularly of the years 1920 and 1921, were unique in the history of Federal Reserve policy up to the time of writing. It has been only during this short period of two years that the Reserve banks have ever attempted to perform the function which they were originally intended to perform—financing the short-term credit needs of industry. Government bonds were not regarded as an ideal bank asset; and investors were encouraged to take them over at such prices as buyers were willing to pay.

The danger of overexpansion of credit through the mechanism of the Federal Reserve system was recognized; and attempts were made to avoid the recurrence of such overexpansion. Governor Harding of the Federal Reserve Board stated in the *Annual Report of the Board* for the year 1919:

> The experience of the past three years has demonstrated the expansive power of the Federal Reserve System. It should be understood, however, that an elastic system of reserve credit and note issue implies capacity to control and the ability to curtail credit.

This passage indicates that the Reserve system had abandoned the theory that credit expansion could be automatically checked, and the idea of control was henceforth emphasized.

In its effort to curtail credit, the Federal Reserve Board authorized the individual Reserve Banks to raise discount rates on a number of occasions beginning in November, 1919. During 1920, the rate on commercial paper and on member bank 15-day notes was raised by steps from 4¾ per cent to 7 per cent at the larger Reserve banks. In the beginning of 1921, this rate stood at 7 per cent at six Reserve banks and at 6 per cent at the remaining six banks. Beginning in April, 1921, all Reserve banks commenced lowering rates until they stood between 4½ per cent and 5½ per cent at the close of the year. Rates ruling on paper secured by Government obligations were lowered less than were commercial paper rates, so that by October 5, there were uniform rates on all types of paper at every Reserve bank. Since that time preferential rates have not been used.

The volume of bills discounted rose and fell with the rates charged on them. This was the cause of comment by some Reserve banks which had expected the opposite to be the case.[7] The high point for bills discounted for the system as a whole was reached on November 5, 1920, when they totaled 1,827 million dollars, although discounts at some Reserve banks continued to rise during 1921. This indicates the uneven nature of the liquidation. Such liquidation was effected first in the eastern industrial sections, notably in the Boston district where discounts reached their high point at the end of 1919 and in the New York, Philadelphia, Chicago, and St. Louis districts, where the liquidation after the peak in the autumn of 1920 was rapid. It came later in the agricultural districts.

The composition of the discount portfolio of the Reserve banks was altered substantially, indicating the extent to which the banking system was successful in its effort to drive Government bonds out of the banks into the hands of investors. Increases in the volume of bills discounted during 1920 consisted entirely of rediscounts of commercial and agricultural paper. Discounts collateraled by Government obligations declined steadily in amount.

The Reserve banks were successful in their plan of driving

[7] See reports of Federal Reserve Agents to the Federal Reserve Board. Report for District No. 7, Chicago, for 1920, *Annual Report of the Federal Reserve Board, 1920*, p. 479, is one example.

Government bonds from bank portfolios, but this action was accomplished at the expense of the holders of these bonds; for their price declined rapidly during 1920, and regained but little of the previous loss in 1921. In the year 1921 the Reserve banks noted a great improvement in investment demand for both long-term Government bonds and certificates of indebtedness. Some signs of a separate money market in Chicago began to appear. While Government securities had previously been bought and sold in New York only, the Federal Reserve Agent at Chicago reported, in 1921, that there were five recognized local dealers in that place who gave daily quotations of prices. Boston also began to develop a separate market both in Government securities and in bankers' acceptances, although a majority of the latter were still bought by Reserve banks.

Beginning in May, 1920, gold imports upon an unprecedented scale commenced. By January, 1922, they had amounted to 844 million dollars. The member banks deposited the gold with their Reserve banks, as they received it, thus repaying their borrowings. Because of the lack of demand for discounts, the Reserve banks purchased $400,000,000 worth of Government securities during the first five months of 1922. Doing this to enable themselves to earn dividend requirements, they also profoundly influenced money-market conditions. This was the first occasion on which the Reserve banks had purchased Government securities to any great extent, their open-market operations having been before 1922 almost entirely in bankers' acceptances, trade acceptances and municipal warrants.

The period of development of independent open-market operations, 1923-1927.—This period marked a new attitude toward central-banking policy. The difference between this period and previous periods was in the methods of control used rather than in the aims of control. Where the open-market operations of the system had previously been used to earn expenses and dividends for the Reserve banks, when their resources were not otherwise invested, or to aid in the establishment of regional discount markets, they were now used as a major instrument of credit control. How the control over open-market purchases of Government securities was centralized in the Open Market Investment Committee in 1923, is outlined in the next chapter.

Discount rates during this period came to be of minor importance in the shaping of Federal Reserve policy. Rates were kept consistently below the rates ruling in the open market. Furthermore, the fact that the discount rate was not expected to act as a means of expressing Federal Reserve policy is attested by the fact that rates were infrequently changed, and sometimes after open-market interest rates—even rates charged by banks in larger cities to their customers—had changed. Open-market operations came to be the major instrument of credit control. They were used as an independent entity, rather than as a method of support of the discount rate, as had been done in England before the War. At the same time the Bank of England was developing an independent open-market policy.[8] Other central banks still depended upon the discount rate to exercise control over their banks and money markets.

The effects of Federal Reserve policy during the period may be measured by the effect which purchases and sales of Government securities had upon bank credit, during three periods of purchase of Government bonds as follows:

1. January, 1922, through May, 1922 — purchase of $400,000,000

2. December, 1923, through September, 1924—purchase of $510,000,000

3. May, 1927, through November, 1927—purchase of $230,000,000

Each period was coincident with an approximately equal increase in the volume of loans to brokers made by New York City banks for their own account.

1. February, 1922, through October, 1922, brokers' loans made by New York City reporting banks increased by $427,000,000.

2. Between December, 1923, and September, 1924, brokers' loans made by New York City banks increased by $502,000,000.

[8] *Report of the Committee on Finance and Industry,* presented to Parliament, June, 1931, par. 358.

3. Between May 11, 1927, and November 16, 1927, brokers' loans made by New York City banks increased by $293,000,000.

This relationship was owing to the fact that purchases of securities for all Federal Reserve banks were made by the Open Market Investment Committee in New York City, resulting in an excess of funds at that point. Since New York City banks make most of their loans on security collateral, and since their loans to brokers represent the flexible part of their loan portfolios, it was natural for the free credit thus released to find its way into the brokers' loan market.

Periods of open-market purchase were followed by corresponding periods of open-market sale of the securities in the portfolios of the Reserve banks, but these sales did not result in a shrinkage of the volume of loans to brokers. While open-market purchases of Government securities increased loans to brokers by New York City banks, open-market sales of the securities raised open-market interest rates, and the effect of these high rates was to attract the funds of out-of-town banks and others to the brokers' loan market. Loans by New York City banks did contract at these times, but the gap caused by their withdrawal was more than filled by outside funds. In addition to this, the contractions in the volume of loans to brokers which took place in 1923, 1926, and later on in 1929, resulted in increases in security loans to customers by banks, so that the total amount of bank credit outstanding based on security collateral did not materially diminish at these times. Thus, even though the Reserve banks sold 525 million dollars' worth of Government securities between June, 1922, and July, 1923, 260 million dollars' worth between November, 1924, and March, 1925, and 405 million dollars' worth between January, 1928, and April, 1929, no reduction in the total volume of brokers' loans ensued. Once banks had been induced to commence lending to brokers, the effect of both purchases and sales of Government securities by Reserve banks was to increase loans to brokers.

Other credit extended, as a result of open-market purchases by the Reserve banks, was nil. Beginning in 1925 there was a rapid decline in the unsecured loans of banks. Although all unsecured loans do not represent truly commercial loans, it may safely be assumed that loans secured by stocks and bonds or by mortgage collateral do not generally represent loans for commercial purposes.[9]

The effect of the great open-market operations of the Reserve banks in Government bonds between 1922 and 1927 was to alter the composition of Reserve bank portfolios. Government securities became an increasing proportion of the earning assets of the Reserve banks.

The *period of inflation, 1928-1929.*—In so far as concerns the use to which credit built up on the basis of Reserve Bank credit was put—the financing of stock speculation—this period differed from the preceding one only in intensity. But it was a period in which the Reserve system attempted to pursue a vigorous deflationary policy—in fact, it stated on frequent occasions that it was doing so—but this policy was counteracted by other forces. The reasons for the failure of the deflationary policy of the Federal Reserve system can be looked for in two places. The first is the large volume of funds available from new banking lenders for the purpose of making security loans, which the Reserve banks wished to discourage. The second was the unwillingness of the Reserve system itself to concentrate all its efforts upon the accomplishment of its main purpose.

Beginning in January, 1928, the Reserve banks sold their holdings of open-market paper in order to curtail credit. By the first week in September their holdings of United States securities had declined by over 400 million dollars and their holdings of bills bought in the open market had been allowed to mature without replacement so that they stood at a figure 200 million dollars below that of the beginning of the year. Discounted

[9] A questionnaire sent to commercial banks by the Subcommittee of the Senate Committee on Banking and Currency and answered by 30 banks, indicates that the majority of loans secured by stocks and bonds were made to enable the borrower to carry these securities. Only 12 out of the 30 banks estimated that more than 20 per cent of their loans to customers secured by stocks and bonds were made for commercial, industrial or agricultural purposes. The remaining 18 banks estimated the proportion of their security loans for such purposes at negligible percentages. *Hearings Pursuant to S. Res. 71*, Part 7, App., p. 1012.

bills, however, rose by more than 500 million dollars during the same period. Therefore, the net effect of the open-market policy of the Reserve banks during the first eight months of 1928 was to change the composition of the portfolios of the Reserve banks, substituting discounted bills for Government securities and bills bought in the open market, most of which were member bank 15-day notes secured by Government obligations. This increase in the volume of discounted bills took place in spite of increases in the rates of discount charged by the Reserve banks from 3.5 per cent in January, 1928, to 5 per cent in August of that year.

In September, 1928, the Reserve banks, fearing that legitimate business would lack funds to move crops, did not raise their buying rates on bankers' acceptances as much as open-market rates on that type of paper had risen. The result of this rate policy was that the holdings of bills bought in the open market by the Reserve banks increased during the autumn of 1928 by 300 million dollars. Since the volume of bills discounted and of Government securities held was the same at the end of the year as at the beginning of September, there was an increase of over 300 million dollars' worth of Reserve-bank credit during the course of the year.

The effect of this increase in Reserve-bank credit upon member-bank credit was to increase bank loans on securities. Loans on securities of reporting member banks increased by about 400 million dollars between the last report date in 1927 and the same date in 1928. In the same period of time, loans to brokers by others than banks increased from 1,006 million dollars to 2,322 million dollars.

In 1929 the situation became worse. This was in spite of the fact that the Federal Reserve system began the year with a more intensive deflationary policy. When 5 per cent discount rates and low holdings of Government securities did not prove sufficient to check the use of Federal Reserve funds in the stock market, the Federal Reserve Board resorted to moral suasion to check the growth in discounted bills. On February 7, 1929, the Board wrote to all the Federal Reserve banks asking them to refuse discount accommodation to any bank which might be increasing its security loans. There was much complaint from both Reserve banks and member banks concerning this step, but measures were taken by all Reserve banks to put it into effect. At the same time, they further disposed of some 50 million dollars' worth of United States securities; and allowed their bill holdings, which had been close to 500 million dollars at the beginning of the year, to run off until they stood below 100 million in the summer. In spite of the moral suasion policy, bills discounted increased by about 100 million dollars. During the first week in June, the policy was unofficially abandoned. It is difficult to determine whether or not the policy was successful.

Mr. Charles H. Hamlin, a member of the Federal Reserve Board, testified that the policy of moral suasion was successful because Reserve bank credit declined between February 9, 1929, and June 8, 1929, while security loans of New York City reporting member banks declined during that period.[10] At the same time, "all other loans" of reporting member banks increased by amounts greater than they had in any previous four-month period. This extraordinary increase leads us to believe that there was some shift of security loans to the "unsecured" category by banks which were accommodating those of their customers who were in need of funds to carry securities which they had purchased but were not yet able to pay for.

On August 9, 1929, the Board changed its tactics and permitted the Federal Reserve Bank of New York to raise its discount rate to 6 per cent, a step the Bank had been attempting to take since February 14. At the same time the Reserve Bank of New York lowered its buying rate on acceptances of all maturities from 5¼ percent to 5⅛ percent. The result of this action was an increase in bills bought in the open market by all Reserve banks of close to 300 million dollars up to the end of October, and a consequent increase in loans on securities of reporting member banks of about 200 million dollars. With the continuing increase in loans to brokers by others than banks,

[10] *Hearings Pursuant to S. Res. 71*, App., Part 6, pp. 167-69.

which reached 3,823 million dollars on October 23, the stock exchange continued to be active, although business had already begun to decline. At the end of October, the stock market "boom" fell under the weight of its own excesses. This leads up to the next period of Federal Reserve policy.

Depression policies of the Reserve banks, 1929-1933.—The panic of October and November, 1929, brought great strains to bear on the New York City banks. "Others" withdrew their funds from the brokers' loan market, the total amount withdrawn before the end of the year amounting to about 2,300 million dollars. In order not to intensify the panic, New York banks increased their loans to brokers by a billion dollars in the first week of the liquidation, and at the same time increased their security loans to their customers. The New York Federal Reserve Bank assisted them in the process by purchasing 115 million dollars' worth of Government securities outright. By the end of the year, the twelve Reserve banks had increased their holdings of securities by 375 million dollars. Thus they departed, for the time being, from the rule that they could not directly assist the banks in lending to speculators.

In the following years, the Reserve banks attempted to give artificial stimulus to business and to the stock market, through the establishment of low rates of interest by whatever means were at hand. By September 16, 1931, United States securities held by the system increased by 231 million dollars beyond the amount held at the end of 1929, despite the fact that the cash reserves of the system were increasing, owing to gold imports, and had reached a figure almost 650 million dollars greater than the reserves held at the end of 1929. The Federal Reserve Bank of New York lowered its discount rate a number of times until it reached 1.5 per cent on May 8, 1931. The rates ruling at the other Reserve banks were as low as 2.5 and 3 per cent through the summer of 1931. In spite of these low rates, the volume of bills discounted at Reserve banks shrank steadily. At the height of the speculative era in 1929, they had stood at 1,084 million dollars in spite of the 5 and 6 per cent rates then ruling. On September 16, 1931, when rates at Reserve banks were at their lowest, the volume of bills discounted was only 263 million dollars; and it had been lower in the preceding summer.

On September 21, 1931, an event occurred which completely altered the policies of the Reserve banks for a short period of time. The abandonment of the gold standard by Great Britain caused a drain on the gold reserves of the Federal Reserve system owing to the withdrawal of dollar balances held in New York for the account of foreign banks, principally the Bank of France. The latter institution feared that the United States would also abandon the gold basis—an event which took place a year and a half later. The Reserve banks made but little effort to counteract the gold movement by means of purchases of United States securities, but they kept their bill rates low so that the volume of bills held by them stood, in the middle of October, at a point 700 million dollars above the lowest level for the year. At the same time, the volume of bills discounted rose to over 1 billion dollars by the end of the year, and discount rates at all Reserve banks were raised—the New York Bank having a rate of 3.5 per cent at the end of the year.

In 1932, the Reserve banks once again attempted to stimulate credit and business through the establishment of low money rates, in spite of the continued hoarding of currency, which had commenced to appear on an extended scale late in 1931, and the repetition of gold exports in May and June, 1932. The fact that the Treasury had been forced to increase its indebtedness, ever since the close of the fiscal year 1930, may have been one factor inducing the Reserve banks to purchase a billion dollars' worth of Government securities in the spring of 1932. The ostensible reason for this great purchase of Government securities was, however, to release credit for business and industry. Actual effects of the purchase were the piling up of reserves in excess of those required by law by member banks, and an increase in the balances held by member banks for the account of other banks. The bankers' balances held by reporting member banks alone increased 626 million dollars during 1932. The excess reserves of member banks were only 584 million dollars in January, 1933. Consequently, reporting member banks were in a position of great vulnerability in case of any mass demands for currency on the part of smaller banks. Thus, the open-market purchase of securities by Reserve banks in 1932 was one factor leading to the crisis and the closing of all banks in 1933.

In the meantime, the Reserve banks had again lowered their discount rates—the rate ruling at the New York Bank having been reducd to 2.5 per cent during the first six months of 1932. These, as was the case with previous low rates, did not serve as stimulants to borrowing, either by member banks from Reserve banks or by customers of member banks from them.

The 1932 open-market policy of the Reserve system was dictated with a view to encouraging business borrowing by making rates of interest low. Since rates ruling in the short-term money markets were the only rates influenced by the policy—rates ruling in the long-term markets remaining high notwithstanding—the policy was ineffective as a stimulant to business borrowing. The open-market policy of 1932 failed, therefore, because it was predicated upon the assumption, either that low short-term rates would stimulate borrowing in the short-term money markets, or that long term rates of interest would always follow short-term rates in their movements.

Beginning in 1922 the Reserve banks extended more and more credit on the basis of the Government debt. While United States securities purchased by Reserve banks, or pledged to them as collateral for discount advances, represented only 44 per cent of total Reserve bank credit in the middle of 1921, they represented 70 per cent of Reserve bank credit in the middle of 1930 and 84 per cent of Reserve bank credit in the middle of 1932, after the huge security-purchase operation of that year had taken place. At the end of the period the Reserve banks were in a condition less liquid than at the beginning, because a larger part of their assets were based on paper, the repayment of which had nothing to do with the movement of goods from producer to consumer. The likelihood of repayment of discounts based on government security collateral depends more upon the strength of the banking endorsement carried by the paper than upon the solvency of the original borrower. The Government securities held by Reserve banks were not repaid. As a result the Reserve banks were unable to meet drains on them for gold and for new currency which occurred during February and March, 1933, as they might have done, had their advances to the market consisted of discounts for strong member banks which would have been settled at maturity.

Changes in the rediscount provisions of the Federal Reserve Act have been instituted during 1932 and 1933 which, if made permanent, will completely eliminate the commercial character of that part of Reserve bank assets which has withstood the pressure of the changes of the decade 1922 through 1932.

Because of the complaint that many banks no longer had eligible assets, the Glass-Steagall Act of February 27, 1932, provided (1) for the discount of the notes of groups of 5 or more member banks which have no eligible assets, with the consent of at least 5 members of the Federal Reserve Board, and (2) for the discount for any member bank with a capital of less than $5,000,000, in exceptional and exigent circumstances, of ineligible assets, provided the assets pledged are satisfactory to the Federal Reserve bank and the consent of at least 5 members of the Federal Reserve Board be obtained. Since few Federal Reserve funds were put into circulation by this means, the Emergency Relief and Construction Act of July 21, 1932, permitted the rediscount by Reserve banks of notes, drafts and bills of exchange of the kinds and maturities made eligible for discount for member banks for individuals, partnerships, or corporations, with the consent of at least 5 members of the Federal Reserve Board, provided such individuals, partnerships or corporations have no other sources of funds. Both the 2d part of the Glass-Steagall Act and The Emergency Relief and Construction Act were made temporary, but subject to renewal. The Glass-Steagall Act, whose one-year lease on life has already expired at the time of writing, has been renewed for another year.

The Emergency Bank Act of March 9, 1933, further broadened the discount powers of the Federal Reserve banks. Under exceptional and exigent circumstances Federal Reserve banks were empowered by this Act to make advances to member banks which have no eligible assets on their own promissory notes "secured to the satisfaction of such Federal reserve bank." This provision was also of one year's duration but to be extended for such periods as the president might prescribe.

The effects of the legislation of 1932 and 1933 cannot as yet be judged. If availed of to any great extent, they will have to be renewed upon frequent occasions. The protection afforded to bank reserves by the liquidity of the Federal Reserve banks will be lost. There will be substituted for this protection a new type of assurance of payment—the assurance based upon the power to issue currency without limit provided by the suspension of the gold standard by the United States. This means inflation of the currency.

III. An Evaluation of Discount Policy

Obstacles to effective discount policy.—The discount rate policy of the Federal Reserve system has been ineffective in bringing about changes in the volume of bills discounted as long as the system has been in operation. The volume of bills discounted has increased at times when discount rates were high, and has declined when discount rates declined. Rates are changed most frequently at the New York Bank; and the changes are usually made earlier than corresponding changes at other Reserve banks.

The fault in discount policy making rates ineffective to stimulate or to check borrowing may have been fundamental, or it may have been one of method. If the fault is one of method, it might be remedied by maintaining rates of discount above market rates of interest on loans of the type expanded on the basis of discount accommodation, by changing rates more promptly, or by unifying the discount and open-market policies of the system.

The Federal Reserve banks have made no attempt to maintain their rates above market rates of interest, except in the first two years of their operation. Even at that time, they held their rates below those charged to the best customers by banks in larger centers—the lowest customer rates charged. After the close of the War, their rates were constantly below the rates on prime commercial-paper ruling in the open market. The Reserve banks made some efforts to defend this position by pointing out that their rates were consistently above the rates on prime bankers' acceptances. The Federal Reserve agents and the Federal Reserve Board reminded the public, on frequent occasions, that rediscounted paper resembled a bankers' acceptance rather than open market commercial paper, because it had a bank endorsement as well as commercial endorsements. This argument is rationalization rather than a statement of fact, for two reasons. First, the Reserve banks do not fix their rates with a view to charging for the risk involved but with a view to accommodating commerce and industry. Second, the Reserve banks do not in practice rediscount bankers' acceptances, although they are permitted to do so, because they purchase bankers' aceptances in the open market at lower rates. The rate at which they purchase bankers' acceptances determines the open-market rate on such paper.

Any effort to maintain discount rates above market rates of interest presupposes the existence of a money market in each Federal Reserve district. Very few centers have what might be called "money markets." But if the element of competition is present in the granting of loans by banks to their customers, there is a market in bank loans. In 1931, a subcommittee of the Committee on Banking and Currency of the United States Senate sent a questionnaire to the Federal Reserve banks, asking their opinions on discount rates and other rates.[11] Reserve banks outside the great financial centers—New York, Boston, Chicago, and San Francisco—thought that customer rates at banks and rates on mortgages could be taken as indicative of market rates in their districts. Some held that rates ruling in the New York market should be followed because funds of banks in outside districts are invested in the New York market, which amounts to an admission that there is no market rate in the districts in

[11] *Hearings Pursuant to S. Res. 71*, Part 6, App., pp. 748-93.

question. Some Reserve banks made the suggestion that rates charged by banks to customers who can obtain accommodation in more than one district, or at more than one bank, be taken as indicative of market rates of interest. Reserve banks in districts where bankers' acceptances are available, with the exception of the Federal Reserve Bank of Chicago, thought that the bankers' acceptance rate should be included in any computation of open-market interest rates, although the Reserve banks themselves had always constituted the market for such paper. While there was disagreement as to whether Reserve-bank discount rates influenced customer rates in financial centers, all Reserve banks agreed that discount rate changes are not passed on to customers of country banks.

In spite of the opinion of most Reserve banks that there were some rates ruling in their districts which could be taken as measures of market rates, only three Reserve banks—those of Chicago, Cleveland, and St. Louis—thought that discount rates should be held above market rates. While eight Reserve banks were against the practice, the Federal Reserve Bank of New York held that if rates were raised to that level, it would be necessary for the Reserve banks to release more credit through open-market operations so that member banks would seldom have to rediscount. This proposal condones the practice of member banks in extending credit on the basis of borrowed reserves—a practice contrary to the previously-stated objectives of the Federal Reserve system.

Even though discount rates were held above customer rates at banks, they would be ineffectual in preventing rediscounting for profit, unless they were always above rates ruling in markets where banks invest their secondary reserves. It is not difficult to hold discount rates above the yields of Government securities. But a large part of the secondary reserves of banks are loaned on call in the New York market; and the call loan rate is subject to fluctuations so violent that discount rates would have to show more extreme cyclical "swings" in order to be at all times above call-loan rates. Since discount rates have never been held at that high point, it is impossible to judge from past experience whether the volume of bills discounted would be contracted when rates are raised under this plan. The experiment might be worth attempting.

The greatest obstacle to effective discount policy has been the excessive use of open-market operations as separate instruments of credit control. Since discount policies and open market policies of the Federal Reserve system have not always had the same end in view, and since changes in the rate of discount charged have not had an appreciable effect upon the volume of funds borrowed from Reserve banks, discount policy has been ineffective as a means of controlling the total volume of member-bank credit. Furthermore, if the Reserve banks had been able to control the discounting of their member banks through rate changes, the member banks could still have circumvented their policies by encouraging their depositors to hold their funds as time deposits instead of as demand deposits, thus economizing in reserves owing to the low reserve requirements for time deposits. This type of economy was practiced during the years 1928 and 1929, enabling member banks to extend more credit than the additions to their reserves would indicate.

The purely negative aims of Federal Reserve policy—the avoidance of the use of Federal Reserve credit for permanent additions to member-bank credit and for speculative uses—have failed completely of attainment, because of the open-market policies of the system. The fact that open-market purchases led to extensions of speculative credit by member banks prevented the member banks from liquidating this credit at all. If the new credit injected by Reserve-bank operations had been used to finance the nation's trade in goods, the short maturity of the loans granted combined with the fact that fluctuations in the prices of goods were less than would have guaranteed repayment at maturity. At the time of maturity of these loans, the Reserve banks could have, by a vigorous rate policy, made certain that too many of them were not replaced.

SUMMARY

Reviewing the experience of the past twenty years, the discount policies of the Federal Reserve system have been rendered ineffectual by a growing dependence upon the government debt as a source of Reserve-bank credit. This trend arose at the time of the World War, although it was brought to an abrupt halt by subsequent efforts to make investors take over the debt. But four years after the cessation of hostilities the government debt once again became the principal Reserve-bank asset. The policy of the Treasury to retire long-term bonds, substituting for them short-term issues, forced the Government debt back into the hands of the banks. When the Treasury once again became an active borrower, the open-market powers of the Federal Reserve system were used to aid the Government in floating its issues. A close relationship of the Reserve banks and the Treasury results in an equally close relationship of the Reserve banks and the speculative markets for member-bank credit may be extended on the basis of assets which do not yield eligible paper. Consequently it is the duty of the Reserve banks to extend no Reserve-bank credit to groups which they cannot control—by buying large blocks of securities in the open market—and to supervise the internal loan policies of banks which borrow from them on the basis of Government bonds. That is, the Reserve banks should exercise banking policy.

Future policies.—If the Reserve banks are to rectify their condition so that they can once again begin lending to their members for the purpose of commercial extensions of credit, they must carry one step further the policies which they followed during the period of post-war deflation. To free their resources of the Government bonds they must permit the price of these bonds to seek its natural level. At such a level investment funds, at present tied up in the form of hoarded money or of stock speculation, will be placed at the disposal of the Government.

Having accomplished the preliminary step of driving Government bonds from bank portfolios, the Reserve banks must extend credit in the future in such a manner that the member-bank credit extended on the basis of Reserve bank credit will be used to accommodate commerce and industry rather than to accommodate Wall Street or to relieve the United States Government of the necessity of collecting taxes in proportion to its expenditures. In view of the greater potential control over the

TABLE 149

CHANGES IN SELECTED ITEMS FROM BALANCE SHEETS OF FEDERAL RESERVE BANKS BEFORE THE ENTRY OF THE UNITED STATES INTO THE WORLD WAR

(In millions of dollars)

	DATES	BILLS DIS-COUNTED	BILLS BOUGHT	U. S. SECURI-TIES	MUNI-CIPAL WARRANTS	GOLD RE-SERVES	MEMBER BANK RESERVES	F. R. NOTES
Beginning with organization of Reserve Banks	6/25/15	26	10	8	12	324	303*	72
	3/30/17	20	84	48	16	938	711	358
	change	− 6	+74	+40	+ 4	+614	+408*	+286

* Net deposits. Data for member-bank reserves not available at that date. Therefore, the change in member-bank reserves is not accurate.

TABLE 150

PERIOD OF THE WORLD WAR

(In millions of dollars)

	DATES	BILLS DISCOUNTED On U. S. sec.	BILLS DISCOUNTED Other	BILLS DISCOUNTED Total	BILLS BOUGHT	U. S. SEC.	WAR-RANTS	GOLD RE-SERVES	MEMBER BANK RESERVES	FED. RES. NOTES
Duration of	3/30/17	0	20	20	84	48	16	938	711	358
the War	11/29/18	1413	403	1815	375	122	*	2065	1489	2569
	change	+1413	+383	+1795	+291	+ 74	—16	+1127	+ 778	+2211
Post-war	11/29/18	1413	403	1815	375	122	*	2065	1489	2569
Era of Govt.	12/26/19	1510	685	2195	585	300	*	2078	1787	3058
Financing	change	+ 97	+282	+ 380	+210	+178	0	+ 13	+ 298	+ 489

* Less than $500,000.

TABLE 151

PERIOD OF DEFLATION OF BANK CREDIT BASED ON GOVERNMENT DEBT

(In millions of dollars)

DATES	BILLS DISCOUNTED On U. S. Sec.	BILLS DISCOUNTED Other	BILLS DISCOUNTED Total	BILLS BOUGHT	U. S. SEC.	GOLD RE-SERVES	MEMBER BANK RESERVES	FED. RES. NOTES
12/26/19	1510	685	2195	585	300	2078	1787	3058
12/31/21	485	659	1144	145	234	2875	1753	2409
change	—1025	— 26	—1051	—440	— 66	+ 797	— 34	— 649

TABLE 152

PERIOD OF DEVELOPMENT OF INDEPENDENT OPEN MARKET OPERATIONS

(In millions of dollars)

	DATES	BILLS DISCOUNTED On U. S. Sec.	BILLS DISCOUNTED Other	BILLS DISCOUNTED Total	BILLS BOUGHT	U. S SECURITIES	OTHER SEC.	GOLD RESERVES	MEMBER BANK RESERVES	FED. RES. NOTES
Purchase	12/31/21	485	659	1144	145	234	*	2875	1753	2409
	5/31/22	171	300	471	118	603	*	3008	1782	2141
	change	—314	—359	— 673	— 27	+369	0	+ 133	+ 29	— 268
Sale	5/31/22	171	300	471	118	603	*	3008	1782	2141
	7/31/23	392	434	826	183	98	*	3101	1878	2178
	change	+221	+134	+ 355	+ 65	—505	0	+ 93	+ 96	+ 37
Purchase	7/31/23	392	434	826	183	98	*	3101	1878	2178
	10/31/24	119	146	264	200	584	4	3037	2138	1799
	change	—273	—288	— 562	+ 17	+486	+4	— 64	+ 260	— 379
Sale	10/31/24	119	146	264	200	584	4	3037	2138	1799
	10/31/26	360	330	690	323	301	2	2799	2223	1756
	change	+241	+184	+ 426	+123	—283	—2	— 238	+ 85	— 43
Purchase	10/31/26	360	330	690	323	301	2	2799	2223	1756
	12/31/27	418	164	582	392	617	1	2733	2487	1790
	change	+ 58	—166	— 108	+ 69	+316	—1	— 66	+ 264	+ 34

* Less than $500,000.

TABLE 153

PERIOD OF STOCK MARKET INFLATION THROUGH THE MEDIUM OF DISCOUNTS, 1928 AND 1929

(In millions of dollars)

	DATES	BILLS DISCOUNTED On U. S. Sec.	BILLS DISCOUNTED Other	BILLS DISCOUNTED Total	BILLS BOUGHT	U. S SECURITIES	OTHER SEC.	GOLD RESERVES	MEMBER BANK RESERVES	FED. RES. NOTES
Deflation	12/31/27	418	164	582	392	617	1	2733	2487	1790
	7/31/28	622	409	1031	162	215	*	2597	2267	1615
	change	+204	+245	+ 449	—230	—402	—1	— 136	— 220	— 175
Straddle Policy, 1928	7/31/28	622	409	1031	162	215	*	2597	2267	1615
	12/31/28	659	397	1056	489	228	10	2584	2389	1838
	change	+ 37	— 12	+ 25	+327	+ 13	+10	— 13	+ 122	+ 223
Moral suasion	12/31/28	659	397	1056	489	228	10	2584	2389	1838
	7/31/29	593	483	1076	75	147	10	2924	2355	1779
	change	— 66	+ 86	+ 20	—414	— 81	0	+ 340	— 34	— 59
Straddle policy, 1929	7/31/29	593	483	1076	75	147	10	2924	2355	1779
	9/30/29	458	500	958	293	162	15	2971	2326	1863
	change	—135	+ 17	— 118	+218	+ 15	+ 5	+ 47	— 29	+ 84

* Less than $500,000.

TABLE 154: THE PERIOD WHEN DEPRESSION WAS ATTACKED BY LOWERING INTEREST RATES

(In millions of dollars)

		BILLS DISCOUNTED								
	DATES	On U. S. Sec.	Other	Total	BILLS BOUGHT	U. S SEC.	OTHER SEC.	GOLD RE-SERVES	MEMBER BANK RESERVES	FED. RES. NOTES
Financing the stock-market crash	9/30/29	458	500	958	293	162	15	2971	2326	1863
	10/31/29	526	474	1000	355	321	25	3004	2666	1899
	change	+ 68	— 26	+ 42	+ 62	+159	+10	+ 33	+ 340	+ 36
Easy credit	10/31/29	526	474	1000	355	321	25	3004	2666	1899
	6/30/31	47	102	149	106	668	9	3409	2381	1723
	change	—479	—372	— 851	—249	+347	—16	+ 405	— 285	— 176
Gold exports, 1931	6/30/31	47	102	149	106	668	9	3409	2381	1723
	10/31/31	362	366	728	681	727	30	2746	2167	2429
	change	+315	+264	+ 579	+575	+ 59	+21	— 663	— 214	+ 706
Period without policy	10/31/31	362	366	728	681	727	30	2746	2167	2429
	2/29/32	463	365	828	109	740	15	2938	1849	2651
	change	+101	— 1	+ 100	—572	+ 13	—15	+ 192	— 318	+ 222
Security purchase, 1932	2/29/32	463	365	828	109	740	15	2938	1849	2651
	7/31/32	205	334	538	43	1841	6	2635	2052	2859
	change	—258	— 31	— 290	— 66	+1101	— 9	— 303	+ 203	+ 208
Gold imports, 1932	7/31/32	205	334	538	43	1841	6	2635	2052	2859
	1/31/33	72	202	274	31	1763	3	3256	2446	2725
	change	—133	—132	— 264	— 12	— 78	— 3	+ 621	+ 394	— 134
Period of mora-toria	1/31/33	72	202	274	31	1763	3	3256	2446	2725
	3/ 8/33	*	*	1414	417	1881	*	*	1776	*
	change			+1140	+386	+ 118			— 670	

* Data not available.

use of funds created through discounts than through purchases of securities in the open market from whomever may hold them, the Reserve banks should in the future emphasize discount policy rather than open-market policy. As long as discount rates are established at a level higher than that of open-market paper the incentive to member banks to borrow for the sake of unwise credit extensions will be minimized. But if the amendment to the Federal Reserve Act of 1916, permitting the use of a bank's investments in Government securities as a source of Reserve-bank credit, remains on the statute books, greater emphasis will have to be placed upon banking policy than formerly. A member bank seeking advances will have to submit its portfolio for close scrutiny, unless such advances be in the form of rediscounted commercial or agricultural paper. Otherwise a new speculative era will be built upon the wreckage of the old one.

CHAPTER XXXI

THE BANKERS' ACCEPTANCE MARKET[1]

The bankers' acceptance market in the United States is a recent innovation introduced as a result of the provisions of the Federal Reserve Act. Since the passage of this Act by Congress, the acceptance market was developed, not by virtue of the need for it, but on the basis of the support given by the operations of the Federal Reserve banks in the open market.

Two undesirable effects, according to some, had been directly traceable to the absence of authorization to accept in the United States. The first was the loss to American banks of a profitable source of business which carried little risk. Before the passage of the Federal Reserve Act, most foreign trade of the country, both with England and with other foreign countries, was financed by means of sterling drafts. The desire on the part of American bankers to finance foreign trade led to their replacement by dollar drafts.

The second undesirable effect of the inability of American banks to accept had to do with the consequence of the lack of dollar acceptances available in the American money markets upon bank-portfolio policies' resulting in the use of bank funds in more speculative investments. Banks had been accustomed to investing their secondary reserves in brokers' call loans. The needs of brokers were considerations secondary to the availability of funds in determining the extent to which brokers borrowed. Disturbances in security prices and in the volume of capital directed to industrial use were the result. The provision of liquid-credit instruments at an attractive yield was urged to direct the secondary reserves of banks into a more useful form of investment. In order to give the banks a place where they might convert their secondary reserves into cash before the maturity of the bills held by them, it was hoped that regional discount markets would develop in Reserve bank cities.

[1] Written by Caroline Whitney.

The nature of bankers' acceptance credit.—Bankers' acceptance credit differs from bank credit arising out of loans and discounts, in that the accepting bank assumes no immediate responsibility for conversion—that is, it does not increase its deposit liabilities. Where loans and discounts result in the substitution of a bank's demand liabilities for time or demand liabilities of borrowers, the acceptance of drafts by the same bank entails the substitution of the bank's time liabilities for time liabilities of the borrowers with the same maturity. The borrowers agree to supply the bank with funds to meet the drafts before they are due; consequently, there is no immediate reason why accepting banks should not by this means expand without limit. In direct loans the bank is deterred from over-expansion by the fear of being called on for conversion of its newly created liabilities. The possibility that clients in whose favor drafts are accepted will not deposit funds to meet the maturing drafts is more remote and so is a less effective deterrent to the bank. If drawers of drafts wish to increase their power to purchase goods immediately they must arrange for the discount of the drafts which banks have accepted for them. In such cases discounting banks substitute for the time liabilities of accepting banks, represented by the drafts, their own demand liabilities.

The marketing mechanism.—Because of the fact that at least two banks are involved in any advance of immediate credit by means of the bankers' acceptance, an elaborate system of marketing accepted drafts among discounting banks has grown up in London—the oldest financial center. Bill brokers purchase drafts from drawers or endorsers, add their own endorsements and then pass them on to banks of discount. Since bill brokers are often men of little capital, they borrow heavily at banks to carry their portfolios. In times of stringency in the money market, they borrow at the Bank of England. Thus they are the first to feel the effects of increased money rates. Rapid and orderly marketing of the bills depends upon knowledge by dealers and by banks of discount of the value of the acceptors' names, consequently, the business of accepting is concentrated in a few banks.

The Federal Reserve Act simply authorized the acceptance of time drafts by national banks—a privilege not previously accorded them—and the rediscount or purchase of such accepted drafts by Federal Reserve banks. Thus, the Act made possible the existence of this type of paper. The establishment of a mechanism for marketing the drafts after acceptance was left in the hands of private business.

In 1917 the Discount Corporation of New York was organized by a group of accepting banks to deal in bankers' acceptances. Other dealers soon became active; but, in the early years, demand from discounting banks was so slight that a market could not be said to exist. The Federal Reserve banks assisted the dealers to market their bills by buying them outright or by purchasing them under 15-day repurchase agreements. They used this means to insulate the dealers against the effects of increased interest rates. Drawers and endorsers of drafts in the United States never became accustomed to marketing their own bills. Dealers generally bought direct from the accepting banks.

The second purpose of introducing the dollar bankers' acceptance into the money market—to give banks an outlet for their secondary reserves—can be accomplished on a nationwide scale only if dealers are scattered throughout the country. Some dealers, therefore, made attempts to establish branches in cities other than New York. These branch offices have either been closed or have turned their attention to Treasury bills. Centers in which there have in the past been markets are Boston, San Francisco, Cleveland, Fort Worth, Houston, and Philadelphia. At present there are only eight well-recognized dealers in bankers' acceptances, all located in New York City.[2]

The accepting banks.—Acceptances of large banks are preferred in the market to those of out-of-town, or smaller metropolitan, banks. In fact there are times when no bills will be bought in large volume by any of the discounting banks other

[2] The dealers are The New York and Hanseatic Corporation, Salomon Bros. and Hutzler, The Discount Corporation of New York, The First of Boston Corporation, The Shawmut Corporation of Boston, The M. and T. Securities Corporation, Alexander T. Stephan, and The Bankers' Discount Co. The First of Boston Corp. and the Shawmut Corp. deal in Boston but have their head offices in New York City.

than perhaps three to five large new York banks. Dr. B. H. Beckhart, of Columbia University, has estimated that of all acceptances, from 70 to 80 per cent are executed by banks in New York City at all times.[3]

The Reserve banks themselves have encouraged the concentration of the businesses of accepting and dealing in bankers' acceptances in the hands of a small group of New York City banks and dealers by means of their Open Market Investment Committee (formerly the Open Market Policy Conference.) This Committee buys bills in New York City for the account of out-of-town Reserve banks. The eleven other Reserve banks have tended more and more to buy their bills through the Committee and less and less to buy them direct from banks in their own localities.[4] Foreign funds going into the bankers' acceptance market are for the most part invested by the Federal Reserve Bank of New York.[5] These tendencies have strengthened the position of New York, and have weakened the positions of other cities, both from the point of view of the broadening of the market and of that of the encouragement of the practice of accepting by local banks.

Discounting banks.—In the past a large part of the task of extending immediately available bank credit through the discount of bankers' acceptances has consisted in Reserve bank credit, as shown by the distribution of the bankers' acceptances outstanding as reported to the American Acceptance Council between different types of investors.[6]

[3] B. H. Beckhart, *The New York Money Market,* Vol. III, p. 333. The American Acceptance Council has estimated that, for the last few years, 40 of the first 100 accepting banks have been located in New York City, 7 in Boston, 6 each in Philadelphia and San Francisco, 5 in Chicago, and 4 in Los Angeles. The remainder are scattered. In Oct., 1932 there were only 118 accepting banks in the United States. *Acceptance Bulletin,* Nov., 1932, p. 1; and April, 1933, pp. 1-3.

[4] Most of the Reserve banks gave information as to the source of bankers' acceptances which they purchased each month from 1922 through 1930 to the Senate Committee on Banking and Currency. Tables are published in *Hearings Pursuant to S. Res. 71,* Part 6, App., pp. 886-98.

[5] Some foreign banks invest in bills which are ineligible for discount at or purchase by Reserve banks. These bills are few in number and are never marketed to American banks.

[6] A graphic presentation of the total volume of dollar bankers' bills outstanding can be found in *New York Money Market,* Vol. III, p. 319, by B. H. Beckhart.

In the first four years for which data are available, the Reserve banks supported the bankers' acceptance market to such an extent that this means was used to contribute to the current inflation of credit based on Reserve bank credit. Beginning in 1928 when the French franc was stabilized and a large volume of French funds was put out at interest in New York, foreign banks supplied the funds to support the American bill market. It was not until 1930 that American banks began discounting bills with their own funds. After that, the Reserve banks stepped in only in times of great stringency—in the autumn of 1931 and again just before the banking holiday of March, 1933.

The decline in the amount of acceptances held by "others, including dealers," indicates a decrease in the holdings of banks other than accepting banks. The member bank *Call Reports* sent to the Federal Reserve Board indicate that at the end of 1928 all member banks held $212,000,000 worth of purchased acceptances, while only $49,000,000 was so held by the group of accepting banks. By the end of 1932, the amount held by all member banks was worth $405,000,000, that held by the group of accepting banks, totaling $380,000,000.

The uses of acceptance credits.—In order to enhance the marketability of bankers' acceptances, it is desirable that they possess great uniformity of quality. For this reason they are drawn only for the best types of transactions and consequently are marketed at a low rate of interest. A transaction may be defined as satisfactory if it fulfills one of two conditions: either it must represent a sale of goods passing through the channels of trade between producer and consumer, or it must be of such a nature that the goods underlying the credit may be stored in such a manner that the accepting bank may appropriate and probably sell theirs at once for enough to meet the obligation. Both types of transactions have been used as a basis for acceptance credit. In the early years of the system, the Federal Reserve Board attempted to limit the use of acceptance credits to cases where there had been a sale of goods for foreign trade. Later the Board introduced the secured draft and placed great emphasis upon restrictions of the type of security employed to protect it.

Legal regulations.—Authorization to accept time bills of exchange was granted to member banks by a provision of Section 13 of the Federal Reserve Act. Such bills were limited to those arising out of transactions involving the importation or exportation of goods and having not more than six months' sight to run. In view of the fact that the accepting bank lends only a guarantee, the aggregate amount which any member bank might accept was limited to one-half of the paid up capital and unimpaired surplus of the bank.

Federal Reserve banks were permitted, by Section 13, to rediscount acceptances of the kinds authorized for acceptance by member banks, with a maturity of not more than three months, and endorsed by a member bank. Under Section 14, they were permitted to purchase such bills in the open market, with or without the endorsement of a member bank. The Board interpreted Section 14 as permitting the purchase of acceptances based on imports and exports, with a maturity up to six months.

On March 3, 1915, the Act was amended to permit the acceptance by member banks of bills up to an aggregate amount of 100 per cent of their capital and surplus, if they had previously been granted this privilege by the Federal Reserve Board.

On September 7, 1916, the purposes for which banks were allowed to accept drafts drawn upon them were widened by an amendment to the Act. The domestic shipment draft was introduced, as was also the draft drawn against goods stored in warehouses. The maturity of these drafts was limited to six months, and they were to be fully secured by shipping documents or warehouse receipts still attached at the time of acceptance. This change in the Act represented a departure from the previous practice of limiting the bankers' acceptance to credit transactions involving an actual sale of goods and substituting the secured draft. The aggregate amount of acceptance liability which a member bank might assume on account of these new types of drafts was limited to 50 per cent of its paid up capital and unimpaired surplus.

Another type of bankers' acceptance authorized by the amendment to the Federal Reserve Act of September 7, 1916, not tied to a specific transaction, is the draft drawn by banks and bankers in foreign countries for the purpose of creating dollar exchange. The regulation of such acceptance powers was vested in the Federal Reserve Board and it has since authorized them only in the cases of countries which it has named—principally located in South America. These drafts were intended to furnish the means of stabilizing the seasonal variations in the rates of exchange of the currencies of countries which exported only one or two crops.

The limited experience with bankers' acceptances in the United States made the Federal Reserve Board lay down rather definite rules by regulations, and by opinions of counsel regarding methods which member banks should follow in accepting, and as to the methods which Federal Reserve banks should follow in discounting or purchasing them. Fear that member banks would accept drafts based on the shipment of goods between domestic points in order to provide manufacturers with working capital made the Board rule that they could not be discounted or purchased if their maturities exceeded, not three months, but the time required to finance the underlying transaction, provided this time did not exceed three months. Similarly, the length of time a warehouse acceptance was to run was limited to the "time ordinarily necessary to effect a reasonably prompt sale, shipment, or distribution into the process of manufacture or consumption."[7]

Domestic shipment drafts were further limited by rulings of the Federal Reserve Board. In the case of a draft drawn by a purchaser of goods, the maturity was limited to the time of shipment of the goods, whereas a draft drawn by the seller might have a maturity sufficient to cover sale as well as shipment, providing the terms of sale conformed to those customary in the trade.[8] In cases where there was no bona fide sale, as in a sale by corporation to its agent, the maturity of the draft was to cover the time of shipment only.[9] In 1929 the Federal Reserve Board

[7] Regulations A and B, Series of 1920, *Annual Report of the Federal Reserve Board*, 1920, pp. 289-293.

[8] *Federal Reserve Bulletin*, 1922, p. 52.

[9] *Ibid.*, 1917, p. 690.

reversed these rulings by permitting domestic shipment acceptances, whether drawn by a buyer or by a seller, to be used to cover both shipment and sale.[10] This ruling was of great significance because it gave industry the right to raise working capital through the bankers' acceptance market; and, because of the prominent part played in that market by the Reserve banks, based a part of Reserve bank credit upon the working capital needs of industry.

Bankers' acceptances based on goods stored in warehouses were at first assumed to apply to goods stored in domestic warehouses only; but the Board ruled in 1919 that they might be used to cover goods stored in foreign countries if payable in the United States in dollars, and that such drafts might be rediscounted by Reserve banks though not purchased by them in the open market.[11] Regulation B, Series of 1923, admitted such paper to the privilege of purchase by Reserve banks while Regulations A and B, Series of 1923, removed the restriction that they be payable in the United States in dollars.[12] These changes of the regulations covering warehouse acceptance credits laid the groundwork for inflation of foreign credits in later years.

The rulings and regulations, as to bankers' acceptances based on imports and exports, remained strict until 1927, when, for the first time, member banks were allowed to accept drafts after the imported or exported goods had reached their final destination, thus allowing this instrument to be used by foreign manufacturers for the provision of working capital.[13]

Data on bankers' acceptances outstanding.—The American Acceptance Council receives reports from all accepting banks of any considerable size of the volume of their acceptance liabilities at the end of the month. Since December, 1924, these reports have been received monthly. They were made occasionally before that date—March 31, 1920, through 1924, and at the end of every year. The reports of the condition of member banks on call dates give the total acceptance liabilities of these banks. The data of the American Acceptance Council are more inclu-

[10] *Ibid.*, 1929, p. 811. [11] *Ibid.*, 1919, p. 740.
[12] *Annual Report of the Federal Reserve Board*, 1923, pp. 266-71.
[13] *Federal Reserve Bulletin*, 1927, p. 860.

sive, owing to the fact that many drafts are accepted by specialized acceptance corporations—particularly the International Acceptance Bank, recently merged with the Bank of the Manhattan Co.—which is one of the banks reporting to the American Acceptance Council. Furthermore, small banks—the majority of the nonmember banks—do very little accepting. For these reasons the data published by the American Acceptance Council are nearly representative of the total amount of bankers' acceptances outstanding. The data published by the Council exceed the total of acceptances executed for customers of all member banks, including the amount executed by such corporations as the International Acceptance Bank.

Changes in the volume of bankers' acceptances outstanding.[14]—In the period for which monthly data are available, the period since December, 1924, the volume of dollar bankers' acceptances increased substantially, reaching a peak at the end of 1929. At that date, more than twice as many bills were outstanding as at the end of 1924. After 1929 the decline was rapid. At the beginning of the period under consideration, most of the bills drawn were for exports or imports. There was a gradual increase in the use of domestic warehouse acceptances, continuing until 1932, and a very rapid increase in the use of foreign storage and shipment acceptances. In 1933 these two classes of bills together accounted for more than half of the bankers' acceptances outstanding. This change in the make-up of the acceptance liabilities of banks reflects the more liberal rulings of the Federal Reserve Board, permitting greater latitude in the use of such drafts for financing the holding of goods thus keeping them off the markets.

The fact that the foreign bankers' acceptance was used to cover up loans made for nonproductive purposes is evident from figures indicating that the greatest growth of this type of credit instrument occurred in 1928, 1929, and 1930, the years when foreign long-term bonds could not be sold in American markets. Some of these credits were liquidated after the financial

[14] A graphic presentation of the total volume of acceptances outstanding distributed by purchases can be found in *New York Money Market*, Vol. III, p. 410, by B. H. Beckhart.

crisis in central Europe in 1931, but over $200,000,000 worth is still outstanding. Many of these are included in the "Stillhaltung Agreement," consummated with German banks in 1931 and renewed in 1932 and 1933, and have not been repaid. They represented, not goods in storage pending reasonably immediate sale, but credit extensions anticipatory to the flotation of long-term bond issues, which flotations never took place.

Dollar exchange drafts had a growth parallel to that of drafts drawn against goods stored in or shipped between foreign countries. The former were used in South America for the same purpose which gave rise to the latter in Central Europe.

Bankers' acceptances based on domestic transactions arise for the most part from goods stored in warehouses. There is a marked seasonal variation in this type of bill, indicating that much of this credit is liquid; but the amount outstanding each August, the month in which the seasonal variation is a minimum, increased after the decline in wholesale prices had set in in 1930. This is proof that part of these credits was used to hold goods off the market rather than to hold them over short periods of time pending orderly marketing.

Bankers' acceptances based on transactions involving the importation and exportation of goods have shown the same seasonal, and almost the same cyclical, variations as the transactions underlying these credits. Export credits increased more sharply in and after 1927 than did exports, probably reflecting the fact that export bills were being allowed with a maturity longer than formerly. Bankers' acceptances based on import and export transactions declined as rapidly as did imports and exports after 1929, indicating that the credits were liquid.

Seasonal variations in bankers' acceptances.—There is a pronounced seasonal movement in the volume of bankers' acceptances outstanding—the shape of the seasonal curve depending upon the type of transaction underlying the acceptance. All reach their low points at the end of July or August of each year. Domestic shipment acceptances and acceptances based on exports are at their maximum at the end of the year. Those based on imports rise until the end of March, while dollar exchange drafts are at their maximum at the end of January. There is no visible seasonal variation in acceptances based on goods stored in or shipped between foreign countries. The Reserve bank holdings of bankers' acceptances vary with the seasons in the same manner as do the total amount of bankers' acceptances outstanding, but the change from the low point in the summer to the high point at the end of the year is far steeper. The Reserve banks definitely intend to carry the seasonal load, freeing the funds of discounting banks for other purposes.

The use of the bankers' acceptance for inflation.—Reserve bank purchases of bankers' acceptances may be undertaken merely to stabilize the acceptance market, or as a method of releasing Federal funds to be used as bank reserves. Purchases of the former type are typified by the seasonal policy of the Reserve banks, but purchases of the latter type—except in periods of great stress such as 1931 and 1933—may serve to provide the banks with reserves upon which to expand their loan portfolios.

In the summers of 1928 and 1929, although the Reserve banks had embarked upon restrictive credit policies, their buying rates on acceptances were held so low that they absorbed more than the customary seasonal purchases of bills. In both these periods loans to brokers for the account of New York City banks rose, showing that the Reserve bank purchases of bankers' acceptances had an inflationary effect.

Proper acceptance buying policy of the Reserve banks requires that their buying rates be kept consistently a little above the open-market rate on the same kind of paper. In that case the unloading of bankers' acceptances upon Reserve banks will take place only in times of emergency, when banks are not increasing their loans for other reasons.

Relative success or failure of objectives of acceptance policy.—The intention of the framers of the Federal Reserve Act to build up a series of discount markets in Reserve-bank cities has failed to materialize although there is an active market in New York. For the first fifteen years of Federal Reserve operation, the willingness of the Reserve banks to buy acceptances in unlimited amounts prevented the use of this market as an outlet for secondary reserves of banks. Since that time Reserve-bank buying rates have been held slightly above market rates on bankers' acceptances and banks have bought bills with a view to turning them into cash by sale to Reserve banks at times of stringency. Their success with this policy in October, 1931, and February, 1933, and the rapidity with which the member banks undertook to carry the burden of discounting acceptances should be a recommendation of that policy. There is some hope that large metropolitan banks may invest their secondary reserves in bankers' acceptances. Unless out-of-town Reserve banks buy all their bills locally, there is no prospect that outside markets will develop.

The purely nationalistic aim of establishing the bankers' acceptance in the United States—to finance foreign trade at home—has been a partial success. However in their great haste to establish the dollar bankers' acceptance, the Federal Reserve Board has permitted these bills to be used to finance frozen and capital transactions not foreseen at the time when the Act was passed. Import and export bills have elsewhere represented the best credit risks and have responded most to changes in trade. Warehouse credits—particularly foreign warehouse credits—have been misused. By their very nature they are fitted for use for speculative purposes. If granted in large amounts they will bring about a decline in the confidence of bankers in the dollar acceptance as an investment, and will prevent the establishment of a permanent discount market.

CHAPTER XXXII

OPEN-MARKET OPERATIONS[1]

In the course of its adjustments to the ever-changing conditions in American banking and finance, the Federal Reserve system has experimented with various instruments of credit control. While attempting to bolster their respective earnings, several of the Reserve banks purchased $400,000,000 of government securities during the first five months of 1922.[2] These purchases, much to the surprise of the banks, failed to accomplish their purpose, for the net earnings of the system dropped from $82,000,000 in the previous year, to $16,000,000 in 1922.[3] The result was something quite unexpected. According to the Federal Reserve Bank of New York,

> The consequences of this operation, together with large gold imports, was to reduce discounts to member banks at the Federal Reserve banks from over $1,000,000,000 to $400,000,000 and thus put the banks in a position to advance funds more freely to their customers and to increase their investments. It seems likely that this step aided in some measure the recovery of business and agriculture from the depressed conditions of 1921. Purchases were also followed by reductions in discount rates at several reserve banks and by increases in the total volume of bank credit.[4]

The Cleveland Reserve bank thought that the purchases also resulted in an increase in brokers' loans.[5]

In June the Reserve banks began disposing of their over-filled portfolios of government securities, mainly in order to aid the Federal Treasury to carry out its redemption program as inex-

[1] Written by Eli Tash.

[2] *Hearings before a Subcommittee of the Committee on Banking and Currency of the United States Senate,* 71st Cong., 3d sess., pursuant to S. Res. 71, 1931, pp. 794-894, questionnaire no. 9, question no. 2; and Strong, B., *Interpretations of Federal Reserve Policy,* ed. by W. R. Burgess, New York, 1930, p. 235.

[3] *Annual Report of the Federal Reserve Board,* 1928, p. 162.

[4] *Hearings Pursuant to S. Res. 71,* 1931, pp. 803-4.

[5] *Ibid.,* pp. 800, 812.

pensively as possible.[6] By July, 1923, $525,000,000 of government securities had been dumped on the market. The several Reserve banks conducted their sales separately until October, 1922, when the Committee of Governors of Reserve banks took over the duty of supervising the execution of orders for the individual banks.[7]

The impetus that had developed in trade and commerce continued at a steady growth, apparently in spite of the 1922-1923 sales of securities by the Reserve banks. These sales appeared to be offset by an increase in the volume of rediscount accommodations sought by member banks. The juxtaposition of events made it appear as if the new purchases of Government securities during the early months of 1922 had, by relieving the member banks of the responsibility of increasing their rediscount obligations to the Reserve banks, checked the prolonged liquidation which followed the midsummer collapse of prices in 1920. Then when the Reserve banks were disposing of part of their security portfolios, rediscounts were again rising. As business activity continued to increase in volume and intensity toward the close of the year, the Reserve officials were faced with the urgent question as to whether they could put a damper on excessive speculative activities by more sales of Government securities, which would again force member banks to rediscount, and thus take upon themselves the responsibility for further credit expansion.

It was the resolution to attempt to answer this question empirically, as well as to aid the Treasury, that led the Reserve banks to create a more efficient centralized supervision of open-market operations. On April 1, 1923, the Committee of Governors was superseded by the Open-Market Investment Committee for the Reserve system.[8] The new committee consisted of five members from the eastern Reserve banks, and was under the general supervision of the Federal Reserve Board. Its duty was to devise and recommend plans for the purchase, sale, and distribution of the open-market portfolios of the Reserve banks.

[6] *Ibid.*, pp. 795 ff; 804; and Strong, *Interpretations*, p. 86.
[7] *Op. cit.*, Strong, p. 236; also, *Hearings Pursuant to S. Res. 71*, 1931, p. 804.
[8] Strong, *Interpretations*, pp. 238-39.

The Committee did not interfere with the local operations of the several banks, its dealings being confined strictly to system accounts or joint dealings for all the banks as a unit. All actions of the Committee were subject to ratification by the directors of each Reserve bank before becoming effective as to that bank. Since all purchases and sales of any considerable amount, however, had to be made in New York City through the local Reserve bank, because of the nonexistence of any other market for "governments," the banks in the financial hinterlands had no alternative in practice to the program adopted by the Committee, which could always plead peculiar and intimate knowledge of the market in favor of its decisions. On April 13, 1923, the Open-Market Investment Committee held its first meeting.[9] From that date on, until superseded by the Open-Market Policy Conference on March 25, 1930, it supervised the purchases and sales for system account.

In this fashion did the Reserve system enter upon its career of open-market operations. During 1922 and 1923 the Reserve banks discovered, quite by accident, the possibilities of open-market dealings in Government securities as an instrument of credit-control. The fortuitous manner of revealing the efficiency of open-market correctives in bringing pressure upon the credit positions of member banks is of great significance in interpreting the apparently aimless wanderings of subsequent open-market policies. Two facts appeared to be clear to the Reserve authorities as they emerged from their 1922-1923 operations. First, it was shown that purchases and sales of Government obligations by the Reserve banks directly influenced the reserve position of the members banks. Secondly, they were convinced that open-market operations constituted a potent instrument of credit-control only when administered jointly by all the Reserve banks. The remaining characteristics of the open-market instruments would unfold themselves with further experimentation.

Indeed at the very outset of its *Annual Report,* for 1923, the Board informed the Speaker of the House of Representatives that the new developments of the past two years had been of

[9] *Hearings Pursuant to S. Res. 71,* 1931, p. 799.

such a nature as to warrant a dismissal of the customary technical summary of the activities of the year in favor of a purely theoretical analysis of central bank credit-control as administered by its newly found instrument.[10]

When one-name commercial paper had been made ineligible for open-market purchases, it was generally believed that the open-market powers of the Reserve banks had been rendered impotent as a medium of credit control; and so it was, but during the World War the United States Government borrowed some $26,000,000,000 from its banks and citizens. The Reserve banks had considered their dealings in Government bonds and certificates, at best, a patriotic duty which they must perform as an adjunct toward winning the War. When these securities remained within the banking structure after the termination of hostilities, they correctly viewed them with alarm as containing a dead weight of long-term loans upon the banking assets of the country. The habit of securing advances at preferential rates by offering their Government securities as collateral had placed the member banks in the position from which they entered the inflationary post-armistice period.

The Reserve system had found a new banking technique. Its immediate task resolved itself into determining the use which it wished to make of the open-market instrument. As Federal Reserve policy vacillated from objective to objective, it became increasingly difficult to gauge the effectiveness of the open-market technique. Counterbalancing actions on the part of the Reserve banks themselves, and improper promulgation of their operations, made it appear that at times open-market transactions were a vital part of the Administration's credit policies, while in other instances they were quite impotent.[11] It is necessary to inquire into the actual effectiveness of open-market dealings in Government securities as an instrument of central-bank policy. Out of the maze of activity with Government bonds since 1923, two challenging questions present themselves: Can they

[10] *Annual Report of the Federal Reserve Board,* 1923, p. 1.

[11] Cf., Chamber of Commerce of the U.S.A.; *Report of the Banking and Currency Committee on the Federal Reserve System;* and also, *Auxiliary Statements,* Washington, 1929.

aid in the efficient promulgation of any program which the Reserve system seeks to impose upon the nation's banking and financial business? Do they possess any power over the national credit fund? If we have answered these questions in the affirmative, we must pursue the further inquiry: Have open-market operations unduly fostered speculation, especially in securities, while failing to exercise the necessary curb upon credit expansion when the process is reversed?

In order to determine the potential capacity of open-market operations to affect the credit structure of the nation, it will be necessary to analyze first the nature of the instrument itself and observe the manner in which it operates upon the banking and credit institutions of the country. We must follow this with an analysis of the application of the instrument by the Reserve banks, observing, meanwhile, the limitation upon the functions that it can perform; and, finally, we shall note the effectiveness of the open-market technique as actually applied. Having examined the open-market instrument in this fashion, we shall attempt to formulate principles of open-market policy and lend a word of caution against attributing too much potency to the unsupported instrument. This caution applies both to the capacity to aid, as well as to harm, business and commerce. Put specifically, we must beware of attributing sole responsibility for the catastrophic speculative expansion of the 1920's to the purchases of Government securities in 1922, 1924, and 1927, just as we must not expect open-market policies to be able, alone, to check the economic and financial stagnation which set in at the closing of the third decade of the century. Nevertheless, our findings will prompt us to ask: Were the open-market policies of the Federal Reserve system in any way responsible for the national banking moratorium which followed the inauguration of the President of the United States on March 4, 1933?

Nature of the open-market instrument.—The essential characteristic of the open-market powers of the Reserve banks is the capacity to go directly into the money market either to purchase or sell bills and Government securities.[12] The important aspect

[12] *Annual Report of the Federal Reserve Board,* 1923, p. 11.

of this power is that the Reserve banks may (1) deal with any one within the market, and (2) buy and sell at their own discretion without being forced to wait until dealers or banks come to them to buy or sell. This freedom of action is limited only by the types of paper in which the banks may deal. They may buy and sell any obligation of the United States without restriction. They may deal in only those municipal tax-anticipation notes which mature within six months of the date of purchase.[13] Trade- and bank-acceptances also are eligible for purchase by the Reserve banks. Although the original Reserve Act required that acceptances be based on imports and exports,[14] a later amendment permitted their use in domestic shipments, the storage of readily marketable staples, and for the express purpose of creating dollar exchange. The Reserve banks are further authorized to deal in cable transfers and gold coin or bullion at home or abroad. Each of the twelve Reserve banks has formulated its own standards which recognized dealers must attain in order to do business with the Reserve bank. They have developed also the practice of purchasing Government securities and acceptances under agreement with their dealers to repurchase them within fifteen days.[15] These agreements, according to the Reserve banks, have played only a minor rôle in the open-market dealings of the system.

The open-market portfolio contains paper of varying maturities. The holdings of United States securities range from one-day certificates of indebtedness, through 30-, 60-, and 90-day Treasury notes, to long-term bonds.[16] The predominant proportion of "governments" is well over thirty days' maturity. Many of the acceptances, on the other hand, have maturities of less than thirty days, so that it is possible for the Reserve banks to reduce their holdings by simply refraining from further pur-

[13] Section 14, Federal Reserve Act.

[14] Willis, H. P., and Steiner, W. H., *Federal Reserve Banking Practice*, New York, 1926, pp. 487-89; see also, *op. cit.*, Chamber of Commerce of U.S.A., *Auxiliary Statements*, p. 18.

[15] *Hearings Pursuant to S. Res. 71*, 1931, pp. 794-947 for complete statements of Open-market operations and Bankers Acceptances.

[16] *Annual Report of the Federal Reserve Board*, 1928, pp. 73-75; *Ibid.*, 1931, pp. 51-54.

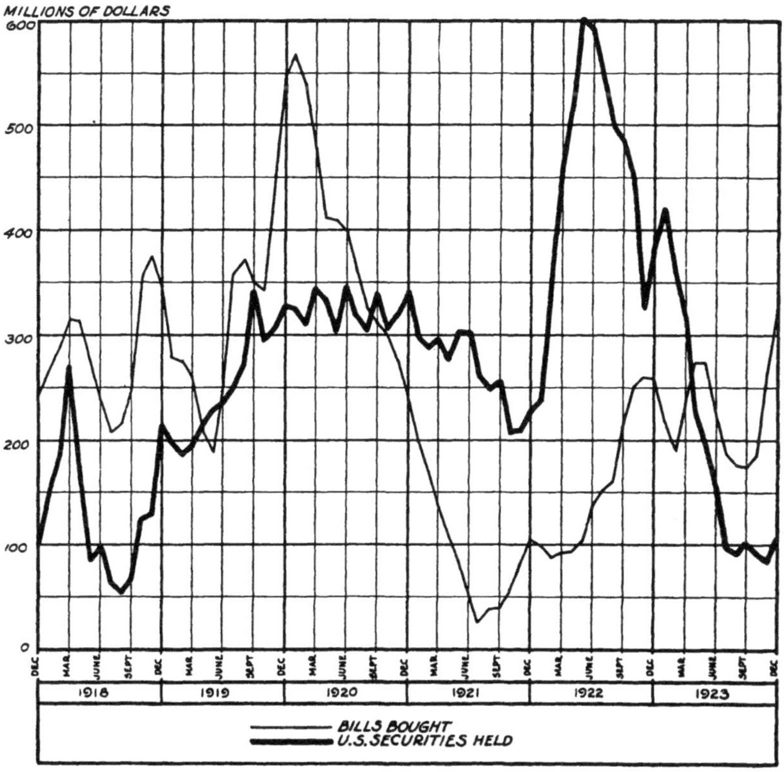

CHART XX. BILLS BOUGHT AND UNITED STATES SECURITIES HELD BY THE FEDERAL RESERVE SYSTEM

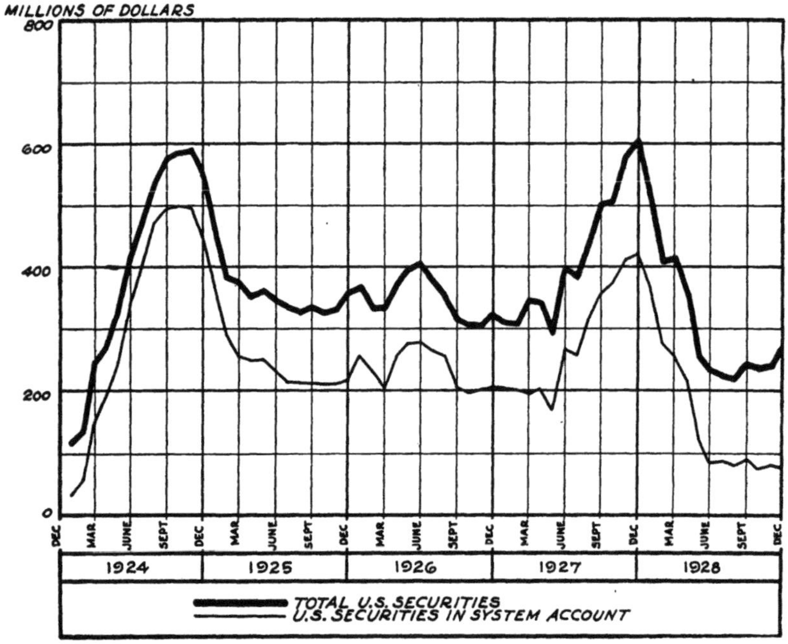

CHART XXI. UNITED STATES GOVERNMENT SECURITIES HELD BY FEDERAL RESERVE BANKS: TOTAL AMOUNT AND AMOUNT HELD FOR THE ACCOUNT OF THE SYSTEM chases. As their portfolios tend to be filled with government securities and foreign and domestic short-term paper based on the storage of goods, their easy liquidity is lost. When goods fail to move or foreign exchange cannot be secured to liquidate the paper, the Reserve banks are forced to renew the instruments. This, together with the tying up of funds in "governments," seems to have been the cause of the "frozen" condition of the Reserve banks which forced them to seek a national moratorium on banking in March, 1933.

Prior to December 15, 1923, each of the Reserve banks operated in the open market independently of the others. In October, 1922, efforts were made to coördinate their sales of Government securities, but it was not until the former date that joint purchases were undertaken for "System" account.[17] After the establishment of this joint account, all major operations in Government securities were conducted through it. A glance at Chart XX readily reveals how completely the open-market policies of the Reserve banks were executed through the joint account of the system. The Federal Reserve Bank of New York acted as the agent and handled the system's orders which were executed in New York. To that extent this bank assumed an undue importance in determining the open-market policy of the group.

Controls in operating the open-market instrument.—In conducting its buying and selling campaigns in the open market, the Reserve system can exercise four possible controls: (1) over the volume of credit; (2) over the timing of the change in volume; (3) over the "rate" to be charged or paid; (4) over the "selection" of credits that it will grant.

Volume control.—This is the regulation of the total volume of purchases and sales. By increasing its purchases, the Reserve system can make an equivalent amount of credit available for reserves of member banks. The payments which it makes for the securities acquired through open-market purchases eventually find their way back to the Reserve banks in the form of member-bank deposits. These deposits are the legal reserves of the

[17] *Ibid.*, 1928, p. 74; Also, *Hearings Pursuant to S. Res. 71*, pp. 825-840.

member banks, and may be used as a basis for further loans by them. Similarly, by increasing its sales in the open-market, the Reserve system may curtail the amount of credit available to member banks or force them to rediscount an equivalent amount of paper. Should member banks not have paper eligible for discount, they would have to resort to direct loans, or "advances," from the Reserve banks in order to maintain their previous level of reserves.

As a matter of practice, the Reserve banks have restricted their control over the volume of open-market operations to dealings in Government securities. In order to carry out their policy of supporting the domestic acceptance market, they were forced to relinquish their initiative in their purchases of bills. It has been the policy of the Reserve banks to buy any bills brought to them by accredited dealers at the established rates. The Committee of the Chamber of Commerce of the United States of America concluded regarding this plan:

> Except in recent months, therefore, open-market dealings in acceptances by reserve banks have resembled rediscount operations more than open market dealings in government securities. In bill purchases the reserve banks have assumed at least as passive a rôle as in the granting of rediscount accommodations.[18]

It has been commonly assumed that the Reserve system has an unlimited capacity to make purchases in the open market. Not only is it limited by the amount of eligible paper available, but also it is unable to make purchases for more than a given percentage of its total assets. It has been estimated that 35 per cent of the total assets of the system are available for open-market purchases.[19] Although certain writers have argued to the contrary, it seems to the present writer that the only restriction upon the extent to which the Reserve system could divest itself of its entire portfolio, if an emergency required such action, is the capacity of the market to absorb the sales. It seems to be the case dur-

[18] Chamber of Commerce of the U.S.A.; *Report of the Committee on Federal Reserve System, Auxiliary Statements*, p. 21; see also, *Hearings Pursuant to S. Res. 71*, p. 841.

[19] Shaw, W. A. *The Theory and Principles of Central Banking, in England and the United States*, London, 1930, p. 215.

ing a crisis, when the Reserve banks find it necessary to mobilize their assets, that the panicky condition of the market, which is creating the need for liquid funds in the first instance, will wipe out most of the buyers as such. Thus, we are inevitably drawn to the conclusion that the capacity of the Reserve banks to sell their open-market securities is dependent to a great extent upon the conditions prevailing in the chief money markets of the nation. In particular, the state of the New York money market will determine the limits to the volume of securities that can be sold at any given time. When the facts of the banking crisis of February-March, 1933, are released to the public, it is quite likely that the truth of the above argument will be illustrated. When the panicky demands for currency flooded the Reserve banks, the $2,000,000,000 of their assets invested in United States securities proved to be quite solidly frozen. By making unprecedented purchases of these securities in the early part of 1932, the Reserve banks deliberately made themselves vulnerable to just such a "squeeze."

Aside from abandoning the legal reserve requirements, the only manner in which the Reserve banks could meet the demand for additional currency was to turn back to the stricken market and ask it to produce the funds which it was itself demanding. The capacity of the Reserve banks to decrease their open-market portfolios is, thus, quite inextricably linked with the time element, which will be discussed below. Over a period of time, the entire holdings of United States securities could be driven out of the Reserve system into the hands of private investors, and, judging from the experience with the 1924, 1927, and 1932 purchases, this seems to be a most advisable policy for the Reserve system to pursue.

The absolute deterrents upon the volume of open-market purchases, which the Reserve system can make, are, aside from the dictates of sound policy, the willingness of the market (or the Treasury) to sell, plus the total of available assets of the system.[20] The supply of government securities and bills offered by dealers is a function of money-market conditions and the fiscal policy of

[20] *Ibid.*, pp. 215-19.

the United States Treasury, over both of which the Reserve system has very little, if any, control. The Reserve banks, however, can have no assurance that either purchases or sales in the open market will affect the total fund of national credit; nor do they know the extent to which their actions will be countervailed by existing conditions in the national economy. We shall reserve for our discussion below an evaluation of the effectiveness of the "volume" control over the credit available to the community.

Timing control.—The second control over open-market operations is that of timing. It is of vital importance that purchases coincide with the seasonal expansion of business and the harvest demand for foreign exchange to facilitate the flow of exports. The great exodus of farm products each year is accomplished in an orderly procession mainly because of the ready purchase of bills by the Reserve banks. The cyclical timing of purchases and sales is equally as important as, and decidedly more difficult than, the determination of seasonal operations. If the system anticipates a future need to control the money market by substantial sales, it must first build up its portfolio by careful purchases which will not foster the very condition that it seeks to correct. While the fairly even seasonal pulsations of business present the basic elements of a proper seasonal credit policy, the complexities of the relationship between credit and business in the various stages of economic cycles have often led to the adoption of ineffectual and contradictory policies. While open-market purchases in 1927 led to a dangerous period of security speculation, purchases of $1,200,000,000 of government securities in 1932 apparently only served to freeze the assets of the Reserve system. The proper timing of open-market operations is the most difficult and most important problem that the Reserve system must face in the near future. The paramount function of the Open-Market Policy Conference, and the Open-Market Committee,[21] which it superseded, is to determine the proper promulgation of the buying and selling programs of the system. Aside from its general effect upon the credit condition of the country, open-

[21] Chamber of Commerce of the U.S.A.; *Report of the Committee on Federal Reserve System, Auxiliary Statements,* p. 22.

market operations in Government securities must be timed (according to Reserve officials) so as not to embarrass the funding and redemption operations of the Federal Treasury.[22] Whether the Reserve banks should modify their credit policies in deference to Treasury needs will be discussed below when we consider the functional use of open-market operations. It must suffice here merely to point out the importance of timing as an element in open-market control.

Rate control.—Buying rates present an equally difficult and complex control of open-market operations. In so far as purchases are confined to Government issues, the rates have no significant bearing upon the problem of control of banking by regulating the "price" of funds; and in bill purchases, the stated policy of the Reserve system supporting the domestic acceptance market and encouraging the use of dollar exchange has forced the Reserve banks to "follow the open-market rates, established by accepting houses."[23] Thus the rate-making control over open-market operations has been relinquished by the Reserve banks. The only rate problem has been that of determining the Reserve buying rates with reference to the rates prevailing in the market. Not all the banks are in agreement as to whether the Reserve schedule of rates should be maintained slightly above, even with, or below, the prevailing market rates.[24] In general, the practice has been to fix the rates at a point which would discourage extensive unloading, except when dealers found the private markets clogged. At the same time the Reserve system has taken a position of readiness to stand behind the dealers in the event they should find it necessary to dispose of their portfolios. It was in connection with this purpose of the Reserve banks that the repurchase agreement was developed.[25] According to its terms a dealer who is temporarily pressed for funds will dispose of part of his portfolio to a Reserve bank with agreement to repurchase the bills within fifteen days.

[22] *Hearings Pursuant to S. Res. 71*, 1931, p. 804.

[23] *Ibid.*, p. 920 and Questionnaire No. 10, questions no. 9, 12 (especially part *c*), 23, and 24, pp. 841 ff.

[24] *Ibid.*, pp. 879-81.

[25] *Ibid.*, pp. 849, 946, 947 (question no. 33); see also nos. 29, 30, 31 and 32.

Rates on government securities have similarly been an ineffectual means of controlling the outflow of credit into the community. As most of the Government securities are issues of the Federal Government, any raising of the rates would meet with the opposition of the Treasury, which seeks to market its issues as cheaply as possible. During the War the entire rate structure of the Reserve system was subordinated to the desire of the Government to float its bonds. To what extent political pressure has been exerted by the Treasury Department upon the buying rate for Government securities in later years is a moot question. As the Government piles up larger and larger deficits, and as it indulges in extra-budgetary economic experiments requiring repeated resort to the bond market, we can safely assume that the temptation to exert such pressure upon the Reserve system becomes exceedingly powerful.

Another aspect of paramount importance in rate control is the relationship that should exist between the open-market schedules and the rediscount rates established by the Reserve banks. Consideration of this fundamental relationship has been deferred until the analysis of the functional uses of the open-market instrument can be considered.

Selectivity control.—The final control over open-market operations is selectivity in buying paper in the money market. The Reserve banks may seek to restrict the flow of credit to industries which are unduly expanded by refusing to buy paper drawn or accepted by members of the industry. Excess flow of funds to specific areas might be checked by eliminating bills originating in that area from the purchases of the open-market portfolio. Such practices would raise a hue and cry against discrimination and financial dictatorship over industry. It is mainly the fear of such charges of favoritism that has restrained the use of selectivity as an instrument of control by the Reserve banks. The Federal Reserve Bank of New York has stated explicitly that it "does not discriminate in the buying rate for bills on the basis of the transactions underlying the bill, for the market would never discriminate in that way." The bank believes "it would be harmful to the position of dollar exchange bills in world markets as well as at home if such discrimination were attempted. . . . Such a practise, in our opinion, would make for untold confusion in the discount market."[26] Nevertheless, should the Reserve banks have the courage to carry out their convictions regarding the undue expansion that may occur from time to time in different industries, they will have a comparatively powerful weapon against inflation by proper selectivity in their open-market purchases. Similarly, they could sponsor credit-starved industries with preferential rates and direct purchase of their bills. This power, however, is limited by the extent to which overextended industries are financed in the open market. As the Reserve system tends to concentrate its open-market operations in Government securities, its power of discrimination would be restricted to exerting pressure against banks which are financing the expansion in industry. Whether such use of pressure is legal is a debatable matter.

Operation of the open-market instrument.—We have described the construction of the open-market machine and have commented upon the several control "gadgets" that it possesses. Let us observe how it generates power. What happens when a Reserve bank buys or sells in the open market? First, as to a sale, an open-market sale by the Reserve system withdraws funds from the market. When the dealers pay for the securities, which they purchase from the Reserve banks, in checks drawn against their banks, the result is to reduce the amount of reserve deposits of those member banks from which the funds are finally taken. These member banks have the alternative of rebuilding their impaired reserves by rediscounting, securing more gold, or securing advances from their Reserve banks, on one hand; or, on the other, of curtailing their outstanding loans and investments so as to restore their reserve ratios. Whether these banks rebuild their reserve balances or decrease their loans depends upon several factors. The demands for funds exerted by the community for business, financial, and speculative purposes will in part determine their decisions. Their own *feeling* as to the wisdom of trimming their credit sails as well as the ease or difficulty with

[26] *Ibid.*, p. 920.

which they can rebuild their reserves will also affect their ultimate policy. A countervailing flow of gold inward may take the decision out of their hands by rebuilding their reserves automatically. They may not all decide upon the same policy. Underlying these general conditions, which help to determine member-bank credit action, are several specific influences, such as the current phase of the business cycle; the state of business psychology (panicky, cautious, wavering, confident, optimistic, speculative); the demand rates for additional funds; the marginal surplus of unemployed funds of the community; and the ease or difficulty of getting more funds.

Functional use of open-market operations.—With this short review of the nature of open-market dealings in mind, we may now turn to an analysis of the functions which they perform in the American banking structure. What these functions will be depends entirely upon the particular Federal Reserve policy of which the open-market transactions are an instrument in any given situation. As the purpose of Reserve action varies, we naturally may expect to find a changing efficiency of the open-market mechanism. It is not a cure-all for all banking and credit ailments. A considerable degree of the apparent ineffectiveness of open-market operations may be explained in this multiplicity of purposes for which they are used. Often their efficiency has been impaired by a hesitating vacillation between different policies by the Reserve authorities. On other occasions they have been applied for purposes to which they are functionally unsuited in our present banking structure. Sometimes they have been used as instruments of conflicting purposes so that the net effect has been to offset the opposing operations. On other occasions the policies themselves have been faulty and impossible of attainment even with perfect instruments. We shall discover that what, at times, appeared to be a limitation upon the effectiveness of open-market operations was, in reality, owing to the inefficient use of the mechanism by the Reserve banks. This has been particularly true on those occasions when the authorities failed to coördinate their open-market activities with their rediscount policies.

Much of this lack of consistency in the policies of the Reserve system was because of its unfamiliarity with the newly discovered tool and attempts, through experimentation, to gauge its actual effectiveness. The end of a decade of such very costly experiments left the authorities in rather complete disagreement as to the proper functions of the open-market powers of the Reserve banks.[27]

The several functions which have been variously assigned to open-market operations, and which have been advanced as the reasons for many purchases and sales, fall into two general categories. These may be termed broadly (1) institutional and (2) credit-control functions.

The first group comprises those miscellaneous functions not included in the second category. It includes all possible functions of the Reserve system exclusive of the so-called credit-control function. The institutional controls may seek to manipulate the credit instruments of the Reserve system in order to correct the gold flow, the reserve ratio, the earning position of the system, or the fiscal and financial stringencies of the Federal Treasury. They may seek to aid business and commerce or ease a tense political situation.

The credit-control function seeks to augment the supply of credit so as to affect the price level of the country. It is based upon the quantum analysis of money and credit, with the belief that changes in the monetary side of the equation of exchange can be so controlled as to direct the movements in the price level and production factors of the equation. The credit-control concept of central bank operations assumes a causal relationship flowing from the volume of outstanding credit to the price level and the volume of production. It further assumes a central-bank capacity effectively to regulate the volume of credit. We shall presently consider the applicability of such a credit-control function to open-market operations.

Substitute for discount control.—Among the "institutional" functions of open-market transactions, as expounded by several Reserve officials and some economists, is the concept that open-

[27] *Ibid.*, Part VI, pp. 794-825.

market operations may be substituted for discount control by the Reserve banks. This concept arises out of the notion that member banks will follow the hint delicately given by any change in the open-market operations of the Reserve system. The banking community will be persuaded to regulate its credit policies, it is argued, without waiting for the stimulant of an altered rediscount rate. John M. Keynes thinks that open-market operations can influence "the member banks to move in step with one another in the direction indicated and desired by the Central Bank."[28] This point of view has been somewhat extended in the custom among some Reserve banks of regarding an open-market operation as in itself a sufficient check to any undesirable credit tendency. They have repeatedly made sales in the open-market with the avowed intention of curtailing an incipient or already expressed inflationary tendency. They did not follow this policy with an increase in the rediscount rate.

There can be no question that it has become a customary practice of member banks to remain indebted to their Reserve banks by means of rediscounts and "advances" whenever they deem such a course to be profitable. Although John M. Keynes himself seems to be somewhat confused as to whether a change in the volume of purchases will tend to provoke an opposite change in the volume of rediscounts, he is, nevertheless, quite explicit in stating that "the history of the Federal Reserve system since the war has been, first of all, a great abuse of the latitude thus accorded to Member Banks to increase the 'advances' of the Reserve Banks."[29] This has been the case because the Reserve authorities have not seen fit to raise the rediscount rate as a concomitant to open-market sales. They have acted on the assumption that the open-market operation is a substitute for the change in the discount rate.

Control the money market.—The past experience of the Reserve system has disclosed a surprising functional relationship between open-market operations and the money market.[30] The Reserve Act is explicit in its attempt to divorce the system from

[28] Keynes, J. M., *A Treatise on Money*, Edinburgh, 1930, Vol. II, pp. 253-55.
[29] *Ibid.*, Vol. II, p. 239.
[30] *Hearings Pursuant to S. Res. 71*, 1931, p. 7.

the New York money market. The Reserve Board has made repeated efforts to plug the system's credits against the draining influence of the security markets. Yet a bank executive, in a memorandum of December 26, 1924, wrote that the only definite effect of the 1924 purchases was a price advance in the security market.[31] How has it come about that open-market operations are reflected in changes in the amount of brokers' loans, and the only direct effect upon prices is found in the securities markets? The question is of considerable importance. If reserve credits released in the open-market tend to remain there and result in an inflation of security values, the functional effectiveness of this means of credit release is highly questionable. Some have believed that the Reserve banks should seek to control the money market "in the hope that (through it) we can maintain a control that will check or prevent an inordinate use of credit beyond the legitimate demands of commerce and industry."[32] The conclusion, however, is based on the assumption that there is extreme fluidity in the supply of credit as it meets the relative demands of industry, finance, and commerce. A member of the Reserve Board, thinks this fluidity does not exist. He testified before the Senate Hearings as follows: "Where money first tends to go, it has a tendency to stay. . . . It is sometimes very sluggish in its movement and tends to remain where it is first put out—that is, the New York call-loan market. It will stick there if there is a good demand for it."[33] Open-market purchases, for the most part, have consisted of "governments." The New York dealers receive the funds and deposit them with the local banks, thus increasing the New York banks' reserve balances. Upon the basis of these balances the banks place new loans in the New York market. According to this member's testimony, the banks, "finding their reserves increased, are obliged to go out and find some use for this new money." They rarely find it immediately by increasing their commercial loans. They are, therefore, almost of necessity compelled to buy investment securities or open-market paper or to make so-called open-market loans, of which the most familiar type is the call loan.[34]

[31] *Ibid.*, p. 807. [32] *Ibid.*, p. 73. [33] *Ibid.*, p. 149.
[34] *Ibid.*, p. 135. The word "they" is substituted for "it."

Regardless of its effectiveness as such an instrument, the proper function of open-market operations is not to control the money market. The open-market portfolio should primarily serve to reinforce the discount policy of the Federal Reserve so as to aid business and commerce and agriculture. While the state of the money-market and the regulation of market rates is of considerable social importance, the objective of the open-market instrument should lie elsewhere.

Aid and assist business, commerce and agriculture.—Can open-market operations aid and assist business? While the experience of the past decade may seem to point to a negative conclusion, there are several circumstances which lead us to suspect that, under proper conditions, Reserve "purchase" portfolios can be an effective aid to business. Many of the failures in the past have been due to errors in policy or incompetent handling and administration of the open-market technique. The Banking Act of 1933 has unqualifiedly empowered the Reserve system to employ the principle of selectivity in granting credits. The Reserve Board already has the power to regain its lost initiative in the bill market; and the integration of the discount, and purchase activities of the system can be easily accomplished with a courageous and independent board.

In spite of these possibilities, the control of credit to conform to the needs of business is, at best, a very difficult task. The problem of ascertaining the proper credit rations for specific industries and commercial enterprises is fraught with manifold statistical difficulties. Legally, the system cannot extend credit to one industry so as to jeopardize the credit needs of other industries. Administratively, it is difficult to ascertain precisely what credit policy should be adopted. Reliance upon statistical guidance introduces a time-lag that may seriously offset the value of the operation. In the absence of any single definitive guide, the Reserve system has adopted the practice of watching a series of indices through which it expects to discover the trends and needs of industry and commerce; but the very multiplicity of guides proves the haphazardness of the statistical control.

Credit-control functions.—Without in any way seeking to evaluate the theoretical validity of the theorists' claim of a causal relation between credit and prices and production, there are certain practical obstacles to the conversion of such a theory into a working banking policy. According to sundry theorists, the sole guide to credit regulation is the maintenance of a stable price level. Dismissing the difficulty of constructing a satisfactory price index which will be significant for credit regulation without too great a time-lag, we find other difficulties confronting a price stabilization policy for open-market dealings. Central bank credit control should be both qualitative and quantitative. The quantity theorist, focusing attention on general price levels, ignores the specific needs of individual enterprises. He is concerned only with "changes in the value of money" which he assumes to have a uniform effect upon all prices. Qualitative control, such as selectivity in the rationing or release of credit to specific industries, geographic distribution of credit, and the timing of the release of credit, are all relegated to commercial banks. Central banks are to exercise merely quantitative credit control. Some advocates of monetary control have refined the quantitative problem into a dual system of equilibria between production and consumption on one hand, and savings and capital goods on the other; but they, also, have failed to consider the qualitative aspects of credit control.

As at present constituted, the Federal Reserve system cannot achieve quantitative credit control in the theoretic meaning. Although, in their open-market operations, the Reserve banks deal with nonmember banks and institutions as well as with member banks, they by no means have a direct contact with all the private banks in the country. Even with our rather extensive development of banking data in the United States, we have practically no information as to the credit policies of nonmember banks. There is no way of ascertaining whether an inflow of gold into the vaults of these state banks will result in increased deposits. We do not know how much deposits they have outstanding at any particular time. Should the Reserve system adopt a policy of credit restriction, the state banks could adopt one of expansion (as they may well have done in 1928 and 1929), or *vice versa*.

We are inevitably drawn to the conclusion that, even if it were desirable, administrative obstacles would defeat any effort to establish credit control through open-market operations. For an instrument cannot be effective over factors which it cannot control or influence.

Principles and technique of proper open-market policies.—The foregoing analysis of open-market operations, by the process of limitation and exclusion, has defined the proper functioning of the open-market instrument of Federal Reserve policy in terms of the undesirable practices which should not be undertaken. Only negatively has a constructive program for an efficient open-market policy been suggested. An attempt is made below to present in brief a synthesized and positive statement of the proper operation of the Reserve open-market portfolio.

Recognition of the essential characteristic of a Central Bank as the performance of a public service, in contradistinction to a commercial bank which seeks to acquire a maximum of profits, is the first step in a proper understanding of the efficient operation of the open-market instrument. This assumption of the public nature of the Reserve banks does not, however, eliminate the difficulties discussed above. It clarifies the issue, but leaves the fundamental problems to be solved. The task of ascertaining the proper functions of the public service institution remains. Once having selected those functions which are to be performed, we must develop an efficient technique for achieving these ends under the complex shiftings of our financial and economic institutions. We have determined the nature of our organism. There remains the necessity of plotting a course of action for it, and then providing a technique of action with which it can attain its goal.

The primary function of open-market operations is to aid in maintaining the two-fold equilibrium of a balanced production with consumption and a balanced saving with capital needs. These balances should be established in the international as well as the domestic economic and financial activities of the country. As the space-time gap between production and consumption widens with the increasing complexity of our industrial organization, the task of maintaining a fluid equilibrium is rendered more difficult. Similarly, the widening of the space-time interval between the expending of labor and the realization of income has further complicated the problem. The rapidity of the changes in the industrial, economic, and financial arts makes it almost impossible for the *entrepreneur,* worker, or financier to realize the consequences of their economic decisions. The fortuitous element of social accretion, which has contributed to many individual incomes, lends force to the speculative urge to acquire gambling gains. The extensive development of our credit institutions, together with the increasing complexity of industrial processes, permits anticipatory action. We can save before we have earned an income from which we expect to acquire a surplus fund. Production must precede, and often create, consumption demand. This complex system of anticipatory actions offers many openings for uneconomic digressions which result in disturbing our two-fold equilibrium.

Thus we come to our first principle of credit administration: the alignment of production with consumption. Specific production can be controlled by regulating the supply of credit available to industry. To achieve this control two canons of action must be applied. The supply of credit must be adjusted to the demand for funds in the first case. In the second, the demand for funds should be restrained or expanded to adjust to the controlled supply of credit. The first canon has been regularly employed by the Reserve system. It attempts to adjust the supply of credit to the seasonal fluctuations of business. During the periods of heavy movement of goods, roughly coterminous with the spring and fall seasons, additional Reserve credits are released. During the slack seasons, when production declines and trade tends to sag, the surplus funds are withdrawn from the financial markets. This is accomplished chiefly by means of Federal Reserve notes and rediscounts, with an occasional use of open-market operations in bills. The function of adjusting the supply of credit is attained with a fair degree of ease because the movement is in harmony with the prevailing tendencies in the banking and industrial communities. Very little initiative is required from the Reserve authorities. As consumption moves along in its seasonal swing, production adjusts itself with easy spontaneity. The surplus of funds during the slack season is removed from the market by the failure to renew maturing bills which were rediscounted with the Reserve banks, and the return of Federal Reserve notes. Similarly, the demand for additional funds during the active season is met by the sale of bills in the open market to Reserve banks, by rediscounts and advances.

The criteria of the stage of cyclical business activity should be the basic economic conditions characteristic of the country at large and of specific industries rather than the money-market, as heretofore. As the movement toward the trough or the peak of the cycle becomes more pronounced, the difficulty of curbing the movement increases considerably. If the period of expansion has reached a speculative and boom stage, it may be necessary to refuse outright to advance additional credit. Such a policy, coupled with a positive contraction of credit to offset possible countervailing factors, such as gold movements and changes in foreign balances, would have prevented the additional inflation of 1928 and 1929.

The task of formulating a proper technique for the application of the above principle of credit regulation is by no means a simple one. In general, it will be readily recognized that successful control depends upon the promptness and efficiency with which a corrective is applied. The timeliness of Reserve action will depend upon the astuteness and courage of the Reserve authorities. Its efficiency will depend in part upon effective coördination in the use of all credit-control instruments (such as open-market operations and rediscounts), and in part upon certain factors which are mainly beyond the scope of Federal Reserve control.

It must be clearly recognized that although the above principle of consumption-production equilibrium is of necessity applicable to "long run" credit regulation, it should also be a factor in the daily decisions of the Reserve authorities. While it is impossible to weigh the academic niceties of deflation when faced with the imminent danger of the loss of a substantial part of our gold reserves, it is still necessary to bear in mind the possible effects upon business of any step which seeks to check the flow of precious metal. And as soon as the international position has been rectified, fresh steps should be taken to restore the domestic equilibrium. The normal banker shuns so-called academic advice because he is consistently concerned with the immediate problems of day to day banking. However, having been given economic power, he must be held responsible for the ultimate consequences of his acts and decisions. It is therefore not only his business to keep the banking vehicle well oiled and in constant movement, but also to select the road upon which he will travel. The Reserve banker, above all others, must consider the social consequences or long run effects of his actions.

We must not assume from this responsibility of the banker that all maladjustments are attributable to his negligence and faulty guidance. While the banks exercise a considerable influence upon our economic development, the reverse is also true. The regulation of the supply of credit alone is not sufficient to yield a positive control over business and financial enterprises. It is necessary to take into consideration conditions of demand for credits. Now, with only a partial and somewhat faulty control over supply, and no control over demand, it is unreasonable to expect the Reserve system to maintain absolute control over credit conditions in the United States. Changes in rediscount and open-market rates, dealings in bills and government securities and even credit rationing only alter the conditions of supply. The success of any Federal Reserve credit policy is contingent upon two factors: first, the countervailing forces present in the supply of credit (such as gold flows), and second, the elasticity and fluctuations (shifting of demand schedule) of demand. The elasticity and shiftability of demand are rarely separated in analyzing credit conditions; yet it is easily apparent that any credit control through "price" of credit, or changes in rate, manipulations can be effective only by reason of the elasticity of demand. However, should the elasticity change or should the schedule shift, the "price" control will not achieve its desired objective. Elasticity and shiftability (of the demand schedule) are functions of many factors. They can vary over night. In part, they respond to the temper of business prospects, which is a partly psychological and partly an economic factor. The intensity of business activity, the degree of speculation, and in general the demand for goods in process and in storage are further determining factors.

The crux, then, of efficient Federal Reserve credit control lies in the ability of the Reserve banks to gauge the cyclical swings of business activity so as to decrease their amplitude. Should perfect consumption-production and saving-capital needs equilibrium be maintained, the problem would be solved.

The second principle of credit-control is thus one of balanced savings. If any single factor can be isolated and made to bear the burden of the responsibility for the economic-financial debacle of the last five years, we are inclined to believe that the enormous increase in our capital investments through anticipatory savings is the fundamental factor. We might inquire to no end what conditions made possible and caused this increase in capital stock without a concomitant increase in savings. Many factors conspired to bring about the condition, and not least of these have been the speculative urge, the habit of using long-term funds (security issues) to meet short-term needs, and the inability of our business leaders to realize that, despite the intricacies of modern banking, it is impossible to create capital without saving. The time-lag introduced by our credit mechanism makes it possible to save after the capital equipment has been created, but, nevertheless, sooner or later, somebody must save part of his income to meet the expenditure. And as saving must come out of income, the effective purchasing power for consumers' goods is thereby reduced.

If investments are to be properly aligned with savings, it is necessary to check the use of commercial credits for long-term loans. While collateral loans may properly be made by commercial banks, they should not be renewed for long periods. The laxity in renewing bills beyond the life of the underlying transaction tends to create a disparity between capital investments and saving. The indiscriminate acceptance of "storage" bills has allowed much commercial credit to perform what is properly the function of savings. While we cannot go into details of "sound" commercial banking at the present writing, the general proposition of the function of savings as the only supplier of the demand for capital funds should be emphasized.

In any national economy the two-fold equilibrium of consumption-production balance and savings-investment balance is applicable to both the internal and external economy of the nation. Domestic equilibrium must be accompanied by an international adjustment of exports-imports and borrowings-lendings. Quite often the foreign balance of the United States may be upset with the resultant abnormal flow of gold. The proper corrective of such a tendency may not of necessity lie in the granting of additional foreign credits, as was attempted in the last decade, but rather in the lowering of our exceedingly high tariff barriers. The granting of credits merely postpones the inevitable day of reckoning (unless new factors enter to correct the situation). Now, when the gold flow is due to a temporary phenomenon such as the seasonal movement of crops, a credit corrective is quite proper. However, when the fundamental cause lies in the two-fold obstructions of mountainous War Debts and insurmountable tariff walls, a credit adjustment merely aggravates the situation. The Federal Reserve system can neither alter our tariffs nor change the amount of War Debts which we demand should be paid us. It can, however, refrain from glossing over the situation by harmful credit policies.

Had our Reserve system had the breadth of vision to appreciate the absolute necessity of adjusting our foreign economic-financial relations; had it had the fortitude to force the country to solve the situation instead of putting it off; had the Reserve authorities recognized the necessity of discriminating between business transactions; *bona fide* and *legitimate,* and had they had the courage to act upon this knowledge, the present economic collapse could have been avoided for the greater part. It is not essential that the dislocations resulting from a great war should eventuate in a social cataclysm that is world wide in its scope.

The application of sound principles of credit control can not be made by any universal rule. The proper technique is one that varies with the altering immediate situation so as to take into consideration all countervailing forces and tendencies. The functional limitations of the instruments used should be recognized.

CHAPTER XXXIII

OPEN-MARKET POLICY OF THE FEDERAL RESERVE IN 1932[1]

The year 1932 opened under unfavorable omens. The National Credit Corporation, which had been formed in October, 1931, with private capital but Government approval, had been ineffective in halting bank failures, and, according to records of the Federal Reserve Board, 563 banks were forced to close their doors in November and December. At the end of 1931 the long-term capital market was in a state of partial paralysis and the stock and bond markets fluctuated nervously at their bear market lows. Productive activity was receding, the Federal Reserve Board's unadjusted index of industrial production standing in December, 1931, at 68 as compared with 96 in December, 1929, and 126 in May of the same year. Commodity prices, particularly of farm products, were weak and the Bureau of Labor Statistics index of 784 price series (1926 = 100) was 68.6 in December, 1931, as compared with 93.3 in December, 1929. As estimated by the American Federation of Labor, there were 8,300,000 unemployed persons at the end of 1931, a greater number than at any previous time of the depression.

Severe liquidation.—Influencing and influenced by the many deflationary factors holding sway through 1931, there was an unusually severe liquidation of bank credit. As estimated by the Federal Reserve Board, the following changes occurred:

In the atmosphere of panic at the end of 1931 and the start of 1932 there was pressure upon the United States Government and the Federal Reserve banks to "take vigorous affirmative action to stem the forces of deflation." Plans were widely discussed for a Reconstruction Finance Corporation, to be financed through the Treasury for the purpose of extending credit to banks, insurance companies, railroads, and other important institutions. In many quarters a demand was voiced that the

[1] Written by Schroeder Boulton.

Federal Reserve banks should "exert their influence upon the credit situation through a vigorous campaign of purchases of government securities in the open market." Intimations were published that such a policy was considered in official quarters.

On January 11, 1932, according to press advices, the Open Market Policy Committee (Open Market Policy Conference) met with Ogden L. Mills, then an Under-Secretary of the Treasury, and outlined a policy for the next six months. Moreover, it was vaguely indicated that substantial purchases of government securities were agreed upon. However, those who watched

ALL BANKS IN THE UNITED STATES

(In millions of dollars)

DATE	DEPOSITS	LOANS	A) INVESTMENTS
June 30, 1930	54,954	58,108	17,471
Dec. 31, 1930	53,039	56,209	18,074
March 25, 1931	51,427	55,924	19,111
June 30, 1931	51,782	55,021	19,637
Sept. 29, 1931	49,152	53,365	19,615
Dec. 31, 1931	45,821	49,704	18,399

a) The increase of $928,000,000 in investments in the eighteen months to December 31, 1931 was a result of acquisitions of United States Government securities. During this period the Federal budgetary deficit necessitated an increase of $1,606,000,000 in interest-bearing public debt, $1,016,000,000 of which was represented by the shorter term bills and certificates bearing a low interest rate, unattractive to the public, and principally absorbed by banks and institutional investors. All member banks, representing about two thirds of the banking resources of the country, increased their holdings of governments by $1,258,000,000 in the eighteen months to December 31, 1931.

weekly Federal Reserve statements for a sign that the system intended to commence purchases of government securities were given no clue, as holdings were allowed gradually to diminish from $791,000,000 on January 2 to $752,000,000 on January 16 and $740,000,000 on February 27.

Reconstruction Finance Corporation.—Of primary importance in the administration recovery program was creation of the Reconstruction Finance Corporation, authorized by law during the first week of February. Initial capital was to be provided through sale of $500,000,000 in stock to the Treasury, further capital up to $2,000,000,000 in total capitalization to be procured through sale of debentures which the Treasury was authorized to purchase. The corporation was empowered to make loans to banks, life insurance companies, railroads, building and loan associations and other agencies strongly affected with public interest. Administration theorists, in line with their long-held belief that the depression was a temporary distortion from normal Republican prosperity, caused by difficulties abroad and domestic liquidation and lack of confidence, held that if these important institutions were given "needed credit" a basis for confidence would be created such as to give rise to an increase in bank lending, improvement in business, strength in commodity prices and general restoration of more stable conditions.

Glass-Steagall Bill

That open-market operations were not commenced immediately upon formation of the Reconstruction Finance Corporation was surprising to some observers. Explanation of the delay was presented by the terms of the hurriedly enacted Glass-Steagall bill, which became a law in February, 1932. Sections One and Two of the bill provided for emergency borrowing at penalty rates from the Federal Reserve banks on assets previously ineligible, by individual banks having a capital not exceeding $5,000,000, or by groups of five or more banks. Section Three effected a drastic change in the regulations as to required reserves of the Federal Reserve banks. Until enactment of the bill they had been required to maintain a gold and lawful money reserve of 35 per cent against deposits and a gold reserve of 40 per cent against Federal Reserve notes in circulation, with a total reserve of 100 per cent required against notes (whether or not in circulation) and against deposits, the balance above the minimum gold and lawful money reserves consisting of such reserves, or of eligible paper in the form of discounts or acceptances. In addition, a redemption fund of 5 per cent gold was required against that portion of notes not covered by gold. Under Section Three of the Glass-Steagall bill the Federal Reserve banks were authorized to substitute United States Government obligations for eligible paper as backing for notes and deposits.

Purpose of the Glass-Steagall bill.—Section Three of the bill was especially approved by the Reserve authorities in view of their desire for freedom in conducting open-market purchases of Government securities. Purchases of Government securities, resulting in increased deposits with the Federal Reserve banks but creating neither gold nor eligible paper to pledge against these deposits, would have produced strain, especially in a period of gold export, such as early 1932. The granting of permission to pledge Government securities was calculated to relieve this strain.

Defense of the gold standard was not directly involved in the provisions of the Glass-Steagall bill; the question was rather one of enabling open-market operations to be conducted with maintenance of the gold standard. Statistics of the Federal Reserve Board give no substantiation to the oft-repeated statement that the bill was designed to remedy a shortage of eligible paper which was endangering preservation of a safe volume of "free gold." At the end of 1931 member banks made reports showing that they held $2,573,000,000 in eligible commercial paper in addition to $4,694,000,000 in Government securities. In absence of open-market purchases of Government obligations or heavy member-bank excess-reserve balances, in order to secure gold from the Federal Reserve banks member banks must either borrow, or must sell, acceptances; thus gold exports automatically set up an offsetting process. This occurred during the period of gold drain from September 16 to October 28, 1931, when gold reserves decreased by $747,000,000; Government holdings increased by only $15,000,000; discounts increased by $454,000,000; bills bought increased by $507,000,000; Federal Reserve note circulation increased by $378,000,000; and reserve deposits decreased by $189,000,000. During this period discount rates of the Reserve banks were increased by as much as 2 per cent.

In their anxiety to promote credit ease, the Federal Reserve officials desired to prevent in 1932 a repetition of the process of the fall of 1931, when circumstances had forced them to follow more or less the orthodox pre-war central-bank hard-money practices applicable during periods of gold drain. In theory they remained committed to soft money. The Federal Reserve *Bulletin* for March, 1932 (p. 144), after defining "free gold" as the excess of gold holdings over the sum of holdings required under minimum-reserve ratios and holdings needed to complete any deficiency in eligible paper as backing for notes and deposits, stated:

Free gold . . . does not . . . limit the amount of gold that can be exported, because a demand for gold for export, by causing member banks to borrow from the Federal Reserve bank in order to obtain it, serves to increase reserve bank holdings of bills discounted and thus results in the creation of the collateral necessary to replace the gold that has been withdrawn.

The free gold does, however, limit the extent to which the reserve banks by open market operations can enable member banks to meet an external drain of gold or an internal demand for currency without increasing their indebtedness to the reserve banks. When the member banks have to borrow in order to obtain gold or currency, this borrowing becomes an element of tightness in the credit situation, which in existing circumstances would be undesirable because it would make the banks more reluctant to extend loans to their customers. It is true that if acceptances were sold to the reserve banks for the purpose of obtaining currency or gold, there would be no inroad on free gold, because acceptances as well as discounts are eligible as collateral for Federal reserve notes. Acceptances, however, are not always available in sufficient amounts and for this reason cannot be depended upon by the member banks as an adequate basis for obtaining credit from the Federal reserve banks. . . .

The enactment of legislation that enables the Federal Reserve system to pursue a policy based on the assurance that in case of need not merely its "free gold" will be available, but practically its entire gold reserves in excess of legal requirements, has resulted in strengthening the entire credit structure of the country and in increasing the System's power to coöperate in the recovery of business.

Execution of 1932 Open-Market Policy

As soon as the Glass-Steagall Act became law the Federal Reserve system commenced purchases of Government securities. Initial increases in holdings occurred as follows:

Week to March 2	$19,000,000
" " " 9	25,000,000
" " " 16	57,000,000
" " " 23	– 7,000,000 (decrease)
" " " 30	37,000,000
" " April 6	13,000,000

Although proponents of open-market purchases had been careful to state that the effect of such purchases might not significantly be felt until after a lapse of a considerable period of time, perhaps as much as nine months or more, nevertheless deflationary credit phenomena accompanying the original purchases caused some disappointment. However, this disappointment, rather than causing any desire to halt the program, gave rise to a decision to accelerate it. On April 13 a witness then appearing before the Goldsborough subcommittee of the Senate Banking Committee revealed by implication that at a meeting of the Open Market Policy Conference held on April 12 it had been decided to speed up purchases of Government securities from $25,000,000 weekly, agreed upon at a meeting held seven weeks previously, to $75,000,000 or more per week. Subsequent Federal Reserve statements revealed the following increases from the week ending April 13 to that ending May 18:

Week to April 13	$100,000,000
" " " 20	93,000,000
" " " 27	113,000,000
" " May 4	96,000,000
" " " 11	98,000,000
" " " 18	81,000,000

On April 25 Ogden L. Mills, Secretary of the Treasury, in the following words defended the new heavy scale purchases of Government securities:

With the collapse of the banking system indefinitely halted and with commercial and industrial organization still in a state of extreme strain, what would appear to be required now is the stimulus of credit expansion, supported by a liberal policy of the Federal Reserve System, such as it is pursuing at present, and regulated in its development by that system.

In the week ended May 11 the first pledge of government Securities, $98,000,000, was announced as having taken place under the provisions of the Glass-Steagall Act.

Criticism of policy.—Criticism and alarm in connection with the open market purchases were expressed in many quarters. It was decided to reduce the scale of operations and on May 17 the Federal Reserve Board announced that "The Governors of the Federal Reserve Banks met today with the Federal Reserve Board, and it was decided to continue open market operations by the purchase of government securities, the extent and amount to be determined from time to time as conditions justify."

As an implied admission that the unprecedentedly heavy purchases of Governments had not yet produced the desired effect of loosening credit, Governor Meyer disclosed before the Senate Banking and Currency Committee, on May 18, that the Federal Reserve Board had instructed the Governors of the twelve Federal Reserve banks to "go home and find ways and means of spreading credit according to the Board's present policy." On May 19 the then management of the New York bank called together a committee of bankers and industrialists "for the purpose of considering methods of making the large funds now being released by the Federal Banks useful affirmatively in developing business." This step, now almost forgotten, was received at the time with extravagant newspaper acclaim, a New York *Times* headline stating:

TWELVE BANKS AND INDUSTRIALISTS TO FIND WAYS TO USE FEDERAL RESERVE FUNDS—HOOVER APPROVES RECOVERY MOVE—MOST POWERFUL GROUP SINCE WAR FORMED BY GOVERNOR HARRISON—RISE IN PRICES OBJECT—FINANCING HOMES AND AID ON FARM LOANS ARE ALSO EXPANSION POSSIBILITIES—VAST SUMS PILED UP HERE—BANKS HAVE HAD DIFFICULTY IN FINDING GOOD BORROWERS IN TIME OF FEAR.

Committees similar to that of the New York bank were formed in other Federal Reserve districts.

Continuance of Government security purchases.—After the middle of May heavy government security purchases were continued, but at a much slower rate than in the preceding period:

Week to May 25	$59,000,000
" " June 1	50,000,000
" " " 8	70,000,000
" " " 15	47,000,000
" " " 22	38,000,000
" " " 29	71,000,000

Purchases were made at a still slower pace in July, acquisitions aggregating only $50,000,000 from June 29 until purchasing came to a halt on August 10, when holdings totalled $1,851,000,000 as compared with $741,000,000 on February 24, and $817,000,000 on December 31, 1931. Subject to a policy of purchasing only to replace maturities, system holdings of $1,855,000,000 on December 31 remained substantially unchanged from the August 10 total.

Changes in discount and acceptance buying rates of the Reserve banks were not of any particularly important influence in 1932, excepting that they contributed to extraordinary ease in the primary money market. The Federal Reserve Bank of New York on February 24 reduced its discount rate ½ per cent to a level of 3 per cent, and two days later shaded its acceptance buying rate by ⅛ to ¼ of 1 per cent. Respectively on June 24 and 25 the New York and Chicago banks reduced their discount rates to 2.5 per cent, while the Federal Reserve Bank of New York also slashed its buying rate on prime bankers acceptances from 2.5 per cent to a level of 1 per cent on maturities up to 90 days. After these reductions both bills bought and bills discounted of the system continued to run off. Eight Reserve banks in 1932 continued to operate without change under rediscount rates of 3.5 per cent established in 1930 or 1931.

Results of 1932 open-market policy upon the Federal Reserve banks.—In terms of the condition of the Federal Reserve banks and considering solely the period of aggressive purchases from February 29 to July 31, what was the effect of open-market policy upon the Reserve banks? Among other changes, there was an increase in Federal Reserve bank credit of $730,000,000; a decrease of $290,000,000 in bills discounted to a level of $338,000,000, and an increase of $203,000,000 in member-bank reserve deposits. These changes are brought out in the following table:

TABLE 155

CONDITION OF THE FEDERAL RESERVE BANKS

(In millions of dollars)

END OF MONTH		GOLD RESERVES	U. S. SECURITIES	BILLS DIS-COUNTED	TOTAL RES. BK. CREDIT	FED. RES. NOTE CIR.	MEM. BK. RESERVE DEPOSITS	RESERVE RATIO
Dec.	1931	2989	817	638	1853	2624	1961	66.5
Jan.	1932	2976	746	899	1856	2665	1947	66.6
Feb.	"	2938	740	828	1709	2651	1849	68.4
		—open-market campaign						
March	"	3020	872	638	1597	2563	1924	70.7
April	"	3004	1228	556	1850	2566	2124	67.1
May	"	2790	1549	490	2096	2572	2113	62.1
June	"	2578	1784	440	2310	2795	1982	57.6
July	"	2635	1841	538	2439	2859	2052	56.5
		—end of open-market campaign—						
Aug.	"	2773	1852	433	2331	2814	2146	58.9
Sept.	"	2893	1854	332	2233	2750	2225	61.1
Oct.	"	3003	1851	328	2227	2709	2383	62.0
Nov.	"	3049	1851	309	2202	2692	2411	62.6
Dec.	"	3151	1855	235	2145	2739	2509	62.9

1932 Open-market policy and the money markets.—The 1932 purchases of Government securities increased the extreme ease in the primary money markets, which were glutted throughout the year with safety-seeking short-term funds, partially owing their existence to the previous open-market operations of 1930 and 1931. With the heavy 1932 acquisitions, rates on short term securities of the United States Government, stock exchange time and call loans and bankers' acceptances went to practically unprecedented low levels, while rates on other types of paper eased markedly from levels which at the start of the year had already been low. These declines were accompanied by reductions in interest paid by New York and other banks on time and demand deposits.

TABLE 156

OPEN-MARKET RATES, NEW YORK CITY

(Federal Reserve *Bulletin*)

MONTH 1932	PRIME COMMERCIAL PAPER, 4 TO 6 MONTHS	PRIME BK. ACCEPT. 90 DAYS	TIME LOANS 90 DAYS	U. S. TREAS. NOTES AND CERTIFICATES 3 TO 6 MONTHS	TREASURY BONDS
Jan.	3¾–4	2¾–3	3½–4	2.48	4.27
Feb.	3¾–4	2¾–2⅞	3½–3¾	2.42	4.11
March	3½–3¾	2⅜–2⅝	2¾–3½	2.25	3.92
April	3¼–3¾	⅞–2⅛	2 –3	1.11	3.74
May	2¾–3½	⅞–1⅛	1½–2	.31	3.77
June	2½–3	⅞	1½	.34	3.78
July	2¼–2¾	¾	1¼–1½	.22	3.65
Aug.	2 –2½	¾	1¼–1½	.14	3.57
Sept.	2 –2¼	¾	1¼–1½	.03	3.54
Oct.	1¾–2¼	½– ¾	½–1¼	—	3.54
Nov.	1½–1¾	½	½	—	3.55
Dec.	1¼–1¾	⅜	½	.04	3.48

Declines in short-term interest rates were much more severe than in long-term rates (on some occasions short-term Treasury securities sold on a minus yield basis as a result of anxiety of purchasers to be in position to receive favorable allotments on subsequent issues). The Federal Reserve banks helped to drive down short-term as compared with long-term interest rates through concentrating their purchases in the shorter term bills, certificates and notes: of government securities held on July 31, 1932, $1,152,000,000 were bills and certificates, $269,000,000 notes, and $421,000,000 bonds, as compared with, on February 29, 1932, $348,000,000 bills and certificates, $74,000,000 notes and $319,000,000 bonds.

That, despite ease in the primary-money markets, there was a paralysis of investor confidence throughout 1932 is made clear by the following statistics relative to the long-term capital market compiled by the Commercial and Financial Chronicle:

NEW FINANCING IN 1932 (EXCLUDING UNITED STATES GOVERNMENT FINANCING)

(In millions of dollars)

Jan.	$ 199	Aug.	169
Feb.	95	Sept.	138
March	192	Oct.	124
April	143	Nov.	76
May	124	Dec.	158
June	148	Total	$1,721
July	155		

Municipal issues equaled nearly one-half the above total of $1,721,000,000, of which $530,000,000 represented refunding issues. Total issues in 1931 were $4,023,000,000, in 1930, $7,677,000,000, and in 1929, $11,592,000,000.

1932 Open-market policy and member-bank credit.—Study of member bank statistics fails to indicate that any liberalization of lending policies resulted from the 1932 open-market operations. As it happened, the period of aggressive open-market policy coincided with one of the most drastic spasms of credit and business liquidation in the history of the United States. Despite temporary enthusiasm engendered by passage of the Reconstruction Finance and Glass-Steagall acts, a number of events and circumstances early in 1932 served markedly to disturb confidence. Moreover domestic business and world commodity trade and prices were weakly sinking to lower levels despite all attempts at stabilization or stimulation. Further influencing domestic panic was the fact that European central banks and other foreign agencies with short-term funds in the United States, alarmed by the Congressional discussion of inflation measures, by the unbalance of the Government budget, and by our confused political situation, commenced, early in January, to withdraw that portion of their surplus short-term funds which remained in this country after the 1931 gold run. Heavy open-market purchases of Government securities by the Reserve system disturbed the confidence of foreign bankers, and gold loss was exceptionally heavy in May and June. The gold outflow practically ended in June with the reduction of foreign short-term balances, which, at the end of December 1931, had been estimated by the Department of Commerce at $1,462,000,000, to approximately $600,000,000 according to estimates of the Federal Reserve Bank of New York. This latter figure was considered hardly a minimum working balance.

1932 NET EXPORTS AND IMPORTS OF GOLD*

(Federal Reserve Board)

Jan.	Export	$ 73,000,000	Aug.	Import	6,100,000
Feb.	"	90,600,000	Sep.	"	27,900,000
March	"	24,700,000	Oct.	"	20,600,000
April	"	30,200,000	Nov.	"	21,700,000
May	"	195,500,000	Dec.	"	100,900,000
June	"	206,000,000	Net Export		$446,200,000
July	"	3,400,000			

* Releases from earmark in the first four and last six months of 1932 involving a net release during the year of $457,500,000, plus domestic production, etc., of $41,600,000 were sufficient to offset exports and to produce an increase of $53,000,000 in monetary gold stock.

Liquidation of loans.—In spite of large increases in member-bank reserve balances and decreases in indebtedness to the Reserve banks, liquidation of loans was extremely heavy throughout 1932, nor was there at any time evidence of substantial increase in credit for business purposes. This is made clear by the following statistics (because of failure to issue a call for condition statements March, statistics are not available) indicating that in the period from December 31, 1931, to December 31, 1932, when Federal Reserve Bank credit was increased by $292,000,000, member banks reduced their loans to customers by $3,665,000,000.

Other investments lowered.—During the later months of 1931 member banks sharply reduced their holdings of "other investments"; this decrease carried into 1932 when such holdings declined from $5,996,000,000 to $5,726,000,000. Partly because

LOANS OF ALL MEMBER BANKS

(In millions of dollars)

	LOANS TO BANKS	LOANS TO CUSTOMERS				OPEN MARKET LOANS
		Total	Secured by Stocks and Bonds	Sec. by Real Estate	Otherwise Secured	
Dec. 31, 1931	790	17,570	6,290	3,038	8,244	901
June 30, 1932	573	15,267	5,292	2,894	7,081	747
Sept. 30, "	457	14,497	5,086	2,885	6,527	970
Dec. 31, "	444	13,905	4,848	2,862	6,195	855

of heavy Government borrowing on short-term obligations, holdings of Government securities rose in the year from $5,319,000,000 to $6,540,000,000.

TABLE 157

WEEKLY REPORTING MEMBER BANKS IN LEADING CITIES

(In millions of dollars, monthly averages of weekly figures)

MONTH	LOANS ON SECURITIES	ALL OTHER LOANS	INVESTMENTS	
			Total	U. S. Securities
Dec. 1931	5,763	7,441	7,545	4,127
Jan. 1932	5,644	7,331	7,203	3,943
Feb. "	5,497	7,214	7,064	3,856
March "	5,388	6,987	7,059	3,866
April "	5,150	6,820	7,126	3,875
May "	4,975	6,727	7,410	4,121
June "	4,811	6,609	7,457	4,200
July "	4,616	6,455	7,348	4,144
Aug. "	4,578	6,319	7,690	4,499
Sept. "	4,524	6,229	7,986	4,759
Oct. "	4,437	6,168	7,421	5,140
Nov. "	4,280	6,120	8,587	5,279
Dec. "	4,319	6,021	8,500	5,220

Statistics of weekly-reporting member banks in leading cities (101 cities) give evidence of steady credit liquidation, proceeding steadily even through the speculative boom of the late summer and early fall of 1932.

Excess reserves.—Heavy excess reserves over legal requirements resulted from credits caused by purchases of government securities. Excess reserves of all member banks increased from an average of $43,000,000 in February to $204,000,000 in July, and $526,000,000 in December. In prosperous times it is customary for member banks to make full use of reserve balances, expanding credit to the limit allowed by the size of the balances. Although friends of the 1932 open-market policy felt that the creation of excess balances would practically necessitate an expansion of loans, this reasoning bore little relation to bankers, who in a panic year not only desired liquidity, but, with the decline in business, found a real scarcity of good borrowers for new money, or to business men who in a period of uncertainty desired to be as free of debt as possible.

As further clue to the lack of credit expansion it is important to note that excess reserves were not spread evenly throughout the system. Of about $525,000,000 excess reserves estimated on December 28, 1932, about $311,000,000 was to the account of New York banks, and $194,000,000 to the account of Chicago banks, leaving only $20,000,000 for banks in other cities. The tabular data, page 777, of customer loan rates provide some substantiation of the belief that effective excess funds were concentrated mainly in the principal money centers; these data also indicate how slight was the effect of Federal Reserve easy-money policy in influencing substantial change in rates charged to bank customers.

Deflation.—Pumping of Federal Reserve credit into the banking system, and extension of loans by the Reconstruction Finance Corporation were ineffective in fundamentally alleviating the condition of a large percentage of banks, especially interior banks, whose real difficulty lay in that their assets no longer covered their deposits, because of bad loans and declines in market values of investments. The threat involved in the condition of interior banks, known as it was to experienced officers of sound banks, must have served as a considerable check upon any desires they may have felt toward credit expansion. In the case of the insolvent banks their own condition served as a painful prod toward credit liquidation in an effort to pay off loans to the Reconstruction Finance Corporation or borrowings from the Federal Reserve banks or other banks.

RATES CHARGED TO CUSTOMERS BY BANKS IN PRINCIPAL CITIES

(Federal Reserve Board)

MONTH	NEW YORK CITY	8 OTHER NORTHERN AND EASTERN CITIES	27 SOUTHERN AND WESTERN CITIES
Dec. 1931	4.64%	4.91%	5.56%
March 1932	4.72%	5.14%	5.64%
June "	4.61%	5.13%	5.62%
Sept. "	4.30%	5.03%	5.63%
Dec. "	4.22%	4.88%	5.60%

Recurrent panics.—Recurrent public panics, because of bank failures, served as an additional goad toward liquidity. In the early months of the Reconstruction Finance Corporation bank

TABLE 158

BANK FAILURES AND RECONSTRUCTION FINANCE CORPORATION LOANS TO BANKS AND TRUST COMPANIES IN 1932

MONTH 1932	BANKS FAILED (Federal Reserve Board)		INCREASE IN RFC LOANS TO BANKS AND TRUST COMPANIES
	Number	Deposits (In millions of dollars)	(In millions of dollars)
Jan.	342	219	—
Feb.	121	57	40
March	46	15	78
April	74	32	105
May	82	34	96
June	151	133	106
July	132	49	76
Aug.	85	30	46
Sept.	67	14	Decrease 13
Oct.	102	20	40
Nov.	93	43	Decrease 2
Dec.	161	71	22
Total	1456	717	594

failures decreased considerably, probably for the most part because of misleading statements by public officials and others as to the function of the Reconstruction Finance Corporation and as to the soundness of banks. In June, 1932, a wave of bank failures occurred in the Chicago district, where more than forty small and medium-sized banks closed their doors in the few weeks prior to the granting of an $80,000,000 Reconstruction Finance Corporation loan to the Central Republic Bank and Trust Company. The rate of bank failures was at an abnormally high level throughout 1932, the peaks being reached in January and December.

Hoarding had little net effect upon member banks in 1932; currency circulation declined through most of the first half of the year, rose sharply at the end of June, and closed the year with only a slight increase over 1931.

DATE	MONETARY GOLD STOCK	CURRENCY IN CIRCULATION	BILLS DISCOUNTED	RESERVE BALANCES
		(In millions of dollars)		
Dec. 31, 1931	4,460	5,647	638	1,961
March 31, 1932	4,390	5,459	639	1,924
June 30, "	3,919	5,695	440	1,982
Sept. 30, "	4,193	5,653	332	2,225
Dec. 31, "	4,513	5,675	235	2,509

Changes in member position.—The mechanism of 1932 changes in the position of member banks as related to the Reserve banks is shown in Table 159, covering, first, the period of aggressive open-market operations and gold outflow and, second, the period of reduced open-market activity and gold return.

That the apparent banking ease, at the end of 1932, had been fictitious became open knowledge with the development of banking difficulties in late January, 1933 leading to unprecedented increases in currency hoarding, gold hoarding, and gold exports, culminating in the national banking moratorium of March, 1933.

Industrial activity and speculation in 1932.—It had been hoped by sponsors of the Federal Reserve system's open-market policy of 1932, that increases of credit would occur which would assist stock, bond, and commodity prices and give rise to improvement in business. The following changes were those which actually took place:

MONTH 1932	INDUSTRIAL ACTIVITY SEASONALLY UNADJUSTED (F. R. BOARD 1923-25 = 100)	COMMODITY INDEX 784 PRICE SERIES (BUREAU OF LABOR STATISTICS, 1926 = 100)	FLAT AVERAGE OF PRICES OF ALL LISTED SHARES, N. Y. STOCK EX. (FIRST OF MONTH)	AVERAGE PRICE DOMESTIC CORPORATION BONDS, N. Y STOCK EX. (FIRST OF MONTH)
Jan.	71	67	$20.37	$66.53
Feb.	71	66	29.66	67.58
March	68	66	29.89	68.94
April	64	66	28.50	65.79
May	61	64	24.26	61.56
June	59	64	19.48	52.62
July	56	65	18.89	55.63
Aug.	59	65	22.66	60.99
Sept.	67	65	29.57	68.75
Oct.	68	64	28.63	68.77
Nov.	65	64	26.29	65.57
Dec.	60	63	25.61	64.08

Business activity and stock, bond, and commodity prices all declined heavily in 1932, particularly in the spring and again late in the year. A strong speculative boom occurred in the summer, which lifted sharply stock, bond, and speculative commodity prices; according, however, to most indices, business activity was only slightly above the seasonal increase. Inasmuch as restrictive bank-credit policies remained in force throughout 1932, it is necessary to seek elsewhere for an explanation of the occurrences of the summer of 1932. In the security and commodity markets, and, to a certain extent, also in business, the following factors are believed to have been influential:

1. End of gold export panic June, 1932
2. Severely liquidated position of the securities markets—New York Stock Exchange member borrowings only $244,000,000 at end of June
3. Passage of the budget bill, defeat of the bonus, and adjournment of Congress
4. Formation of a bond pool by New York banks—"banking" support to security prices
5. Signing of the Lausanne agreement—strength in foreign security markets
6. Vigorous efforts by political and journalistic forces to encourage optimism

Criticism of 1932 open market policy.—Criticism of the Federal Reserve system's 1932 open-market policy can hardly be divorced from consideration of the general policies of the Republican Administration following 1929. Holding itself largely

TABLE 159

CHANGES IN POSITION OF MEMBER BANKS

FEBRUARY 27—JULY 2, 1932
WEEKLY AVERAGES OF DAILY FIGURES

	(In millions of dollars)
Funds received by member banks through:	
Increase in Federal Reserve holdings of United States Government securities	1051
Decrease in unexpended capital funds of the Reserve banks	2
Decrease in nonmember deposits with the Reserve banks, etc.	5
Increase in Treasury currency adjusted	5
	1063
Disposition of funds:	
Increase in Reserve balances of member banks	84
Decrease in bills discounted by the Reserve banks	358
Decrease in Reserve bank bill holdings	75
Decrease in other Reserve bank credit	11
Decrease in monetary gold stock	437
Increase in money in circulation	98
	1063
JULY 2—DECEMBER 31, 1932	
Funds received by member banks through:	
Increase in Federal Reserve holdings of United States Government securities	61
Increase in other Reserve bank credit	3
Decrease in nonmember deposits with the Reserve banks, etc.	9
Increase in monetary gold stock	584
Increase in Treasury currency adjusted	102
	759
Disposition of funds:	
Increase in Reserve balances of member banks	492
Decrease in bills discounted by the Reserve banks	221
Decrease in Reserve bank bill holdings	31
Increase in unexpended capital funds of the Reserve banks	14
Increase in money in circulation	1
	759

responsible for the extraordinary prosperity in the post-war years, the Republican party was unprepared after 1929 to admit that this prosperity had not been sound and that basic readjustments were needed. Hence in so far as attempts were made to influence recovery, they for the most part were directed toward a return of new era conditions.

In particular, the Federal Reserve management had become addicted to a philosophy of permanent prosperity. In the several years before the 1929 crash, Reserve authorities, in the face of dangerous inflation, refused to inagurate any thorough-going restrictive measures, quixotically hoping to curb speculation while maintaining progress in business activity. After 1929, in defiance of world-wide disturbances which gave rise to a heavy foreign liquidating movement, the Reserve banks attempted to insure continuance of domestic-credit expansion to keep pace with past average yearly increases in domestic business. Following the breakdown of 1931, Administration and Federal Reserve policies were not essentially changed, but extremely vigorous measures were adopted having the same general aim as previously. Chief among these measures were the loan policy of the Reconstruction Finance Corporation and the 1932 Federal Reserve policy of open-market government security purchases.

That the 1932 open-market policy failed to achieve its ends of credit expansion; business stimulation and stock and bond market resuscitation was owing to a variety of factors, all of them important:

1. Absence of general public confidence in business and political leadership; presence of public concern over the political and business outlook

2. Absence of investor confidence and paralysis of the capital market

3. Concern over the heavy Federal budgetary deficit

4. Reluctance of bankers to lend and business men to borrow in a period of uncertainty; universal desire for liquidity

5. Difficulties presented by the instability of the American unit banking system; bank failures

6. Highly unsettled international conditions; increases in tariff barriers and a continuing decline in world trade and world-commodity prices

Arguments in favor of policy.—It has been said, in favor of the 1932 open-market policy, that it enabled a heavy gold drain to be met without an increase in rediscounts. This it did, but by forcing money-market rates to unattractively low levels (unattractive from the standpoint of the lender), and by disturbing the confidence of foreign bankers, 1932 purchases of government securities undoubtedly accelerated the outflow of gold. Further, though in the past having encouraged an attitude that the, under certain circumstances, perfectly normal process of borrowing from the Reserve banks is a thing to be avoided whenever possible and indulged in only temporarily, and to meet emergency needs, the Reserve officials were themselves partially responsible for a situation in which the act of rediscounting assumed an abnormal significance, and in which even a temporary increase in rediscounts necessarily meant rapid contraction of bank credit.

Had the open-market purchases "taken" and resulted in an increase in member-bank credit, it is a moot question whether there would have been business recovery or simply a temporary speculative business boom. No purely mechanical interaction between credit and business, such as the Reserve banks apparently have clung to, can be proved from actual practice. Although over the long-run credit generally increases and decreases with changes in the rate of business activity, efforts to stimulate business through forced manipulative expansions of credit during periods of severe depression have almost always resulted unfavorably.

The 1932 open-market policy failed to achieve its announced purposes, but caused a radical change in the position of member banks, and a considerable weakening in the position of the Reserve banks.

Accordingly it appeared as one result of the heavy market acquisitions, at the end of 1932 member banks possessed an unusual volume of excess reserve balances (standing almost entirely to the credit of banks in New York and Chicago) while the Federal Reserve banks held such an amount of Government securities that to have purchased more would have appeared useless, while to have sold would have had an extremely adverse effect upon the Government security market.

PART VI

PUBLIC FINANCE AND BANKING

BY LOUIS SHERE

CHAPTER XXXIV

THE DEBT SITUATION—BACKGROUND

The study which has thus far been made of banking and of central banking in the United States has emphasized, as already explained, certain phases of the banking situation and of the portfolio position of the banks, and has taken for granted a general background knowledge on the part of the reader concerning the more familiar banking conditions. In this treatment only incidental reference has been made to the important question of the public debt. That has necessarily been referred to as an incident to the treatment, particularly in connection with such questions as discount and open-market policies and speculation. Such treatment has, however, been held to a minimum, in order that the issues involved in it might not be confused with other banking questions.

It is now necessary to devote special attention to a study of the position of the Treasury and its relationship, both to member and to central banking. Such a survey is offered in the following pages which are intended to trace the growth of the present Treasury position and to establish its relationship to existing banking.

The question of the relationship between the Federal Reserve system and the Treasury has, from the very origin of the system, been open to almost constant controversy and discussion. How far the Department should be represented on the Federal Reserve Board, and how far, being so represented, it should be permitted to exert an outside influence upon the discount policy of the system are matters that have been under constant discussion. The controversy about them was urgent during the formulation of the Banking Act of 1933, and was a major question leading to the postponement of the adoption of the Act in its later stages. The problem of official control or direction is, after all, only the smallest of the issues which have centered around the position of the Treasury Department in its banking aspects. This question has passed through three distinct phases.

The first covers the period of the World War and is characterized by the Treasury difficulties which were then thought to necessitate a resort to enormous short-term loans, floated and carried by the aid of the Federal Reserve system. This first period closed with the attempt made by those who had then been in charge of affairs to restore the system to something approximating its original condition, by driving out of Reserve portfolios a large part of the Treasury obligations which had accumulated there. In this endeavor a considerable measure of success was encountered, but the effort so made unavoidably met the antagonism of banking interests, and was succeeded by a period of reversal.

This second period opened with the new Harding Administration in 1922. It was occupied with the effort to reduce the public debt by maintaining the obligations of the Government largely in short-term form to be carried in Reserve banks pending their retirement through the accumulation of surplus income from taxation, which was thus to be applied to the retirement of outstanding bonds. By this process the public debt was reduced from about 27 billions of dollars to rather less than 17 billions; but, to accomplish that result, the Federal Reserve system was given as its primary duty that of floating, trading in, regulating, and retiring the short-term public debt of the United States. It resulted in an almost exclusive devotion of the Federal Reserve system to the satisfaction of the needs of public finance, even at the cost of soundness in the banking system, and at the further cost of developing unsound speculation.

The third period opened immediately after the collapse of 1929, when public revenue began to show the effects of the shrinking income and business volume of the nation. Continuous deficits, amounting to unprecedented sums, imposed upon the Reserve banks enormous new burdens for financing and carrying the obligations of the Government, while the unskillful handling of the Treasury compelled the Reserve institutions to incur dangers from which they had previously been, in some measure, exempt. The final outcome of the period has not yet been reached; it must be deferred until such time as Government finance is restored to a balance, and the Reserve system is rendered less subject to the necessity of seeking by its policy to maintain activity in the market and to strengthen the prices either of securities or of commodities. Meanwhile, the actual management of the Reserve system, in the face of public demands which subject it to greater and greater burdens and requirements, presents one of the fundamental difficulties of contemporary banking in the United States. It is a problem of peculiar difficulty because of the fact that the average man, uninformed about the banking side of public finance, is practically unable to exert the influence of a well-judged opinion, so that fundamental decisions must be taken and policies inaugurated regardless of the point of view of the masses of the community.

This is not a situation which makes for soundness or efficiency in policy, but which, on the other hand, tends to promote irresponsibility and dogmatic self-assurance in management. In approaching it the student needs first of all to inform himself fairly completely of the debt status of the United States; then to follow this discussion with an analysis of the relationship of the banks at large to the requirements of the Treasury. He is then in a position to adjudge the part which must be played by the Federal Reserve system in its support both of the other banks and of the Government.[1]

The public debt of the United States prior to the War was relatively insignificant. In the short space of two and one-half years a huge mountain of debt was absorbed into the economic system of the country with the aid of the fiat credit created by the then recently established Federal Reserve system. The interest-bearing debt outstanding[2] rose from $1,023,000,000 on March 31, 1917, to the peak of $26,349,000,000 on August 31, 1919. In the course of the following decade this mass of debt was whittled down, irregularly, year by year, until it had been

[1] These introductory paragraphs were written by H. Parker Willis.

[2] Unless otherwise indicated the figures for this item in the text of the following chapters exclude special issues to trust funds which are not outstanding in the hands of the public.

reduced by $11,357,000,000. At the end of December, 1930, the interest-bearing debt stood at the post-war low of $14,992,000,000. It has since that time been increased by $8,088,000,000 to $23,080,000,000 as of December 31, 1933. This growth reflects the devastating influence of the depression upon the national income coupled with a series of extraordinary activities undertaken by the Federal Government in its effort to relieve the public from the full impact of the slump in business and the further deterioration of the price structure.

The war-finance episode has been so admirably portrayed by Prof. Jacob Hollander as to require no detailed treatment here.[3] In the period 1919-1930 the Treasury succeeded in rapidly reducing the outstanding Federal debt by establishing a sinking fund for that purpose, and by applying its receipts from foreign governments as well as the surplus revenues collected in each year of that generally prosperous decade. The annual debt reductions continued after the current depression had made considerable headway, because a substantial part of the incoming revenues is always based on the business results of some previous calendar or fiscal year.

The sources of public debt increase or decrease, together with the annual growth or reduction in the gross debt outstanding, are presented in Table 160.

The shrinkage in ordinary receipts.—The total receipts from taxation for the fiscal year 1930 were higher than in any of the seven preceding fiscal years, reflecting the lagging of tax bases relative to the current business situation, because tax collections for any fiscal year are based on the profits and incomes of business done the preceding calendar or fiscal year. Since 1930, however, the decline in receipts from taxation has been extremely rapid. The total tax receipts for the fiscal years 1932 and 1933 amounted to only $1,889,000,000 and $1,855,000,000 respectively, or in each year scarcely 51 per cent of the average for the period 1922-1930 of about $3,400,000,000. Income taxes collected for the fiscal year 1934 will relate for the most part to

[3] Hollander, Jacob Harry, *War Borrowing* (New York: The Macmillan Co., 1919).

TABLE 160

SOURCES OF PUBLIC DEBT INCREASE OR DECREASE FOR FISCAL YEARS 1919-1933 ON THE BASIS OF THE DAILY TREASURY STATEMENTS (UNREVISED)

(In millions of dollars)

		DEBT RETIREMENTS CHARGEABLE AGAINST ORDINARY RECEIPTS							
FISCAL YEAR	TOTAL GROSS DEBT	Sinking Fund	From Foreign Governments	Miscellaneous	Total Chargeable against Ordinary receipts	INCREASE IN THE GENERAL FUND BALANCE	SURPLUS RECEIPTS	PAYMENTS ON ACCT. OF RECONSTRUCTION FINANCE CORP.	REDUCTION IN GROSS DEBT OUTSTANDING
1919	25,485	—	8	—	8	333	—13,371	—	+13,029
1920	24,299	—	73	6	79	—894	212	—	1,185
1921	23,977	261	74	87	422*	192	87	—	322
1922	22,963	276	65	82	423	—278	314	—	1,014
1923	22,350	284	101	18	403	99	310	—	614
1924	21,251	296	149	13	458	—136	505	—	1,099
1925	20,516	306	159	1	467	— 18	251	—	735
1926	19,643	317	170	1	487	— 8	378	—	873
1927	18,512	334	179	7	520	24	636	—	1,131
1928	17,604	355	182	4	540	31	399	—	907
1929	16,931	370	176	3	550	61	185	—	673
1930	16,185	388	160	5	554	— 8	184	—	746
1931	16,801	392	48	—	440	153	— 903	—	+ 616
1932	19,487	413	—	—	413	— 55	— 2,885	268	+ 2,686
1933	22,539	426	34	2	462	445	— 1,791	1,277	+ 3,052

* Exclusive of $4,800,000 written off the public debt Dec. 31, 1930.

SUMMARY OF CHANGES IN GROSS DEBT FROM JUNE 30, 1919 TO JUNE 30, 1933*

Gross debt outstanding:	June 30, 1919	25,485†
	June 30, 1930	16,185
	Total reduction	9,299
Debt retirement:	Cumulative sinking fund	3,187
	From foreign governments	1,489
	Miscellaneous	230
	Total chargeable to ordinary receipts	4,907
	Retirement through reduction in general fund balance	933
	From surplus receipts	3,460
	Total reduction	9,299
Gross debt outstanding:	June 30, 1930	16,185
	June 30, 1933	22,539
	Total increase	6,354
	Deficit of ordinary receipts	5,579
	Advances to Reconstruction Finance Corporation	1,545
	Through increase in general fund balance	543
	Total factors of increase in debt	7,667
	Cumulative sinking fund	1,231
	From foreign governments	82
	Total factors of decrease in debt	1,313
	Increase in gross debt (from June 30, 1930 to June 30, 1933)	$ 6,354

* Source: *Annual Report of the Secretary of the Treasury*, 1932, and *Daily Statement* of the U. S. Treasury, June 30, 1933.

† Discrepancies of a million dollars in the items of this table are attributable to rounding the constituent figures to the nearest million.

TABLE 161: SUMMARY OF EXPENDITURES ON THE BASIS OF THE DAILY TREASURY STATEMENTS (UNREVISED) CHARGEABLE AGAINST ORDINARY RECEIPTS*

(In millions of dollars)

FISCAL YEAR	TOTAL GENERAL EXPENDITURES	REFUNDS OF RECEIPTS	POSTAL DEFICIENCY	AGRICULTURAL MARKETING FUND (NET)	ADJUSTED SERVICE CERTIFICATE FUND	ALL OTHERS INCLUDING TRUST FUNDS†	TOTAL EXPENDITURES EXCLUDING PUBLIC DEBT	INTEREST ON PUBLIC DEBT	RETIREMENTS OF PUBLIC DEBTS	TOTAL PUB. DEBT EXPEND. CHARGEABLE AGAINST ORDINARY RECEIPTS	TOTAL EXPENDITURES CHARGEABLE AGAINST ORDINARY RECEIPTS
1920	3231	—	—	—	—	2152	5383	1020	79	1099	6482
1921	3080	—	—	—	—	1037	4117	999	422	1521	5538
1922	2136	83	64	—	—	98	2381	991	423	1414	3795
1923	1950	154	33	—	—	101	2238	1056	403	1459	3697
1924	1828	148	13	—	—	119	2108	941	458	1399	3507
1925	1837	171	23	—	99	51	2181	882	467	1349	3530
1926	1827	210	40	—	120	69	2266	832	487	1319	3585
1927	1858	138	27	—	115	49	2187	787	520	1307	3494
1928	1953	170	32	—	112	105	2372	732	540	1272	3644
1929	2107	213	95	—	112	93	2620	678	550	1228	3848
1930	2163	158	92	150	112	106	2781	659	554	1213	3994
1931	2390	91	146	191	224	126	3168	612	440	1052	4220
1932	2601	101	203	136	194	760	3995	599	413	1012	††5007
1933	2406	70	117	3§	100	189	2879	689	462	1151	††4030

* *Annual Report of the Secretary of the Treasury*, 1932, and *Daily Statement* of the U. S. Treasury, Jan. 30, 1933. Since July 1, 1932, deductions from salaries credited to certain funds, including the adjusted service certificate fund, have been classified as receipts, whereas prior to that date such items were used to offset expenditures for the respective funds.

† Includes for 1932 an item of $500,000,000 representing stock of Reconstruction Finance Corporation and $125,000,000 additional stock of the Federal Land Banks (See also note ††). For prior years there is here included the Treasury's operations in special accounts which are not separately detailed in this table. For example, in this column is reflected the accounting with railroads, War Finance Corporation, Shipping Board, etc.

†† Expenditures chargeable against ordinary receipts exclude net payments on account of purchases of notes of Reconstruction Finance Corporation, $267,735,209 for 1932 and $1,277,038,168 for 1933.

§ Excess of credits, deduct.

the transactions of the calendar years 1932 and 1933, so that on a given scale of rates, regardless of whether or not there are extremes of inflation, the receipts for the year 1934 cannot be expected to be much better than the discouraging inflow experienced in the fiscal year 1933.

The expansion of expenditures.—If public expenditures had remained constant after the onset of the depression, the shrinkage in revenues from taxation alone would have increased the public debt by something like $3,500,000,000 by the close of the fiscal year 1933. As is shown in Table 161, public expenditures continued the upward trend begun in 1924. The growth in general expenditures throughout the depression cannot be accounted for altogether by the acceleration of the government's public-works program. The importance of public works in expenditures is brought out in Table 162, and to the close of the fiscal year 1932 was not at all commensurate with the volume of public discussion of this item as one of the stimulants to business activity. The general expenditures figures also reflect the costs of emergency relief granted in the drought-stricken areas by the Department of Agriculture; the total expenditures by this department rose from $160,000,000 in 1928 to $319,000,000 for the fiscal year 1932. Veterans' Administration costs also increased in the depression period. Disbursements made from all appropriations by fiscal years 1928 to 1932 amounted to 660, 673, 684, 759, and 841 millions of dollars, respectively.

The important developments on the side of expenditures are to be found outside the category of "general expenditures." Aside from the postal deficiency, the operations of the Treasury under *(a)* the Agricultural Marketing Act, passed on June 15, 1929; *(b)* the World War Adjusted Compensation Act of May 19, 1924, and its amendment of February 27, 1931; *(c)* the Reconstruction Finance Corporation Act of January 22 and the Emergency Relief and Construction Act of July 21, 1932; and the "new deal" have made the greatest contributions to the growth of the Federal deficit and the public debt.

a) The Agricultural Marketing Act of 1929.—This measure was "An act to establish a Federal Farm Board to promote the effective merchandising of agricultural commodities in interstate and foreign commerce, and to place agriculture on a basis of economic equality with other industries."[4] A revolving fund of $500,000,000 was set up for the purposes of this Act, to be administered by the Federal Farm Board. On December 7, 1932, the net assets of the revolving fund amounted to $140,000,000,

TABLE 162

GENERAL EXPENDITURES OF THE FEDERAL GOVERNMENT EXCLUSIVE OF OUTLAYS FOR PUBLIC WORKS 1920-1932

(In millions of dollars)

FISCAL YEAR	TOTAL GENERAL EXPENDITURES	FEDERAL EXPENDITURE ON CONSTRUCTION, REPAIRS AND ALTERATIONS OF PUBLIC WORKS*	GENERAL EXPENDITURES EXCLUDING PUBLIC WORKS
1920	3,231	212	3,019
1921	3,080	246	2,834
1922	2,136	215	1,921
1923	1,950	197	1,753
1924	1,828	235	1,593
1925	1,837	271	1,566
1926	1,827	256	1,571
1927	1,858	256	1,602
1928	1,953	274	1,679
1929	2,107	308	1,799
1930	2,163	324	1,839
1931	2,390	473	1,917
1932	2,601	561	2,040

* Public Works figures do not include naval vessels. These data are the unpublished figures of the Federal Employment Stabilization Board.

representing a loss of $360,000,000[5] in grain, cotton, and other speculations. By executive order, March 27, 1933, the Federal Farm Board was merged with other agricultural credit agencies into one agency—the Farm Credit Administration. Subsequently the remaining assets of the Federal Farm Board were liquidated.

[4] Clark and Weld, *Marketing Agricultural Products* (New York: The Macmillan Co., 1932), Ch. XXVII, especially pp. 639-40.

[5] *Special Report* by Federal Farm Board to Congress (supplementing its *Third Annual Report)* Dec. 7, 1932, Press Service, Nos. 3-43, p. 5.

b) The World War Adjusted Compensation Act, 1924, and the amendment of February 27, 1931.—The World War Adjusted Compensation Act of 1924[6] introduced an invisible item into the public debt of United States, since the full amount of the obligation thereby incurred does not show up in any statement of the public debt. In Section 501, the Director of the Veterans' Bureau was directed

> upon certification of the Secretary of War or the Secretary of the Navy . . . to issue without cost to the veteran designated . . . a non-participating adjusted service certificate . . . of a face value equal to the amount in dollars of a 20-year endowment insurance that the amount of his adjusted service credit increased by 25 per centum would purchase, at his age on his birthday nearest the date of the certificate, if applied as a net single premium, calculated in accordance with the accepted actuarial principles and based upon the American Experience Table of Mortality and interest at 4 per centum per annum, compounded annually.[7]

Table 163 shows the cumulative amount of the face value of the adjusted-service certificates issued and outstanding as of the end of each fiscal year 1925-1933. The gross amount of this obligation outstanding may be expected to increase gradually up to January 2, 1935, because an amendment of June 5, 1930, extended the time for making applications for benefit under the Adjusted Compensation Act to that date.

Perhaps a word of explanation as to the origin of the "adjusted service credit increased by 25 per centum" is necessary.[8] Congress intended "to make some adjustment in the remuneration given to men who served in the Army, Navy, and Marine Corps as against the wages earned by those who labored at home." The Act provided "a basic service credit of $1 a day for each day's service in the United States and $1.25 a day for each day's service overseas." Basic credits of $50 or less were paid in cash. In case of the veterans who had died prior to the enactment of the bill, "the adjusted service credit was paid in 10 equal quarterly installments to the dependents of the veteran if the

[6] *Annual Report of the Director of Veterans' Bureau,* 1924, pp. 665 ff.
[7] *Ibid.,* p. 668.
[8] *Annual Report of the Administrator of Veterans' Affairs,* 1932, pp. 36 ff.

amount was over $50, otherwise in one sum." "In case of a living veteran, to the basic credit . . . there was added 25 per cent, and this sum was used as a single net premium to purchase for the veteran at his then attained age, a paid-up endowment certificate maturing upon the death of the veteran, or at the end of the 20-year period." The 25 per cent was added because the deferred-payment plan was adopted, so as to spread the cost over a considerable period.

TABLE 163

ADJUSTED SERVICE CERTIFICATES ISSUED AND OUTSTANDING, 1925-1932*

(Cumulative amounts in millions of dollars)

TO JUNE 30	FACE VALUE OF ADJUSTED SERVICE CERTIFICATES ISSUED	CLAIMS OF BENEFICIARIES OF ADJUSTED SERVICE CERTIFICATES ISSUED	ADJUSTED SERVICE CERTIFICATES OUTSTANDING
1925	2,733†	5	2,728
1926	3,070	20	3,050
1927	3,249	34	3,215
1928	3,372	51	3,321
1929	3,474	71	3,403
1930	3,493	90	3,403
1931	3,563	108	3,455
1932	3,648	129	3,519
1933	3,668	156	3,512

* Source: *Annual Reports,* U. S. Veterans' Bureau, 1925-1930; and Administrator of Veterans' Affairs, 1931-1933.

† The figures in this table follow the text of the reports which vary slightly from those submitted in the statistical tables.

To redeem the certificates the Act provided for the creation of a fund in the Treasury to be known as The Adjusted Certificate Fund. Authority was given to appropriate

for each calendar year (beginning with the calendar year 1925 and ending with the calendar year 1946) an amount sufficient as an annual premium to provide for the payment at face value of each adjusted certificate in twenty years from its date or on the prior death of the veteran, such amount to be determined in accordance with the accepted actuarial principles and based upon the American Experience Table of Mortality and interest at 4 per centum per annum, compounded annually.

The annual appropriations for this purpose were shown in Table 161, page 791. On June 30, 1932, the value of the reserve fund was $1,214,000,000 or $2,305,000,000 less than the amount necessary to make immediate payment of the maturity value of the certificates. Present worth of outstanding certificates was $1,879,000,000 or $1,640,000,000 less than the maturity value.[9] The Secretary of the Treasury was authorized to invest and reinvest the moneys in the fund in interest-bearing obligations of the United States and to sell such obligations of the United States for the purposes of the fund. The interest on and the proceeds from the sale of any such obligations were to become a part of the fund.

Since there were, at the time when the legislation was initiated, no interest-bearing United States obligations which precisely met the actuarial requirements of the fund, the Treasurer issued to the fund special 4 per cent certificates and notes in the amount of the annual appropriation and accrued interest on the securities held by the fund after allowing for deductions incidental to the operations of the fund, as for example, payments to beneficiaries upon the death of the certificate holders. The moneys actually appropriated, which, of course, came from the regular tax sources, lost their identity in the general fund of the Treasury, but the transactions resulted in effect in substituting these special 4 per cent issues for some equivalent portion of the United States debt otherwise outstanding which was retired. These special issues are included in the Treasury statements of the public debt outstanding although they are not held by the public, but for the interruption of the Amendatory Act of February, 1931, the amount of these special issues placed in the fund would have continued to increase until approximately 1944, when the Treasury would have been faced with the problem of marketing, not necessarily these specific 4 per cent issues, but approximately $3,500,000,000 of the most suitable type of Government obligation, so as to provide the cash for the liquida-

[9] *Ibid.*, p. 37.

tion of the adjusted service certificates which would have been outstanding on the date of final payment.[10]

Prior to the passage of the amendatory legislation of February, 1931, only some $290,000,000 had been borrowed on the security of the adjusted service certificates. The loan provisions of the original Act of 1924 first became effective on January 1, 1927. Loans were not permitted until after the expiration of the second year from date of issue of the certificate, and the amount of the loan was determined actuarially on the basis of a definite percentage of the reserve, so that by February 27, 1931, on average the loan value of the outstanding certificates stood at 22 per cent of the face value.

The total advances to veterans during the fiscal year 1931 amounted to $867,000,000. Over two million loans in the amount of $796,000,000 were made under the provisions of the new legislation in the last four months of that fiscal year. The total loans outstanding on June 30, 1931, amounted to $1,087,000,000 and were made to 2,265,345 veterans. By the close of the fiscal year 1933, "a total of 2,836,922 certificates had been pledged and held by the Veterans' Administration for loans and interest aggregating $1,536,880,479."[11] In addition, loans made by banks to the value of $60,000,000 were outstanding.

This great increase in the loans to veterans was made possible by the amendment of February 27, 1931,[12] which arbitrarily raised the loan basis of the service certificates from 22 to 50 per cent of their face value and which for the first time made available to the Administrator of Veterans' Affairs for loan purposes the resources of both the Adjusted Service Certificate fund and the Government Life Insurance fund. To provide for the additional loans to veterans as authorized by the new legislation, it became necessary for the Treasury to convert into cash the securities held in the Adjusted Service Certificate fund. The special securities were withdrawn from the fund not for sale to the public but for retirement. The Treasury proceeded to sell

[10] For the Treasurer's statement on the method of handling the fund, see *Treasury Annual Report*, 1925, pp. 118-20.

[11] *Annual Report of the Administrator of Veterans' Affairs*, 1933, p. 25.

[12] *Ibid.*, 1931, p. 171.

to the public government obligations in the form of Treasury bills and other short-term debt—types which could be placed with the banks at exceptionally favorable interest rates.

These loan operations, therefore, had the effect of increasing the floating debt outstanding in the hands of the public by over a billion dollars. On June 30, 1932, the value of the reserve fund was $1,214,000,000. The fund held only $105,000,000 of United States Government securities; $1,109,000,000 of the assets of the fund had been transformed from actual or potential investment in United States Government obligations in the form of special 4 per cent obligations into other assets which were almost entirely loans on adjusted service certificates.

In addition, all the funds available for investment from the Government Life Insurance fund during the fiscal year 1932 were used to make loans to veterans. On June 30, 1932, the administrator of Veterans' Affairs had invested from the fund $456,000,000 in the form of loans on policies and on adjusted service certificates.[13]

> Whenever a veteran borrows, the amount advanced stands as a lien against his adjusted service certificate at a rate of interest originally established at 2 per cent above the Federal rediscount rate for 60 days' paper in the Federal Reserve district in which the loan is made. This was modified later so that in no event would the interest charged the veteran exceed 4½ per cent, and at the last session of Congress a further reduction in interest was made to 3½ per cent.[14]

Besides lowering the maximum interest rate from 4.5 per cent compounded annually to 3.5 per cent compounded annually, the amendatory legislation of July 21, 1932,[15] permits veterans to borrow immediately upon the issuance of the certificate. Prior to this amendment a loan could be made only after the expiration of two years from the date of issue.

The several acts amending the World War Adjusted Compensation Act of 1924 have tended in the direction of putting a

[13] *Annual Report of the Secretary of the Treasury*, 1932, p. 115.
[14] *Annual Report of the Administrator of Veterans' Affairs*, 1932, p. 37.
[15] *Federal Reserve Bulletin*, Sept., 1932, p. 598.

billion dollars more of immediate spending power into the hands of veterans at the expense of their future economic status. This legislation synchronized with the general double-barreled policy which coupled the elements of relief with those which were supposed to make for an acceleration of business activity.

c) *The Reconstruction Finance Corporation.*—On the side of expenditures, the activities of the Reconstruction Finance Corporation, established under the Reconstruction Finance Corporation Act of January 22, 1932,[16] and extended as to the scope of its operations by the Emergency Relief and Construction Act of July 21, 1932,[17] have contributed substantially to the recent growth of the public debt.

The aim of the government in establishing the Corporation is perhaps best set forth in the words of President Hoover announcing his approval of the Reconstruction Finance Corporation Act:

> It brings into being a powerful organization with adequate resources, able to strengthen weaknesses that may develop in our credit, banking and railway structure, in order to permit business and industry to carry on normal activities free from the fear of unexpected shocks and retarding influences.
>
> Its purpose is to stop deflation in agriculture and industry and thus to increase employment by the restoration given to their normal jobs. It is not created for the aid of big industries and big banks. Such institutions are amply able to take care of themselves.
>
> It is created for the support of the smaller banks and financial institutions, and through rendering their resources liquid to give renewed support to business, industry, and agriculture. It should give opportunity to mobilize the gigantic strength of our country for recovery.[18]

The Corporation was organized February 2, 1932. Although the last temporary expiration date was placed at the end of January, 1935, under authority granted in section 13 of the Reconstruction Finance Corporation Act, the President can keep the Corporation afloat indefinitely until such time as the turn of events either justifies or permits closing out its accounts

[16] *Ibid.*, Feb., 1932, pp. 94 ff. [17] *Ibid.*, Aug., 1932, pp. 520 ff.

[18] *Ibid.*, Feb., 1932, p. 89.

with the many political jurisdictions, business units of various kinds, and the Treasury itself.

The potential resources of the Reconstruction Finance Corporation now appear to be scarcely distinguishable from those of the Treasury itself. The authorized capital of the Corporation is $500,000,000. In addition, it was allowed to borrow—originally $1,500,000,000, later $3,300,000,000, and now an indefinite amount—through issuing its own obligations.[19] Up to the close of business on December 31, 1933, the Corporation had acquired $2,643,000,000 (net) in cash from the Treasury of the United States—$500,000,000 representing the purchase of the entire authorized capital stock; $268,000,000 representing net payments from credits established on account of purchases of notes which were issued by the Corporation exclusively to the Treasury during the fiscal year 1932; $1,277,000,000 representing similar advances in the fiscal year 1933; and $598,000,000 in the period June 30-December 31, 1933.[20]

The practice had been to allocate from the total pool of funds available to the Reconstruction Finance Corporation certain amounts for definite purposes to be disposed of in accordance with regulations prescribed in one of the sections of the general relief acts. As the scope of its operations widened it became necessary to increase the borrowing powers of the Reconstruction Finance Corporation, until, under the Emergency Banking Act, the limit for this specific purpose was entirely removed, but the other ameliorative legislation of the new administration has otherwise continued the practice of either setting aside from, or adding to, the general pool of available funds definite amounts for the purposes of certain specific relief or emergency projects.[21]

Thus, for example, under Section 2 of the Reconstruction Finance Corporation Act, $200,000,000 was made available to the Secretary of Agriculture to be used by him for the purpose of making loans to farmers in localities where emergency condi-

[19] Sec. 9 of the Reconstruction Finance Corporation Act; Sec. 205[a] of the Emergency Relief and Construction Act (see footnotes 16 and 17); and Sec. 304 of Emergency Banking Law, New York *Times*, March 10, 1933.

[20] *Daily Statement* of the United States Treasury.

[21] Some of these projects, as will be shown later, are also fed by direct appropriations from the Treasury.

tions prevented them from otherwise obtaining loans for crop production in 1932. Only $64,000,000 of the aggregate allotted was used by the Secretary of Agriculture to finance crop production during 1932. An Act of February 4, 1933, authorized the Secretary of Agriculture to make similar loans not in excess of $90,000,000 during 1933. As of the close of business December 31, 1933, $135,000,000 in cash had been advanced to the Secretary of Agriculture for crop loans to farmers, of which $20,000,000 was repaid.[22]

With the unused balance of the original $200,000,000 allotted to the Secretary of Agriculture, the Reconstruction Finance Corporation was authorized in section 201[e] of the Emergency Relief and Construction Act of July, 1932, to purchase the stock of Regional Agricultural Credit Corporations which were to be created in any of the 12 land-bank districts with a minimum capital of $3,000,000 each in order to provide wider credit facilities to farmers and stockmen. Twelve such institutions, with some 20 branch offices, have been created with permission to rediscount with the Federal Reserve banks and the Federal Intermediate Credit banks. Through the aforementioned order of March 27, 1933, the functions of the Secretary of Agriculture with regard to loans in aid of agriculture and those of the Reconstruction Finance Corporation pertaining to the management of regional agricultural credit operations were, together with the Federal Farm Board and the Federal Farm Loan Board, consolidated into one agricultural credit agency—the Farm Credit Administration.

The Reconstruction Finance Corporation has advanced $44,500,000 for capital of the Regional Agricultural Credit Corporations, which leaves $40,500,000 of the original $200,000,000 available (as of December 31, 1933) to the governor of the Farm Credit Administration under the provisions of Section 5[a] of the Farm Credit Act of 1933. Further, under sections 201[c] and 201[d], respectively, of the Emergency Relief and Construction Act, the Reconstruction Finance Corporation is authorized to make loans for the purpose of financing sales of surplus agricultural

[22] *Commercial and Financial Chronicle,* Jan. 20, 1933, p. 443.

products in foreign markets; and to institutions which are engaged in facilitating the orderly marketing of agricultural commodities and live stock produced in the United States. On December 31, 1933, less than $79,000,000 had been disbursed for these purposes. The drain on the Reconstruction Finance Corporation for all agricultural purposes, as may be seen from the above account, has hitherto been relatively unimportant, but

TABLE 164

NUMBER OF LOANS AND NUMBER OF INSTITUTIONS BORROWING FROM RECONSTRUCTION FINANCE CORPORATION FROM FEB. 2, 1932 THROUGH DEC. 31, 1933*

CLASS OF BORROWER UNDER SECTION 5 OF THE RECONSTRUCTION FINANCE CORPORATION ACT	NO. OF LOANS	NO. OF INSTIT.
Banks and trust companies†	11,857	6,663
Building and loan associations	1,201	1,004
Insurance companies†	199	132
Mortgage loan companies	321	260
Credit unions	8	6
Federal land banks	47	12
Joint stock land banks	50	24
Agricultural credit corporations	241	19
Regional agricultural credit corporations	1,032	12
Livestock credit corporations	154	20
Federal intermediate credit banks	8	8
Railroads (incl. receivers)	125	67
Total	15,243	8,227

* Source: *Commercial and Financial Chronicle*, Jan. 20, 1933, p. 444.
† Including loans secured by preferred stock.

promises to assume larger proportions when the full effects of the agricultural relief approved May 12, 1933,[23] the Agricultural Adjustment Act (Title I), and the Emergency Farm Mortgage Act (Title II) have been realized. The Reconstruction Finance Corporation was empowered by the Emergency Farm Mortgage Act to increase the amount of its notes or other obligations outstanding by an additional $300,000,000. In Section 30A the Reconstruction Finance Corporation is directed to make available to the Farm Loan Commissioner $100,000,000

[23] *Federal Reserve Bulletin*, 1933, p. 307.

for the purpose of making loans to the Joint Stock Land banks engaged and doing business under the Federal Farm Loan Act. In Section 32, the Reconstruction Finance Corporation is directed to allocate to the Farm Loan Commissioner $200,000,000 for the purpose of making loans to any farmer secured by first and second mortgages upon his real or personal property, including crops. For the main purpose of the Act, the refunding of farm mortgages, a $2,000,000,000 bond issue guaranteed as to interest by the Government was authorized in Section 21. While no provision of Reconstruction Finance Corporation funds was made for the purposes of Title I, the Agricultural Adjustment Act, which embraces the allotment plan, nevertheless promises to be one of the most expensive relief items; because the disbursements to the agrarians are in no definite way limited to the less certain receipts from proposed processing or sales taxes on agricultural products. No student of the subject can contemplate the successful elevation of the domestic price of a world commodity above the market price except for the briefest of periods and at extraordinary costs, processing taxes notwithstanding. The agricultural adjustment will be ahead of us after the agricultural adjustors are behind us.

The chief functions of the Reconstruction Finance Corporation fall under Section 5 of the Reconstruction Finance Corporation Act. The number of institutions, by classes, borrowing, and the amounts of the loans advanced, repaid, and outstanding, are shown as of December 31, 1933, in tables 164 and 165.

The banks have been the leading clients of the corporation. To December 31, 1933, loans aggregating $1,883,000,000 were authorized to 6,663 banks and trust companies inclusive of loans authorized to receivers and liquidating agents of closed banks. Disbursements to open and closed banks amounted to $1,444,000,000 of which $711,000,000, or 50 per cent, has been repaid, leaving the outstanding advances to banks as of December 31, 1933, at $733,000,000.

The majority of the loans were made to banks located in the smaller centers, but a substantial block of the authorizations to

September 30, 1933, as shown in Table 166, fell to the banks located in the larger cities.

One of the immediate objectives of the Reconstruction Finance Corporation appeared to have been achieved when, in February, 1932, the number of bank suspensions had been reduced from the high levels which prevailed throughout 1930 and 1931 and the peaks which dominated the autumn and winter months of those two years. The number of suspensions had

TABLE 165

OPERATIONS OF THE RECONSTRUCTION FINANCE CORPORATION UNDER SECTION 5 OF THE RECONSTRUCTION FINANCE CORPORATION ACT TO DECEMBER 31, 1933*

(In millions of dollars)

CLASS OF BORROWER	ADVANCES	REPAYMENTS	AMOUNT OF LOANS OUTSTANDING ON OCT. 31, 1933
Banks and trust companies†	1,444	711	733
Railroads (incl. receivers)	394	57	337
Mortgage loan companies	213	36	177
Regional agricultural credit corporations	155	125	31
Building and loan associations	113	46	67
Insurance companies†	92	26	66
Federal land banks	142	—	142
Live stock credit corporations	13	10	3
Joint stock land banks	15	1	14
Federal Intermediate Credit Banks	9	9	0
Agricultural credit corporations	5	3	2
Credit unions	1	—	1
Total	2,596	1,024	1,573

* Source: *Commercial and Financial Chronicle,* Jan. 20, 1933, p. 444.
† Including loans secured by preferred stock.

been growing at an alarming rate, rising from 491 in 1928 to 642 in 1929, to 1,345 in 1930, and to a record of 2,298 in 1931. In the five months prior to the creation of the Reconstruction Finance Corporation, 1,702 banks had failed—342 of these failed in January, 1932. The total failure record for 1932 was 1,456. In December the situation seemed to be getting out of control once more; 161 banks were suspended, followed by 241 more closing in January, 1933, 148 in February, and the banking holiday in March.

The first phase of the Reconstruction Finance Corporation banking activities thus proved a complete failure. The second phase was initiated under the Emergency Banking Act of March 9, 1933.

Before the Emergency Banking Act, the relations of the Reconstruction Finance Corporation to the banks were such as to place the Government in an untenable position. Advances were

TABLE 166

THE NUMBER OF BANK BORROWERS AND AMOUNT OF LOANS AUTHORIZED UNDER SECTION 5 OF THE RECONSTRUCTION FINANCE CORPORATION ACT FROM FEB. 2 TO SEPT. 30, 1933, BY SIZE OF CITIES OR TOWNS*

POPULATION OF CITIES OR TOWNS IN WHICH BORROWERS ARE LOCATED	BANKS AND TRUST COMPANIES			
	BORROWERS		AUTHORIZATIONS	
	Number	Percentage of total	Amount	Percentage of total
Under 5,000	4,466	70.7	$ 209,947,771	13.5
5,000– 9,999	501	8.0	69,763,043	4.5
10,000– 24,999	460	7.3	107,142,628	6.9
25,000– 49,999	223	3.5	93,369,930	6.0
50,000– 99,999	189	3.0	184,000,964	11.9
100,000–199,999	138	2.2	140,351,204	9.1
200,000–499,999	97	1.5	183,519,266	11.8
500,000–999,999	128	2.0	336,506,750	21.7
1,000,000 and over	115	1.8	226,920,249	14.6
Total	6,317	100.0	$1,551,521,805	100.0

* Source: *Quarterly Report of Reconstruction Finance Corporation.*

made to the weakened banks only on their better assets, and, operating with public funds, the directors of the Corporation were inclined toward a conservative lending policy which called for wide margins of safety. Whenever the fresh supply of ready cash failed to resuscitate the borrowing bank and it had lost the confidence of its clients, the Government found itself in the embarrassing position of a preferred claimant upon the assets of the suspended institutions. Accordingly, when failures in large numbers broke out anew, the government could not have been expected to continue the unpopular form of relief which, if unsuccessful, compelled it to enforce its legal rights against the interests of private creditors (depositors) and owners of the suspended banks.

The loan practices of the Reconstruction Finance Corporation were all the more provoking to the borrowing institutions, because of the change in policy on publicity which was effected under the Emergency and Construction Act of July 12, 1932. It required that

> The Reconstruction Finance Corporation shall submit monthly to the President and to the Senate and the House of Representatives (or the Secretary of the Senate and the Clerk of the House of Representatives, if those bodies are not in session) a report of its activities and expenditures under this section and under the Reconstruction Finance, *together with a statement showing the names of the borrowers to whom loans and advances were made, and the amount and rate of interest involved in each case.*[24]

The original requirement was only that a quarterly report be submitted to Congress "stating the aggregate loans made to *each of the classes of borrowers provided for and the number of borrowers by states in each class.*"[25] When the Clerk of the House began to make the more detailed information public, the depositors of the borrowing banks and the public in general, which finally had come to suspect that all was not well with the financial structure of the country, became more definitely panicky and began to test the banks with withdrawals. The searchlight of publicity, therefore, in part destroyed the efficacy of the Reconstruction Finance Corporation as a stop-gap to the tide of bank failures.[26] Sound institutions have nothing to fear from publicity. Only those that have lost the confidence of the community could be adversely affected. The present administration was at least consistent in abolishing the practice of publishing the individual names of borrowing banks, although the wisdom of pouring public funds into these weakened institutions might be questioned.

[24] *Federal Reserve Bulletin,* Aug., 1932, p. 521, Sect. 201[b] of the Act.

[25] *Ibid.,* Feb., 1932, p. 98, Sect. 15 of the Reconstruction Finance Corporation Act.

[26] The American Bankers Assoc. conducted a survey on this point and found the bankers questioned almost unanimously adverse to the new publicity policy.

The emergency banking law of March 9, 1933, which followed the complete breakdown of the banking system of the United States and the temporary closing of all banks in the country, placed the government directly in the banking business. A large part of the capital of all banks had been destroyed in the course of the depression. It was the realization of this fact which contributed to the general state of alarm which existed prior to the banking holiday. Actually, the banks were little worse off prior to the panic than they had been for some considerable time, but the public had not generally realized the corrosive effects of the depression on bank assets. The double liability provisions relating to bank stocks, in many cases, had become practically ineffectual, so that the capital of banks could not always be replenished by assessing the stockholders who might, themselves, have been on the verge of bankruptcy. The emergency banking law enables the Government, through its agency the Reconstruction Finance Corporation, to restore part of the bank capital. Section 304 of the Act[27] provides:

> If in the opinion of the Secretary of the Treasury any national banking association or any state bank or trust company is in need of funds for capital purposes, either in connection with the organization or reorganization of such association, state bank or trust company, or otherwise, he may, with the approval of the President, request the Reconstruction Finance Corporation to subscribe for preferred stock in such association, state bank or trust company, or to make loans secured by such stock as collateral. . . . The Reconstruction Finance Corporation may, with the approval of the Secretary of the Treasury, and under such rules and regulations as he may prescribe, sell in the open market or otherwise the whole or any part of the preferred stock . . . acquired by the Corporation pursuant to this section. *The amount of notes, bonds, debentures and other such obligations which the Reconstruction Finance Corporation is authorized and empowered to issue and to have outstanding at any time, under existing law, is hereby increased by an amount sufficient to carry out the provisions of this section.*

Prior to this emergency the aggregate borrowing power of the Reconstruction Finance Corporation had been definitely

[27] Emergency Banking Law, Bank Conservation Act, New York *Times*, March 10, 1933, p. 2.

limited and, in addition, the allotment was stipulated for expenditure on each new function undertaken. Neither of these restrictions was imposed upon the Reconstruction Finance Corporation in its rôle as a bank stockholder. The Corporation, however, has issued a set of rules governing applications for subscriptions to or loans on preferred stock of banks under the Emergency Bank Act, which would seem to indicate a generally conservative policy. It favors what has come to be known as the Detroit plan. In this case, the National Bank of Detroit, with capital of $25,000,000, was established on March 21 and opened for business on March 24, 1933. One-half of the capital was contributed by the Reconstruction Finance Corporation, in subscriptions to preferred stock, and the remainder by the General Motors Company, in subscriptions to common stock which is subject to assessment and on which no dividends may be paid until the 6 per cent cumulative preferred dividends have been met. This new bank took over the liquid assets of the First National Bank and the Guardian National Bank of Commerce. The remaining assets will eventually be made available to the depositors by the United States Comptroller of the Currency through his agents the "conservators" for the two extinguished banks. If there is a deficiency of assets, the conservators will assess the stockholders of the original banks; or, if there is a balance remaining, after all claims had been discharged, it will be distributed to them.

In the words of one of the directors of the Reconstruction Finance Corporation, "the government will endeavor to help those who help themselves, but cannot be expected to furnish all the new capital required."[28] The national banks were authorized in Section 301 of the Emergency Bank Act to issue preferred stock, but most state laws do not permit such stock and, further, in some states the preferred stocks are assessable. This means that preferred stock offerings to the Corporation will practically be limited to national banks. The corporation requires a margin of protection for its stock purchases represented by local subscriptions to common or other subordinate stock

[28] New York *Times,* March 22, 1933, p. 25.

issues and, where the wiping out of the capital of issuing institutions has impaired the deposits, it will call for a reduction of deposits or other creditor claims on a pro-rata basis so as to bring back a balance between the claims against the institution and the value of its assets. While the Reconstruction Finance Corporation does not aim at dictating the policies of the banks, the preferred stock will have substantial voting rights in all matters affecting the issuing institutions. In addition, the regulators provide for such safeguards as: limitations on common stock dividends so long as the preferred stock remains outstanding; compulsory regular application of a large part of the net profits to the retirement of the preferred stock; consultations between the bank and the Corporation with respect to general policies; and both periodic and special reports.

On March 24, 1933, Section 304, Title III, of the Emergency Banking Act was amended by adding:[29]

> Nothing in this section shall be construed to authorize the Reconstruction Finance Corporation to subscribe for preferred stock in any State bank or trust company if under the laws of the State in which said State bank or trust company is located the holders of such preferred stock are not exempt from double liability. In any case in which under the laws of the State in which it is located a State bank or trust company is not permitted to issue preferred stock exempt from double liability, or if such laws permit such issue of preferred stock only by unanimous consent of stockholders, the Reconstruction Finance Corporation is authorized, for the purpose of this section, to purchase the legally issued capital notes or debentures of such State bank or trust company.

As of December 31, 1933, the Reconstruction Finance Corporation had purchased $475,000,000 of preferred bank stock; had extended loans secured by such collateral in the amount of $30,000,000; and had purchased $342,000,000 capital notes and debentures of banks for the purpose of aiding in the organization or reorganization of banks and trust companies under authority of section 304, Title III, of the Bank Conservation Act, as amended.

[29] *Federal Reserve Bulletin,* April, 1933, p. 247.

The second phase of the Reconstruction Finance Corporation's banking activities promised to be more successful than the first. The policy of reorganizing the weaker banks, segregating the liquid from the slow assets, and drawing in fresh capital partly from the local interests and partly from the government, temporarily providing banking facilities for many communities which might otherwise have been reduced to a state of barter, is on the whole commendable. The frozen assets were to be placed in the custody of the conservators who, presumably, all await some propitious moment for the liquidation of the assets with the least possible loss to the stockholders and the creditors of the supplanted institutions. This policy even if carried through is, after all, only a makeshift. In practice the policy under the Bank Conservation Act has been more to conserve weak institutions than to reorganize and consolidate them into going concerns. Until the last two months of 1933, the Reconstruction Finance Corporation's operations under Section 304 of Title III of this Act were not extensive.

The danger is that the breakdown in the banking system will come to be viewed entirely as the consequence of the extraordinary business depression and that due weight will not be given to its inherent defects. Those more sensitive to the meaning of 9,886[30] bank suspensions in the decade 1923-1932, have for some time been advocating a more permanent and fundamental revision of the banking structure than that forced upon the country in the recent emergency. Perhaps the best example of this more comprehensive viewpoint is afforded by the proponents of the "Banking Act of 1933,"[31] which is popularly known as the Glass bill.[32] As enacted, the bill was a compromise. Among the important proposals of the Glass bill as passed by the Senate were: the establishment of branches by national banks in those states which authorize their state banks to maintain branches; the divorcement of security affiliates from national

[30] Of the 9,886 banks suspended, 1,247 were reopened.

[31] *Federal Reserve Bulletin,* June, 1933, p. 385.

[32] The text of the Glass bill (S.4412) as passed by the Senate is available in the *Commercial and Financial Chronicle.* Feb. 11, 1933, p. 940. See also Federal Reserve Board's comments and recommendations on the Glass bill (S.4115), *Federal Reserve Bulletin,* April, 1932, p. 206 ff.

banks within five years' time; the prevention of the speculative uses of bank funds; and, in general, "the safer and more effective use of the assets of Federal Reserve banks and of national associations." For the purposes of the present discussion, the most interesting feature of the bill is the proposal to create a Federal Liquidating Corporation for the "prompt and economical" liquidation of the assets of closed banks. The procedure for handling the reorganization of the banking system, as outlined in this bill, would have involved the Treasury to a much less extent than the methods actually pursued. It might have prevented the complete collapse, and, in any event, it would have built a solid foundation for progress in American banking.

According to this bill the Treasury would supply $125,000,000 to the capital of the liquidating corporation; the Federal Reserve banks and the member banks of the system would be called upon to provide the balance.[33] It is a plan whereby the banks, themselves, partake in the mechanism devised for cleaning out the decayed parts of the banking structure. Without the branch banking provision the liquidating corporation could not function, for the branches of the stronger institutions must extend into those communities which otherwise might lose all their banking facilities.

Basically the difference between the procedure under the Glass bill and the accomplishments of the Reconstruction Finance Corporation, during what has here been termed the first phase of its banking activities, is this: In the one case, it was recognized that the assets of many banking institutions had been impaired beyond restitution; that these banks could continue neither to hold the confidence of their depositors nor to meet the ordinary calls of every-day business; and that, therefore, reorganizations were inevitable. To continue to loan to a group of tottering banks, as was done by the Reconstruction Finance Corporation, was sheer waste. It was throwing good money after bad. There are no intrinsic values for the assets of banks any more than there is intrinsic worth for anything. The burden of

[33] *Commercial and Financial Chronicle*, Feb. 11, 1933, pp. 941-42.

holding the immense bag full of depreciated bank assets until the increased tempo in business had filled back a portion of the mythical values of the securities, which had been carried off by the depression, was considered by the proponents of the Glass bill to be too great even for the Federal Treasury. It was, therefore, proposed to eradicate the dangerous elements in the banking system, and to provide facilities for reorganizing the extinguished banks so that the successor institutions might be free from the deadening effect of the frozen assets which had destroyed their forebears. The frozen assets were to be purchased by the liquidating corporation and sold, as soon as market conditions warranted, for the benefit of the creditors of the institutions entering the consolidation. The banking system, itself, was deemed to have adequate resources to be able to provide, through a system of branches, all the banking services that the country really needed.

The merit of the Glass bill would seem to be that it coupled permanent reform with the mechanism devised to purge the banking system of its weakest members. In this respect it affords a contrast to the procedure prescribed in the emergency banking act—Bank Conservation Act—under which the Reconstruction Finance Corporation has undertaken its second effort in banking. The emergency law also makes possible reorganizations and the segregation of the liquid assets from the frozen assets of closed banks along lines which outwardly appear to be very similar to the plan contemplated in the Glass bill. In the case of the Glass bill the liquidating corporation takes over the duties of disposing of the frozen assets of failed banks for the benefit of their creditors and owners. According to the Detroit plan the conservators will perform this function for the Reconstruction Finance Corporation. In both cases the liquid assets may be assumed by a newly created or reorganized institution, and in each case banking facilities are assured to the public. Wherein lies the difference?

Present methods have resulted in tying up a large volume of Treasury funds in the banking business, mostly in the form of direct loans secured by the assets of the banks borrowing from the Reconstruction Finance Corporation, and also indirectly through the Corporation's subscription to preferred stocks, capital notes and debentures of numerous banks. If the liquidating corporation had been established at the outset of the depression, only $125,000,000 of public funds would have been involved. At the time of the emergency the bank resources had been so impaired that it is debatable whether the banks as a group were in a position to practice self-help. Coming when it did, the plan of the emergency banking act may have been inescapable—that is, it may have become imperative for the Government to subscribe to part of the bank capital of the country, if for no other purpose than to revive enough confidence so as to render the banking system workable once more.

Not only do the banking activities of the Government promise to be more protracted and expensive than they might have been under the liquidating corporation, but the achievements are sure to be meager. No essential change is taking place in the banking system. It is true that many banks have been wiped out. Many more would have been wiped out by now but for the nourishing diet of public funds fed them by the Reconstruction Finance Corporation, which only delays their fate. The Government is artificially sustaining a batch of feeble banking institutions, and one of its most recent steps has been in the direction of restricting the scope of branch banking as proposed in the Glass bill and of helping to replace unit banks in precisely those places where the toll has been heaviest. When prosperity does come and the banks can stand on their own after repaying all their Reconstruction Finance Corporation loans and retiring all the preferred stock, notes and debentures, the banking system in its fundamental characteristics will revert to the type which has been productive of a long chain of bank failures and which has contributed to several crises but which, despite a country of bounteous resources, has not yet proved satisfactory for any substantial stretch of years. Even if the relief features of the emergency bank legislation could, under the pressure of circumstances, be considered admirable in themselves for immediate purposes, they must be pronounced inadequate otherwise; they must be replaced by, or coupled with, some such measure as the original Glass bill which undertakes to revamp the whole style and pattern of banking, to regulate portfolios, to distinguish between banking and speculation, to provide branch banking, and, perhaps, to do many other things so that the assets of banks henceforth might indeed be "safer and more effective."

Now, the Banking Act of 1933, effective June 16, which developed out of the Glass bill differs essentially in at least two respects: First, it narrowed the scope of branch banking from a state-wide to a county basis, thereby prohibiting any radical reform of the system and, secondly, it substituted in section 12B the Deposit Insurance Corporation for the Federal Liquidating Corporation. Instead of eradicating the weakest banks and making whatever funds remained available to the depositors, the efforts of the Administration were to feed sufficient capital into the banks to render them eligible for membership in the deposit guarantee by January 1, 1934. This attempt to carry the old framework of the banking structure forward on an actuarial basis must result in having the business community served by a less virile group of financial institutions than those which might have been set up under the original bill, and thus retarding recovery to a corresponding degree. While the direct obligations of the Treasury were not increased by thus altering the Glass bill, the banking system remains a greater potential source of drain on account of these changes.

The position of the Administration on the banking situation was clarified by the President in a radio address on October 22, 1933, when he said in part:

First, the Federal Government is about to spend one billion dollars as an immediate loan on the frozen or nonliquid assets of all banks closed since January 1, 1933, giving a liberal appraisal to those assets. This money will be in the hands of the depositors as quickly as it is humanly possible to get it out.

Secondly, the Government bank-deposit insurance on all accounts up to $2,500 goes into effect January 1. We are now engaged in seeing to it that on or before that date the banking capital structure will be built up by the Government to the point that the banks will be in sound condition when the insurance goes into effect.[34]

According to the Federal Reserve Board's figures, "at the end of September there were still more than 2,500 closed banks (exclusive of mutual savings banks and banks in the hands of receivers) with total liabilities approximating $1,750,000,000.[35] In order to release these funds the President announced on October 15, 1933, the establishment of a special division in the Reconstruction Finance Corporation—the Deposit Liquidation Division, administered by a Deposit Liquidation Board consisting of six members. "The object of establishing this Deposit Liquidation Division and trying to stimulate the distribution of frozen bank assets is," according to the President, "First, to place money in the hands of depositors with the least possible delay, and second, to bring about more orderly liquidation of the assets of closed banks; this will prevent dumping of assets at sacrifice prices."[36] As noted above, about a billion dollars will be made available by the Federal Government to the Deposit Liquidation Division for its loan operations.

The Emergency Relief and Construction Act of July 21, 1932, authorized the Reconstruction Finance Corporation to make available to the states and their political subdivisions $300,000,000 for the relief of distress in their respective communities. These advances were authorized under two subsections of Section 1 of the Act, subsections *c* and *e*. Those advanced under subsection *c* "are to be repaid to the Federal Government by deductions from future Federal contributions to states to aid in constructing roads,"[37] and constitute by far the most important element in the loans under this category. Advances under subsection *e* were made to the political subdivisions of states and must be repaid. As of December 31, 1933, $299,000,000 (net) had been disbursed to states, territories, and political subdivisions of states for relief purposes under the Emergency Relief and Construction Act of 1932. According to

[34] *Federal Reserve Bulletin*, Nov. 1933, p. 669.
[35] *Ibid.*, Oct., 1933, p. 595. [36] *Ibid.*, p. 596.
[37] *Commercial and Financial Chronicle*, April, 1933, p. 2167

the Federal Emergency Relief Act of 1933, approved May 12, 1933, applications under Title I of the Emergency Relief and Construction Act of 1932 were placed under a Federal Emergency Relief Administrator and the negligible unexpended balance of the $300,000,000 authorized under Title I was made available to him. In addition the 1933 Relief Act directed the Reconstruction Finance Corporation to make available a fund of $500,000,000 which it is to pay over to the states upon certification of the Federal Emergency Relief Administrator. As of December 31, 1933, $315,000,000 of this fund had been disbursed. These are not loans but outright gifts to the states for relief purposes.

The borrowing powers of the Reconstruction Finance Corporation were extended by another $1,500,000,000 under the Emergency Relief and Construction Act to provide loans to states; to other public bodies and agencies, and to corporations for self-liquidating projects more or less of a public nature. This building program had two aims: (1) to create employment and (2) to create traffic for railroads. Very little was actually spent out of this allotment. As of December 31, 1933, only $64,000,000 had been advanced in cash under section 201[a] of the Act and $153,000,000 of the authorizations remained to the credit of the borrowers. These figures do not represent the scope of Federal government's public-works program, because the entire public works and construction program was by the National Recovery Act of June 16, 1933, placed under a Federal Emergency Administration of Public Works and both loan operations and the funds available under Section 201 of the Emergency Relief and Construction Act were transferred to it.[38] The public-works program has at last become an active factor in the recovery policy. On March 31, 1933, the Reforestation Relief bill was signed, which called for a public-works program of $500,000,000 designed to give direct employment to 250,000 men. The policy of maintaining government corps of workers on Federal projects is to be continued. Altogether the Roosevelt Administra-

[38] National Industrial Recovery Act, June 16, 1933, Title II, Sect. 201-3 and Title III, Sec. 301.

tion has projected a public-works program estimated to involve Treasury outlays of over three billion dollars.

The Government has also come to the relief of the small home owner. The Federal Home Loan Bank Act of July 22, 1932,[39] provided for the organization of from eight to twelve Federal Home Loan Banks, each with a capital of not less than $5,000,000 to be subscribed by institutions eligible for membership and by the Treasury out of a $125,000,000 fund to be provided by the Reconstruction Finance Corporation. These institutions are to make advances to building and loan associations, savings banks, insurance companies, and individuals on the security of first mortgages on dwelling-house property, the value of which does not exceed $20,000. The Home Owners Loan Act of 1933, approved June 13, created the Home Owners Loan Corporation for the purpose of refinancing the mortgages on small homes. The Treasury was authorized to subscribe to the stock of the corporation in amounts not to exceed $200,000,000 from funds provided by the Reconstruction Finance Corporation, whose borrowing powers were correspondingly extended. For the main purpose of the Act a two-billion-dollar bond issue guaranteed as to interest by the Government was authorized.

Such, in broad outline, is the scope of the remedial legislation devised to help pull business out of the trough and to provide relief to various sections of society. It has entailed great strain upon the Treasury[40] and added a large bloc to the public

[39] *Federal Reserve Bulletin,* Aug., 1932, p. 527.

[40] Some statisticians have attempted to appraise the cost of the "new deal." It is not possible at present (December, 1933) to forecast the ultimate cost. Who knows what percentage of the advances to private business concerns, farmers, and state and local governments are recoverable; or to what extent contingent liabilities may become actual liabilities? According to a report in the New York *Times* of Nov. 11, 1933, the National Industrial Conference Board compiled a statement of *liabilities* under the new deal which follows:

(In millions of dollars)

Federal Emergency Administration of Public Works	3,150
Agricultural Adjustment Administration:	
Treasury appropriation	100
Processing taxes, 2 years, estimate	1,000
Farm Credit Administration:	
Government guaranteed bonds	2,000

debt with little apparent effect. Can these efforts be continued on a grander scale without undermining the United States Government bond market and thereby impairing one of the very few undepreciated bank assets?

Changes in the Composition of the Public Debt of the United States

A striking feature of both the war and depression periods of debt increase has been the concomitant growth of the floating and other short-term issues.

By the end of December, 1930, the interest-bearing debt outstanding in the hands of the public, that is, exclusive of the special issues to trust funds, was reduced $11,357,000,000 from the peak of August, 1919. Most of the decrease came in the short-term debt. Treasury notes outstanding declined $3,485,000,000, certificates of indebtedness $3,009,000,000, and Treasury bills—a new issue—were outstanding (increased) in the amount of $127,000,000. Altogether then, the shrinkage in the short-term debt accounted for $6,367,000,000 of the $11,357,000,000 debt retirements for that period.

From December 31, 1930, to December 31, 1933, the interest-bearing debt, as defined in Table 167, increased $8,088,000,000. Not all this growth has been in the form of short-term debt. Treasury notes outstanding increased $3,319,000,000, certifi-

Reconstruction Finance Corporation	300
Treasury appropriation	185
Home Owners' Loan Corporation:	
Reconstruction Finance Corporation	200
Government guaranteed bonds	2,000
Federal Emergency Relief Administration (R.F.C.)	500
Emergency Conservation Works Administration:	
Estimated expenditure, 1 year	250
Tennessee Valley Authority (Government guaranteed bonds)	50
Federal Deposit Insurance Corporation (contingent liability)	2,000
Reconstruction Finance Corporation:	
Total lending ability, minus items stated above	3,400
Grand Total	$15,135

It may be pointed out that the Federal Government guarantees the interest but not the principal of the $2,000,000,000 bond issues for the purposes of the Farm Credit Administration and the Home Owners Loan Corporation.

cates of indebtedness, $436,000,000, and Treasury bills $876,000,000, thus making the aggregate increase of the short-dated debt $4,631,000,000, or nearly 58 per cent of the $8,088,000,000 increase which has taken place since the beginning of 1931.

If we describe outstanding issues with maturities (at issue date) of one year or less, as "floating" debt, as distinguished from the intermediate debt represented by the Treasury notes which usually have terms of three to five years, then it may be pointed out that the floating debt has grown from $1,319,000,000 at the

TABLE 167

INTEREST-BEARING DEBT OF THE UNITED STATES OUTSTANDING (EXCLUSIVE OF SPECIAL ISSUES TO TRUST FUNDS), BY CLASSES

(In millions of dollars)

END OF MONTH	BONDS	TOTAL SHORT-TERM OBLIGATIONS	TREASURY* NOTES	CERTIFICATES OF INDEBTEDNESS	TREASURY* BILLS	TOTAL
March, 1917	1,023	—	—	—	-	1,023
Aug., 1919	17,102	9,247	5,046	4,201	-	26,349
Dec., 1930	12,112	2,880	1,561	1,192	127	14,992
March, 1933	14,230	6,430	3,352	2,261	817	20,660
Dec., 1933	15,569	7,511	4,880	1,628	1,003	23,080

* Including Treasury war-savings securities and Victory notes.

end of December, 1930, to $2,631,000,000 at the end of December, 1933, or that $1,312,000,000 of the total $4,631,000,000 increase in the short-term debt for this period was in the form of obligations maturing one year or less from their date of issue.

At the end of April, 1919, the floating debt stood at over six and a quarter billion dollars. It had been built up by issuing certificates of indebtedness for two purposes: First, to anticipate the receipts from the income and excess profits taxes and, secondly, to anticipate the receipts from the sale of long-term war obligations. The first of the certificates were issued before the United States entered the War. On March 31, 1917, $50,000,000 of 90-day certificates of indebtedness were sold by the Treasury directly to the twelve Federal Reserve banks in anticipation of the internal revenue taxes which were payable in June. After this first issue the Federal Reserve banks served as the media through which the tax and loan certificates were distributed to the banks and through them, so far as possible, to the public. The certificates were then accepted by the Treasury in payment of income and excess profits taxes or in payment of Liberty bonds. Secretary Carter Glass explained the need for floating debt as follows:[41]

This means of temporary financing has provided the government with funds in advance of receipts from the sale of bonds or notes, or in anticipation of revenue from income and profits taxes; and has served the additional helpful purpose of distributing the payments of bonds and note subscriptions and of taxes gradually over extended periods of time, avoiding tremendous transfers of funds on any one date and consequent money stringency.

Commenting on the sharp drop in the floating debt from the peak of six and a quarter billion dollars at the end of April to about three and three-quarter billion dollars on October 31, 1919, he declared:[42]

It will not be desirable to fund all the certificates, for the issue of certificates of indebtedness, in anticipation of income and profits tax installments not only furnish a means of financing requirements of the government temporarily upon easy terms, but constitutes an almost necessary financial expedient, to enable the taxpayer to save and to prepare gradually for the great tax payments, and to relieve the banking machinery of the country of the great strain which would be imposed upon it if these tax installments had to be paid on a single day without such preparation.

In October, 1922, when the certificates of indebtedness outstanding amounted to a little over a billion dollars,[43] Secretary A. W. Mellon expressed the opinion that "it will in any event continue to be desirable, with income and profits tax payments as large as they are, for the Treasury to have outstanding at least one billion dollars of tax certificates in amounts and with maturities conforming to the quarterly tax payments." The in-

[41] *Annual Report of the Secretary of the Treasury*, 1919, p. 54.
[42] *Ibid.*, p. 5.
[43] *Ibid.*, 1922, p. 171.

come and profits taxes for the fiscal year 1922 were around two billion dollars and with the exception of 1932 and 1933, have remained more or less around that level. Therefore, according to Secretary Mellon, the necessary amount of floating debt which normally should be outstanding is in the neighborhood of a billion dollars.

On April 30, 1921, when the intermediate debt outstanding amounted to $4,782,000,000 and the certificates of indebtedness stood at the excessive figure of $2,820,000,000, a new policy for the management of the short-dated debt was first outlined by the Secretary.[44] It involved the retirement of as much short-dated debt as possible from the operation of the sinking fund, the application of miscellaneous sources of revenue, and refunding the remainder into Treasury notes with maturities of from three to five years extending over the period between the maturity of the Victory Liberty Loan on May 20, 1923, and the maturity of the Third Liberty Loan on September 15, 1928, and falling due on tax-payment dates, so as to facilitate the program of debt reduction from excess receipts of revenues which was planned by the Administration.

The first issue of Treasury notes was on June 15, 1921,[45] and was followed roughly, at quarterly intervals, by several issues in accordance with the new policy. It enabled the Treasury to take advantage of declining interest rates to an extent which would have been impossible had the entire surfeit of short-dated debt been converted at one stroke into a long-term bond issue.[46] The policy of rearranging the maturities of the short-dated debt and reducing the floating debt at the beginning of the period 1921-1928, however, had to be supplemented by bond issues, because the total volume of short-term issues was excessive and the heavy maturities of notes and certificates falling due on tax-payment dates proved embarrassing to the Treasury.

[44] *Ibid.*, 1921, p. 4.

[45] In the discussion above and in the tables, "Treasury notes" has been used in the sense of intermediate debt with maturities in excess of one year and not over five years. Prior to June 15, 1921, the intermediate debt was in the form of Victory notes and war-savings securities.

[46] *Annual Report of the Secretary of the Treasury*, 1922, p. 4.

It was this circumstance which led up to the first issue of Treasury bonds in October, 1922, the first long-time government obligations offered since the Fourth Liberty Loan of September, 1918.[47]

Toward the end of the period 1921-1928, when despite tax-rate reductions the Treasury was annually realizing surplus receipts, and the short-term debt had been whittled down to a relatively low point so that the maturities falling due on tax dates could no longer be relied upon to take up the excess revenues, the Government was enabled to persist in its established debt-retirement policy by refunding a large portion of the unretired issues of the Second and Third Liberty Loans into Treasury notes with maturities arranged to meet the requirements of its program.[48] The main motive for this refunding operation was the reduction of the interest rates from the 4¼ per cent which applied to almost all of $5,300,000,000 of Second and Third Liberty Loans which remained outstanding as of February 28, 1927.

To sum up: the policy adopted by the Treasury with reference to the public debt prior to the current depression was to adjust it for purposes of retirement and management by converting, at first, some floating debt, and later, some long-time Liberty bonds into intermediate issues and spacing the maturities of new issues, which were arranged to fall on tax-payment dates, over an extended period, so as to facilitate the retirement of the securities from the surplus receipts of the Treasury without violent disturbance of the money market. The primary objective was a debt structure which would "assure the gradual liquidation of the debt and put the nation in shape to meet future emergencies,"[49] but the cost of the different types of financing also entered largely into the choice of government offerings during this period.[50]

From the very beginning of the depression the cost of borrowing came to be the chief determinant of the character of the government securities which have been offered to the public.

[47] *Ibid.*, 1922, p. 5.
[48] *Ibid.*, 1928, p. 28.
[49] *Ibid.*, 1922, p. 9.
[50] *Ibid.*, 1925, p. 29.

Chiefly for the purpose of taking better advantage of the rapidly declining interest rates a new issue—the Treasury bill—was introduced in December, 1929.[51]

The greater part of the revenue receipts are concentrated in the quarterly income tax-payment months, whereas the disbursements are distributed more evenly throughout the year as the various governmental activities call for payment. Unless the short-dated public debt were skillfully managed, the money market would periodically be subject to violent disturbances on account of this disparity. In practice, the effects of the heavy withdrawals of funds for tax-payment purposes are offset by arranging the maturities of the short-term issues so as to coincide with the quarterly peaks in revenue; also, in accordance with the Treasury's estimates of receipts and cost requirements until the next quarterly tax-payment month, it was customary to offer some new issue of certificates of indebtedness to provide the Treasury with new credits at the depositing banks wherewith to supplement its revenues and to tide it over until the next quarterly tax-payment month. This method of financing brought the Treasury's current receipts and expenditures into approximate balance and served to reduce the disturbances in the money market to a minimum.

Beginning with the last quarter of 1929, certificates of indebtedness were not issued in amounts adequate to cover fully the estimated requirements of the Treasury between quarterly tax-payment dates. Treasury bills were sold for cash at relatively frequent intervals to supplement the regular quarterly issues of certificates of indebtedness. Since short-term interest rates fell very rapidly after the stock exchange collapse of October, 1929, the cost of government borrowing was substantially lower for the period of the depression than it would have been without the use of the Treasury bill. It is possible for the Treasury bill to yield another advantage to the Treasury. When the government borrows enough funds on a quarterly tax-payment date to carry it through until the next quarter, a large but diminishing portion of the loan rests idle in the banks at the disposal of the

[51] *Ibid.*, 1929, pp. 38-41.

Treasury. The Government pays interest on this idle money or credit. The Treasury bill permits a hand-to-mouth borrowing policy and therefore can reduce the costs of financing. Actually the Treasury carried such large balances throughout the depression that this benefit was not reaped from the use of the Treasury bill. It would appear, however, that a large part of the balance was carried at a profit, in so far as the borrowing rate was under the statutory 2 per cent allowed the Government on its deposits.

The Present Delicate Position of the Government Securities Market

The Liberty bonds broke under par soon after they were issued in 1917. By the Third Liberty Bond Act of April 4, 1918, the Secretary of the Treasury was authorized to purchase Liberty bonds in order to stabilize their market prices.[52] The bond purchase fund, operated by the War Finance Corporation as an agency of the Treasury, came into existence as early as April 12, 1918, and expired on July 2, 1922. It purchased securities with an aggregate face value of $1,966,000,000 at the cost of $1,876,000,000. Despite its activities, Liberty bond prices which had held on average around 96 during the years 1918-1919 broke by May, 1920, to 88.8, and averaged 90.9 for the year.[53] It was not till April, 1924, that the average for Liberty bond prices again attained the par level of 100. The post-war disintegration of the government-securities market was largely attributed to the sharp shrinkage of the national income. The public had subscribed to much of the public debt with the aid of fiat bank credit and found it impossible to earn enough income during the post-war depression to meet their urgent requirements and at the same time to continue what were in effect installment payments on government bonds. They were forced to sell out their holdings, and Liberty bond prices slumped off.

The pool of investors' money which is available to the capital markets has never been definitely determined nor very ac-

[52] *Ibid.*, 1919, p. 82, and 1922, p. 46.
[53] *Base Book*, Standard Trade and Securities Service, 1930-31, p. 47.

curately estimated, but is known to be of substantial size at any point of time. The supply of funds for capital purposes must have undergone considerable diminution during the current protracted depression. Many people have been forced to live on their savings rather than their incomes. Much of the fund held for investment has been diverted to current consumption. At the same time the demand for capital may be expected to become more insistent in the near future. Many of the industrial plants whose capacities have exceeded and may continue to exceed requirements for some time to come, nevertheless have not been fully maintained in the past three or four years. If efficient production standards are to be maintained, a large part of the available supply of capital funds must soon be diverted into industrial channels for replacements, betterments, repairs, and working capital; also, from the above it is clear that the Government is not yet through with the capital market. With all the remedial legislation which has been enacted and the huge public-works program undertaken, the Treasury, or what in fact are its agencies, will be compelled to offer for public subscription several billions of government bonds. The inevitable result of the combined industrial and governmental demand for capital must be a hardening of interest rates which would depress bond prices. Only a patriotic public disregarding its immediate business interests by maintaining and purchasing parcels of the public debt can prevent the crumpling of the government-security prices, if in present circumstances the burden of federal financing is heaped up to the extent of many more billions.[54]

As will be shown in the following chapter, much of the public debt is now held by the banks. Those banks which will be compelled to realize upon their government securities in the near future will find it extremely difficult to do so except at a loss. If the policy of issuing a large volume of new debt is undertaken and the public is encouraged to take up the securities not with their savings but with the aid of fiat bank credit, as was done during the War, there is a real danger that, despite the

[54] The Treasury estimates the increase in the public debt for the fiscal year 1934 at $6,141,297,168. New York *Times*, Jan. 5, 1934.

powers bestowed upon the Treasury to support the Federal securities with the $2,000,000,000 Stabilization Fund provided in the "Gold Bill" of January 30, 1934,[55] price deterioration of government securities may become an independent disturbing factor in the banking field which is already crowded with ailments.

If the above analysis is correct, then one is compelled to draw two conclusions with reference to the present status of the public debt: First, it is dangerous for the Treasury to pursue further the policy of maintaining a large floating debt, because even from the narrowest point of view, there is nothing to gain except higher costs of financing and possible embarrassment through failure to place refunding issues. The Treasury appeared once to have realized this point, for it issued $500,000,000 three-year 2⅞ per cent notes dated May 2, 1933, "with the right reserved . . . to increase the offering by an amount sufficient to allot in full all subscriptions up to $10,000."[56] A portion of the proceeds of this issue ($239,000,000) was used for the retirement of certificates of indebtedness falling due on May 2, and the balance represented an increase in the public debt. Subsequently this policy of reducing floating debt was discontinued. Second, conditions have not been suitable for a huge conversion project. As of March 31, 1933, there were outstanding the following Liberty bonds which had become redeemable:[57]

First Liberty Loan of 1932-1947		
3½% bonds	$1,392,000,000	
4% bonds (converted)	5,000,000	
4¼% bonds (converted)	536,000,000	
		$1,933,000,000
Fourth Liberty Loan of 1933-1938, 4¼%		6,268,000,000
		$8,201,000,000

The Fourth Liberty Loan would have been redeemable on October 15 if the Treasury had given the required six months' notice on April 15, 1933. The next call for the bonds will be on

[55] *Commercial and Financial Chronicle,* Feb. 3, 1934, p. 742 (Gold Reserve Act of 1934).
[56] New York *Times,* April 25, 1933.
[57] *Daily Statement* of the United States Treasury, March 31, 1933.

April 15, 1934. The Treasury gave the required notice on October 11 for a partial redemption of about $1,875,000,000 of the Fourth 4¼'s.[58]

Simultaneously, the Treasury announced a new series of 1943-1945 bonds dated October 15, 1933, bearing 4¼ per cent interest to October 15, 1934, and 3¼ per cent thereafter. This issue was offered for cash in the amount of $500,000,000 or thereabouts, and in exchange for the Fourth Liberty Loan Bonds, whether or not called for redemption. As of December 31, 1933, there were outstanding $1,398,000,000 of the new issues of 4¼-3¼ per cent bonds of 1943-1945. As of September 30, 1933, there were $6,268,000,000 of Fourth Liberty Loan of 1933-1938 4¼'s outstanding. This had been reduced by $898,000,000 to $5,370,000,000 by the end of December, 1933. It appears, therefore, that $500,000,000 of the 4¼-3¼'s of 1943-1945 were purchased with cash and $898,000,000 exchanged for the 4¼'s of 1933-1938.

It is very questionable whether it is wise to attempt to convert the seven and a half billion dollars of Liberty bonds now outstanding on a lower interest basis. At a lower interest rate the depreciation in prices of government securities which is here anticipated will merely be all the more severe and the problems created thereby so much more difficult of solution. It would be far better if, in the announcements of fresh bond issues in the near future the Secretary of the Treasury were to stipulate a higher interest rate, so that the public debt of the United States might be more largely placed in the hands of the investing public rather than the banking institutions. Then, whenever the money market once more begins to reflect the actual situation in the capital market and there is a hardening of interest rates, the United States Government securities will be better able to resist depreciation.

The composition of the interest bearing debt of the United States by types of security for the period 1917 to 1933 is shown in the following Chart XXII.

[58] New York *Times*, Oct. 12, 1933, p. 28.

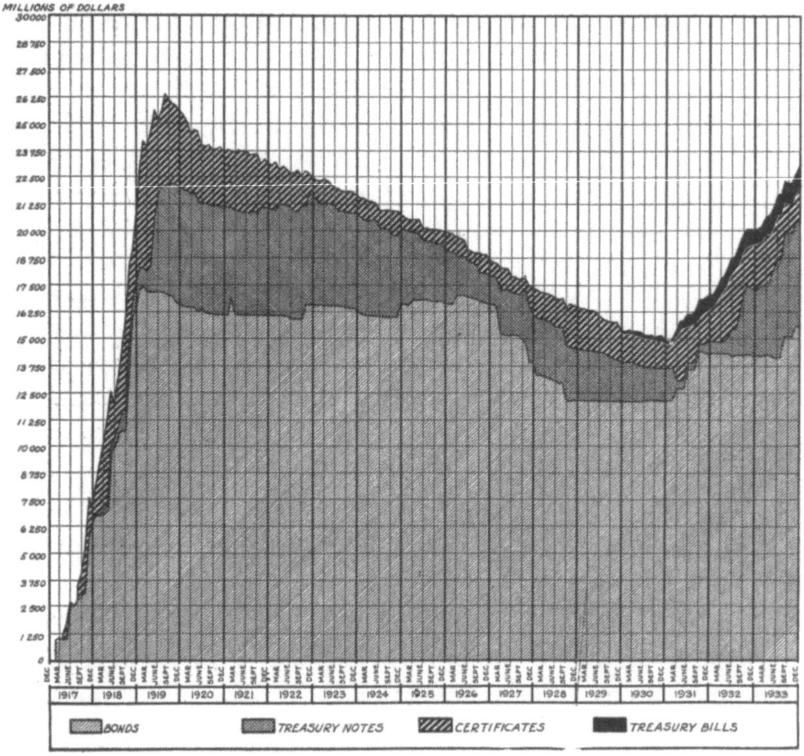

CHART XXII. INTEREST-BEARING DEBT OUTSTANDING, 1917-1933

(Exclusive of special issues to trust funds.)

Source: *Treasury Department, Monthly Statement of the Public Debt of the United States.*

CHAPTER XXXV

PUBLIC DEBT AS A BANK ASSET

Before the War United States government securities found a place among bank resources chiefly in their rôle as backing for the national bank-note issues. The War increased the volume of these securities to several billions of dollars. The services of the banks had been enlisted by the Treasury in placing the numerous issues incidental to financing the War, and ever since then they have held substantial blocks of the public debt. It is a type of investment which the banks have favored because it is thought more secure and "shiftable" than any other type of security and because it is the basis for public deposits. While the banks are at present holding more government obligations than they have ever held, the practice of investing heavily in the United States public debt has by no means originated within the last two or three years of the current depression.

Public Debt Held by All Banks Reporting to the Comptroller of the Currency

Over $8,300,000,000 out of $18,900,000,000, or some 44 per cent of United States Government securities outstanding in the hands of the public as of June 30, 1932, were held by banks, inclusive of the Federal Reserve banks. This represented an increase of about $3,750,000,000 over the amount held two years before. The record of the banks' holdings of United States Government securities so far as made available by them to the Comptroller of the Currency, is presented in Table 168. These data, unfortunately, contain an indeterminate but probably wide margin of error, in the nature of an understatement, which may run into something like a half-billion dollars in the aggregate of any one year. The error arises from the fact that several of the banks, other than national banks reporting to the Comptroller of the Currency, group some of their United States Government securities which are not long-term bonds with their

TABLE 168: UNITED STATES GOVERNMENT SECURITIES HELD BY CLASSES OF BANKS*

(In millions of dollars)

ON OR ABOUT JUNE 30	NATL. BANKS (INCL. BONDS DEPOS. TO SECURE CIRCULATION)	STATE COMMERCIAL BANKS	LOAN & TRUST COMPANIES	STOCK SAVINGS BANKS	MUTUAL SAVINGS BANKS	PRIVATE BANKS	ALL BANKS OTHER THAN NATIONAL	TOTAL ALL REPORTING BANKS	FEDERAL RESERVE BANKS	FEDERAL FARM LOAN SYSTEM‡	GRAND TOTAL U. S. SECURITIES HELD IN BANKS	INTEREST BEARING DEBT OUTSTANDING§	PERCENTAGE OF PUBLIC DEBT IN BANKS
1913	796	3	3	5	18	†	30	825	—	—	825	966	85.4
1914	799	3	3	1	17	†	24	823	—	—	823	968	85.1
1915	783	3	2	5	17	†	28	811	8	—	819	970	84.4
1916	731	1	1	†	5	†	7	739	57	—	796	972	81.9
1917	905	30	32	1	13	1	77	982	71	10	1,063	2,713	39.2
1918	2,117	180	158	31	78	9	455	2,572	259	17	2,848	11,986	23.8
1919	3,176	528	197	4	245	11	986	4,162	232	43	4,437	25,234	17.6
1920	2,270	413	249	34	370	8	1.074	3,344	352	9	3,705	24,061	15.4
1921	2,019	454	450	29	909	11	1,852	3,872	259	33	4,164	23,735	17.5
1922	2,285	391	318	21	477	6	1,215	3,500	555	68	4,123	22,711	18.2
1923	2,694	460	382	137	533	4	1,517	4,211	102	77	4,390	22,008	19.9
1924	2,482	463	350	139	1,167	14	2,133	4,614	431	60	5,105	20,982	24.4
1925	2,537	525	349	162	604	6	1,645	4,182	353	61	4,596	20,116	22.9
1926	2,469	564	345	174	503	5	1,591	4,060	385	54	4,499	19,179	23.5
1927	2,596	530	371	108	221	3	1,233	3,829	370	27	4,226	17,892	23.6
1928	2,891	551	379	123	203	5	1,262	4,153	235	33	4,420	16,854	26.2
1929	2,804	572	364	101	178	4	1,219	4,023	216	23	4,262	16,032	26.6
1930	2,754	490	370	79	153	2	1,093	3,847	591	26	4,463	15,157	29.4
1931	3,256	668	1,545	89	157	2	2,461	5,718	668	23	6,409	16,230	39.5
1932	3,353	552	1,925	93	531	1	3,103	6,456	1,784	105	8,345	18,852	44.3

* Source: *Annual Reports of the Comptroller of the Currency, Federal Reserve Bulletin,* and *Annual Reports of the Secretary of the Treasury.*

† Less than $500,000.

‡ Includes Federal land banks, joint-stock land banks, and Federal intermediate credit banks, as of the end of Sept. or Oct.

§ Exclusive of special issues to trust funds which were not outstanding in the hands of the public.

miscellaneous or unclassified investments. In addition, there are deviations in the data of Table 168 which arouse suspicion. For example, the 1924 item appearing under mutual savings banks is about twice the size of the amount shown for either the preceding or the following year. There is, also, a question as to what extent the remarkable growth in United States government securities held by loan and trust companies during the years 1931-1932 over 1930 is owing to the vagaries in accounting; furthermore, the classes of banks listed in Table 168 are not mutually exclusive. Those designated as national banks, and perhaps also the mutual savings banks, actually include no other varieties; however, the banks included under the other captions in Table 168 must be regarded as impure, even though approximating to "total population," samples of their respective types of banks. While, therefore, the figures in Table 168 are not strictly accurate, they do afford the basis for the general conclusion that the banks have in the aggregate absorbed an increasingly larger portion of the total United States Government securities outstanding. In other words, they have become more and more important factors in the market for United States Government securities.

Not all of the United States Government securities found among the resources of the banks represent their voluntary investments in the public debt. A certain amount of these holdings grow out of legal requirements and are incidental to the performance of regular banking functions. Thus, the Treasurer of the United States holds in trust, year by year, from eight hundred million to a billion dollars of United States Government securities which are pledged by the banks to secure national bank circulation, to secure Federal Reserve bank notes, postal deposits, and postal savings funds.

It is clear that the Treasury has become increasingly dependent upon the banks for its financing, but it is not so easy to appraise the change in bank policy, if any, which is involved on account of the growth in the absolute amount of the Federal debt held by the banks, without at the same time undertaking an inquiry into the variations among the other bank assets and without relating the growth in their holdings of United States Government securities to the growth in other securities and to loans. This basic information is submitted in Tables 169, 170, and 171.

Of the total loans and investments by all banks reporting to the Comptroller of the Currency, an extraordinarily large portion, ranging from 26.6 to 39.3 per cent, has for the period 1913-1932 always been in the form of investments. There are, of course, some variations in this respect as between the different classes of banks, but even those banks which presumably might have been expected to conform closest to the ideal commercial banking institution, that is, the national banks, have habitually invested very heavily in a wide variety of securities. Investments constituted from 23 to 41 per cent of the total loans and investments made by national banks during the period under consideration.

Most of the investments for all types of banks were for most of the period made in so-called "other securities," that is, securities other than those of the Federal Government. The national banks seem to show the greatest preference for United States Government securities. From 30 to 63 per cent of their investments, usually about 40 per cent, were of this type, whereas for banks other than national only from 12 to 28 per cent, usually about 20 per cent, of their investments were in Federal obligations. In interpreting, however, the data of Table 169 from which the above figures were extracted, it will be remembered that involuntary investments in Government securities, that is, the requirement to pledge government bonds with the Treasurer of the United States for purposes itemized elsewhere, would tend toward increasing the national banks' holdings of the Federal bonds more than it would those of the remaining classes of banks which, unlike the national banks, are without the privilege of note issue.

Further, the data contained in Tables 169, 170, and 171 are subject to limitations similar to those stated above in connection with Table 168, but they probably are sufficiently accurate to gauge the relative importance of United States Government

TABLE 169: UNITED STATES GOVERNMENT SECURITIES AS A PERCENTAGE OF TOTAL INVESTMENTS BY CLASSES OF BANKS

ON OR ABOUT JUNE 30	NATIONAL BANKS	STATE COMMERCIAL BANKS	LOAN AND TRUST COMPANIES	STOCK SAVINGS BANKS	MUTUAL SAVINGS BANKS	PRIVATE BANKS	ALL BANKS OTHER THAN NATIONAL	ALL BANKS IN THE U. S.
	%	%	%	%	%	%	%	%
1913	42.1	1.0	.2	3.5	1.0	3.5	.8	15.3
1914	41.7	.7	.3	.4	.9	1.6	.7	14.7
1915	37.9	.7	.2	3.5	.9	2.1	.7	13.8
1916	31.1	.2	.04	.03	.3	1.5	.2	10.9
1917	30.0	3.3	1.8	.3	.6	7.0	1.5	12.3
1918	53.5	14.3	7.5	14.7	3.6	32.6	7.9	26.4
1919	62.9	23.2	9.5	1.5	9.8	27.1	13.7	34.0
1920	54.2	18.6	13.1	10.5	13.6	26.0	14.9	29.4
1921	50.2	18.6	23.2	49.6	31.4	36.7	25.2	34.0
1922	50.1	17.0	13.8	6.6	15.9	18.3	15.2	27.9
1923	53.1	17.8	15.8	37.0	16.7	11.6	17.6	30.8
1924	48.3	17.0	12.7	37.9	36.3	39.8	23.5	32.4
1925	44.3	17.2	12.5	37.6	18.0	16.3	17.0	27.2
1926	42.3	17.5	12.3	34.5	14.8	15.0	16.0	25.7
1927	40.6	15.6	10.6	25.8	6.3	11.3	11.4	22.2
1928	40.5	15.6	9.8	28.7	5.4	17.2	10.9	22.1
1929	42.1	18.5	10.6	26.5	4.7	13.2	11.4	23.2
1930	40.0	16.6	9.6	20.8	3.9	8.7	9.9	21.4
1931	42.4	22.7	33.6	24.4	3.5	11.5	19.9	28.5
1932	46.6	24.4	45.8	26.6	12.7	11.9	28.1	35.4

• Source: *Annual Reports of the Comptroller of the Currency.*

TABLE 170: UNITED STATES GOVERNMENT SECURITIES AS A PERCENTAGE OF TOTAL LOANS AND INVESTMENTS BY CLASSES OF BANKS*

ON OR ABOUT JUNE 30	NATIONAL BANKS	STATE COMMERCIAL BANKS	LOAN AND TRUST COM-PANIES	STOCK SAV-INGS BANKS	MUTUAL SAV-INGS BANKS	PRIVATE BANKS	ALL BANKS OTHER THAN NATIONAL	ALL BANKS IN THE U. S.
	%	%	%	%	%	%	%	%
1913	9.9	.1	.1	.6	.5	.3	.2	4.1
1914	9.6	.1	.1	.1	.4	.2	.2	3.9
1915	9.0	.1	.05	.5	.4	.2	.2	3.7
1916	7.3	.03	.01	.005	.1	.2	.1	3.0
1917	7.6	.6	.5	.1	.3	1.0	.5	3.4
1918	15.0	3.0	2.4	3.1	1.7	5.1	2.5	8.0
1919	19.4	5.9	3.2	.4	5.1	5.8	4.6	11.1
1920	12.4	3.7	3.8	2.6	7.0	5.2	4.4	7.8
1921	12.4	3.9	7.2	5.9	15.9	8.0	7.7	9.6
1922	14.3	3.8	4.8	1.6	7.9	4.5	5.0	8.6
1923	15.8	4.1	5.1	8.8	8.1	3.3	5.6	9.5
1924	14.4	4.0	4.3	8.3	16.7	12.6	7.5	10.1
1925	13.6	4.2	3.9	9.0	8.0	5.0	5.4	8.5
1926	12.7	4.4	3.6	9.1	6.3	4.1	4.9	7.8
1927	12.8	4.1	3.4	6.9	2.6	2.7	3.6	7.0
1928	13.0	4.2	3.1	8.3	2.2	4.3	3.5	7.1
1929	13.1	4.2	2.9	7.3	1.9	3.0	3.3	6.8
1930	12.6	4.0	2.8	6.1	1.6	2.2	3.0	6.6
1931	15.6	6.5	12.4	7.9	1.5	3.2	7.2	10.3
1932	19.2	7.5	19.0	9.9	5.1	3.6	10.8	14.0

* Source: *Annual Reports of the Comptroller of the Currency.*

TABLE 171: INVESTMENTS AS A PERCENTAGE OF TOTAL LOANS AND INVESTMENTS BY CLASSES OF BANKS*

ON OR ABOUT JUNE 30	NATIONAL BANKS %	STATE COMMERCIAL BANKS %	LOAN AND TRUST COMPANIES %	STOCK SAVINGS BANKS %	MUTUAL SAVINGS BANKS %	PRIVATE BANKS %	ALL BANKS OTHER THAN NATIONAL %	ALL BANKS IN THE U. S. %
1913	23.5	11.3	30.1	15.7	47.1	7.3	29.4	27.0
1914	22.9	11.8	30.3	15.2	46.6	11.5	29.2	26.7
1915	23.7	12.6	30.7	15.7	46.3	11.8	29.5	27.2
1916	23.4	16.9	30.2	15.5	47.4	10.9	30.4	27.6
1917	25.2	17.8	29.3	17.3	47.4	13.9	29.9	27.9
1918	28.1	20.9	32.5	21.0	48.4	15.5	31.8	30.1
1919	30.8	25.4	33.6	27.5	51.6	21.2	33.8	32.5
1920	22.9	19.9	29.2	24.9	51.2	20.0	29.4	26.6
1921	24.7	21.1	31.2	11.8	50.7	21.9	30.5	28.2
1922	28.5	22.4	34.7	23.6	50.0	24.8	32.6	31.0
1923	29.7	22.8	32.4	23.8	48.7	28.7	31.8	31.0
1924	29.8	23.4	34.2	22.0	46.0	31.6	31.9	31.1
1925	30.8	24.7	31.4	23.9	44.5	30.4	31.5	31.2
1926	30.0	24.9	29.3	26.3	42.4	27.6	30.6	30.4
1927	31.4	26.2	31.9	26.8	41.0	23.9	31.8	31.6
1928	32.0	27.2	31.8	29.0	40.5	25.0	32.2	32.2
1929	31.0	22.9	26.9	27.5	39.4	22.7	28.7	29.5
1930	31.6	24.2	28.8	29.2	39.6	24.9	30.2	30.7
1931	36.8	28.7	36.8	32.5	42.5	27.5	36.0	36.3
1932	41.2	30.6	41.6	37.2	40.6	30.5	38.2	39.3

* Source: *Annual Reports of the Comptroller of the Currency.*

securities among investments over the period 1913-1932; and the defect that some of the short-term Government securities are reported in the miscellaneous category rather than under United States Government securities does not invalidate the comparison of total investments with any or all of the remaining bank assets.

So far as reliable, the figures reveal the interesting fact that although in absolute amounts there has been a definite upward trend or growth both in the amount of United States Government securities and in other investments held by banks, still the relative importance of investments and of United States Government securities among the bank assets cannot be said to have undergone sufficient continuous change in the same direction to warrant the conclusion that the banks have been consistently revising their policies with reference to portfolios and investments. The percentages which United States Government securities formed of all investments, and which investments were of all loans and investments, have fluctuated from year to year throughout the period 1913-1932, but there is no general drift either upward or downward.

In the years 1931 and 1932 investments, and especially United States Government securities have come to constitute increasingly greater proportions of the resources of all classes of banks. Especially pronounced in this respect are the changes recorded for trust and loan companies. Of the $2,609,000,000 increase in United States Government securities held by all banks reporting to the Comptroller of the Currency during the two-year period June 30, 1930 to June 30, 1932, $1,555,000,000 went into their portfolios; the national banks absorbed $599,000,000; the mutual-savings banks $378,000,000; and the balance was distributed over the other classes of banks.

In the two-year period from June 30, 1930 to June 30, 1932, the banks added nearly $1,100,000,000 of state, county, and municipal bonds to their portfolios. Of this increase $628,000,000 went into the mutual-savings banks, $239,000,000 into the national banks, and the balance was distributed over the other types of banks as shown in Table 172.

TABLE 172

STATE, COUNTY, AND MUNICIPAL BONDS HELD, BY CLASSES OF BANKS, BY YEARS*

(In millions of dollars)†

ON OR ABOUT JUNE 30	NATIONAL BANKS	STATE COMMERCIAL BANKS	TRUST COMPANIES	STOCK SAVINGS BANKS	MUTUAL SAVINGS BANKS	PRIVATE BANKS	ALL BANKS OTHER THAN NATIONAL	TOTAL ALL REPORTING BANKS
1913	175	89	114	51	809	2	1,065	1,240
1914	176	91	211	24	848	4	1,177	1,353
1915	244	102	241	54	849	4	1,250	1,494
1916	278	31	68	1	250	1	352	630
1917	316	54	67	1	236	2	360	676
1918	320	42	38	1	214	1	297	617
1919	323	97	21	1	178	2	299	622
1920	338	78	37	1	186	2	304	643
1921	394	189	139	4	640	3	975	1,368
1922	414	221	87	5	252	2	567	981
1923	402	203	72	10	205	2	493	894
1924	506	202	76	6	612	1	896	1,401
1925	595	221	88	5	156	1	473	1,067
1926	648	266	126	4	226	1	623	1,271
1927	744	286	211	23	458	2	980	1,724
1928	840	325	235	8	479	2	1,050	1,890
1929	757	318	154	5	509	2	989	1,746
1930	792	289	140	6	474	1	910	1,702
1931	997	313	437	3	514	2	1,269	2,266
1932	1,031	261	399	7	1,102	1	1,770	2,802

* Source: *Annual Reports of the Comptroller of the Currency.* † Discrepancies in last digit owing to round figures.

Loans and discounts began to contract during the fiscal year 1930, but it was not until 1931 that liquidation became general. The shrinkage in loans was partly compensated in 1931 by an increase in investments, and even in 1932 when both loans and investments were declining the loans receded more precipitately than the investments. Throughout the recession the banks kept increasing their holdings of Federal, state, county, and municipal securities, thereby providing themselves with earning assets to replace their loans. They had little opportunity to shift out of either foreign securities or the domestic industrial and railroad bond market, for these classes of securities had either become so depreciated early in the depression or their market so restricted that any attempt at realization would have spelt bankruptcy. So long as the banks were able to carry their miscellaneous securities at fictitious values on their balance sheets, and so long as they had the confidence of the public, the majority of them were able to remain open despite frozen portfolios, but too many banks were not in a position to withstand the strain of the slightest test of their liquidity, hence the collapse of March, 1933.

The banks usually fail to distinguish between a mortgage and a bill of exchange. They try to combine investment trust functions with deposit banking, and the wonder is not that the system is perpetually floundering about, as evidenced by the large number of annual bank failures, nor that it periodically develops crises in a country which affords the optimum industrial potentialities, but that it has been able to render any effective service whatsoever to the community. The basic principle of the investment trust is diversification, and diversification assumes a business of considerable size with facilities enabling it to gather independently a wide body of information which affects the profitableness of the institutions represented in its portfolio. The small unit bank, with low capitalization, is ill-adapted for the conduct of an investment business. In practice, the depositor, through the policy of the banks, has been converted into a stockholder with all the responsibilities and none of the rights, for his funds have been used by the banks for the purpose of carrying excessive investments in miscellaneous high yielding bonds. These could in many cases be "unloaded" by unscrupulous issuing houses with ease because the small-unit

TABLE 173

UNITED STATES GOVERNMENT SECURITIES HELD BY ALL MEMBER BANKS ON CALL DATES*

(In millions of dollars)

CALL DATE		NEW YORK CITY	OTHER RESERVE CITY BANKS INCLUDING CHICAGO	COUNTRY BANKS	ALL MEMBER BANKS
1926—April	12	864	1,568	1,399	3,831
June	30	902	1,490	1,353	3,745
Dec.	31	809	1,293	1,288	3,389
1927—March	23	926	1,589	1,321	3,835
June	30	907	1,581	1,308	3,796
Oct.	10	887	1,645	1,324	3,856
Dec.	31	948	1,728	1,302	3,978
1928—Feb.	28	1,082	1,839	1,294	4,216
June	30	1,102	1,810	1,312	4,225
Oct.	3	1,130	1,894	1,362	4,386
Dec.	31	1,094	1,836	1,382	4,312
1929—March	27	1,135	1,896	1,424	4,454
June	29	1,006	1,765	1,384	4,155
Oct.	4	989	1,671	1,361	4,022
Dec.	31	1,112	1,484	1,267	3,863
1930—March	27	1,150	1,662	1,273	4,085
June	30	1,147	1,686	1,229	4,061
Sept.	24	1,091	1,785	1,219	4,095
Dec.	31	1,239	1,727	1,159	4,125
1931—March	25	1,466	2,313	1,224	5,002
June	30	1,656	2,408	1,279	5,343
Sept.	24	1,830	2,301	1,433	5,564
Dec.	31	1,768	2,133	1,418	5,319
1932—June	30	2,008	2,187	1,432	5,628
Sept.	30	2,429	2,466	1,471	6,366
Dec.	31	2,603	2,462	1,474	6,540
1933—June	30†	2,551	2,867	1,469	6,887

* Source: Member bank *Call Reports*.
† Licensed banks (banks operating on an unrestricted basis).

bank cannot afford to pay for the executive ability and the facilities which are required for skillful independent investigation into the soundness of the issues.

Public Debt Held by Member Banks

More reliable figures on the amount of United States Government securities held by member banks of the Federal Reserve

TABLE 174

UNITED STATES GOVERNMENT SECURITIES AS A PERCENTAGE OF INVESTMENTS, BY ALL MEMBER BANKS*

CALL DATE		NEW YORK CITY	OTHER RESERVE CITY BANKS INCLUDING CHICAGO	COUNTRY BANKS	ALL MEMBER BANKS
		%	%	%	%
1926—Apr.	12	52.6	47.8	33.8	42.3
June	30	52.6	45.6	32.7	41.0
Dec.	31	49.8	41.0	30.6	37.7
1927—March	23	51.9	45.1	30.6	39.9
June	30	49.4	44.5	29.5	38.7
Oct.	10	51.9	45.0	28.8	38.7
Dec.	31	51.5	44.8	27.9	38.4
1928—Feb.	28	55.7	46.6	27.5	39.8
June	30	54.8	45.4	27.5	39.3
Oct.	3	58.2	48.1	28.8	41.4
Dec.	31	56.6	47.8	29.1	41.0
1929—March	27	57.5	50.7	30.0	42.6
June	29	55.3	48.9	29.9	41.3
Oct.	4	54.8	49.3	29.9	41.3
Dec.	31	53.2	45.6	28.5	39.5
1930—March	27	56.2	48.7	28.5	41.1
June	30	52.1	45.7	27.0	38.9
Sept.	24	49.6	45.2	26.6	38.2
Dec.	31	50.9	42.8	25.7	37.5
1931—March	25	55.1	49.5	26.9	42.1
June	30	59.1	50.7	28.1	44.1
Sept.	24	60.4	50.4	31.1	45.6
Dec.	31	65.6	50.5	32.3	47.0
1932—June	30	66.2	52.7	33.9	49.3
Sept.	30	69.3	55.7	35.1	52.5
Dec.	31	68.7	56.5	35.8	53.3
1933—June	30†	68.8	62.0	40.8	57.7

* Source: Member bank *Call Reports*.
† Licensed banks (banks operating on an unrestricted basis).

system are made available by the Federal Reserve Board on call dates several times a year, than the Comptroller of the Currency has been able to make public once a year for all reporting banks. In addition, the data for member banks are subdivided broadly according to the size of the city in which the member banks are located, so that it is possible not only to check against the general tendencies revealed by the comptroller's more inclusive but

TABLE 175

UNITED STATES GOVERNMENT SECURITIES AS A PERCENTAGE OF TOTAL LOANS AND INVESTMENTS, BY ALL MEMBER BANKS*

CALL DATE		NEW YORK CITY	OTHER RESERVE CITY BANKS INCLUDING CHICAGO	COUNTRY BANKS	ALL MEMBER BANKS
		%	%	%	%
1926—April	12	14.1	12.6	11.3	12.3
June	30	14.1	11.9	10.9	11.9
Dec.	31	12.1	10.2	10.3	10.6
1927—March	23	14.2	12.2	10.5	11.9
June	30	13.0	12.0	10.2	11.5
Oct.	10	12.8	12.2	10.2	11.5
Dec.	31	12.1	12.5	10.0	11.5
1928—Feb.	28	14.8	13.4	9.9	12.3
June	30	14.1	12.8	9.7	11.9
Oct.	3	15.0	13.3	10.0	12.4
Dec.	31	12.9	12.9	10.1	11.9
1929—March	27	14.0	13.5	10.4	12.4
June	29	11.8	12.7	10.1	11.5
Oct.	4	11.5	11.9	9.9	11.0
Dec.	31	11.9	10.7	9.5	10.5
1930—March	27	13.1	12.1	9.6	11.5
June	30	12.4	12.2	9.3	11.2
Sept.	24	12.1	12.7	9.4	11.4
Dec.	31	13.7	12.4	9.3	11.6
1931—March	25	16.5	16.4	10.0	14.2
June	30	19.2	17.6	10.6	15.5
Sept.	24	21.6	17.5	12.1	16.7
Dec.	31	23.0	17.5	12.9	17.2
1932—June	30	29.8	19.8	14.0	20.1
Sept.	30	34.1	22.4	14.8	22.7
Dec.	31	35.5	23.4	15.4	23.8
1933—June	30†	35.8	29.3	18.7	27.8

* Source: Member bank *Call Reports*. The Loans include overdrafts and acceptances of other banks and bills of exchange or drafts sold with indorsement.
† Licensed banks (banks operating on an unrestricted basis).

less satisfactory figures, but also to ascertain whether the changes which have taken place in the relative importance of investments generally and of United States securities among those investments were uniformly characteristic of banks regardless of their location; or whether there are significant differences as between the investment practices of banks located in the city and those located in the country.

TABLE 176

INVESTMENTS AS A PERCENTAGE OF TOTAL LOANS AND INVESTMENTS BY ALL MEMBER BANKS*

CALL DATE		NEW YORK CITY	OTHER RESERVE CITY BANKS INCLUDING CHICAGO	COUNTRY BANKS	ALL MEMBER BANKS
1926—April	12	26.7	26.3	33.3	29.2
June	30	26.8	26.1	33.2	29.1
Dec.	31	24.2	24.9	33.7	28.2
1927—March	23	27.3	27.0	34.2	29.9
June	30	26.4	26.9	34.6	29.8
Oct.	10	24.6	27.1	35.2	29.8
Dec.	31	23.6	28.0	35.7	29.9
1928—Feb.	28	26.6	28.7	35.9	31.0
June	30	25.8	28.1	35.2	30.3
Oct.	3	25.7	27.7	34.7	30.0
Dec.	31	22.8	27.1	34.8	29.0
1929—March	27	24.3	26.7	34.5	29.1
June	29	21.3	26.0	33.7	27.8
Oct.	4	20.9	24.1	33.0	26.7
Dec.	31	22.3	23.4	33.2	26.7
1930—March	27	23.4	25.0	33.8	27.9
June	30	23.8	26.7	34.6	28.8
Sept.	24	24.4	28.0	35.4	29.8
Dec.	31	26.8	29.0	36.1	30.9
1931—March	25	30.1	33.2	37.0	33.7
June	30	32.5	34.7	37.7	35.2
Sept.	24	35.8	34.8	39.0	36.5
Dec.	31	35.1	34.6	39.9	36.6
1932—June	30	45.0	37.5	41.3	40.7
Sept.	30	49.3	40.3	42.1	43.2
Dec.	31	51.7	41.4	42.8	44.7
1933—June	30†	52.0	47.2	45.7	48.1

* Source: Member bank *Call Reports.* The Loans include overdrafts and acceptances of other banks and bills of exchange or drafts sold with indorsement.

† Licensed banks (banks operating on an unrestricted basis).

On December 31, 1932 the member banks held $6,540,000,000 of the Federal debt. This represented a growth of $2,677,000,000 in three years. The tendency toward larger holdings of Federal issues has been characteristic of all groups of member banks regardless of their location. The New York City member banks absorbed $1,491,000,000, those in other reserve cities $978,000,000, and the country member banks $208,000,000 during the three years ended December 31, 1932 (Table 173). Not only has the greatest amount of increase been in the banks located in the larger centers, but as is shown in Tables 174, 175, and 176, although United States Government securities became generally more important among member bank investments, and investments came to play a more important rôle among bank assets from 1929 to 1932, these changes were more marked for the member banks of New York City and of other reserve cities than for country banks. On December 31, 1929, the percentages which United States securities were of all investments by member banks of New York City, other reserve cities, and country districts, amounted to 53.2, 45.6, and 28.5 respectively. By December 31, 1932, these percentages grew to 68.7, 56.5 and 35.8. The corresponding increase for all member banks was from 39.5 to 53.3 per cent. Similarly, on December 31, 1929, the percentages which all investments were of total loans and investments by member banks of New York City, other reserve cities, and country districts amounted to 22.3, 23.4, and 33.2, respectively. By December 31, 1932, these percentages advanced to 51.7, 41.4, and 42.8. The growth for all member banks was from 26.7 to 44.7 per cent. The different rates of change in the composition of bank assets according to the location of the member banks is further illustrated in the summary Table 177.

In the prosperous period preceding the current depression investments were consistently a more important element in the assets of country banks than in those of New York or other reserve cities; however, as may be seen in Table 176, in the September, 1931, call the importance of investments in New York banks overcame that of other reserve city banks. By June 30, 1932, and thereafter investments in New York banks became of even more relative importance than for country banks. At the same time the relative importance of investments in member banks of other reserve cities had also been increasing more rapidly than in the case of the country member banks. The explanation of this reversal of the position of investments among the assets of the three classes of member banks is to be sought in the different rates of decline in the loans extended by these respective groups of banks as well as in the variety of investment policies pursued by them. It may be added that while the banks had control over and could direct their new investments into Government or other securities, they could in no manner set the pace for the liquidation of loans which attended the shrinkage

TABLE 177

CHANGES IN THE RELATIVE IMPORTANCE OF UNITED STATES GOVERNMENT SECURITIES AND OF ALL INVESTMENTS AMONG MEMBER BANK ASSETS, BY GROUPS OF MEMBER BANKS, FROM DECEMBER 31, 1929, TO DECEMBER 31, 1932*

(In percentages)

	NEW YORK CITY	OTHER RESERVE CITIES	COUNTRY DISTRICTS	ALL MEMBER BANKS
U. S. Government securities as a percentage of all investments	+15.5	+10.9	+7.3	+13.8
U. S. Government securities as a percentage of total loans and investments	+23.6	+12.7	+5.9	+13.3
Investments as a percentage of total loans and investments	+29.4	+18.0	+9.6	+18.0

* Source: Derived from Tables 174, 175, and 176.

in the volume of business. The country loans were on the whole more frozen than those of the larger urban centers. This is reflected in the less rapid decline of loans in the country and in reserve cities other than New York, where the loans were more largely liquid.

In the three years from December 31, 1929, to December 31, 1932, the reduction of loans by all member banks of the Federal Reserve system amounted to almost $11,700,000,000. While the largest absolute decline took place in the loans of member banks of other reserve cities, including Chicago, the liquidation measures proceeded most rapidly in New York. The banks there ex-

TABLE 178

CHANGES IN LOANS, UNITED STATES GOVERNMENT SECURITY HOLDINGS, AND INVESTMENTS (INCLUSIVE OF UNITED STATES GOVERNMENT SECURITIES) BY ALL MEMBER BANKS, FROM DECEMBER 31, 1929, TO DECEMBER 31, 1932*

(In millions of dollars)

	NEW YORK CITY		OTHER RESERVE CITIES (INCLUDING CHICAGO)		COUNTRY BANKS		ALL MEMBER BANKS	
	Amount	%	Amount	%	Amount	%	Amount	%
Decline in loans	3,749	51.4	4,473	42.0	3,445	38.5	11,666	43.4
Increase in investments	1,698	81.1	1,109	34.1	— 325	— 7.3	2,482	25.3
Increase in United States Government Securities	1,491	131.1	978	65.9	208	16.4	2,677	69.3

* Source: Member bank *Call Reports*. The loans include overdrafts and acceptances of other banks and bills of exchange or drafts sold with endorsement.

perienced a shrinkage to the extent of 51.4 per cent of their loans. The declines for other reserve cities, including Chicago, and for the country banks were 42.0 and 38.5 per cent, respectively. Meanwhile investments of all member banks increased $2,500,000,000. Again the most marked changes were in the larger centers as is shown in Table 178.

The increase in the aggregate investments by all member banks in this period is more than accounted for by the increase in their holdings of United States Government securities. They added $2,677,000,000 to their holdings of Federal issues, but all investments grew only $2,482,000,000. In other words, altogether the banks unloaded the small sum of $195,000,000 miscellaneous bonds which they had carried in their portfolios. The pressure on the security market would have been much greater had not the member banks in the larger centers absorbed a part of the securities which the country banks either were compelled to cash in or were converting into Government securities. The country banks sold $533,000,000 of "other securities," while the banks in New York and the other reserve cities purchased $338,000,000 in the three years 1929-1932.

The reader will realize that this analysis turns somewhat upon the choice of the period selected for investigation. There is some evidence that the banks in the larger centers did not act together altruistically. If one chooses the period of June 30, 1930, to June 30, 1932, for study it becomes clear that the pressure on the security market resulting from country-bank sales of miscellaneous bonds assumed more substantial proportions than would appear from the above discussion. During this interval the country banks sold $531,000,000 of "other securities." The member banks in New York City also sold $31,000,000 of their "other securities" and the member banks in other reserve cities, including Chicago, sold $32,000,000. In other words the market was at one time called upon to absorb about $600,000,000 of bonds released for the most part by the country banks. It was only after June 30, 1932, that the banks in the larger centers, presumably, in part, as the result of bargain hunting, added to their investments outside of the Government securities field.

TABLE 179

CHANGES IN LOANS AND DISCOUNTS, UNITED STATES GOVERNMENT SECURITIES, AND ALL INVESTMENTS (INCLUSIVE OF UNITED STATES GOVERNMENT SECURITIES), JUNE 30, 1930-JUNE 30, 1932; BY GROUPS OF MEMBER BANKS OF THE FEDERAL RESERVE SYSTEM AND BY ALL BANKS REPORTING TO THE COMPTROLLER OF THE CURRENCY

(In millions of dollars)

	NEW YORK CITY MEMBER BANKS	MEMBER BANKS OF OTHER RESERVE CITIES, INCLUDING CHICAGO	COUNTRY BANKS	ALL MEMBER BANKS	ALL BANKS REPORTING TO COMPTROLLER OF CURRENCY
Loans and discounts	—3323	—3217	—2589	—9130	—12,420
United States Government securities	+ 861	+ 501	+ 203	+1567	+ 2,609
All investments, inclusive of United States Government securities	+ 830	+ 469	— 328	+ 972	+ 278

* Source: Member bank *Call Reports* and *Reports of the Comptroller of the Currency.*

Taking the statistics of the Comptroller of the Currency's reports at their face value, it would appear (Table 179) that in addition to the pressure which came to the lower-grade bond market from the sales of $595,000,000 of other securities, chiefly by member banks of country districts, nonmember banks "dumped" over $1,700,000,000 of their other investments in the two years ending June 30, 1932. While, for reasons already

TABLE 180

STATE, COUNTY, AND MUNICIPAL BONDS HELD BY ALL MEMBER BANKS ON CALL DATES*

(In millions of dollars)

CALL DATE	NEW YORK CITY	OTHER RESERVE CITY BANKS INCLUDING CHICAGO	COUNTRY BANKS	ALL MEMBER BANKS
1929—March 27	146	460	563	1,169
June 29	118	464	562	1,144
Oct. 4	130	431	555	1,116
Dec. 31	214	461	549	1,224
1930—March 27	177	441	551	1,168
June 30	184	480	569	1,232
Sept. 24	269	544	566	1,379
Dec. 31	306	605	582	1,493
1931—March 25	350	611	592	1,554
June 30	275	644	616	1,535
Sept. 29	322	631	630	1,583
Dec. 31	203	575	610	1,388
1932—June 30	320	595	599	1,514
Sept. 30	359	598	592	1,549
Dec. 31	431	597	586	1,615
1933—June 30†	467	623	534	1,624

* Source: Member bank *Call Reports.*

† Licensed banks (banks operating on an unrestricted basis).

stated and others to follow the data must not be implicitly relied upon, there can be little doubt but that much of the deterioration of the bond market may be attributed to this source. The country member banks as a group resemble the nonmember banks more closely than any other group of member banks and it may reasonably be assumed that the same forces which led to their sales operated to bring about the dumping of bonds on the part of nonmember banks.

The same general contingencies and policies which led the member banks into the United States Government securities appear to have directed their investments also into state, county, and municipal bonds. On December 31, 1932, this type of investment amounted to $1,615,000,000, representing a growth of over $390,000,000 in three years.

To summarize, the liquidation of loans in 1930-1932 proceeded most rapidly in the urbanized regions and there, too, the shrinkage was more largely compensated through an increase in investments. Of this increase, United States Government securities comprised a larger proportion in the member banks of New York City and other urbanized regions than in those of the country districts.

Public Debt Held by the Federal Reserve System

On June 30, 1919, when the public debt was near its peak, the Federal Reserve system, that is, the member banks together with the twelve Federal Reserve banks, held $4,035,000,000 out of $25,234,000,000, or 16 per cent of the interest-bearing debt of the United States, exclusive of special issues to trust funds, which was outstanding in the hands of the public. On June 30, 1921, only about 12 per cent of the public debt was in the Federal Reserve system. Thereafter, because the holdings by the member banks increased steadily at the same time that the Government was pursuing its debt-reduction policy, the portion of the debt held within the Federal Reserve system grew year by year (Tables 181 and 182). By June 30, 1930, $4,652,000,000, or nearly 31 per cent of the public debt was within the system. Of this aggregate the Federal Reserve banks held $591,000,000 or less than 4 per cent and the members $4,061,000,000 or about 27 per cent of the $15,157,000,000 interest-bearing debt which was then outstanding. During the depression the banks absorbed huge blocks of the issues which the Treasury was compelled to float in order to meet the deficit and to finance its extraordinary operations, so that the portion of the public debt held within the Federal Reserve system continued to grow. On December 31, 1932, the Federal Reserve banks held $1,855,000,000 or over

9 per cent; the members $6,540,000,000 or 32.5 per cent, and the system as a whole $8,395,000,000 or nearly 42 per cent of the $20,098,000,000 of United States Government securities outstanding. On June 30, 1933, the Federal Reserve banks held

TABLE 181

UNITED STATES GOVERNMENT SECURITIES HELD IN AND OUT OF THE FEDERAL RESERVE SYSTEM*

(In millions of dollars)

ON OR ABOUT JUNE 30, EXCEPT WHERE OTHERWISE INDICATED	U. S. GOV'T SECURITIES HELD BY FEDERAL RESERVE BANKS	U. S. GOV'T SECURITIES HELD BY MEMBER BANKS	TOTAL HELD IN FEDERAL RESERVE SYSTEM	TOTAL HELD OUTSIDE OF FEDERAL RESERVE SYSTEM	TOTAL INTEREST-BEARING DEBT OUTSTANDING†
1915	8	749	757	213	970
1916	57	703	760	212	972
1917	71	1,065	1,136	1,577	2,713
1918	259	2,465	2,724	9,262	11,986
1919	232	3,803	4,035	21,199	25,234
1920	352	2,811	3,163	20,898	24,061
1921	259	2,561	2,820	20,915	23,735
1922	555	3,205	3,760	18,951	22,711
1923	102	3,835	3,937	18,071	22,008
1924	431	3,575	4,006	16,976	20,982
1925	353	3,780	4,133	15,983	20,116
1926	385	3,745	4,130	15,049	19,179
1927	370	3,796	4,166	13,726	17,892
1928	235	4,225	4,460	12,394	16,854
1929	216	4,155	4,371	11,661	16,032
1930	591	4,061	4,652	10,505	15,157
1931	668	5,343	6,011	10,219	16,230
1932	1,784	5,628	7,412	11,440	18,852
1932—Sept. 30	1,854	6,366	8,220	11,928	19,922
1932—Dec. 31	1,855	6,540	8,395	11,703	20,098
1933—June 30	1,998	6,887‡	8,885	12,949	21,834

* *Annual Reports of Federal Reserve Board, Federal Reserve Bulletin,* and *Treasury Reports.*

† Exclusive of special issues to trust funds which were not outstanding in the hands of the public.

‡ Licensed banks (banks operating on unrestricted basis).

$1,998,000,000 and the licensed member banks (operating on an unrestricted basis) $6,887,000,000 of the $21,834,000,000 United States Government securities outstanding. If to the holdings of the licensed banks were added the United States Government securities held by those not licensed, at least 42 per cent of the public debt would still be found in the Federal Reserve system on June 30, 1933.

TABLE 182

UNITED STATES GOVERNMENT SECURITIES HELD IN AND OUT OF THE FEDERAL RESERVE SYSTEM EXPRESSED AS A PERCENTAGE OF THE TOTAL AMOUNT OUTSTANDING*

ON OR ABOUT JUNE 30, EXCEPT WHERE OTHERWISE INDICATED	U. S. GOV'T SECURITIES HELD BY FEDERAL RESERVE BANKS	U. S. GOV'T SECURITIES HELD BY MEMBER BANKS	TOTAL HELD IN FEDERAL RESERVE SYSTEM	TOTAL HELD OUTSIDE OF FEDERAL RESERVE SYSTEM
	%	%	%	%
1915	.8	77.2	78.0	22.0
1916	5.9	72.3	78.2	21.8
1917	2.6	39.3	41.9	58.1
1918	2.2	20.6	22.7	77.3
1919	.9	15.1	16.0	84.0
1920	1.5	11.7	13.1	86.9
1921	1.1	10.8	11.9	88.1
1922	2.4	14.1	16.5	83.4
1923	.5	17.4	17.9	82.1
1924	2.1	17.0	19.1	80.9
1925	1.8	18.8	20.5	79.5
1926	2.0	19.5	21.5	78.5
1927	2.1	21.2	23.3	76.7
1928	1.4	25.0	26.5	73.5
1929	1.3	25.8	27.3	72.7
1930	3.9	26.6	30.7	69.3
1931	4.1	32.6	37.0	63.0
1932	9.4	29.5	39.3	60.7
1932—Sept. 30	9.2	31.6	40.1	59.9
1932—Dec. 31	9.2	32.5	41.8	58.2
1933—June 30	9.2	31.5†	40.7	59.3

* Computed on the basis of data abstracted from *Annual Reports of the Federal Reserve Board, Federal Reserve Bulletin,* and *Treasury Reports.*

† Licensed banks (banks operating on an unrestricted basis).

Unfortunately, it is not possible to ascertain what the holdings of United States Government securities by nonmember banks are, because the basic data which are made available by the Comptroller of the Currency are defective. If the United States Government securities held by member banks are deducted from the amount held by all banks reporting to the Comptroller, one finds, in the years 1928, 1929, and 1930, the part exceeding the apparent whole, or, in other words, that the members hold more public debt than all the banks of the United States (Tables 168 and 183). The explanation is that some of the banks or, perhaps, whole classes of banks, report only long-term bonds, whereas the national banks include all the United States Government securities held under "United States bonds." Some of the banks, other than national, report their short-term Government securities in the category of "unclassified" securities. The practice of grouping short-term government securities with miscellaneous investments of lower grades is not designed to throw the maximum amount of light upon the portfolio position of the nonmember banks.

It would have been interesting to compare the relative importance of United States Government securities among the assets of member and nonmember banks and to see whether there has been any divergence in portfolio policy of members and nonmembers since the close of the War. Thus, if a tendency on the part of the member banks to retain United States Government securities to a greater degree than do nonmembers could have been established, then a partial explanation for the preference which member banks have shown for Government securities might have been sought in the privilege accorded them to borrow from the Federal Reserve banks on their own fifteen-day notes secured by United States Government obligations. Inquiry along these lines will be impossible unless the Comptroller of the Currency, or some other Governmental authority is empowered to obtain from all banks data supplied according to a definite set of instructions and on a basis sufficiently uniform to permit of their legitimate combination.

However, one cannot maintain that the privilege to borrow on their own notes with United States Government securities as collateral is the major reason for the accumulation and retention of substantial blocks of government securities in the portfolios of member banks. In the years immediately following the War, it does appear that a considerable portion of this

TABLE 183: UNITED STATES GOVERNMENT SECURITIES HELD BY MEMBER BANKS RELATED TO TOTAL INVESTMENTS AND TOTAL LOANS AND INVESTMENTS 1915-32*

(In millions of dollars)

ON OR ABOUT JUNE 30, EXCEPT WHERE OTHERWISE INDICATED	U. S. SECURITIES HELD	TOTAL INVESTMENTS	TOTAL LOANS & INVESTMENTS	PERCENTAGE U. S. GOV'T SECURITIES OF LOANS & INVESTMENTS	PERCENTAGE INVESTMENTS OF LOANS & INVESTMENTS	PERCENTAGE U. S. GOV'T SECURITIES OF INVESTMENTS
1915	749	2,044	8,764	8.5	23.3	36.6
1916	703	2,351	10,315	6.8	22.8	29.9
1917	1,065	3,083	12,453	8.6	24.8	34.5
1918	2,465	5,274	18,507	13.3	28.5	46.7
1919	3,803	6,827	22,242	17.1	30.7	55.7
1920	2,811	6,026	25,559	11.0	23.6	46.6
1921	2,561	6,002	24,121	10.8	24.9	42.7
1922	3,205	7,017	24,182	13.3	29.0	45.7
1923	3,835	7,757	26,507	14.5	29.3	49.4
1924	3,575	7,963	27,167	13.2	29.3	44.9
1925	3,780	8,863	29,518	12.8	30.0	42.6
1926	3,745	9,123	31,184	12.0	29.3	41.1
1927	3,796	9,818	32,756	11.6	30.0	38.7
1928	4,225	10,758	35,061	12.1	30.7	39.3
1929	4,155	10,052	35,711	11.7	28.1	41.3
1930	4,061	10,442	35,656	11.4	29.3	38.9
1931	5,343	12,106	33,923	15.8	35.7	44.1
1932	5,628	11,414	28,001	20.1	40.8	49.3
1932—Sept. 30	6,366	12,121	28,045	22.7	43.2	52.5
1932—Dec. 31	6,540	12,265	27,469	23.8	44.7	53.3
1933—June 30†	6,887	11,928	24,786	27.8	48.1	57.7

* Source: *Annual Reports of the Federal Reserve Board,* and *Federal Reserve Bulletins.*
† Licensed banks (banks operating on an unrestricted basis).

class of investment was tied up with their borrowings at the Federal Reserve banks on their own notes. For example, on June 30, 1920, about 35 per cent of their United States Government securities were used to secure notes discounted at the Reserve banks (Table 184). By 1922 this percentage had declined to around 10 and thereafter has consistently remained so low that it is no longer probable that the determining influence on member-bank policy, with reference to their holdings of United States Government securities, can be the advantage which discounting their own notes holds over rediscounting some of their other eligible assets at the Reserve bank.

Of all the bills discounted by Federal Reserve banks, something under one-half are usually member-bank collateral notes secured by United States Government obligations. This relationship has been fairly uniform throughout the period since 1920 when detailed information on this point was first made available. All other types of bills discounted at the Federal Reserve banks, such as commercial and agricultural paper, bankers' and trade acceptances, demand and sight drafts, bills secured by United States Government obligations pledged by the original borrowers from the banks, and member-bank collateral notes secured by collateral other than United States Government obligations, together make up the remainder, that is, usually a little over 50 per cent of all bills discounted by the Reserve banks. In seeking an explanation of the large holdings of the public debt by member banks, the significant comparison would seem to be, not the larger percentage which member bank collateral notes secured by United States Government obligations and discounted at the Reserve banks is of all bills discounted, but the smaller percentage which the amount used for collateral purposes is of all the United States Government securities held by member banks. The disparity in the magnitude of these two factors—United States Government securities held by member banks, and member-bank collateral notes discounted and secured by United States Government obligations —has widened steadily. There must be other and controlling reasons to explain why member banks continue to hold government securities on a large scale.

If one studies superficially the growth in the absolute amounts of United States Government securities held by member banks (Table 181) or again the increase in the proportion of the total interest-bearing debt which has been absorbed into the Federal Reserve system (Table 182) the impression is formed that the banks more and more have come to be institutions engaged in the business of financing the Treasury of the United States and less devoted to the cause of providing credit facilities to industry. While this is true of the depression years, when the legitimate credit demands from business are relaxed and governmental bodies finding their revenues from taxation inadequate are compelled to borrow, it has not been characteristic of the entire post-war period. For the major part of the last fifteen years, the growth of other investments and loans has matched in some rough degree the increase in the amount of public debt held by the member banks (Table 183).

It cannot be said, therefore, that the various claimants for bank credit were at any time confronted by a banking system which had incapacitated itself by letting out a disproportionate amount of its resources to the treasuries of the United States and the several subordinate political jurisdictions. In the light of the past policy pursued by the banks, no one imagines that, but for their increased holdings of public debt, the banks would have permitted the cash to pile up in their vaults until such time as it might be called for by business enterprises. It seems reasonable to suggest that the banks would have selected more largely from the "bargain counter" of corporate securities and that the condition of all classes of banks would have been very much more alarming than it is at the present time, and this despite the uncertain position of the Government-security market which was sketched in Chapter XXXIV.

The large volume of public debt which has gone into the banks might not in and of itself have created a serious situation. In the circumstances, however, the banks are least able to face with equanimity the probable deterioration of the government bond market. Many banks would be driven into bankruptcy. The fundamental defect of the American banking system is that in practice it permits the mixture of investment trust functions with the acceptance of deposits. The banks hold too many miscellaneous corporate and foreign bonds. They have facilitated the tremendous overcapitalization of American industries through the purchase and flotation of these issues and it is altogether likely that the capital equipment of the country would not today be so far ahead of requirements and have fallen into

TABLE 184

HOLDINGS OF BILLS DISCOUNTED BY FEDERAL RESERVE BANKS SECURED BY U. S. GOVERNMENT OBLIGATIONS, COMPARED WITH TOTAL HOLDINGS OF BILLS DISCOUNTED AND UNITED STATES GOVERNMENT SECURITY HOLDINGS OF MEMBER BANKS

CALL DATES		MEMBER BANK COLLATERAL NOTES SECURED BY U. S. GOVT. OBLIGATIONS AND DISCOUNTED AT FEDERAL RESERVE BANKS AS A PERCENTAGE OF TOTAL HOLDINGS OF U. S. GOV'T SECURITIES	MEMBER BANK COLLATERAL NOTES SECURED BY U. S. GOVT. OBLIGATIONS AND DISCOUNTED AT FEDERAL RESERVE BANKS AS A PERCENTAGE OF ALL BILLS DISCOUNTED BY MEMBER BANKS AT FEDERAL RESERVE BANKS
		%	%
1920—May	4	37.6	43.9
June	30	34.2	39.6
Nov.	15	34.4	33.4
Dec.	29	33.2	32.0
1921—April	28	29.1	35.0
June	30	20.5	29.9
Dec.	31	17.2	38.8
1922—March		9.9	37.4
June	30	5.1	35.4
Dec.	29	8.7	53.1
1923—April	3	9.6	52.9
June	30	10.5	48.2
Sept.	14	11.1	47.1
Dec.	31	9.7	48.4
1924—Mar.	31	6.4	43.7
June	30	3.2	34.1
Oct.	10	2.9	39.9
Dec.	31	4.8	59.1
1925—April	6	5.3	51.9
June	30	6.5	50.8
Sept.	28	8.4	49.9
Dec.	31	10.2	59.9

* *Annual Reports of the Federal Reserve Board.*

TABLE 184 *(Continued)*

DATES CALL		MEMBER BANK COLLATERAL NOTES SECURED BY U. S. GOVT. OBLIGATIONS AND DISCOUNTED AT FEDERAL RESERVE BANKS AS A PERCENTAGE OF TOTAL HOLDINGS OF U. S. GOVT. SECURITIES	MEMBER BANK COLLATERAL NOTES SECURED BY U. S. GOVT. OBLIGATIONS AND DISCOUNTED AT FEDERAL RESERVE BANKS AS A PERCENTAGE OF ALL BILLS DISCOUNTED BY MEMBER BANKS AT FEDERAL RESERVE BANKS
1926—April	12	8.1	48.9
June	30	6.7	48.8
Dec.	31	10.7	57.2
1927—March	23	6.3	53.4
June	30	6.4	54.7
Oct.	10	5.9	52.4
Dec.	31	10.5	71.8
1928—Feb.	28	7.3	62.1
June	20	17.7	68.2
Oct.	3	15.1	62.0
Dec.	31	15.3	62.3
1929—March	27	15.2	61.7
June	29	13.8	55.3
Oct.	4	11.4	47.7
Dec.	31	9.1	55.8
1930—March	27	4.2	55.3
June	30	2.7	39.8
Sept.	24	2.6	38.7
Dec.	31	2.2	35.4
1931—March	25	2.6	51.5
June	30	0.9	30.7
Sept.	24	2.4	40.0
Dec.	31	6.0	49.7
1932—June	30	2.7	35.1
Sept.	30	1.6	30.8
Dec.	31	.9	25.5

such bad repair through idleness if these miscellaneous securities had been compelled to go more directly into the hands of the public without the encouragement which it derived from the purchases of financial houses and banks. In this way the banks helped to undermine, not only the industrial system, but the financial structure of society as well. So long as the member banks, without regard to business conditions, follow the policy of lending or investing every idle dollar so as to prevent the growth of cash in vault, and so long as the nature of the investments and the composition of the portfolios remain largely without Governmental regulation, the practices of member and nonmember banks may be depended upon to nullify the efforts of the best central bank leadership and the wisest Secretary of the Treasury. With confusion in officialdom, lack of sagacity on the part of the Board and directors of the Federal Reserve banks and the inherently unstable and treacherous investment policies pursued by the rank and file, the banks were carried through, without interference, to the disastrous finale of March, 1933.

If there were a corps of commercial banks, free from the encumbrances of holding miscellaneous bond issues, whose principal assets were in the nature of loans to business, then it would be entirely feasible for them to purchase substantial blocks of whatever United States or other Government securities might have to be offered in the market during depression periods. These would be precisely the periods when their ordinary loans undergo some shrinkage; but where the banks are always carrying many high-yielding bonds of one kind or another, they are not in a position to take up the slack in the decline of their loans with purchases of Government securities. These are usually not sufficiently "shiftable" to be relied upon too extensively as secondary reserves, especially where, in practice with the low level of cash in vault, they must serve for the most part as primary reserves. If the banks were otherwise more or less in a high state of liquidity they would not need to look so much to the prospect of having to "dump" their Government securities at a loss. They could count on working off their extra holdings over the years of late depression and early business revival, and in that way place themselves in a position ready to meet the gradually rising demand for bank accommodation for commercial and industrial purposes.

Since a very large part of the resources of the banks are at present tied up in miscellaneous and depreciated investments and frozen loans, it would appear that the demand for bank credit which might arise with the revival of business can only be met through the immediate liquidation of some considerable part of their Government securities. This process will bring pressure to bear in the bond market and will tend toward depressing the prices of the Federal issues. The Federal Reserve banks, through their open-market policy can somewhat mitigate the severity of the decline, but they are themselves overstocked with Federal securities and are, therefore, not in the best condition to take up much of the approximately seven billions of dollars in United States Government securities now held by the member banks. In view of the unsatisfactory condition of the underlying banking structure, the central banks must preserve a wide margin of potential Federal Reserve bank credit. If the Treasury and the member banks both call upon the Federal Reserve banks to subscribe to or absorb additional amounts of United States Government securities it is difficult to see when they would be able to return to the performance of their regular central-banking functions. As explained in Chapter XXXIV, great difficulty might be expected in placing the forthcoming refunding and new issues with the public so that the situation promises to become exceedingly embarrassing to business, to the banks, to the central banking authorities and to the Treasury, alike.

The banks have attempted to combine the long-term financing of industry in prosperous periods with the financing of the Federal Government in depression. Only a small part of the demand deposits of a bank can be tied up in the form of long-time assets, because while, on the average, not all of the rights inherent in the demand liabilities will be exercised at any one time, the maturities of the assets must, for the most part, be such as to permit the bank to meet those calls whenever they do occur. A certain amount of investment in easily marketable securities, without particular regard to their maturities, may be substituted for liquid assets of proper or manageable maturities on the ground that the selected securities are of the shiftable variety and, therefore, readily convertible into cash. Many of the current difficulties have developed because the banks are left too largely to their own judgment in the selection of the types of securities to put into their portfolios. There is always a tendency to invest an excessive amount of the deposits because it seems profitable to do so and for the same reason also to invest in high-yielding bonds. Lack of governmental regulation as to the amount and kind of securities eligible for bank investments has resulted in excessive subscriptions to corporate bonds and has brought all classes of banks too far into the field of long-term financing of industry. This represented a gross misuse of depositors' funds, brought about unparalleled overcapitalization of industry, and ultimately wiped out a large portion of both bank capital and the savings of the community.

The banks in this weakened condition, which resulted largely from their attempts at long-term financing of industry, were ill prepared to assume the responsibilities of financing the Treasury. Yet the complications arising from the manner in which the Federal deficit was financed, and which have yet to be faced in their most acute form, must not be allowed to distort one's appraisal of United States Government securities as a bank asset. To the extent that banks may legitimately invest in any type of security, Government issues afford them the most secure and shiftable asset. However, unless there is a fundamental reorganization of the banking structure so that the banks may be expected to emerge from periods of prosperity in more liquid condition and with less of a burden of miscellaneous bonds, then it would seem undesirable for them to invest in Government bonds whatever loose funds they may have in their tills. On the other hand, if by doing something which approaches commercial banking business, and if through regulation, the banks could be kept out of the corporate and high-yielding foreign bond market so that they might be expected to enter depression periods in fairly liquid condition, then there does not appear to be any reason why the slack of declining business loans might not be taken up by advances to the Treasury through the purchase of United States Government securities. These securities have become a dangerous asset, chiefly because the banking system had been honeycombed through the misuse of bank credit in the boom which terminated in 1929, and because the administration does not appear to recognize any limits to bank capacity.

Types of United States Government Securities Held by Banks

The aggregate requirements of the Government on account of extraordinary outlays brought about by the slump in business were at first greatly underestimated. The Administration then in power expected the business recession to be of short duration. The Treasury, therefore, chose to finance the Government through the depression by increasing the floating and short-dated debt of the United States. Subsequently it became clearer that the cost of carrying the country through the economic doldrums would reach into several billions of dollars, but interest rates fell so sharply that the Treasury was encouraged to continue the policy of following the money market downward in the price for funds in order to keep the cost of public borrowing as low as possible. It has been suggested in Chapter XXXIV that the Treasury has, purely from its own narrow point of view, overstayed the market and that it would have been wiser temporarily to forego some of the benefits of borrowing at low interest rates and to have offered a long-term bond issue to the market in order to forestall the possibility of later having to pay excessive rates in refunding the shorter maturities.

When one considers the habits of investment which have prevailed among bank managements in the past many years, it does not appear certain that the choice of issue by the Treasury would necessarily have affected the extent to which the banks have found it desirable to go into the United States Government securities market. This conclusion is supported by the fact that the banks have not purchased short-dated and floating debt exclusively during the depression. They have absorbed large amounts of long-term bonds in addition to the large blocks of floating debt. By allowing their shorter maturities to run off without renewing their subscriptions to refunding issues, the banks may be in a better position to get out of the Federal bond market than they would have been if the Treasury had chosen long-term rather than short-term financing. This is not, of course, meant to justify the Treasury's policy. It is questionable, however, whether the Treasury, through choice of maturities alone, is responsible for the important rôle which United States Government securities play in the portfolios of the member and nonmember banks. Nevertheless, if the banks had not taken liberal portions of the Treasury's offerings of their own free will, perhaps the familiar methods of the war-finance period might have been resorted to, and the banks stocked with much Government paper in any event. During the War the Treasury at least tried to interest the public in its issues because at that time there were both a business boom and the Treasury to finance, whereas in this depression the banks have been relatively free from the pressure of business loans and, therefore, have extensively collaborated with the Treasury. Unfortunately, this coöperation has obscured the desirability of interesting the investing public in Government bonds, until conditions had reached a point where it became very difficult to do so on a straight investment basis.

There is no continuous record of the amount of the public debt, by classes, which the member banks have held in their portfolios. Up to 1926 the Federal Reserve Board published this information for the reporting member banks of leading cities. These data are presented in Chart XXIII.

On December 31, 1932 all member banks held $6,540 millions of United States Government securities. Of this amount $4,096 million were bonds; $1,649 million were Treasury notes; $551 million were certificates of indebtedness; and $244 million were Treasury bills. In other words some 63 per cent of the aggregate holdings was in long term debt; 25 per cent was in securities maturing from within three to five years of their issue dates; and about 12 per cent represented investment in the floating debt of the United States. If these figures are compared with the amounts of each type of security held by the member banks before the depression, a considerable shift to the shorter maturities is noticeable. Thus, on October 4, 1929, the call date just prior to the break in the security market, the member banks held $2,992 million of bonds, $665 million of Treasury notes and $365 million of certificates; that is, 74 per cent of $989 mil-

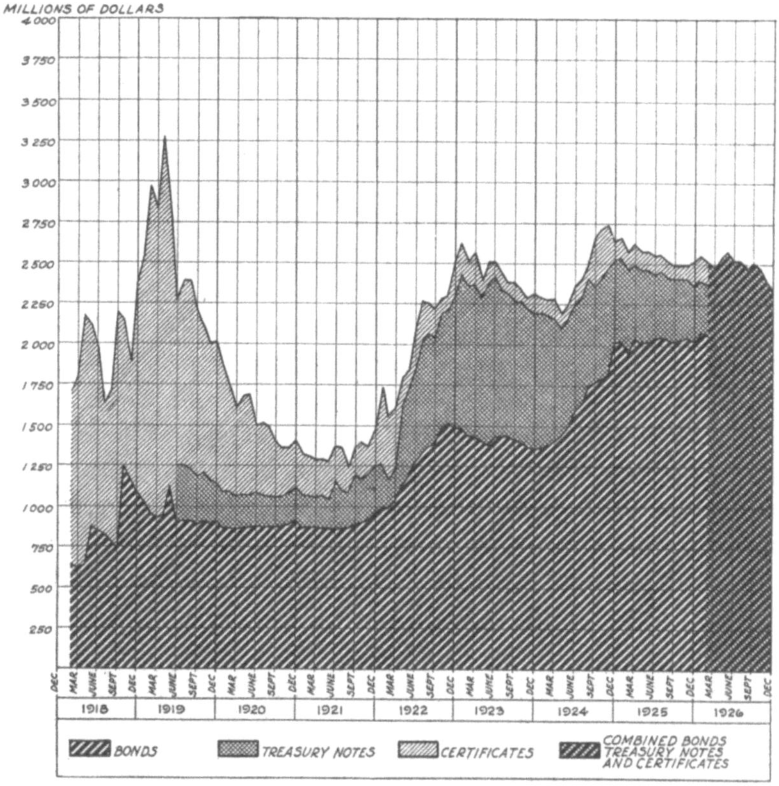

CHART XXIII. UNITED STATES GOVERNMENT SECURITIES HELD BY REPORTING MEMBER BANKS, BY CLASSES, 1918-1926

(Last ten months of 1926 separate figures not available.)
Source: *Federal Reserve Board Annual Reports.*

lion of United States Government securities held by the member banks was in long term issues, 17 per cent in intermediate debt and 9 per cent in floating debt.

The shift towards the shorter maturities was greatest in the more highly urbanized regions. This fact is clearly brought out in the summary Table 185. For example, the member banks located in New York City held on December 31, 1932, $2,603 million of the federal debt—$1,121 million in bonds, $971 millions in Treasury notes, $355 millions in certificates of indebtedness and $157 millions in Treasury bills. Only 43 per cent of their holdings was in long-term bonds, whereas 63 per cent of all member bank investments in United States Government securities was of this class. About 37 per cent of the $2,603 million was in intermediate securities compared with 25 per cent for all member banks; and nearly 20 per cent in floating debt as against 12 per cent for all member banks. On October 4, 1929 there did not appear to be a great deal of difference in the maturity distribution of the United States Government securities held by the various groups of member banks. The member banks of the other reserve cities increased their holdings of Government bonds to a greater degree than did the banks of New York City. The policy pursued by the country member banks, however, appears to be the reverse of that followed by the New York banks. A larger percentage of the United States Government securities which they held on December 31, 1932 was in long term bonds than on October 4, 1929 (Table 185). Altogether the member banks absorbed $2,518 million of public debt during the period October 4, 1929 and December 31, 1932, including $1,104 million of bonds, $984 million of Treasury notes and $430 million of certificates and bills. Since 43.8 per cent of the total increase took place in long term bonds, it is not easy to explain the growth, in aggregate holdings in terms of the type of issue selected by the Treasury.

Another indication that the shift into short-term debt has been furnished principally by operations of the member banks located in the urban regions is given in Table 186. The distributions of the holdings between the three groups of member banks,

TABLE 185

INCREASE IN INVESTMENTS IN UNITED STATES GOVERNMENT SECURITIES, BY CLASSES OF SECURITY AND GROUPS OF MEMBER BANKS FROM OCTOBER 4, 1929 TO DECEMBER 31, 1932*

(In millions of dollars and percentages)

MEMBER BANKS IN NEW YORK CITY

	Held October 4, 1929		Held December 31, 1932		Increase	
	Amount	Per cent	Amount	Per cent	Amount	Per cent
Bonds	732	74.0	1,121	43.1	389	24.1
Treasury notes	226	22.9	971	37.3	745	46.2
Certificates and bills	31	3.2	511	19.6	480	29.7
Total United States Govt. securities	989	100.1	2,603	100.0	1,614	100.0

MEMBER BANKS IN OTHER RESERVE CITIES, INCLUDING CHICAGO

	Held October 4, 1929		Held December 31, 1932		Increase	
	Amount	Per cent	Amount	Per cent	Amount	Per cent
Bonds	1,239	74.1	1,753	71.2	514	64.9
Treasury notes	238	14.2	457	18.6	219	27.7
Certificates and bills	194	11.6	253	10.3	59	7.5
Total United States Govt. securities	1,671	99.9	2,462	100.1	791	100.1

COUNTRY MEMBER BANKS

	Held October 4, 1929		Held December 31, 1932		Increase	
	Amount	Per cent	Amount	Per cent	Amount	Per cent
Bonds	1,021	75.0	1,222	82.9	201	177.9
Treasury notes	201	14.8	221	15.0	20	17.7
Certificates and bills	139	10.2	31	2.1	—108	—95.6
Total United States Govt. securities	1,361	100.0	1,474	100.1	113	100.0

ALL MEMBER BANKS

	Held October 4, 1929		Held December 31, 1932		Increase	
	Amount	Per cent	Amount	Per cent	Amount	Per cent
Bonds	2,992	74.4	4,096	62.6	1,104	43.8
Treasury notes	665	16.5	1,649	25.2	984	39.1
Certificates and bills	365	9.1	795	12.1	430	17.1
Total United States Govt securities	4,022	100.0	6,540	99.9	2,518	100.0

* Source: Member bank *Call Reports.*

by classes of security, for the call dates of October 4, 1929 and December 31, 1932 were compared. No substantial change took place relatively in the amounts of bonds held. In the case of all classes of the short-dated securities a much greater percentage of the aggregate held by all member banks was found to be lodged with the banks in New York City at the close of 1932 than at the beginning of the depression. On October 4, 1929, 34 per cent of the intermediate debt held by all members was in the member banks of New York City; on December 31, 1932, 59 per cent. The change in certificates of indebtedness for the corresponding period was from 9 per cent to 64 per cent. Of course,

TABLE 186

UNITED STATES GOVERNMENT SECURITIES, BY CLASSES, HELD BY GROUPS OF MEMBER BANKS AS A PERCENTAGE OF THE TOTAL AMOUNT HELD BY ALL MEMBER BANKS ON CALL DATES OCTOBER 4, 1929 AND DECEMBER 31, 1932*

CLASS OF SECURITY	NEW YORK CITY		OTHER RESERVE CITIES INCLUDING CHICAGO		COUNTRY DISTRICTS	
	Oct. 4 1929	Dec. 31 1932	Oct. 4 1929	Dec. 31 1932	Oct. 4 1929	Dec. 31 1932
Bonds	24.5	27.4	41.4	48.8	34.1	29.8
Treasury notes	34.0	58.9	35.7	27.7	30.3	13.4
Certificates and bills	8.8	64.3	53.2	31.8	37.9	4.0
Total of all classes	24.6	39.8	41.6	37.7	33.8	22.5

* Source: Member banks *Call Reports.*

the other groups of member banks necessarily held a smaller percentage of the aggregate of these securities held by all members. For other reserve city banks the percentage of treasury notes held declined from 36 to 28 and of certificates of indebtedness from 50 to 30; whereas the decline for banks in country districts was still sharper being from 30 to 13 and 41 to 5 per cent, respectively.

The member banks of the Federal Reserve System have always been an important factor in the market for United States Government securities. They have become especially important in the marketing of the short-dated securities. On October 4,

1929 nearly 25 per cent of all long-term Federal bonds, 33 per cent of the Treasury notes, and 18 per cent of the floating debt outstanding in the hands of the public was in the portfolios of member banks. By December 31, 1932, about 29 per cent of the bonds, as much as 54 per cent of the intermediate debt, and 28 per cent of the floating debt had been taken in as member bank investments. It will be shown in Chapter XXXVI that the Federal Reserve banks themselves have constituted a still more important element in the marketing of the recent increase in the short-dated public debt.

It is difficult to interest the investor in government securities of very short maturities. The public holds floating issues largely as a convenient way of building up tax reserves. Since the increase in taxation has not kept pace with governmental expenditures during the past few years and budgeting deficits have been the rule, corporations and large individual taxpayers could not be relied upon to create a market for the large volume of short-term securities issued by the Treasury. The banks have filled the breach for the Treasury; it is less certain that they can continue to absorb large portions of the projected increase in Federal issues.

CHAPTER XXXVI

PUBLIC DEBT AS THE BASIS FOR FEDERAL RESERVE BANK CREDIT

Introduction

The investment practices of the member banks do not fit into a central-banking structure which was designed as an integral part of commercial banking. For more than a decade prior to the formation of the Federal Reserve system, the investments of national banks (perhaps the most ideal or liquid of American banking institutions) were around a quarter of their total loans and investments. In addition, many of the loans have never been of the self-liquidating variety. That is, they were not advanced against goods in the final steps of the production process or against merchandise in stock awaiting the market. A good part of the loans by all banks are reported by investigators in the field to be for long-term capital purposes; not for working capital, but for the betterment and extension of business enterprises. This type of bank loan is inferior to investment in common stocks of the businesses, for it is usually less negotiable. It does entail, however, all the responsibilities of a common stockholder; yet, while the legislation in most states prohibits all classes of banks from purchasing junior securities, it does not regulate the quality of the loans permissible to banks. True commercial banking hardly exists, or can, in recent years at least, be said ever to have existed in the United States. A haphazard fusion of bank functions without much regard to their economic affinity is characteristic of banking in the United States. That was the situation when the Federal Reserve system was organized. It has become more pronounced since then; a larger part of bank assets is now invested in securities and a greater portion of the bank loans are made on the basis of safety, well collateraled by securities, but not necessarily liquid.

It is doubtful whether by maintaining high standards of

liquidity the Federal Reserve banks could within a few decades, by example and through their restricted service, have brought the unwieldly banking system with its many thousands of separate units to relinquish their unsound practices and to maintain themselves in a higher state of liquidity. Education is a slow process. For that reason one is driven to the conclusion that the best results cannot be obtained merely by purging the central banks of evil practices. It may be more essential to cut up the present pattern of the underlying banking structure and to create a group of truly commercial banks conforming to the standards presupposed in the Federal Reserve Act. The portfolios of these banks and their loans should be strictly regulated to comply with the requirements of sound commercial banking. The Federal Reserve banks can serve only such a group of banks. These should be the member banks. The security investment business lies outside the scope of the Federal Reserve system. It is not clear why many eminent authorities have fostered the notion that it is desirable for the Federal Reserve system to include any and every institution which has something to do with finance. Such procedure can but perpetuate the impotency of the system.

It may be desirable to establish a second central institution to guide and control the flow of long-term capital and to perform the discount function for those institutions which are primarily holders of securities. It certainly is not desirable to require of the Federal Reserve banks, as at present constituted, that they engage in this enterprise; yet, that is precisely what in effect has recently been accomplished through successive ameliorative enactments, although some have come to see more clearly that unless the underlying banking system is reorganized so as to raise the quality of bank credit, at least for those banks afforded the privilege of becoming members of the Federal Reserve system, then the quality of Federal Reserve bank credit must be dragged down to the level of member bank credit. The quality of Federal Reserve bank credit, and also of the assets backing the Federal Reserve notes, have undergone a process of continuous deterioration through amendment of the eligibility features of the Federal Reserve Act. The fact that the process was completed in the emergency of 1932-1933 must not be allowed to obscure the more fundamental factors in the situation. Whether the generalship of the central-banking authorities has been of the best is another matter. When the rank and file of the banks are so far out of step with the accepted tenets of deposit banking, perhaps the most excellent bank leadership must fail. It is not possible, by withholding from member banks the services of the Federal Reserve banks, to punish separately the bank stock-holders who had permitted their managements to misuse the people's money. The interests of the depositors also are brought into jeopardy. The government interfered in the public interest to break down the eligibility standards of the central banks so that they might the better go to the rescue of their members and rediscount classes of assets hitherto ineligible. A central-banking system which, on account of the feebleness of its clientele, must stand ready in depression to yield a large supply of cash against frozen assets, must retain a condition of supreme liquidity.

What the Federal Reserve banks can do for the Treasury in depression depends on what the member banks have been doing for business in prosperity. If the member banks emerge in good condition, not only can they legitimately absorb a substantial volume of the public debt to take up the slack in their commercial loans, but they leave the central banks free to utilize their wide margin of potential credit for Treasury purposes, if necessary, without fear that, through lack of confidence in the member banks, some unforseen demand for Federal Reserve bank credit or notes might arise. If in prosperity the member banks make loans for capital purposes and buy high-yielding second-grade bonds, then, considering the weakened condition of the banking system, the Federal Reserve banks are not in any position to act as a receptacle for the Treasury issues. They enter the depression, first and foremost, as rescue institutions and as such must avoid freezing their resources in United States Government securities. With a more durable group of member banks, however, there is no reason why the wide margins of potential Federal Reserve credit could not be made available to the Government.

Larger bank units, perhaps with branches, guided by proper banking principles may be expected to come out of prosperous periods in fairly liquid condition, so that in business recession and depression the demand for central bank credit from banking sources should be low. Purchase of United States Government securities by the Federal Reserve banks under these circumstances will, it is true, create excess reserves of member banks, but these are not dangerous if a sound underlying banking structure is assumed, because the banks must await the demand for loans for business, and business demands for loans do not arise unless the prospect for profits comes into evidence. Nevertheless, the perpetuation of a very large pool of outstanding Federal Reserve bank credit after the resumption of business activity could not be countenanced because, when the demand for business loans is once forthcoming, the banks through providing excessively cheap credit might facilitate a fresh overexpansion. Even with the soundest banking system there is a limit to the amount of Federal Reserve bank credit which it is safe to build up in depressions through the purchase of United States Government securities, because it is quite conceivable that if a huge amount of credit is created in the lean years, perhaps when the money lever is more or less inoperative, the Federal Reserve banks could not "mop up" the supply in early revival without breaking the bond market. Under these circumstances the foundation would be laid for the next collapse.

The danger in the current open-market operations of the Federal Reserve banks, and in those projected for them by the Government, is, first, that there appears to be no recognition of a limit to the capacity which the central banks have for the absorption of United States Government securities, and second, it is not clearly grasped that what the Federal Reserve banks can properly do for the Treasury is in important ways, linked with the condition of the member banks and the state of industry and trade.

TABLE 187

INCREASE IN UNITED STATES GOVERNMENT SECURITIES HELD BY FEDERAL RESERVE BANKS, BY TYPES OF ISSUE FROM OCTOBER 31, 1929, TO DECEMBER 31, 1933*

(In millions of dollars)

TYPE OF ISSUE	HELD OCT. 31, 1929	HELD DEC. 31, 1930	HELD DEC. 31, 1932	HELD DEC. 31, 1933	INCREASE FROM Oct. 31, 1929, to Dec. 31, 1930	Dec. 31, 1930, to Dec. 31, 1932	Dec. 31, 1932, to DEC. 31, 1933	Oct. 31, 1929, to DEC. 31, 1933
Bonds	81	164	422	443	83	258	21	362
Treasury notes	120	227	300	1053	107	73	753	933
Certificates of indebtedness	91	315	719	941 (certificates and bills combined)	224	404	193 (certificates and bills combined)	850 (certificates and bills combined)
Treasury bills	—	24	415		24	391		
Total	293	730	1855	2437	437	1125	582	2144

* Source: *Annual Reports of the Federal Reserve Board* and *Federal Reserve Bulletin.*

TABLE 188

INCREASE IN INTEREST-BEARING DEBT OF UNITED STATES OUTSTANDING, COMPARED WITH INCREASE IN UNITED STATES GOVERNMENT SECURITIES HELD BY FEDERAL RESERVE BANKS BY TYPES OF ISSUE, FROM OCTOBER 31, 1929, TO DECEMBER 31, 1933*

(In millions of dollars)

TYPE OF ISSUE	OUTSTANDING				INCREASE FROM DEC. 31, 1930, TO DEC. 31, 1933	INCREASE IN HOLDINGS BY FEDERAL RESERVE BANKS FROM DEC. 31, 1930, TO DEC. 31, 1933	INCREASE IN FEDERAL RESERVE HOLDINGS AS PERCENTAGE OF THE INCREASE IN AMOUNT OUTSTANDING
	Oct. 31, 1929	Dec. 31, 1930	Dec. 31, 1932	Dec. 31, 1933			
Bonds	12,116	12,112	14,223	15,569	3,457	279	8.1
Treasury notes	2,020	1,561	3,075	4,880	3,319	826	24.9
Certificates of indebtedness	1,658	1,192	2,158	1,628	436	602 (Certificates of indebtedness and Treasury bills combined)	46.0 (Certificates of indebtedness and Treasury bills combined)
Treasury bills	—	127	642	1,003	876		
Total	15,794	14,992	20,098	23,080	8,088	1,707	21.1

* Source: *Annual Reports of the Federal Reserve Board; Federal Reserve Bulletins;* and *Treasury Reports.*

Public Debt Held by the Federal Reserve Banks

On December 31, 1933, the Federal Reserve banks held \$2,437,000,000 of United States Government securities. From the middle of 1932 they have held, almost without exception, at least \$1,800,000,000 of United States Government securities, which is more than three times the maximum amount ever held by them, not excluding the years of war finance. In the summer and autumn of 1922, in the autumn of 1924, and the autumn and winter of 1927, the peak amounts held approached, or slightly exceeded, \$600,000,000. In general more of the public debt was retained in the portfolios of the Federal Reserve banks during the period 1924-1927 than formerly, and a far larger volume of securities has been consistently retained by the central institutions throughout the current depression than ever before. Not less than \$500,000,000 has been held since March, 1930, and not less than \$1,500,000,000 since May, 1932.

At the end of October, 1929, the Federal Reserve banks held less than \$300,000,000 of United States Government securities. Up to December 31, 1933, the central banks had increased these holdings by over \$2,100,000,000; but not all of the increase took place after the Federal debt began to expand. Between October 31, 1929, and December 31, 1930, over \$400,000,000 of the public debt had been absorbed by the Federal Reserve banks. This was before the Treasury began to meet its deficit and the extraordinary outlays of the depression by borrowing. This part of the open-market operations, therefore, was for purposes other than creating a market for the new Federal issues. About \$1,700,000,000 of the increase, however, came after the Federal debt began to grow and although professedly made for a number of reasons, such as will be discussed later, doubtless was not unaffected by the requirements of the United States Government securities market.

Over one fifth of the entire increase in the interest-bearing debt outstanding in the hands of the public since December 31, 1930, went into the portfolios of the Federal Reserve banks (Table 188). A larger portion of the newly issued short-term maturities was absorbed than of the increase in bonds. Almost one-half of the increase in the floating debt and one-fourth of the increase in intermediate debt, but only 8 per cent of the increase in bonds, was lodged with the central institutions.

At the close of 1932 the Federal Reserve banks held $415,000,000 of Treasury bills, $719,000,000 certificates of indebtedness, about $300,000,000 of the intermediate debt and about $422,000,000 of long-term bonds. That is, they held over $1,100,000,000 of floating debt representing over 60 per cent of their entire holdings of the public debt (Table 187). In 1933 the amount of shorter maturities held had been somewhat reduced, but still hovered around the level of $1,000,000,000. An interesting feature of the composition of the public debt held by the Federal Reserve banks is the important place occupied by Treasury bills, especially after April, 1932. This issue was created in the early stages of the depression, as explained in Chapter XXXIV, with a view toward adjusting the Treasury financing more closely to the rapidly changing money-market conditions. It is, therefore, a little surprising to find that as of December 31, 1932, over 60 per cent of the outstanding amount was retained by the Federal Reserve banks (Table 189).

Not only do the Federal Reserve banks constitute the chief market for the 90-day Treasury bills, but they also play an important rôle in the market for certificates of indebtedness. Toward the close of 1932 they held fully one-third of the entire amount of certificates of indebtedness oustanding. Altogether the central banks have become increasingly important in the market for United States Government securities since the beginning of the depression. On October 31, 1929, they held less than 2 per cent of the public debt, whereas on December 31, 1933, they held about 11 per cent, but their holdings of floating debt have come to be more and more important both relative to their aggregate holdings (Table 189) and to the total amount of the issues outstanding.

The Illiquidity of the Federal Reserve Banks

Circumstances related to the outstanding economic position of the United States among nations have provided the Federal

Reserve banks with wide margins of potential, but unused, Federal Reserve bank credit. The existence of this reservoir of credit has provoked considerable speculation as to whether some legitimate use could not be made of it for Treasury purposes when the state of business and the Federal finances were both at low ebb.

The position here taken is that it is perfectly proper for the Federal Reserve banks to freeze part of their potential Federal Reserve bank credit in United States Government securities in

TABLE 189

UNITED STATES GOVERNMENT SECURITIES HELD BY FEDERAL RESERVE BANKS, AS A PERCENTAGE OF THE INTEREST-BEARING DEBT OUTSTANDING, BY CLASSES OF SECURITY*

DATE	BONDS	TREASURY NOTES	CERTIFICATES	BILLS	CERTIFICATES AND BILLS	TOTAL
Oct. 31, 1929	.7	6.0	5.5	—	5.5	1.9
Dec. 31, 1930	1.4	14.5	26.4	19.1	25.6	4.9
Dec. 31, 1931	2.5	5.5	16.3	26.5	19.0	4.8
Dec. 31, 1932	3.0	9.7	33.3	64.6	40.6	9.3
Oct. 31, 1933	2.9	20.2	—	—	42.5	10.8
Dec. 31, 1933	2.8	21.5	—	—	35.8	10.5

* Source: *Reports* and *Bulletins* of the Federal Reserve Board, and *Treasury Reports.*

recession and depression, provided that at all times their relationship with the member banks and the general condition of these members are satisfactory. If the eligibility requirements call for high standards of liquidity, then the bills bought and the rediscounts made by the Federal Reserve banks will be related to active business transactions and that portion of Federal Reserve bank credit which grows out of the direct relationship with the member banks will be liquid. These standards, if rigidly adhered to, must have a salutary effect upon the banking practices of the members, because they could hope for access to the central banks only if their portfolios contained strictly liquid commercial paper. For this reason the practice of permitting the member banks to borrow on their own notes secured by

United States Government bonds is vicious in its effect upon the banking system—not because it induces the member banks to hold United States Government securities, which some believe to be inherently bad bank assets, but because it allows the members to pay too little attention to the quality of their other assets. They have a ready means of access to Federal Reserve bank credit even though their investment and lending policies do not warrant it. Their day-by-day contacts with the central banks should for the members be object lessons in good banking practice. This principle grows out of the concept of liquidity. Now, it may be inquired, if the Federal Reserve banks are permitted to purchase substantial amounts of United States Government securities in recession, does not this provide the member banks without regard to their individual condition with excess reserves, and would not this come to the same thing as throwing down the eligibility barriers? Not at all. The member banks go astray not in periods of depressed business, but in the booming *milieux* of revivals and prosperity. Then the leadership of the central bank is most essential because the demand for bank credit is pressing in upon the member banks from all sides. The problem is one of wise selection from the multitude of claimants.

If the guiding and restraining influence of the Federal Reserve banks made evident through its discount rate and open-market operations prevails under these circumstances, then the members may be expected to come out of prosperity without too intimate associations with industrial enterprises and with their demand liabilities more largely matched by commercial loans of quick turnover. They could then bear the slackening of trade without emergency support from the central bank. To provide such a group of member banks with excess lending power cannot be dangerous because the demand for business loans is very low and bankers must engage in considerable scouting to ferret out worthwhile loan prospects. It is, perhaps, in the public interest that they should during such times be induced to find clients with possibilities for profitable business activity. It is scarcely conceivable that any bank management should be able to weather the temptations of rising prosperity only to throw away idle cash in vault on worthless ventures during depressions. The complaint against those few banks which did put themselves into liquid condition soon after the break in the security market is not that they played fast and loose with trust funds but rather a reflection on conservatism. On the other hand, if the Federal Reserve banks fail to adhere in their discount policy and in their open market purchase of bills to the spirit of the eligibility features and otherwise through lack of leadership and because inadequately supported by Government regulation of portfolios, they do not succeed in bringing their members through active business periods in satisfactory shape, then they can do but little for the Treasury in depression; for their first duty is to the banks, and banks loaded with excessive holdings of miscellaneous bonds and with other frozen assets stand in need of relief, especially if for some reason they should lose the confidence of the public—as they must if the public is at all enlightened.

While the type of open-market policy selected by the Federal Reserve banks in collaboration with the Treasury during the depression now prevailing is, therefore, not disastrous, it was undertaken with a substructure of banking, and after an era of central-bank leadership, which was vastly different from the ideal projected for the future and without regard to the many dangers which must flow from such deviation. It may not have been possible for any central-banking system to meet successfully the pressure for cash which originated with the public when it once lost confidence in the quality of the bank credit extended by the member banks, but the Federal Reserve banks, on account of their large holdings of United States Government securities had rendered themselves powerless. They found it especially difficult to come to the rescue of their members because of the fixed reserve and collateral requirements against their deposits and notes. It was impossible to dislodge huge blocks of United States Government securities without at the same time disrupting the entire market and thus reflecting upon Federal credit and creating a stringency which would perhaps have precipitated the wildest of panics. The Federal Reserve Board had authority to revise the reserve ratio required of the Federal Reserve banks, but seemingly dared not exercise this right for fear of aggravating a delicate situation. When the limits of the legal ratios were approached, gold payments were suspended and subsequently the country with the largest gold stock in the world and also with a favorable balance of trade saw fit to remove itself completely from the gold standard.

The impotency of the Federal Reserve banks within the limits of the legal fixed reserve and collateral ratios and on account of their record purchases of United States Government securities, during the banking emergency of 1933, is illustrated in Charts XXIV and XXV and tables 190, 191, 192, and 193.

In only three earlier periods during the history of the Federal Reserve system had United States Government securities constituted as much as or exceeded 10 per cent of the combined resources of the central institutions—namely, April-August, 1922; July-December, 1924; and September-December, 1927. At the end of September, 1929, United States Government securities were as low as 3 per cent of the total resources of the Federal Reserve banks, but thereafter the importance of this asset steadily increased to 16 per cent by the end of March, 1932, 22 per cent at the end of April, 28 per cent at the end of May, and 32 per cent by the close of June, 1932. From then on United States Government securities comprised substantially a third of the combined resources of the Federal Reserve banks. At the end of October, 1933, United States Government securities amounted to the record of 36 per cent of total Federal Reserve bank resources (Table 191). Federal Reserve bank credit steadily deteriorated in quality. It was being based less and less on bills discounted and bills bought and more largely on United States Government securities (Table 192). In October, 1929, on the average, 60 per cent of Federal Reserve bank credit was based on bills discounted, 23 per cent on bills bought, 11 per cent on United States Government securities held, and about 5 per cent on miscellaneous assets. In December, 1932, on the average, 13 per cent of Federal Reserve bank credit was based on bills discounted, 2 per cent on bills bought, and as much as 85 per cent of the central bank's credit was frozen in United States Government securities. By October, 1933, as much as 95 per cent of Federal Reserve bank credit was based on Federal issues.

TABLE 190

PRINCIPAL ASSETS OF THE FEDERAL RESERVE BANKS, 1918-1933*

(In millions of dollars)

END OF YEAR OR MONTH	TOTAL RESERVES	BILLS DISCOUNTED: Secured by U. S. Gov't Obligations	BILLS DISCOUNTED: Total	BILLS BOUGHT	U. S. GOV'T SECURITIES	TOTAL RESOURCES
1918	2,146	1,400	1,703	304	311	5,252
1919	2,136	1,510	2,195	585	300	6,325
1920	2,254	1,533	2,687	260	287	6,254
1921	3,010	659	1,144	145	233	5,151
1922	3,177	332	618	272	436	5,252
1923	3,169	354	723	355	134	5,066
1924	3,047	187	314	387	540	5,096
1925	2,824	382	635	374	375	5,109
1926	2,948	365	637	381	315	5,150
1927	2,867	418	582	392	617	5,345
1928	2,709	659	1,056	489	228	5,352
1929	3,011	354	632	392	511	5,458
1930	3,082	89	251	364	729	5,201
1931	3,158	321	638	339	817	5,672
1932	3,331	61	235	33	1,855	6,115
1933—Jan.	3,457	72	274	31	1,763	6,033
Feb.	3,126	325	582	336	1,866	6,464
March	3,455	137	426	305	1,838	6,610
April	3,633	119	435	171	1,837	6,606
May	3,807	66	302	20	1,890	6,466
June	3,813	34	164	48	1,998	6,531
July	3,793	41	167	9	2,028	6,442
Aug.	3,820	38	153	7	2,129	6,607
Sept.	3,805	30	128	7	2,277	6,735
Oct.	3,817	27	116	7	2,421	6,889
Nov.	3,778	37	119	24	2,432	6,865
Dec.	3,794	27	98	133	2,437	7,041

* Source: *Annual Reports of the Federal Reserve Board* and *Federal Reserve Bulletins.*

In the 1920-1921 crisis United States Government securities figured as a basis of Federal Reserve bank credit in an indirect manner. They were used very largely to secure member bank notes discounted at the Federal Reserve banks (See Chart

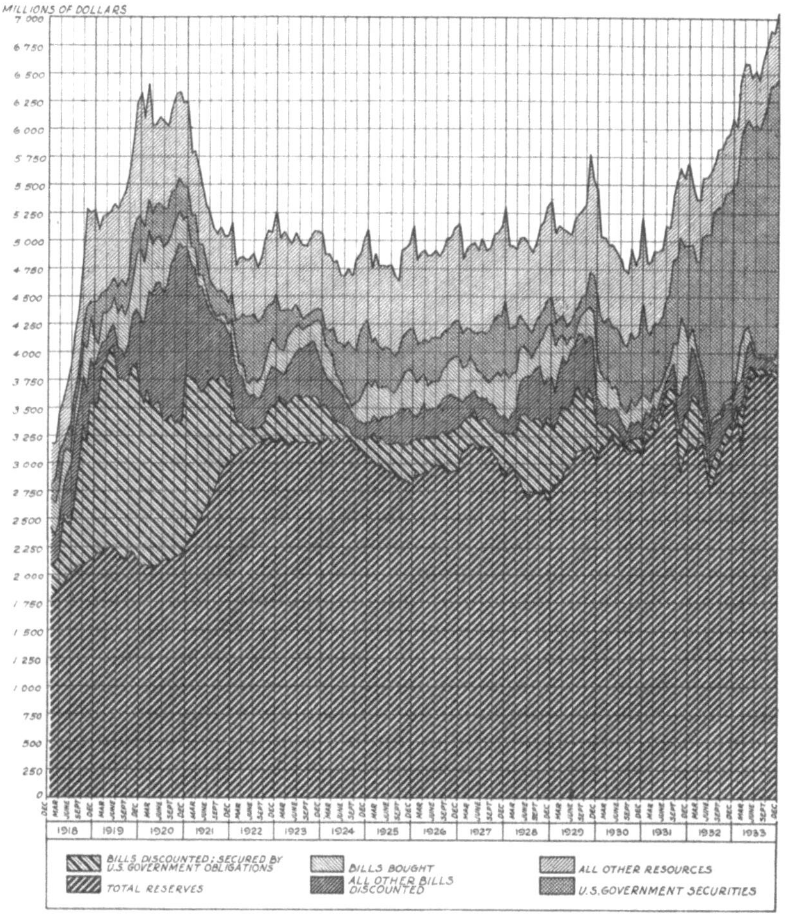

CHART XXIV. DISTRIBUTION OF FEDERAL RESERVE BANK ASSETS, 1918-1933

Source: *Federal Reserve Board Annual Reports and Federal Reserve Bulletins.*

XXIV). Throughout the entire period, September, 1918, to June 1921, over a billion dollars of Federal Reserve bank credit was thus to be accounted for. In so far as the member banks resort to this method of gaining access to the central banks because they

TABLE 191

PERCENTAGE DISTRIBUTION OF PRINCIPAL ASSETS OF THE FEDERAL RESERVE BANKS, 1918-1933*

END OF YEAR OR MONTH	TOTAL RESERVES	BILLS DISCOUNTED SECURED BY U. S. GOV'T OBLIGATIONS	TOTAL BILLS DISCOUNTED	BILLS BOUGHT	U. S. GOV'T SECURITIES
	%	%	%	%	%
1918	40.9	26.7	32.4	5.8	5.9
1919	33.8	23.9	34.7	9.2	4.7
1920	36.0	24.5	43.0	4.2	4.6
1921	58.4	12.8	22.2	2.8	4.5
1922	60.5	6.3	11.8	5.2	8.3
1923	62.6	7.0	14.3	7.0	2.6
1924	59.8	3.7	6.2	7.6	10.6
1925	55.3	7.5	12.4	7.3	7.3
1926	57.2	7.1	12.4	7.4	6.1
1927	53.6	7.8	10.9	7.3	11.5
1928	50.6	12.3	19.7	9.1	4.3
1929	55.2	6.5	11.6	7.2	9.4
1930	59.3	1.7	4.8	7.0	14.0
1931	55.7	5.7	11.2	6.0	14.4
1932	54.5	1.0	3.8	0.5	30.3
1933—Jan.	57.3	1.2	4.5	0.5	29.3
Feb.	48.4	5.0	9.0	5.2	28.9
March	52.3	2.1	6.4	4.6	27.8
April	55.0	1.8	6.6	2.6	27.8
May	58.8	1.0	4.7	.3	29.2
June	58.4	.5	2.5	.7	30.6
July	58.9	.6	2.6	.1	31.5
Aug.	57.8	.6	2.3	.1	32.2
Sept.	56.5	.5	1.9	.1	33.8
Oct.	55.4	.4	1.7	.1	36.0
Nov.	55.0	.5	1.7	.1	35.4
Dec.	53.9	.4	1.4	.2	34.6

* Source: Computed on basis of data in Table 188.

do not possess other eligible assets this portion of the Federal Reserve bank credit must be considered frozen, along with that based on actual United States Government securities held, because the member banks cannot liquidate their obligations to the central banks from the ordinary activities of business enterprises. Where the banks possessing other eligible assets, however, resort to this method of direct discount as more convenient

TABLE 192

PERCENTAGE DISTRIBUTION OF FEDERAL RESERVE BANK CREDIT OUTSTANDING, 1917-1933*

YEAR	BILLS DISCOUNTED	BILLS BOUGHT	U. S. GOV'T SECURITIES	OTHER FEDERAL RESERVE BANK CREDIT	TOTAL FEDERAL RESERVE BANK CREDIT
	%	%	%	%	%
1917	58.3	20.7	8.7	12.4	100.1
1918	70.9	13.9	8.6	6.7	100.1
1919	66.0	17.1	10.2	6.6	99.9
1920	79.0	7.0	9.8	4.2	100.0
1921	76.2	6.8	14.6	2.4	100.0
1922	47.9	18.8	27.6	5.7	100.0
1923	61.2	25.7	8.4	4.7	100.0
1924	23.4	27.8	43.0	5.8	100.0
1925	45.7	24.5	23.8	6.0	100.0
1926	46.2	26.6	22.3	4.8	99.9
1927	33.7	24.1	38.6	3.5	99.9
1928	55.6	26.5	14.4	3.6	100.1
1929	48.9	19.5	27.1	4.5	100.0
1930	27.5	20.2	50.6	2.7	100.0
1931	39.7	17.4	39.8	3.0	99.9
1932	12.9	1.6	84.6	1.0	100.1
1933—Jan.	12.1	1.5	85.6	0.8	100.0
Feb.	13.8	4.6	81.1	0.5	100.0
March	30.7	11.7	58.0	0.5	100.9
April	16.9	9.2	73.2	0.7	100.0
May	14.8	3.8	80.8	0.6	100.0
June	11.3	.5	87.5	0.6	99.9
July	7.7	.7	91.2	0.5	100.1
Aug.	7.1	.4	92.2	0.4	100.1
Sept.	5.9	.3	93.4	0.5	100.1
Oct.	4.8	.3	94.5	0.4	100.0
Nov.	4.4	.5	94.7	0.3	99.9
Dec.	4.4	3.8	91.7	0.7	100.0

* Source: *Annual Reports of the Federal Reserve Board* and *Federal Reserve Bulletins.* (Based on average of daily figures for month of December, except where otherwise indicated.)

than rediscounts, the Federal Reserve bank credit based on collateraled member bank notes may be thoroughly liquid in fact if not in form. It is impossible to ascertain what portion of the direct discounts represent illiquid central bank credit of the

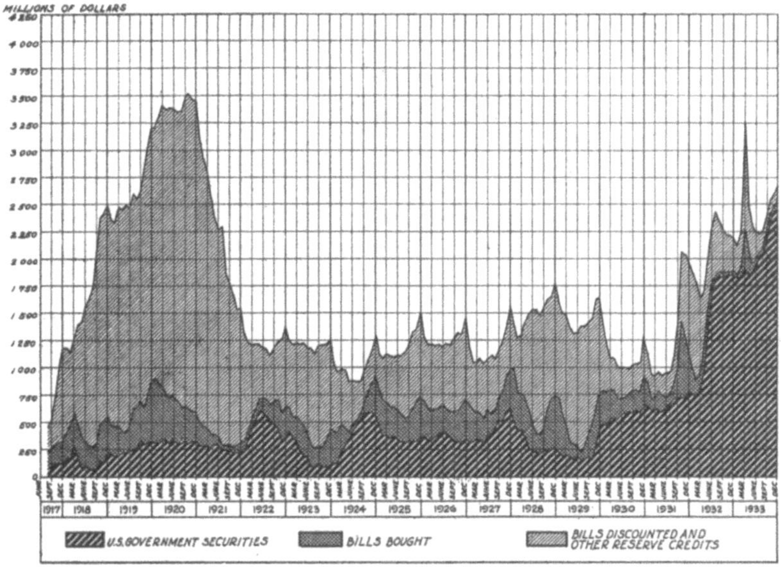

CHART XXV. RESERVE BANK CREDIT OUTSTANDING, 1917-1933

(Average of Daily Figures)

Source: *Annual Reports of the Federal Reserve Board and Federal Reserve Bulletin.*

same class as that based on United States Government securities actually held by the Federal Reserve banks and dependent upon the shiftability of these assets for final means of payment. To be conservative, one is perhaps warranted, therefore, in adding these two items together in appraising the illiquidity of the Federal Reserve banks.

In the depression now prevailing the Federal Reserve banks purchased the securities directly. In October, 1929, bills discounted secured by United States Government obligations amounted to about $500,000,000; but it is true that, between that date and the weeks of the crisis, this indirect use of the public debt as a basis for Federal Reserve bank credit has been relatively unimportant, amounting, as of the end of the month for the period October, 1929, to December, 1932, to less than $200,000,000 in 26 out of the 38 months. Temporarily in the crisis of 1933, as for example, in the March 8, 1933, Federal Reserve bank statement, this basis for Federal Reserve bank credit again reached toward a billion dollars, but the latest statements since the banking holiday do not indicate that United States Government securities have become in this indirect fashion an important basis for Federal Reserve bank credit (See Chart XXIV).

THE VOLUME OF FEDERAL RESERVE BANK CREDIT

The purchase of United States Government securities by the Federal Reserve banks built up the daily average amount of Reserve bank credit outstanding to a record total of $3,661,000,000 for the week ended March 11, 1933, and to an average for the entire month of March of over $3,250,000,000 which was somewhat under the previous peak of the period February-December, 1920 (Chart XXV).

What were the circumstances which brought this unusual amount of Federal Reserve bank credit into existence?

For the most part the policy which the Federal Reserve banks could pursue throughout the depression 1929-1933 had already been shaped by the policies that they and their members in fact did pursue during the preceding decade.

The need for a large portion of the record, or near-record, volume of Federal Reserve bank credit which had been accumulated during the last few years arose when both the nationals of the United States and foreign interests lost faith in the financial stability of the country and thereupon began to convert various forms of wealth into gold and other types of cash, either to hoard domestically or to transfer to other lands for safekeeping. Through purchase of United States Government securities, the Federal Reserve banks attempted somewhat to offset the effects of the gold drains and currency withdrawals upon the money market. This was no time to punish the member banks for making excessive investments and extending credit on improper bases. The volume of Federal Reserve bank credit could have been permitted to contract to a point where the members would have found it necessary to meet all requests for cash and their reserve requirements by means of rediscounting eligible paper or discounting their own notes secured by United States Government obligations. Many of the banks were so thoroughly frozen that perhaps they had no choice except to discount their own notes secured by United States Government securities. No one will deny that it would have been imprudent through central bank aloofness to bring about a money-market stringency at a time when the depositors were already fretful over the condition of their banks.

Changes in the monetary gold stock and money in circulation, however, were not the sole determinants of the open-market operations of the Federal Reserve banks. The volume of Federal Reserve bank credit based on open-market resources—bills bought and United States Government securities—did not expand and contract in sufficiently close conformity with changes in these factors to warrant the conclusion that the central banks were nothing but shock absorbers during the trying period since 1929. The system was very definitely committed to the policy of sustaining or creating excess reserves for member banks on the theory that somehow the banks might be able to force out into business the potential credit which these reserves could legally support. The important place which the prospect for profits and the relatively unimportant place occupied by interest charges—especially open market rates—among business expenses was apparently forgotten in the enthusiasm for cheap money which prevailed in political and banking circles.

Between September, 1929, and August, 1931, according to data in Table 193, monetary gold stock increased $607,000,000 and money in circulation increased $136,000,000. There is here indicated, therefore, a reduction in open-market resources of the Federal Reserve banks equal to the difference between those two quantities, or $471,000,000. Actually the Federal Reserve banks added $453,000,000 represented by an increase of $547,000,000 of United States Government securities and a reduction of $94,000,000 in bills bought in the open market. Altogether the volume of Federal Reserve bank credit fell off by $320,000,000 during this period, but it is clear that if the open-market policy had been guided purely by changes in the aforementioned factors, the decline would have amounted to $1,244,000,000,[1] unless indeed the member banks under these circumstances had found it impossible to reduce their discounts and rediscounts with the Federal Reserve banks by as much as $747,000,000.

Between August, 1931, the peak, and July, 1932, the trough of monetary gold stock, it declined $1,034,000,000 and money in circulation increased $804,000,000, indicating an increase in open-market resources of Federal Reserve banks equal to the sum of these two quantities, or $1,838,000,000. The open-market resources actually increased $1,031,000,000; represented by an increase of $1,106,000,000 of United States Government securities, and a decline of $75,000,000 of bills bought in the open market. Bills discounted increased $301,000,000.

From February, 1933, to March, 1933, monetary gold stock declined $231,000,000 and money in circulation increased $1,106,000,000 indicating an increase in the open-market resources of the Federal Reserve banks equal to the sum of $1,337,000,000. The actual increase was only $348,000,000 represented very largely by bills bought in the open market. Bills discounted rose sharply to $687,000,000.

[1] 471 + 453 + 320 = 1,244.

TABLE 193: CHANGES IN MONETARY GOLD STOCK AND MONEY IN CIRCULATION RELATED TO CHANGES IN VOLUME OF FEDERAL RESERVE BANK CREDIT OUTSTANDING, 1929-1933*

(Average of daily figures in millions of dollars)

	BILLS DISCOUNTED	BILLS BOUGHT	U. S. GOV'T SECURITIES	TOTAL OPEN-MKT. RESOURCES	TOTAL F. R. BANK CREDIT	MONETARY GOLD STOCK	MONEY IN CIRCULATION
Sept., 1929	969	229	165	394	1427	4368	4811
Aug., 1931	222	135	712	847	1107	4975	4947
July, 1932	523	60	1818	1878	2422	3941	5751
Feb., 1933	307	102	1804	1906	2224	4491	5892
March, 1933	994	379	1875	2254	3233	4260	6998
April, 1933	425	230	1837	2067	2511	4301	6137
Oct., 1933	119	7	2355	2362	2492	4324	5656
Change:							
Sept., 1929, to Aug., 1931	—747	— 94	+ 547	+ 453	— 320	+ 607	+ 136
Aug., 1931, to July, 1932	+301	— 75	+1106	+1031	+1315	—1034	+ 804
July, 1932, to Feb., 1933	—216	+ 42	— 14	+ 28	— 198	+ 550	+ 141
Feb., 1933, to March, 1933	+687	+277	+ 71	+ 348	+1009	— 231	+1106
March, 1933, to April, 1933	—569	—149	— 38	— 187	— 722	+ 41	— 861
Sept., 1929, to Oct., 1933	—850	—222	+2190	+1968	+1065	— 44	+ 845

* Source: *Annual Reports of the Federal Reserve Board* and *Federal Reserve Bulletins.*

Table 193 shows that while open-market resources of the Federal Reserve banks expanded very roughly in response to changes in monetary gold stocks and money in circulation, they did not contract in conformity therewith. Bills discounted fluctuated primarily as a balancing item, but had the Federal Reserve banks exposed their members to the disturbing influences, such as gold exports and increases in the demand for currency without shielding them from their full impact, the fluctuations in bills discounted would have been much more violent.

A considerable amount of criticism has fallen upon the Federal Reserve authorities for failure to adjust their open-market holdings in such a manner as to prevent excess reserves of member banks. It will be clear from the above analysis that much of the slack created in one period was more than taken up during some subsequent period of emergency. The excess reserves of the member banks did not precipitate the banking crisis. This crisis had been slowly fashioned for more than a decade in the faulty investment and loan policies of the thousands of banks. Excess reserves were built up in the hope that they might stimulate business. This policy, it is true, reflects a complete misapprehension of the rôle of money and credit in business depressions. That is another matter; but once the banking system had got itself into a more or less completely frozen condition and thereby had ultimately undermined the confidence of the depositors, central bank accommodation was no longer optional. In a certain sense these excess reserves anticipated the accommodation which would have been forced from the Federal Reserve banks in one way or another. It made it a little easier for the member banks with a supply of excess reserves to face the storm which broke upon them. Otherwise the borrowings would have been heavier and their difficulties correspondingly greater.

This explanation however offers no brief for excess reserves which might have had a bad psychological effect upon some bank managements, which otherwise might have taken some steps the better to prepare themselves for contingencies. As it was, they may have been unduly affected by the existence of a few thousand dollars of excess reserves and too forgetful of the millions of frozen assets. The policy, too, may have fostered further investments in United States Government securities at a time when, considering the decadent state of the banks, they should have conserved a larger cash-in-vault position. In other words, while excess reserves may have helped to perpetuate the member banks' policies which brought them to the brink of disaster, the foundation for the crisis had been laid long before the Federal Reserve banks permitted these idle reserves to pile up to any appreciable amount. The existence of the excess reserves made it easier for the member banks to obtain access to the gold stocks and currency of the Federal Reserve banks. The climax was reached quicker. It was easier to modify the Federal Reserve system and to reshape the bases of its currency and credit to conform to the quality of the assets held by the member banks. Had the weaker banking institutions been gradually eliminated over the period 1929-1932 and the losses realized upon and fairly distributed between the stockholders and unfortunate depositors, perhaps the banking system could have withstood the *malaise* brought on by the destructive practices of prosperity days. The attempt to carry the weak banks with the strong through the depression and to rely upon the "reflation" of bank assets for salvation finally undermined the confidence in sound and unsound institutions alike. Under these circumstances the drain on the gold stocks and resources of the central banks could not be prevented. All the eligibility features of the Federal Reserve Act went first. Finally, because the Federal Reserve banks in the emergency were fettered by the legal reserve and collateral requirements, and it would seem for this reason alone, the gold standard was abandoned.

The Treasury was subjected to criticism in Chapter XXXIV for failure to explore the market for its long-term securities. It was there suggested that it has overstayed the short-term market and that serious difficulties were in prospect both on account of the type and volume of its offerings; but the Treasury cannot be held responsible for the banking emergency. Even if the Federal Reserve Board had been prevailed upon by one of its

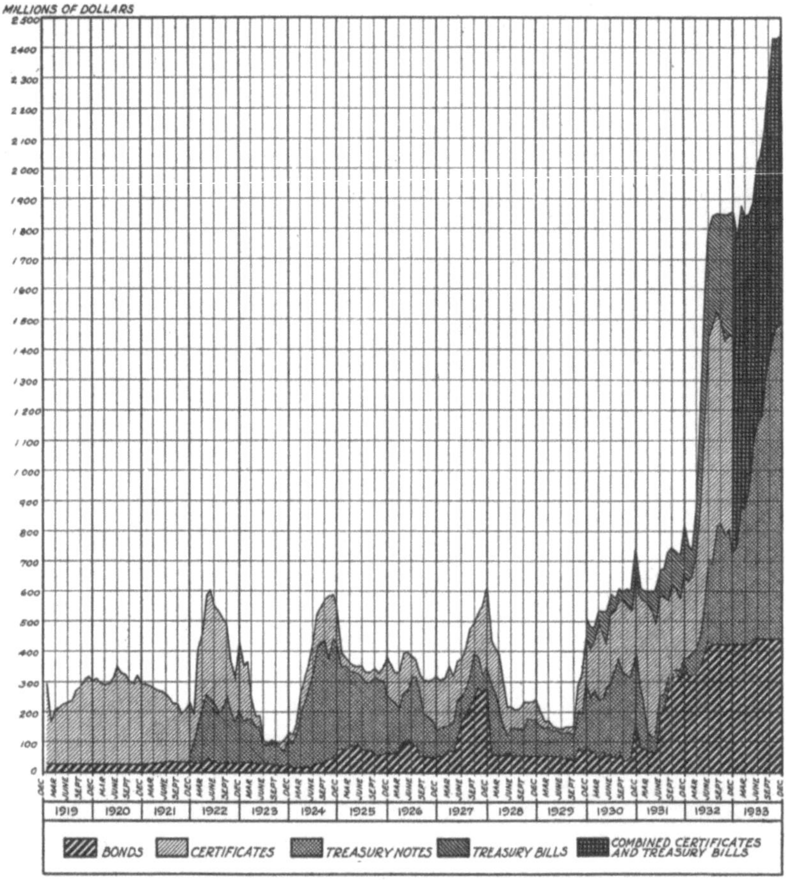

CHART XXVI. UNITED STATES GOVERNMENT DEBT HELD BY FEDERAL RESERVE BANKS, 1919-1933

(For year 1933 separate figures Treasury notes and Treasury bills not available.)

Source: *Annual Reports of the Federal Reserve Board* and *Federal Reserve Bulletin*.

members—the Secretary of the Treasury—to view the benefits of excess reserves to business in the light of its helpfulness to the market for United States Government securities and of the importance of maintaining the country's credit (that is, keeping the issues around par) such responsibility could not be placed with the Treasury because excess reserves are too superficial an element in the banking situation during depression periods. Federal Reserve bank credit has been called "the heart of the money market." It may be that during revival and prosperity periods, but in inactive business conditions Federal Reserve bank credit plays a much less romantic rôle.

The cheap money policy of the Federal Reserve banks failed to start the expected business revival. It affected essentially the open-market rates, but those rates apply to a relatively small volume of business loans. The rates charged customers did not respond to the open-market operations of the Federal Reserve banks to anything like the same extent. This deliberate creation of excess reserves brought about artificially low open-market rates but did not lower the price demanded for the bulk of the advances by banks. The bankers may have been more diligent in seeking out prospective clients but they were not very willing to let out their funds at bargain rates except for very short periods. Even if the demand for loans were primarily governed by interest rates and not by the prospect for profits, the policy of stimulating business activity by means of manipulating the reserves of member banks through Federal Reserve bank operations had to fail unless in some way or other the central banks could at the same time have induced the member banks to lower the rates on the bulk of their loans.

The Treasury took advantage of the bankers' preference for short maturities and supplied them with a volume of floating issues which was at times more than adequate to fill the gap left through the shrinkage of bankers' acceptances and open market commercial paper. The Federal Reserve banks themselves were at hand to absorb any oversupply of these floating issues which the Treasury's misjudgment may have been responsible for, as indicated in the accompanying Chart XXVI. This was finance made easy and permitted the Treasury to take full advantage of the very low rates for short maturities. The decline of the rates for long-term funds, whether corporate or government, was not at all commensurate with the fall in open-market rates or the yield on the short-term United States Government securities.

In conclusion it would seem that while the open-market operations of the Federal Reserve banks had no especially beneficial effects upon business and although excess reserves did not ruin the banking system, the cheap-money policy did encourage a rather short sighted Treasury policy of financing too largely by means of short-term issues and through the creation of artificially low open-market rates did make it possible for the Treasury to save interest, but has brought about a situation in the Federal finances which threatens to become extremely embarrassing. The Treasury has overstayed the short-term market and now in the least favorable circumstances is about to be compelled to go to the public.

CHAPTER XXXVII

PUBLIC DEBT AND NOTE CURRENCY

The Emergency Banking and Currency Legislation of 1932-1933

The Federal Reserve banks can lead but not control their members. A central bank can gather information on production and prices of the more important types of commodities. It may try to fathom the proper relationships between the various groups and according to its light indicate to the banking community the evidences of maladjustments as they appear. This in itself is a very complex task which has hitherto baffled economic analysts. The "weather signs" of the Federal Reserve banks are the discount rate and the open-market operations, but weather signs do not make the weather; neither can full responsibility for banking conditions be placed with the Federal Reserve banks. Its instruments cannot be too drastically applied. They are in practice delicate instruments, only slightly punitive even when the members have behaved in the most outrageous manner and in violation of all sound banking principles. Unless the rank and file of the banks have formed the habit of looking to the weather signs, control is impossible except perhaps by general regulations, circumscribing their more fundamental activities.

It has been suggested in Chapter XXXVI that had United States Government securities been ruled out as eligible assets, member banks might have kept themselves in more liquid condition, because they could no longer rely upon this means of access to Federal Reserve bank credit. Nevertheless, the elimination of this eligible asset cannot prevent the misuse of bank funds, because it is precisely in the prosperity years that eligible assets (exclusive of United States government securities) are most plentiful; also, these eligible assets are concentrated more largely in the larger centers, where speculative proclivities are most in evidence. Eligibility runs in terms of the current business situation and member banks can obtain access to Federal Reserve bank credit in largest amounts just when corrective measures of central bank control would seem to be most urgent. The speculative use of Federal Reserve bank credit, therefore, cannot be prevented by prohibiting the member banks from borrowing on their own notes with United States Government securities as collateral, although the elimination of this feature of the law may lead to an increase of the cash-in-vault position and to a relative reduction of investments made by banks. Once the member banks succeeded in getting themselves into a more or less completely frozen condition, the Government did not stand behind the higher standards of Federal Reserve bank credit. It devised ways and means for dragging the quality of the Federal Reserve bank credit down to the level of the member banks. The trend of the "remedial" legislation all has been in that direction and in the direction, too, of shifting over toward an "inelastic" currency based not upon commercial paper but more and more upon United States Government securities. Despite the fact that the member banks were well stocked at least with United States Government securities, the cry went up that they were suffering from a shortage of eligible assets, or that the several billion of eligible assets were so badly distributed among the banks that many really could not obtain access to Federal Reserve bank credit. The government did not repeat, after the old-fashioned schoolmaster, "No licking, no learning," but proceeded to break down the eligibility barriers and to admit whatever types of assets the members actually did possess to the rediscount privilege. The public interest might have been better served by eliminating many of the unit banks which had got themselves into such thoroughly illiquid condition, by consolidating many units, perhaps in a network of branches, by throwing some institutions out of the Federal Reserve system and by strictly regulating the loans and investments of those retained as members. In other words, a major operation in the underlying banking structure might have been performed during the crisis, tending to lift the quality of member-bank credit. Instead, the quality of the Federal Reserve bank credit was lowered.

TABLE 194: HOLDINGS OF ELIGIBLE ASSETS* (UNITED STATES GOVERNMENT SECURITIES† AND ELIGIBLE PAPER‡) COMPARED WITH BORROWINGS AT FEDERAL RESERVE BANKS

(In millions of dollars)

	By Reserve City Banks			By Country Banks			By All Mem. Banks			Member Bank Borrowings at Federal Reserve Banks
	U. S. Govt. Sec.	Eligible Paper	Total	U. S. Govt. Sec.	Eligible Paper	Total	U. S. Govt. Sec.	Eligible Paper	Total	
1926—June 30	2210	2825	5035	884	2100	2984	3094	4925	8019	516
1927— "	2299	2775	5074	847	1922	2839	3146	4767	7913	441
1928— "	2714	2680	5394	862	1967	2829	3576	4746	8223	1096
Oct. 3	2823	2551	5374	914	1817	2731	3738	4368	8106	1020
Dec. 31	2730	2349	5079	932	1811	2744	3662	4160	7822	1041
1929—March 27	2832	2582	5414	974	1761	2735	3807	4343	8150	981
June 29	2577	1688	5265	929	1773	2702	3506	4461	7968	1029
Oct. 4	2469	2865	5334	912	1733	2645	3381	4598	7979	899
Dec. 31	2403	2713	5116	814	1684	2498	3217	4397	7614	646
1930—March 27	2619	2542	5161	818	1662	2480	3438	4204	7642	206
June 30	2640	2285	4925	772	1620	2392	3412	3905	7317	274
Sept. 24	2682	2271	4953	764	1541	2305	3446	3812	7258	173
Dec. 31	2777	2700	4877	708	1438	2146	3485	3538	7023	248
1931—March 25	3584	2045	5629	776	1373	2149	4360	3418	7778	165
June 30	3871	1870	5741	836	1328	2164	4707	3198	7905	147
Sept. 29	3942	1787	5729	994	1209	2203	4936	2996	7932	323
Dec. 31	3706	1505	5211	989	1068	2056	4694	2573	7267	623
1932—June 30	3985	1457	5442	994	971	1965	4979	2428	7407	440
Sept. 30	4623	1508	6131	1003	916	1919	5626	2424	8050	331
Dec. 31	4776	1403	6179	987	844	1831	5763	2246	8009	235

* Source: *Annual Reports of the Federal Reserve Board,* 1931, and *Federal Reserve Bulletins.*

† Exclusive of approximately $650,000,000 of government securities pledged against national bank-note circulation.

‡ Including paper under rediscount.

Prior to the formation of the Federal Reserve system, one of the major defects of the currency was its inelasticity. In other words the national-bank notes were based, not upon gold and commercial paper, but upon United States Government securities, so that fluctuations in business frequently brought embarrassment to the banks through their inability to supply the community with the requisite amounts of cash. The Federal Reserve Act attempted to provide for an elastic bank-note issue. Accordingly, certain provisions were inserted calling for a 40 per cent reserve against Federal Reserve notes in circulation. The balance of the Federal Reserve notes issued by Federal Reserve agents to Federal Reserve banks (a somewhat larger amount than the notes in actual circulation because some of the notes issued by the agent were always to be found in the vaults of the Federal Reserve banks) was to be covered by eligible assets of the Federal Reserve banks, bills bought and discounted, and by non-gold reserves represented by lawful money held by the Federal Reserve banks. With the ebb and flow of business the volume of commercial paper would change, and it was believed that the amount of the currency in circulation would alter in response to the fluctuations of its primary base. This logic did not reckon with the loan-and-investment practices of the majority of banks which undermined the confidence of the public in bank credit and which in the trough of a record-breaking depression brought the depositors clamoring for currency in amounts that ultimately outstripped the base for the currency.

The volume of eligible assets possessed by the Federal Reserve banks did not keep pace with the volume of notes in circulation, because the basis of Federal Reserve bank credit which kept growing larger and larger was not the borrowings at the Federal Reserve banks resulting in bills discounted but United States Government securities which were purchased in the open market. If the Federal Reserve banks had stood aloof and waited for the member banks to come for Federal Reserve bank credit, their volume of eligible assets would have kept pace with withdrawals of Federal Reserve notes and a uniform "elastic" currency could have been maintained at least until the wide margin of potential Federal Reserve bank credit had been consumed by the demand for cash.

As was seen above, the Federal Reserve banks did not deem it expedient to remain detached from the financial situation and attempted to save the members from certain shocks and even tried to induce a revival of business by creating excess reserves of member banks. The result was that by May, 1932, the Federal Reserve banks had actually run out of free gold, and as early as February, 1932, the first of the legislation was enacted tending to shift the currency back to a government bond basis and to unfetter the Federal Reserve banks. In the face of the fixed reserve and collateral requirements for its note issue, the central banks had become completely frozen. Up to the emergency of 1933 there still remained a wide margin of potential Federal Reserve bank credit, the excess reserves of the Federal Reserve banks themselves over and above the reserves required for deposits and notes were still substantial, but, because of the small holdings of eligible assets, so much gold was required to cover the notes that by May, 1932, despite the very large volume of gold in the vaults of the Federal Reserve system, there was actually, according to the law, insufficient gold to cover the Federal Reserve notes issued by the Federal Reserve agents to the Federal Reserve banks.

From a certain point of view, it is misleading to refer to the admittance of United States Government securities as collateral for Federal Reserve notes; to the creation of a new-style Federal Reserve bank note based on United States Government securities and on other assets of member banks; and to the permission granted national banks to utilize United States Government bonds of higher than 2 per cent interest as the basis of their note issues, as a drift back to an inelastic currency. Perhaps it would be more accurate to call the present currency "super-elastic." As a matter of fact the so-called elastic currency devised by the Federal Reserve Act became highly inelastic on account of the practices of the member banks.

Broadening the basis of the currency tended to make it more elastic in the emergency. Except that the new legislation has made a patchwork of the currency system of the country and that it makes provision for outright fiat money, there is little danger in these features as temporary measures. The public will ordinarily use only a certain amount of currency in relation to the volume of business transactions depending on the monetary habits of the people. These habits and practices vary from nation to nation and within any nation only when for some special reason there is cause for alarm. There is no reason to believe, therefore, once the source for agitation has been removed, that there will remain outstanding a volume of notes at all commensurate with the vastly extended base. This assumes that the Government will not meet its current expenses by some variant of printing-press methods.

Much of the legislation tending to broaden the base for the currency was made necessary, given the general condition of the banks, by the fact that the Federal Reserve Act had fixed legal reserve and collateral ratios for the Federal Reserve notes. Although the Board is empowered to alter these provisions whenever circumstances warrant, this right cannot be exercised without at the same time somewhat aggravating a delicate situation. If the Board, however, had had the courage to suspend the reserve requirements and had supplied the member banks liberally with Federal Reserve notes against the collateral of their better assets, it is altogether likely that the run on the banks would not have become so general; and both a uniform currency (mostly Federal Reserve notes) and the gold standard could have been preserved. The legal fiction of a high gold backing of the Federal Reserve notes was saved, but this currency was supplemented with issues which were not similarly backed with gold, and United States Government securities had to be admitted as part backing even for the Federal Reserve notes themselves. The purpose of much of the current legislation is difficult to fathom. Any shortage of currency could have been met more easily by the removal of the legal reserve and collateral requirements. True, this would have frightened many depositors; so did much of the new currency legislation.

The evil which comes from embodying fixed reserve and collateral ratios in the banking law was well illustrated in the sudden drop of both excess reserves and free gold of the Federal Reserve banks between the end of February, 1933, and March 8, 1933. Excess reserves dropped from $1,093,000,000 to $440,000,000 and free gold computed according to the provisions of the Glass-Steagall act fell from $972,000,000 to $297,000,000. By the end of March, 1933, excess reserves of the Federal Reserve banks were again up to the high level of $1,326,000,000 and there was $1,194,000,000 of free gold. These wide swings in the gold position of the Federal Reserve banks, partly artificially produced by government decree and at great sacrifice of the dollar's prestige, can hardly actually reflect the changes in the banking and financial situation of the country.

The trouble is that many, not well versed in the minutiae of finance, come to place undue weight upon the fluctuations of these fixed legal ratios of gold cover, so that any approach to the fixed limits tends to undermine confidence and prevent the central banks from marshaling their full strength in such emergencies. The central banking authorities and the public alike are apt to formulate a mechanistic conception of banking and currency affairs without proper regard to the more fundamental considerations affecting the safety of the depositors. There can be little doubt that the existence of wide margins in the reserve ratio of the Federal Reserve banks over and above the legal fixed ratio of gold against both notes and deposits fostered a false sense of security among central bank and government officials alike in a period when the underlying banking structure should have been receiving more serious attention.

The Glass-Steagall Act of February 27, 1932, was the first attempt to save the legal ratios of the Federal Reserve banks in the emergency of 1932-1933. The free gold of the Federal Reserve banks declined rapidly toward the end of 1931 and remained at a low level in the first few months of 1932. As already explained this situation was brought about by the conjuncture of an unusual internal drain of gold and currency and large purchases of United States Government securities by the central banks undertaken with a view to obviate the necessity of member-bank borrowing and in the hope that easy money conditions could somehow stimulate business activity. Had the member banks been forced to borrow at the Federal Reserve banks in order to obtain gold for export purposes in response to the foreign demand and in order to obtain, chiefly, currency to meet the more insistent internal drain, the Federal Reserve banks would have had enough eligible assets to pledge with the Federal Reserve agents for the requisite supplies of Federal Reserve notes and for reserve purposes. The total reserves of the Federal Reserve banks had not become seriously depleted by the end of February, 1932. It was not till toward the end of June, 1932, when they stood at $2,800,000,000, or some half-billion dollars less than at the beginning of the year, that the gold drain from abroad had made serious inroads upon the gold holdings of the central banks. The Federal Reserve notes in circulation, however, grew from an average of less than $1,500,000,000, for the first three months of 1931, to over $2,500,000,000 for the corresponding period of 1932, even though business conditions were much slacker.

Meanwhile, the total deposits of the central banks, mostly member-bank balances, contracted but little, so that the reserve requirements on their account were reduced by a small amount compared with the growth in reserve and collateral requirements against the greatly expanded volume of Federal Reserve notes outstanding. The choice of policy lay between selling a portion of the United States Government securities held by the Federal Reserve banks, thereby forcing the member banks to borrow (which would at the same time have increased the eligible assets held by the central banks) or, if the legal ratios must be preserved, alternatively to admit United States Government securities as legal collateral against Federal Reserve notes issued by Federal Reserve agents to Federal Reserve banks, and in this manner making it possible for the Federal Reserve banks both to perpetuate the easy-money policy and to supply their members with plenty of cash to turn over to their excited depositors.

Prior to the enactment of the Glass-Steagall bill, only gold and eligible paper could be pledged by the Federal Reserve banks with the Federal Reserve agents, so that, when the borrowings at the central banks were low or, in other words, the eligible assets held by the Federal Reserve banks were small, it was necessary for them to tie up gold. This tied up both a 40 per cent reserve against Federal Reserve notes in circulation, for the 35 per cent of their total deposits, and also the 5 per cent redemption fund against that portion of the Federal Reserve notes issued by Federal Reserve agents to Federal Reserve banks which was not covered by gold. Gold was also required to cover notes not covered with eligible paper to equal the entire balance of Federal Reserve notes issued by the Federal Reserve agents outstanding. In a period when Federal Reserve credit was largely based on United States Government securities and eligible assets held were correspondingly low, it meant that much of the gold holdings of the Federal Reserve banks were tied up for collateral requirements against their notes.

Even though the reserve ratio still remained high, the free gold—that is, the amount of gold required, neither for reserves against notes and deposits, nor for collateral against notes—was running down toward the limit. It was permissible for the board to revise the reserve ratios in order to carry through its easy money policy without embarrassment from the technical gold position of the Federal Reserve banks. The Glass-Steagall act made it possible for the Federal Reserve banks, at least for the time being, to adhere to the fixed gold ratio. It admitted United States Government securities as collateral for Federal Reserve notes. To gold and eligible paper were added, United States Government securities which the Federal Reserve banks could pledge as collateral with the Federal Reserve agents against Federal Reserve notes. The potential increase in Federal Reserve bank credit was not directly affected by this act, for it did not change the reserve requirements of the Federal Reserve banks, but it did increase the amount of free gold, because United States Government securities could now be substituted for all the gold in excess of 40 per cent of Federal Reserve notes in circulation which formerly was pledged as collateral against Federal Reserve notes issued by Federal Reserve agents to the

Federal Reserve banks. According to the provisions of the Fedral Reserve Act, by May, 1932, all the free gold would have been exhausted and a deficit of $62,000,000 gold would have existed for reserve and collateral purposes. Under the Glass-Steagall Act, with United States Government securities admitted as collateral for Federal Reserve notes, the free gold then amounted to $1,087,000,000. Excess reserves of the Federal Reserve banks are always a little above the free gold when computed according to the Glass-Steagall Act, because it is still necessary to maintain a 5 per cent reserve with the Treasury against that portion of the Federal Reserve notes, issued by the Federal Reserve agents, which is not covered by gold.

The unhealthy condition of the banking system is clearly reflected in Table 195. If the demand for central-bank credit had been an outgrowth of the business situation, the member banks, as borrowers at the Federal Reserve banks, would have supplied them with adequate eligible assets to back the currency. The demand for central-bank credit which manifested itself in the years 1932-1933 had nothing to do with the state of business. It grew out of the decay of confidence in a deteriorating banking system. The central banks attempted to buoy up a sinking flotilla of member banks through purchase of United States Government securities and the creation of easy credit conditions. They were enabled by the new legislation to use any available assets which consisted, aside from gold, mostly of Government securities, to provide central-bank credit in the form in which it was demanded—not primarily as member-bank balances to form the base for larger extension of bank credit to business (although those too became excessive) but as Federal Reserve notes to satisfy the disgruntled depositors of weak member banks. On December 31, 1933, $601,000,000 of United States Government securities, $188,000,000 of eligible assets, and $2,625,000,000 of gold were pledged with the Federal Reserve agents against Federal Reserve notes which they had issued to the central banks. In other words, over 19 per cent of the Federal Reserve notes were backed by United States Government securities.

It was argued elsewhere that it may be perfectly legitimate

TABLE 195: FEDERAL RESERVE NOTE STATEMENT, AS OF THE END OF EACH MONTH, 1932-1933*

(In millions of dollars)

	FEDERAL RESERVE NOTES			COLLATERAL HELD BY AGENT AS SECURITY FOR NOTES ISSUED TO BANKS		
	Issued to Federal Reserve Bank by Federal Reserve Agent	Held by Federal Reserve Bank	In Actual Circulation	Gold	Eligible Paper	U. S. Gov't Securities
1932—Jan.	2923	257	2665	2058	1006	—
Feb.	2912	261	2651	2069	892	—
March	2817	253	2563	2211	667	—
April	2774	208	2566	2275	562	—
May	2765	193	2572	2101	485	205
June	3028	233	2795	1956	453	635
July	3080	221	2859	1969	525	611
Aug.	3052	238	2814	2082	417	578
Sept.	2984	234	2750	2189	315	499
Oct.	2918	209	2709	2192	312	455
Nov.	2914	221	2692	2242	294	414
Dec.	2987	248	2739	2352	220	428
1933—Jan.	2937	212	2725	2407	256	313
Feb.	3679	262	3417	2225	856	617
March	4036	340	3696	2578	599	885
April	3679	251	3428	2649	435	640
May	3437	234	3203	2814	190	481
June	3337	243	3094	2784	134	443
July	3265	253	3012	2760	103	469
Aug.	3250	262	2988	2758	98	450
Sept.	3242	241	3002	2695	80	538
Oct.	3226	260	2966	2636	73	567
Nov.	3265	235	3030	2618	96	598
Dec.	3350	270	3080	2625	188	601

* Source: *Federal Reserve Bulletin.*

to build up a large volume of central-bank credit during depression periods, for secondary purposes, such as would follow from a policy of close coöperation with the Treasury, provided that the underlying banking structure proved sound. It was also suggested that the powers of the central banks to create a demand for credit were rather definitely limited, although an easy rate policy appears most logical in depression periods. In this recent crisis, however, in the depth of one of the most inactive of business periods, there was actually a very urgent demand for central-bank credit. It is the existence of this demand for central bank credit in the form of currency, and not the large supply of Federal Reserve bank credit which marks the dangerous state of the banking system.

In other circumstances, the central banks could properly increase the volume of their credit if this were held to be in the broader interests of society. With a sound banking system, a large volume of central-bank credit might be created in slack business periods without destroying the gold and commercial paper basis of the currency. In this latest crisis the basis for the currency was undermined, not because the Federal Reserve banks built up a huge portfolio of United States Government securities and a record volume of central bank credit, but because there was no confidence in the member banks which had forfeited the good will of the depositors through undesirable loan and investment practices. The result was that this large supply of Federal Reserve bank credit was drawn upon to supply currency. So great was this internal drain that the Federal Reserve banks without the Glass-Steagall act would have had to exceed the legal limits for reserves and collateral; but it may be stressed that this internal drain was ready-made by the rank and file of the banks, and had little to do at least with the latest policies of the Federal Reserve banks, whatever one may think as to their general culpability.

The currency was only one of the principal features of the Glass-Steagall Act which foreshadowed the essential characteristics of later banking and currency legislation. A second point of interest is that the eligibility barriers to Federal Reserve bank credit were lowered. This was in fact a necessary complement to the currency provisions. The crux of the matter was to let the member banks convert whatever assets they had accumulated into Federal Reserve bank notes. Notes were what their depositors wanted. Eligible assets were shown above to be many times the total borrowings from the Federal Reserve banks, but the distribution of these eligible assets, it was feared, was such that some poor individual bank might be caught short during a run and forced to the wall. To assure all members of the maximum amount of solicitation, the Glass-Steagall Act provided for borrowing by groups of not less than five member banks on hitherto ineligible assets at a rate at least one per cent above the prevailing rate at the Federal Reserve bank. Provisions were made also for borrowing by the individual banks with capital not in excess of $5,000,000 on their own promissory notes secured to the satisfaction of the Federal Reserve bank. Indirectly, the nonmember banks were to share in the liberal dispensations of the Glass-Steagall Act. The member banks, having freer access to Federal Reserve bank credit could, in turn, be of greater assistance to their nonmember correspondents.

The Glass-Steagall Act became the pattern for subsequent currency legislation. An addendum, it would seem, is found in a section in the Federal Home Loan Bank Act of July 22, 1932, dealing with national-bank currency. The Act extended for three years the circulation privilege to all bonds of the United States bearing interest at a rate not in excess of 3⅜ per cent. Formerly any bonds of 2 per cent interest had the circulation privilege. The Act added almost $3,000,000,000 of bonds to the potential base for national bank notes. Actually this type of currency could not legally expand beyond the paid-in capital of national banks, which on December 31, 1932, amounted to $1,631,000,000. On that date there were $777,000,000 of national-bank notes outstanding, so that it was permissible for the national banks to increase their note circulation, backed by United States Government securities, some $854,000,000. On June 30, 1932, the call date prior to the extension of the note issue privilege of national banks, their note liability amounted to $650,000,000. In other words, their note circulation had grown $127,000,000 in the six months ended December 31, 1932. Those national banks which had to borrow at Federal Reserve banks in order to obtain large supplies of notes for their depositors will now find it cheaper to expand their own issues. Central bank control over its member banks appears to be more remote than ever with this perhaps temporary extension of the note-issue privilege to the national banks. These notes are "first cousins" to that portion of the Federal Reserve notes backed by United States Government securities. On December 31, 1932, there was $428,000,000 of notes and $776,000,000 of the national bank currency. The Federal Reserve bank notes, still closer "kin," had then not yet come into existence. On December 31, 1933, Federal Reserve notes were backed by United States Government securities to the extent of $601,000,000. On the other hand, the national-bank currency did not expand during 1933. The licensed national banks reported $727,000,000 of their notes outstanding as of June 30, 1933.

The Emergency Banking Act of March 9, 1933, startling in some of its other provisions, brought no fundamentally new features in the currency and Federal Reserve bank credit sections.[1] The policy of shifting the currency more largely to a basis of United States Government securities and of lowering the quality of Federal Reserve bank credit to accommodate the weaker member banks is continued. The Glass-Steagall Act of February 27, 1932, and an incidental section of the Federal Home Loan Bank Act of July 22, 1932, as explained above, had already increased the use of United States Government securities as a basis for the currency. Under this legislation a portion of the Federal Reserve notes were, for the first time, to be backed by United States Government securities and issues of higher interest rates were admitted as backing for national bank notes. The Emergency Banking Act provided for still another way of enlarging the currency. The Federal Reserve banks could now obtain Federal Reserve bank notes from the Treasurer of

[1] *Federal Reserve Bulletin*, March, 1933, pp. 117-18.

the United States by depositing either United States Government securities or "any notes, drafts, bills of exchange or bankers' acceptances acquired under the provisions of this Act."

If United States Government securities are deposited as security, circulating notes equal to the face value of the obligations are issued; otherwise, notes only in the amount of 90 per cent of the estimated value of the security pledged. This legislation admitted to the circulation privilege practically any asset possessed by the member banks which the Federal Reserve authorities and the Treasury could adjust to the rather elastic provisions of the law. While this legislation is quite consistent with the general policy of debasing the quality of the central bank credit and of the currency of the country, it is not at all clear why this fresh appendage to an already unduly complex currency system was at all necessary, especially after United States government securities had been admitted to the collateral privilege for Federal Reserve notes. The only possible explanation would seem to be the desire to create anew a favorable impression as to the impregnability of the gold position of the Federal Reserve banks.

This new issue requires no gold backing whatever, not even a 5 per cent redemption or safety fund. If the Federal Reserve bank notes could be substituted for Reserve notes in circulation, the gold ratios could once more become an object of pride. This is a further illustration of the vicious influence of legally established fixed reserve and collateral ratios. If this were the purpose for which the new Federal Reserve bank notes were created, it is extremely ludicrous in the light of the action taken by the United States government on the gold question.

The Federal Reserve bank notes have moved into circulation rather slowly. At the end of December, 1933, there were $234,000,000 of Federal Reserve bank notes outstanding, against which was pledged as collateral $257,000,000 of United States Government securities and $2,000,000 of discounted and purchased bills. The Federal Reserve banks held $25,000,000 in their vaults and there was actually in circulation only $209,000,000 of Federal Reserve bank notes.

The sections of the Glass-Steagall Act of February 27, 1932, which liberalized the basis of Federal Reserve advances to member banks, were to expire on March 3, 1933, but by an Act of February 3, 1933, were renewed for one year, to March 3, 1934. This strand in the legislation is strengthened by a section in the Emergency Banking Act, also effective to March 3, 1934. Any Federal Reserve bank under rules and regulations prescribed by the Federal Reserve Board, may make advances to such member banks as find themselves without a supply of eligible and acceptable assets on their own time or demand notes secured to the satisfaction of the Federal Reserve bank. The rate charged to member banks borrowing on these collateraled notes is one per cent higher than the rediscount rate. The eligibility features of the Federal Reserve Act have thus been completely removed and the basis for Federal Reserve bank credit left largely to the discretion of the Federal Reserve Board.

Two additional steps have been taken in keeping with the policy of broadening the bases of Reserve bank credit. The Emergency Relief and Construction Act of July 21, 1932, for the first time permitted the Federal Reserve banks to make direct advances to the public. They were empowered to discount for individuals, partnerships, or corporations which could furnish evidence that they were unable to secure adequate credit accommodations from other banking institutions. The Emergency Banking Act of March 9, 1933, permitted advances to such parties on their own promissory notes not exceeding 90-day maturity and secured by direct obligations of the United States. Secondly, the Emergency Banking Act was promptly amended so as to permit direct loans by Federal Reserve banks to state banks and trust companies not members of the Federal Reserve system,[2] provided that during the period of indebtedness they complied with the provisions of the Federal Reserve Act applicable to member state banks. Thus, individuals and nonmember banks, as well as the member banks were given access to Federal Reserve bank credit on liberal terms which were left largely to the discretion of the Federal Reserve Board.

[2] *Federal Reserve Bulletin*, April, 1933, p. 247.

The sketch of recent legislation confirms the view that, once the underlying banking structure gets out of gear, there is little hope even for the best of central banks. The Government has adopted measure after measure tending to adjust the quality of Federal Reserve bank credit to the assets possessed by the member banks. It has also made more than reasonably certain that there shall be no shortage of currency by admitting the United States Government securities and other assets hitherto ineligible to the circulation privilege.

It was suggested that a large volume of Federal Reserve bank credit may be justifiable in depression periods given sound banking conditions, but that considering the feebleness of the majority of the banks the Federal Reserve banks either had not adopted or were not permitted by the Government to follow out a cautious policy. It is very disturbing, therefore, to find the Administration moving further along in the direction of closer coöperation between the Federal Reserve banks and the Treasury, despite the unsatisfactory banking situation. Authentic evidence of the Federal Government's faith in manipulations of the currency and credit system is presented in the Agricultural Relief Act of May 12, 1933.[3]

> The President is authorized by this act to direct the Secretary of the Treasury to enter into agreements with the Federal Reserve banks and with the Federal Reserve Board whereby . . . they will, conduct . . . open market operations in obligations of the United States government or corporations in which the United States is the majority stockholder, and purchase directly and hold in portfolio for an agreed period. . . . Treasury bills or other obligations of the United States government in an aggregate sum of $3,000,000,000 in addition to those they may then hold, unless prior to the termination of such period or periods the Secretary shall consent to their sale.[4]

If this action should necessitate the suspension of the reserve requirements of the Federal Reserve banks, the restrictive features provided for in the Federal Reserve Act are to be held in

[3] *Federal Reserve Bulletin*, May, 1933, pp. 306-18.
[4] *Ibid.*, p. 317.

abeyance. That is, no tax shall be imposed upon any deficiency in reserves nor shall the interest rates charged by the Federal Reserve banks be automatically advanced. The President is further authorized to direct the Secretary of the Treasury to issue United States notes in amounts not exceeding $3,000,000,000 to be used "only for the purpose of meeting maturing Federal obligations to repay sums borrowed by the United States and for purchasing United States bonds and other interest-bearing obligations of the United States." The Secretary of the Treasury is directed to retire annually 4 per centum of any such notes. Also, according to the Act, "such notes and all other coins and currencies heretofore or hereafter coined or issued by or under the authority of the United States shall be legal tender for all debts public and private."[5] Another section authorized the use of farm-loan bonds, issued by Federal land banks, as security for advances by Federal Reserve banks to member banks for periods not exceeding 15 days. In this respect they are given the same status as United States Government securities. It must be admitted that the Act closes very fittingly with a further amendment of the Federal Reserve Act: "the Federal Reserve Board, upon the affirmative vote of not less than five of its members and with the approval of the President, may declare that an emergency exists by *reason of credit expansion,* and may by regulation during such emergency increase or decrease from time to time, in its discretion, the reserve balances required to be maintained against either demand or time deposits."[6]

After the Act was passed, Federal Reserve banks continued for some weeks open-market purchases of United States Government securities at the rate of almost $25,000,000 per week. The money market reflects this easy money policy of the Federal Reserve system and the Treasury has been able to borrow at exceptionally favorable rates. These rates are altogether artificial. The country, along with the rest of the world, has passed through three and a half years of business inactivity during which the accumulated savings of the population have been deeply eaten into for consumptive purposes. The depression has

[5] *Ibid.*, May, 1933, p. 317.

[6] *Ibid.*, p. 318.

created a shortage of capital as truly as did the War. With the resumption of increased business activity there can be no escape from higher interest rates, which will tend to depress the price of United States Government securities. The Government requires some three billions for its 1934 public-works program; several thousand odd million for numerous other laudable, public purposes. The danger which flows from an artificial money market is that it is very difficult for the Treasury to make any proper appraisal of what the country can really afford.

No criticism of the close coöperation between the Treasury and the Federal Reserve banks would ordinarily be called for; but, when the member banks and the rest of our banking institutions have been engaged in dissipating a large fraction of the accumulated savings of their depositors through unregulated and little-understood investment policies, so that even today, after several years of more or less violent banking shifts and changes, the situation has not yet by any means been cleared up, the duties of the Federal Reserve banks would seem to be found primarily with their members. These members hold large blocks of United States government securities which threaten to undergo depreciation unless indeed the mechanism provided for by the Agricultural Relief Act of May 12, 1933, proves effective. The Federal Reserve banks, themselves, hold over $2,430,000,000 of United States Government securities. Despite the flexibility introduced into the Federal Reserve Act, another banking emergency, if it should come, will force the Treasury to assume the responsibility for many of the unfortunate misdeeds of private banking concerns, and compel it to underwrite substantially the book values of the assets of the banks. The Treasury, having become closely involved with the Federal Reserve Banks and their members, would seem to have some moral obligation to stake the depositors, even if it were not forced to do so in the public interest. There is no danger in tying in closely with a sound banking system, but it is different where the banks are undermined. The Treasury is trying to extract services from a banking system which is scarcely strong enough to carry on its ordinary functions of financing the business community. There is just as much danger that the banks will ruin the Treasury as there is of the Treasury wrecking the banks. It is an unfortunate partnership unless the banking structure proves sounder than it has been for many generations.

SOME CONCLUSIONS

By H. Parker Willis

We have reached the end of this survey of the banking situation; and are now in position to summarize the situation as we have found it. The present brief chapter will accordingly be devoted to that purpose.

Let us first summarize, point by point, the state of things which we have established, by statistical comparison and general reasoning, as prevailing today in the banking system of the United States:

1. Our banks have been reduced to less than half their number of ten years ago; through failures, retirements, receiverships, and by refusal of the authorities to permit them to continue.

2. The access of the population to the banks is correspondingly hampered, and their convenience correspondingly reduced. Branch banking has expanded slowly to take the place of closed institutions, but the advance has been hampered by delays in legislation, and by prejudice on the part of the people, the banks and the politicians.

3. The banks, moreover, have suffered, and are still suffering from asset deterioration. This deterioration is the result of bad current management, private and governmental, as well as of unwise lending and speculation before 1930. Today, it is the result of the effort of the government to force its bonds and short-term notes upon the banks. They now have in portfolio nearly ten billion of dollars of such short-term debt.

4. The banks are thus slowly being "frozen" to death, and it is largely because of this fact that the government has thought it needful to become a stockholder in nearly 5,000 of them, with current interest estimated now as high as $850,000,000 in preferred shares and debentures. Thus, there is an imminent danger that the banks may pass into the hands of the government for management, either directly or indirectly.

5. While these conditions have been developing, the suspension of specie payments, and the further suspension of nearly all the limits formerly set upon note issue, have tended to promote bad and careless banking and to lay the ground for possible credit expansion of a dangerous and uncontrollable type.

6. The attack upon standards of value and the devaluation of the dollar has destroyed the old basis of redemption, and has correspondingly "extended" the banks.

7. The transfer of central banking powers under the act of January 30, 1934, to the Treasury, has paved the way for the further weakening of the Federal Reserve system, already badly weakened by earlier events.

8. The Federal Reserve system itself has become "frozen" and is unable to resist, by the usual money market methods, the disorganization of American finance growing out of the plan of filling the banks with illiquid government obligations.

9. In these circumstances, the banking system is passing through a time of critical emergency from which it may emerge either as a government system, or as a greatly weakened privately-owned system.

10. Should it emerge in either position, there remains the question what shall be the form to be given to the system in the future. It must, in either case, be rescued from a possible repetition of the evils which have brought it to its present position.

11. Such rescue is proposed in various ways—perhaps through the assumption of control of deposit banking by the Federal government, while trust and savings functions are left to the states; perhaps through new legislation which shall bring all banking under Federal supervision, but with fresh safeguards against bad and dangerous banking.

12. Among such safeguards those most urgently demanded are measures designed to restore the sound management of trust funds and the elimination of long-term assets from behind deposit liabilities.

13. The provisions of the Banking Act of 1933 are likely to be helpful as far as they go, but they do not go far.

14. Complete reorganization of the banking laws is needed

in order to eliminate all contradictory and uneconomic or obsolete provisions, and to install such amendments and changes as seem requisite.

15. Among such amendments should be included, provisions designed to make banking a profession to be conducted only by men of probity and experience.

The summary of conclusions which have thus been presented might be very greatly lengthened were we to continue the discussion beyond the major points which are considered essential in a general banking reorganization. The selection of any one of the main courses of action which have thus been indicated, immediately involves a choice between a number of alternatives for its complete application and working out. Hitherto one of the greatest difficulties encountered in the process of amending the banking laws of the United States has been found in the fact that great differences of opinion existed with respect to technique and selections of particular methods for obtaining given objects. In many cases these problems of detail have been allowed to take precedence over the major issues themselves and have thus tended to obscure the outstanding questions of policy. A time has now arrived when this haphazard method of procedure must be abandoned, and in place of it there must be effort to select general policies which will permit the laying of a foundation for a growth in strength and soundness. It will be necessary in so doing to subordinate the immediate interests of special groups and of given regions of the country to the general welfare of the banking system as a whole.

With this thought in mind this chapter has been confined to an enumeration merely of the principal major issues that present themselves in connection with the present reorganization question. A development of the details may be pursued by the use of the statistical and other data furnished or indicated in the preceding chapters, which have been so arranged as to deal specifically and in detail with the various topics.

INDEX

INDEX

COLUMBIA UNIVERSITY PRESS
COLUMBIA UNIVERSITY
NEW YORK

FOREIGN AGENT
OXFORD UNIVERSITY PRESS
HUMPHREY MILFORD
AMEN HOUSE, LONDON, E.C. 4

Bei Fragen zur Produktsicherheit wenden Sie sich bitte an:
If you have any questions regarding product safety,
please contact:

Walter de Gruyter GmbH
Genthiner Straße 13
10785 Berlin
productsafety@degruyterbrill.com